SEBASTIÃO SALGADO

GENESIS

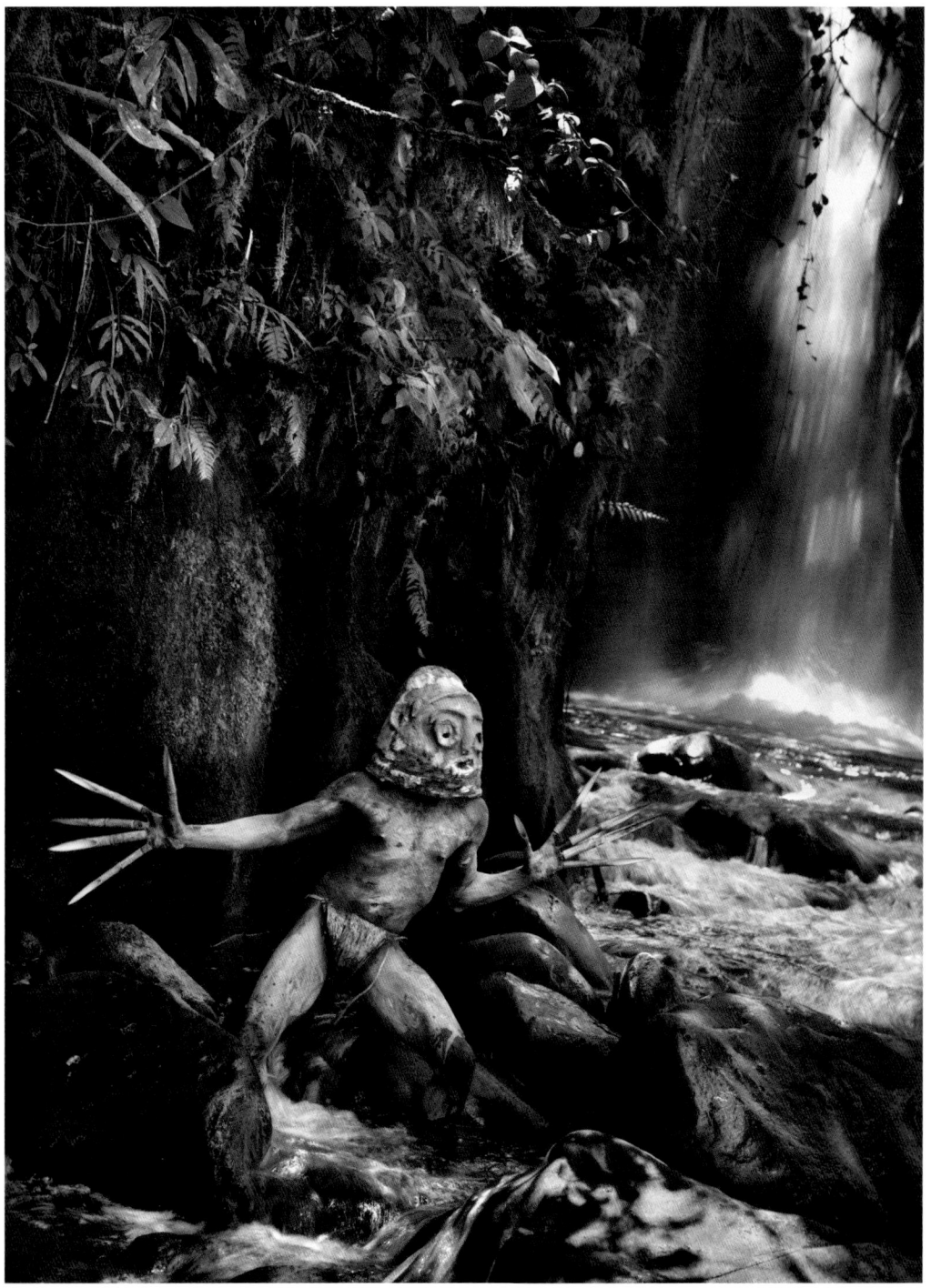

SEBASTIÃO SALGADO

GENESIS

Editing, Concept & Design
LÉLIA WANICK SALGADO

TASCHEN

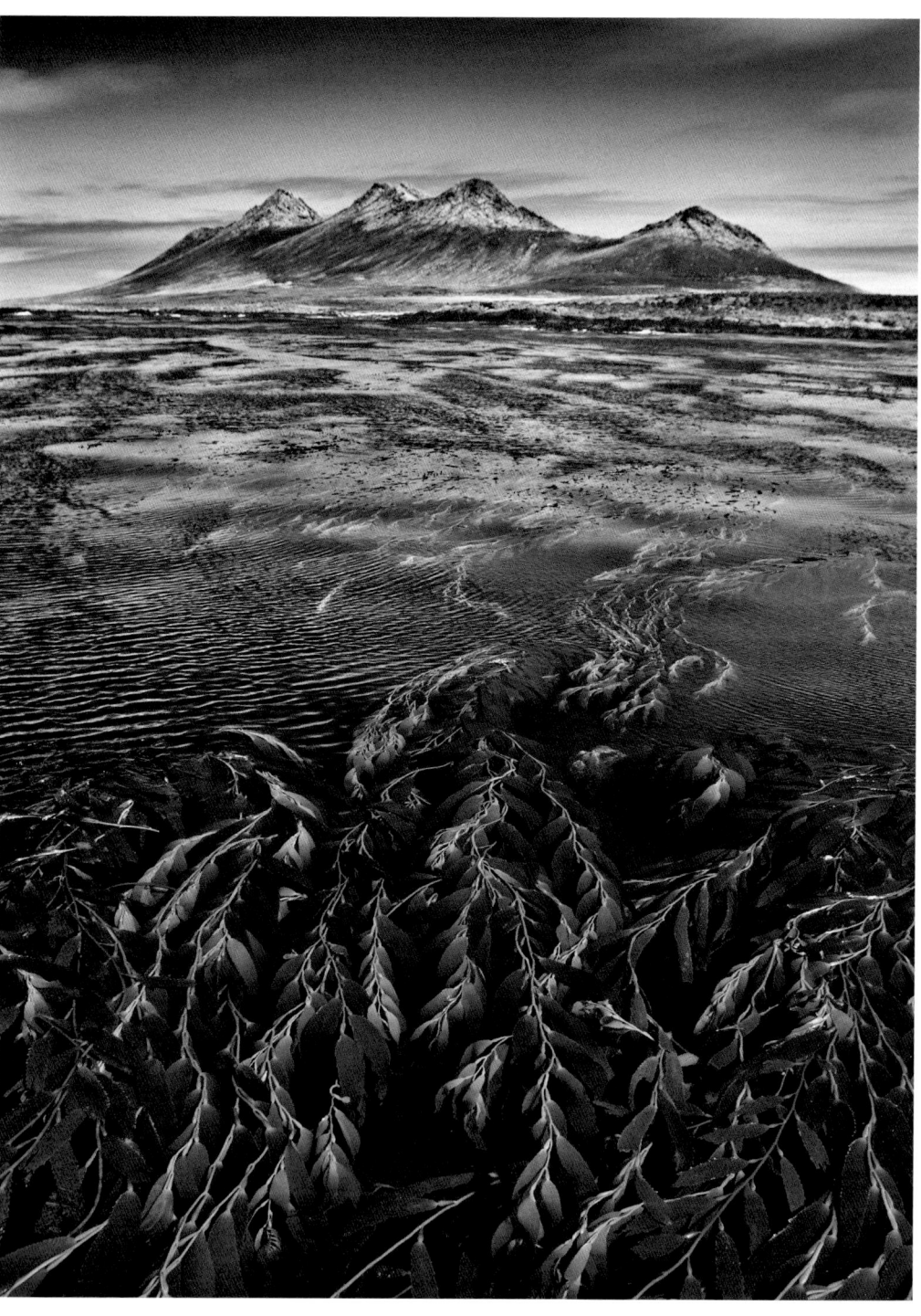

FOREWORD

At the end of the 1990s, I completed a long series of photo essays on the unparalleled movement of peoples across the globe. It involved recording the massive migration of peasants from rural areas to cities on several continents. It led me to follow destitute refugees fleeing armed conflicts and natural disasters and I accompanied young men willing to risk all in the hope of finding a better life in some far-off land. I witnessed much suffering and great courage, but most of all I saw violence and brutality such as I had never even imagined before. By the time the project was over, I had lost all faith in the future of humanity.

Yet these same years brought a happy coincidence. My father asked me and my wife, Lélia Deluiz Wanick, to take over a property in the Vale do Rio Doce in Brazil's Minas Gerais state that had once been our family's cattle ranch. We accepted reluctantly. It was there that I grew up with my seven sisters, surrounded by tropical vegetation alive with birds and wild animals, by rivers full of fish and by rolling hills that set us imagining the world beyond. But this paradise had vanished. By the mid-1990s, as with so many farms in the region, deforestation and erosion had left the land lifeless.

It was then that Lélia, my partner in every adventure of my life, had the bold idea of recreating a forest with the very same local species that once prospered there. We hoped for nothing less than the rebirth of the small ecosystem that I knew as a child. We planted over 300 different species of trees and, as saplings slowly turned the land green, we watched in wonder as birds, butterflies, beetles and tropical flowers returned. With reforestation, instead of turning into flash floods, heavy seasonal rain was also absorbed by the soil and, in time, allowed rivers and creeks to flow year-round. And to our delight, fish and even alligators reappeared.

Marveling at nature's ability to restore itself, we grew more anxious about the fate of the planet at large. We understood the absurdity of the idea that nature and humanity can somehow be separated. We also recognized that the breakdown in our links to nature poses a genuine threat to humanity. Through the rapid urbanization of the past 100 years, we have lost touch with the wilderness, animals and plants that represent the very essence of life on Earth. We may know how to subjugate nature, but we easily forget that we depend on it for our very survival.

These reflections became the seeds for a new long-term photographic project, focused on nature. Initially, we conceived it as a protest against how we are abusing our planet. We planned to show how pollution of our air, water and land has become the price of development; how global warming is bringing climate change with alarming consequences; how industrial farming, large-scale cattle ranching and logging are decimating rainforests.

But after we saw life returning to what was once our property and has since become a national park, we changed our minds. With our faith restored by the spectacle of hundreds of thousands of new trees and the fresh life they rekindled, we decided instead to explore the beauty of our planet. So, over the next eight years, I made 32 trips to distant corners of the globe, often joined by Lélia, sometimes by our son, Juliano, and most of the time accompanied by my invaluable colleague Jacques Barthélemy. Our mission was to seek out the land and seascapes, the animals and ancient communities that have escaped the long—and often destructive—arm of modern man.

We called the project *Genesis* because we imagined turning back the clock to the volcanic eruptions and earthquakes that shaped the Earth; to the air, water and fire that gave birth to life; to the oldest animal species that still resist domestication; to remote tribes whose way of life is largely unchanged; and to extant early forms of human organization. I wanted to examine how humanity and nature have long coexisted in what we now call ecological balance.

This work is the record of my journey, a visual ode to the majesty and fragility of Earth. But it is also a warning, I hope, of all that we risk losing.

My approach was not that of a journalist or scientist or anthropologist. In *Genesis*, I followed a romantic dream to find and share a pristine world that all too often is beyond our eyes and reach. My goal was not to go where man had never before set foot, although untamed nature is usually to be found in pretty inaccessible places. I simply wanted to show nature at its best wherever I found it. And I found it in boundless spaces of immense biodiversity which, amazingly, cover almost half the Earth's surface: in giant, largely untouched deserts; in the frozen lands of the Antarctic and the north of the planet; in vast expanses of tropical and temperate forest; and in mountain ranges of awe-inspiring splendor. Discovering this unspoiled world has been the most rewarding experience of my life.

My earlier projects, *Workers, Migrations* and many others, were voyages through the trials and tribulations of humanity. This one was my homage to the grandeur of nature. Traveling on foot, in boats, small planes or balloons, all the while photographing volcanoes, icebergs, deserts or jungles, I beheld a world unchanged over millennia. And with animals in the wild, from the penguins, sea lions and whales of the Antarctic and South Atlantic to the lions, wildebeests and elephants of Africa, I felt privileged to watch the endlessly repeated cycles of life.

My search for ancient communities proved more complex. There are still "uncontacted" tribes in the jungles of the Amazon and New Guinea, but of the remote peoples I visited, only the Zo'é Indians in the Amazon and the Stone Korowai in West Papua have barely been touched by the outside world. Many others maintain strong identities and have kept the age-old shapes of their wooden homes, their languages, religious rituals, hunting methods and diets. But they no longer live in total isolation. Visits by missionaries and even by groups of ecotourists are bringing the frontier of our consumer society ever closer to them.

My aim was to portray these peoples as close as possible to their ancestral way of life. Some might wear secondhand clothes distributed by evangelical groups, but I wanted to show the ceremonial attire and tribal customs of which they are most proud and which in a few decades may survive only in photographs. Sooner or later, the modern world will touch them—or they will go looking for it. I wanted to capture a vanishing world, a part of humanity that is on the verge of disappearing, yet in many ways still lives in harmony with nature.

The subjects of our research—landscapes, animals and peoples—often overlapped. In designing this book, we have therefore opted for five broad chapters, each representing a large region that may also embrace several major ecosystems. The result is a mosaic, the mosaic presented by nature itself. It is this that *Genesis* celebrates.

Sebastião Salgado
Paris

Page 2 The mudmen performers are among the most striking figures of the imaginative world of the Highlands. Paya, Western Highlands Province. Papua New Guinea. July and August 2008.

Page 4 These marine algae, known as giant bladder kelp (*Macrocystis pyrifera*), spread like garden weeds in the extremely cold waters of the South Atlantic. The mountains of Steeple Jason Island are visible in the background. Falkland Islands. November and December 2009.

BEHIND THE PICTURE

Genesis was born of a meeting of minds. After almost three decades of working together on the dramas and tragedies of humanity, Sebastião Salgado and I turned our attention to the planet on which we live. The change of focus was not accidental. After completing *Workers* and *Migrations*, we founded the Instituto Terra with the aim of reforesting a rural property belonging to Sebastião's family in Brazil. Once a cattle ranch, the land had been badly degraded by deforestation and erosion, yet nature responded quickly to young saplings and seasonal rain. As we watched this rebirth with a mixture of awe and delight, the idea for our next long-term project came to us: to explore the beauty of nature across the globe.

But where should we start? We embarked on extensive research to identify broad regions and specific sites with landscapes, animals and peoples that remained largely untouched by the modern world. Along with our team at Amazonas Images in Paris, Sebastião and I studied books, consulted experts and benefitted immensely from the advice of both UNESCO's World Heritage Centre in Paris and Conservation International in Washington. Given the difficulty of reaching and working in many naturally blessed locations, we understood that, at most, Sebastião could make four two-month trips per year. And once we had defined more than 30 important destinations, we braced ourselves for an eight-year project.

Defining the calendar for these trips was complex. Many places could ideally be visited only at certain times of the year, such as the short dry season in Indonesia or the flood months in Brazil's Pantanal or summer in the Arctic and Antarctic. In many cases, we also needed special permission to work in national parks or protected islands. For Sebastião to move long distances over difficult terrain, we went in search of boats, planes, balloons, trucks and trains of mules as well as experienced guides. And in many cases, he set off with his own food as well as all kinds of medicine.

Finally, with a detailed project in place, we began looking for backers.

We turned first to magazines that had supported *Workers* and *Migrations*. Although some had already been badly hit by the print-media crisis, we signed agreements with *Rolling Stone* in the United States, *The Guardian* in Britain, *Paris Match* in France, *Visão* in Portugal, *La Vanguardia* in Spain and *La Repubblica* in Italy. We also received generous financial help from Susie Tompkins Buell, the Christensen Fund and the Wallace Global Fund in the United States, all already engaged with Instituto Terra. Further, from 2005 for two years, we enjoyed support from Brazil's Companhia Siderúrgica de Tubarão, now ArcelorMittal Tubarão. All this help enabled us to embark on *Genesis*.

Sebastião's first trip in 2004 took him to the Galápagos Islands, in many ways the logical starting point for a look back at our planet's earlier life. For those of us involved in preparing his trips, it was in turn the starting bell for an uninterrupted artistic, logistical and technological marathon. From 2005, Jacques Barthélemy, a fearless mountain guide, became Sebastião's traveling companion and assistant. Determined to share the experience in situ,

I joined them on half of the journeys. Our son, Juliano, who was preparing a documentary on the making of *Genesis*, also accompanied Sebastião on several trips.

When Sebastião was traveling alone with Jacques, we spoke almost daily by satellite telephone, a vital connection when problems arose. On one occasion, with Sebastião already on a boat off the southern tip of South America, from Paris we obtained Chilean government permission for him to land on the Diego Ramírez Archipelago. On another, we had to arrange for Jacques to be evacuated from the tropical forest of Papua New Guinea after a bee sting badly infected his leg. And even after taking all precautions, Sebastião fell ill with malaria, disrupting one of his voyages.

One complication came when Sebastião switched to using digital cameras, which required not only different handling of the images from each trip, but also new printing techniques so that photos shot with film and digitally were indistinguishable. In our Paris office, Françoise Piffard and Marcia Navarro Mariano played a crucial role in every stage of production, while Valérie Hue and Olivier Jamin managed the archives and digital copies. Beyond our in-house team, Adrien Bouillon prepared contact sheets and working prints, while Dominique Granier worked on analog copies producing silver prints and verifying the negatives made by the Dupon laboratory from digital images. We are especially indebted to Philippe Bachelier for advising us on the move from analog to digital images.

Each of the trips involved a complex follow-up process. At first, Sebastião would return with hundreds of rolls of film which had to be developed; from contact sheets, images were selected to be made into work prints; and from these, we chose the photos to be provided, along with an accompanying text, to our partner magazines. After Sebastião began using digital cameras, he returned to Paris with memory cards that we transferred to contact sheets and made work prints. In that sense our routine changed little, while Sebastião could carry on working in exactly the same way as before.

By 2011, with Sebastião's travels close to completion, the time came to start preparing the next stage—that of designing and selecting the photographs for this book and accompanying exhibitions. And as with *Workers* and *Migrations*, the exciting prospect of showing *Genesis* around the world posed new challenges of planning and organization.

We are indebted to an array of people, notably to those in our Paris office who have been engaged throughout and those who played vital roles at crucial moments, including our old friend Alan Riding, who helped prepare the texts in this book. We also cannot forget those too numerous to name who helped Sebastião as ship captains, bush pilots, guides, drivers and porters in remote corners of the planet.

Many organizations provided vital assistance: the Galápagos National Park, the Charles Darwin Foundation, the Fundación Vida Silvestre, Kluane National Park and Reserve, Fundação Nacional do Índio (FUNAI), UNICEF, UNEP, Conservation International,

Wildlife Conservation Society of New York, Géo-Découverte, UNESCO's World Heritage Centre, and Tara Expéditions. To all, we express our thanks.

Whether organizations, sponsors or individuals, what brought us together at different moments was our faith in this project. Now that it is completed, I believe we can all take pride in what is not only an inspiring overview of the splendor of the Earth, but also a call to arms to protect it.

Lélia Wanick Salgado
Amazonas Images director

We owe our gratitude to the Brazilian company, VALE. Founded in the 1940s, this enterprise has been a central part of the life of the region where both of us were born and raised. When we created Instituto Terra, VALE played a very important role by providing seedlings from its own reforestation program as well as other timely assistance. And it has continued to support Instituto Terra ever since, most recently working with us on the recovery of hundreds of water sources across the watershed of the Rio Doce. Given this close relationship, we turned to VALE when part of our original editorial partners could no longer sustain *Genesis* and the company again responded with enthusiasm. Without its participation, our project could not have been completed as planned.

Sebastião Salgado and *Lélia Wanick Salgado*

MESSAGE FROM UNESCO

Sustainability is the great challenge of the 21st century and, to achieve this, we must start with the way we see the world, with how we think about it, how we act towards it.

This goal underpins all of UNESCO's work in education, the sciences, culture and communication: Peace and sustainability must be crafted in the minds of women and men, and especially young minds.

This is the power of *Genesis*, this new book by Sebastião Salgado. It has the power to open our eyes, to change how we see the world. This is the first step towards changing our behavior.

Sebastião Salgado's photographs capture the majesty and the mystery of life. They also express the complexity of the challenges we face. Working in his signature black and white, he has produced an inspiring testament to the fragile beauty of the world.

UNESCO and Sebastião Salgado have often collaborated, guided by our shared commitment better to understand humanity and our natural environment and to share this understanding as widely as possible. In this context, UNESCO's World Heritage Centre helped to provide guidance and advice during the early stages of *Genesis*. Focusing on sites and regions around the globe, Salgado's work highlights landscapes, animals and peoples that remain almost untouched by the modern world.

The result is a tribute to the breathtaking and precious wealth of our planet and its sometimes forgotten corners. I see these images as a call to action—for UNESCO to continue its work laying foundations for sustainability; and for us all to recognize the role that each of us must play in safeguarding the world and ways of life that nourish us. For this inspiration, I wish to thank Sebastião Salgado.

Irina Bokova
Director-General of UNESCO

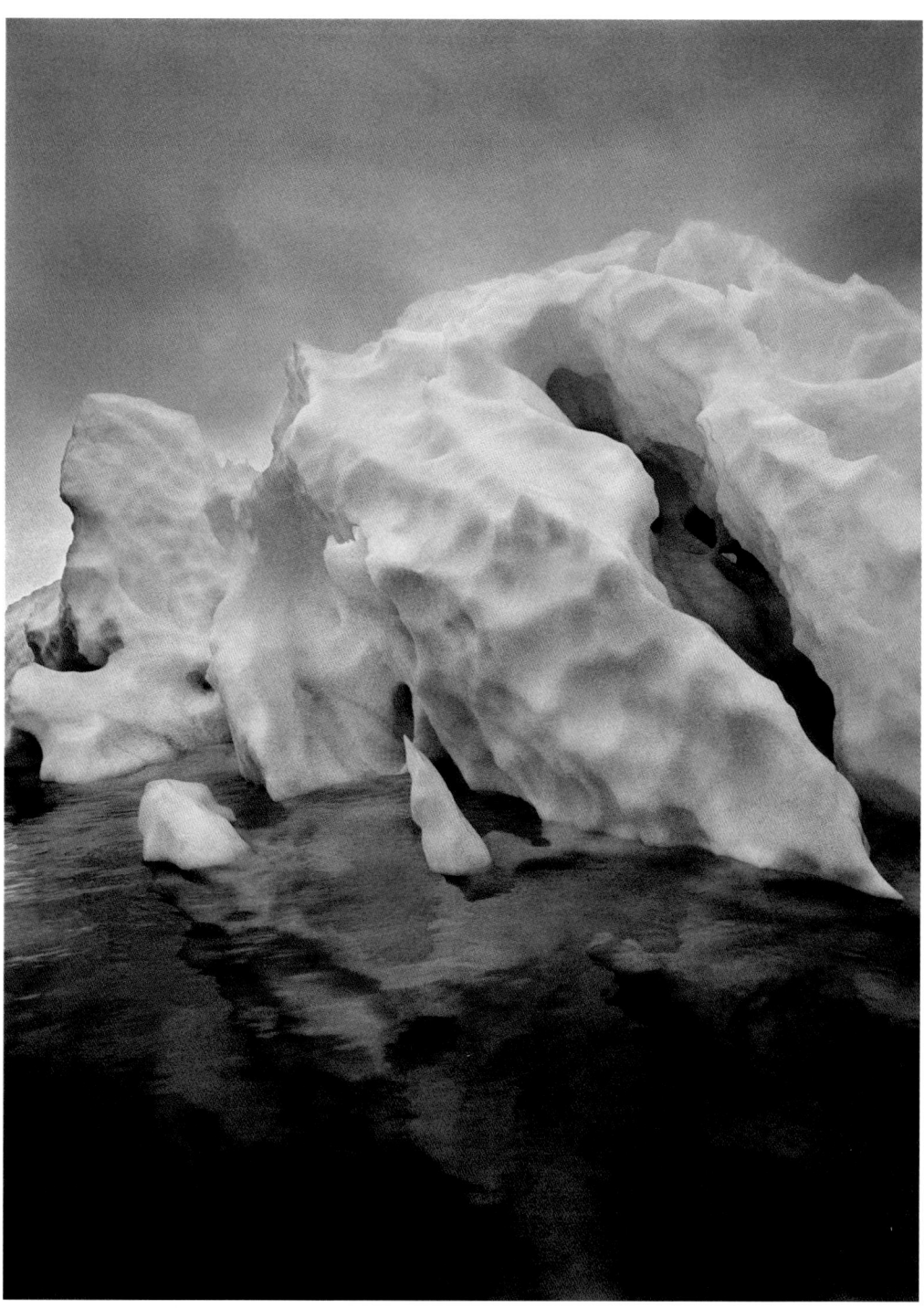

PLANET SOUTH

Twice the size of Australia, Antarctica seems even larger on maps because its landmass lies hidden beneath a vast frozen blanket that stretches hundreds of miles into the southern oceans. The coldest, driest and windiest of the world's five continents, Antarctica's fierce ecosystem reaches as far as the Falkland Islands, South Georgia and the South Sandwich Islands, and the southern mountains and coasts of Argentina and Chile. And yet in this harsh environment, the cycle of life goes on. How could it not be part of *Genesis*?

The only viable time for non-scientists to visit the region is during the southern hemisphere's summer. Heading by boat south from Cape Horn, we stopped briefly at the Diego Ramírez Archipelago, miniscule islands absolutely crammed with albatross. Some 500 miles (800 kilometers) of wild sea later, as we approached the Antarctic itself, I was stunned by the sheer size of the icebergs, the islands and the mainland beyond. Its mountain range, 2,200 miles (3,500 kilometers) long, with peaks above 14,500 feet (4,500 meters), was beyond our reach. But we landed on Deception Island, an almost perfect ring, which is entered through a narrow passage. And on King George Island, we found a colony of Gentoo and Adélie penguins cohabiting comfortably with herds of elephant seals, the world's largest seals, some weighing five tons.

On some islands, the snow cover melts in the summer, but we were warned of the perils of walking on the ice and glaciers of the mainland because of hidden crevasses. And the weather can change without notice. Our 120-foot (36-meter) boat was designed so that it would rise above rather than be crushed by ice, but we were still trapped for three days before the wind changed and the ice pack moved away. Sailing into the Weddell Sea was particularly hazardous because of the number of icebergs, some barely visible, others almost alarmingly large. Several had flat surfaces as long as an airport runway. One stood out because it was topped by a massive cube of ice, a sight so monumental that we called it "the cathedral."

Another trip to the south took us on a smaller vessel, from the Falkland Islands, home to huge concentrations of giant albatross, to South Georgia. On this lonely island, with its tiny human population, we found royal and macaroni penguins as well as the Antarctic cormorant and the southern giant petrel. Along with native sea lions and sea elephants, the island even has reindeer, introduced by Norwegian whalers a century ago. It then took us four days of rough seas to reach the South Sandwich Islands, nine tiny uninhabited volcanic islands, in the main covered in ice. Since they have no beaches, we approached them in a Zodiac inflatable boat and literally leapt ashore to find huge colonies of penguins. I really felt I was at the end of the world.

On the South American mainland, Antarctica still felt close, with the 48 glaciers of the Southern Patagonian Ice Field filling valleys that span the borders of Chile and Argentina. This area of the southern Andes is so inaccessible that, to this day, it has been only partly explored. We traveled on foot, camping in subzero temperatures and accompanied by the constant growl of the glaciers as they drag along stones and rocks deep under the ice. Across the globe, scientists are monitoring the shrinking of glaciers as global temperatures rise. We saw this happening at the edge of Lake Argentino, where large pieces of the Perito Moreno Glacier near Calafate break off and tumble into the water continuously.

I could not leave the South Atlantic without recording the southern right whale, which migrates to the Antarctic during the summer, then heads north to breed. One of the largest breeding grounds is off the Valdés Peninsula on Argentina's Atlantic coast, a natural sanctuary shaped like a crab with two sheltered gulfs. To spend several weeks in a boat among these whales was one of the most poignant experiences of my life. While we waited for the best light to photograph, 50-foot (15-meter) whales and their young played around us, sometimes coming so close that we could have stroked them. And who would not be moved by one of nature's grandest spectacles: a 40-ton animal leaping into the sky and then crashing back into the water?

Other creatures come to the peninsula to breed, including elephant seals, which become very aggressive during the mating season. The orca, commonly known as the killer whale, also hunts close to shore. It is a majestic and terrifying animal and, here, its chosen prey is the sea lion, which comes to breed on the beaches of the peninsula. Half a century ago, local fishermen stopped hunting sea lions, but these animals still fear humans. So to photograph them, I hid in a sand hole, knowing that the orcas were lying in wait should I frighten any sea lions into the sea. But, sooner or later, they must lead their young to the water and, inevitably, on several occasions, I saw an orca seize a baby in its teeth and swim away. I was saddened, but how could I question nature's ways?

Page 12 Iceberg moving on the Weddell Sea. Antarctic Peninsula. January and February 2005.

Opposite Mount Français on Anvers Island, beside the Gerlache Strait, offers one of the most spectacular views of the Antarctic Peninsula. January and February 2005.

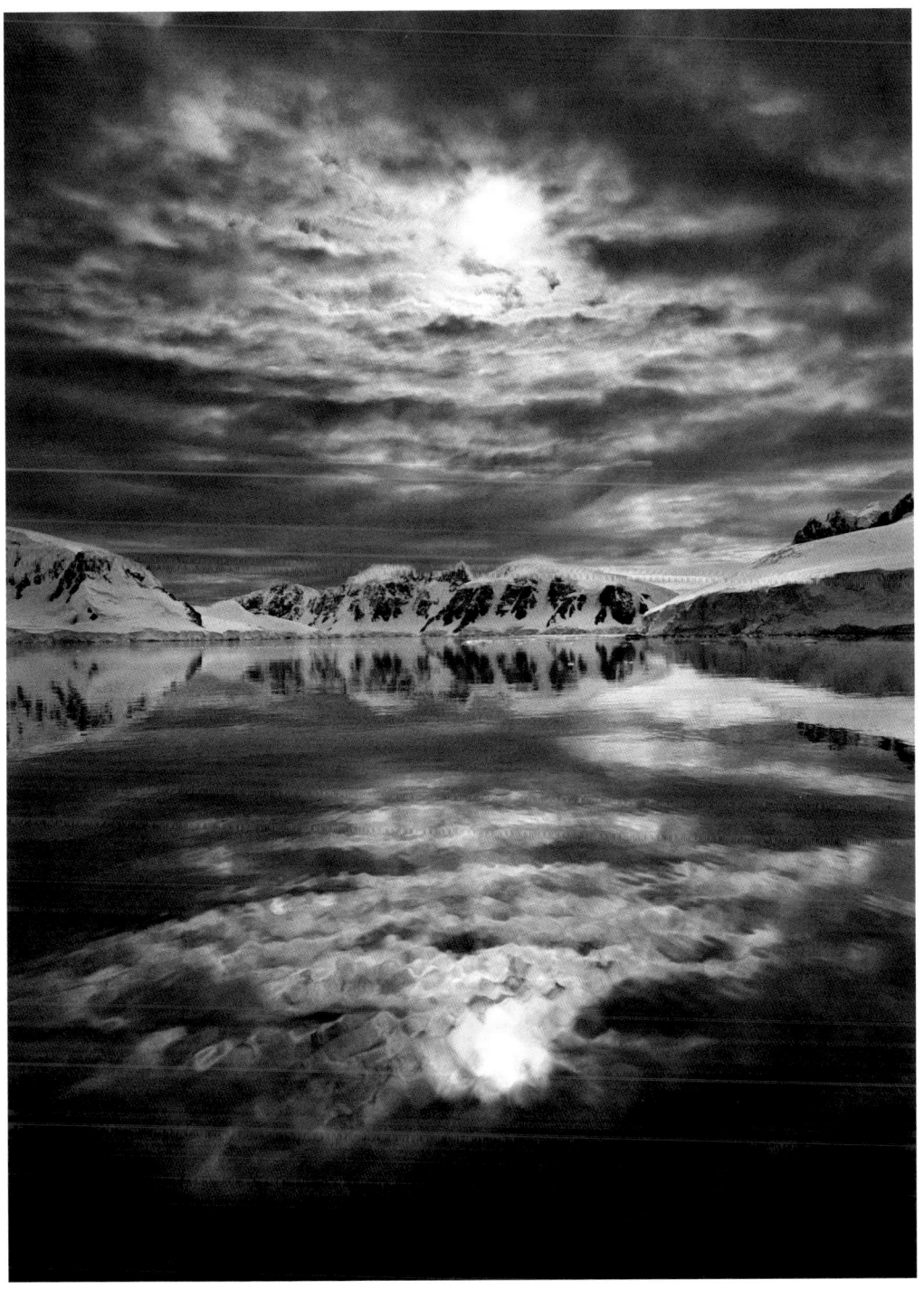

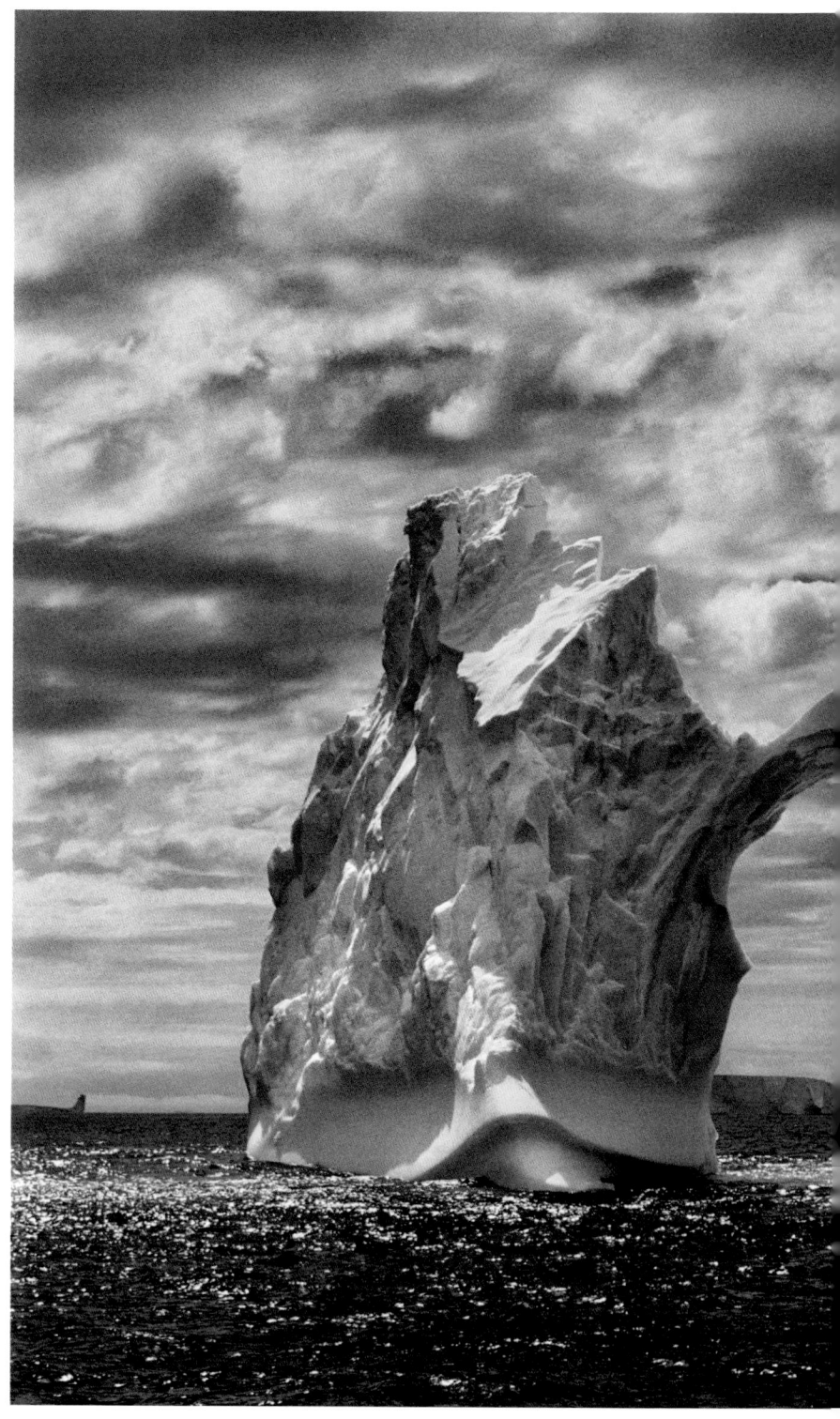

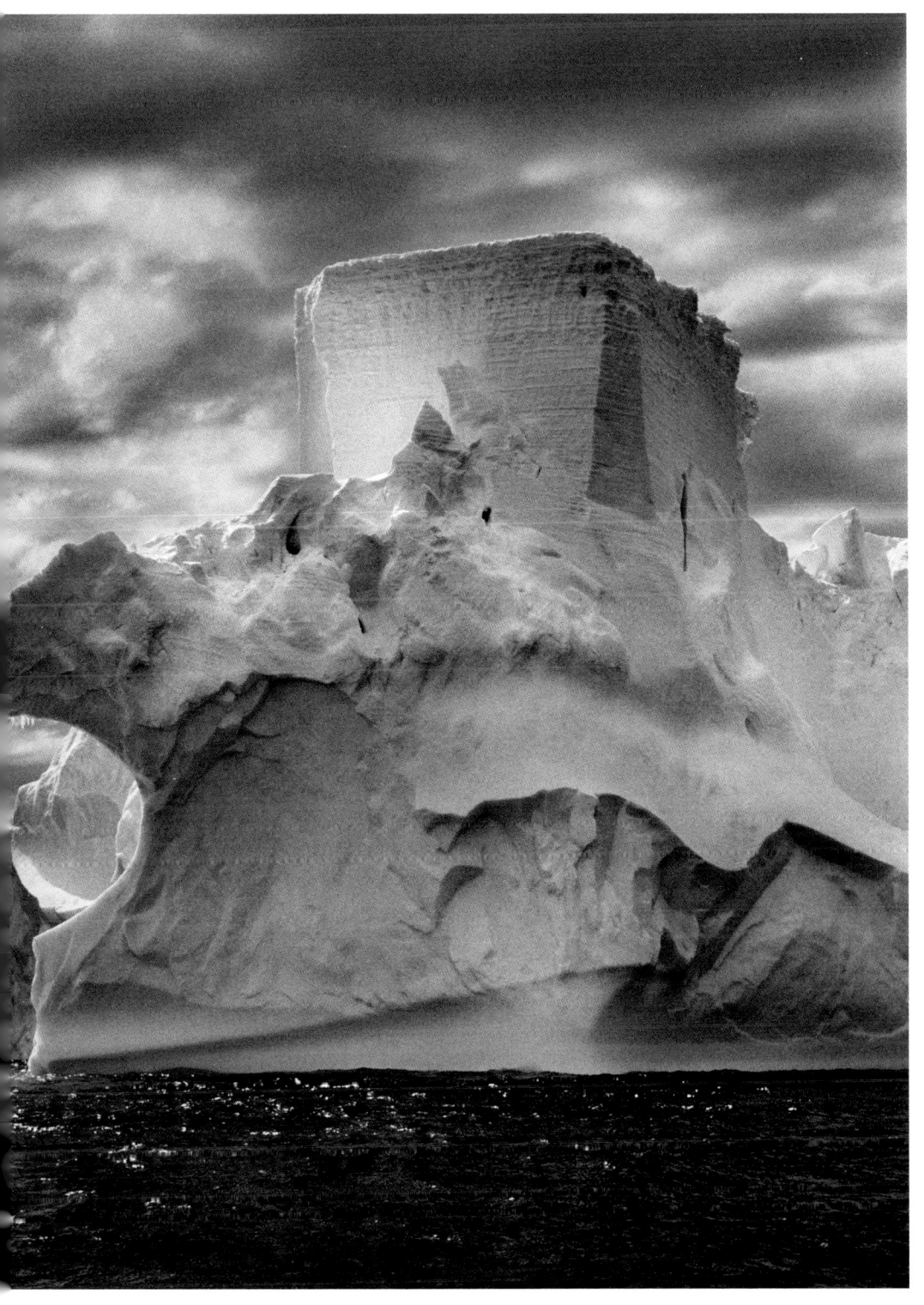

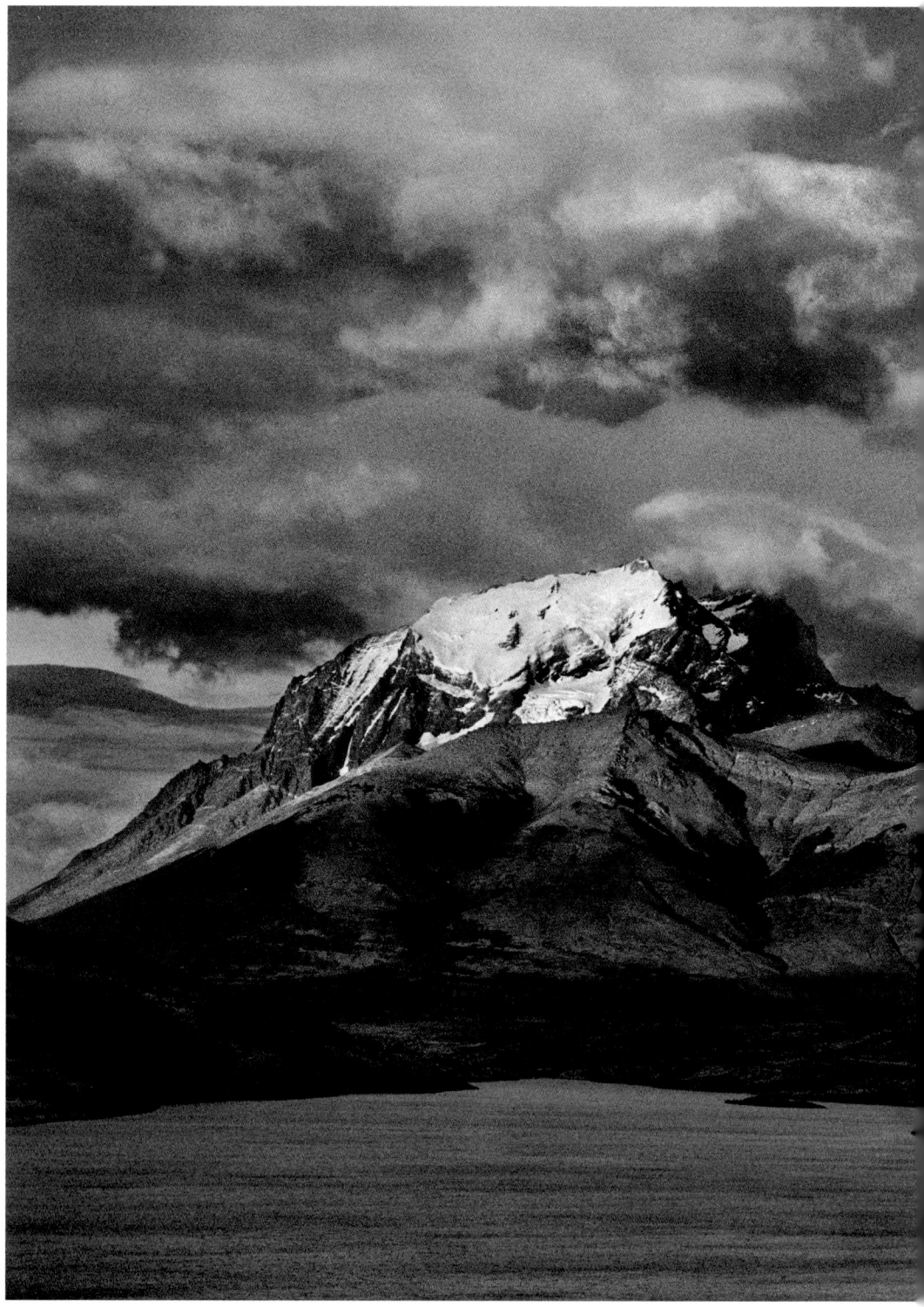

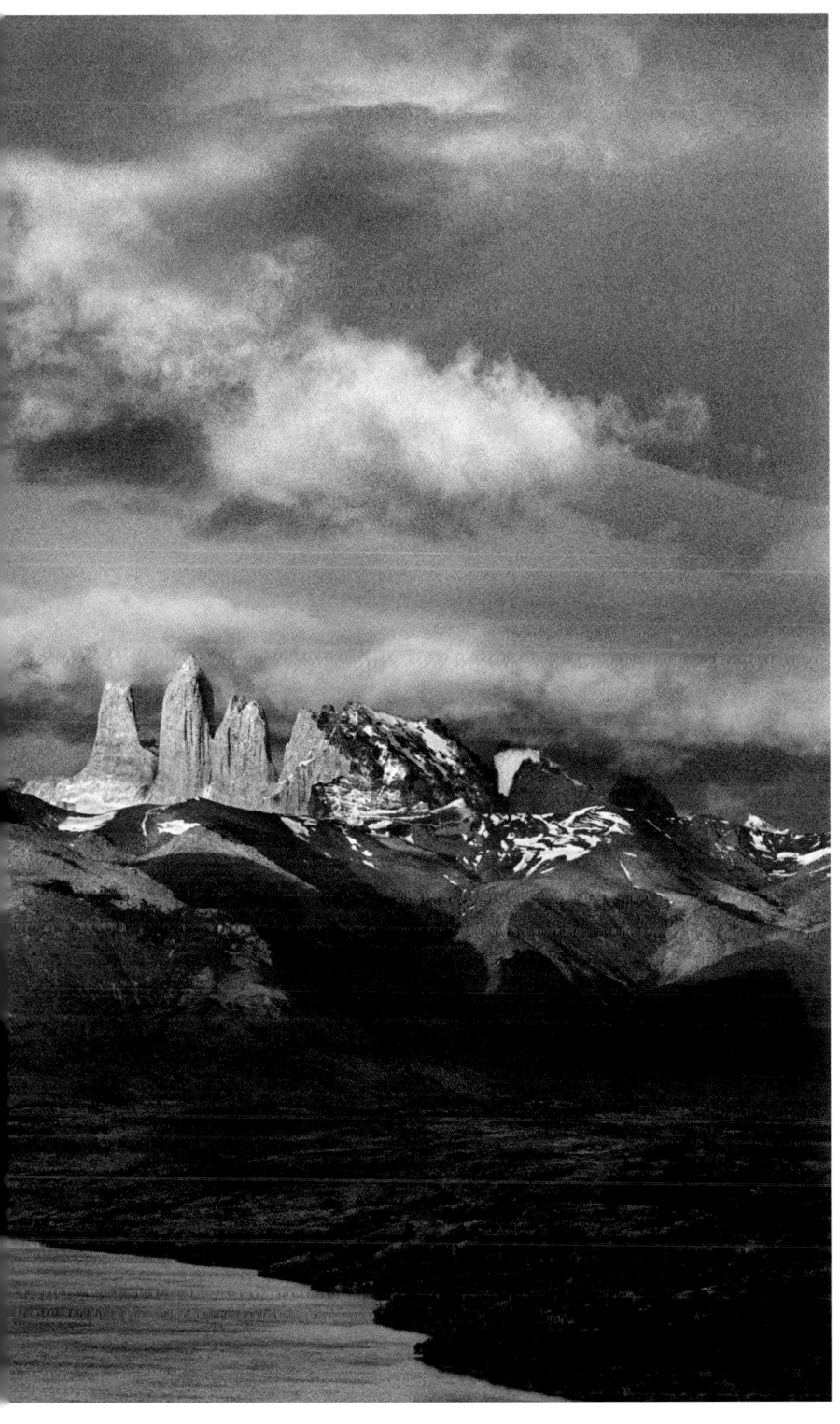

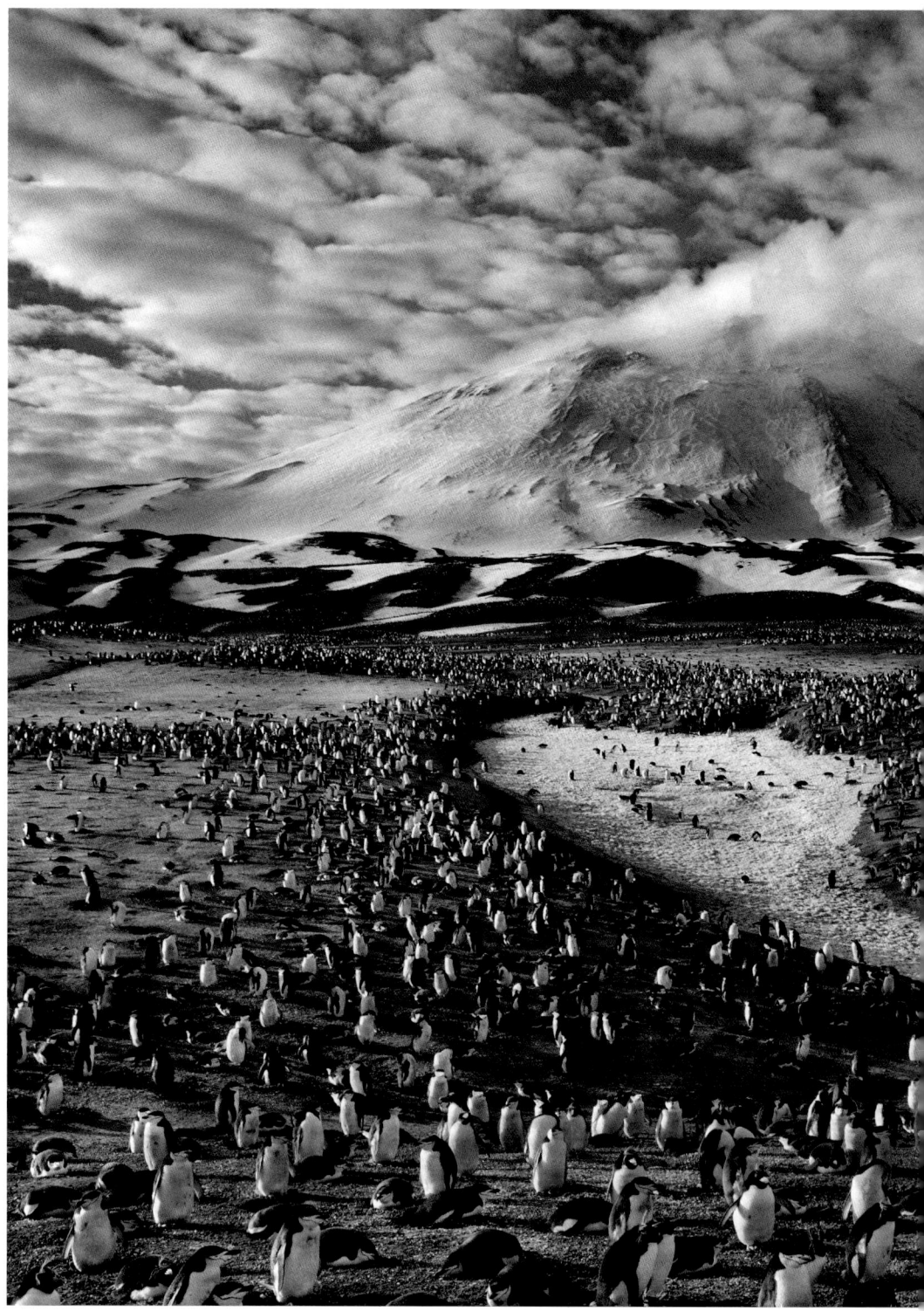

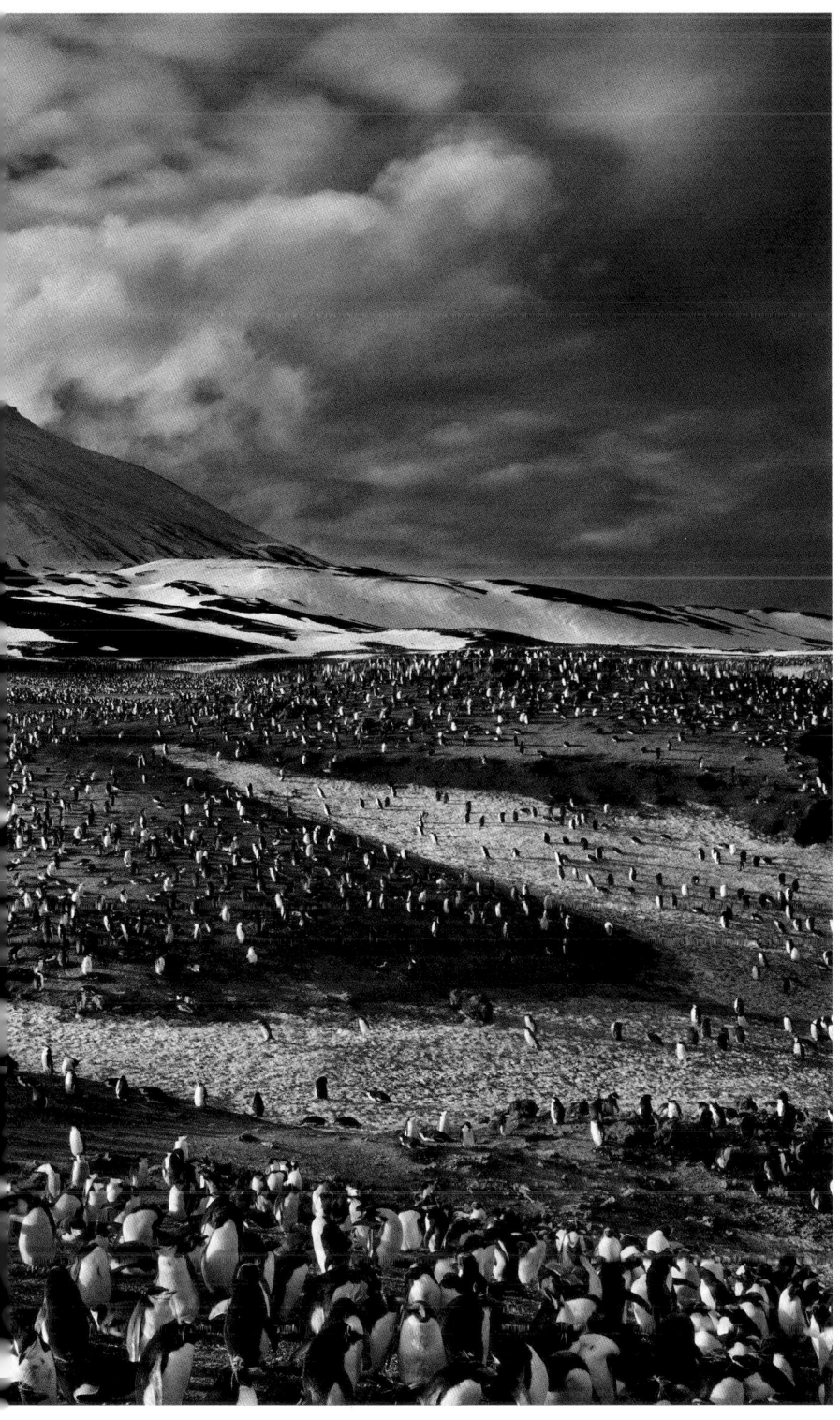

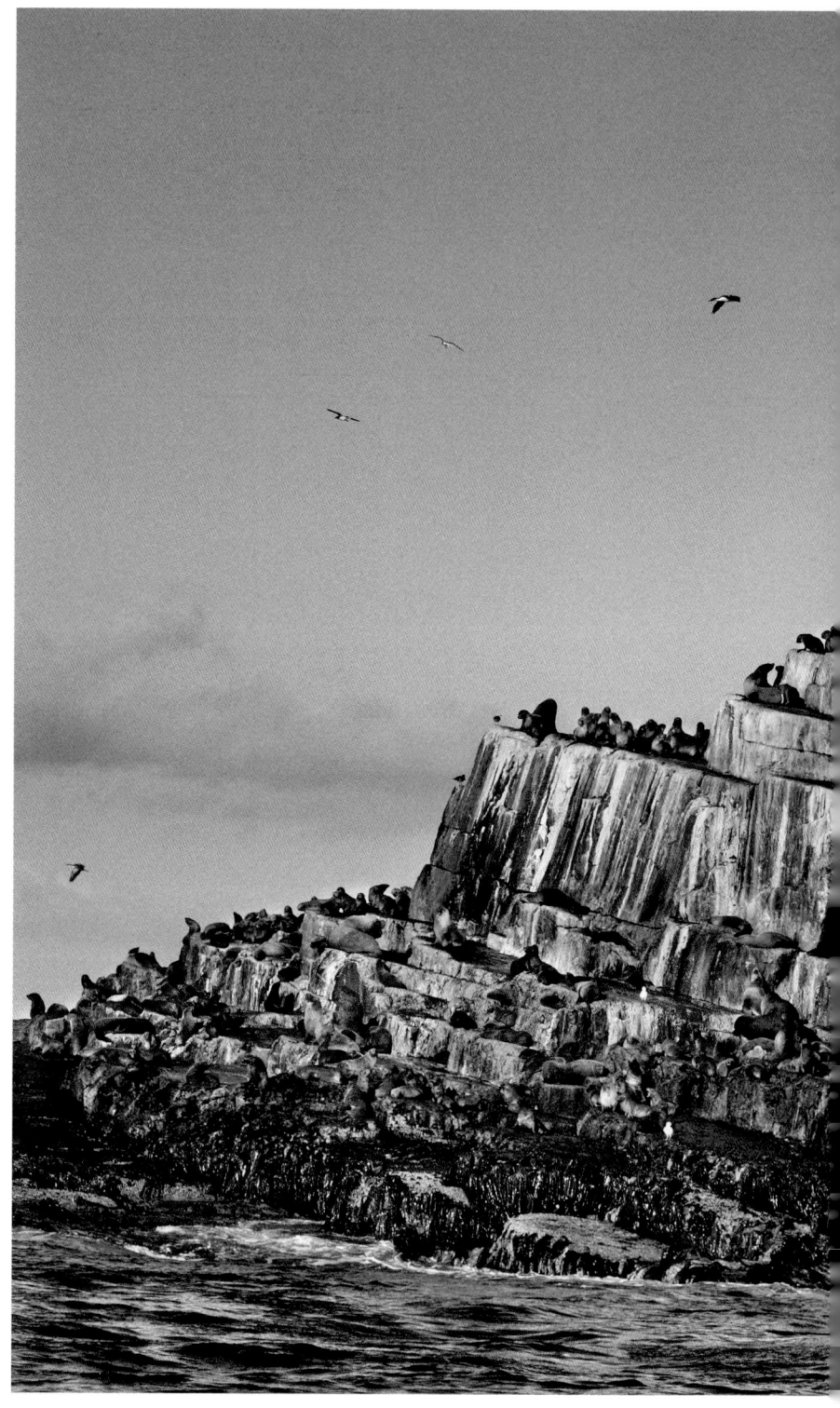

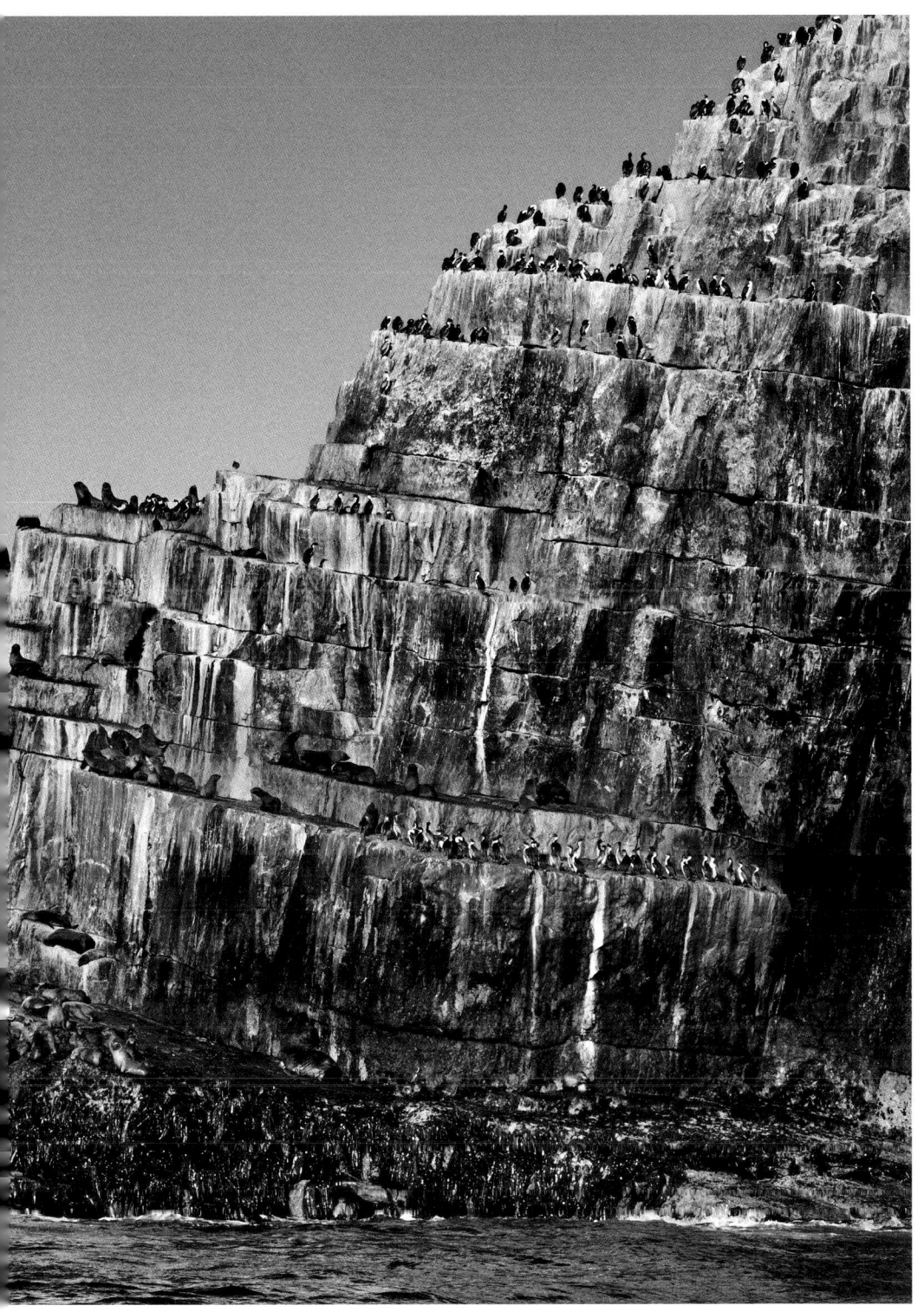

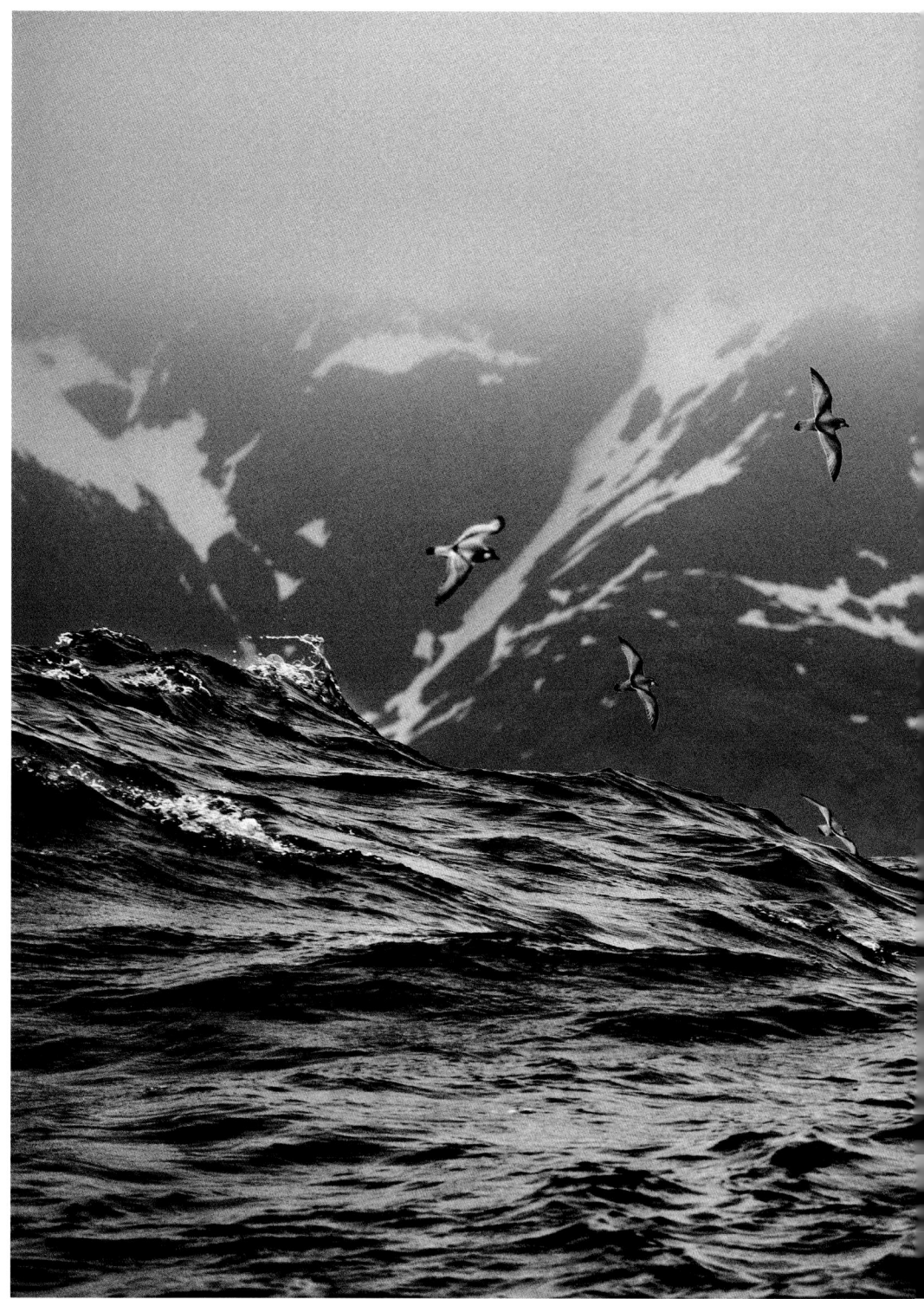

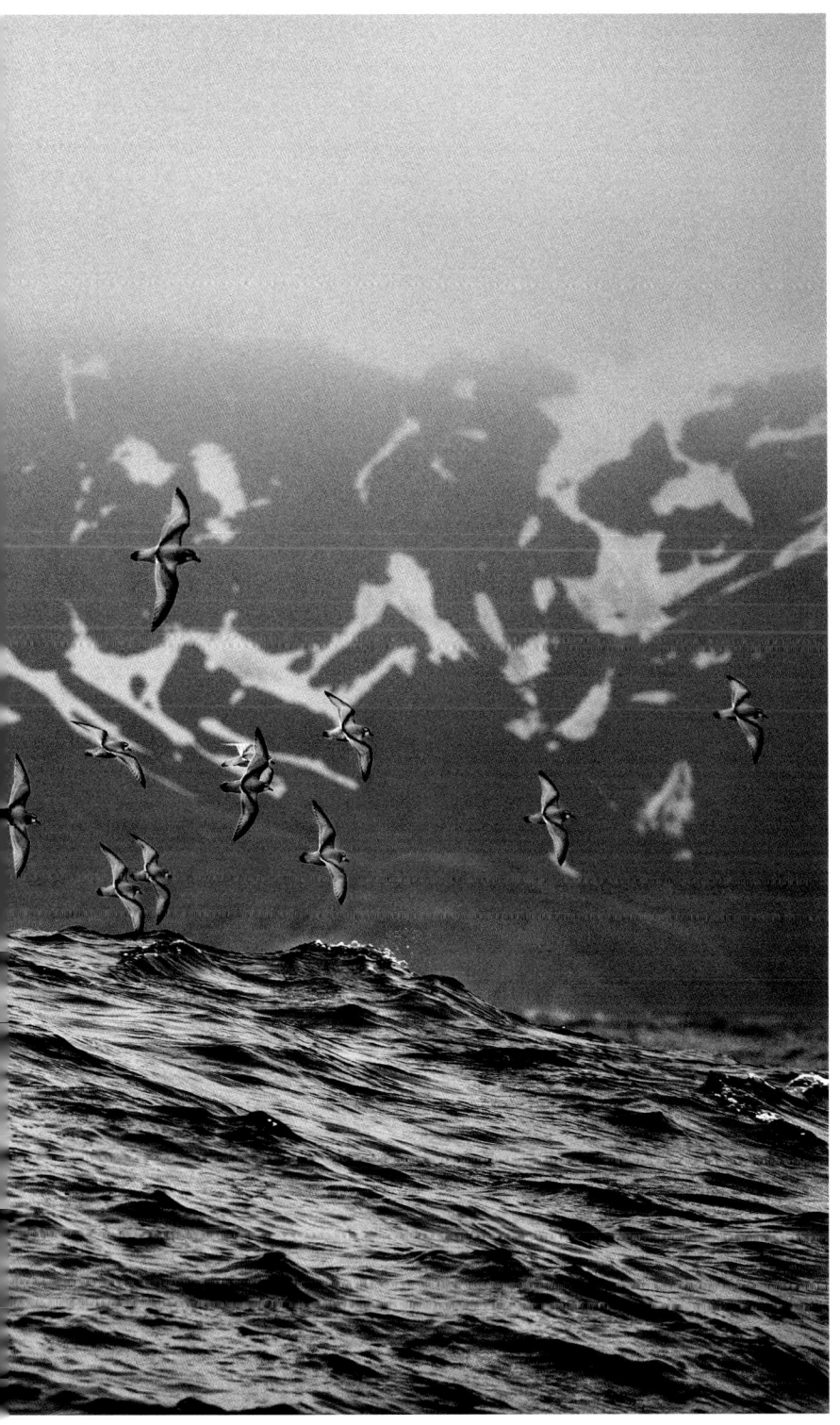

Pages 16/17 Iceberg between Paulet Island and the South Shetland Islands on the Weddell Sea. At sea level, earlier flotation levels are clearly visible where the ice has been polished by the ocean's constant movement. High above, a shape resembling a castle tower has been carved by wind erosion and detached pieces of ice. Antarctic Peninsula. January and February 2005.

Pages 18/19 The Torres del Paine mountain range near the southern end of the Southern Patagonian Ice Field contains some of the most spectacular and distinctive peaks to be found in the Patagonian Andes. Huge granite monoliths rise abruptly from the steppes, adding drama to the landscape. Chilean Patagonia. April 2007.

Pages 20/21 Zavodovski Island is the most accessible of the nine tiny volcanic South Sandwich Islands. A 1997 survey estimated that it is home to some 750,000 couples of chinstrap penguins (*Pygoscelis antarctica*) as well as a large colony of macaroni penguins (*Eudyptes chrysolophus*). This island boasts the largest concentration of penguins on Earth. The island's active volcano is visible in the background. South Sandwich Islands. November and December 2009.

Pages 22/23 Eddystone Rock. Colonies of fur seals (*Arctocephalus gazella*) and rock shags, or Magellanic cormorants (*Phalacrocorax magellanicus*), are grouped on the eroded terraces of the rock, the northernmost point of the Falkland Islands. November and December 2009.

Pages 24/25 Antarctic prions (*Pachyptila*) on Bird Sound, the 1,600-foot (500-meter) wide channel separating Bird Island from the South Georgia Island mainland. This petrel is common in the Antarctic Circle. South Georgia. November and December 2009.

Opposite and pages 28/29 Southern right whales (*Eubalaena australis*), drawn to the Valdés Peninsula because of the shelter provided by its two gulfs, the Golfo San José and the Golfo Nuevo, often navigate with their tails upright in the water. When a tail stands immobile for tens of minutes, it is probable that the whale is completely vertical in the water in a kind of resting position; it has also been claimed that the whales use their tails as a sail, allowing the wind to do the work. After close observation, it is possible to predict when a whale will jump: a sudden and swift movement of the tail provides the burst of energy that enables the whale to project its massive body out of the water. Valdés Peninsula. Argentina. September and October 2004.

Pages 30/31 Unusually, the southern right whale (*Eubalaena australis*) has two separate blow holes. As a result, a cloud of vapor in a distinctive V-shape appears when these whales surface. This makes them vulnerable to whale hunters, who can easily identify them from afar. Further, because of their natural curiosity, southern right whales will often approach boats, making the task of hunters still easier. Valdés Peninsula. Argentina. September and October 2004.

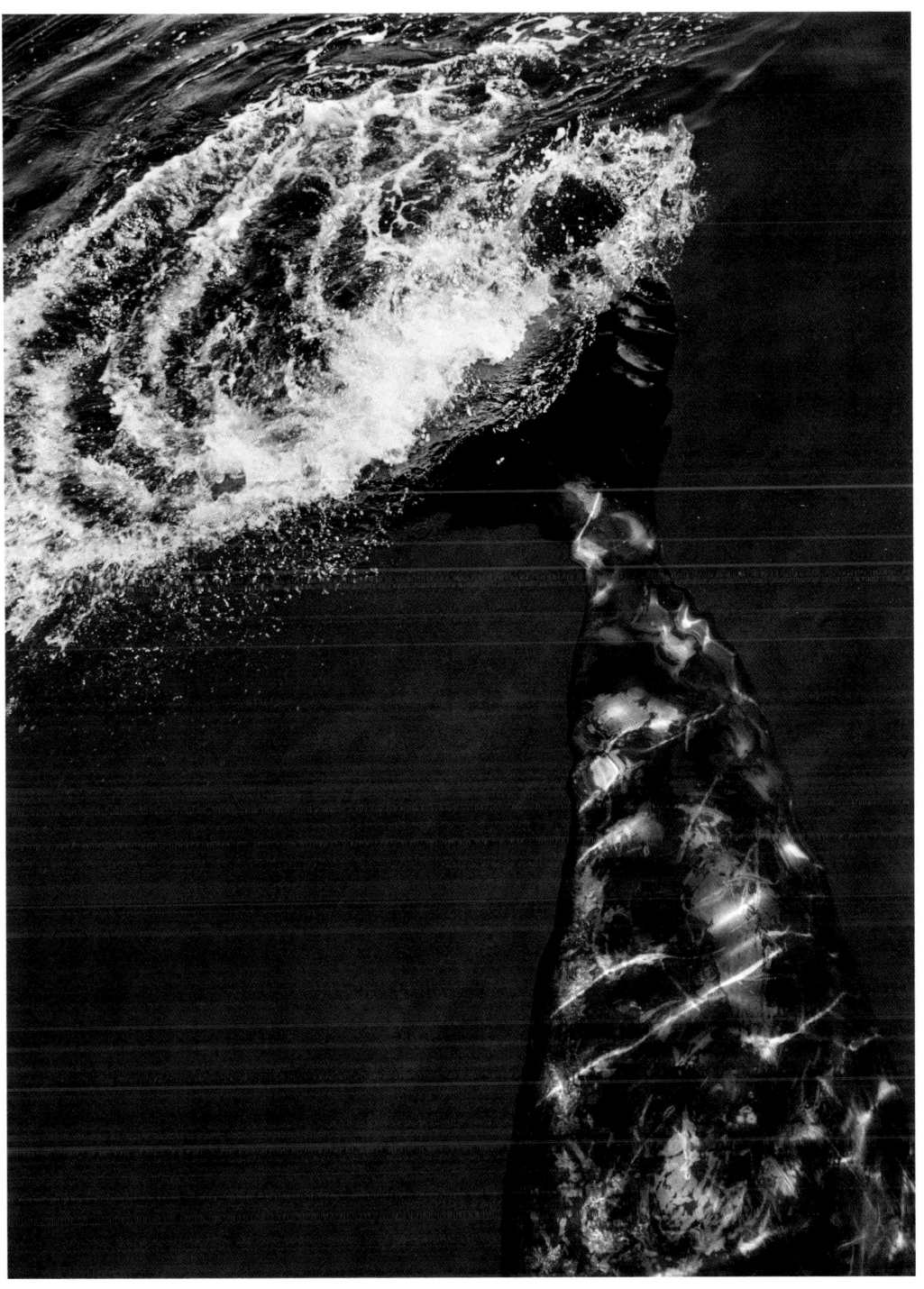

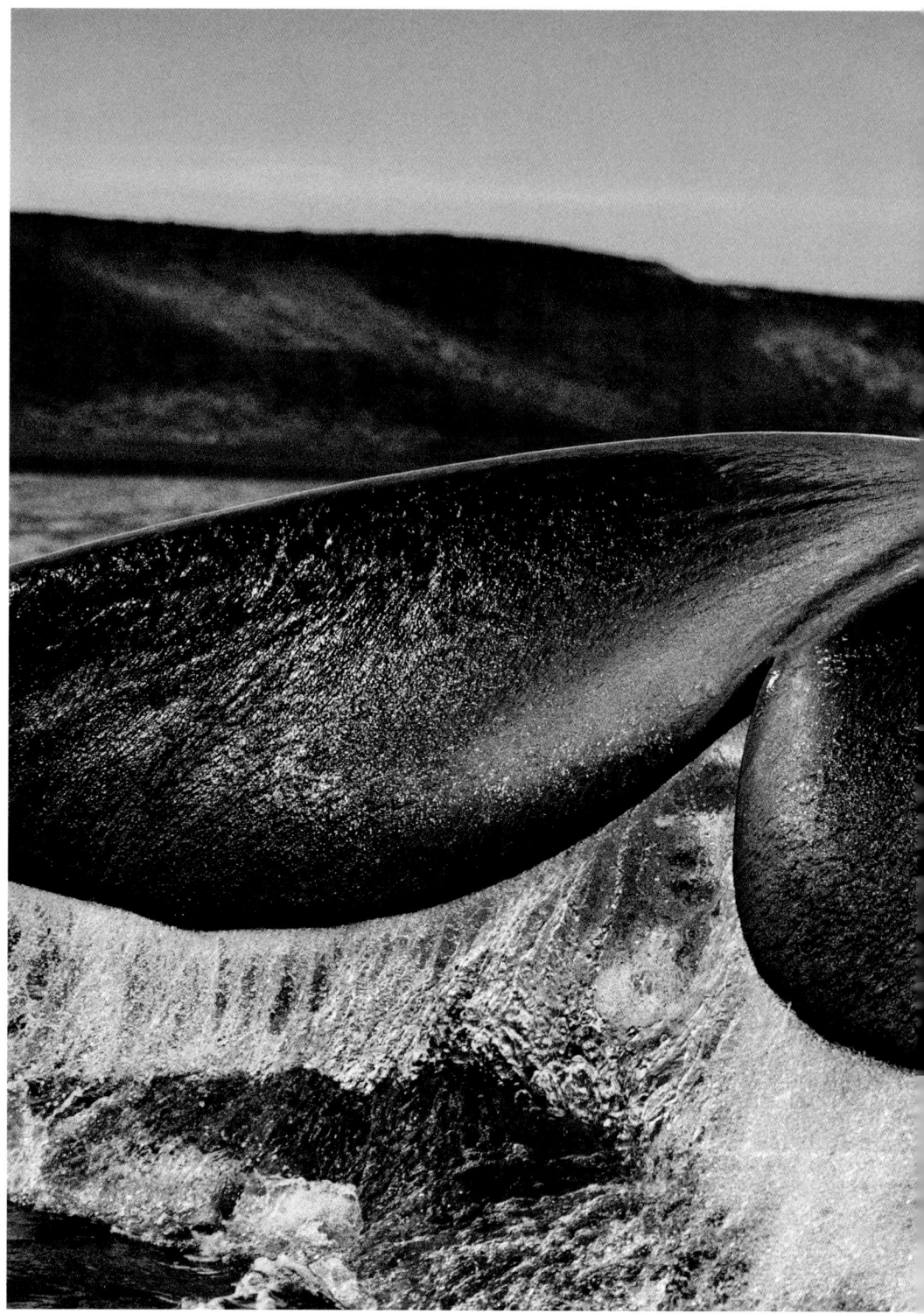

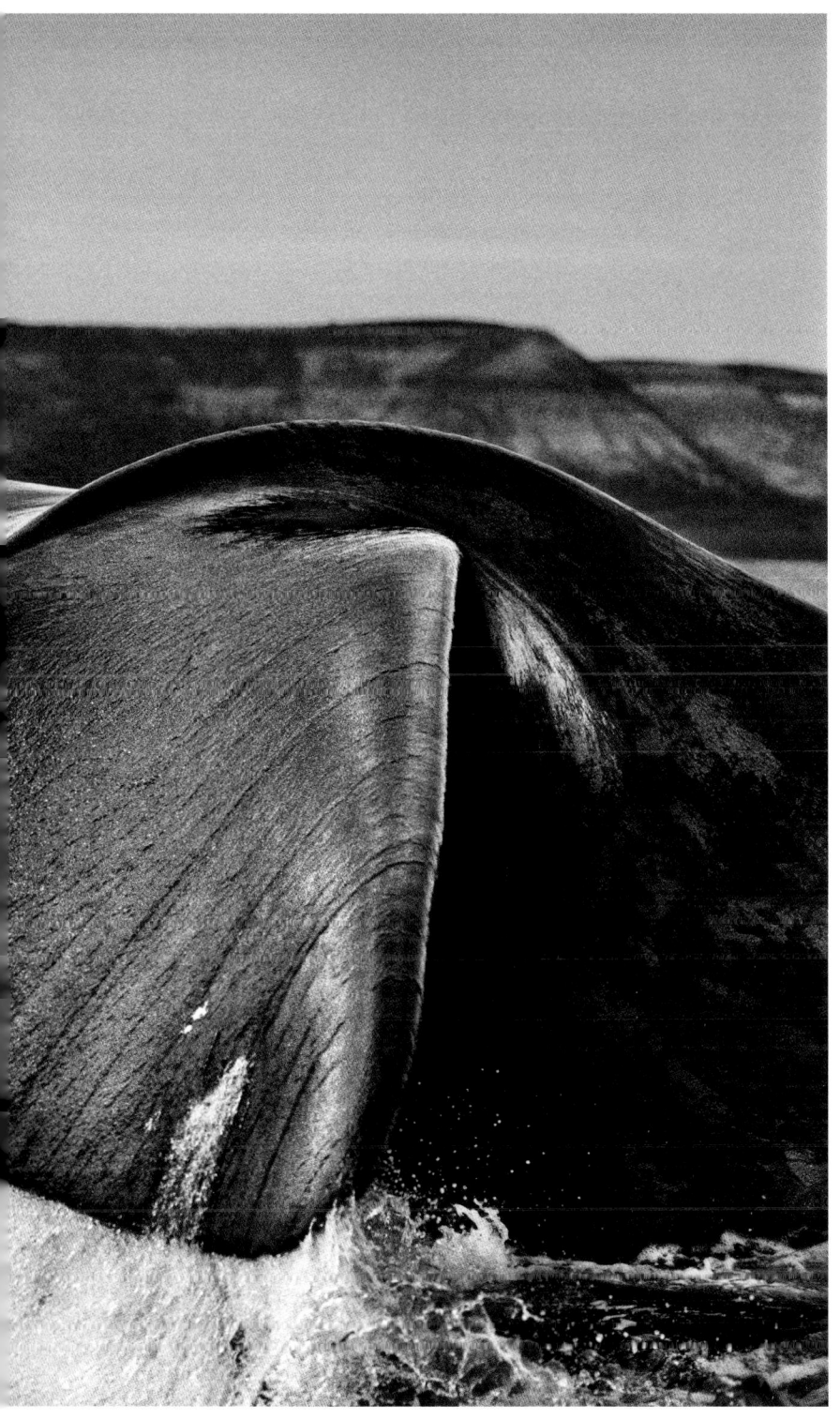

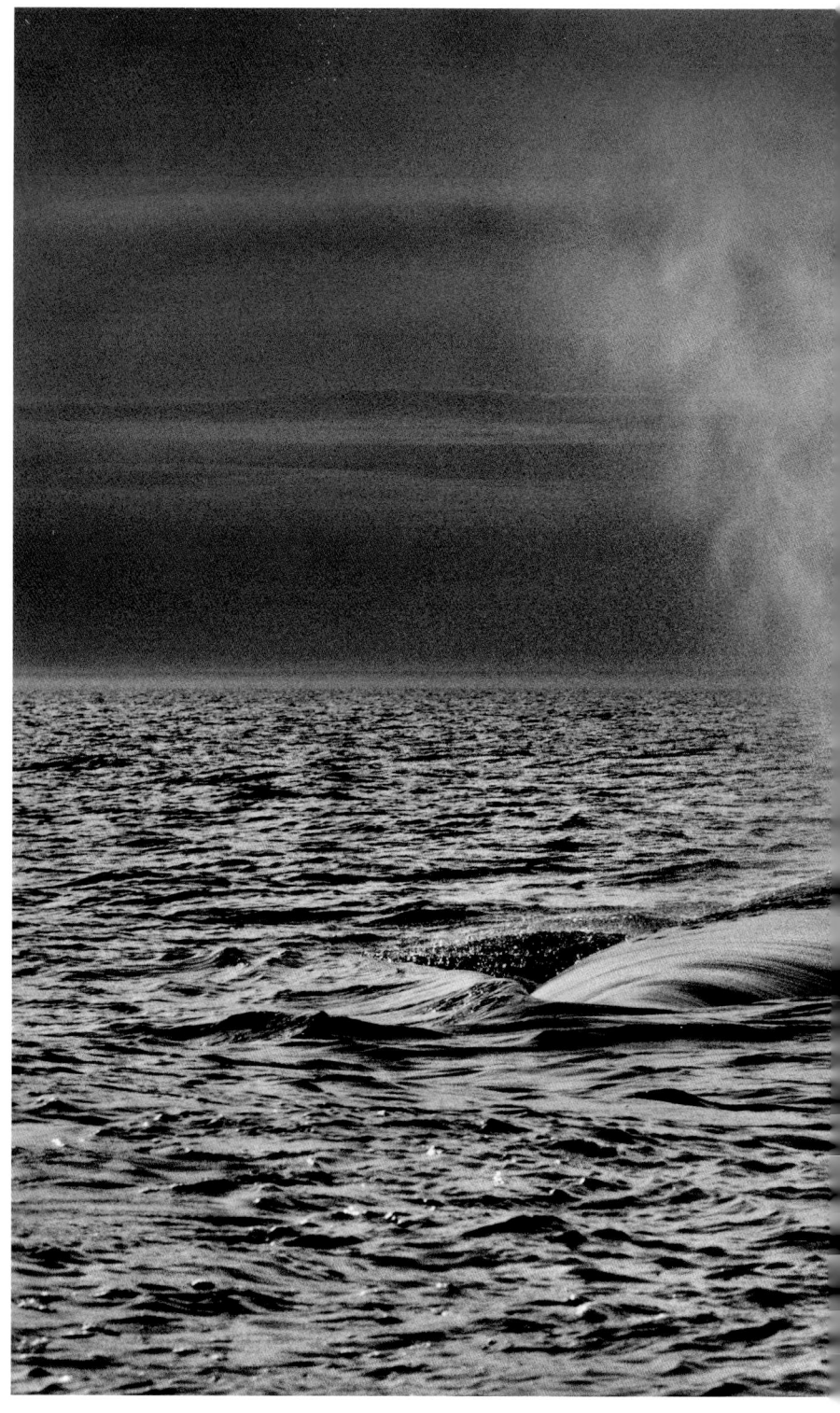

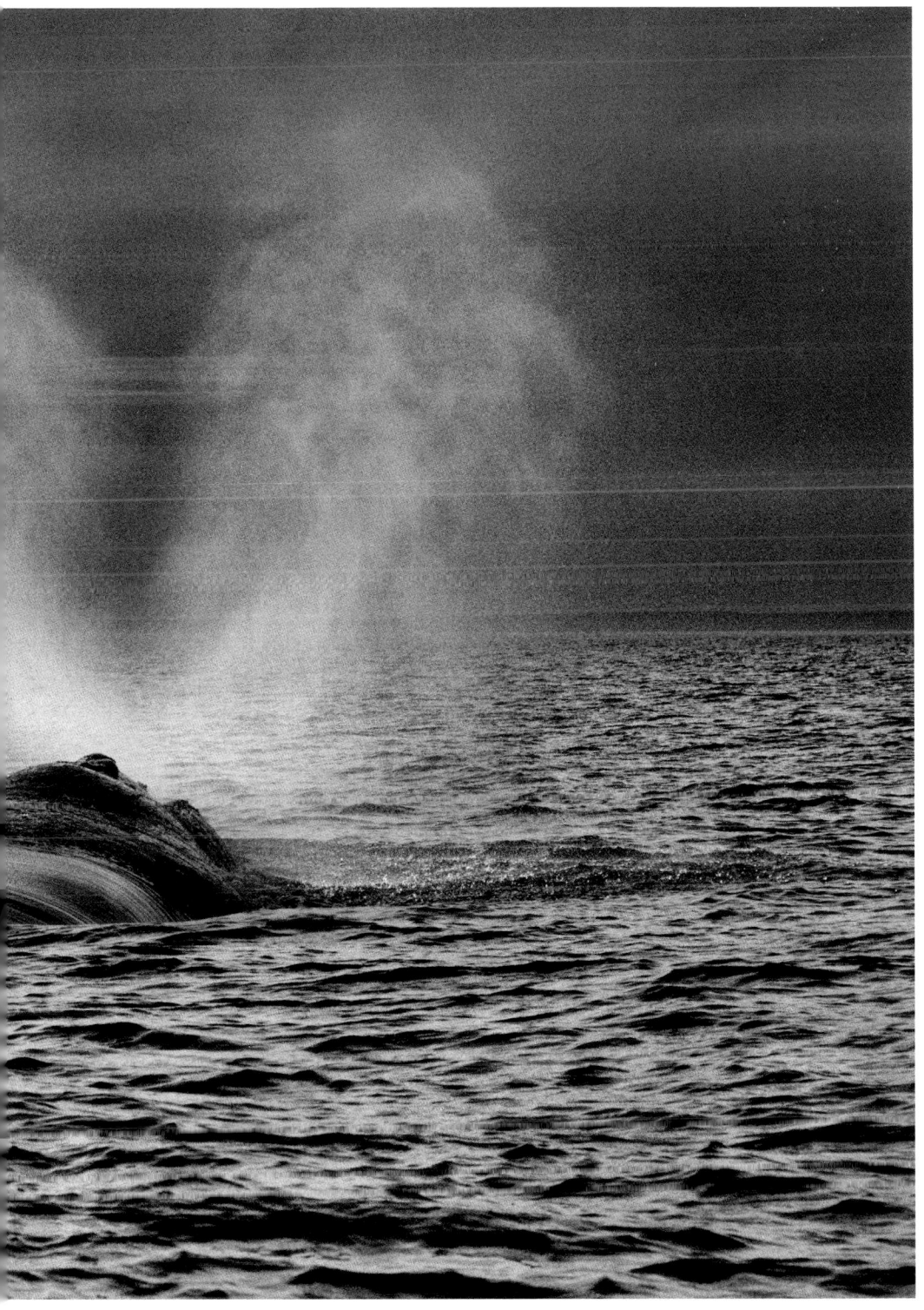

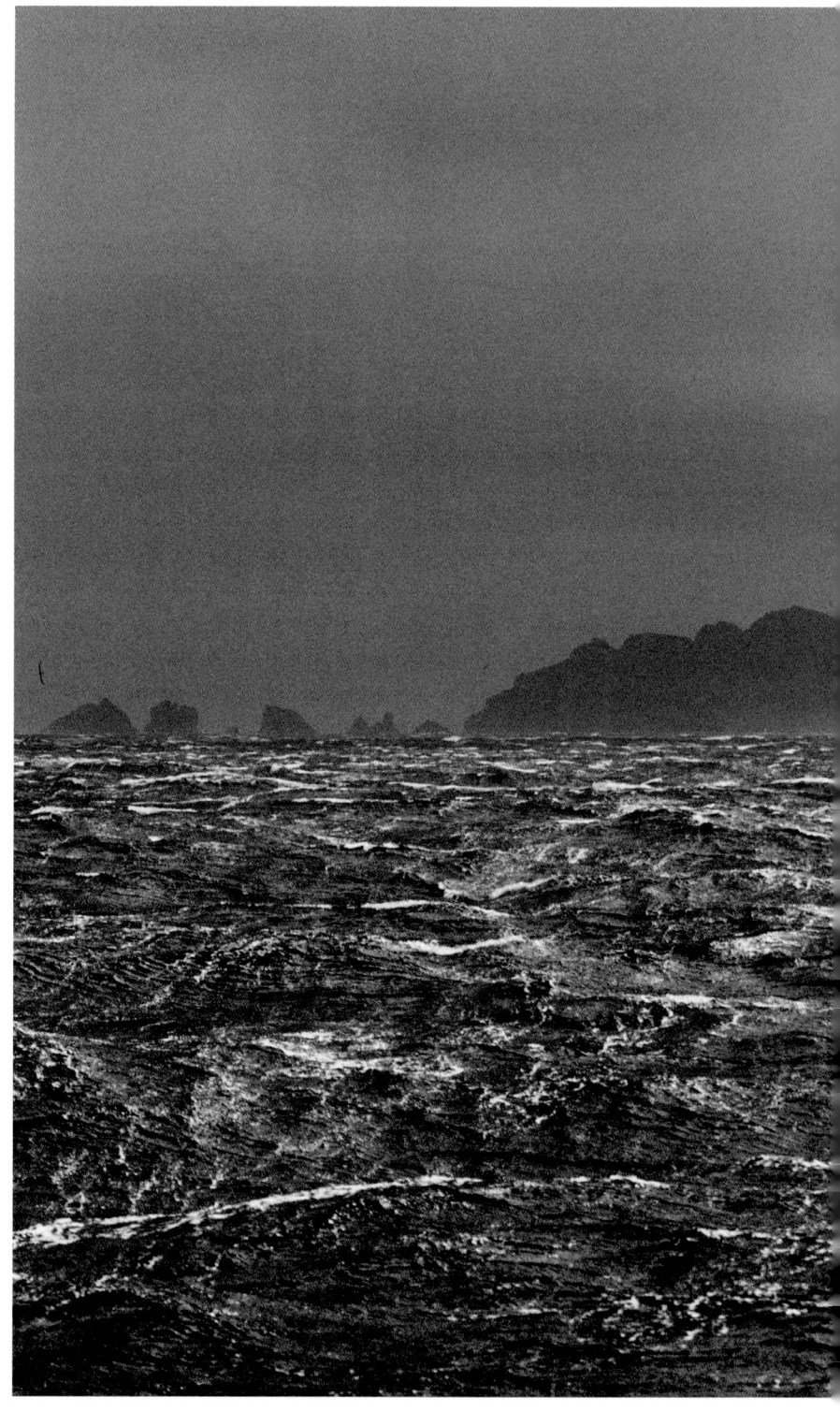

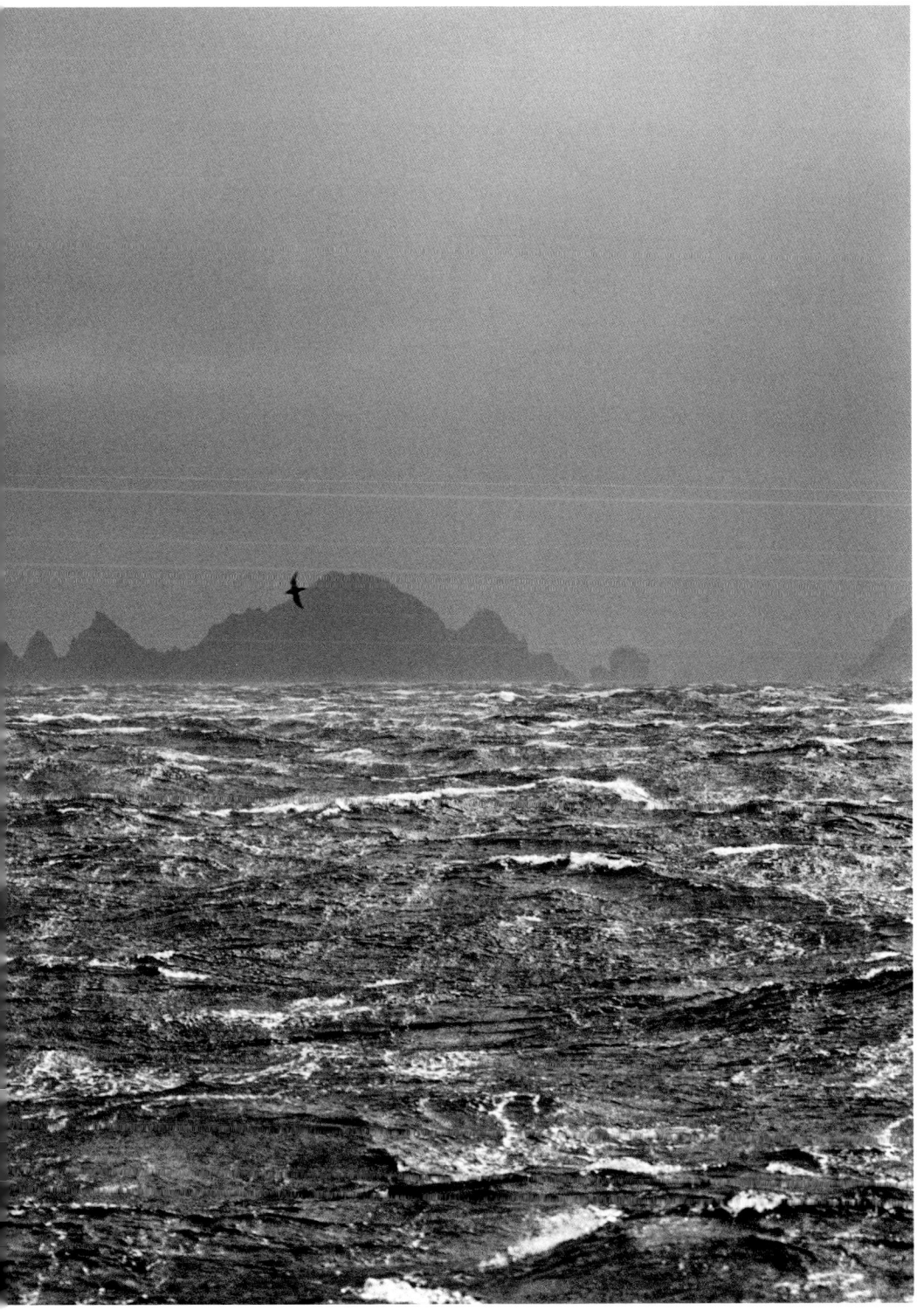

Pages 32/33 The Drake Passage, which separates the islands of Cape Horn from the South American mainland, also links the Atlantic and the Pacific Ocean and provides the route from Tierra del Fuego to the Antarctic. Unsurprisingly, it is often very stormy, with winds gusting at over 50 knots per hour. Here the rough seas around Cape Horn. Chilean waters. January and February 2005.

Opposite At times, only the tails of the southern right whales (*Eubalaena australis*) are visible. Measuring as much as 20 feet (6 meters), they glide through the water erect, as if announcing a surfacing submarine. Other times, the whales remain completely still for several minutes at a time, their bodies under water and their tails spread like huge sails. Then, quite suddenly, in a noisy display of strength, they may strike the surface with their tail, sending shock waves through the water, which other whales presumably know how to interpret. Valdés Peninsula. Argentina. September and October 2004.

Pages 36/37 Off the Valdés Peninsula on Argentina's east coast, whales are victims of an unusual ecological imbalance provoked by fish factories. Fish remains, thrown back into the sea or dumped on land, have made food easily available to seagulls and have encouraged their reproduction. But there are now so many seagulls in the area that they have found a new source of nourishment in whales themselves. They land on the backs of surfacing whales, puncture the skin with their strong beaks and eat the flesh of the whale. The resulting wounds then make it easier for other seagulls to increase the size of the lesion. Some injuries become so serious that they endanger the whales when they travel to much colder waters further south. Valdés Peninsula. Argentina. September and October 2004.

Pages 38/39 On King George Island, off the Antarctic Peninsula, there is a large concentration of elephant seals (*Mirounga leonina*). As adults, these animals, weighing four to five tons, are the largest seals in the world. Young males gather in small groups and practice harmless combat. This training is crucial preparation for the mating season: their aim is to gather a large number of females in a harem, but they must be ready to fight off other males who try to separate a female in order to mate with her. On the Antarctic islands or on the coasts of Patagonia, a male elephant seal may control as many as 100 females. Antarctic Peninsula. January and February 2005.

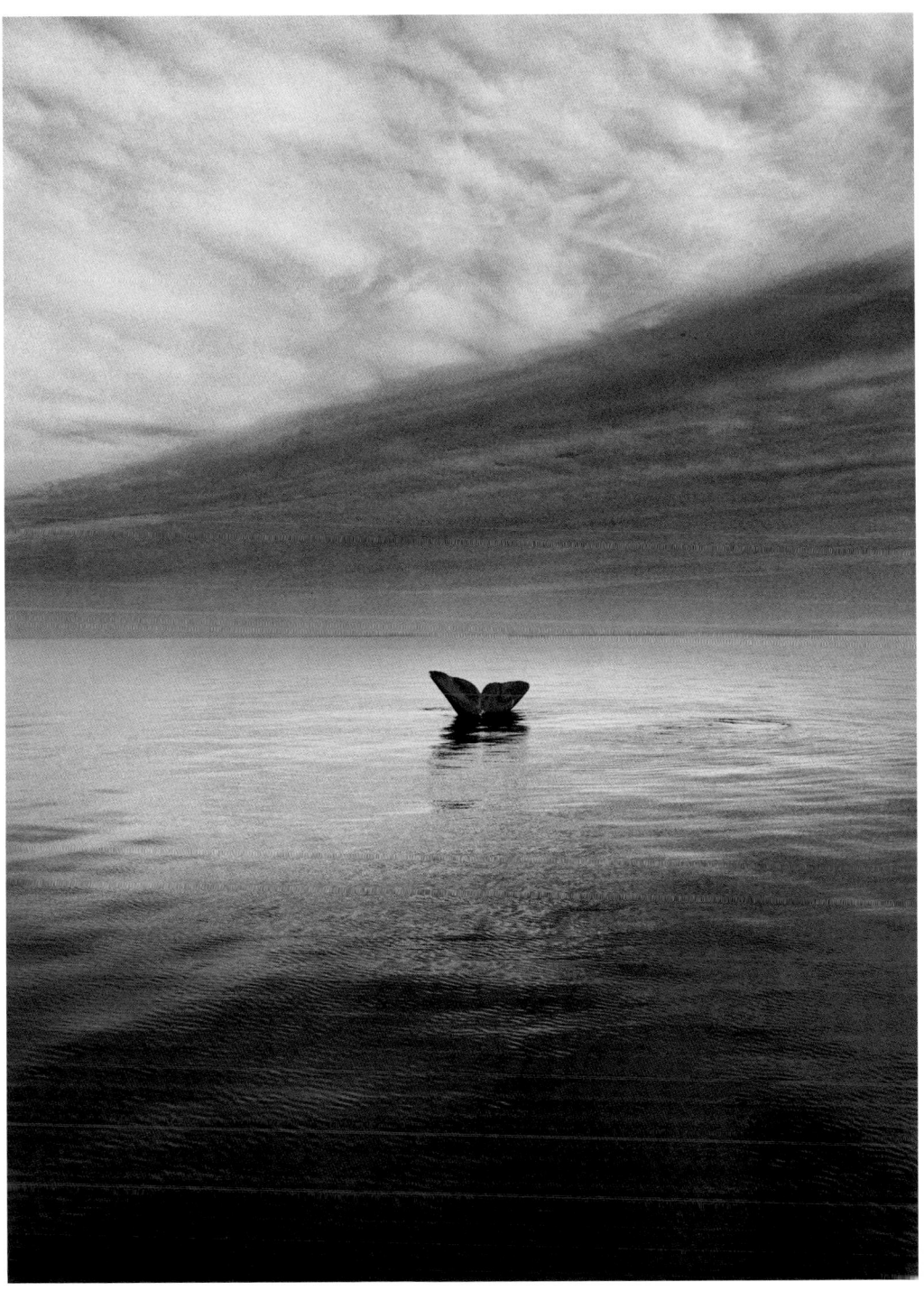

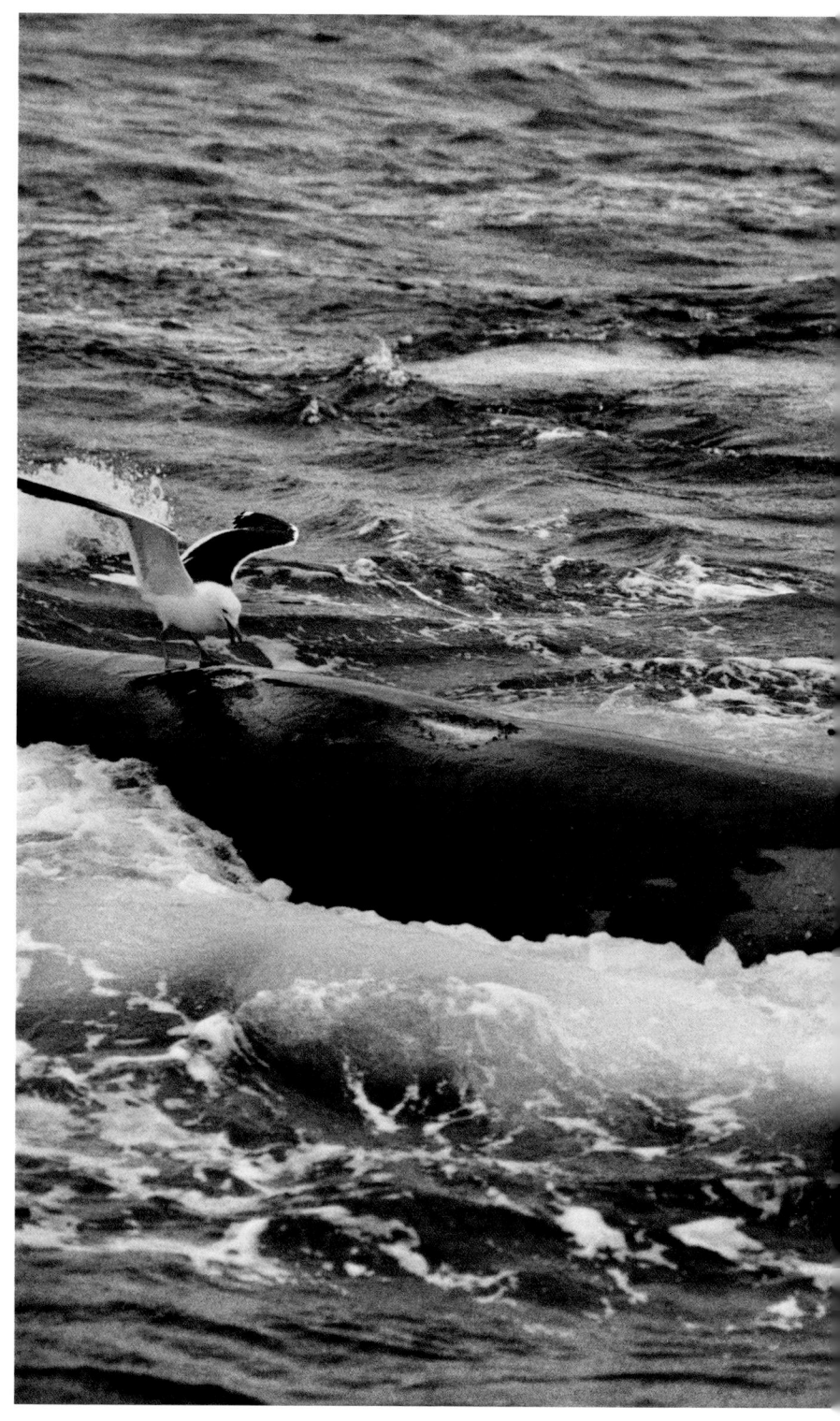

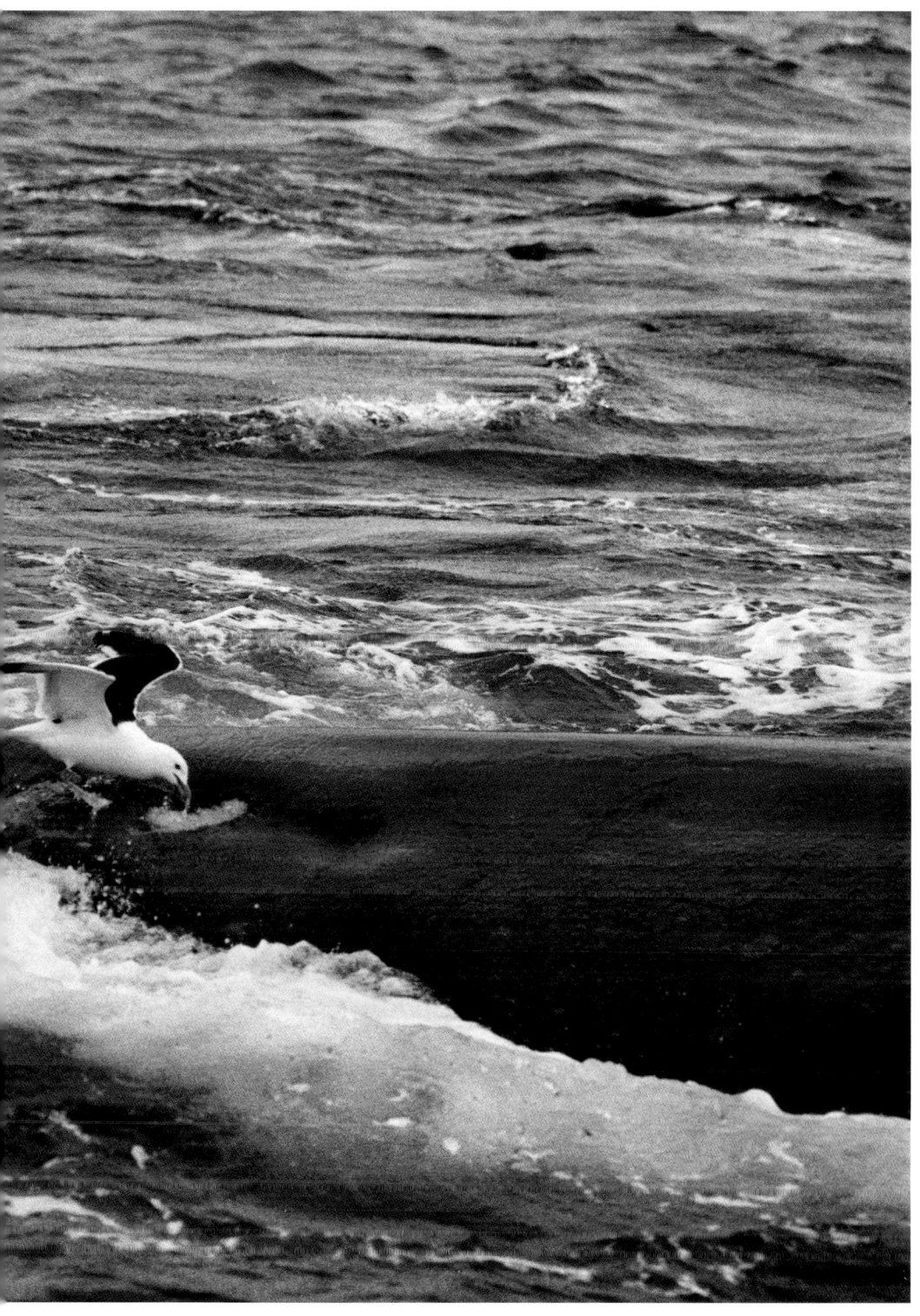

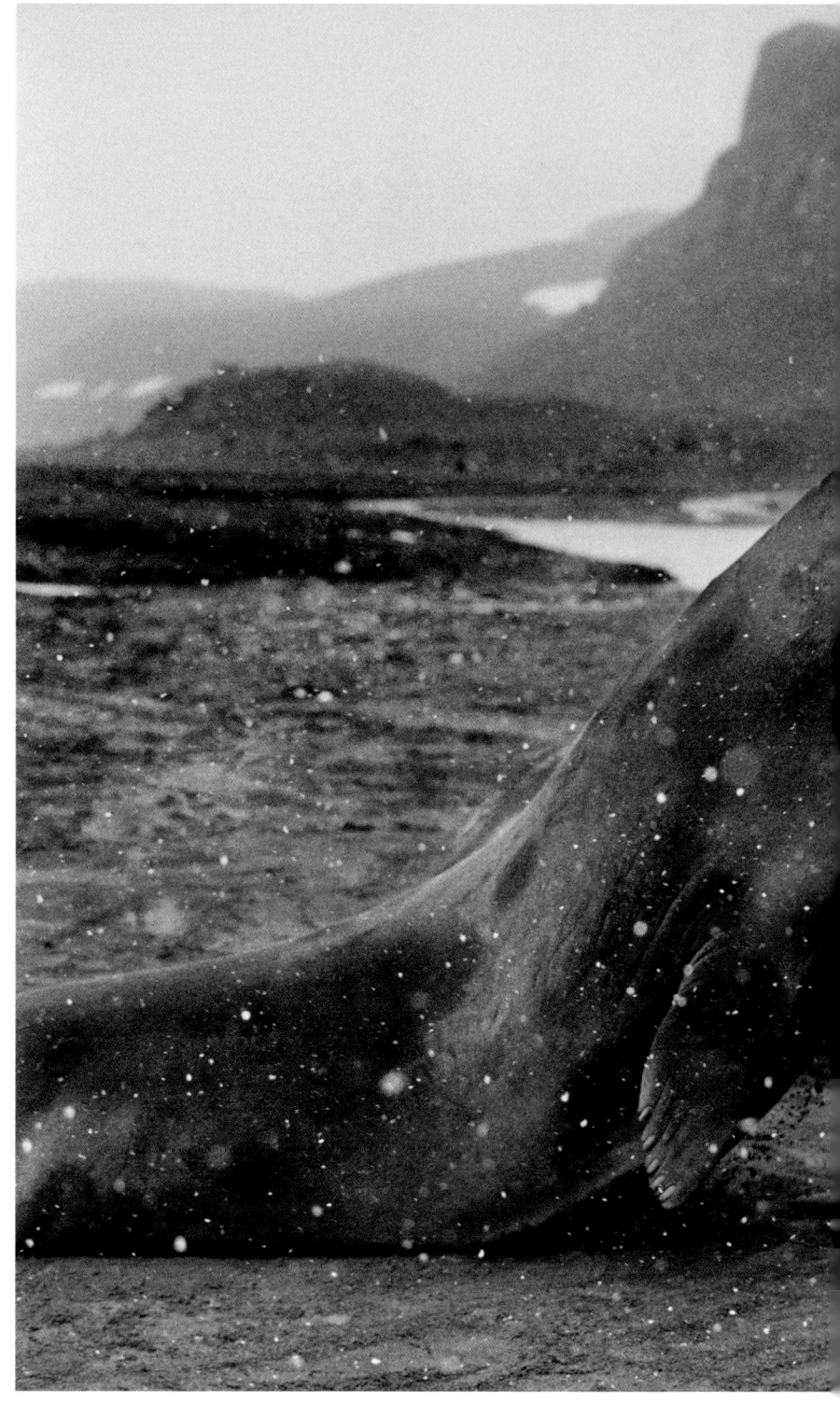

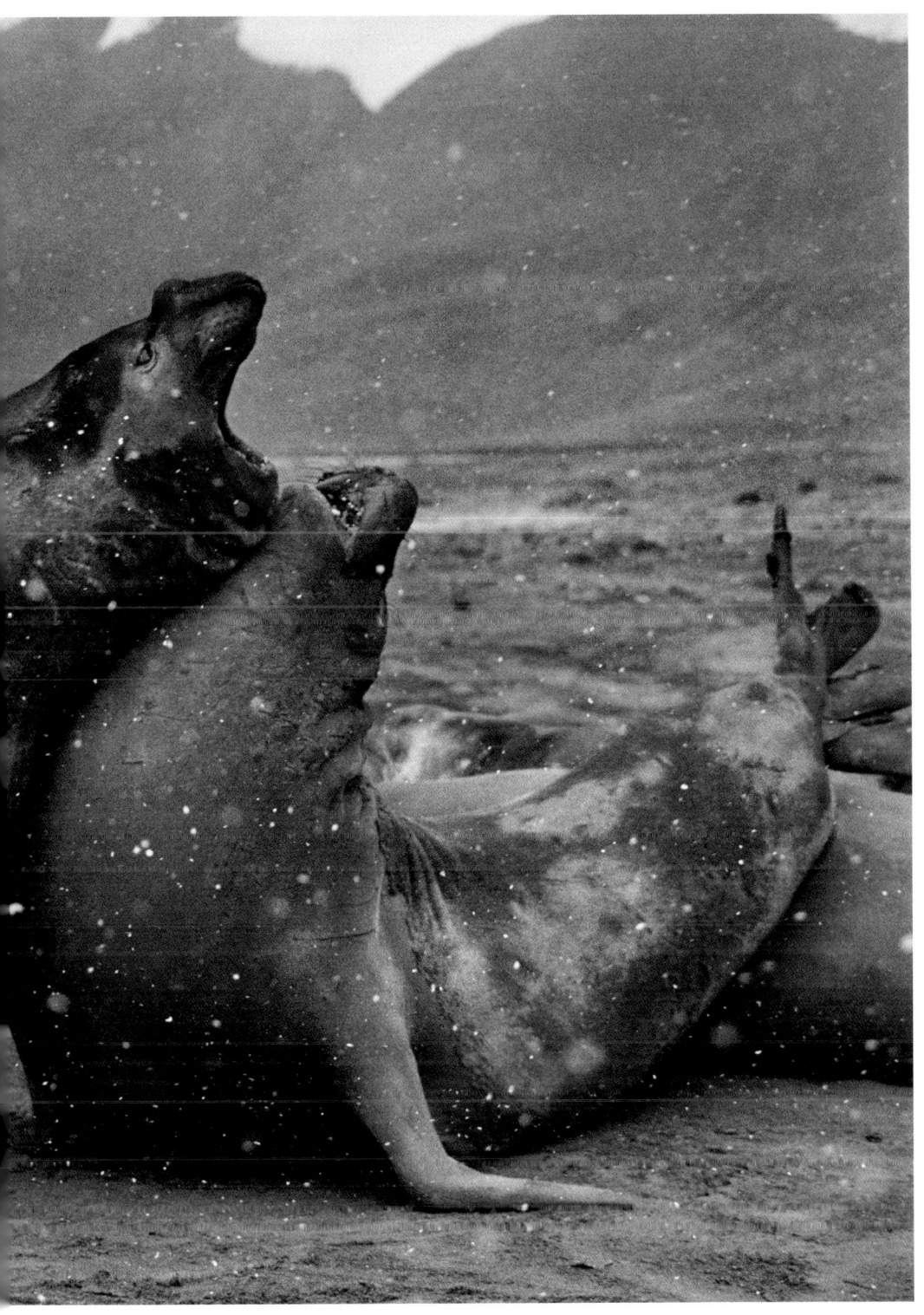

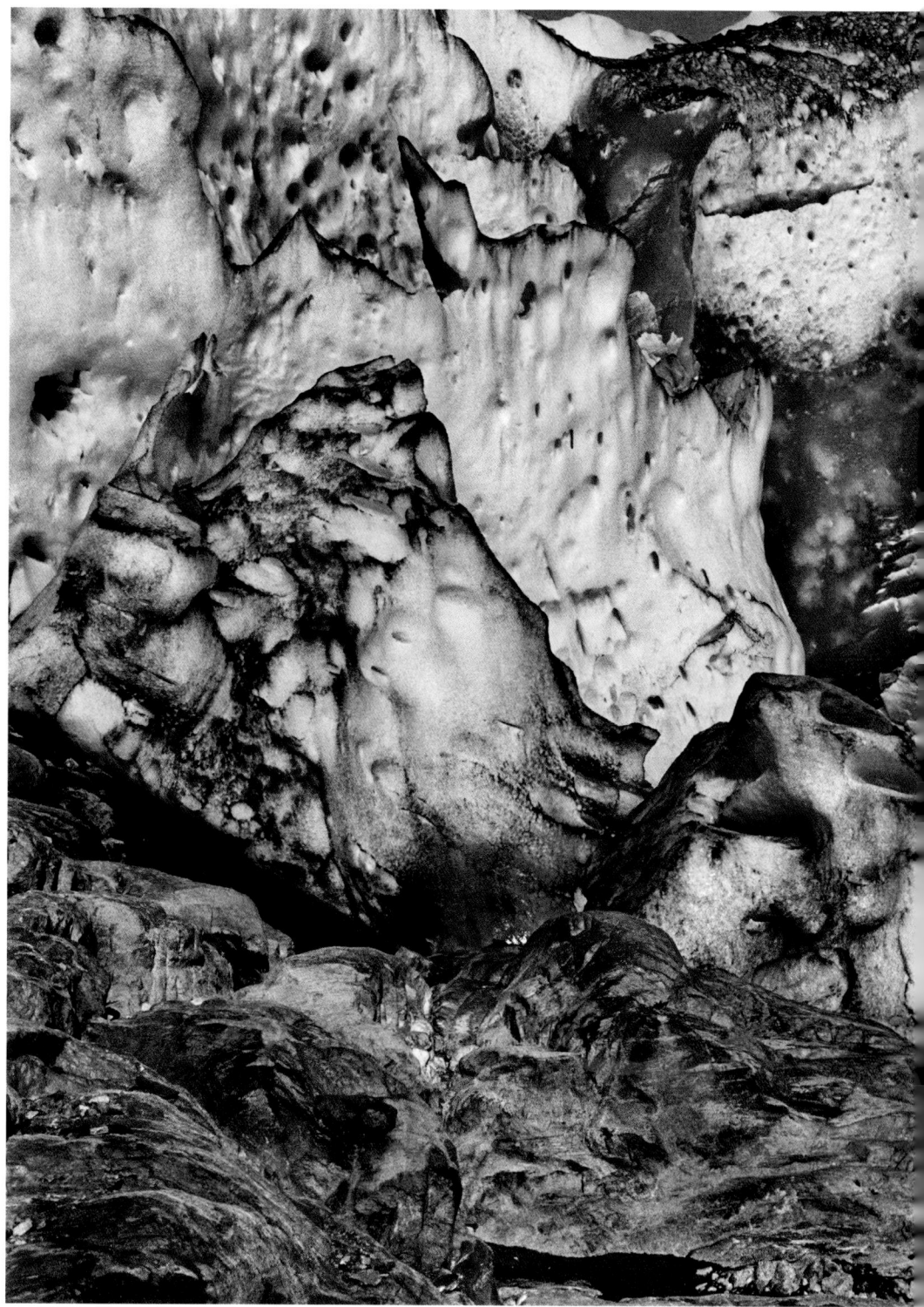

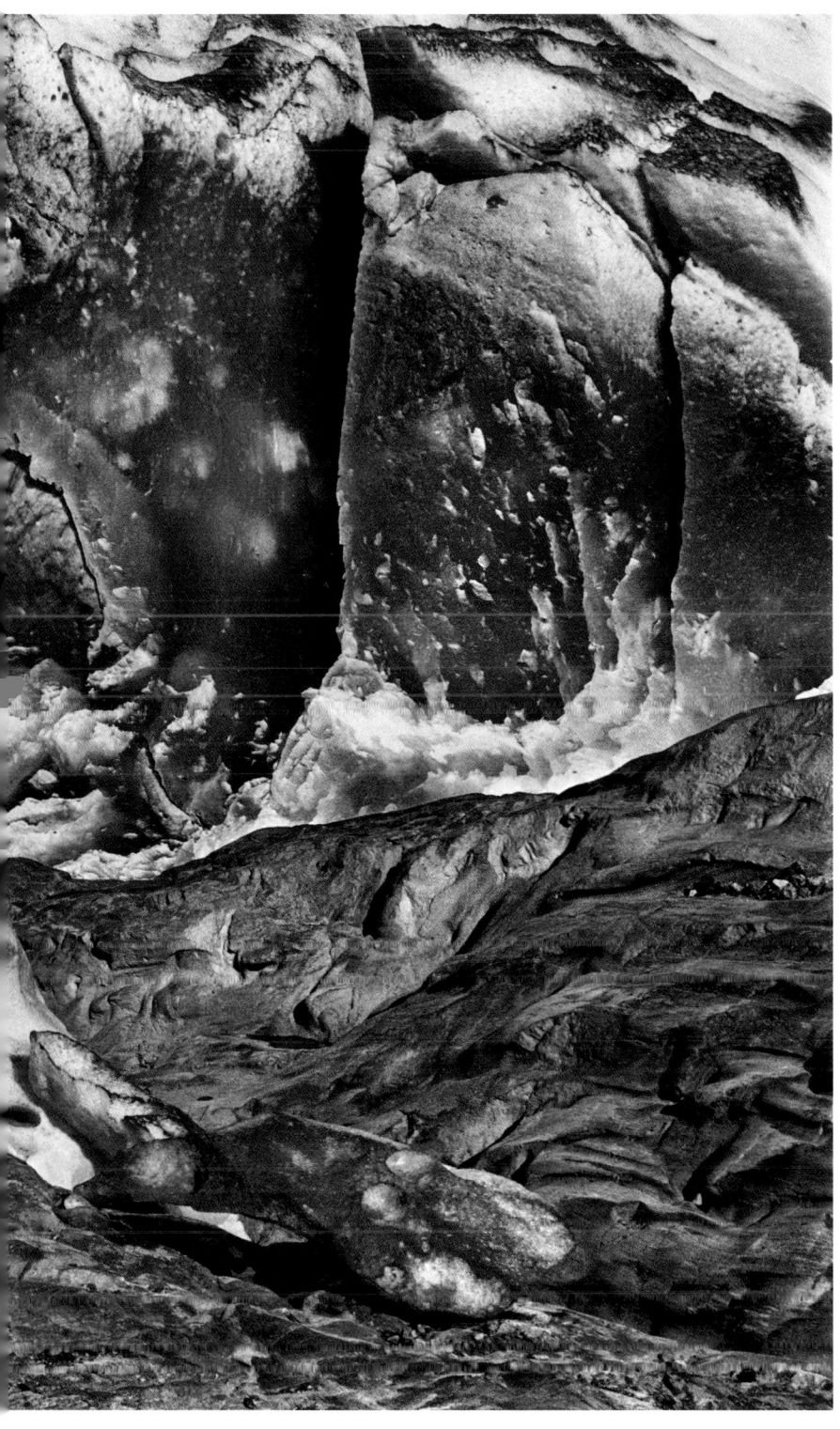

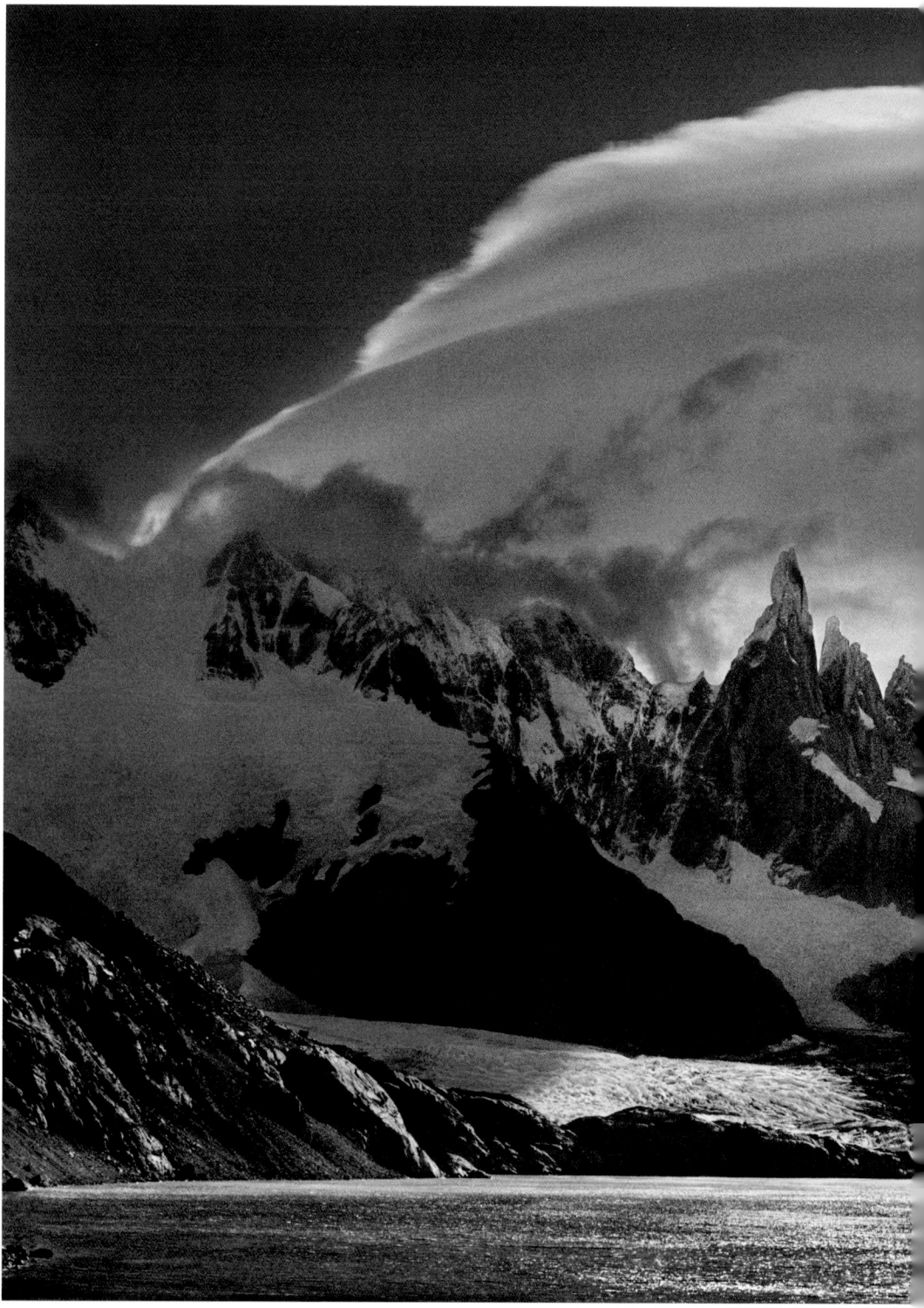

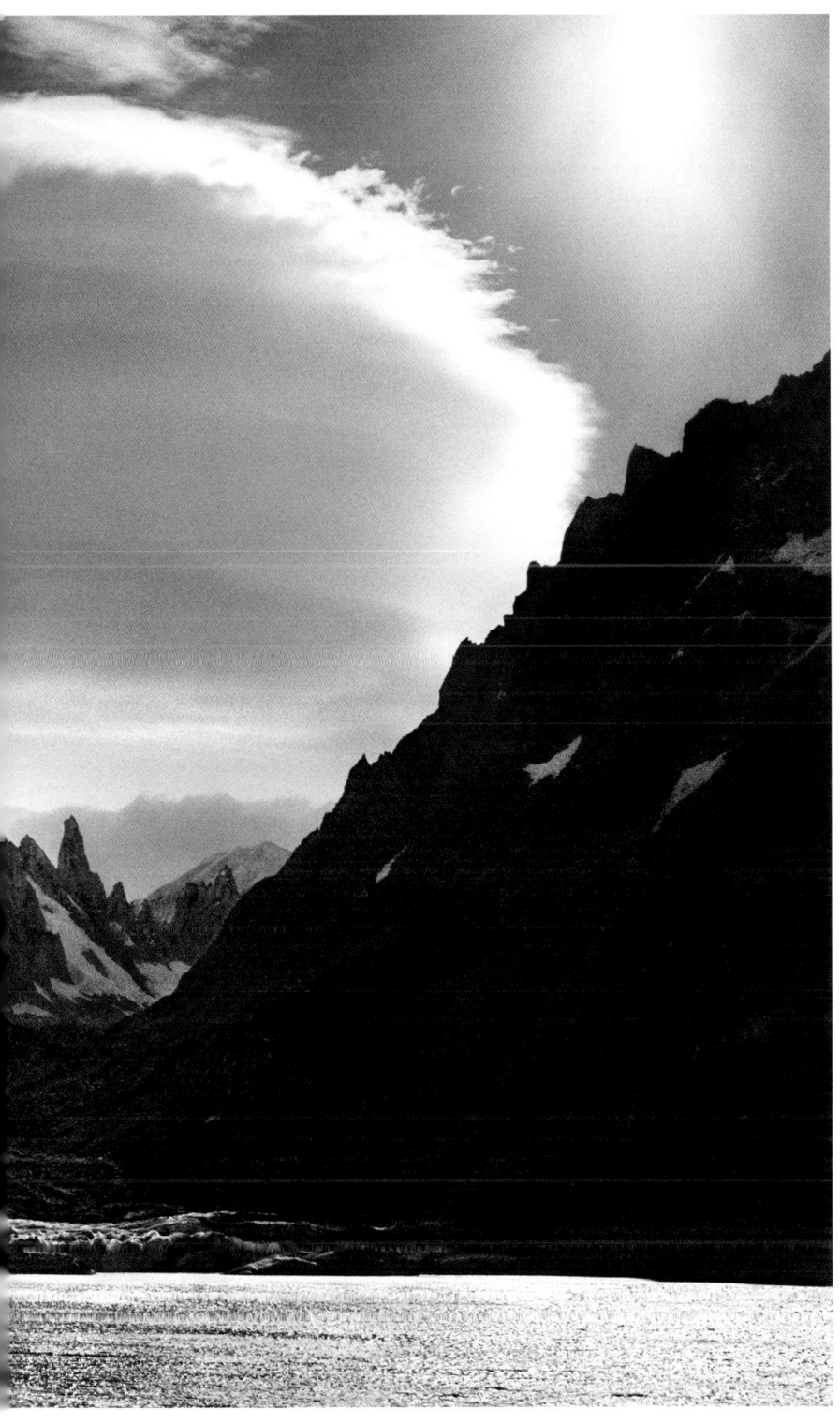

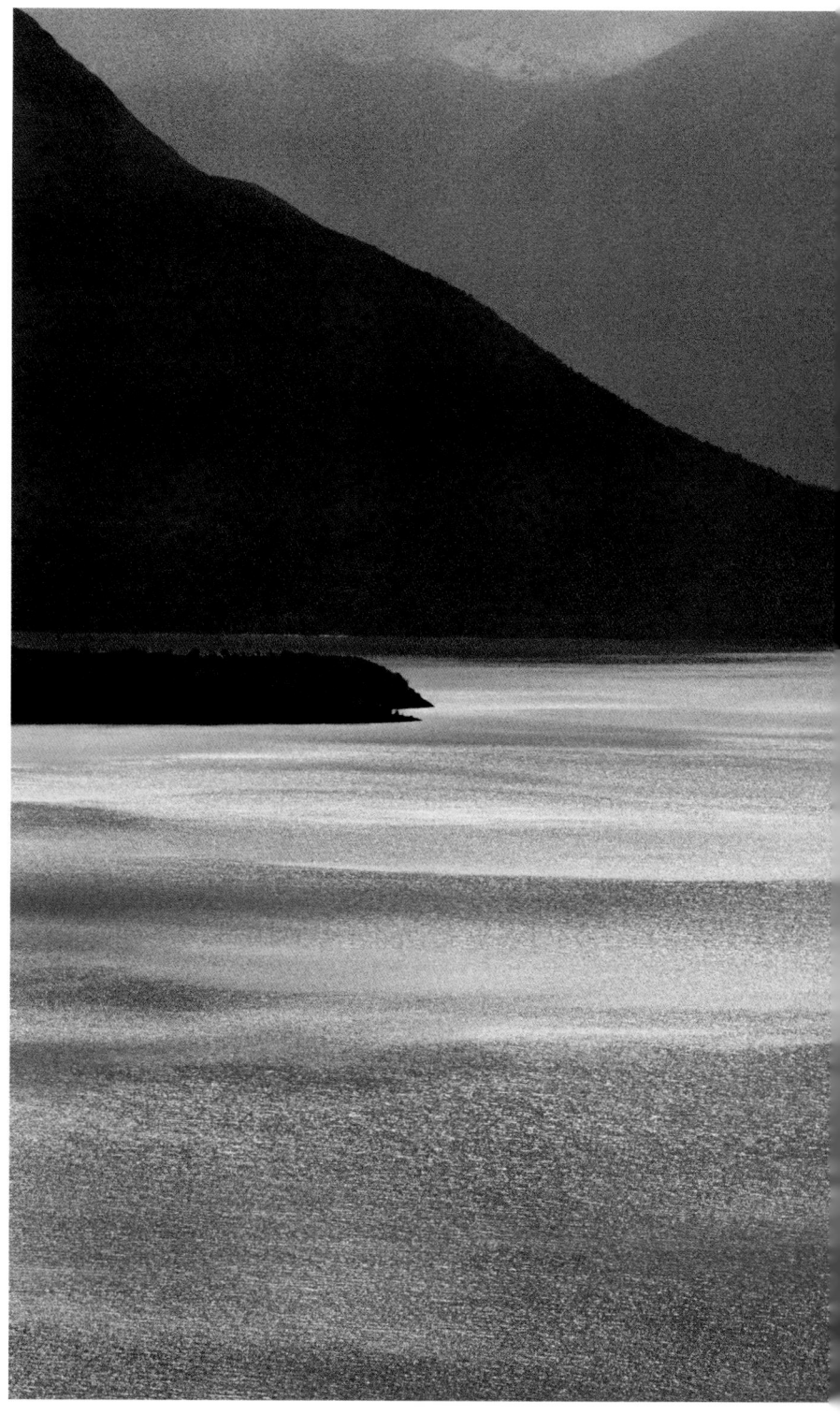

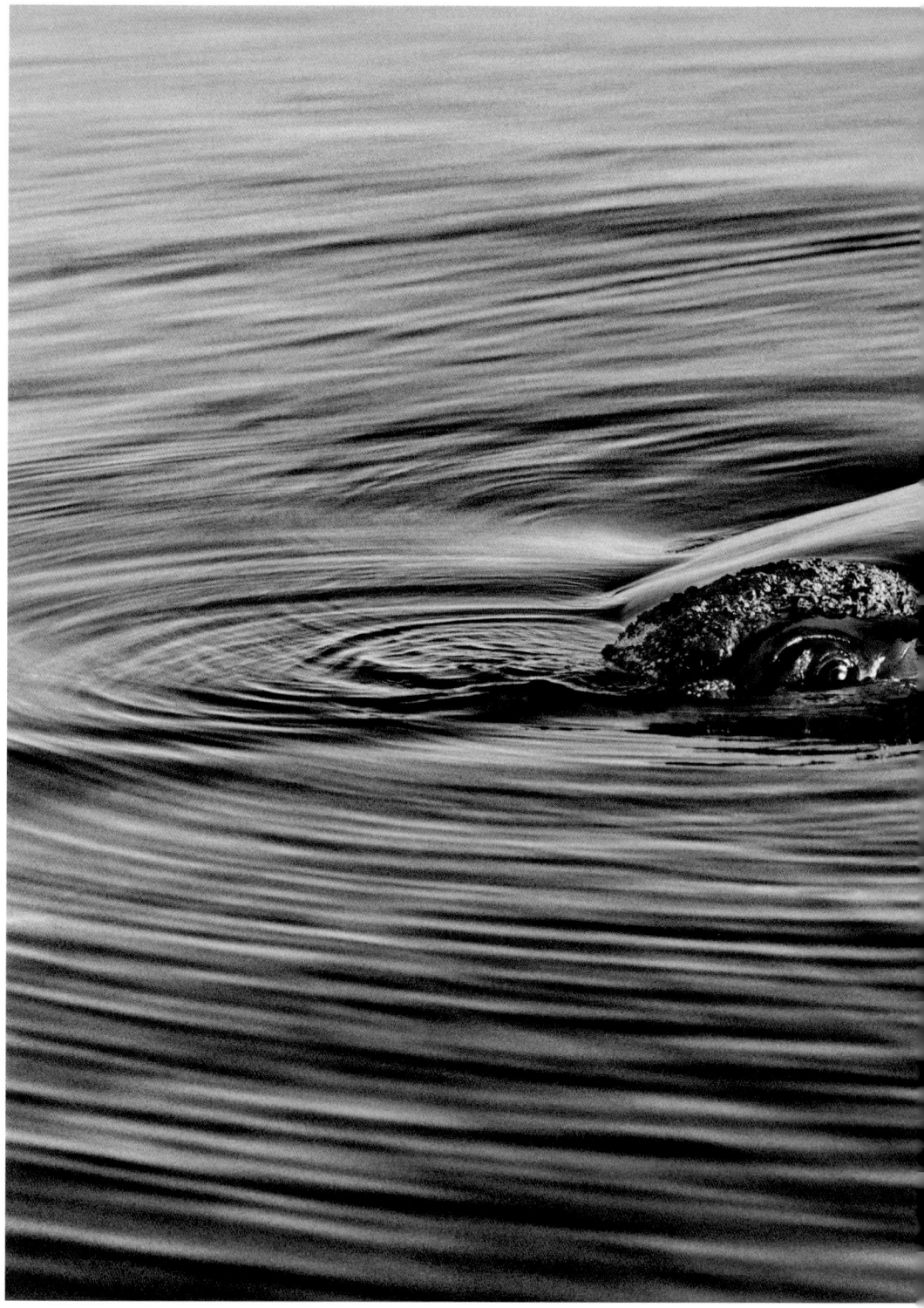

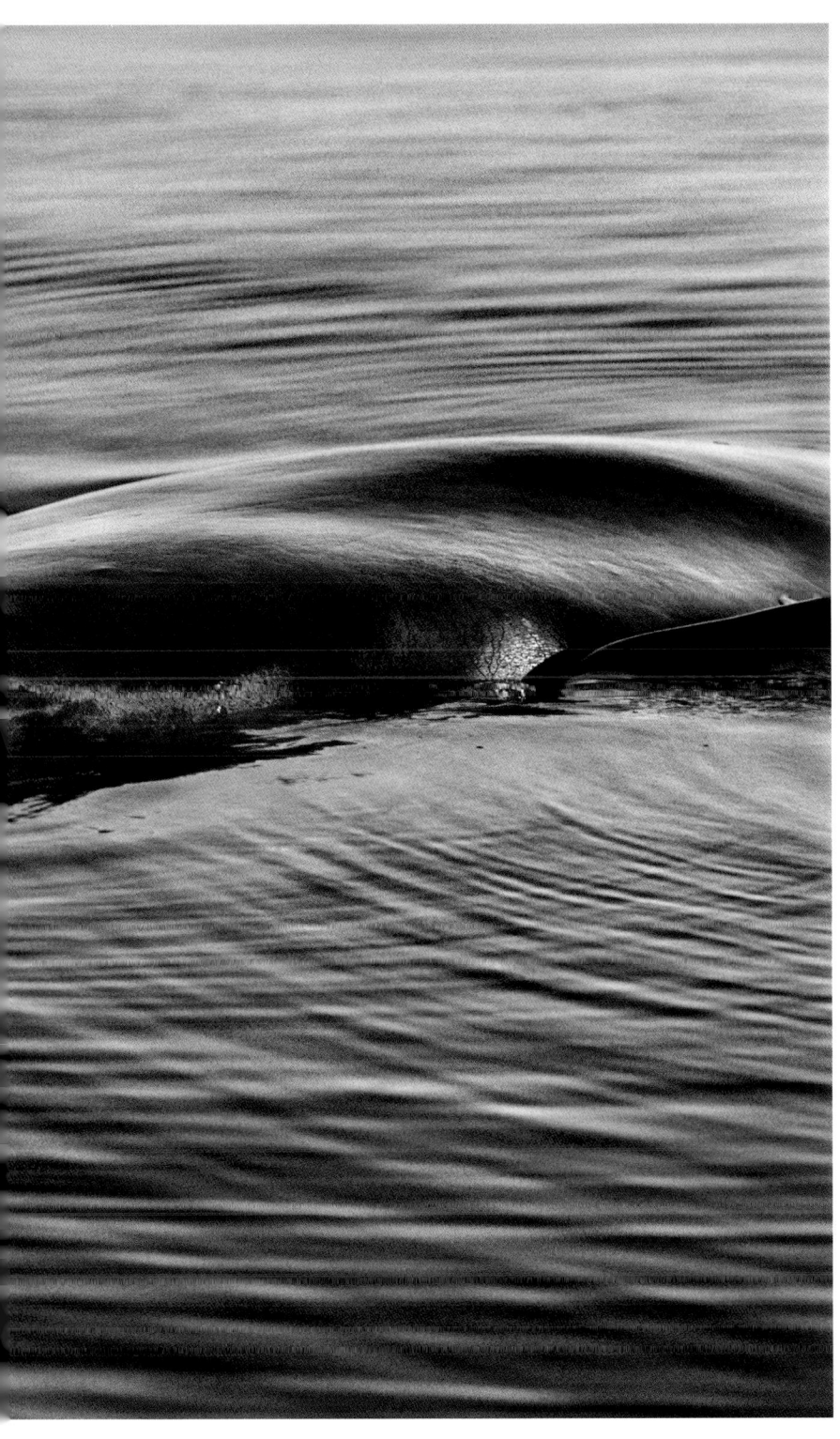

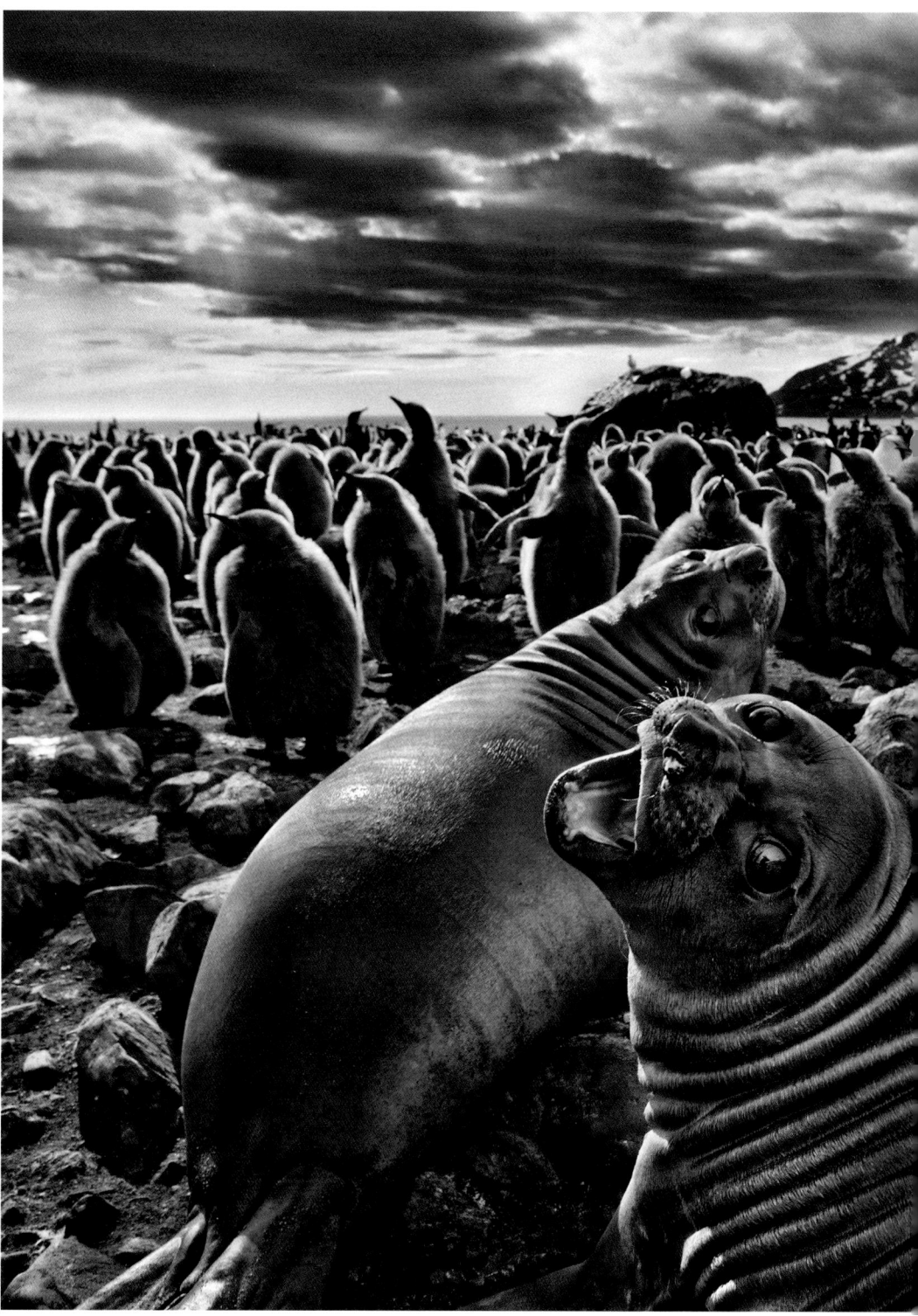

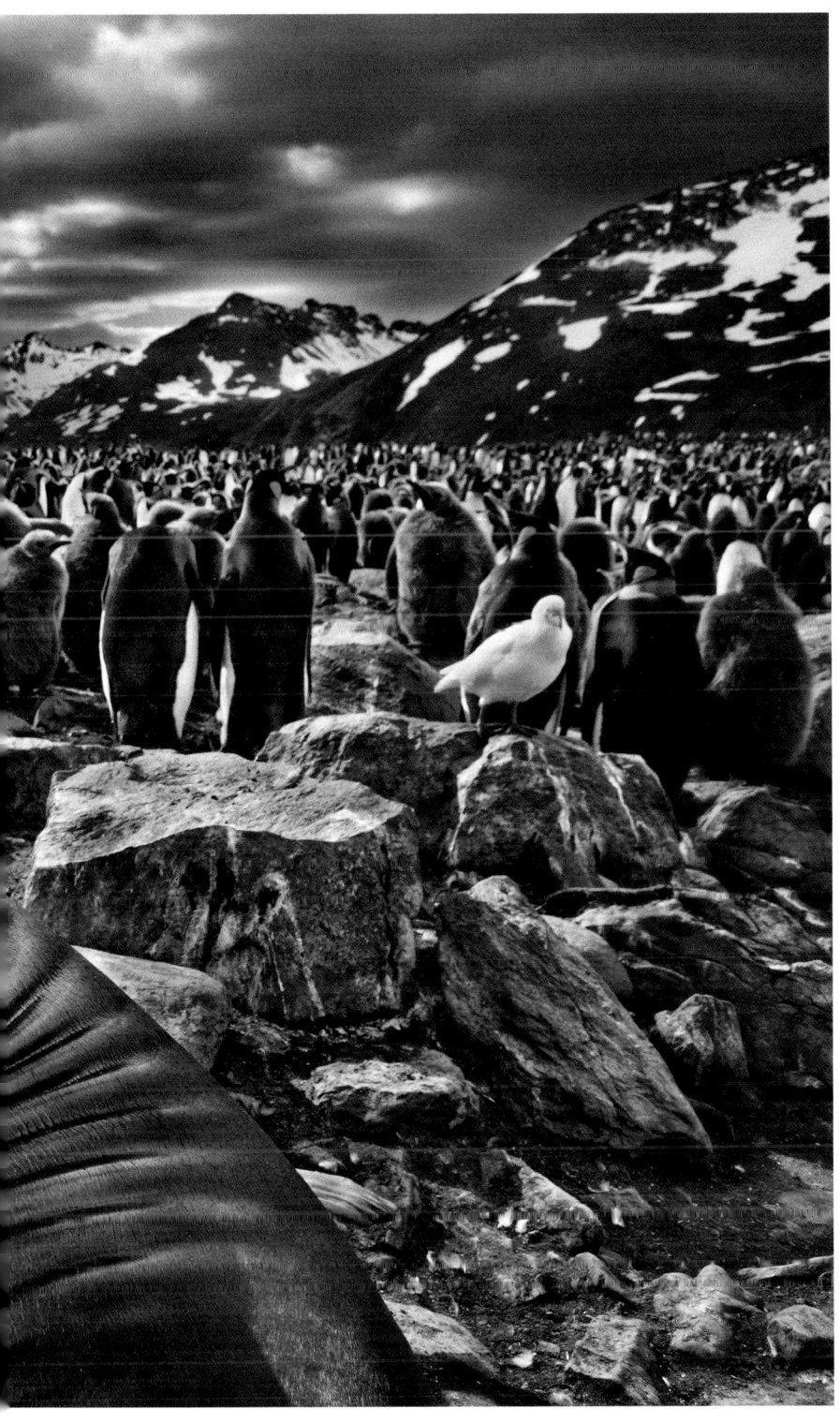

Pages 40/41 The face of Viedma Glacier. The Viedma Glacier is one of the largest of the 48 glaciers of Southern Patagonia Ice Field, which itself covers an area of between 14,000 and 16,800 square kilometers (5,400 and 6,500 square miles). The Viedma, which is 2 kilometers (1.2 miles) wide when it enters Lake Viedma, constantly topples large chunks of ice into the water. While the glacier as a whole is slowly moving towards the lake, the glacier's face has retreated by several hundred meters in recent decades. Argentine Patagonia. March and April 2007.

Pages 42/43 Cerro Torre, part of a mountain chain in the Southern Patagonian Ice Field, stands out for its elegant and slender peak. The mountain itself is 10,200 feet (3,128 meters) high, but its summit rises like a jagged knife, with vertical drops of between 3,600 and 4,900 feet (1,100 and 1,500 meters) on three sides. Often hidden by swirling clouds, Cerro Torre has proved an immense challenge to mountain climbers, few of whom have ever conquered it. Adding to their difficulties, fierce westerly winds blowing across the icecap have covered its rock face with a thick mantle of ice and a slippery mushroom of rime ice. Argentine Patagonia. March and April 2007.

Pages 44/45 Lake Argentino. Los Glaciares National Park, located in the Argentine Andes straddling the border with Chile, covers an area of high-altitude lakes and embraces a snow-capped sector of the Southern Patagonian Ice Field. Glacial activity is con-centrated around two main lakes, namely Argentino and Viedma, which drain into the Atlantic Ocean via the Santa Cruz River. Argentine Patagonia. March and April 2007.

Pages 46/47 This southern right whale (*Eubalaena australis*) became very friendly after we had accompanied her for several days. When the ocean was calm, she would rise to investigate who was approaching, turning on her side so that one eye looked straight at us. The eyes of southern right whales are set behind the lower jaw. Valdés Peninsula. Argentina. September and October 2004.

Pages 48/49 Southern elephant seal calves (*Mirounga leonina*) at Saint Andrews Bay. South Georgia November and December 2009.

Opposite A colony of black-browed albatrosses (*Thalassarche melanophris*) on the archipelago of Willis Islands; visible in the background is Bird Island. South Georgia. November and December 2009.

Pages 52/53 and 54/55 The Jason Islands are a cluster of 12 islands on the westernmost point of the Falkland Islands. These photographs were taken on Steeple Jason Island, home to more than 500,000 couples of black-browed albatrosses (*Thalassarche melanophris*), the largest colony of albatrosses in the world. Falkland Islands. November and December 2009.

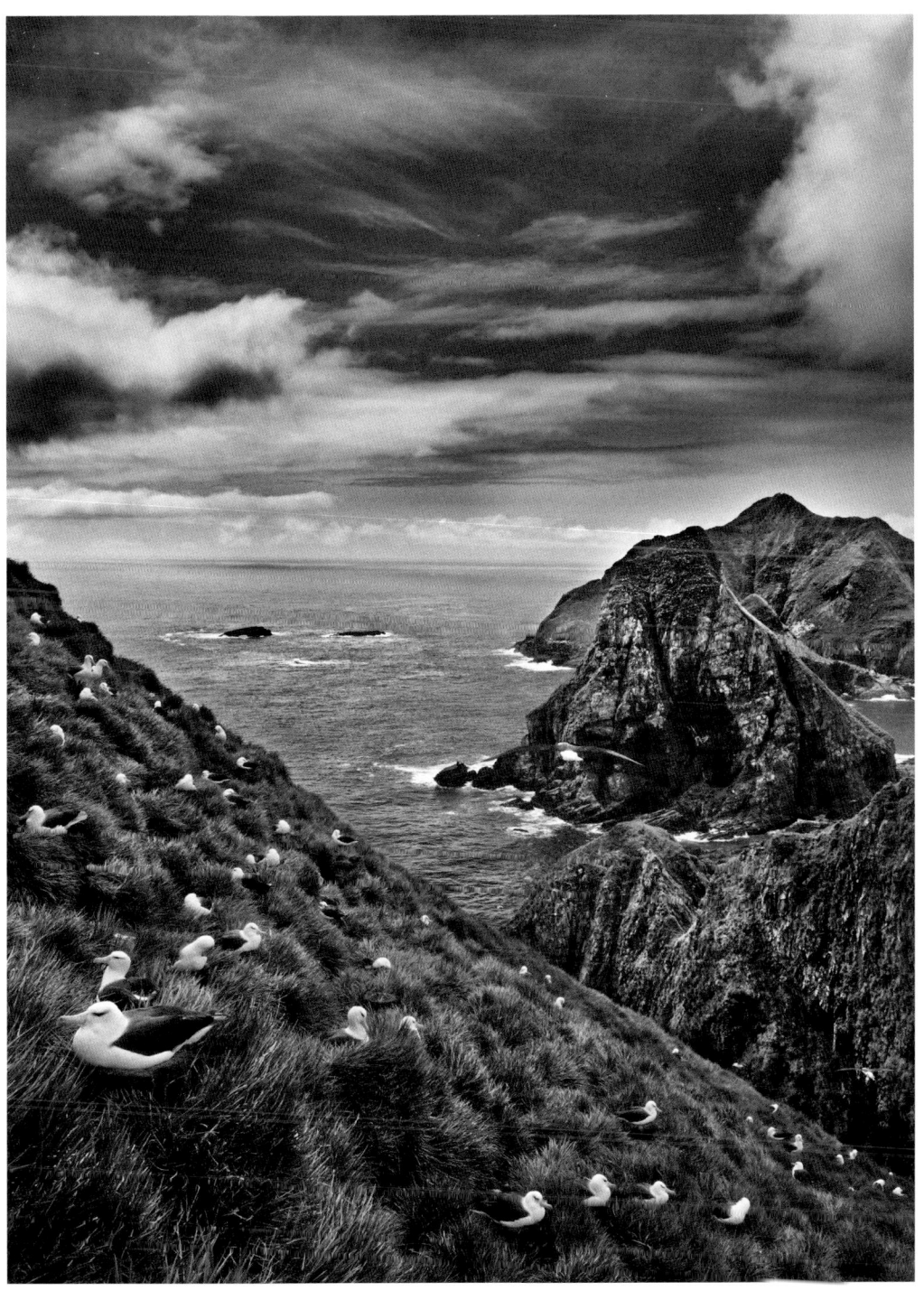

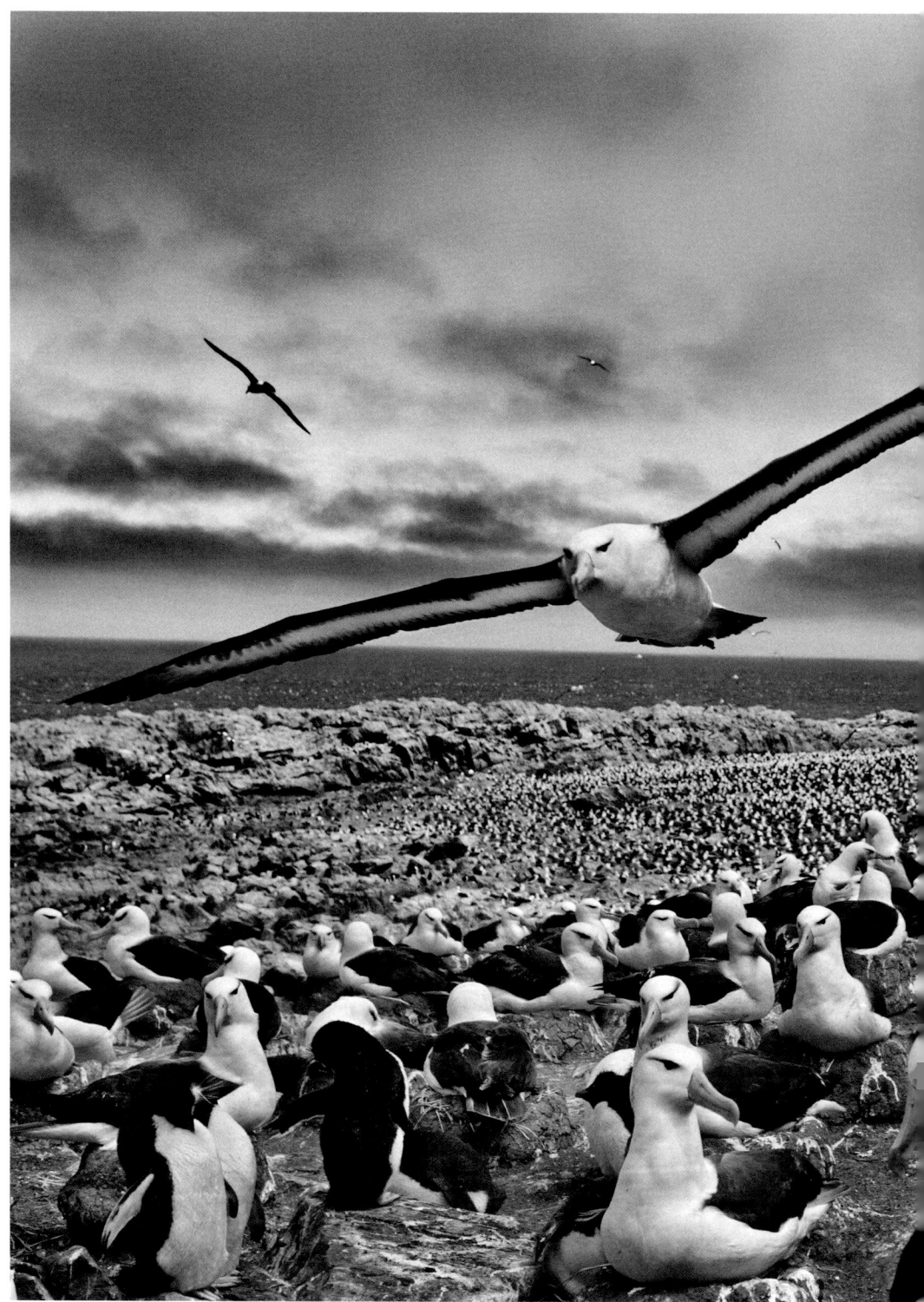

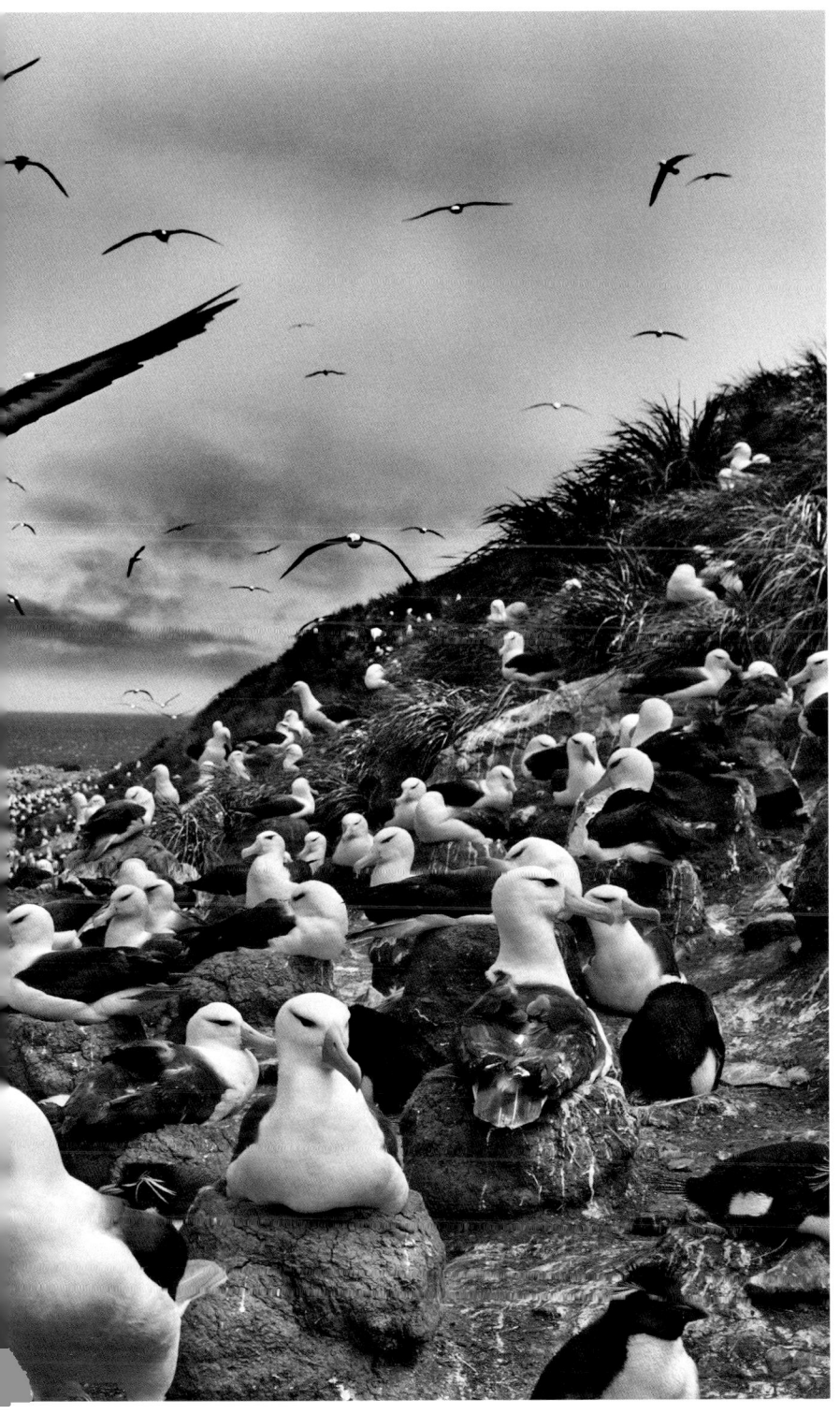

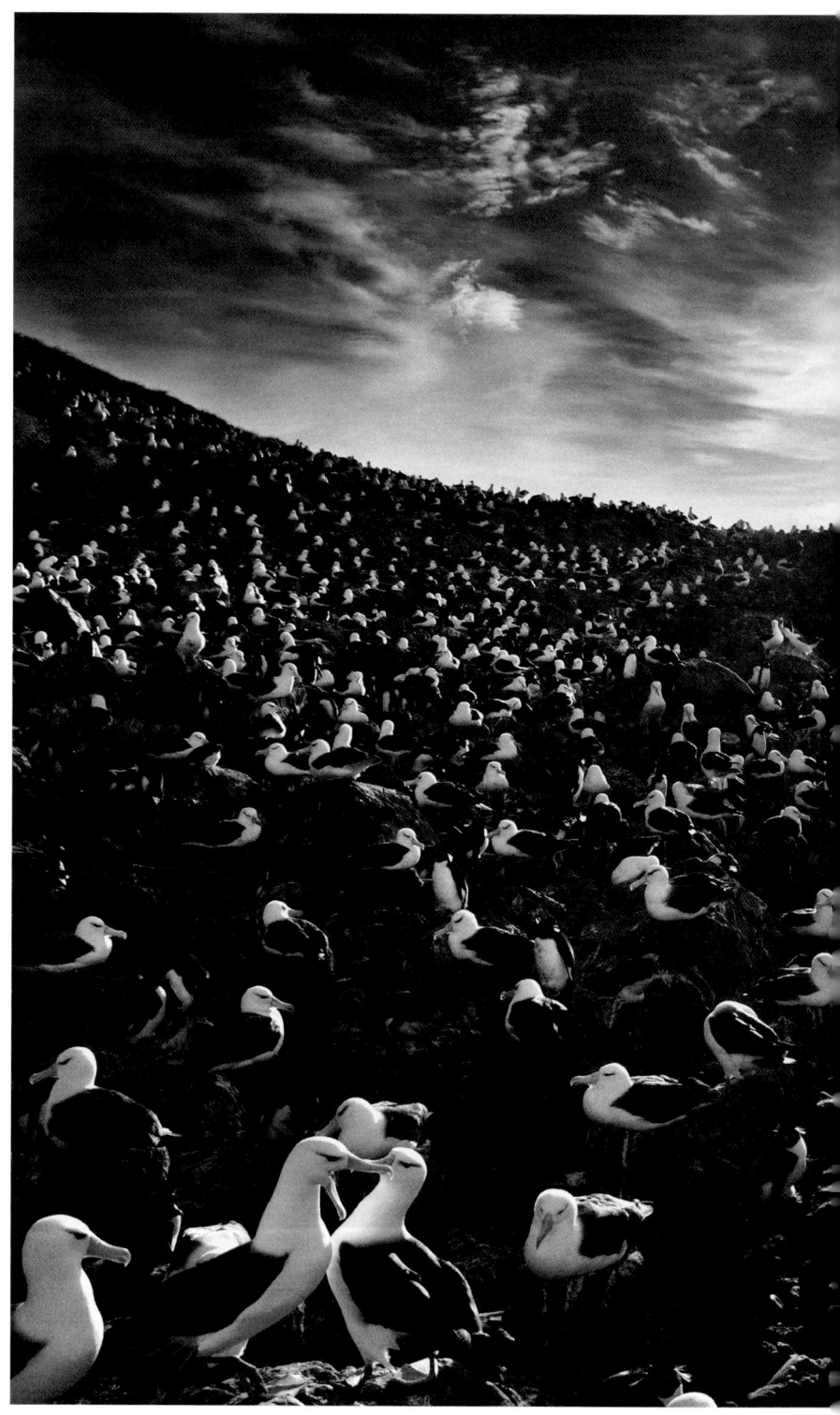

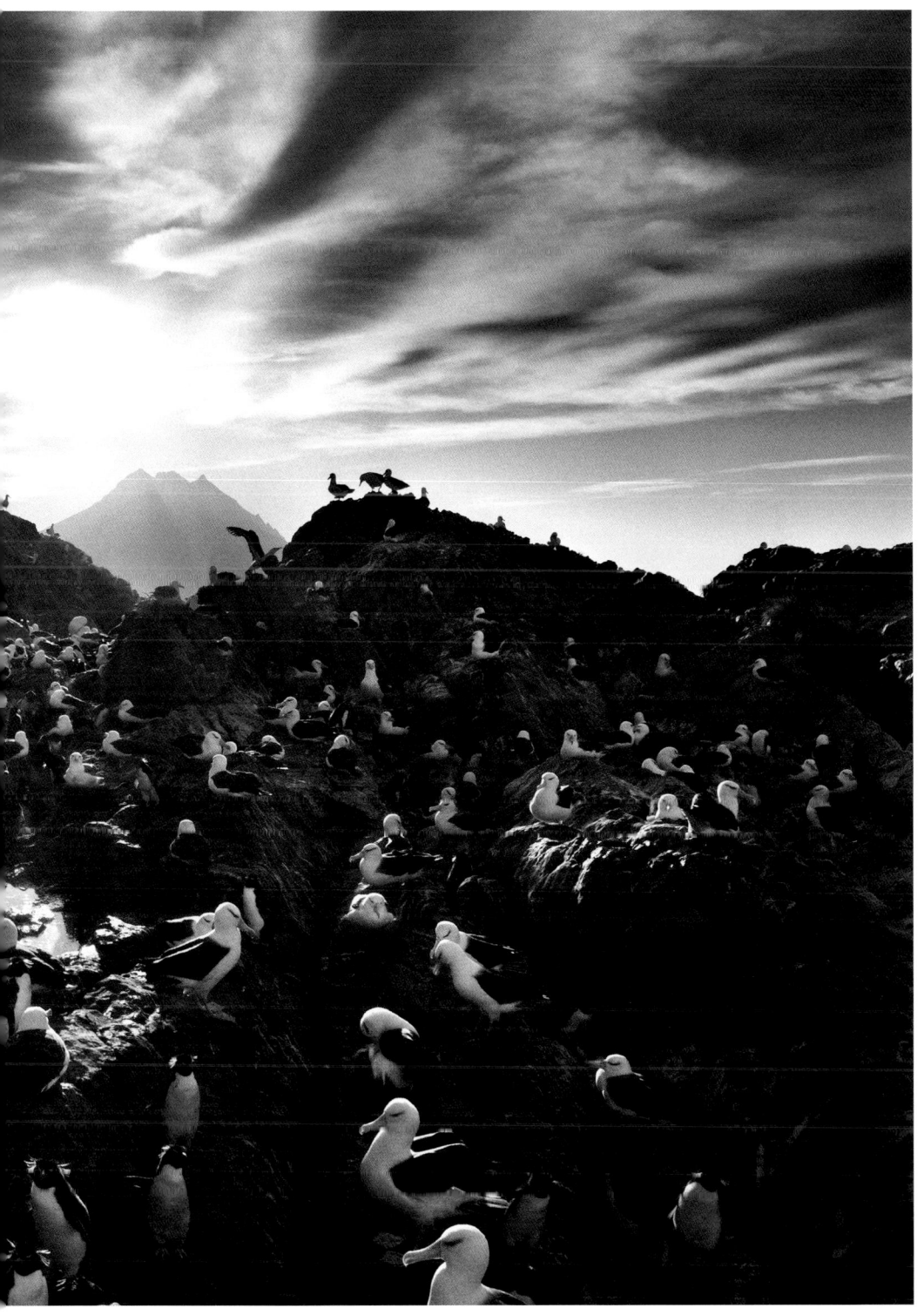

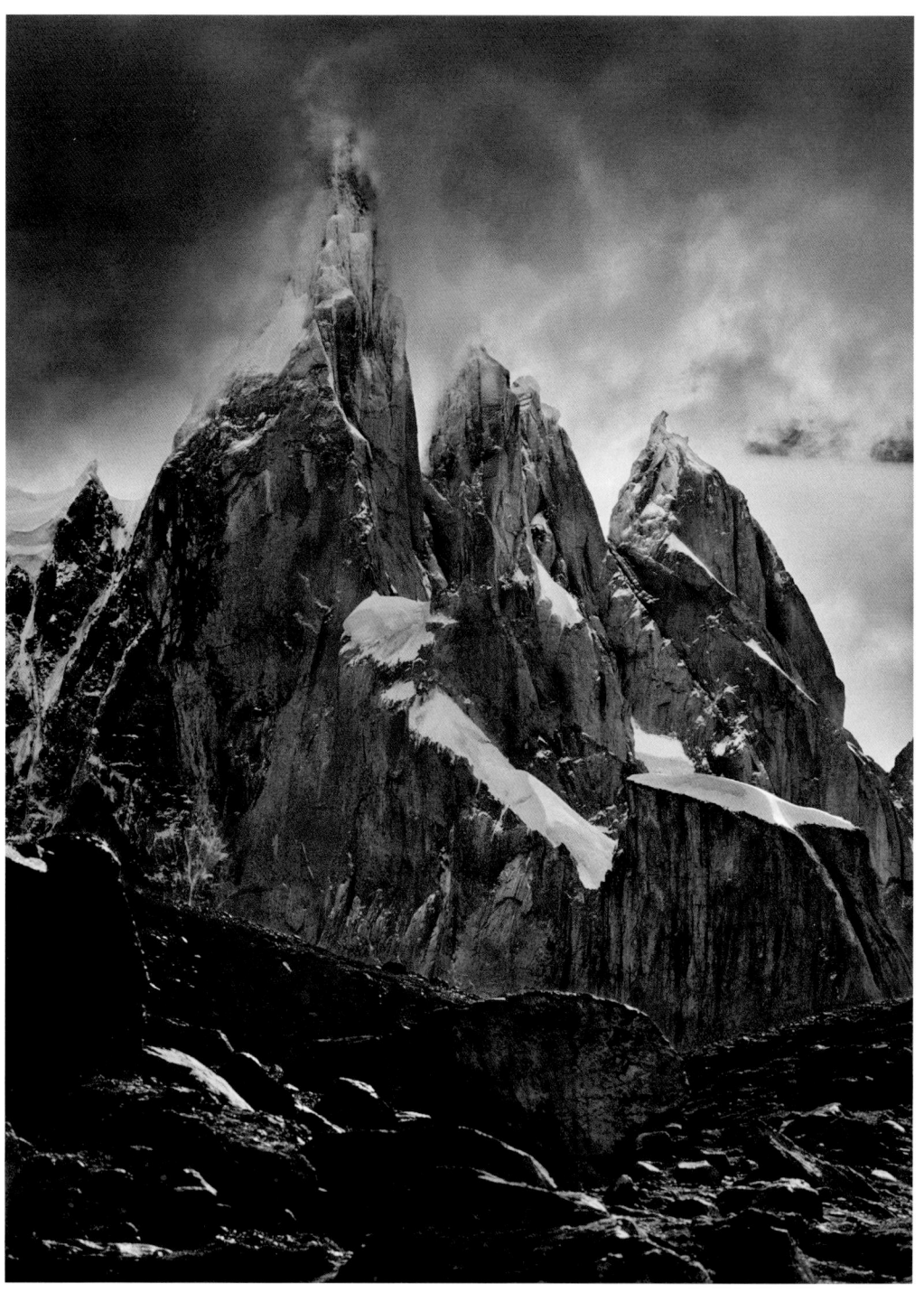

Opposite Cerro Torre, part of a mountain range in the Southern Patagonian Ice Field, stands out for its elegant and slender peak. The mountain itself is 10,200 feet (3,128 meters) high, but its summit rises like a jagged knife, with vertical drops of between 3,600 and 4,900 feet (1,100 and 1,500 meters) on three sides. Often hidden by swirling clouds, Cerro Torre has proved an immense challenge to mountain climbers, few of whom have ever conquered it. Adding to their difficulties, fierce westerly winds blowing across the icecap have covered its rock face with a thick mantle of ice and a slippery mushroom of rime ice. Argentine Patagonia. March and April 2007.

Pages 58/59 A colony of black-browed albatrosses (*Thalassarche melanophris*) on the hills of Elsehul Bay in the far north of South Georgia. November and December 2009.

Pages 60/61 On Deception Island. The feeling of reaching another planet is particularly intense on Deception Island, at the northern tip of the Antarctic Peninsula. The island is almost a complete circle, with only Neptune's Bellows providing a narrow entrance to the caldera, a 7-mile (12-kilometer)-wide bay created by the collapse of a volcano.

This photograph shows the Bailey Head penguin colony on the eastern edge of the island, which can be reached only by scaling a 1,900-foot (582-meter)-high ridge. Speckled black and white, the slopes of the crater are a glacier, which is hidden by rocks in many places, thus making for a hazardous climb; in some places, soil runs down like lava. Once on the other side of the ridge, a 4.2-mile (7 kilometer) walk is still necessary to reach this extraordinary colony of hundreds of thousands of chinstrap penguins (*Pygoscelis antarctica*). Antarctic Peninsula. January and February 2005.

Pages 62/63 An iceberg located between Bristol and Bellingshausen islands. South Sandwich Islands. November and December 2009.

Pages 64/65 King penguins (*Aptenodytes patagonicus*) at Saint Andrews Bay. This immense bay, with spectacular mountains to one side, is home to the largest colony of king penguins in the world (approximately 300,000 couples). South Georgia. November and December 2009.

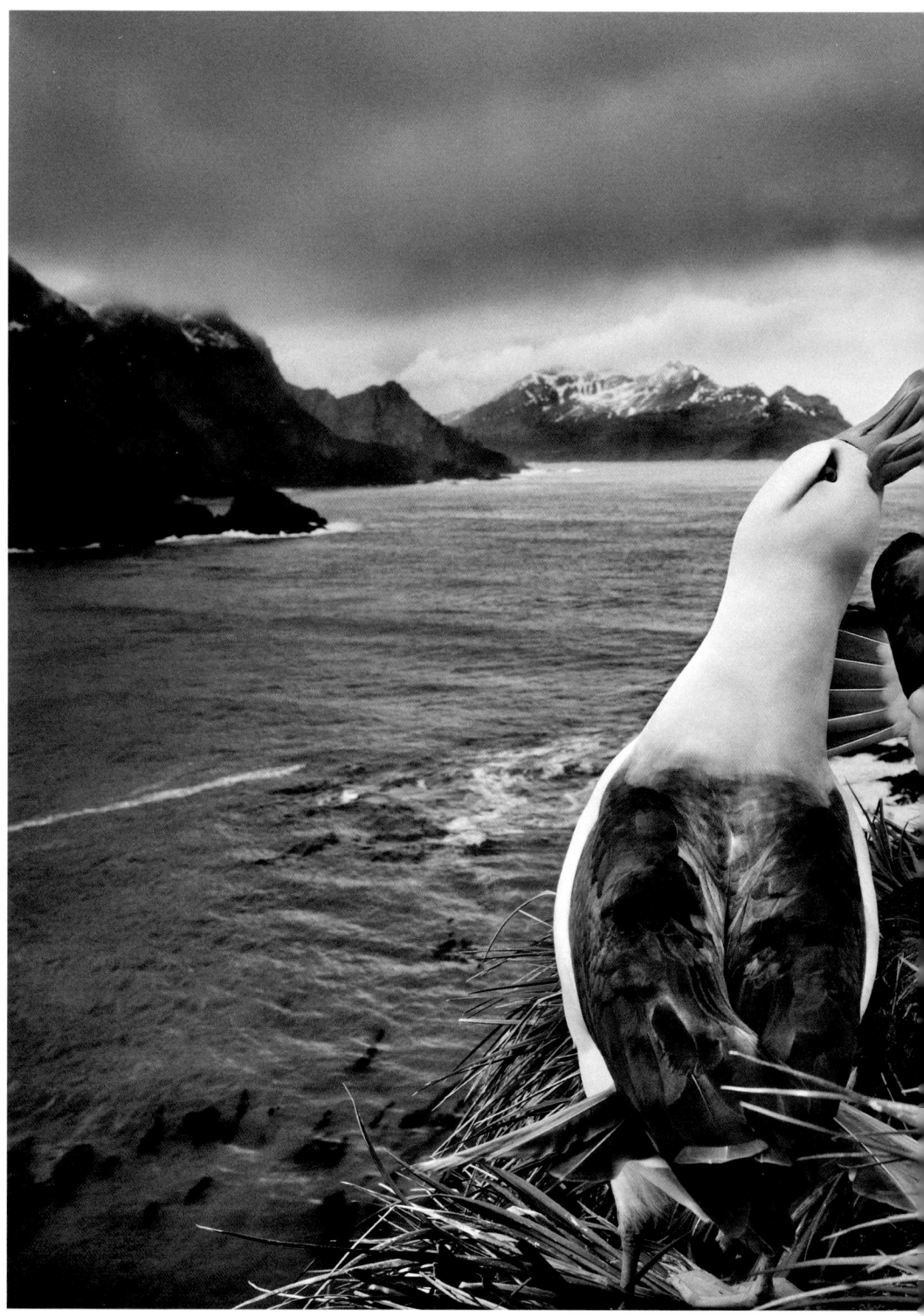

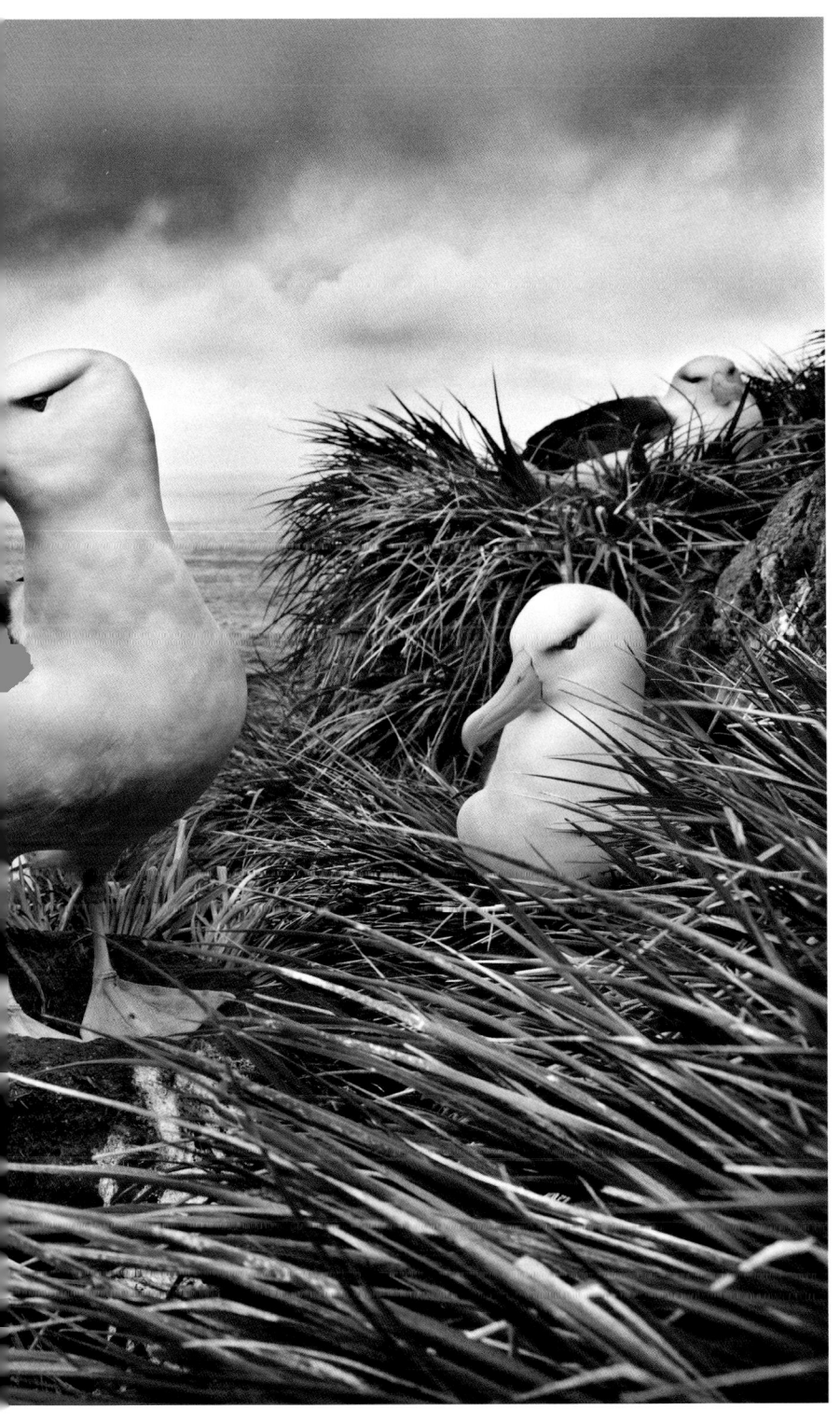

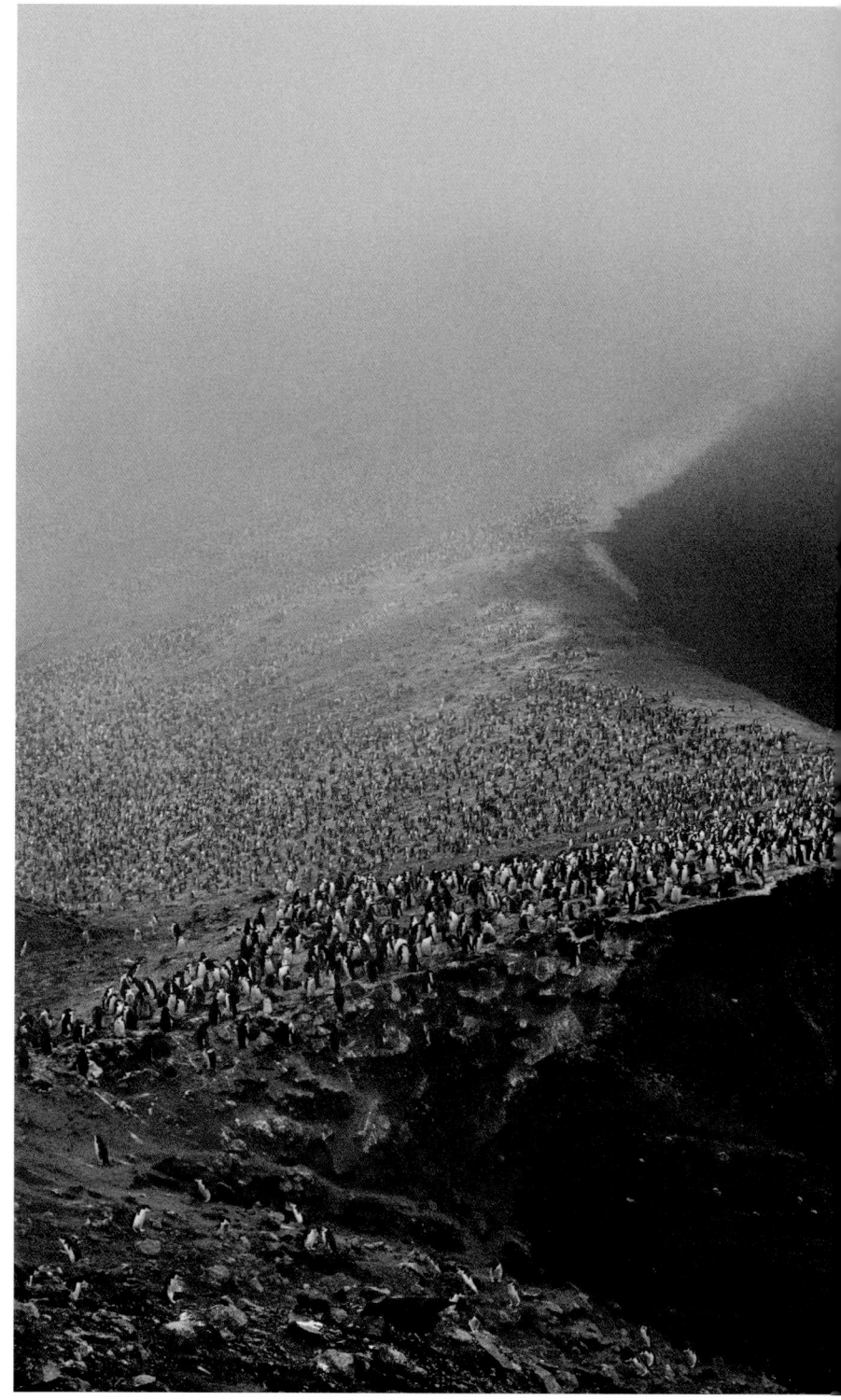

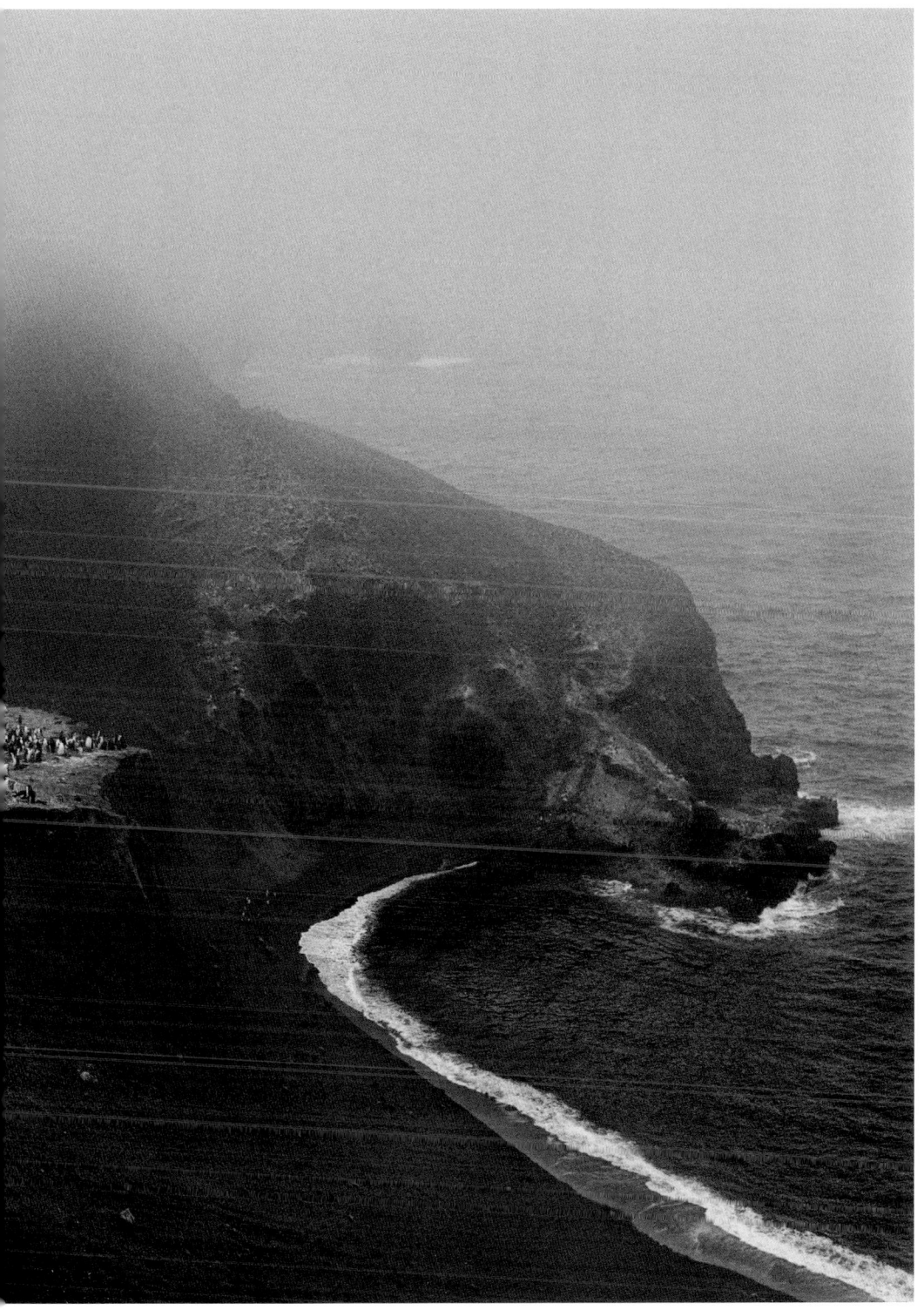

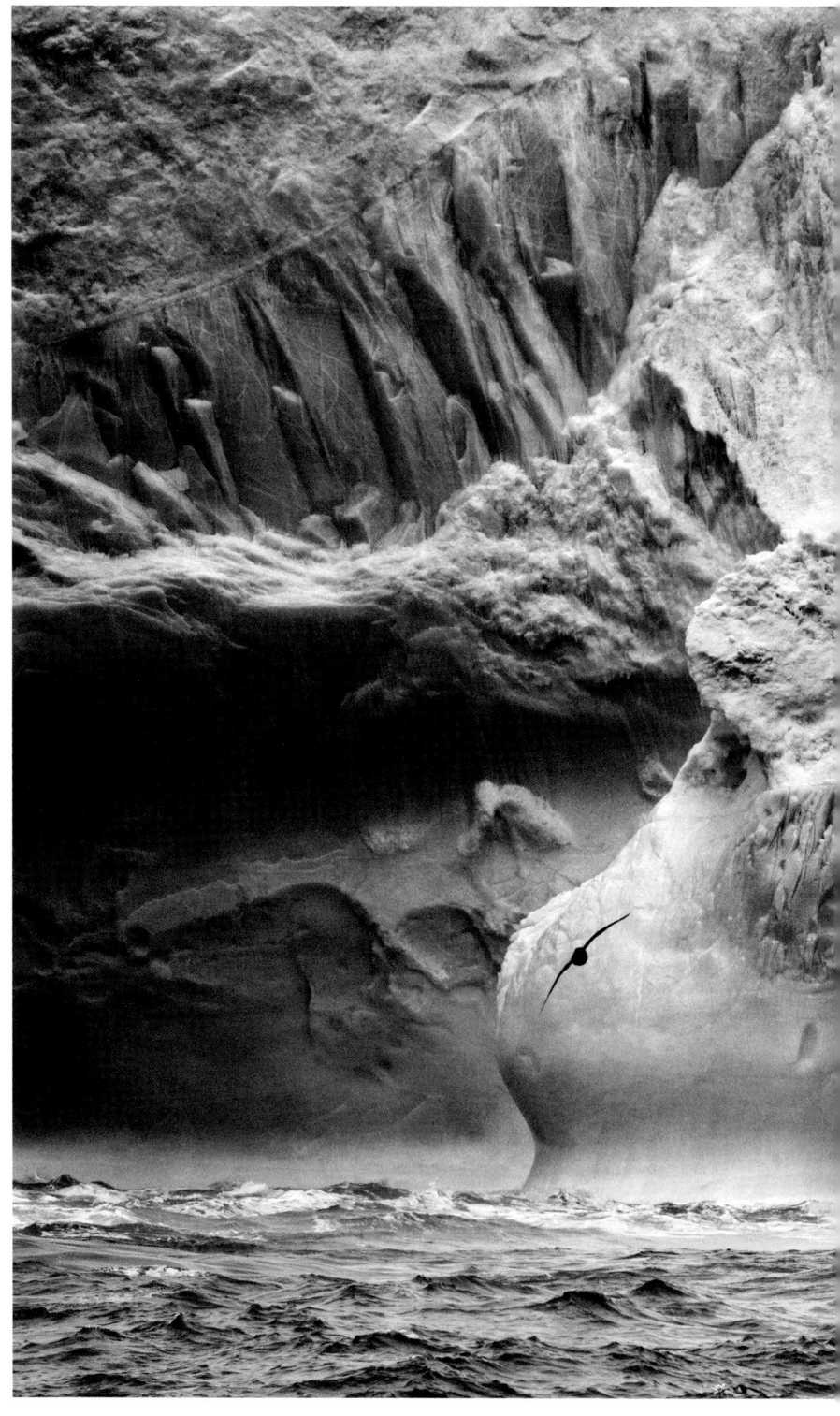

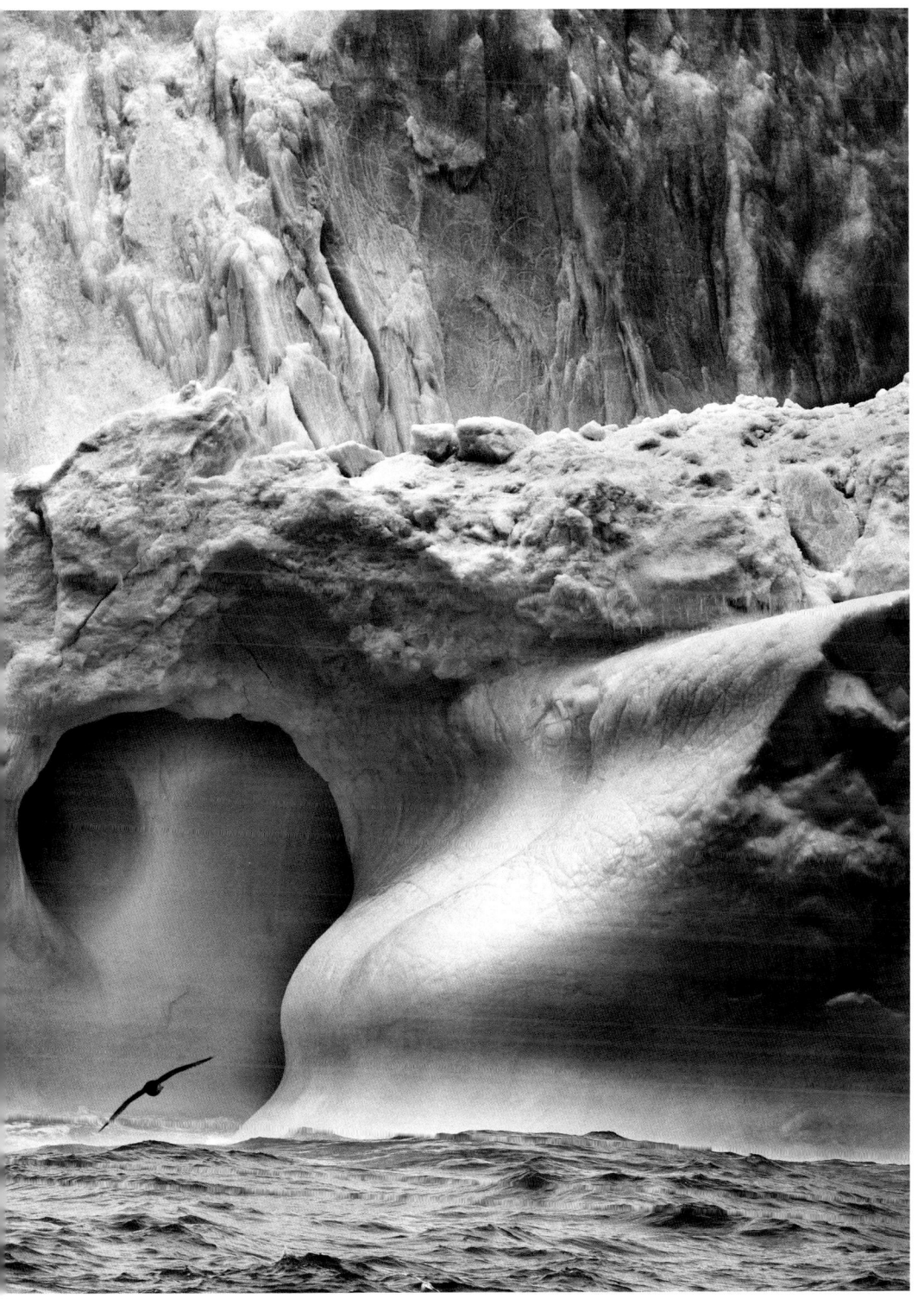

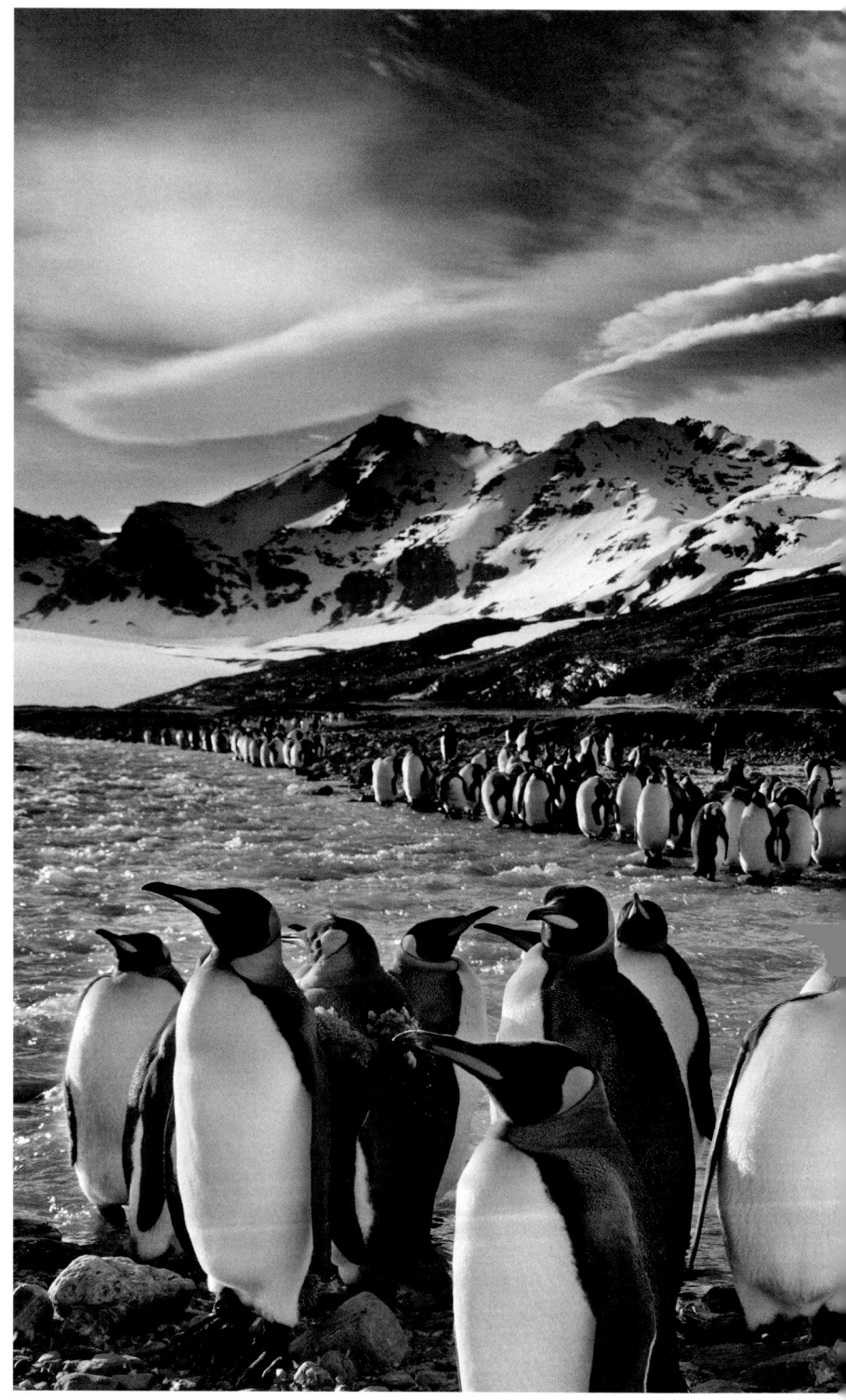

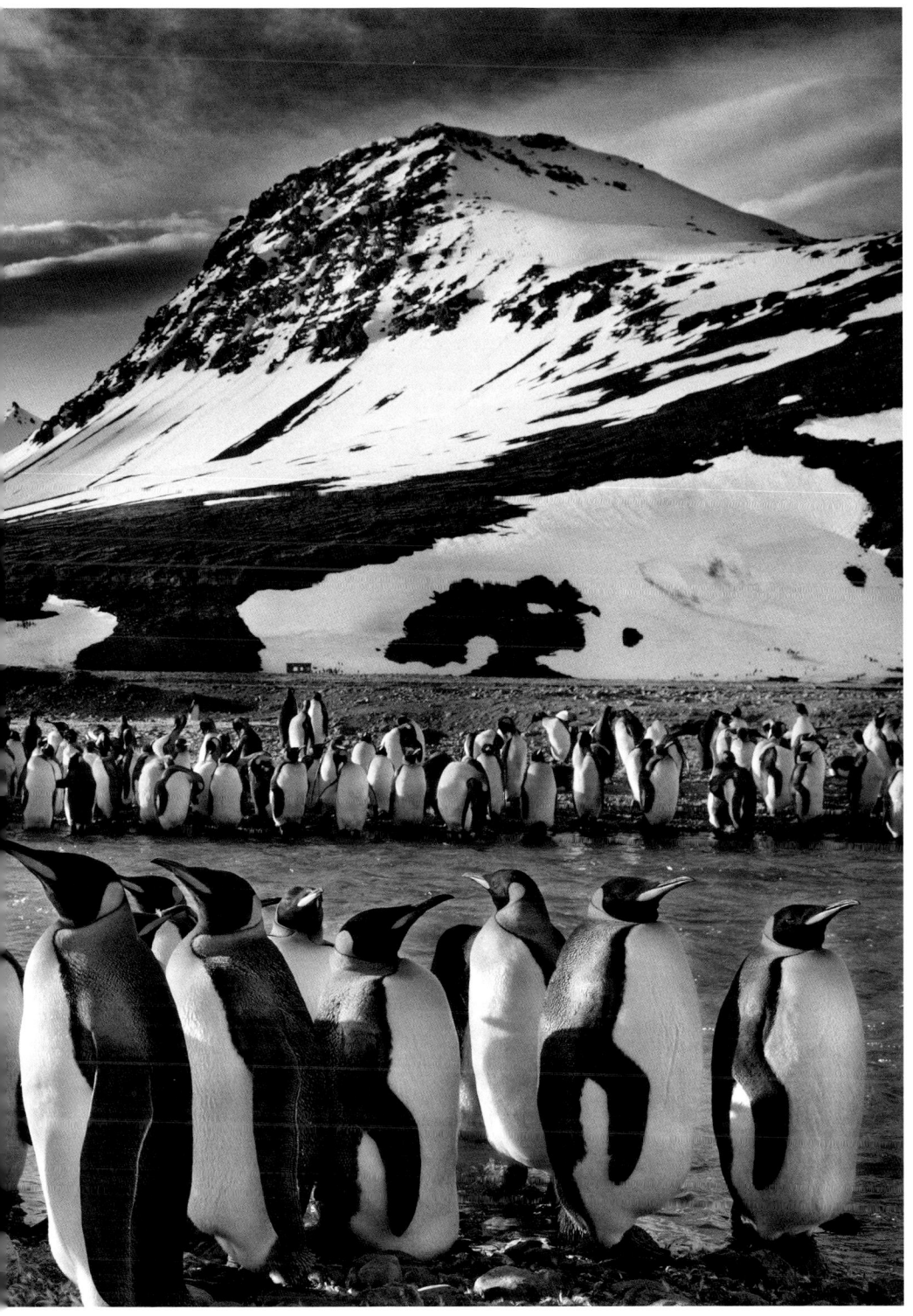

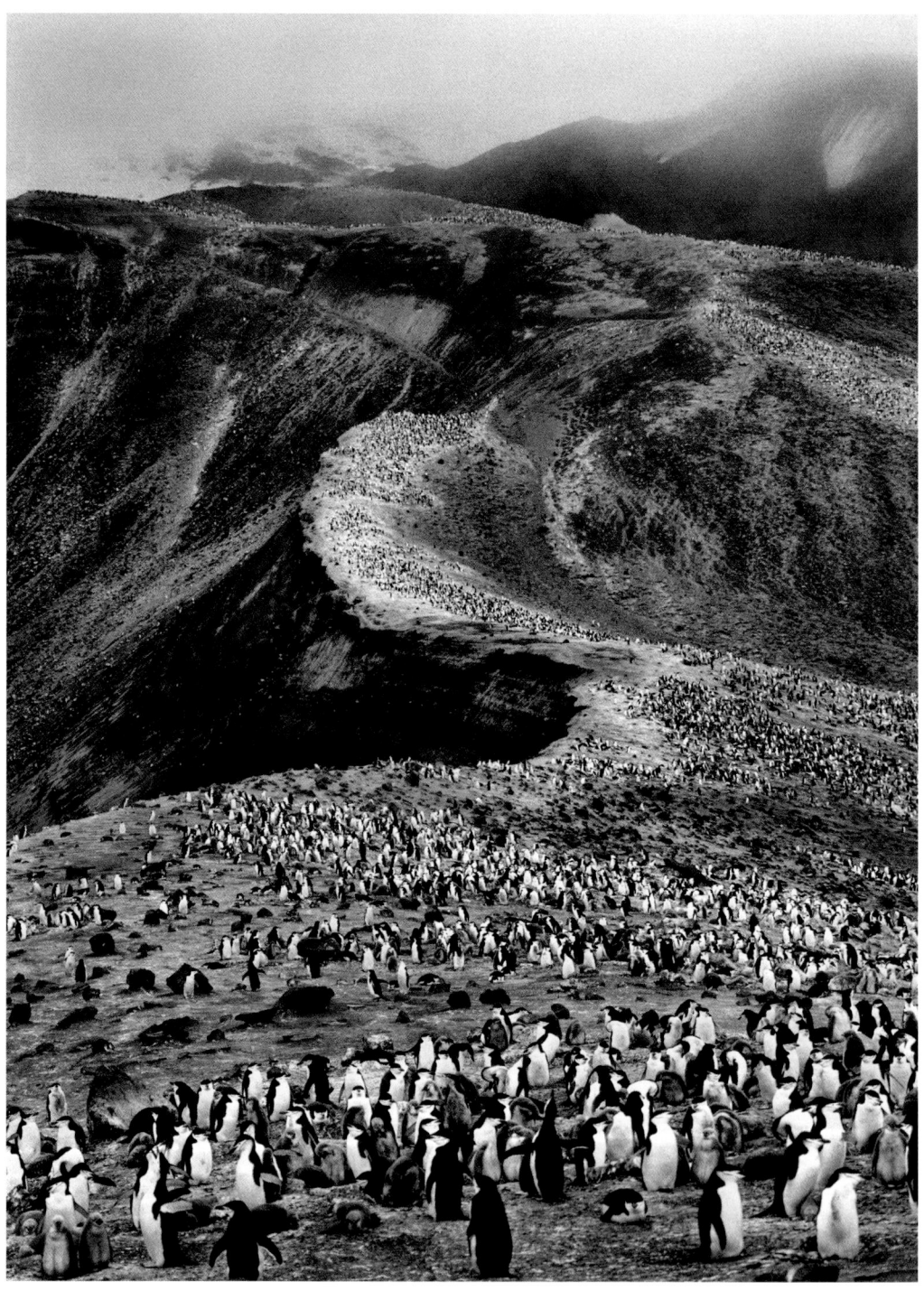

Opposite On Deception Island. The feeling of reaching another planet is particularly intense on Deception Island, at the northern tip of the Antarctic Peninsula. The island is almost a complete circle, with only Neptune's Bellows providing a narrow entrance to the caldera, a 7-mile (12-kilometer)-wide bay created by the collapse of a volcano. This photograph shows the Bailey Head penguin colony on the eastern edge of the island, which can be reached only by scaling a 1,900-foot (582-meter)-high ridge. Speckled black and white, the slopes of the crater are a glacier, which is hidden by rocks in many places, thus making for a hazardous climb; in some places, soil runs down like lava. Once on the other side of the ridge, a 4.2-mile (7-kilometer) walk is still necessary to reach this extraordinary colony of hundreds of thousands of chinstrap penguins (*Pygoscelis antarctica*). Antarctic Peninsula. January and February 2005.

Pages 68/69 Like all nine of the South Sandwich Islands, Saunders Island has an active volcano. Mount Michael, on the eastern part of Saunders Island, is totally inaccessible. Hills to the west are, in turn, completely covered by ice and ash. Over many years, the erosion of this compacted ash has created a surreal landscape. The island is also inhabited by penguins of several different species, notably the chinstrap (*Pygoscelis antarctica*), which number over 150,000 couples. South Sandwich Islands. November and December 2009.

Pages 70/71 The Perito Moreno Glacier. This glacier, 19 miles (30 kilometers) long and 2,300 feet (700 meters) deep, is one of 48 fed by the South Patagonian Ice Field, itself the world's third largest reserve of fresh water. Covering an area of 97 square miles (250 square kilometers), it is one of only three

Patagonian glaciers that are not retreating. Periodically, the glacier advances into Lake Argentino forming a natural dam. Water builds up at Brazo Rico until the pressure is so great that, every three years or so, in a spectacular display, it bursts through a 200-foot (60-meter)-high wall of ice. Where the Perito Moreno Glacier reaches Lake Argentino, it is 3 miles (5 kilometers) wide and 560 feet (170 meters) deep. It advances at roughly 2,300 feet (700 meters) per year, but its front has barely moved in 90 years since it loses mass at almost the same rate. Argentine Patagonia. March and April 2007.

Pages 72/73 King penguins (*Aptenodytes patagonicus*) and southern elephant seals (*Mirounga leonina*) at Saint Andrews Bay. This immense bay is home to the largest colony of king penguins in the world (approximately 300,000 couples) as well as at least 10 percent of the globe's southern elephant seals, estimated to total between 650,000 and 750,000. South Georgia. November and December 2009.

Pages 74/75 Chinstrap penguins (*Pygoscelis antarctica*) on an iceberg located between Zavodovski and Visokoi islands. South Sandwich Islands. November and December 2009.

Pages 76/77 At 11,290 feet (3,441 meters), Mount Fitz Roy is the highest peak visible here. To its right are the Mermoz and Guillaumet group of mountains; and to its left stands the Poincenot peak, rising to 9,850 feet (3,002 meters), as well as the Raphael and Saint-Exupéry peaks. Fitz Roy dominates the area, its pyramid-like summit visible from the plains more than 75 miles (120 kilometers) to the east. Viewed from Lake Viedma, its towering scale is breathtaking. Argentine Patagonia. March and April 2007.

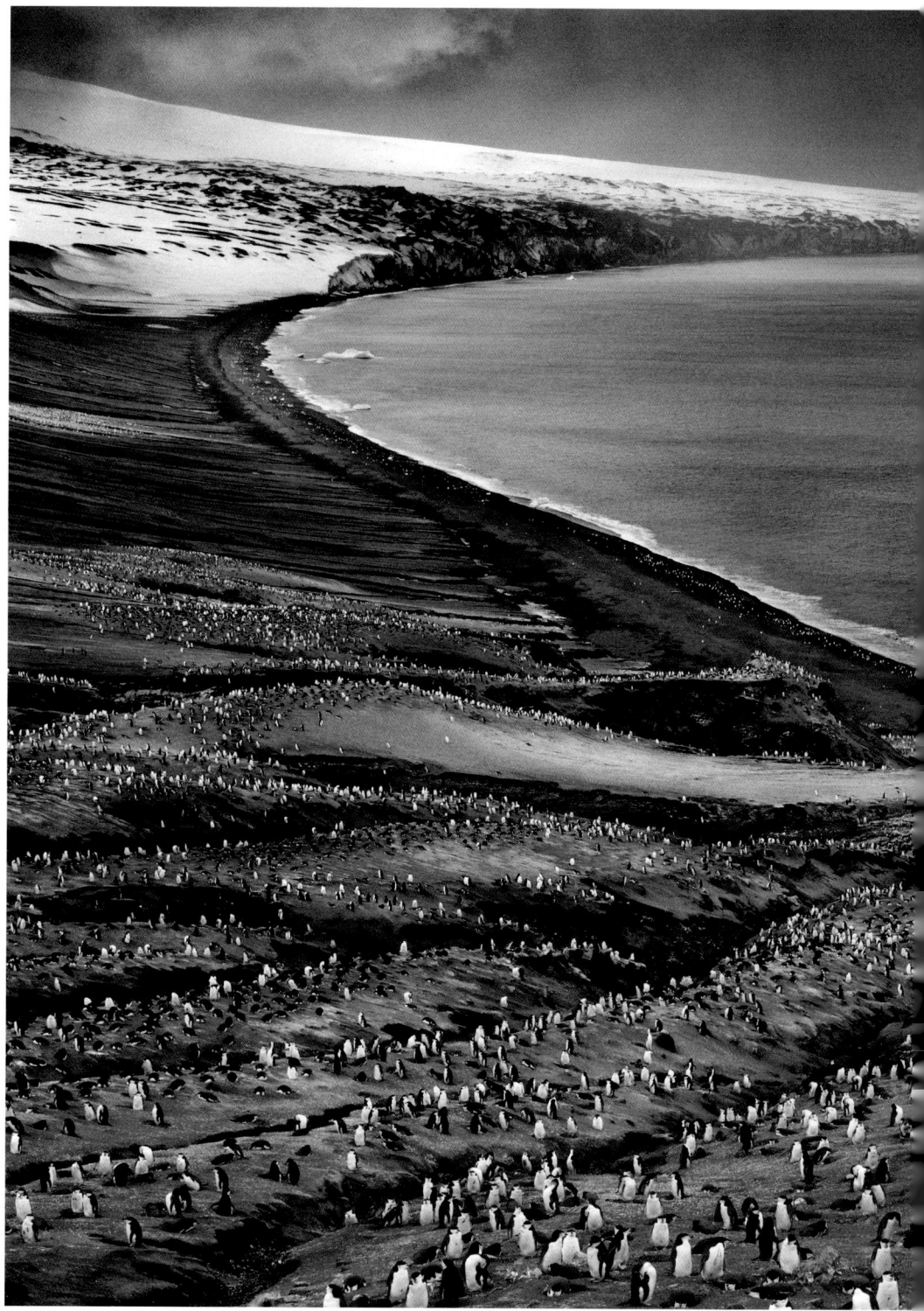

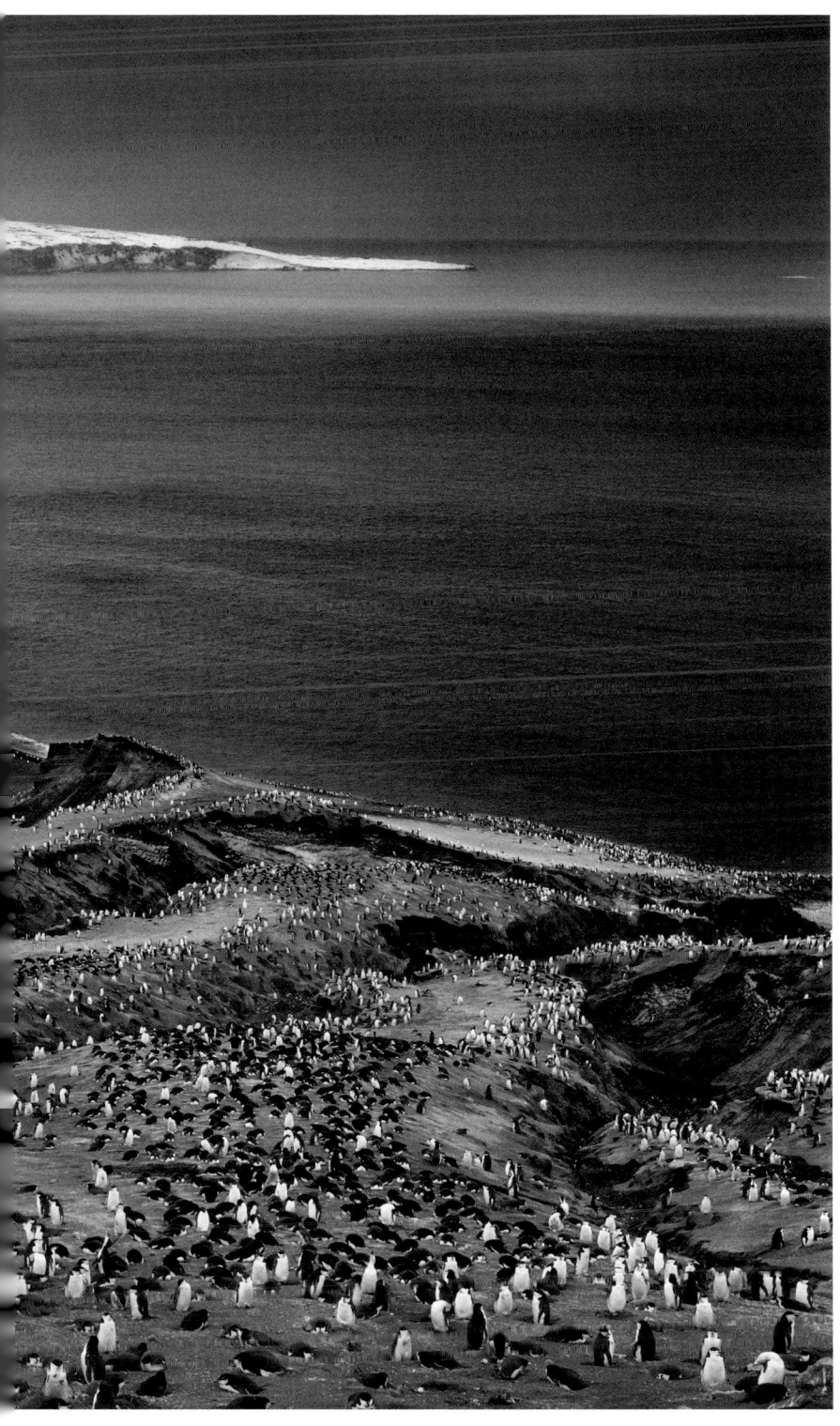

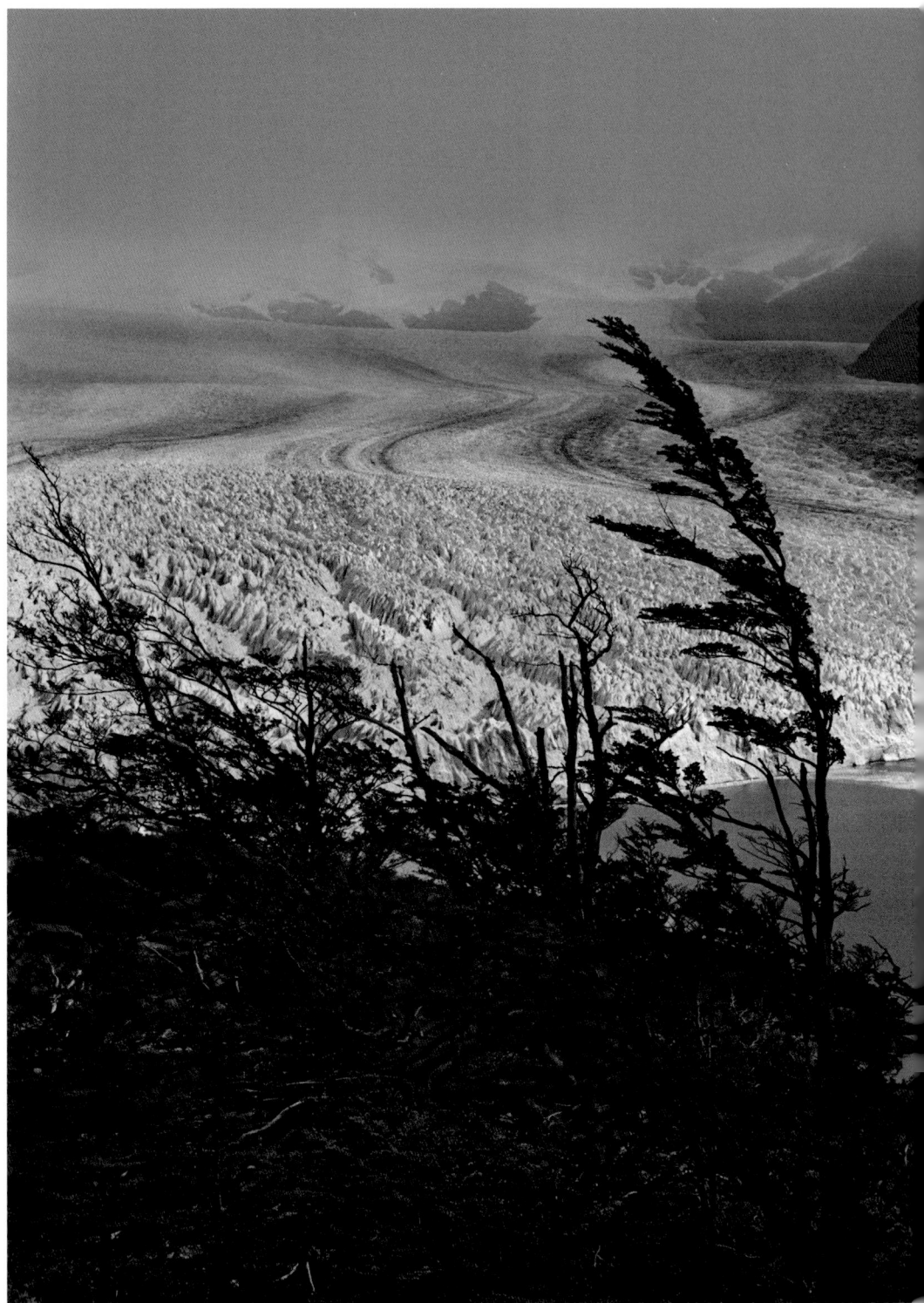

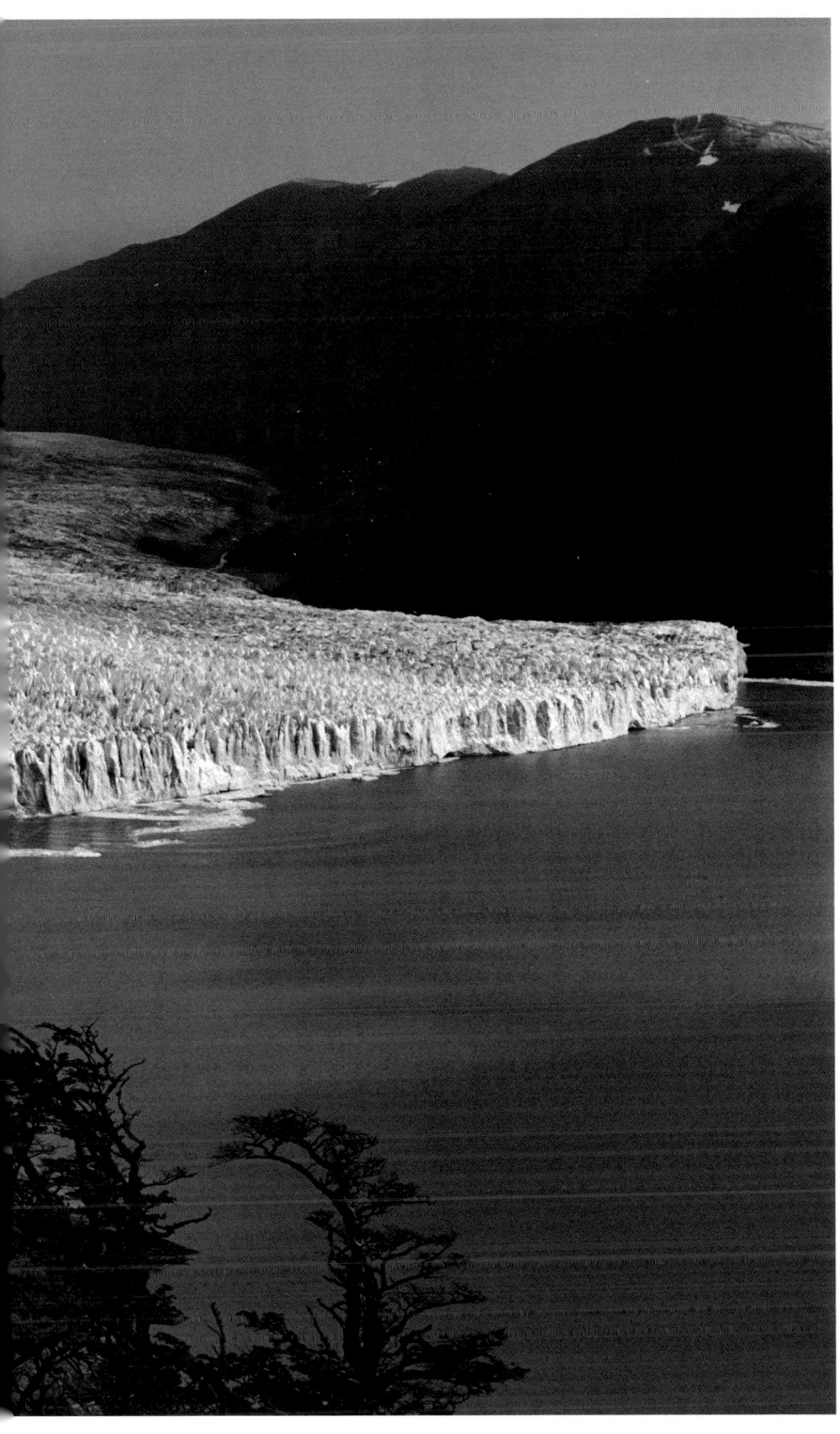

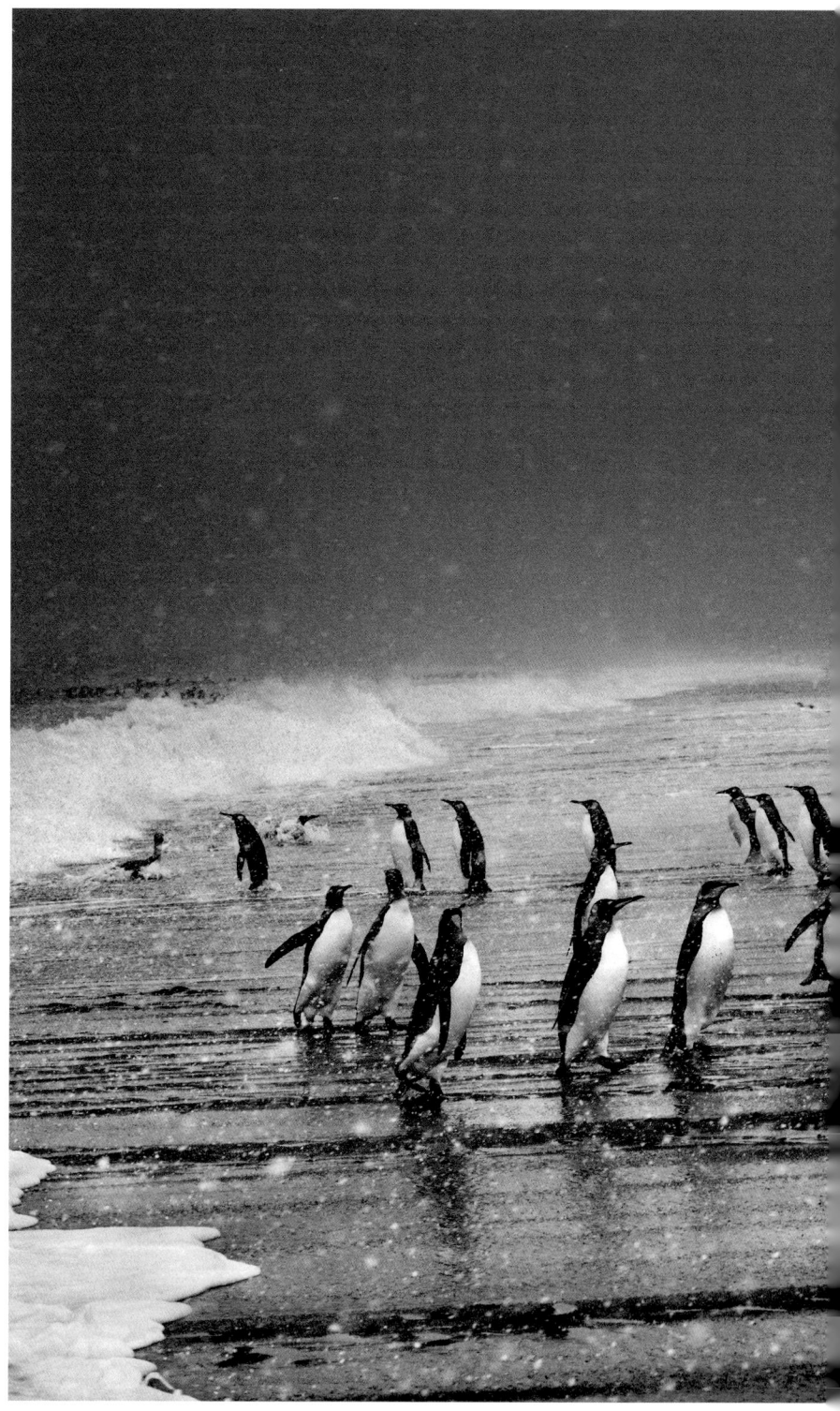

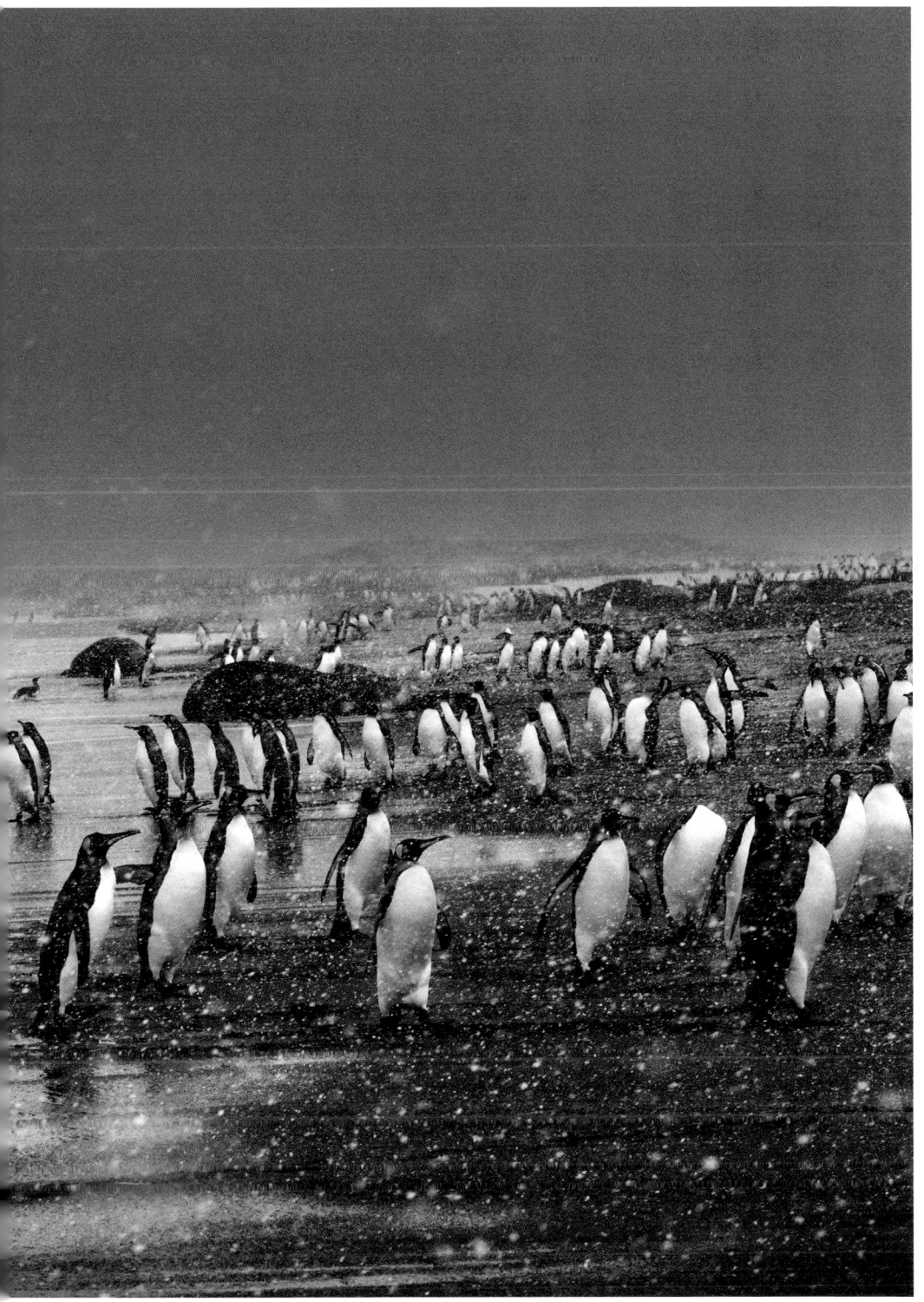

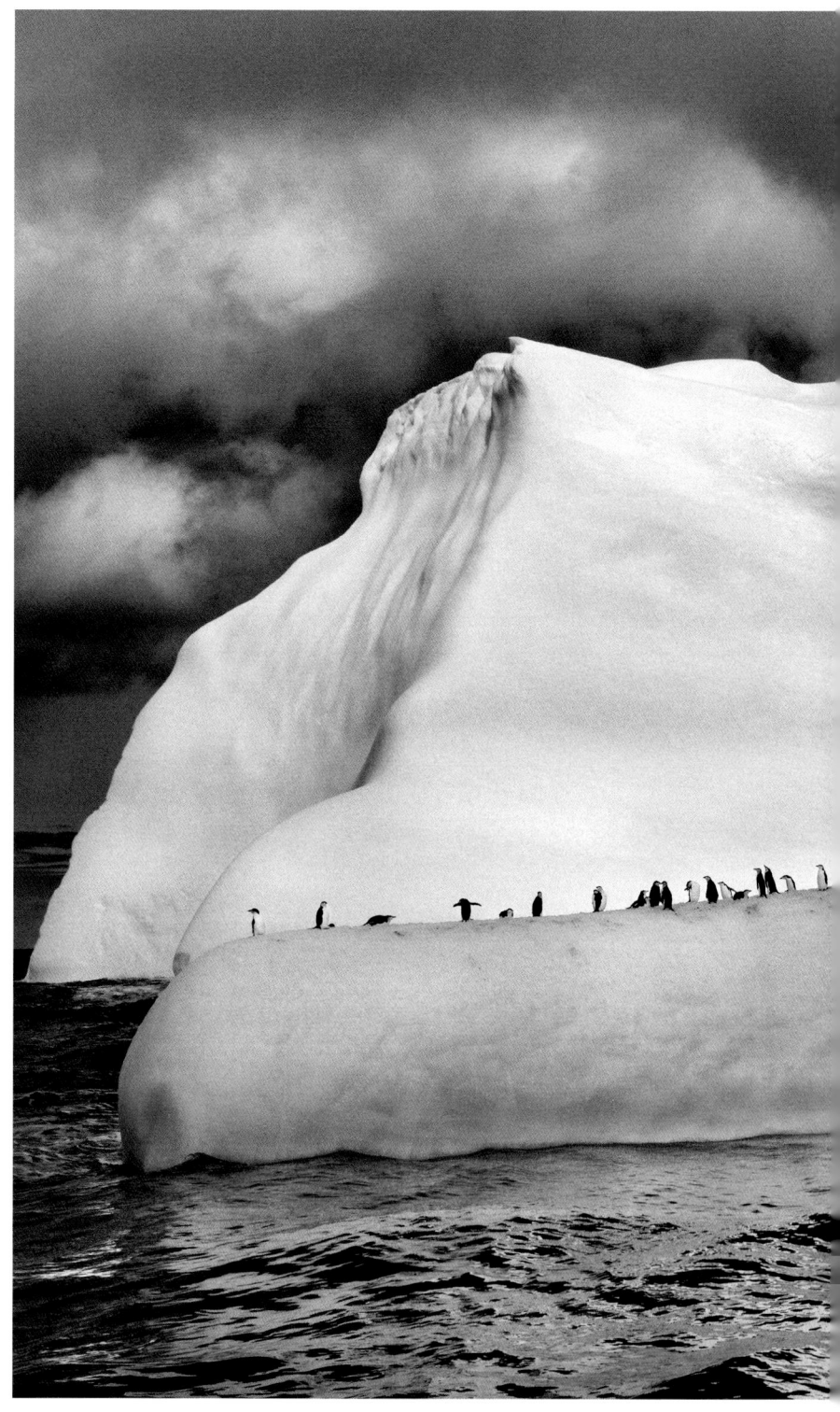

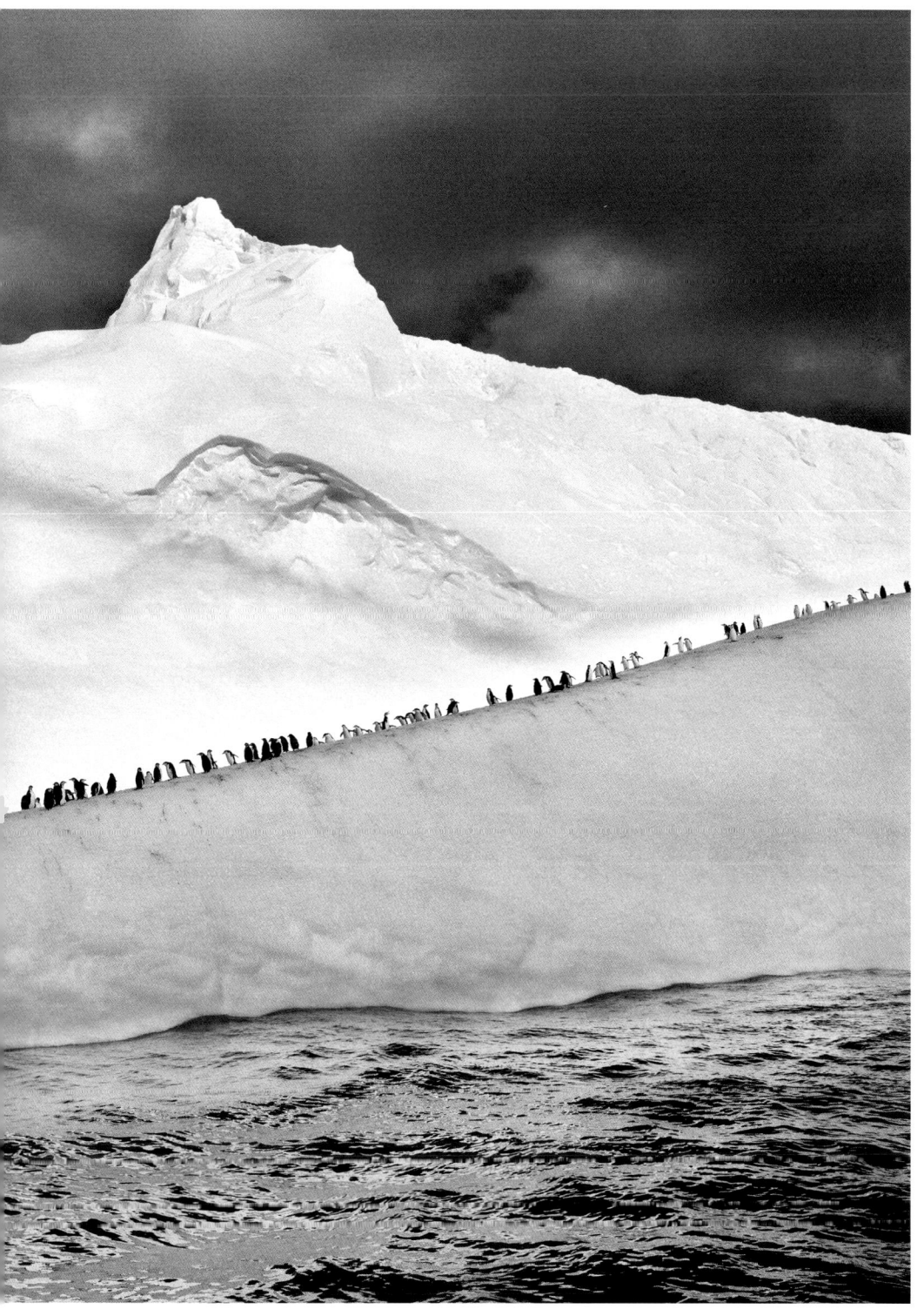

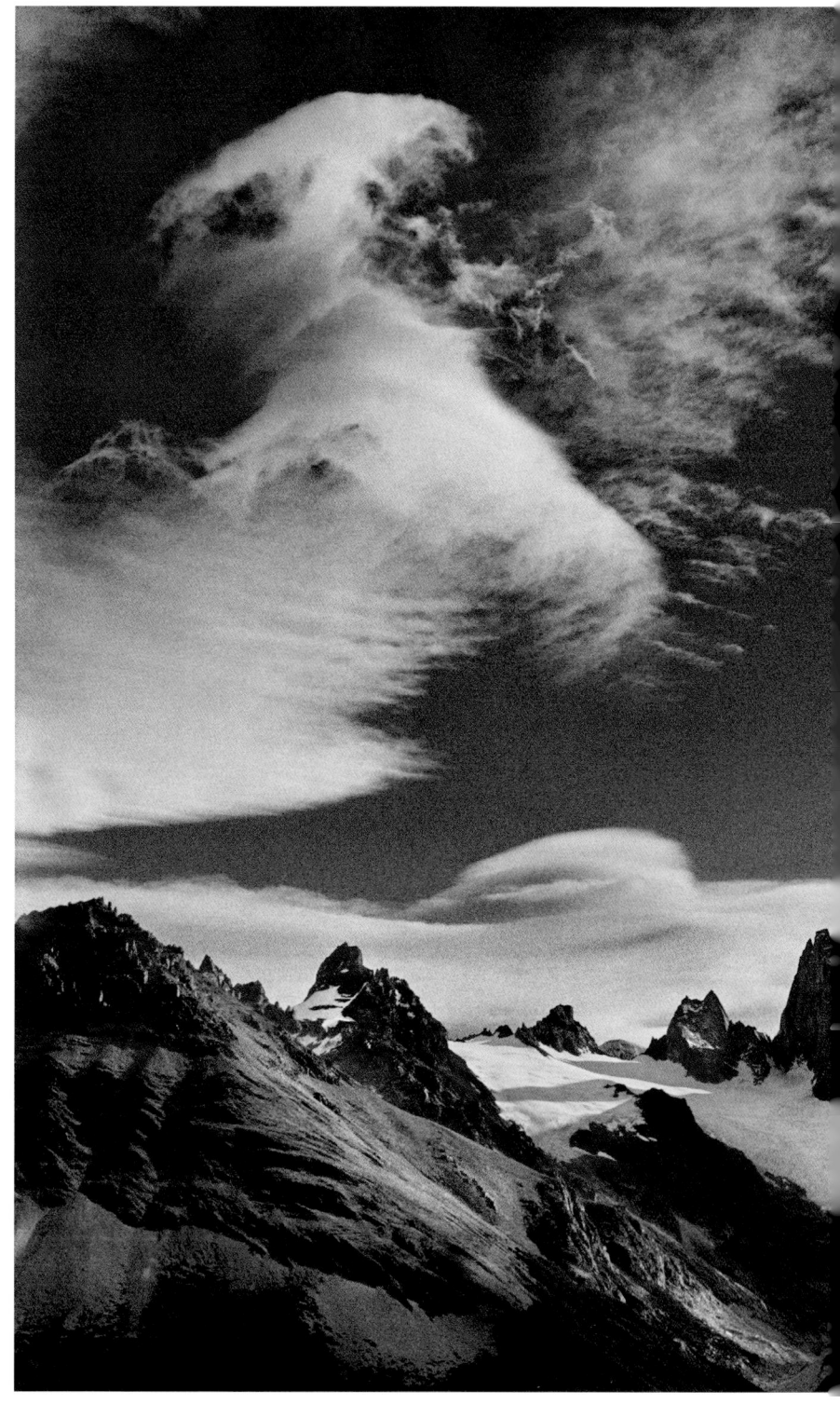

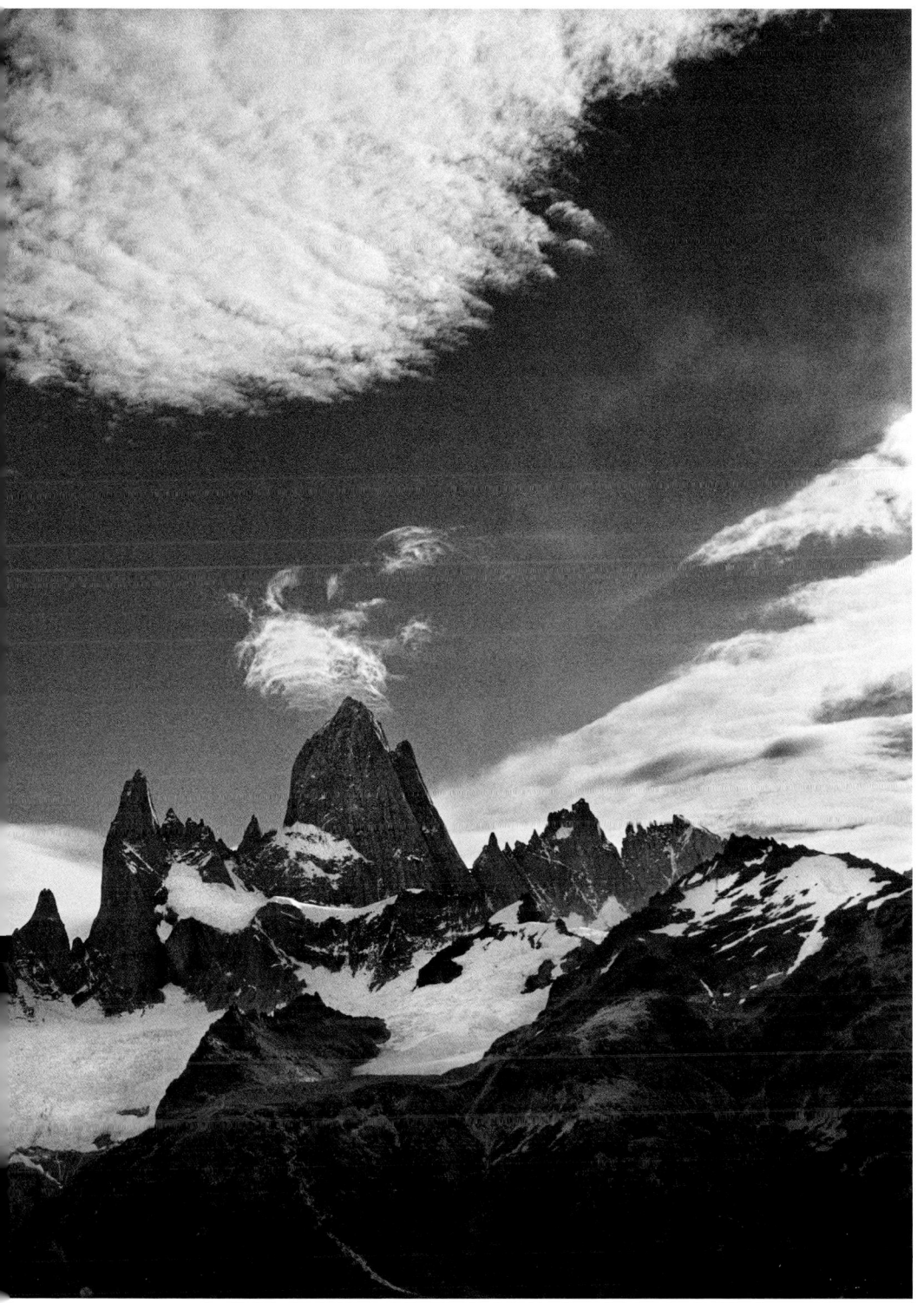

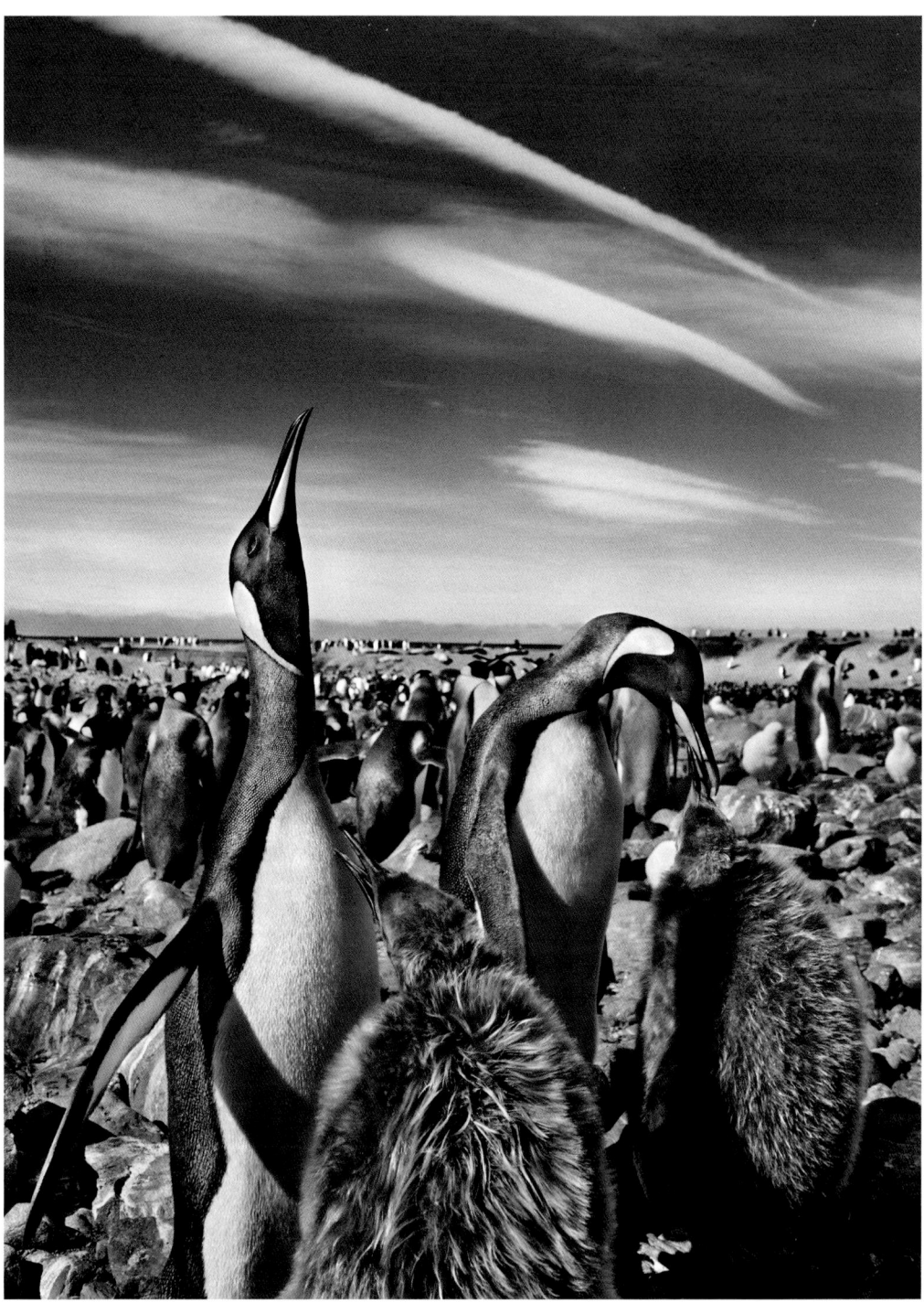

Opposite A colony of king penguins (*Aptenodytes patagonicus*) at Saint Andrews Bay. South Georgia. November and December 2009.

Pages 80/81 Like all nine of the South Sandwich Islands, Saunders Island has an active volcano. Mount Michael, on the eastern part of Saunders Island, is totally inaccessible. Hills to the west are, in turn, completely covered by ice and ash. Over many years, the erosion of this ash has created a surreal landscape. The island is also inhabited by penguins of several different species, notably the chinstrap (*Pygoscelis antarctica*), which number over 150,000 couples. South Sandwich Islands. November and December 2009.

Pages 82/83 Macaroni penguins (*Eudyptes chryslophus*) at Pacific Point on Zavodovski Island. South Sandwich Islands. November and December 2009.

Pages 84/85 Large quantities of bull kelp, or Durvillaea antarctica (*Durvillaea fucales*), are found on the Falkland Islands and on islands north of South Georgia. They are seen here at Boulder Point on Beaver Island in the west of the Falkland Islands. November and December 2009.

Pages 86/87 The Diego Ramírez Archipelago embraces two groups of islands and islets. Their cliffs, covered with a grassy plant called tussock, are home to large colonies of albatrosses and penguins. It is a stunningly beautiful place, with its thick vegetation undulating like waves in the constant wind. The archipelago, about 10 hours' navigation from Cape Horn in the direction of the Antarctic, carries the name of the leader of Portuguese expedition that discovered it on February 12, 1619. The Chilean Navy installed a meteorological station there in 1951. The photograph shows nesting albatrosses on Diego Ramírez Island. Two kinds of albatross live here, the gray-headed albatross (*Thalassarche chrysostoma*) and the black-browed albatross (*Thalassarche melanophris*), both majestic. They coexist peacefully on this island, sometimes even nesting next to each other. Chile's Diego Ramírez Archipelago. January and February 2005.

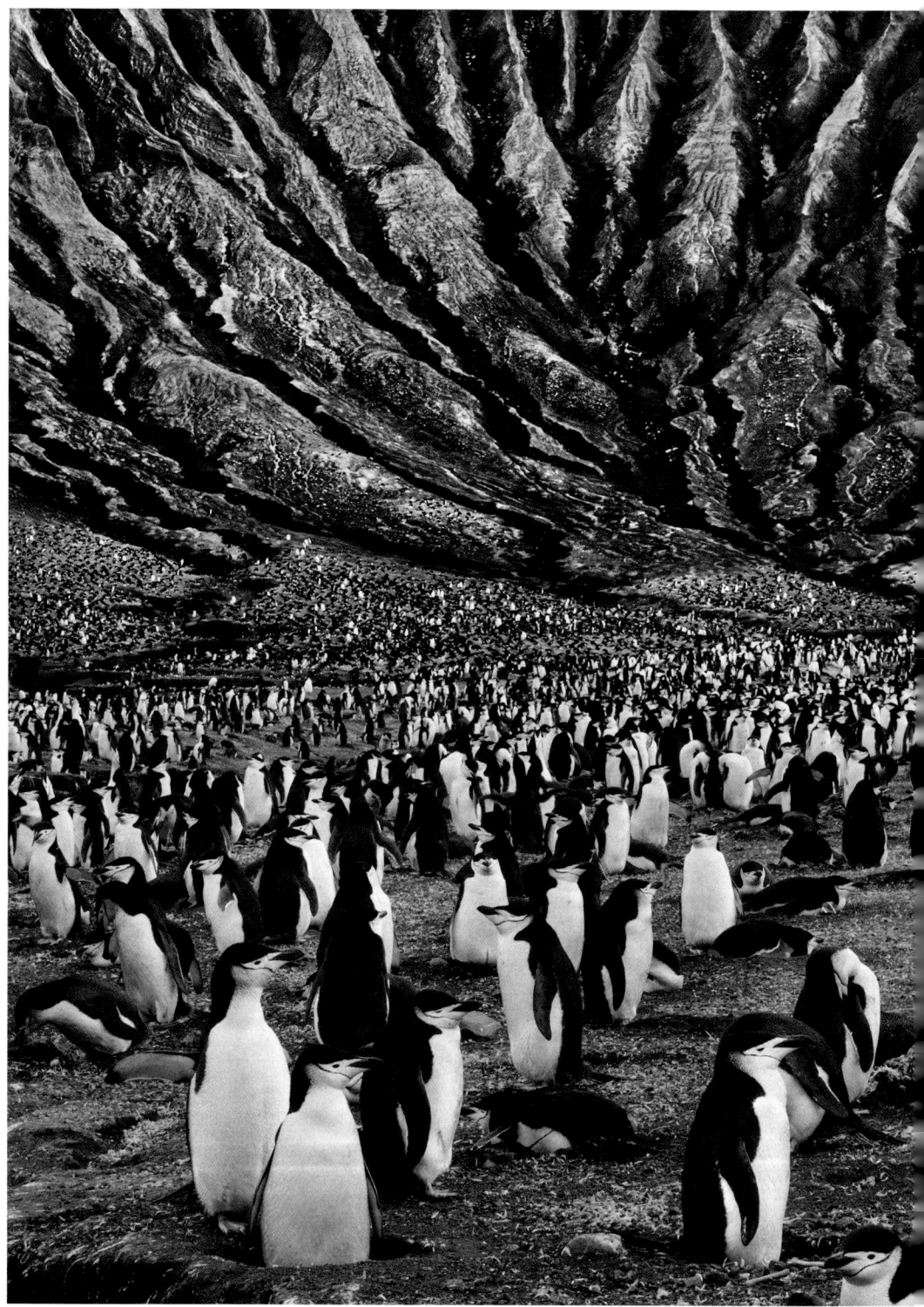

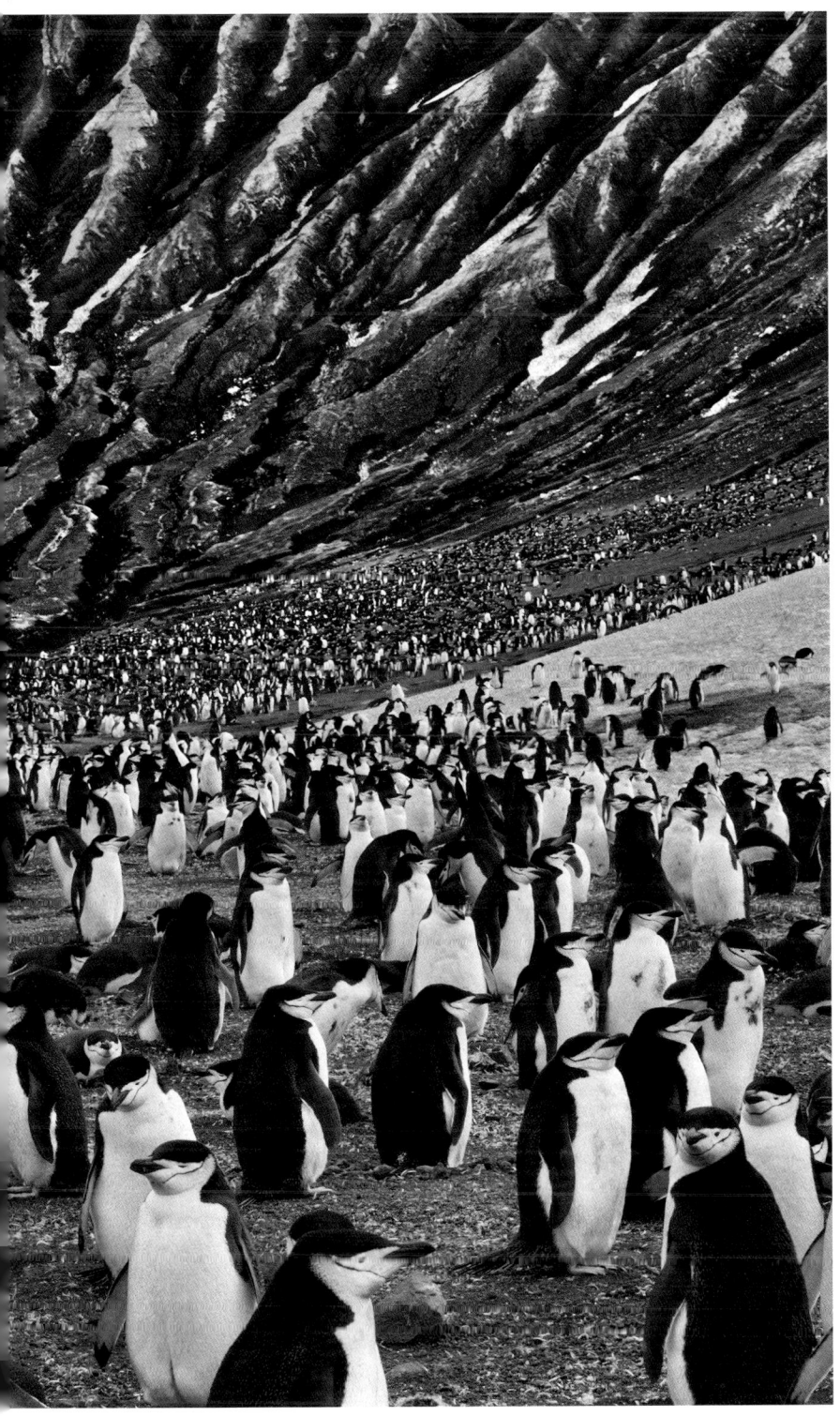

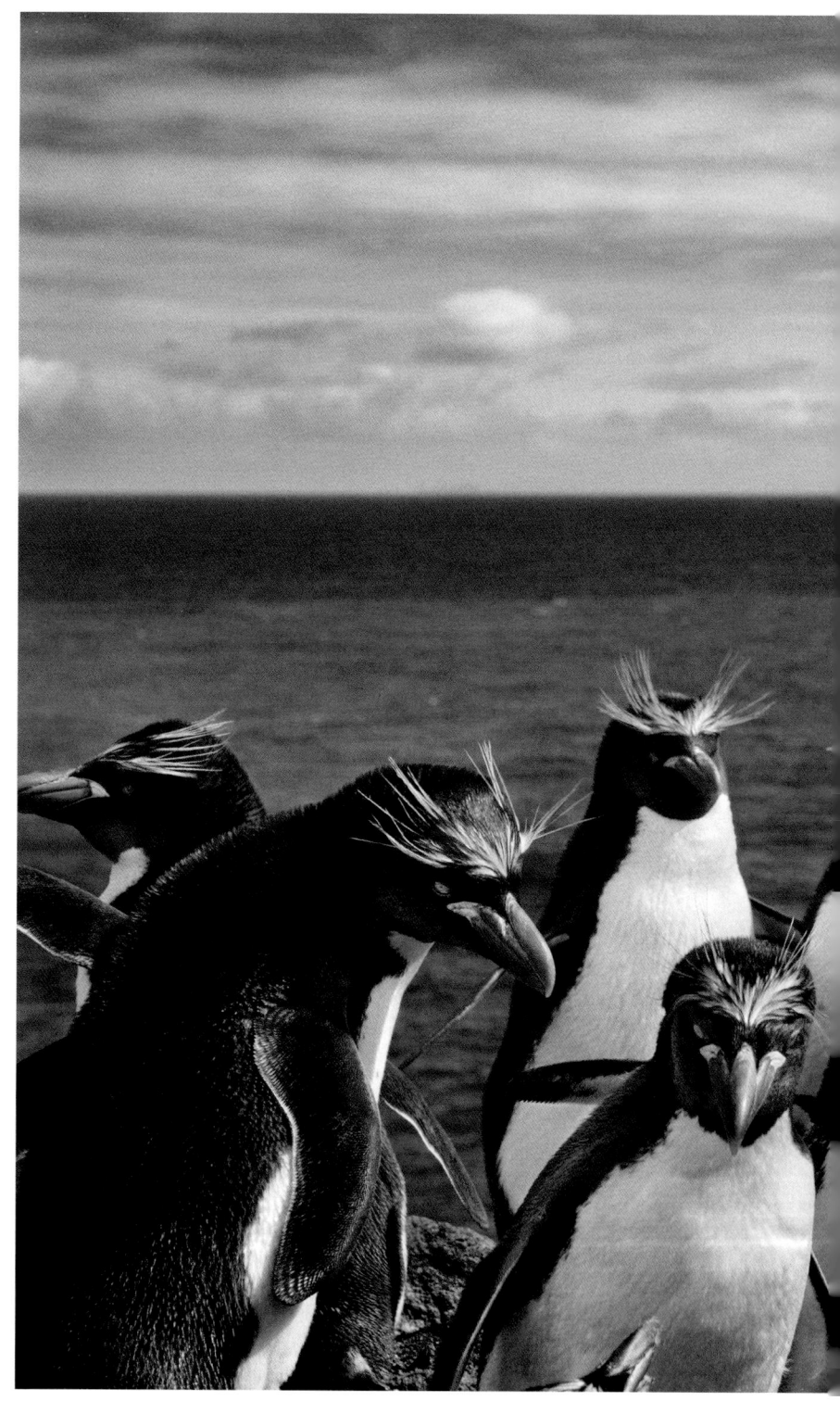

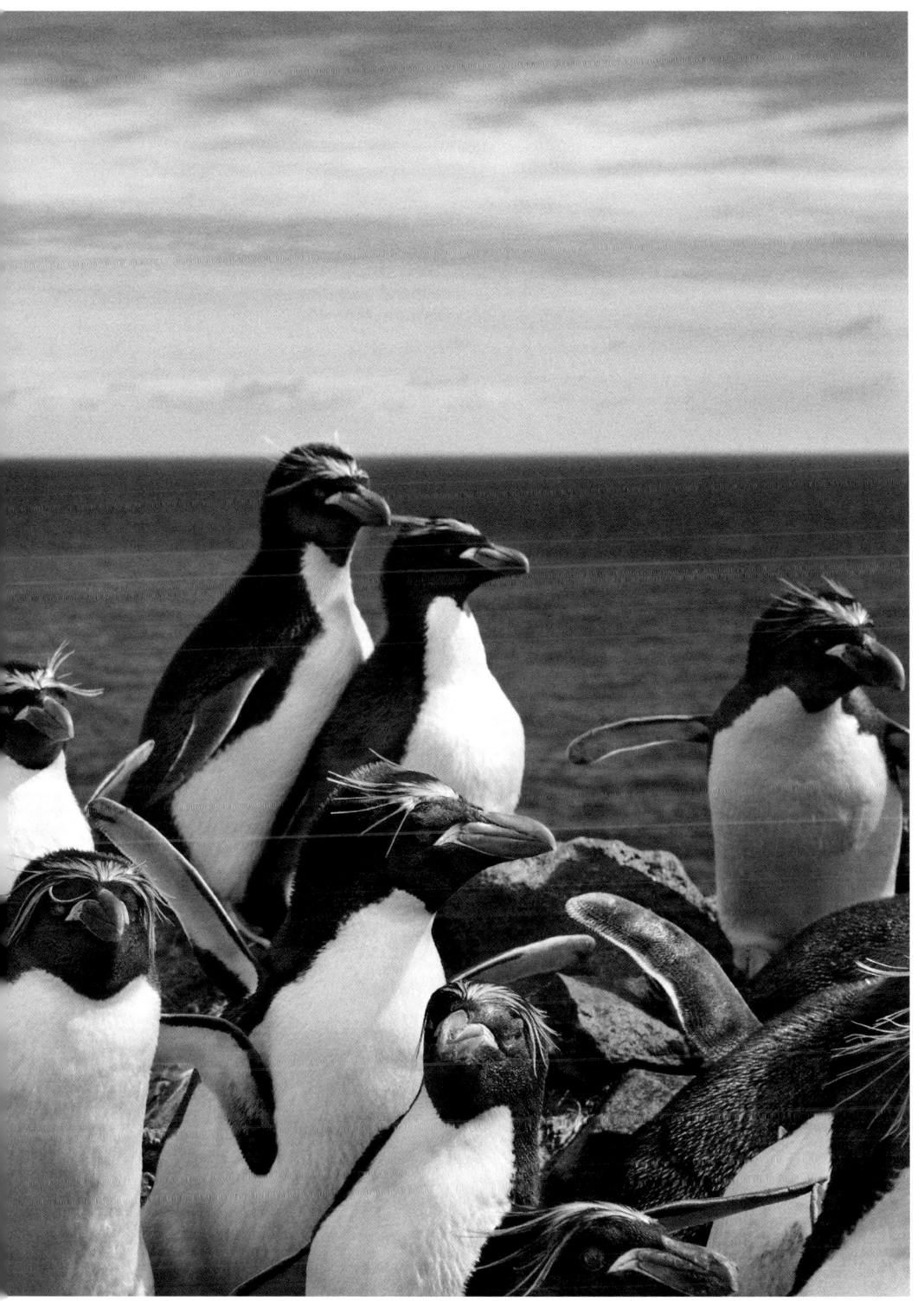

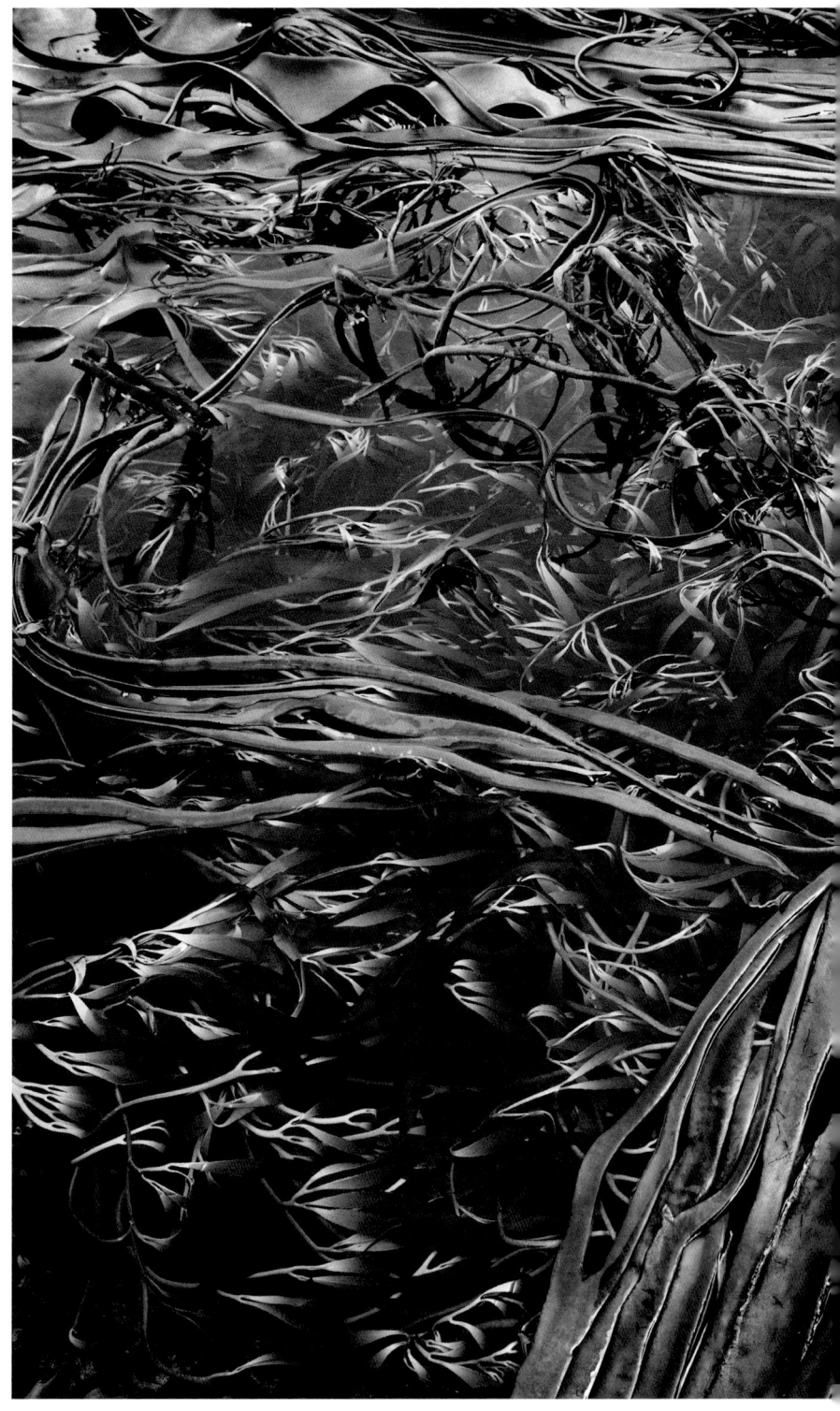

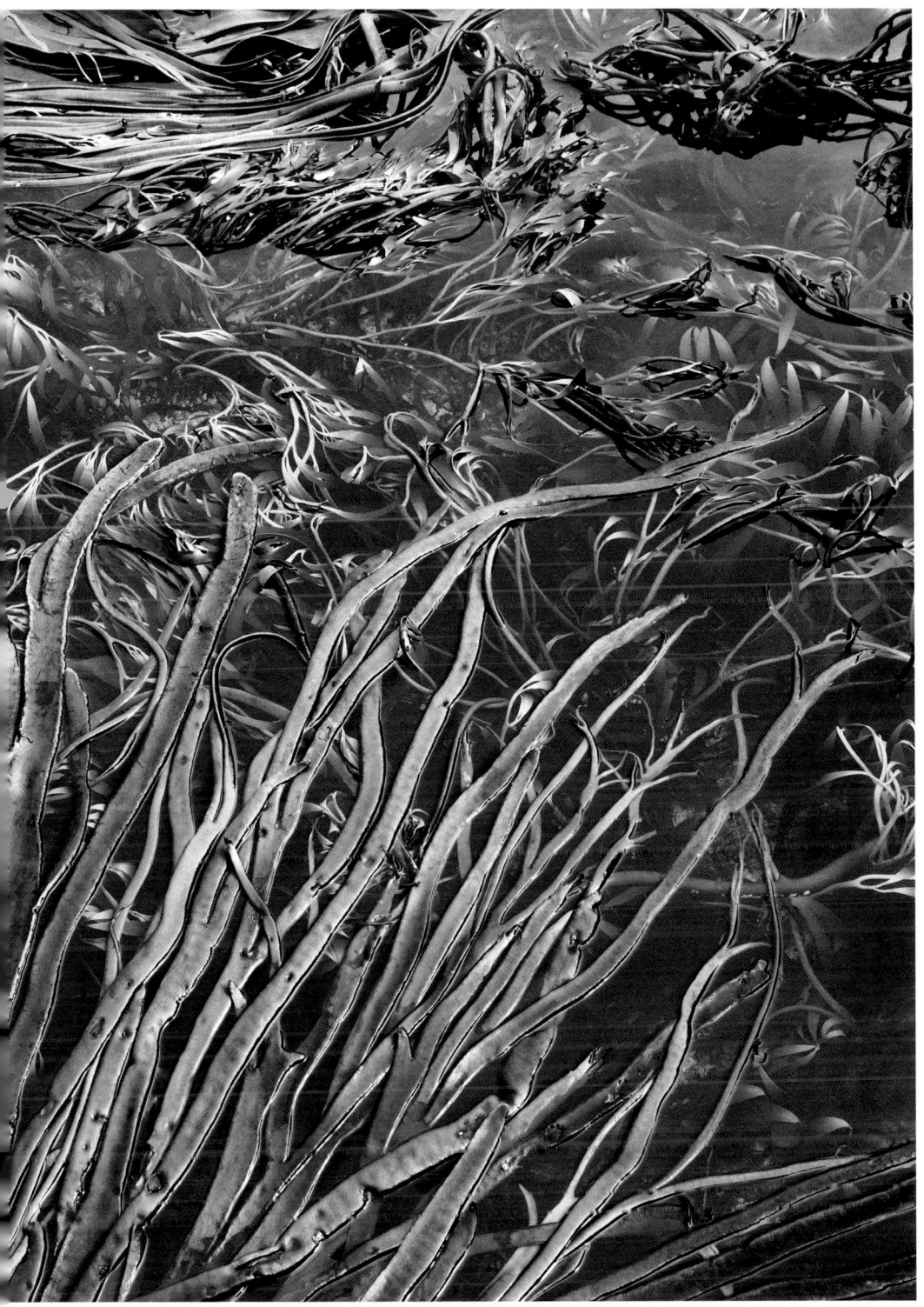

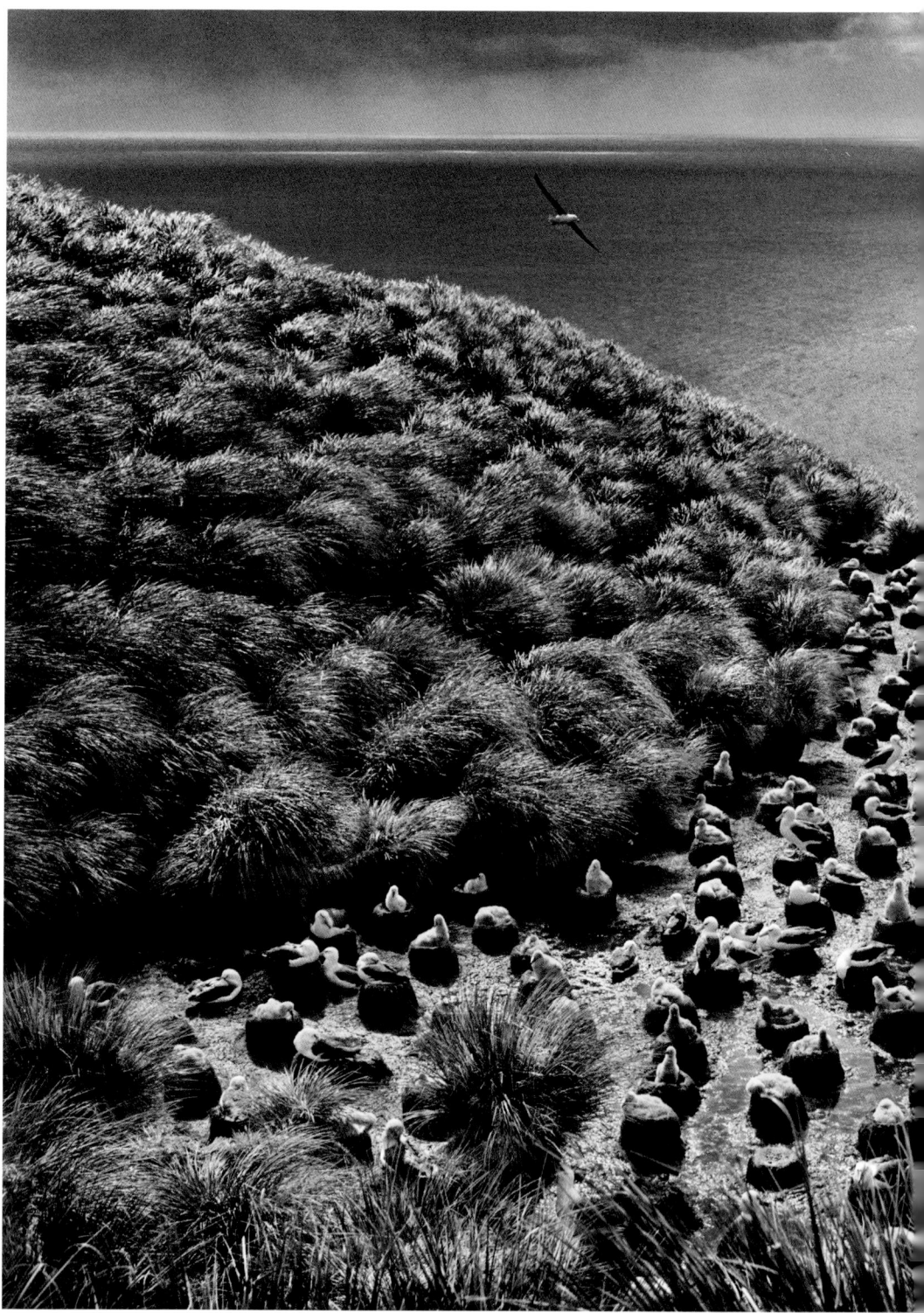

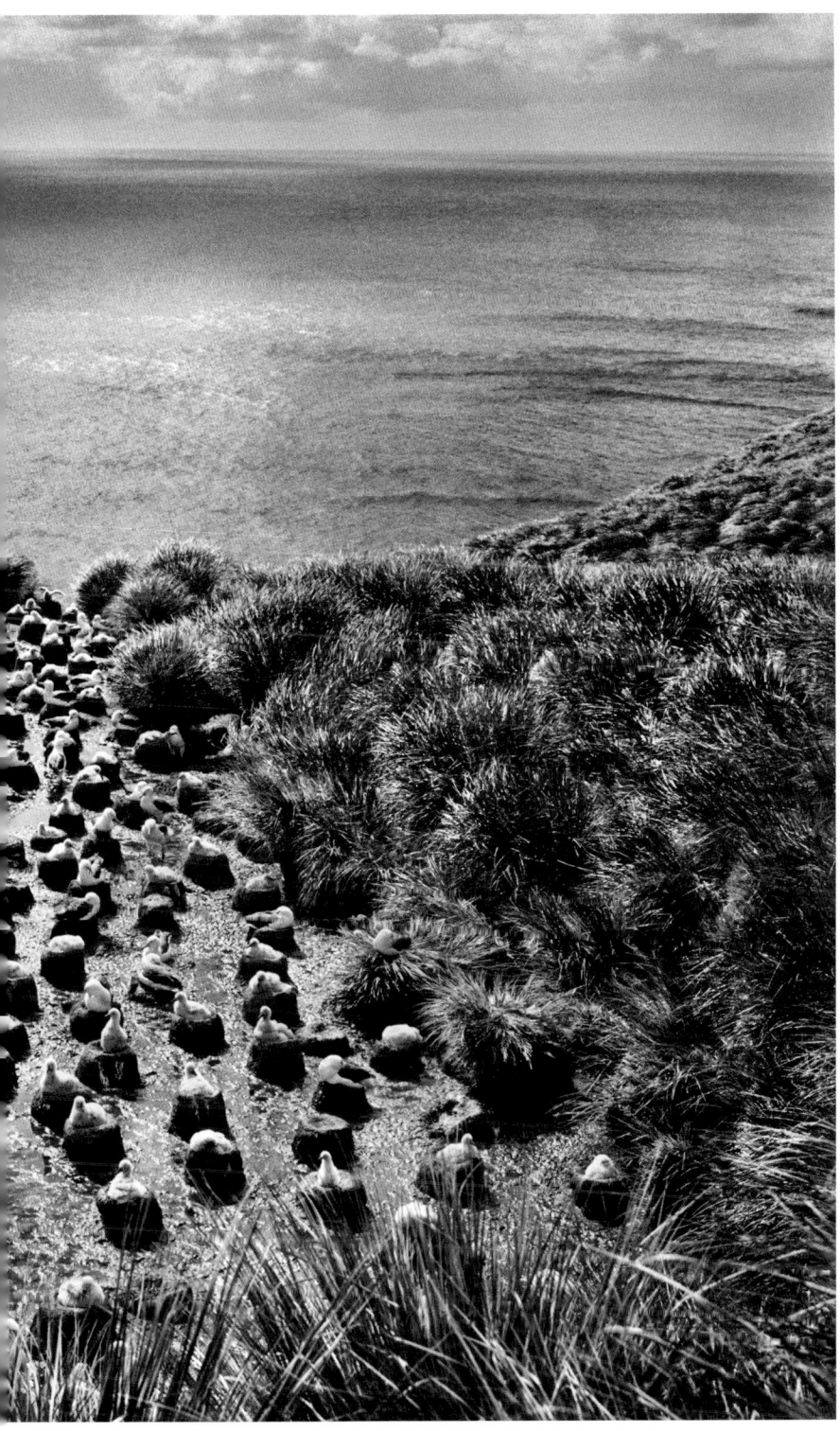

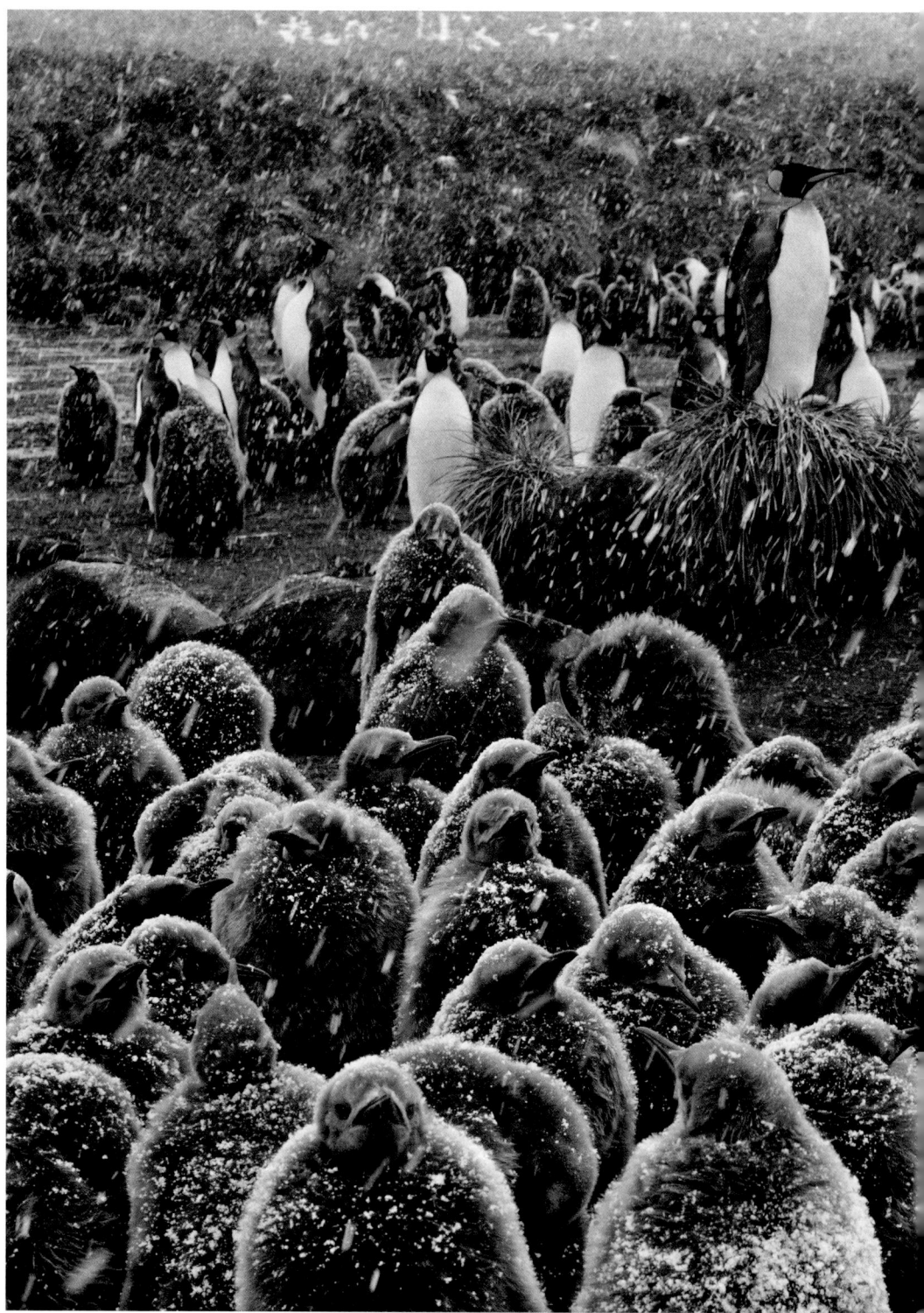

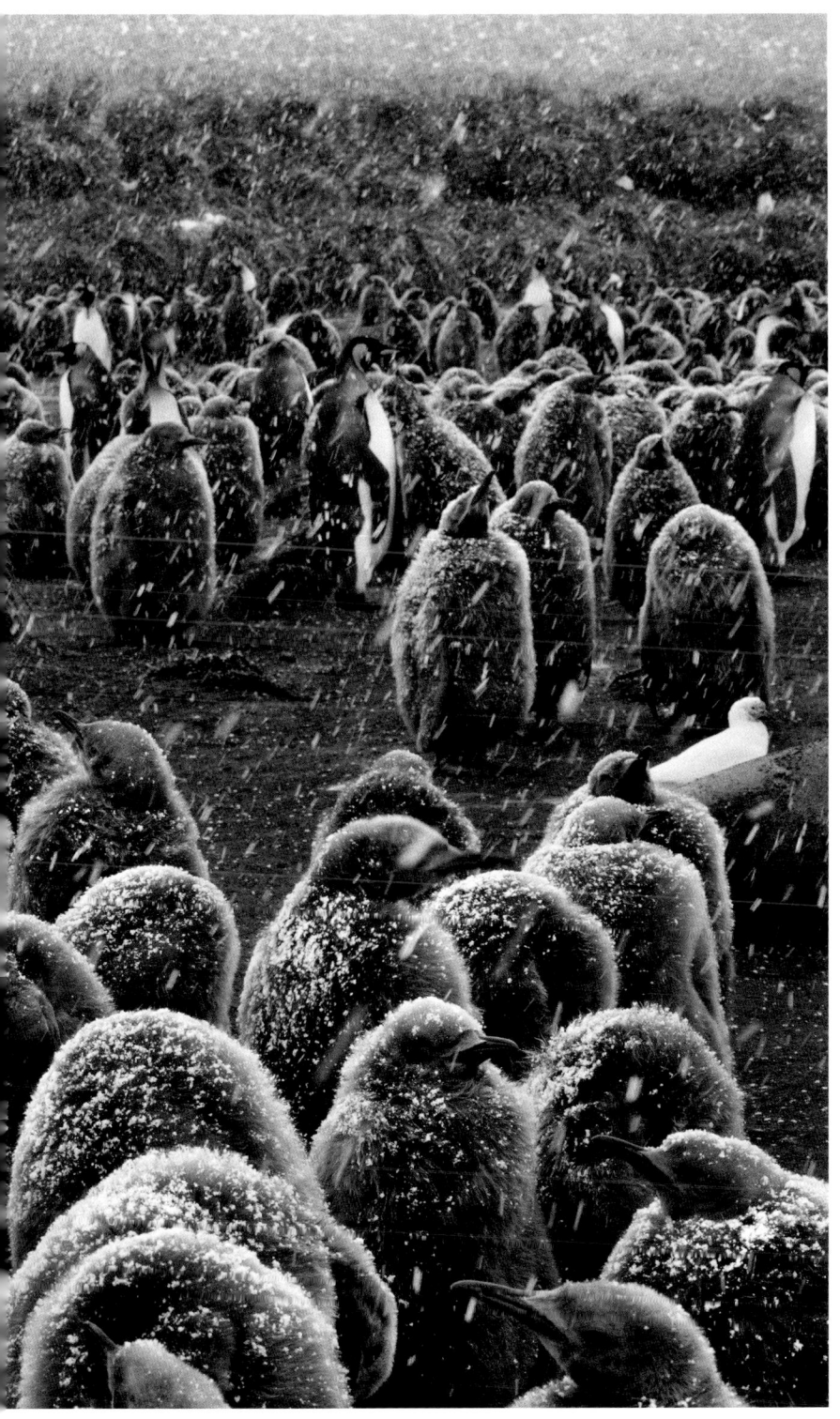

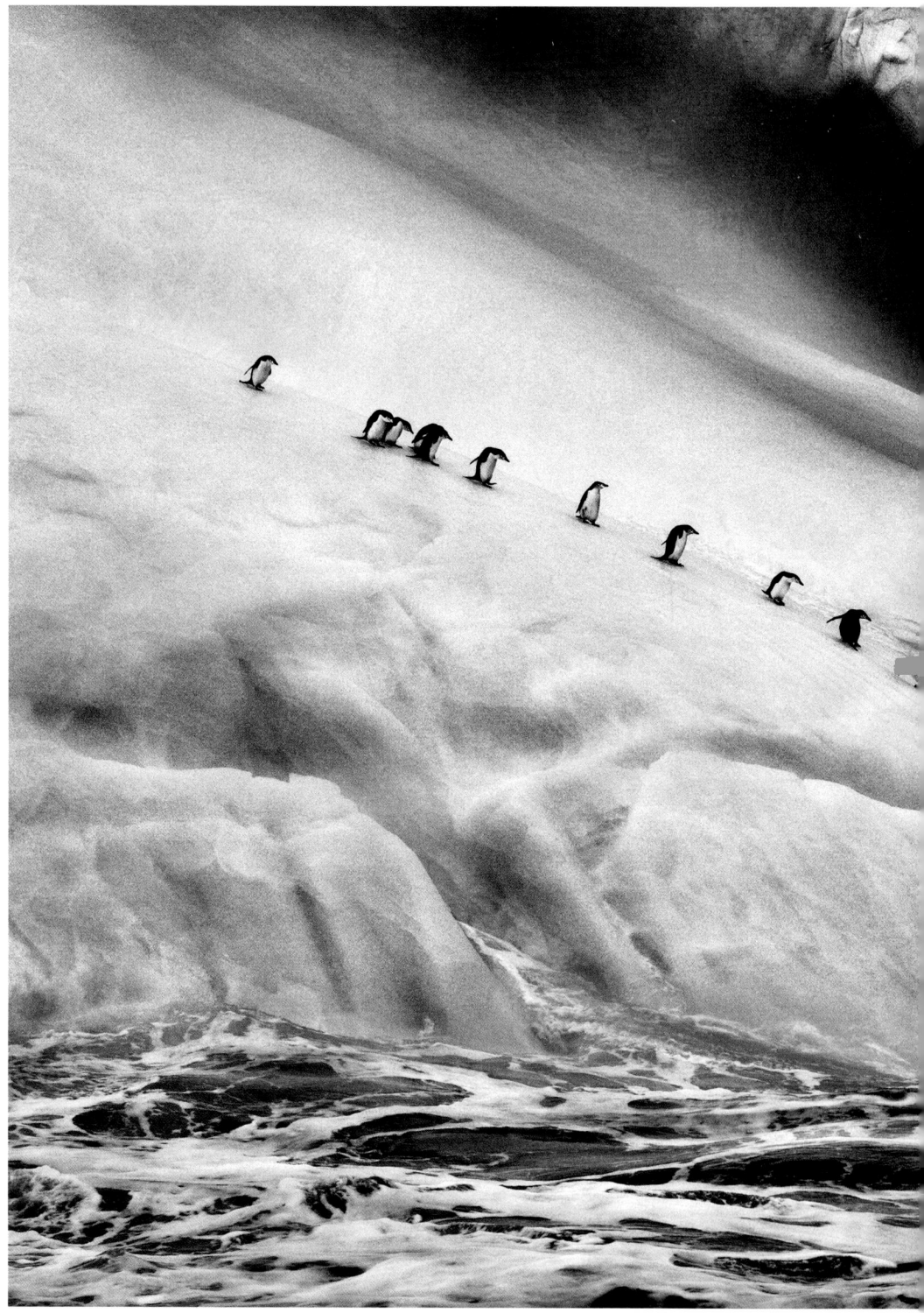

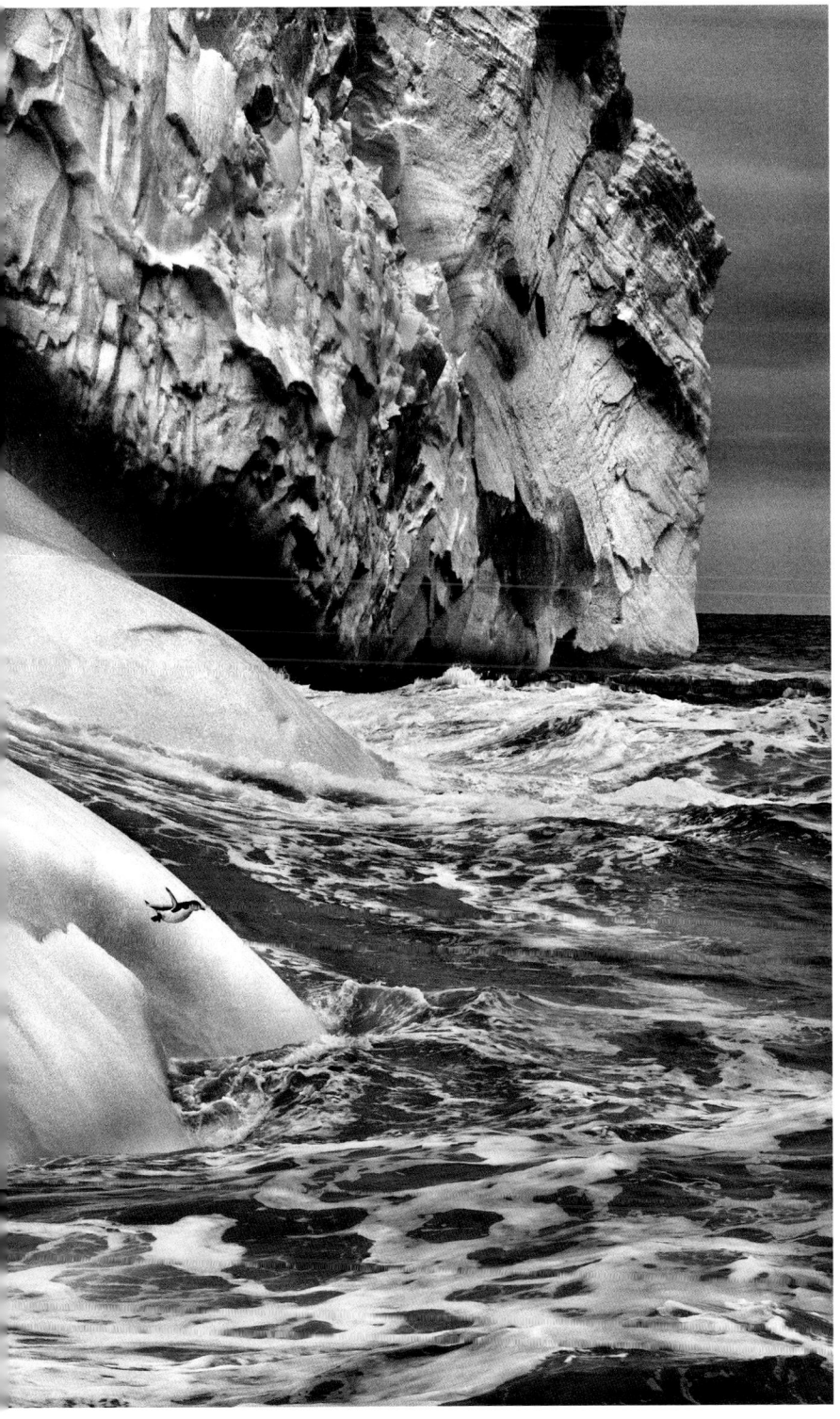

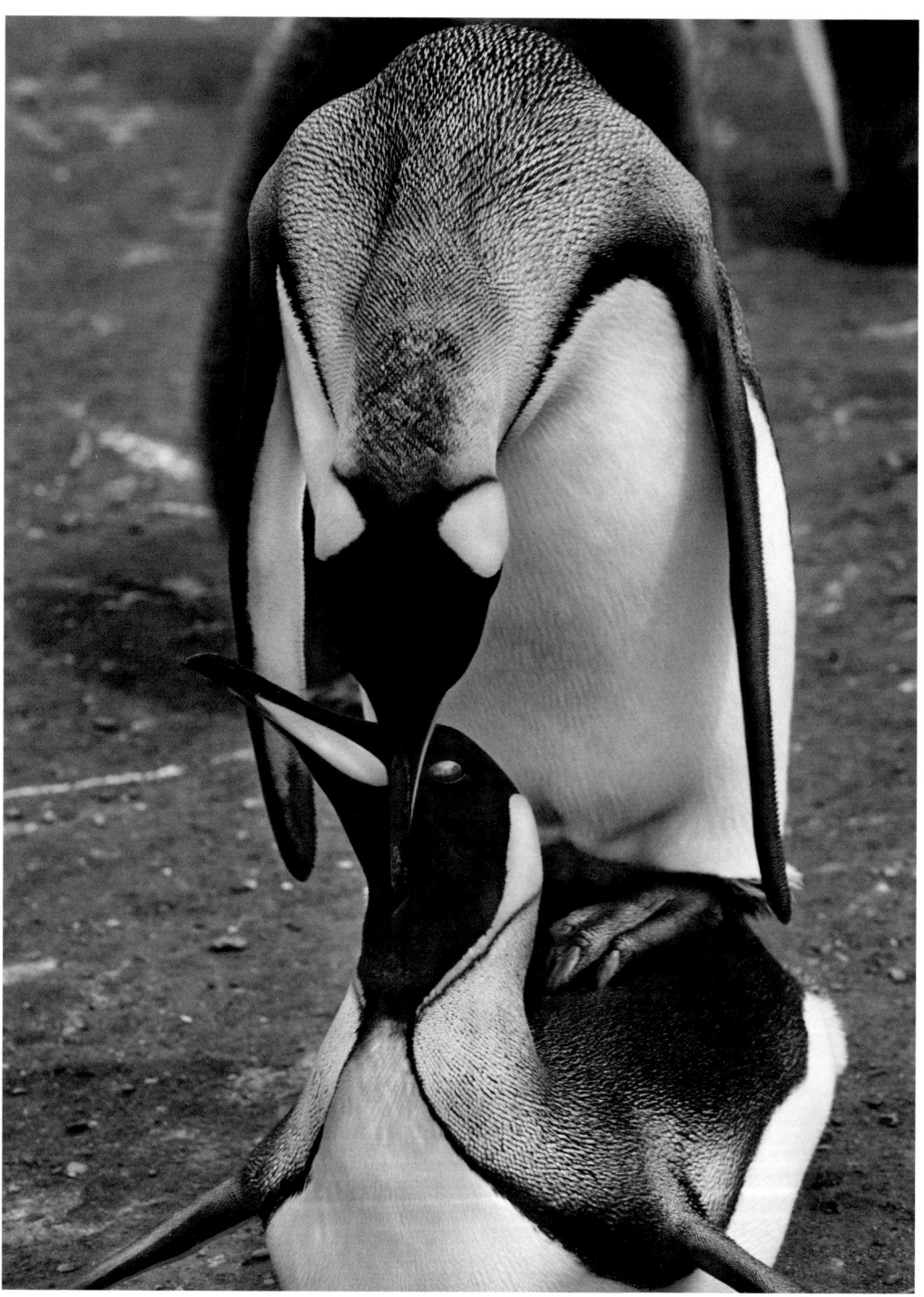

Pages 88/89 A colony of king penguins (*Aptenodytes patagonicus*) at Gold Harbour Bay. South Georgia. November and December 2009

Pages 90/91 Chinstrap penguins (*Pygoscelis antarctica*) on an iceberg located between Zavodovski and Visokoi islands. South Sandwich Islands. November and December 2009.

Opposite King penguins (*Aptenodytes patagonicus*) at Gold Harbour Bay. South Georgia. November and December 2009.

Pages 94/95 A group of fur seals (*Arctocephalus gazella*) on the coast between Punta Delgada and Punta Caleta on Argentina's Valdés Peninsula. This outstanding sanctuary for marine fauna is also excep

tionally beautiful, with strong winds creating huge sand dunes and, outside its two sheltered gulfs, turning the sea into one of the roughest on Earth. Valdés Peninsula. Argentina. September and October 2004.

Pages 96/97 This view of the Grey Glacier from John Gardner Pass reveals the erosion of rocks caused by the constant movement of the glacier. The Southern Patagonian Ice Field, which straddles Chile and Argentina, boasts several spectacular glaciers, including Grey Glacier in the Torres del Paine National Park in Chile. This glacier, which covers 100 square miles (270 square kilometers) and, when measured in 1996, was 17 miles (28 kilometers) long, begins in the Patagonian Andes to the west and enters Grey Lake in three tongue-like lobes. Chilean Patagonia. March and April 2007.

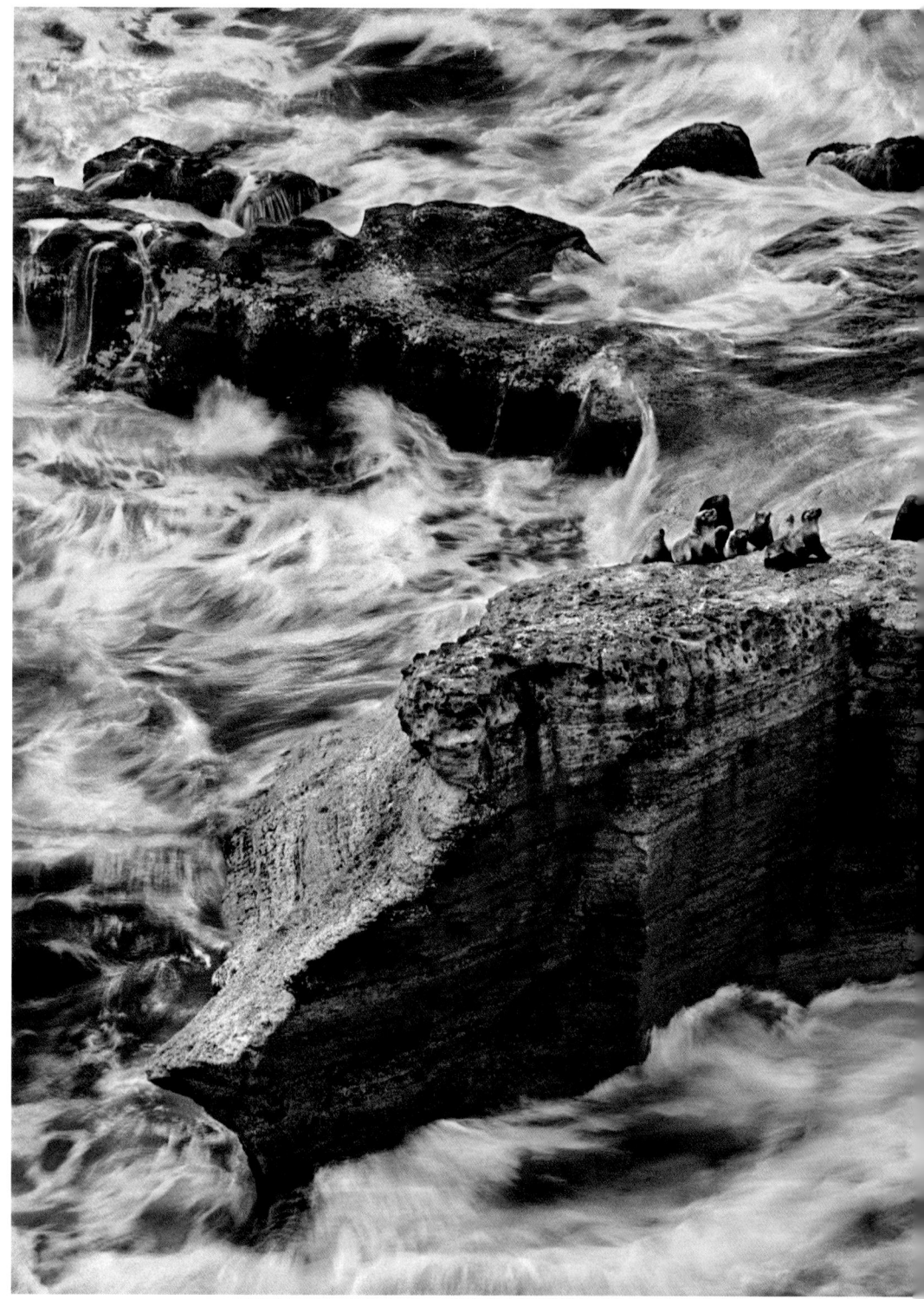

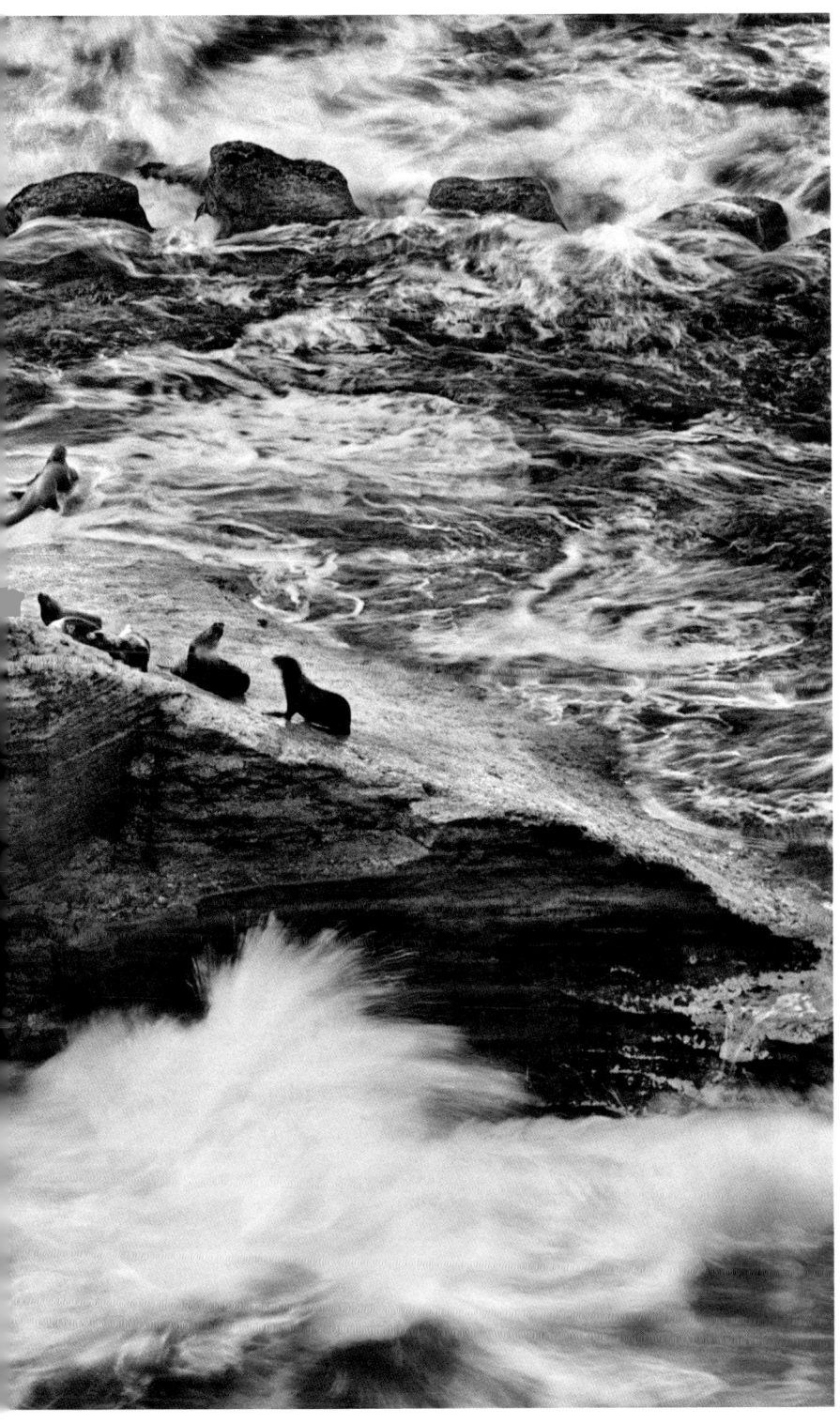

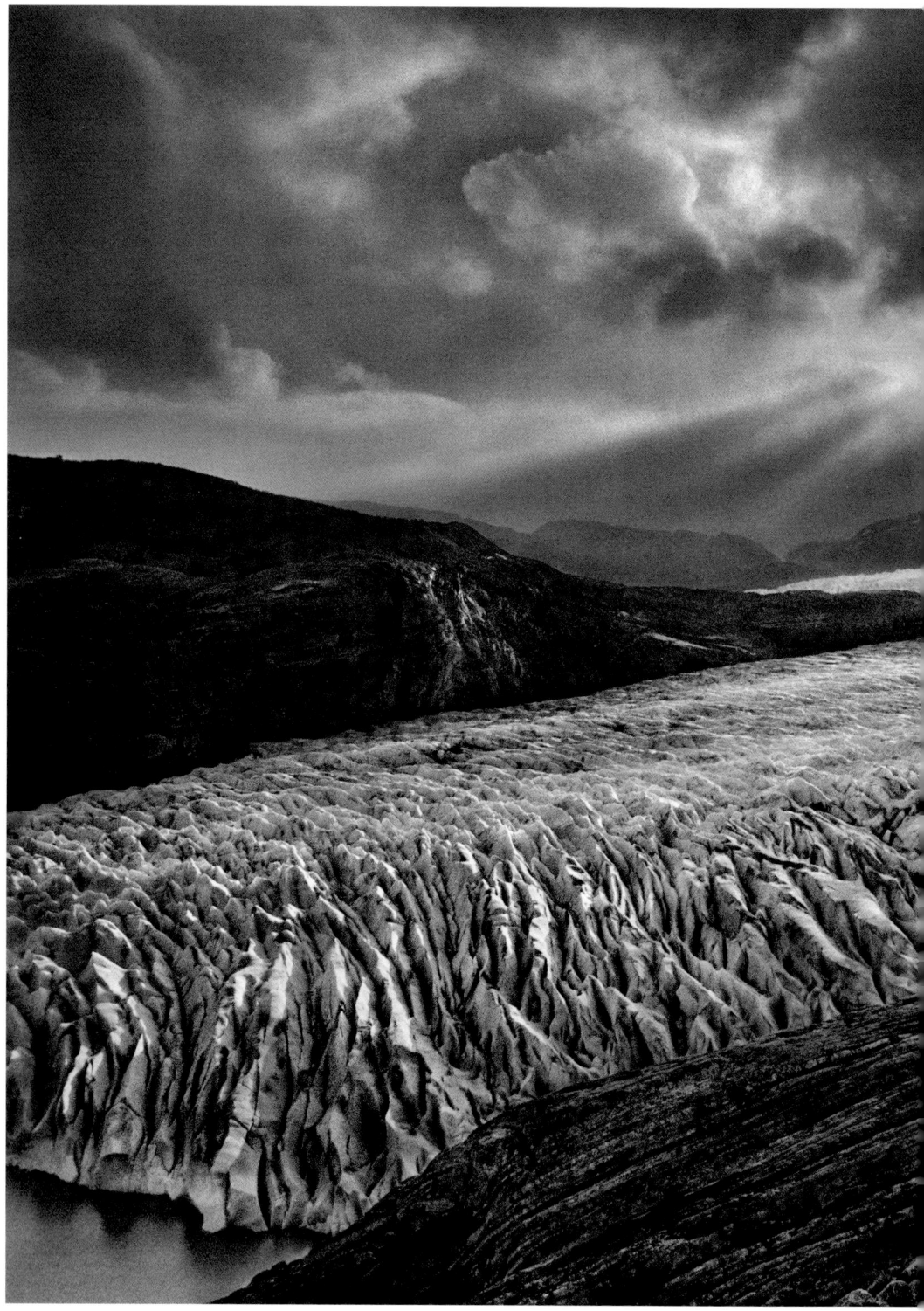

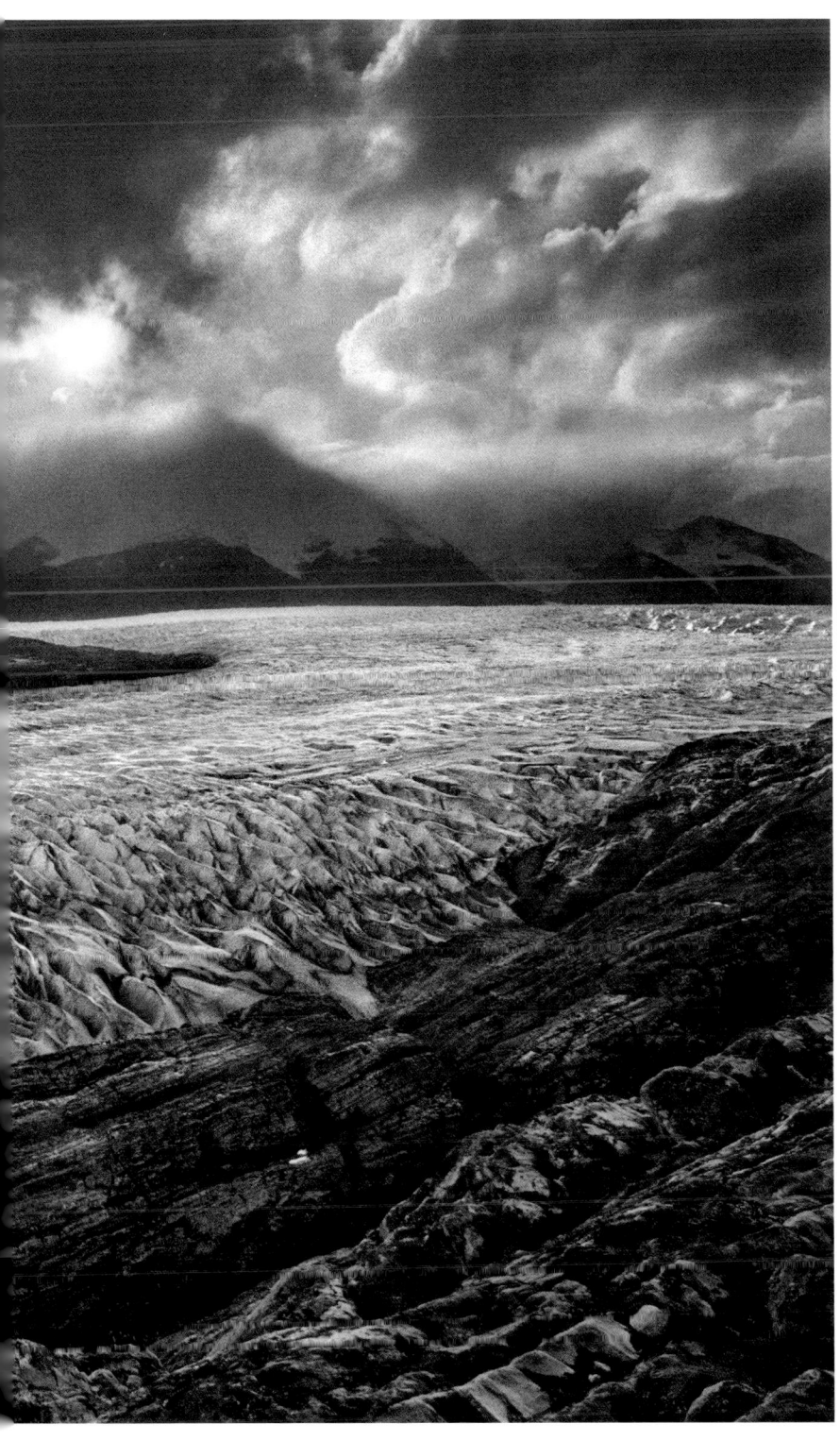

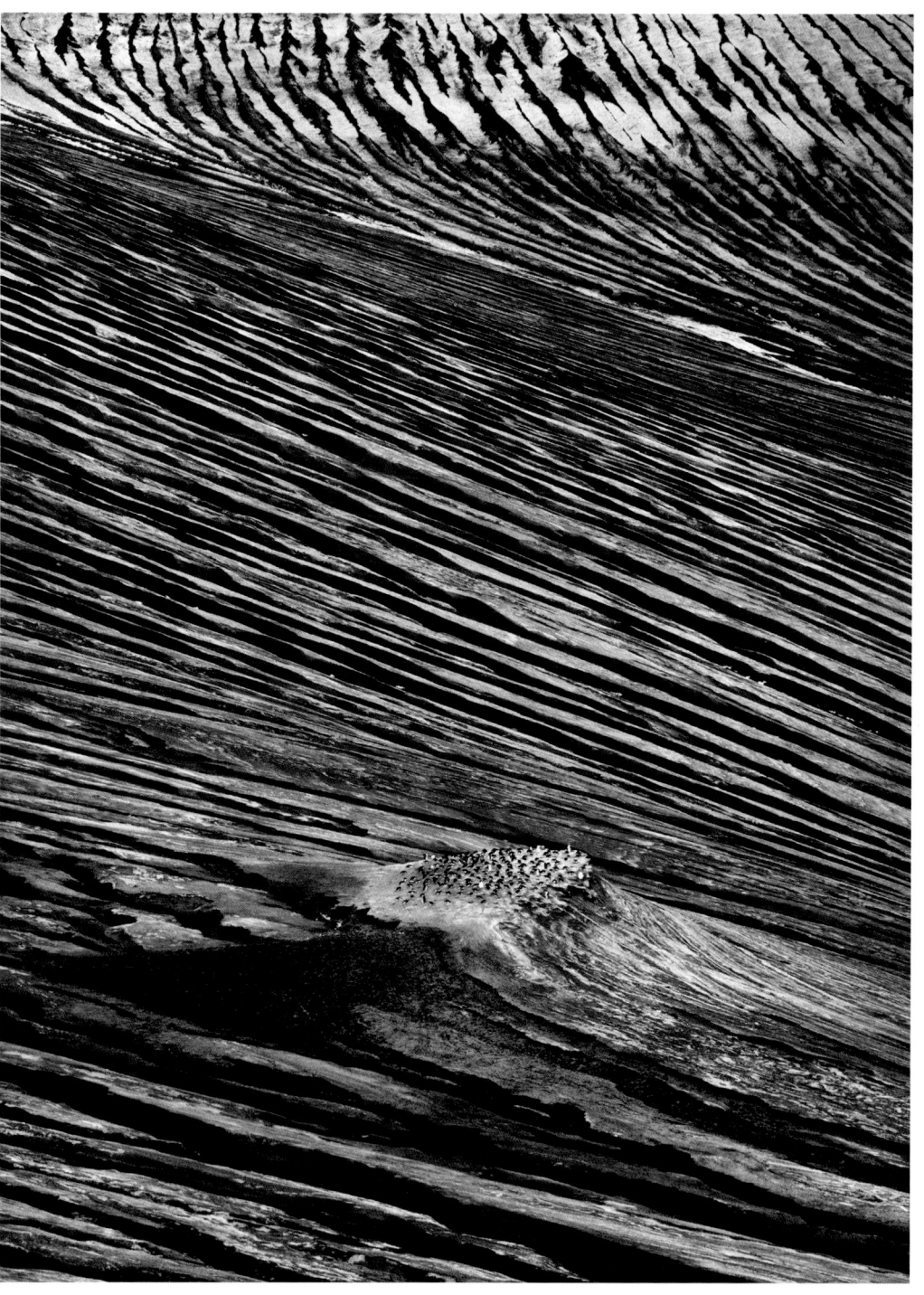

Opposite Like all nine of the South Sandwich Islands, Saunders Island has an active volcano. Mount Michael, on the eastern part of Saunders Island, is totally inaccessible. Hills to the west are, in turn, completely covered by ice and ash. Over many years, the erosion of this ash has created a surreal landscape. The island is also inhabited by penguins of several different species, notably the chinstrap (*Pygoscelis antarctica*), which number over 150,000 couples. South Sandwich Islands. November and December 2009.

Pages 100/101 The Golfo San José where the dunes meet the sea. Valdés Peninsula. Argentina. September and October 2004.

Pages 102/103 Two Weddell seals (*Leptonychotes weddellii*) on an iceberg close to Foyn Harbour on Enterprise Island. Foyn Harbor, named after the inventor of the harpoon gun using black powder, is the site of a former whaling station, which, like others in the Antarctic, would be used only in summer months. A few abandoned barracks remain, partly covered by snow, while the half-sunken wreck of a whaling factory ship can still be seen offshore. Antarctic Peninsula. January and February 2005.

Pages 104/105 A southern elephant seal (*Mirounga leonina*). Males can weigh more than 6,600 pounds (3,000 kilos), although females rarely exceed 2,000 pounds (900 kilos). Large numbers of southern elephant seals come to the Valdés Peninsula in August and early September, when the mating season starts after the females give birth. The females arrive first, after having spent about six months at sea; since they come alone, it seems that they also live alone at sea. On land, they join large harems, numbering as many as 100 females, who "belong" to one adult male. They, in turn, attract solitary males who patrol the periphery of the harem in the hope of pulling away a female with whom they can mate. Several times a day, a dominant male is forced to chase away a potential poacher and fierce battles often ensue. Valdés Peninsula. Argentina. September and October 2004.

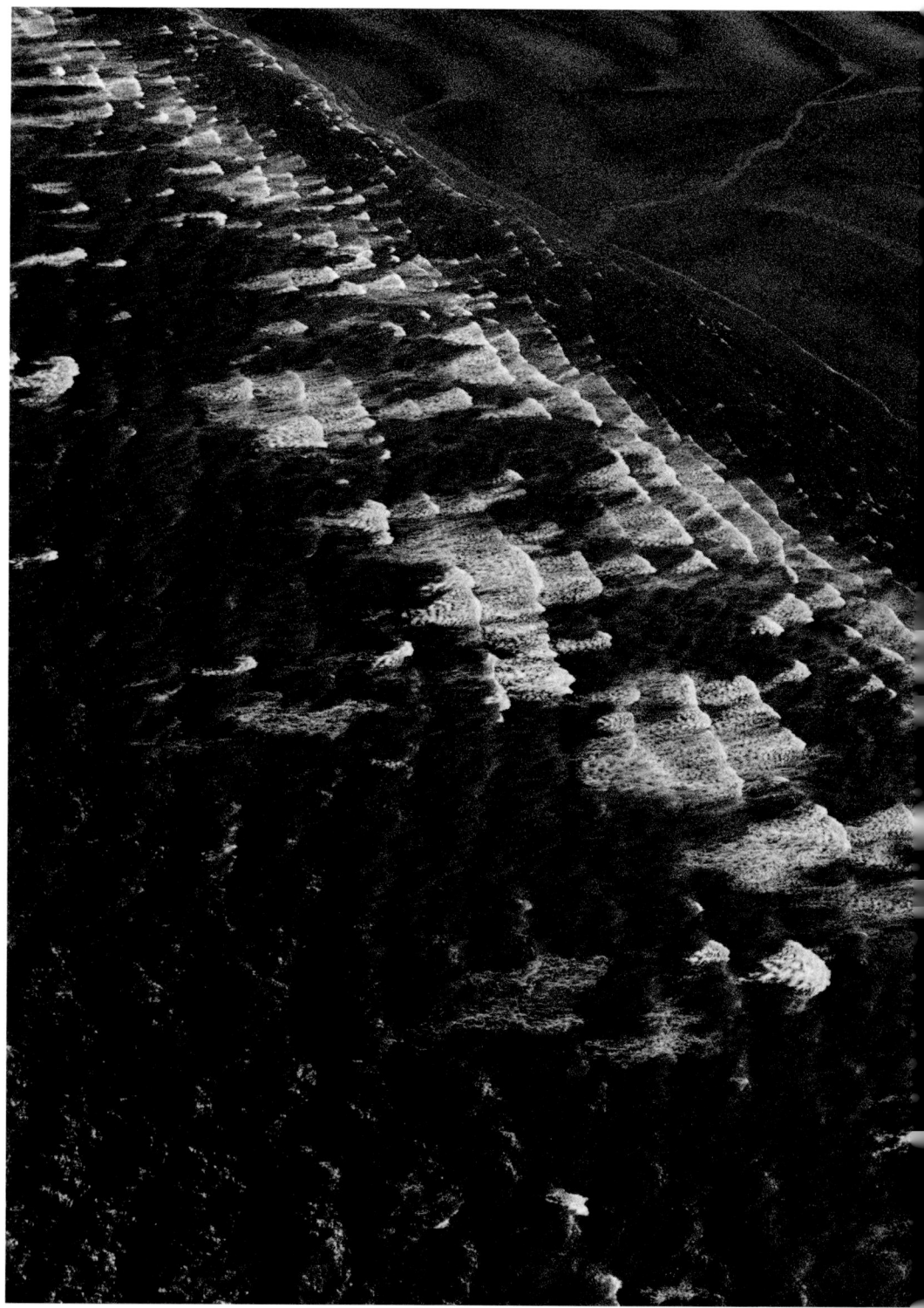

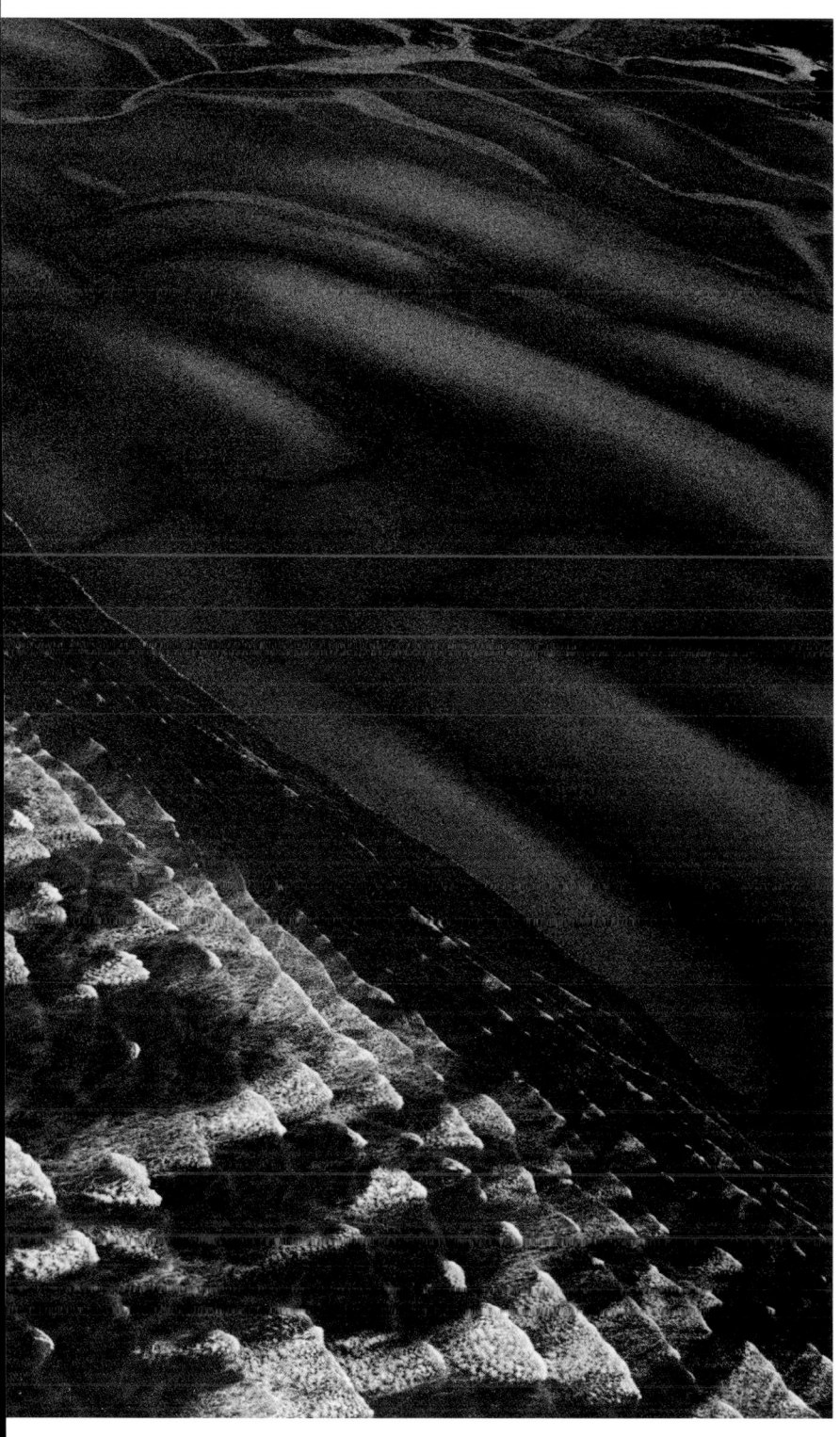

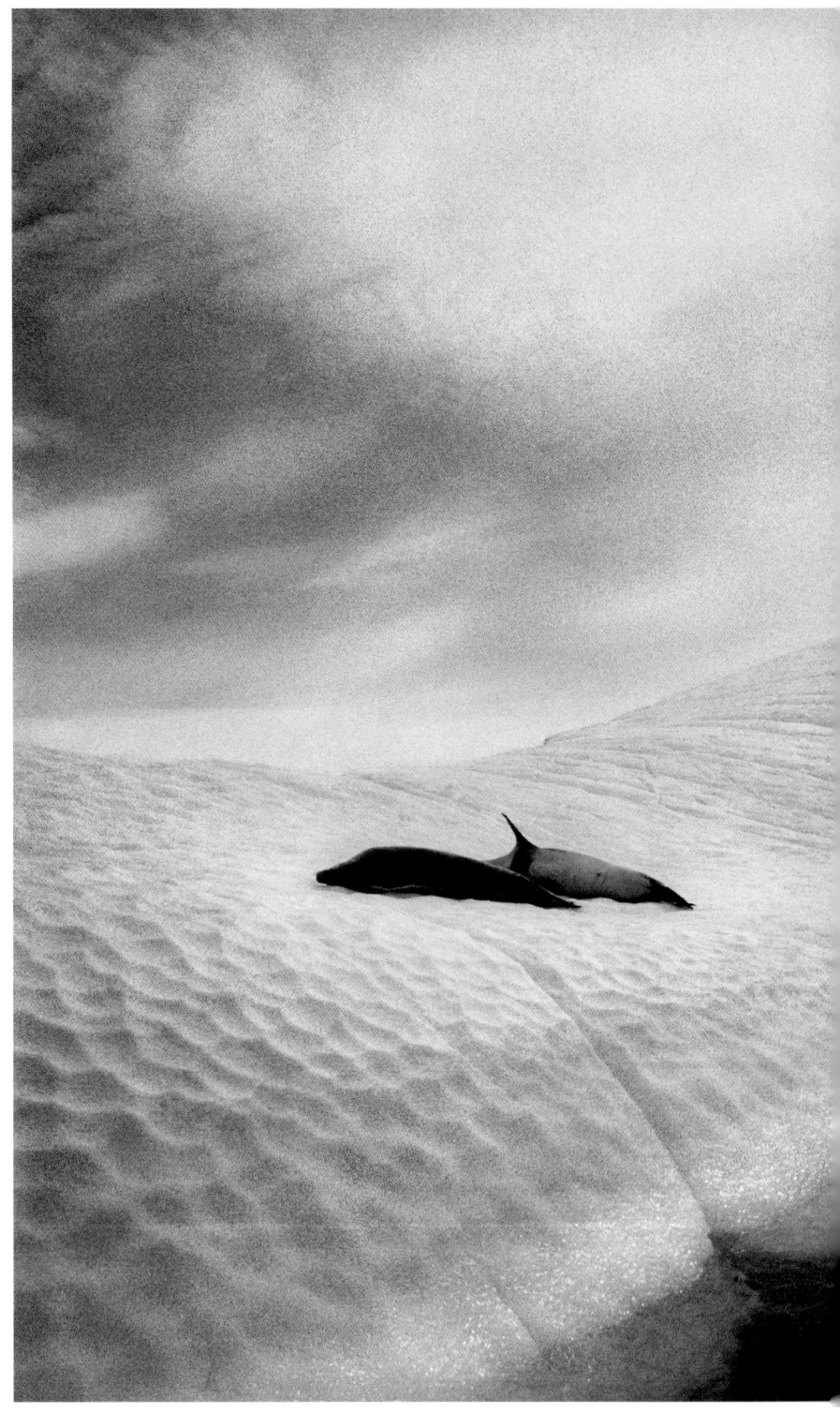

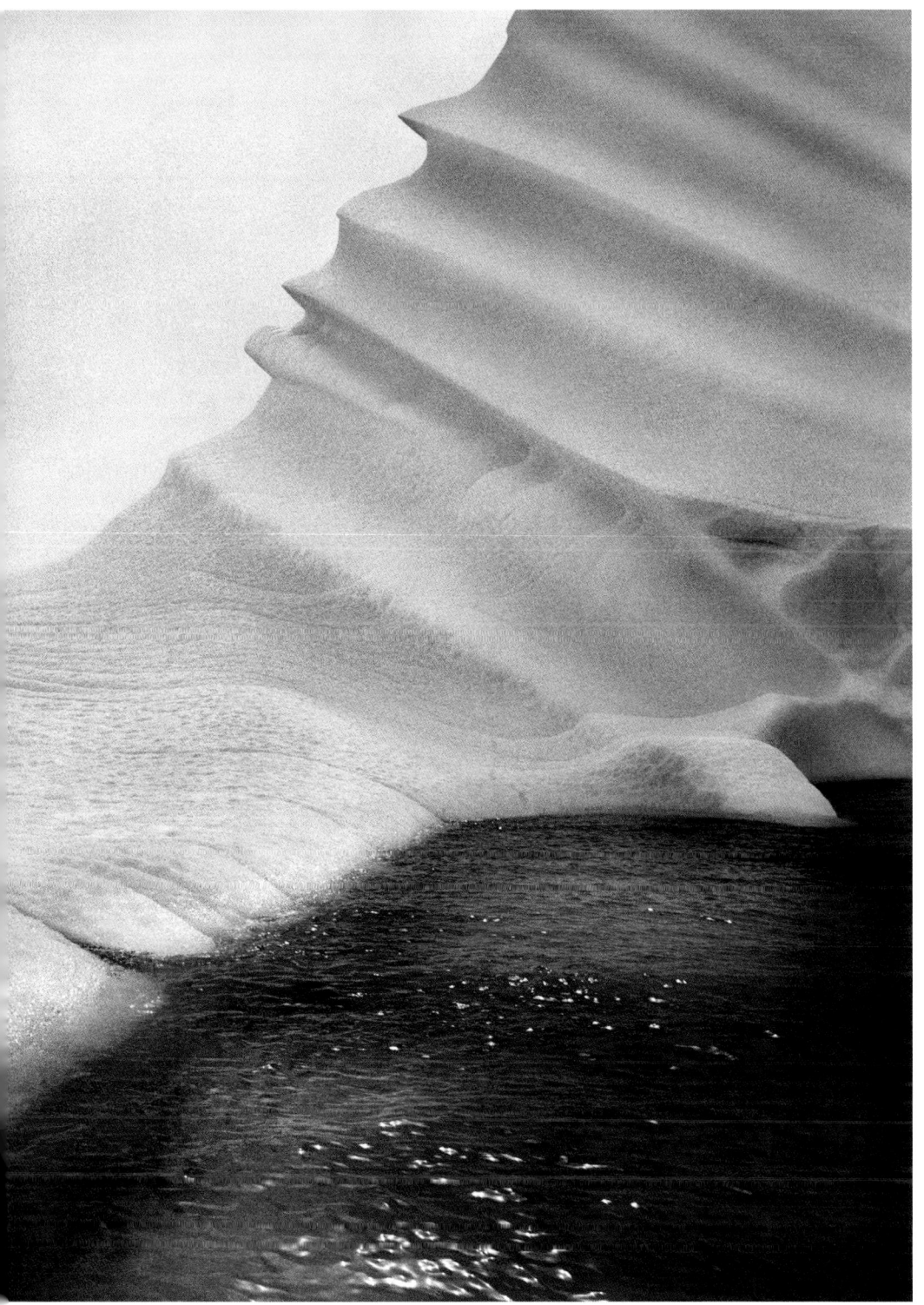

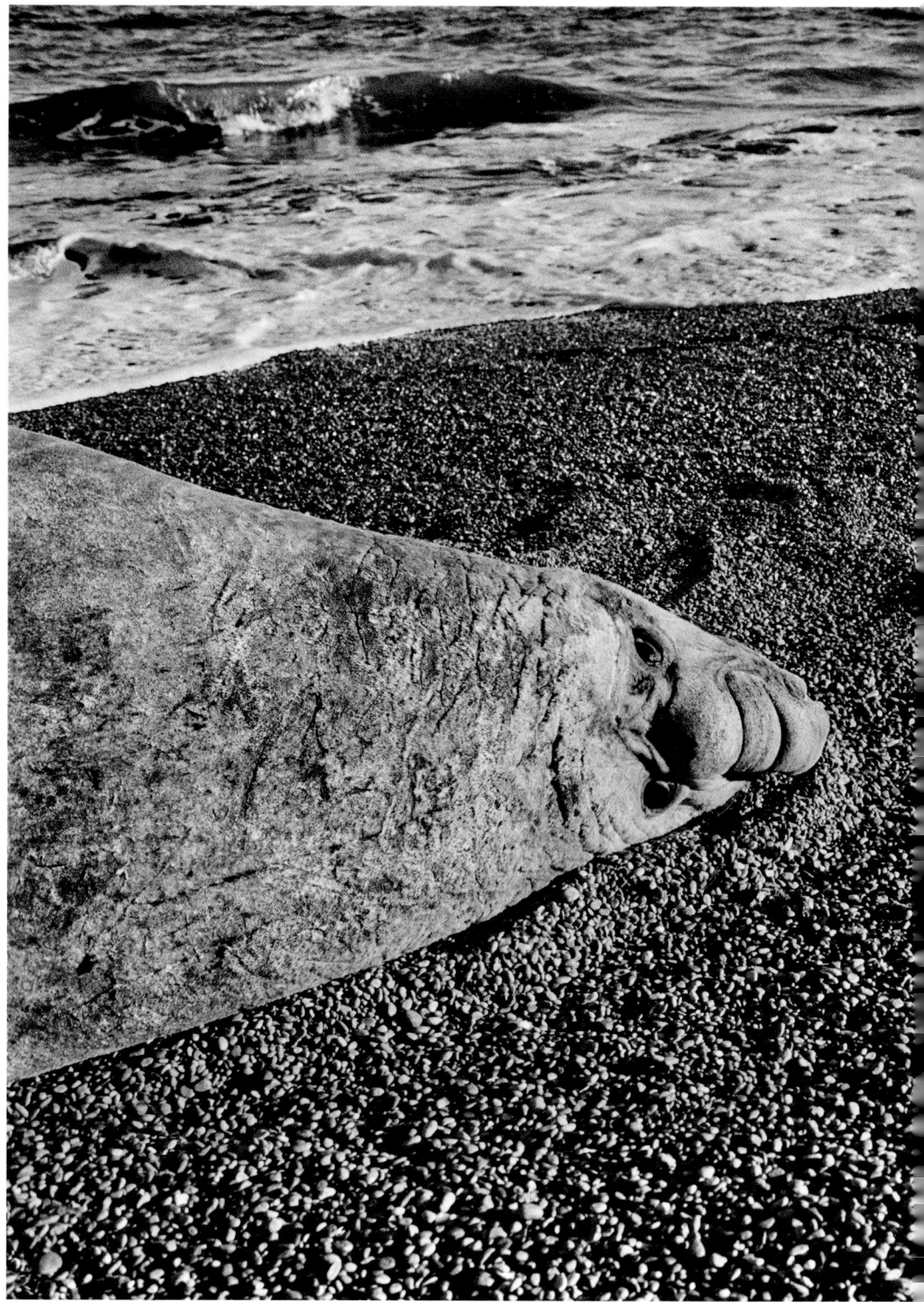

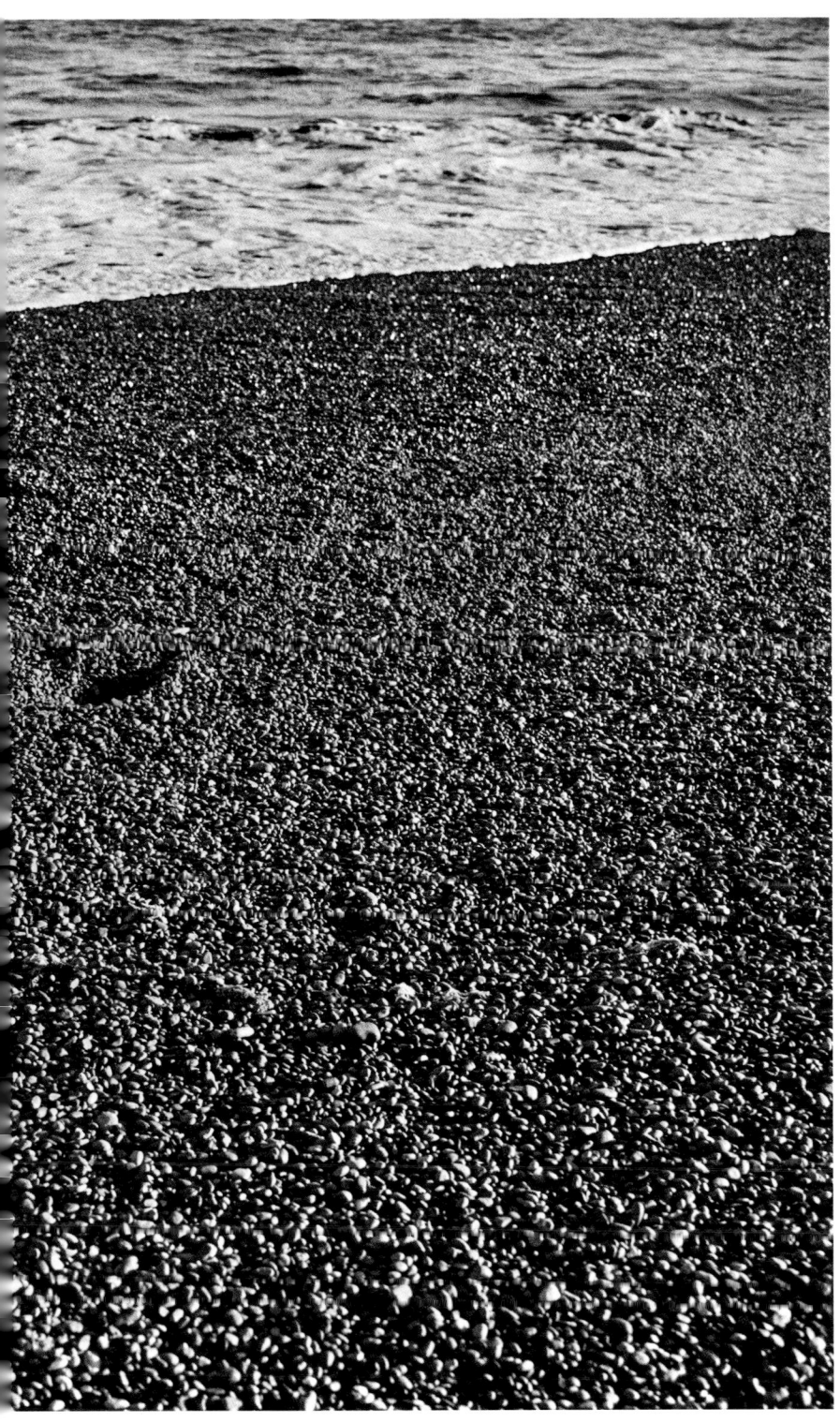

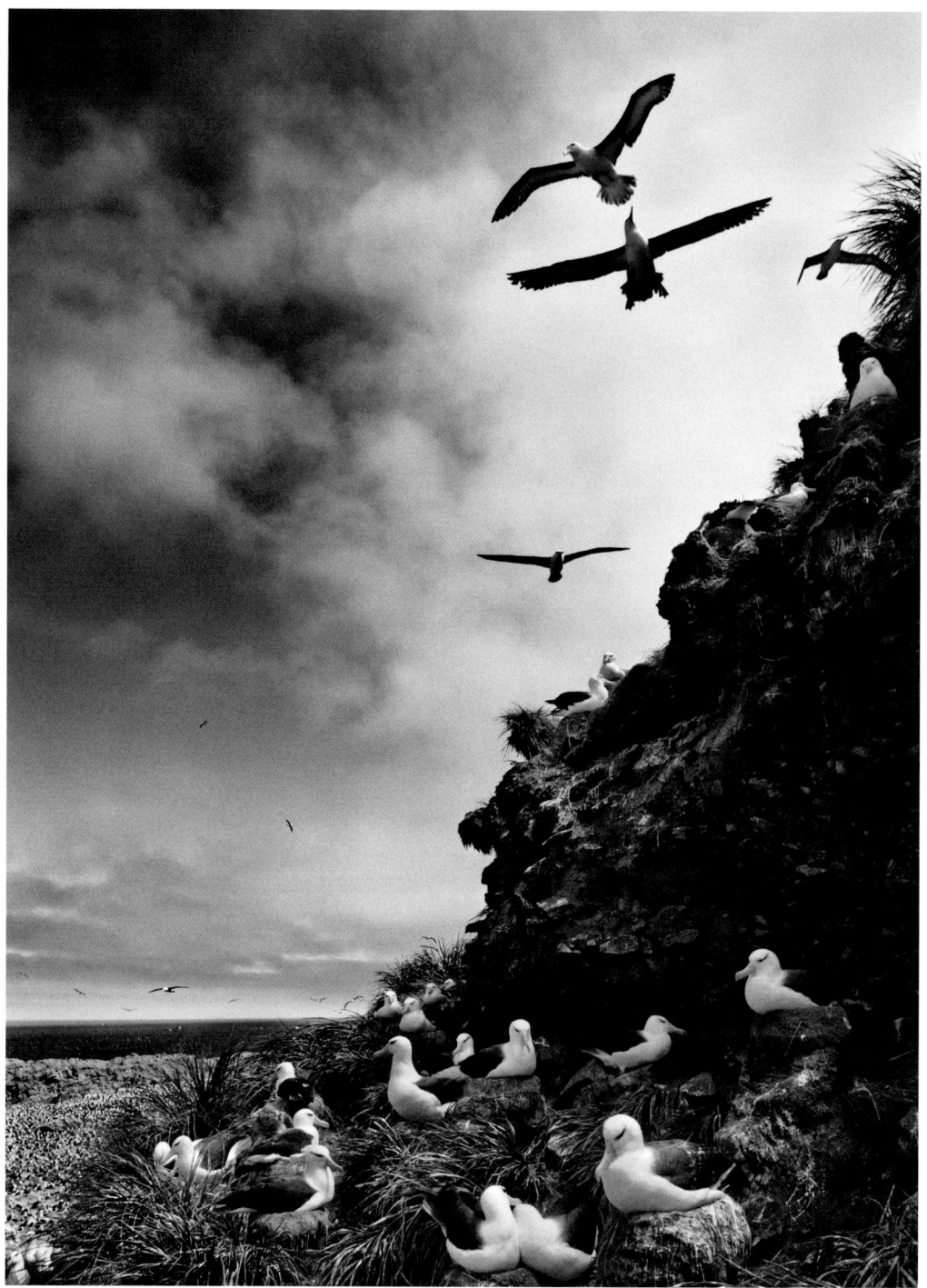

Opposite The Jason Islands are a cluster of 12 islands on the westernmost point of the Falkland Islands. These photographs were taken on Steeple Jason Island, home to more than 500,000 couples of black-browed albatrosses (*Thalassarche melanophris*), the largest colony of albatrosses in the world. Falkland Islands. November and December 2009.

Pages 108/109 Southern giant petrels (*Macronectes giganteus*). This petrel, with a wing span exceeding 7 feet (2 meters) and a body length of 34 to 37 inches (86 to 95 centimeters), is one of the largest flying predators of the Antarctic and sub-Antarctic regions. Saint Andrews Bay. South Georgia. November and December 2009.

Pages 110/111 A group of Dominican gulls, also known as the kelp gull (*Larus dominicanus*), on Bellingshausen Island, with Cook Island in the background. South Sandwich Islands. November and December 2009.

Pages 112/113 A colony of black-browed albatrosses (*Thalassarche melanophris*) on the archipelago of Willis Islands; in the background one can see Trinity and Bird Island. South Georgia. November and December 2009.

Pages 114/115 Lake Argentino, the source of the Santa Cruz River. In 1834, Vice-Admiral Robert Fitz Roy, who was captaining the HMS *Beagle* on its famous trip around the globe, led an expedition to explore the Rio Santa Cruz in the Argentine Patagonia. His dream was to reach the Andes, but the current was too strong for his longboat and, after 18 days, he turned back. Charles Darwin, a scientist on the *Beagle* and a member of this unsuccessful trip, later recalled his regret at not reaching the snow-clad peaks he could see in the distance:

From some high land we hailed with joy the white summits of the Cordillera, as they were seen occasionally peeping through their dusky envelope of clouds. During the few succeeding days we continued to get on slowly, for we found the river-course very tortuous, and strewed with immense fragments of various ancient slaty rocks, and of granite.

May 4 – Captain Fitz Roy determined to take the boats no higher. The river had a winding course, and was very rapid; and the appearance of the country offered no temptation to proceed any further. Everywhere we met with the same productions, and the same dreary landscape. We were now one hundred and forty miles distant from the Atlantic, and about sixty from the nearest arm of the Pacific. The valley in this upper part expanded into a wide basin, bounded on the north and south by the basaltic platforms, and fronted by the long range of the snow-clad Cordillera. But we viewed these grand mountains with regret, for we were obliged to imagine their nature and productions, instead of standing, as we had hoped, on their summits.

CHARLES DARWIN, from *The Voyage of the Beagle*, 1834. Argentine Patagonia. March and April 2007.

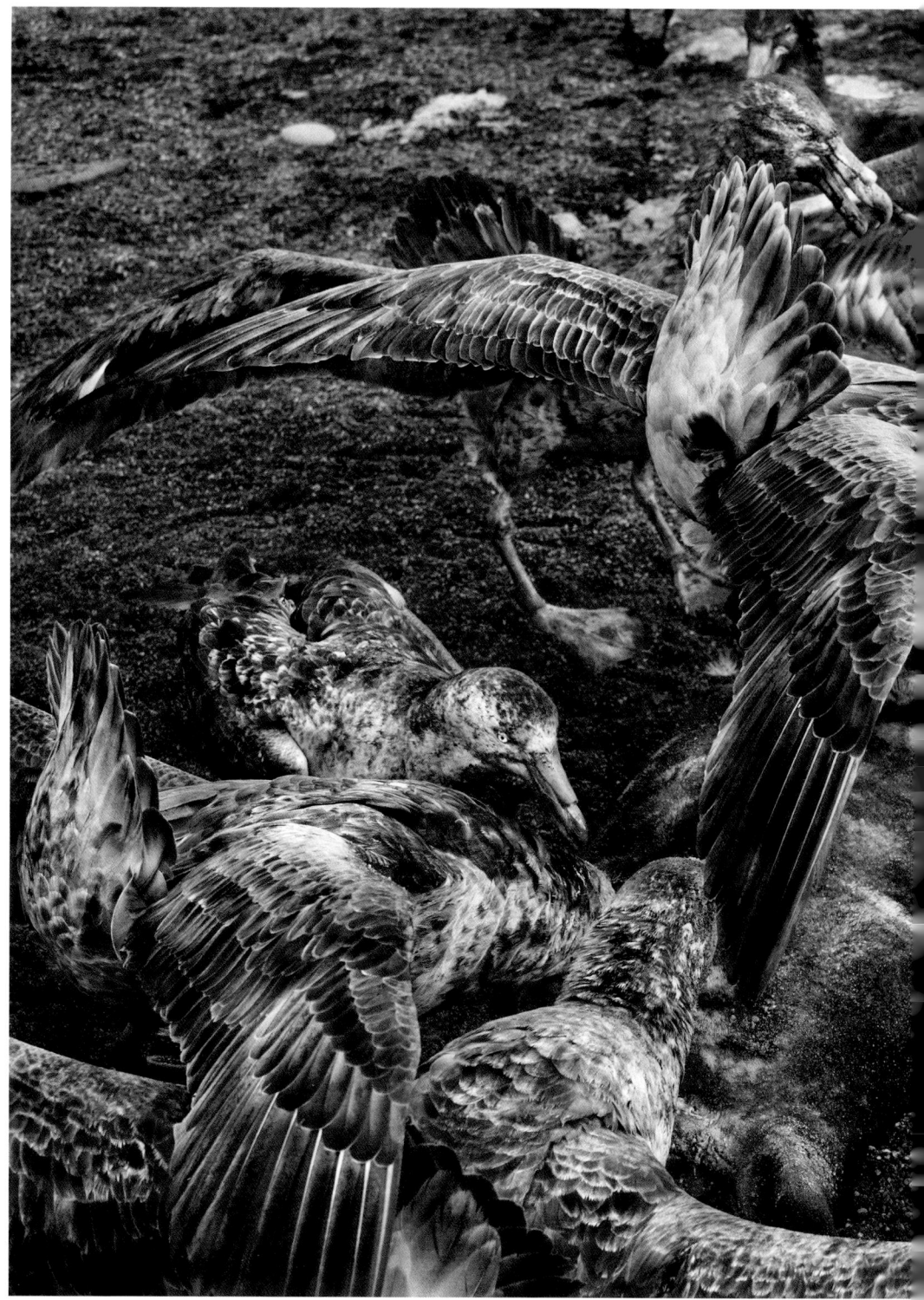

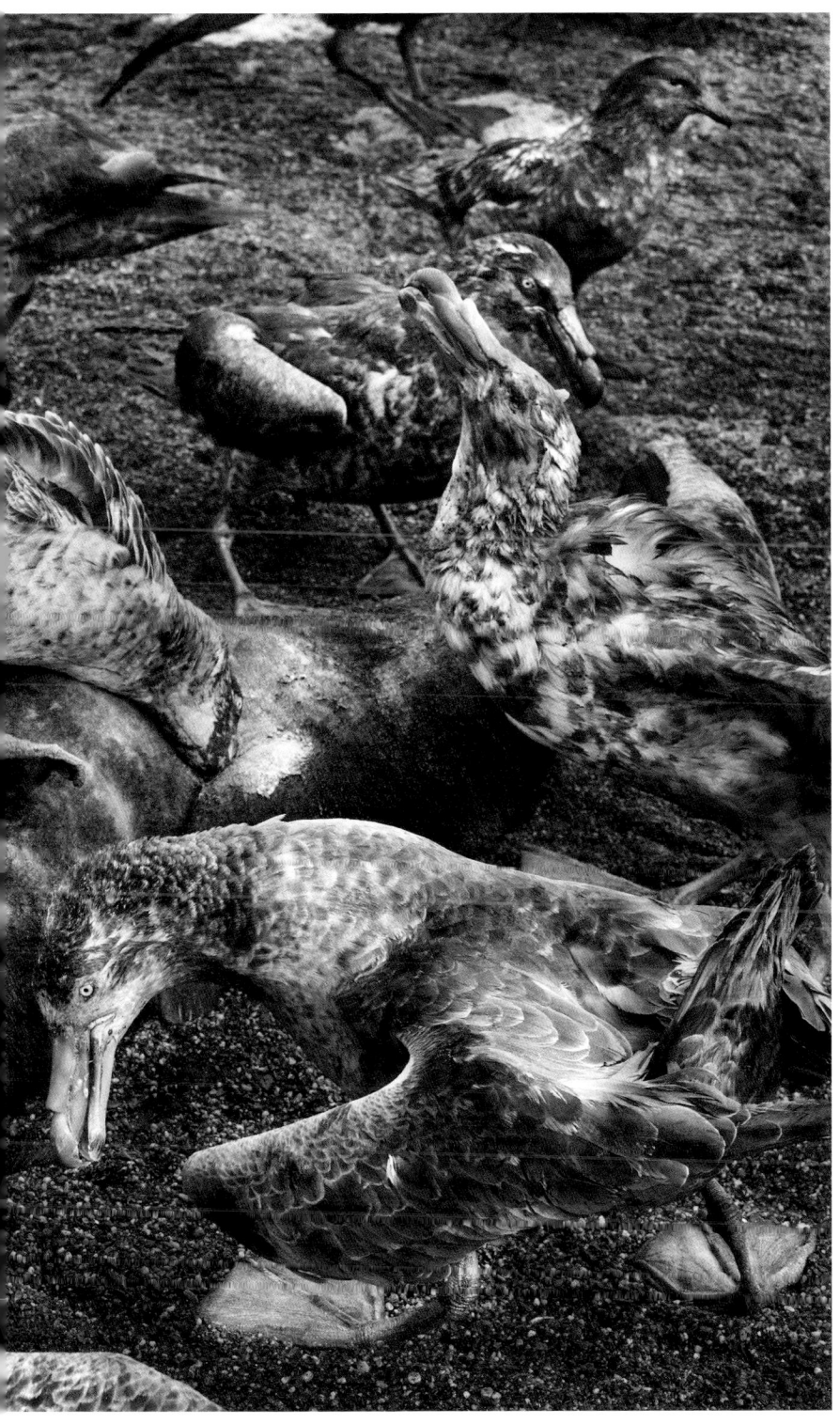

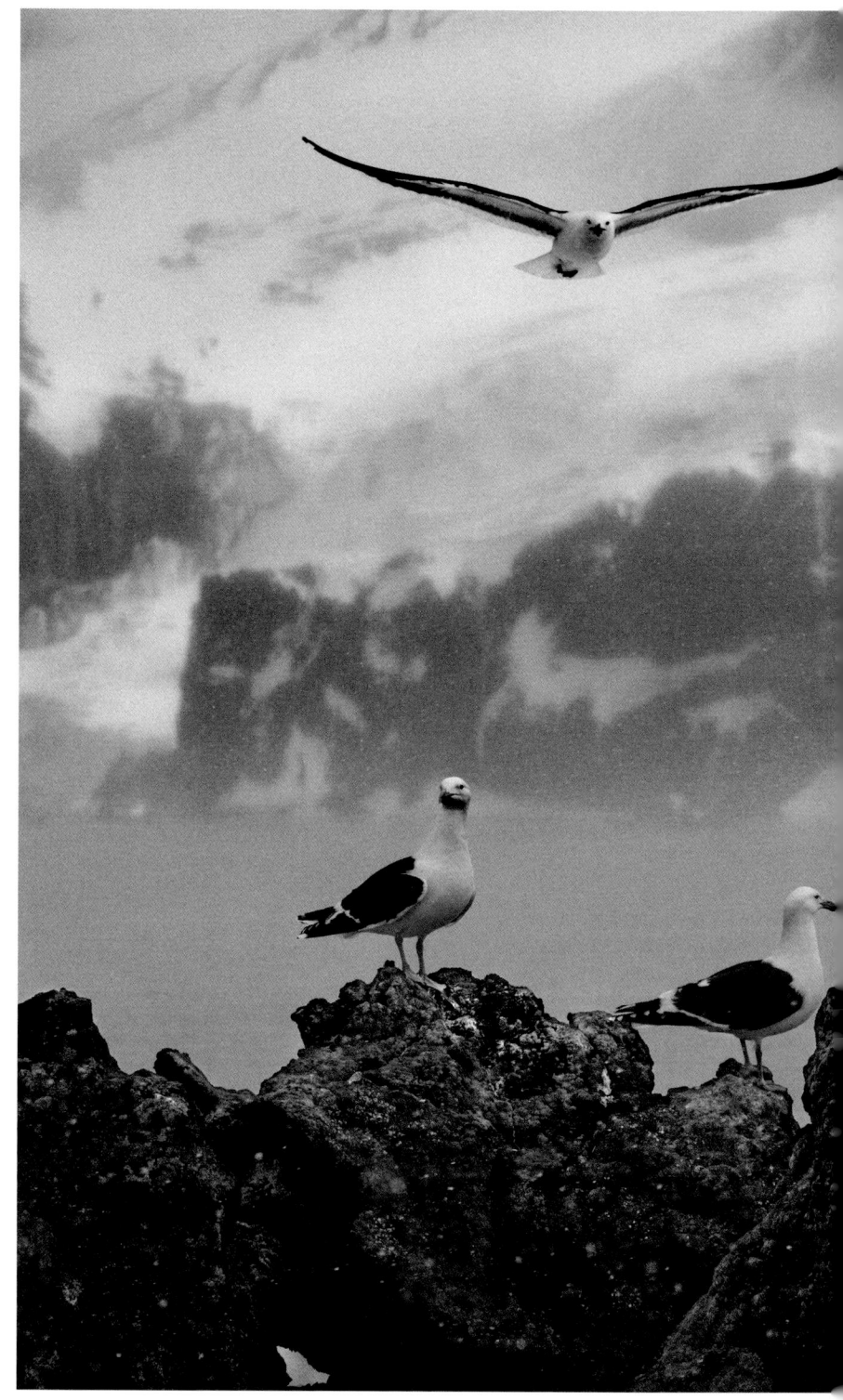

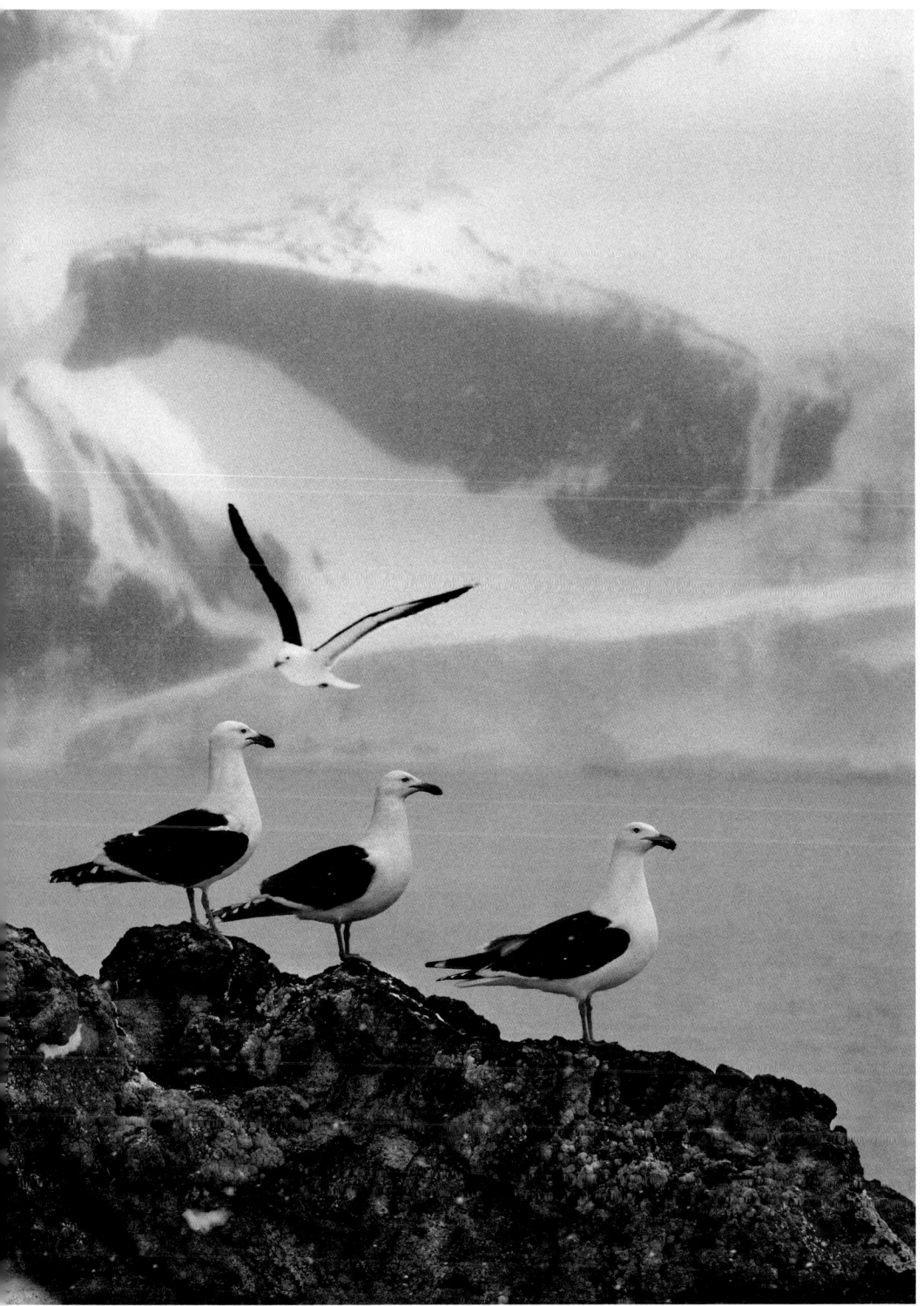

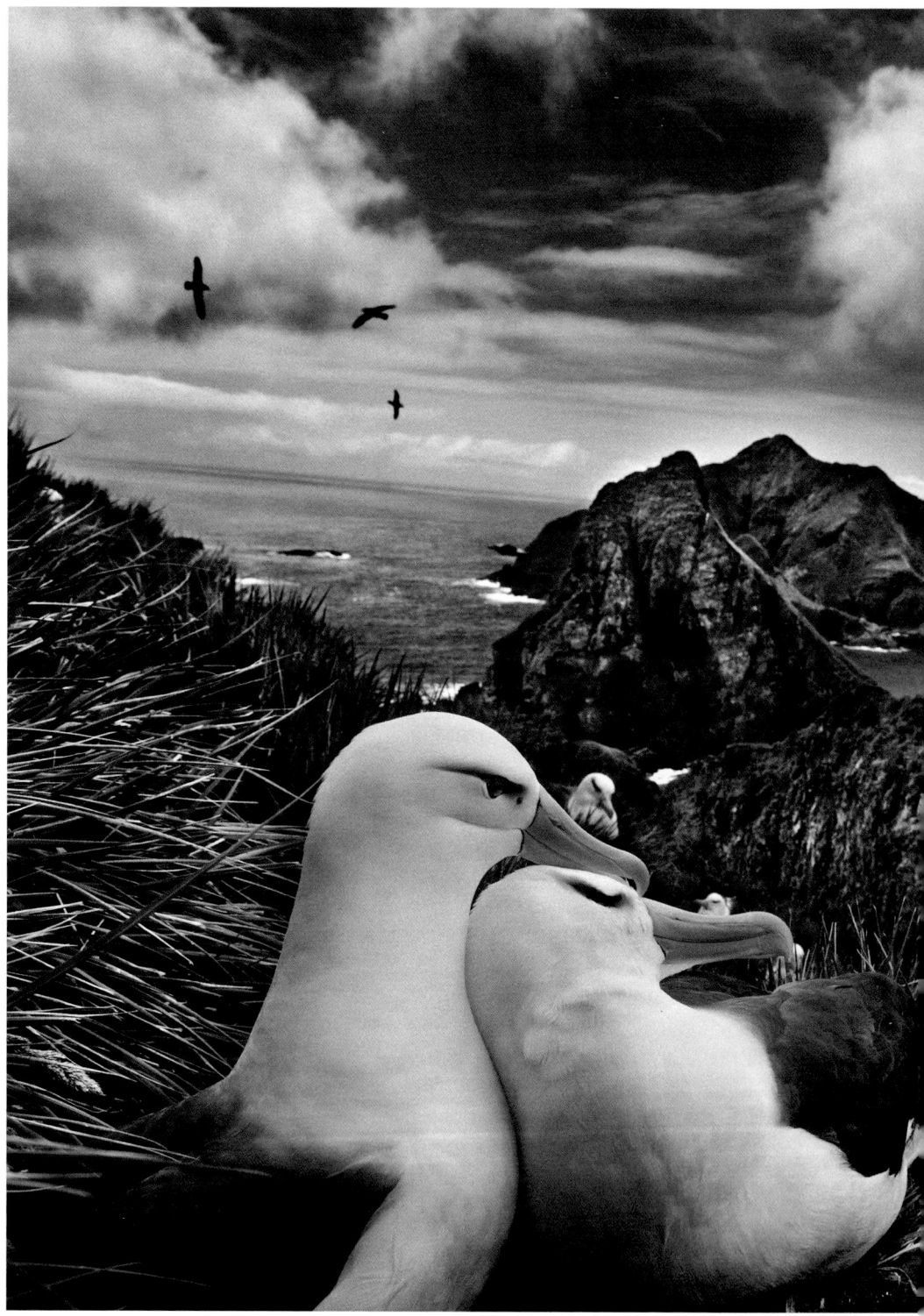

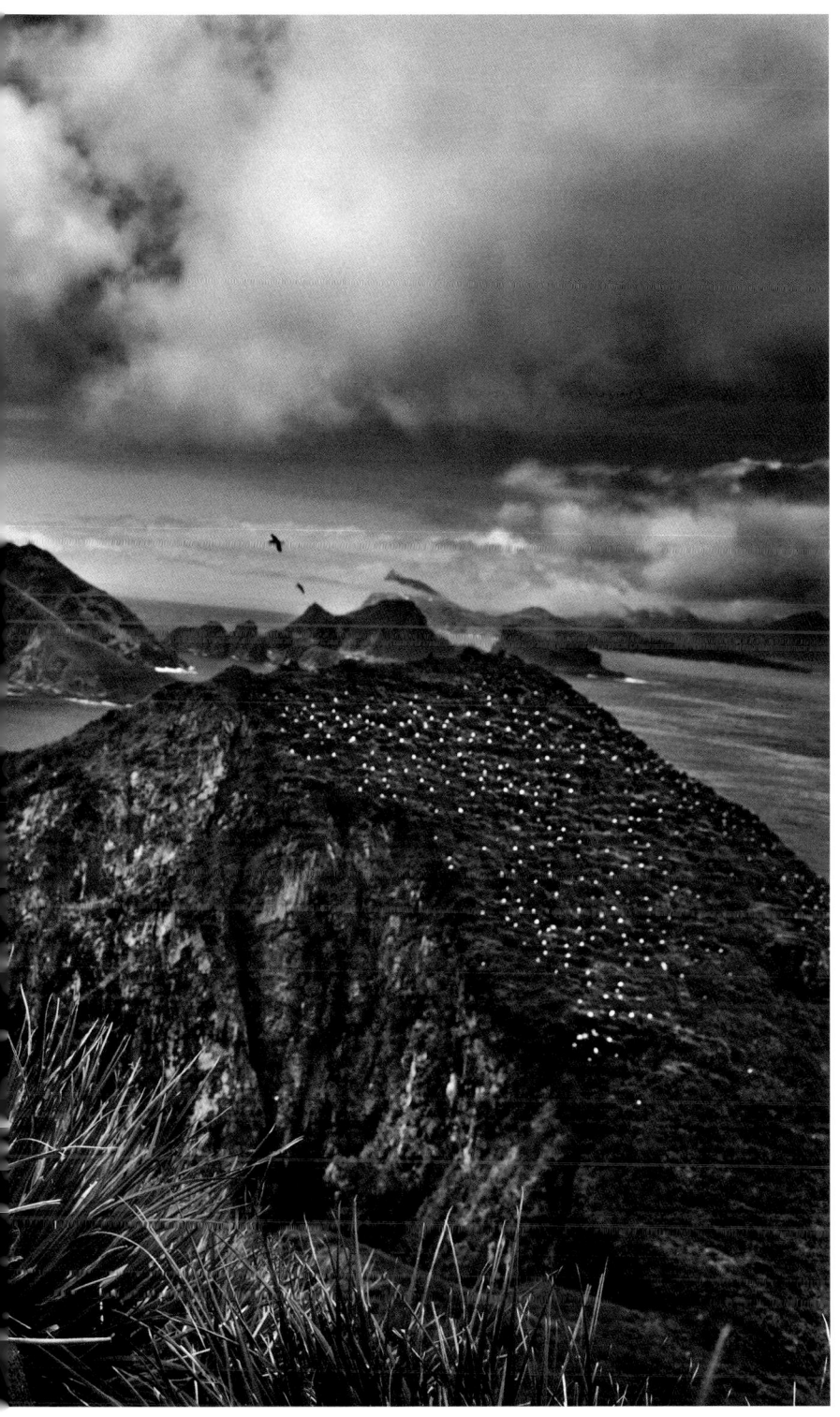

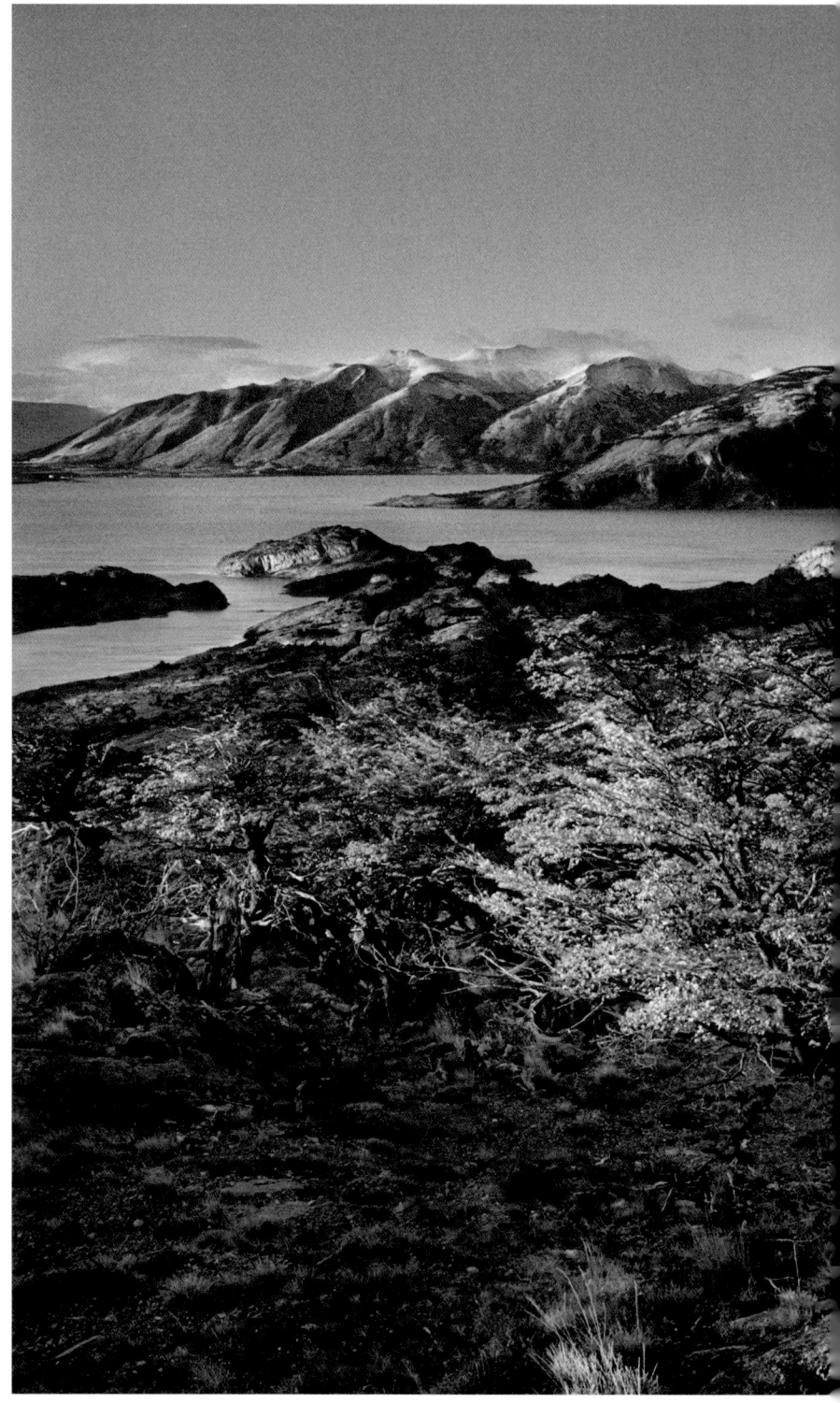

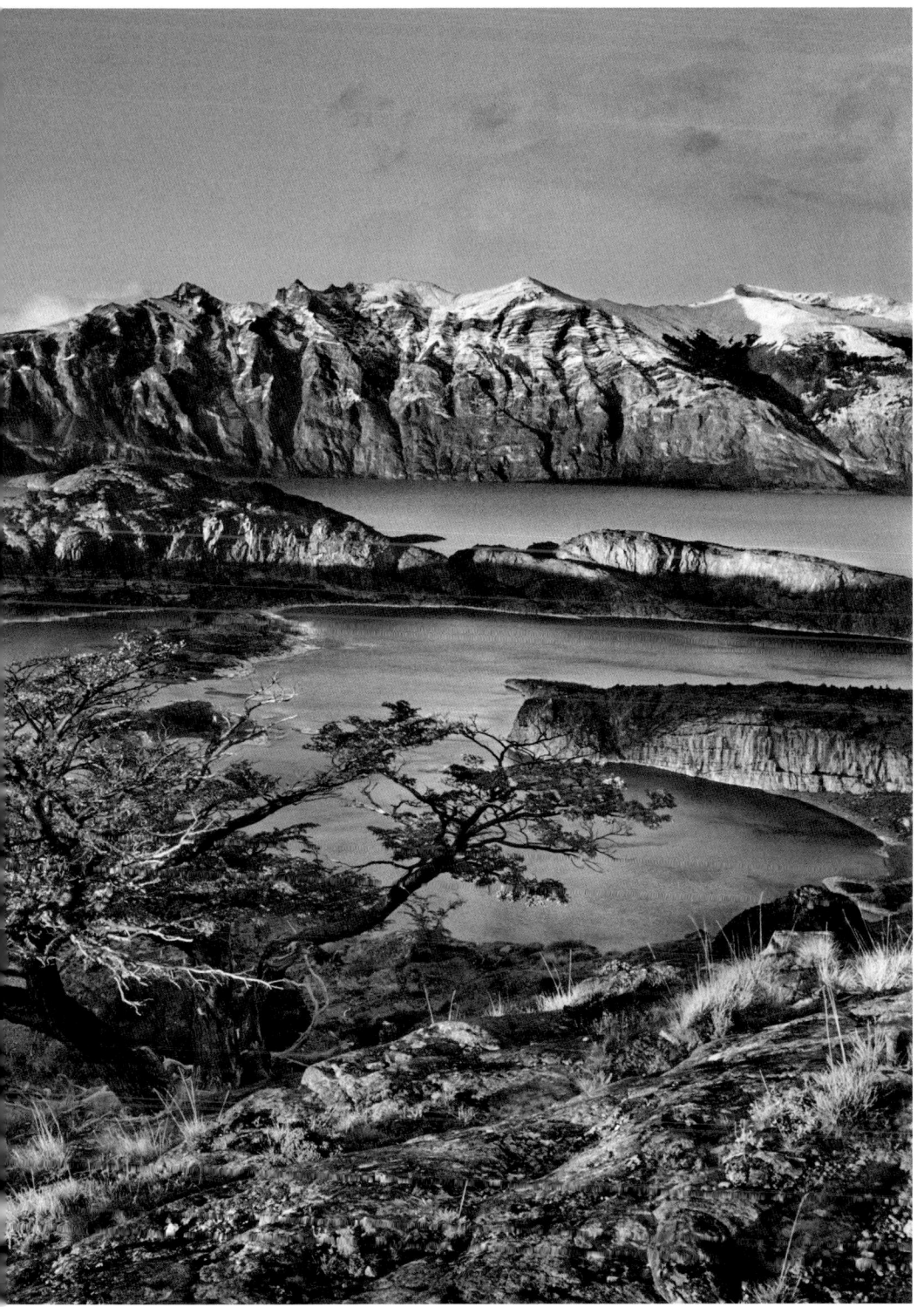

SANCTUARIES

Isolated islands offer ideal conditions for the development and survival of endemic flora and fauna. As a result, unique animal and plant species are often concentrated in small geographical areas. Their principal threat is the encroachment of human settlements. While some ancient tribes still live "inside" nature much as their forebears did, this harmony is also often disturbed by modern man. Thus, in what were once safe refuges, ancestral ways of life, rare animals and unique plants are inescapably threatened with extinction.

I started my voyage on the Galápagos Islands, that extraordinary natural laboratory that inspired Darwin's theory of evolution. Its multiple creatures have survived in good measure because they have had no predators, except during the 18th and 19th centuries, when passing seamen hunted the giant tortoise for food. Today, the tortoises are protected, along with the other animals I was able to photograph, from marine iguanas, fur seals and sea lions to brown pelicans, great frigate birds and flightless cormorants. And, astonishingly, all this life flourishes beside fields of lava and at the base of active volcanoes.

Madagascar, the large island off the east coast of southern Africa, is another of the world's biodiversity "hotspots." Close to 90 percent of its tens of thousands of animal and plant species can be found nowhere else on Earth. It has no fewer than 860 varieties of orchids and 170 of palm trees. The lemur, a monkey-like primate that is the island's most distinctive animal, appears in over 100 different subspecies.

Traveling up the arid west coast, we drove past stunning sand dunes formed by broad riverbeds which are dry much of the year. The baobab tree, with its distinctive bloated trunk, is quite the strangest of the flora. Madagascar boasts six of the eight species of baobab trees found on Earth. Further inland, I came across the *tsingy*, among the most bizarre geological formations I have ever seen. Formed over millions of years by crushed shells, their surfaces as sharp as broken glass, they rise 160 to 330 feet (50 to 100 meters) out of the undergrowth like huge stalagmites.

In the humid northeast of the island, vast stretches of rainforest remain. But I often saw tell-tale plumes of smoke where jungle is being cleared by fire to make room for cattle farms. As a memory bank of evolution, Madagascar is at risk.

On islands off the west coast of Sumatra, the sanctuaries of several ethnic groups are also being invaded. From the 1960s, the Indonesian government decided to bring these traditional hunter-gatherers into settlements. It required adults to convert to either Islam or Christianity. Many did, but a few clans stayed in the jungles of Siberut Island. Those were the Mentawai people we wanted to meet.

Noted for their spirituality and body art, the Mentawai still build everything out of natural products of the rain forest, including their *uma*, which serves as dormitory, kitchen and temple. In the jungle, men usually wear only tree-bark loincloths and some women cover themselves with dresses of woven leaves. They have no need to grow their food since they are surrounded by abundant animal and plant life. Every clan has several shamans, each with a different responsibility, such as dance and song rituals and foretelling the future.

New Guinea, the mountainous island north of Australia, is one of the world's most pristine natural habitats, with over 1,000 known languages and ethnic groups. The island is divided politically, with independent Papua New Guinea to the east and the Indonesian province of West Papua, also known as Irian Jaya, to the west.

In Papua New Guinea, we traveled into the fertile valleys, wild rivers and untamed saw-toothed mountains of the southern highlands. Several ethnic communities allowed us to record their *singsings*, elaborate ceremonies for which the people decorate their bodies with paint, plants, shells, beads and animal teeth. The Huli, the region's largest group, now wear Western clothes. But for fiestas, Huli wigmen also paint their faces and wear wigs made with their own hair. In the Asaro region, the mudmen frighten their enemies by covering themselves in mud and donning large, white masks made of packed mud.

The island's least assimilated group is Irian Jaya's Stone Korowai, also known as "gentle cannibals" because they hunt down and eat those deemed to be sorcerers. Men are naked except for a penis sheath and women wear only a short grass skirt. Since clan warfare is common, their chief lives in a house built 100 feet (30 meters) above the ground.

The Mek tribe, on the other hand, has had more contact with Western missionaries and, for Christian religious services, tribesmen often wear old Western clothes. Even the local pastor, who wears nothing but a long penis sheath during the week, puts on a donated Western shirt for church on Sunday.

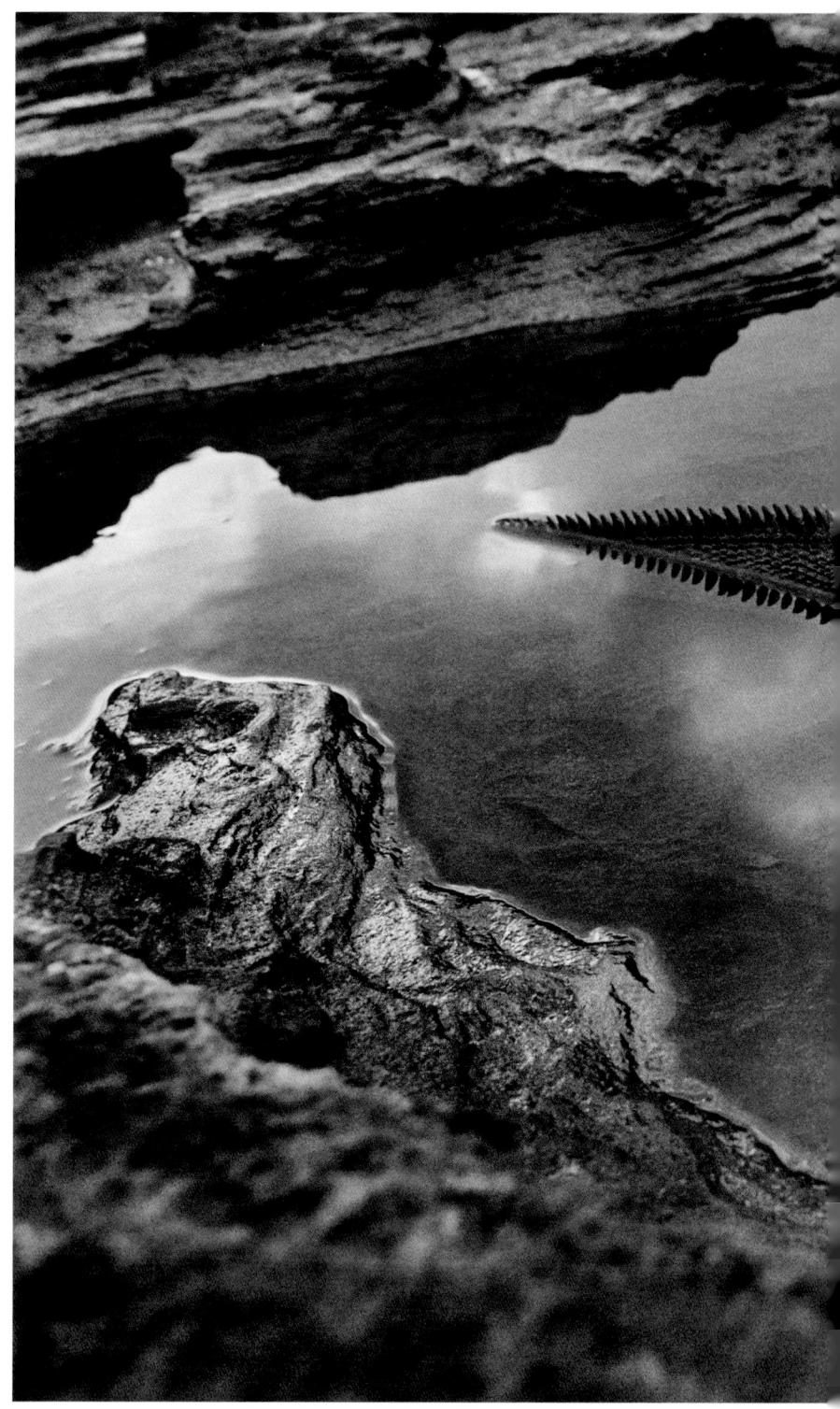

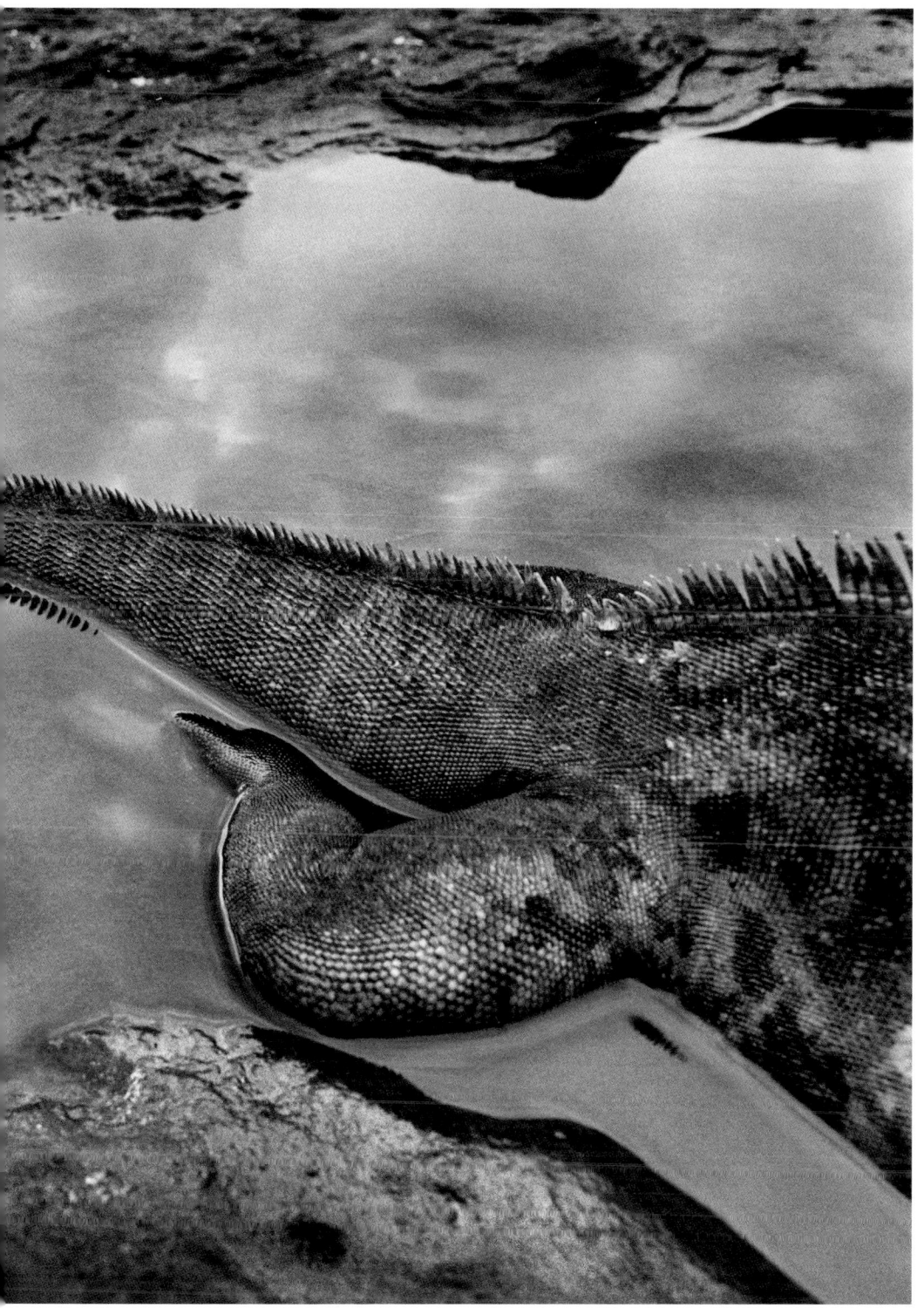

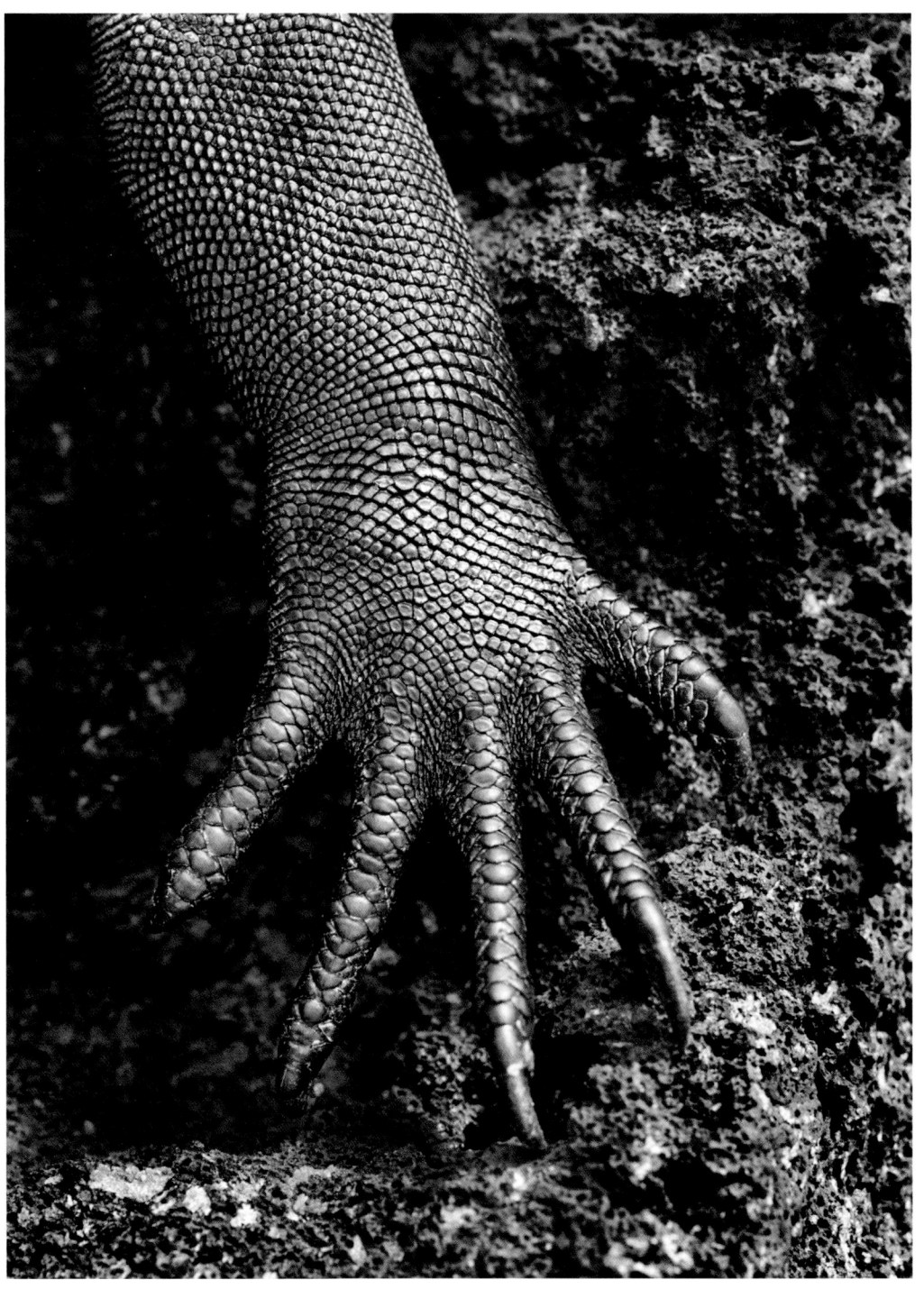

Pages 118/119 Marine iguana (*Amblyrhynchus cristatus*). This animal is a perfect example of adaptation and evolution. The first marine iguanas apparently came to the archipelago from the American mainland, almost 620 miles (1,000 kilometers) to the east. They were probably transported by sea currents atop tree trunks, pieces of land with foliage and other objects floating on the water and, once here, they were forced to adapt to local conditions. A smaller number of these migrants remained land iguanas and can be found on only a few islands, but the majority evolved into marine animals: they learned to swim, to feed on seaweed, to dive and to remain submerged for long stretches; they even developed special glands to excrete excess salt from their food intake. It is the only type of iguana in the world able to live in salty waters. Galápagos. Ecuador. January, February and March 2004.

Opposite Marine iguana (*Amblyrhynchus cristatus*). Like other ectothermal reptiles, the marine iguana must regulate its own body temperature: as soon as the sun rises, it lies flat, warming as much body area as possible until the temperature reaches 95.9° Fahrenheit (35.5° Celsius); it then changes position to avoid overheating. The marine iguana needs a high body temperature in order to swim, to move about and to digest. Galápagos. Ecuador. January, February and March 2004.

Pages 122/123 Punta Cormorant, Floreana Island. Despite its name, there are no cormorants in this area of the island. But I did find 21 greater flamingos (*Phoenicopterus ruber*) on a salty lagoon behind the beach. The flamingos fly from island to island, seeking out small lagoons where they can find their main food, water boatmen (*Trichocorixa reticulata*) and shrimp (*Artemia salina*). The greater flamingos' population in the Galápagos stands at around 500. Galápagos. Ecuador. January, February and March 2004.

Pages 124/125 Lava cactus (*Brachycereus nesioticus*). The *Brachycereus*, as it is known in the Galápagos, is the only true colonizer plant to be found on recent lava flows, as seen in this photograph. It displays creamy-white flowers and, with its soft-as-fur spines, it is the only cactus that can be touched without harm. Some plants are 24 inches (60 centimeters) high. Galápagos. Ecuador. January, February and March 2004.

Page 126 Giant tortoise (*Geochelone elephantopus*) on the rim of the crater of Alcedo Volcano on Isabela Island. These antediluvian animals are in every way impressive: they may measure 5 feet (1.5 meters) and weigh up to 550 pounds (250 kilos); they can live for more than 150 years; and, outside the mating season, they choose to live in solitude. While their tiny young, weighing just 3 ounces 80 grams at birth, are easy prey for hawks (*Buteo galapagoensis*), the giant tortoises have no predators today. But in the 18th and 19th centuries, they were hunted mercilessly by pirates, whalers, sealers and settlers to the point that, on some islands where they were once numerous, they were completely exterminated. Their value aboard ship was that they could survive for a long time without food or water and provided fresh meat when none was available. Galápagos. Ecuador. January, February and March 2004.

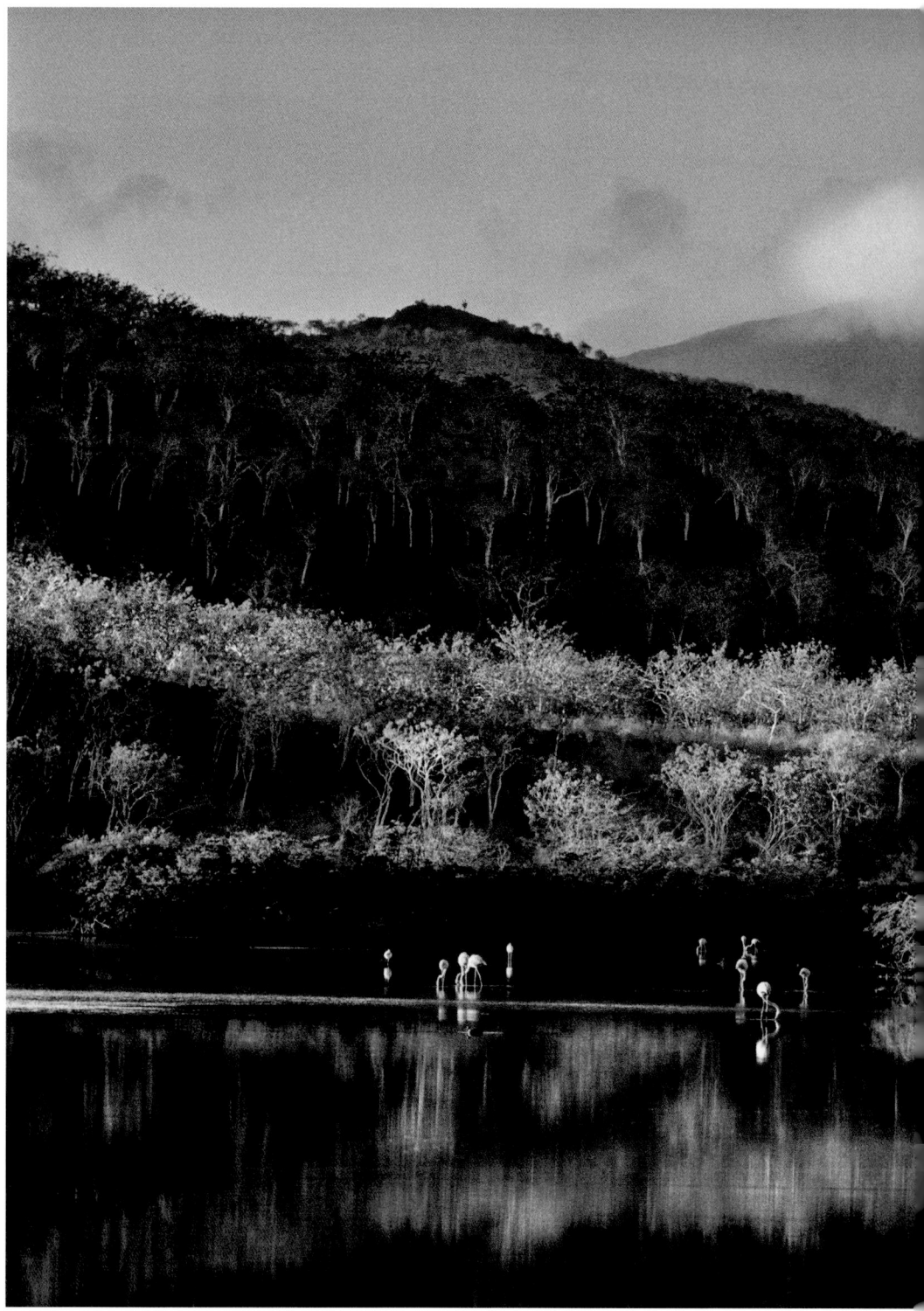

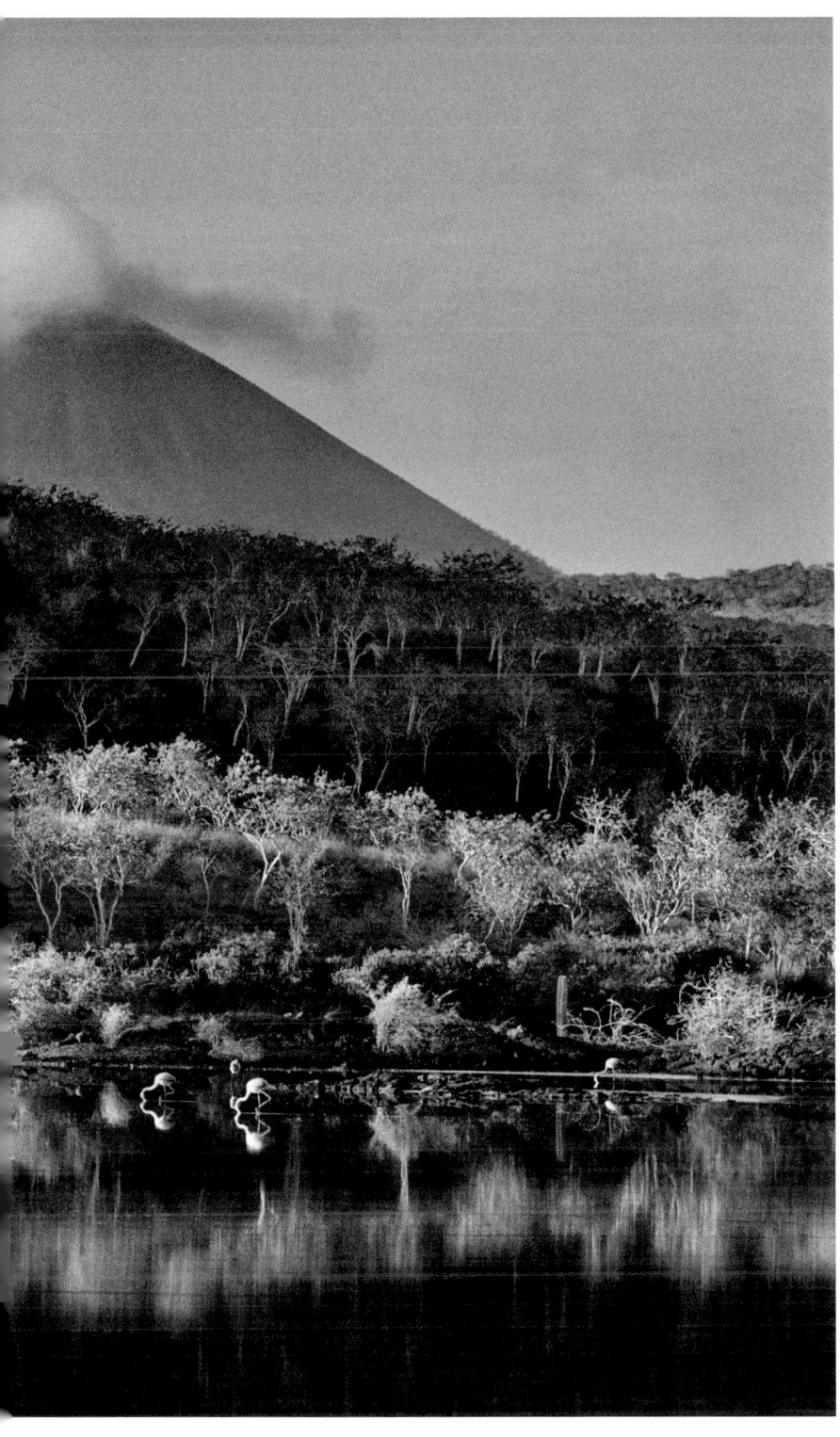

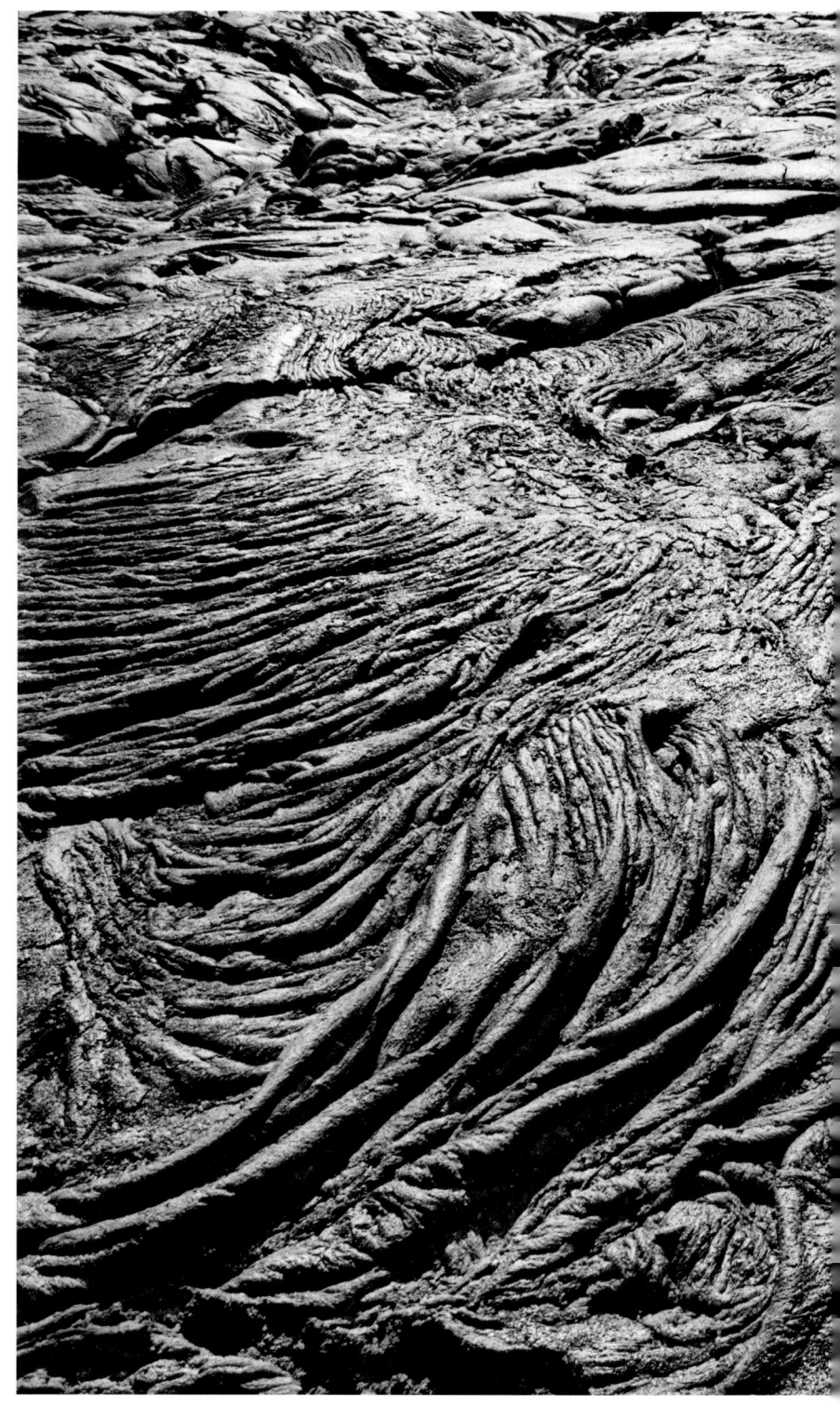

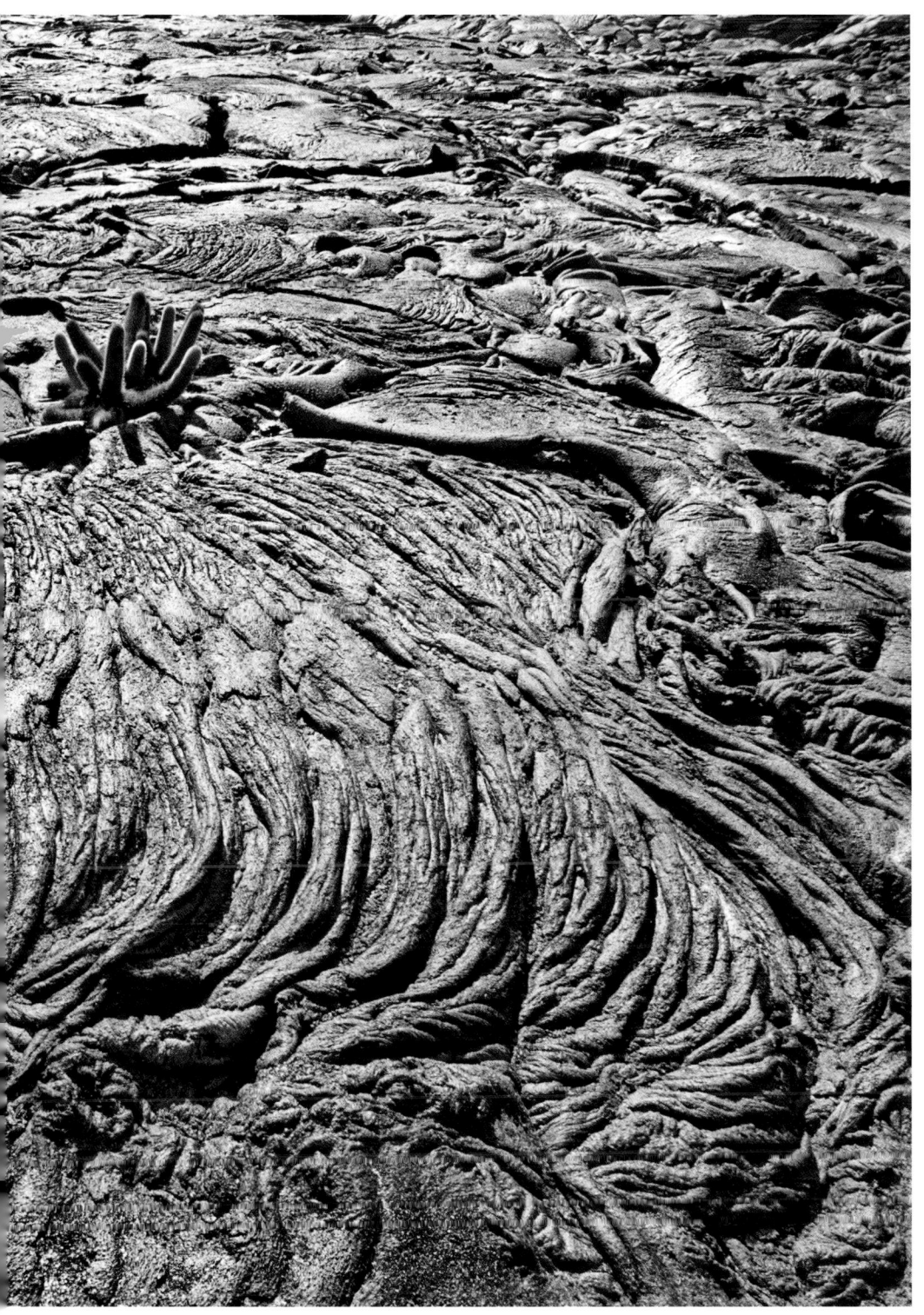

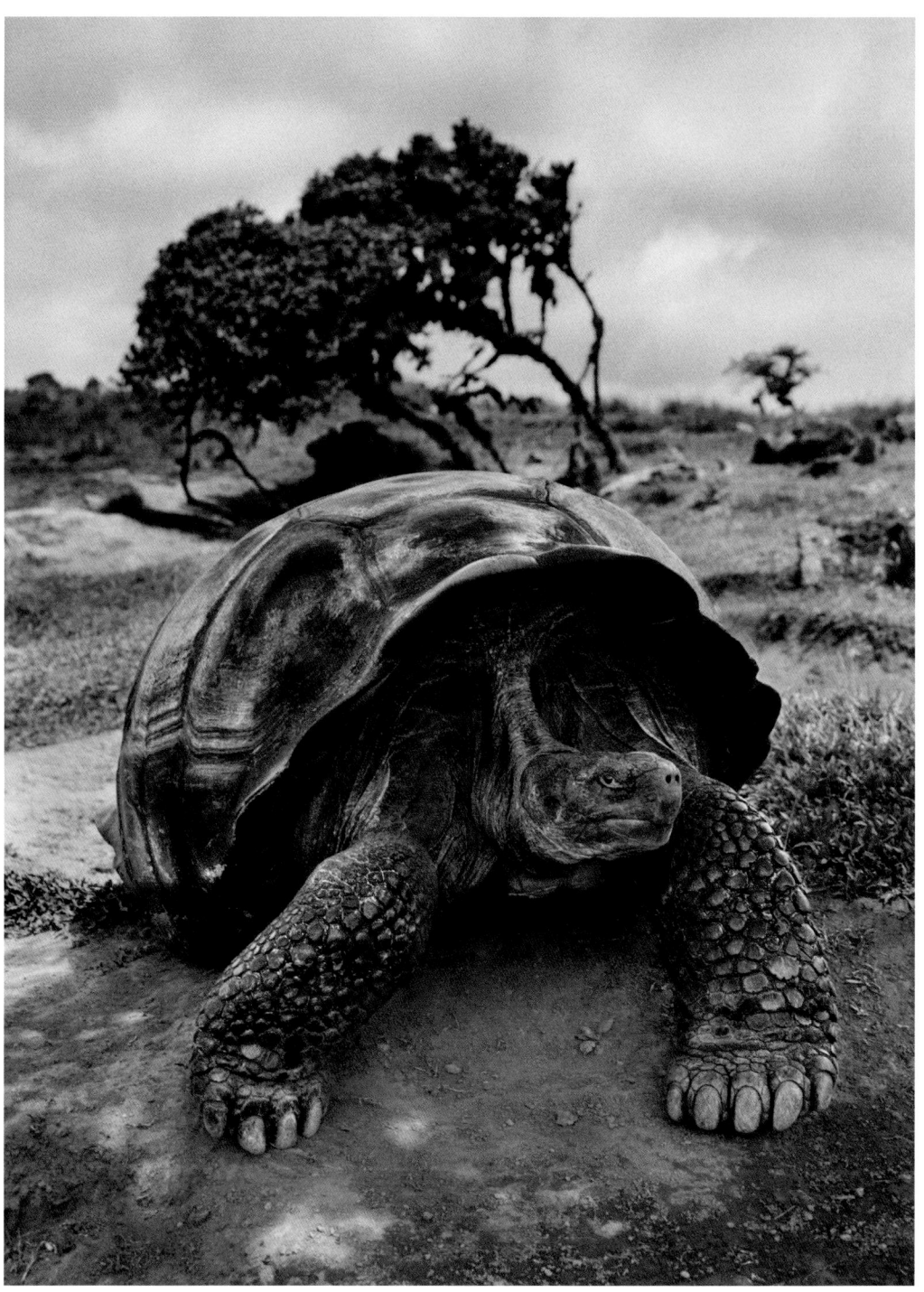

THE GALÁPAGOS

The Galápagos, celebrated for their extraordinary number of rare endemic species, form an archipelago of volcanic islands in the Pacific some 605 miles (970 kilometers) west of Ecuador. Today, the islands and their surrounding waters form a national park and a biological marine reserve. But their importance was first drawn to the world's attention by the English naturalist Charles Darwin, who visited the Galápagos in 1835 during his round-the-world voyage on the HMS *Beagle*. His observations and the specimens he collected played a fundamental role in shaping his groundbreaking theory of evolution by natural selection.

Geologically speaking, the archipelago is still unstable. It is located on the Nazca Plate, a tectonic plate that is moving very gradually under the South American Plate to the east. It is thought that some islands were formed as far back as 90 million years ago, but they have since disappeared. The 15 main islands and three smaller islands visible today are much newer, dating back between one and five million years. In fact, two of the newest islands, Isabela, the archipelago's largest, and Fernandina, each barely a million years old, are still being formed by volcanic activity, with Fernandina's volcano having erupted as recently as April 2009.

The Galápagos are spread over 17,000 square miles (45,000 square kilometers), with the northernmost island 137 miles (220 kilometers) from the southernmost. They also vary enormously in size and altitude, some with peaks of close to 9,800 feet (3,000 meters), which has further added to the diversity of species on the different islands. But some generalizations are possible. Vegetation is usually to be found beside shores, salt-water lagoons and boulder-strewn beaches, while protected coves and lagoons are dominated by mangrove swamps. Inland areas near sea level are arid, but fog banks throughout the night and into the morning provide humidity at higher elevations, even during the dry season. In some places, moisture is retained in temporary pools, allowing a fern-grass-sedge to grow in the upper reaches of some islands.

The reptiles, insects, birds and other animals found on the islands may at first sight appear familiar, but most belong to species endemic to the Galápagos. For instance, all the reptiles, except for two marine tortoises, are endemic. These include the Galápagos giant tortoise, the monarch of the islands, with 11 subspecies found on different islands, all of which are endangered. Also endemic are terrestrial iguanas, marine iguanas, three racer species, several species of lava lizards and geckos. The variety of birds is no less extraordinary. There are, for example, 13 species of Darwin's finches, including the Floreana tree finch and the mangrove finch. Other noteworthy species include dark-rumped petrels, Galápagos flightless cormorants, Galápagos penguins, lava gulls, Floreana mockingbirds, Galápagos hawks, lava herons, nocturnal swallow-tailed gulls, Galápagos rails, thick-billed flycatchers, Galápagos martins and Galápagos doves. Six species of native mammal are also known: Galápagos fur seal, Galápagos sea lion, two species of rice rat, bat and hoary bat.

Marine fauna include several species of shark, ray and cetacean, while green turtles and hawksbill turtles are also common, with green turtles nesting on sandy beaches.

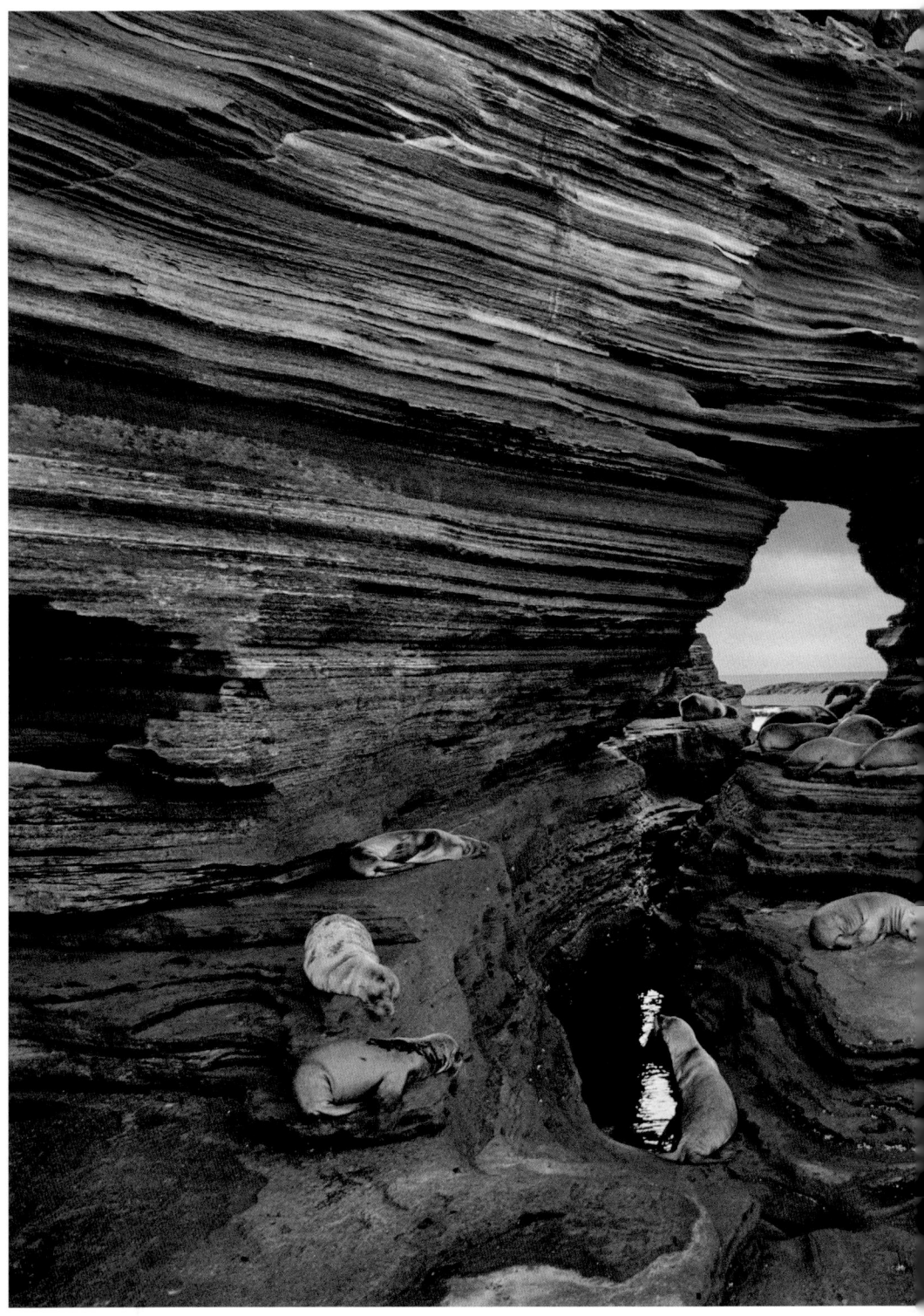

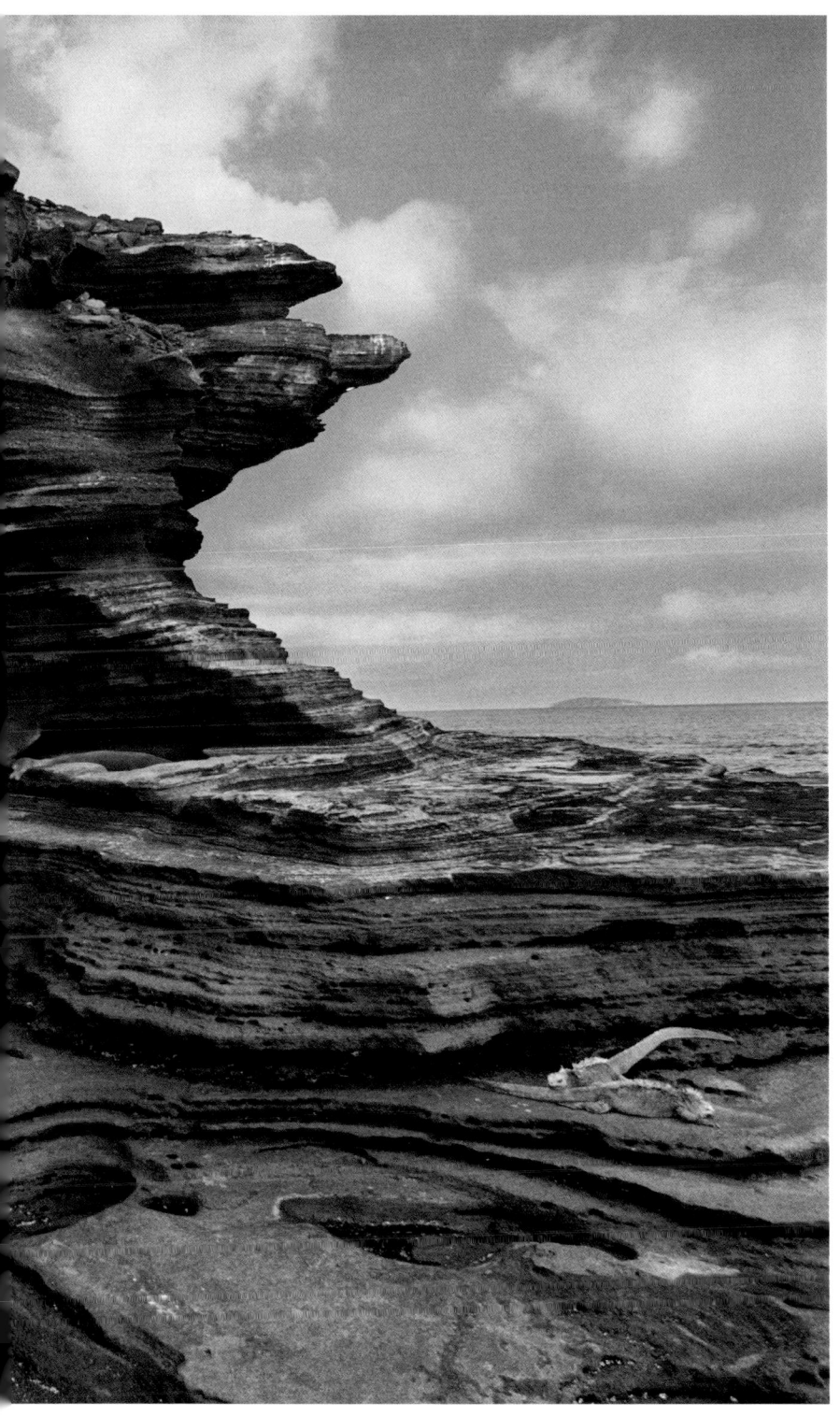

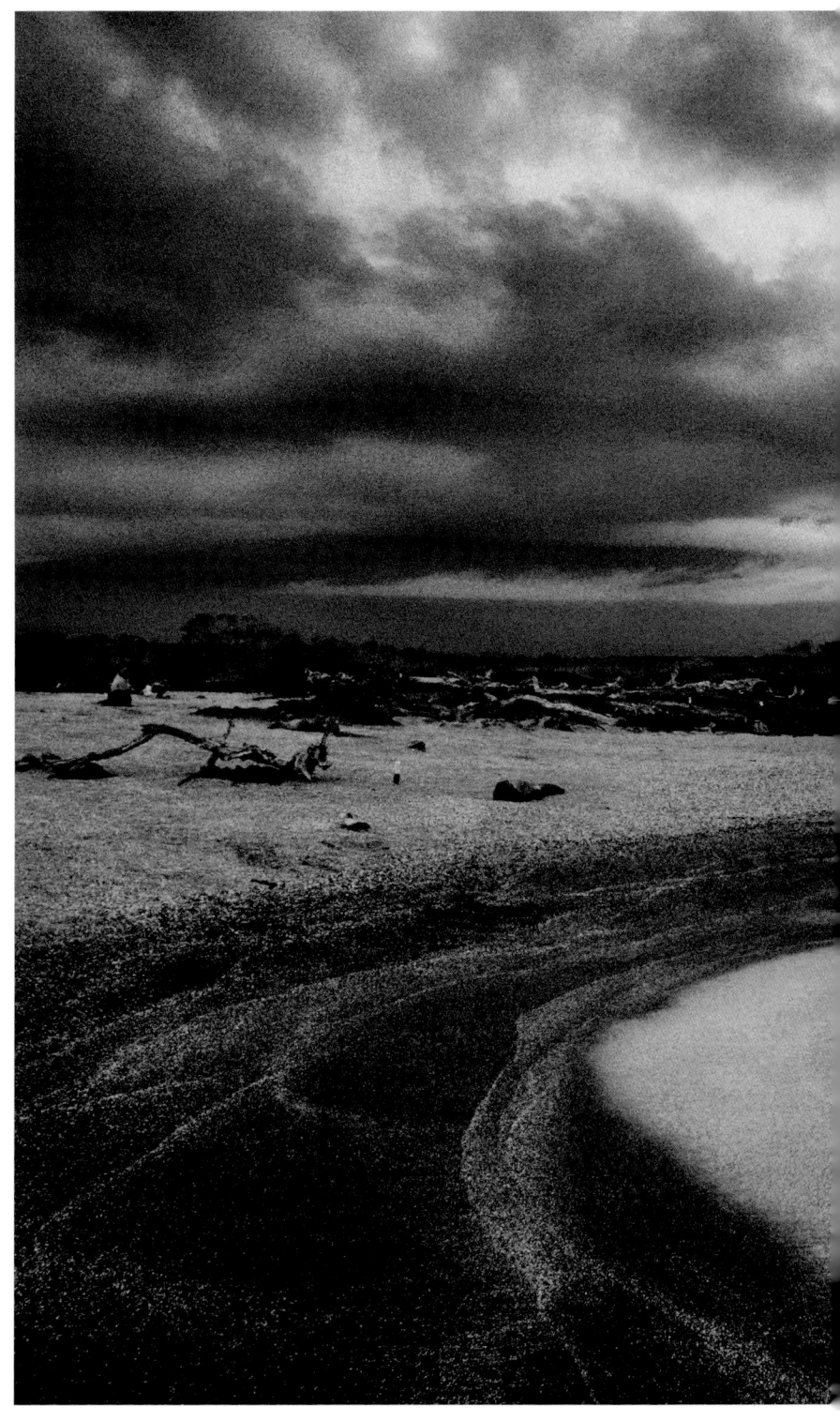

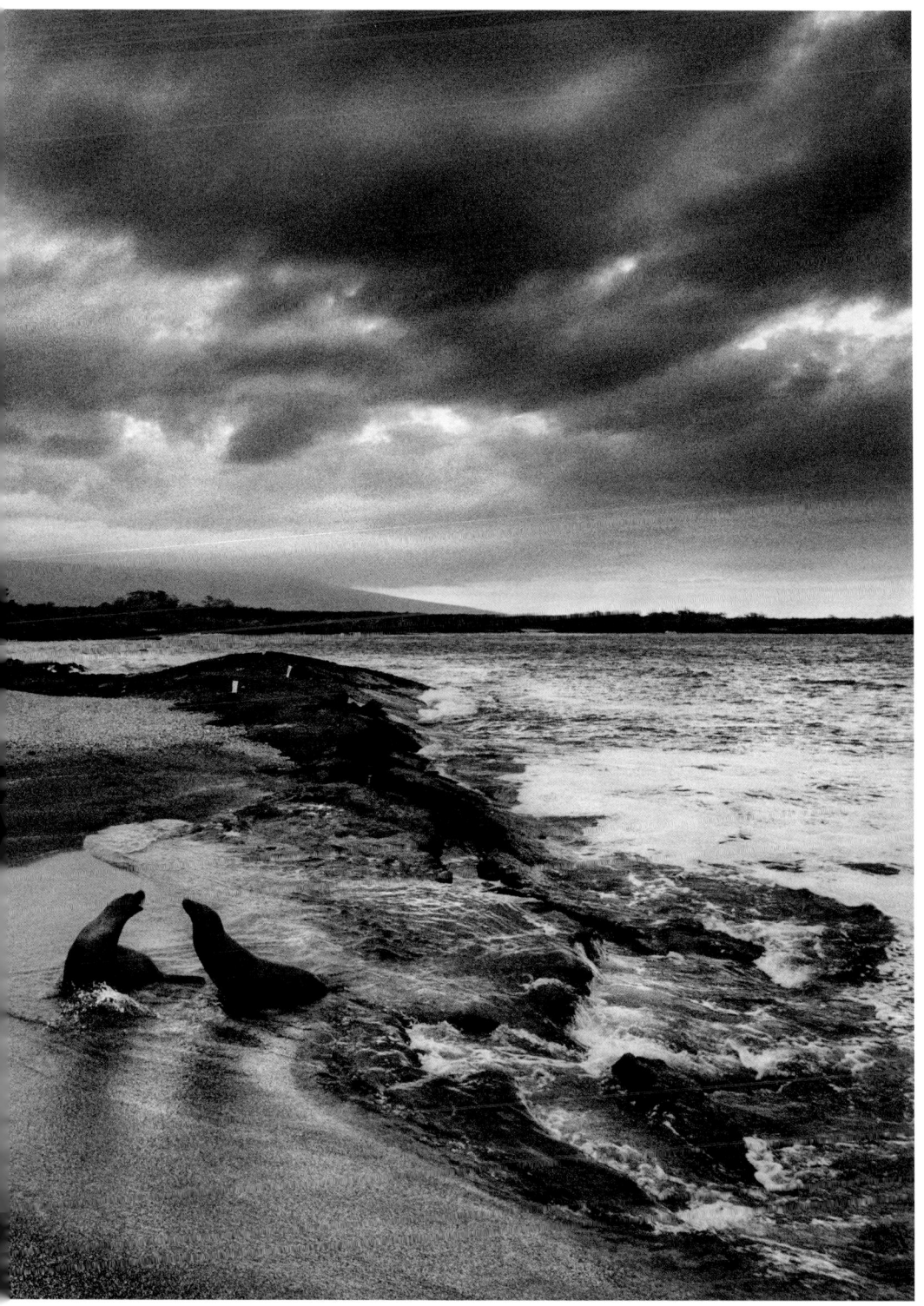

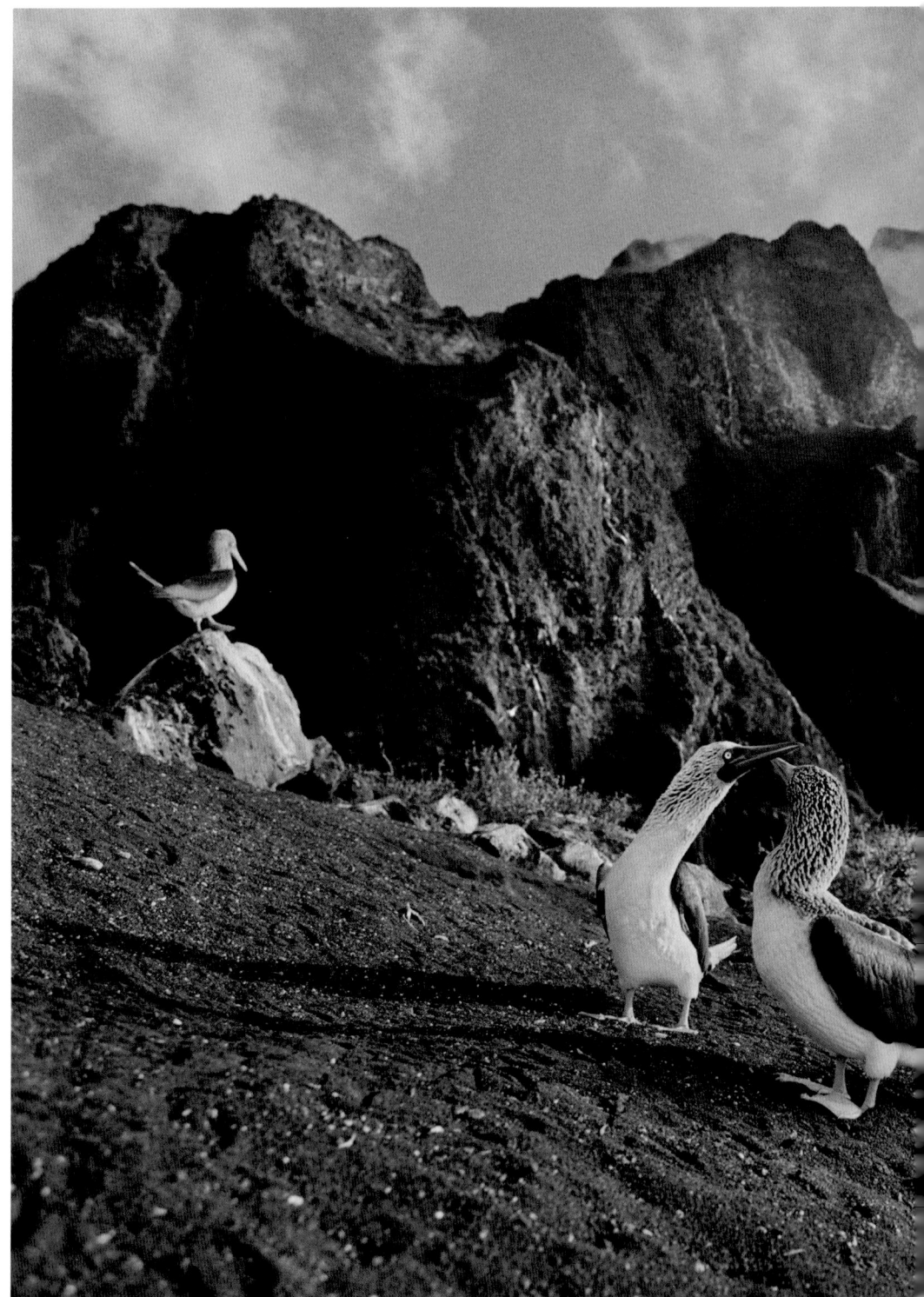

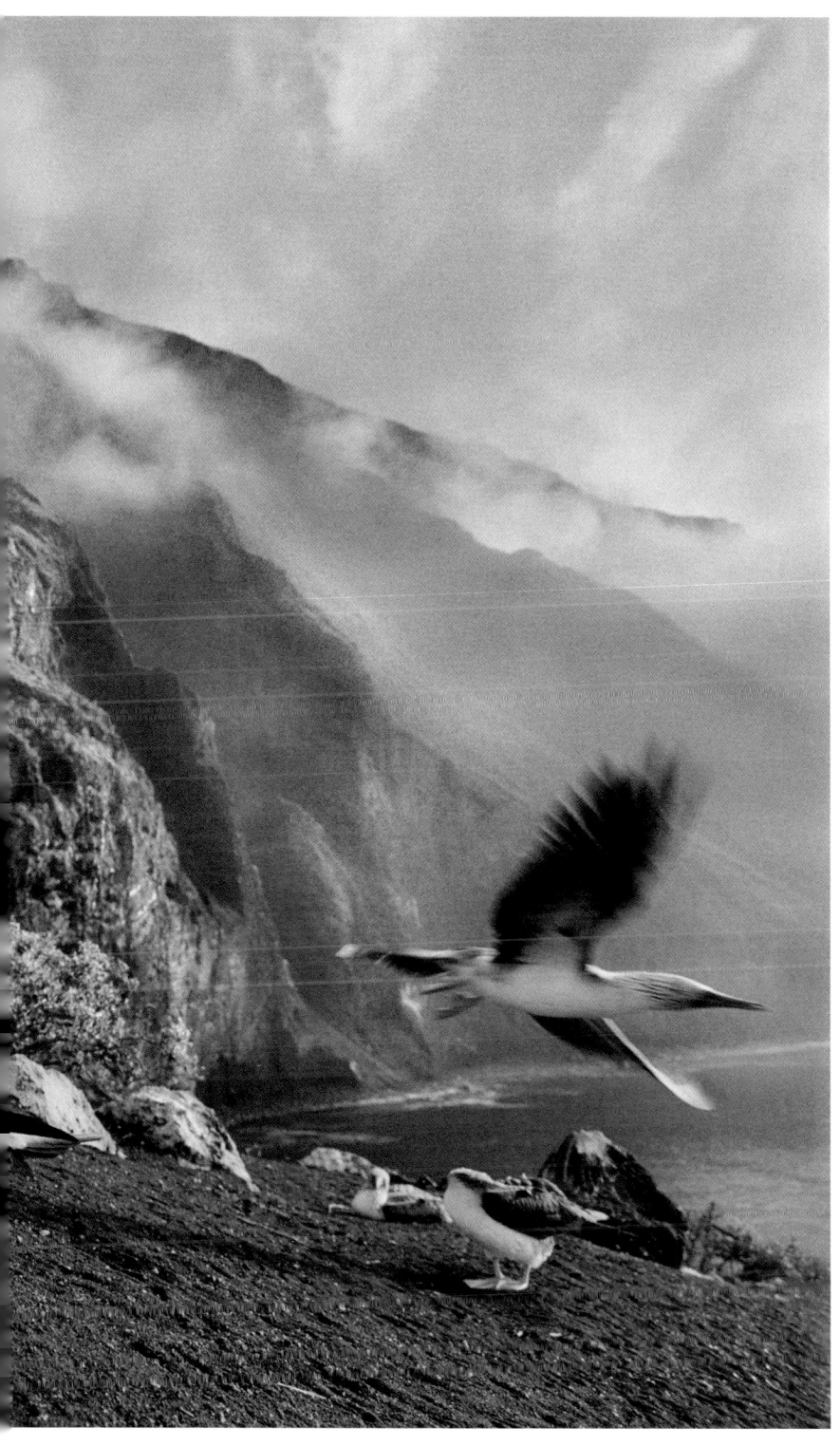

ETHNIC GROUPS OF
IRIAN JAYA, INDONESIA

Pages 135 through 165

West Papua, which was known as Irian Jaya until 2000, is the Indonesian-ruled western half of the island of New Guinea, one of the most pristine refuges for ancient human settlements on Earth. The independent state of Papua New Guinea, occupying the eastern half of the island, is also of great ethnographic significance. The western half has a population of some three million, dominated by ethnic Papuans, Melanesians and Austronesians, but also embracing numerous traditional groups living in dense forests and inaccessible mountains, among these the Korowai, who lived in total isolation until the 1970s. In fact, while Indonesian is the official language, spoken in towns and major cities like Jayapura (renamed Port Numbay) estimates of the number of indigenous languages still spoken in the region range from 200 to over 700, with Dani, Yali, Ekari and Biak among the most widely used.

The Netherlands granted Indonesia independence in 1949, but held onto the western half of this island as Dutch New Guinea until 1962. This explains why the predominant religion is Christianity (often combined with traditional beliefs), followed by Islam. For many years after Indonesia took over the territory, West Papua faced a violent separatist movement, but some calm has returned since the Jakarta government promised greater regional autonomy. The province's main industries include agriculture, fishing, oil production and mining.

Pages 128/129 Sea lions (*Zalophus californianus*) at Puerto Egas in James Bay. Santiago Island. The Galápagos sea lion is one of the largest of the archipelago's animals, weighing up to 550 pounds (250 kilos), although it is still smaller than the sea lions of California, where it originated. This group is resting in the shadow of beautiful rocks formed by piled and compacted volcanic ash; these formations, known as tuff, are rather soft and are easily eroded by the wind and sea. Galápagos. Ecuador. January, February and March 2004.

Pages 130/131 Sea lions (*Zalophus californianus*) at Punta Espinoza. Fernandina Island. This island's 4,900-foot (1,495-meter)-high volcano towers in the background. At certain times of the year, sea currents bring very cold waters to the archipelago, resulting in thermal shocks, which produce strange and beautiful blankets of fog. Galápagos. Ecuador. January, February and March 2004.

Pages 132/133 Blue-footed boobies (*Sula nebouxii*), Roca Vicente. Isabela Island. I visited this large colony twice, in mid-February and then three weeks later. During the first visit, the blue-footed boobies were flying around in their hundreds searching for mates; during the second visit (when this photograph was taken), few were in flight since by then pairs had been formed and breeding was underway. In the background stands Ecuador Volcano, so named because it is located only a few hundred meters from the equator. Galápagos. Ecuador. January, February and March 2004.

Opposite and page 139 The Korowai spend their days in the forest collecting all they need to survive. Since wild pigs are a delicacy difficult to find, the Korowai eat almost any animal as well as insects and fruit. West Papua. Indonesia. February and March 2010.

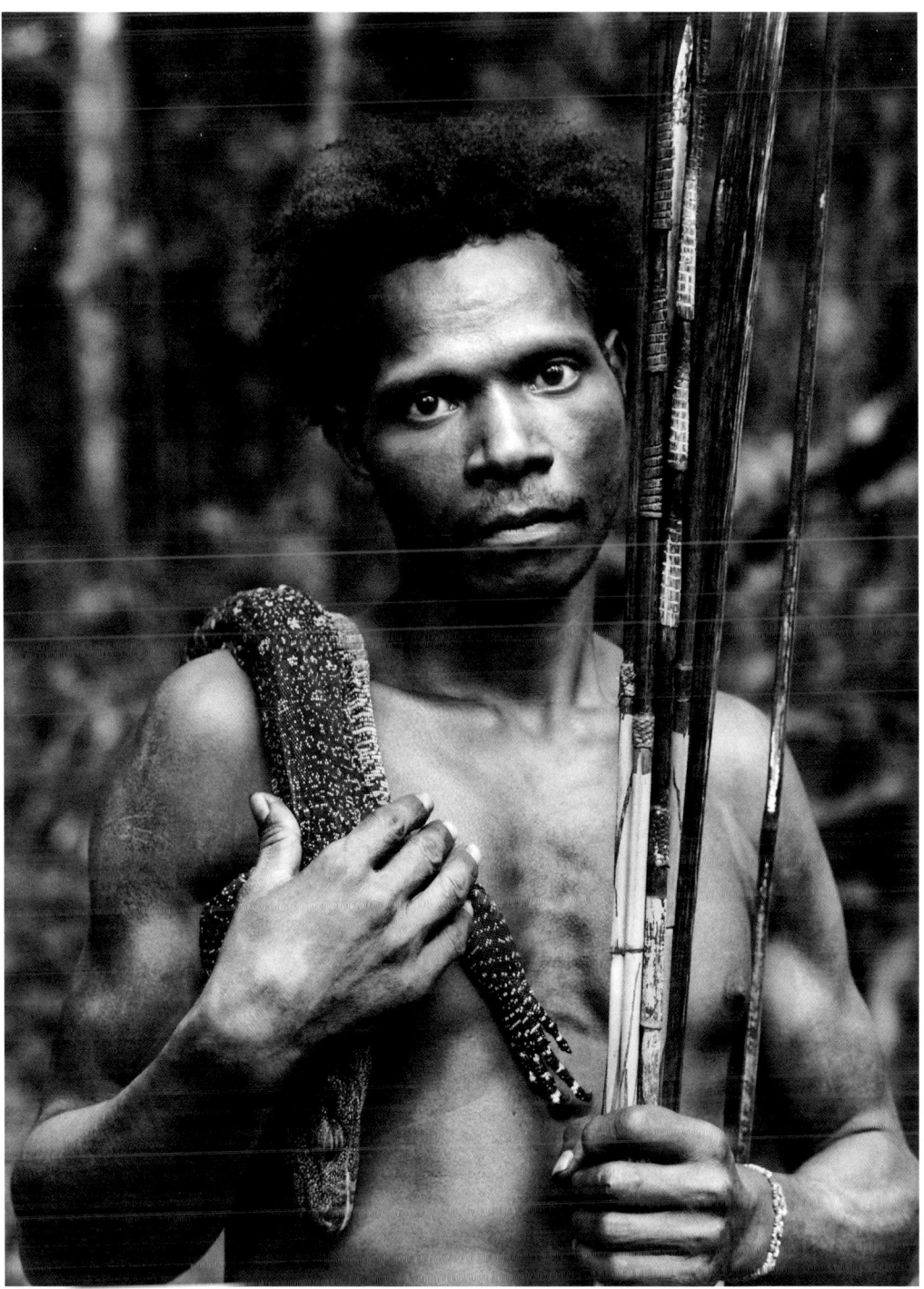

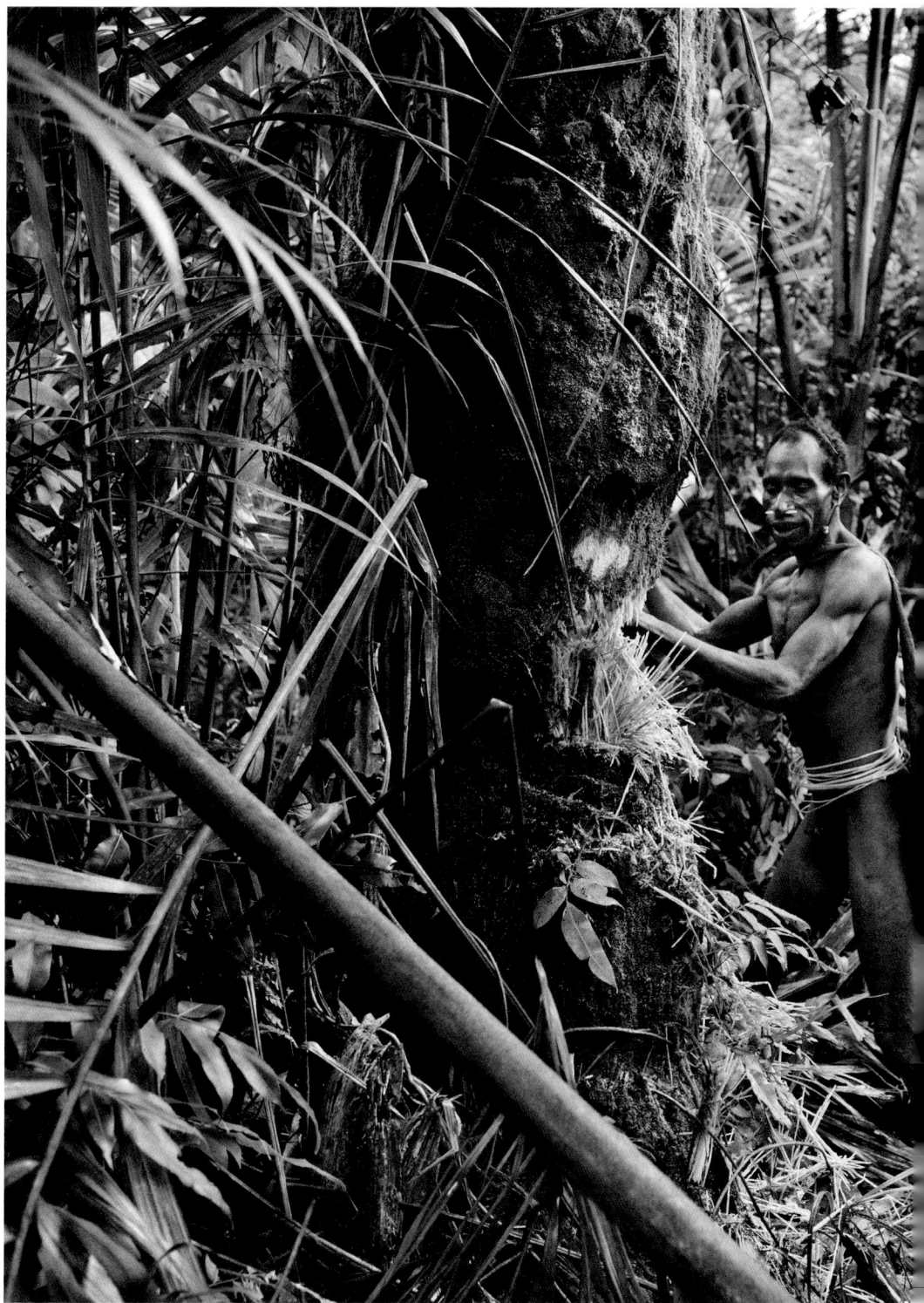

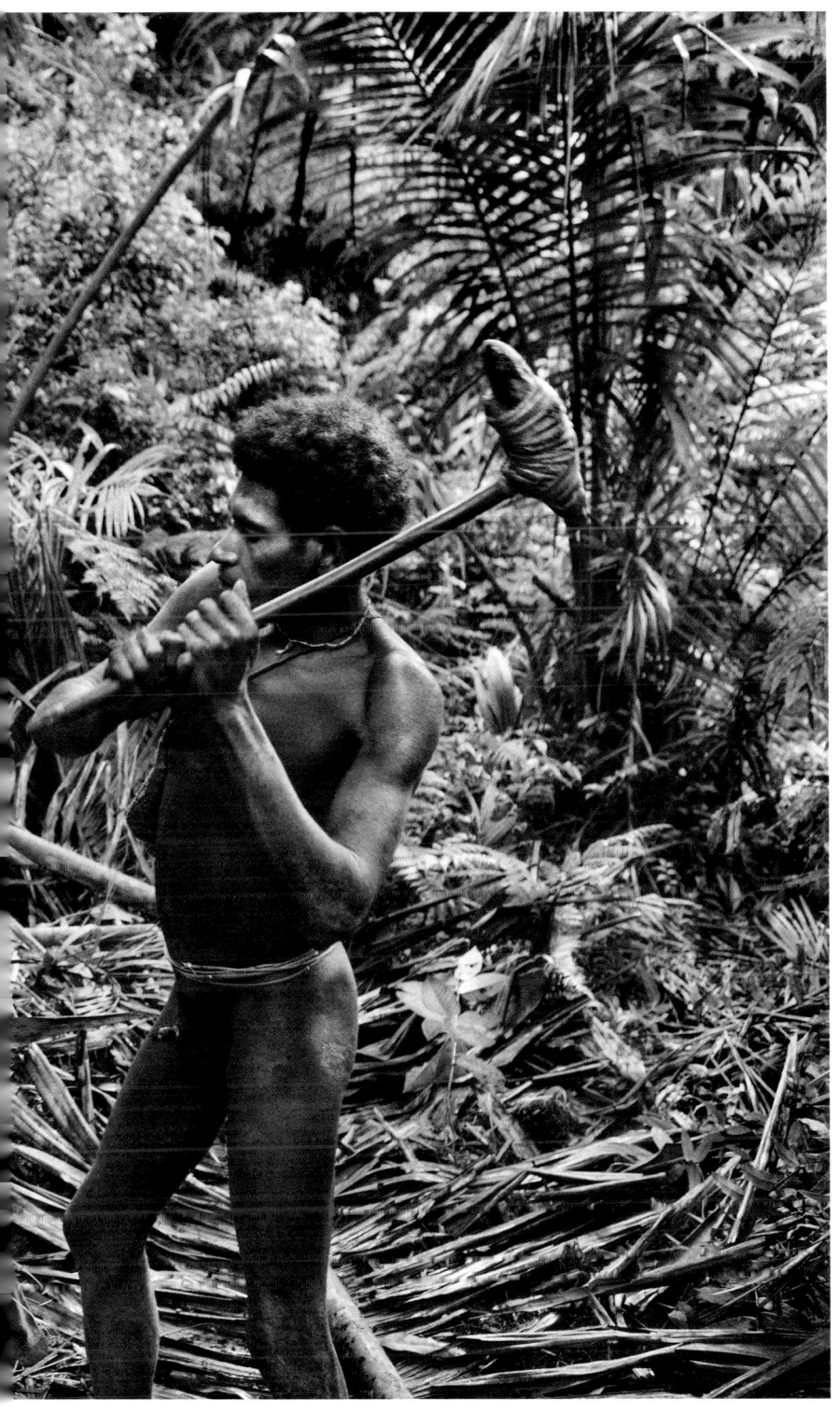

Pages 136/137 Since most of the Korowai still use stone tools in their daily life, they have become known as the Stone (Age) Korowai. The Korowai are hunter-gatherers, with much of their cuisine based on sago, a starch extracted from the center of palm-tree trunks, which is then ground into flour. This photograph shows the Korowai using stone axes, bone knives, wooden hammers and other ancient tools in stripping the bark off the sago tree. West Papua. Indonesia. February and March 2010.

Pages 140/141 The Korowai inhabit a 230-square-mile (600-square-kilometer) territory, a swampy tract in the southwest of the country, defined by the sea, the Becking and Eiulanden rivers and mountains in the north. Some 2,500 Korowai live in this difficult terrain in small family groups. West Papua. Indonesia. February and March 2010.

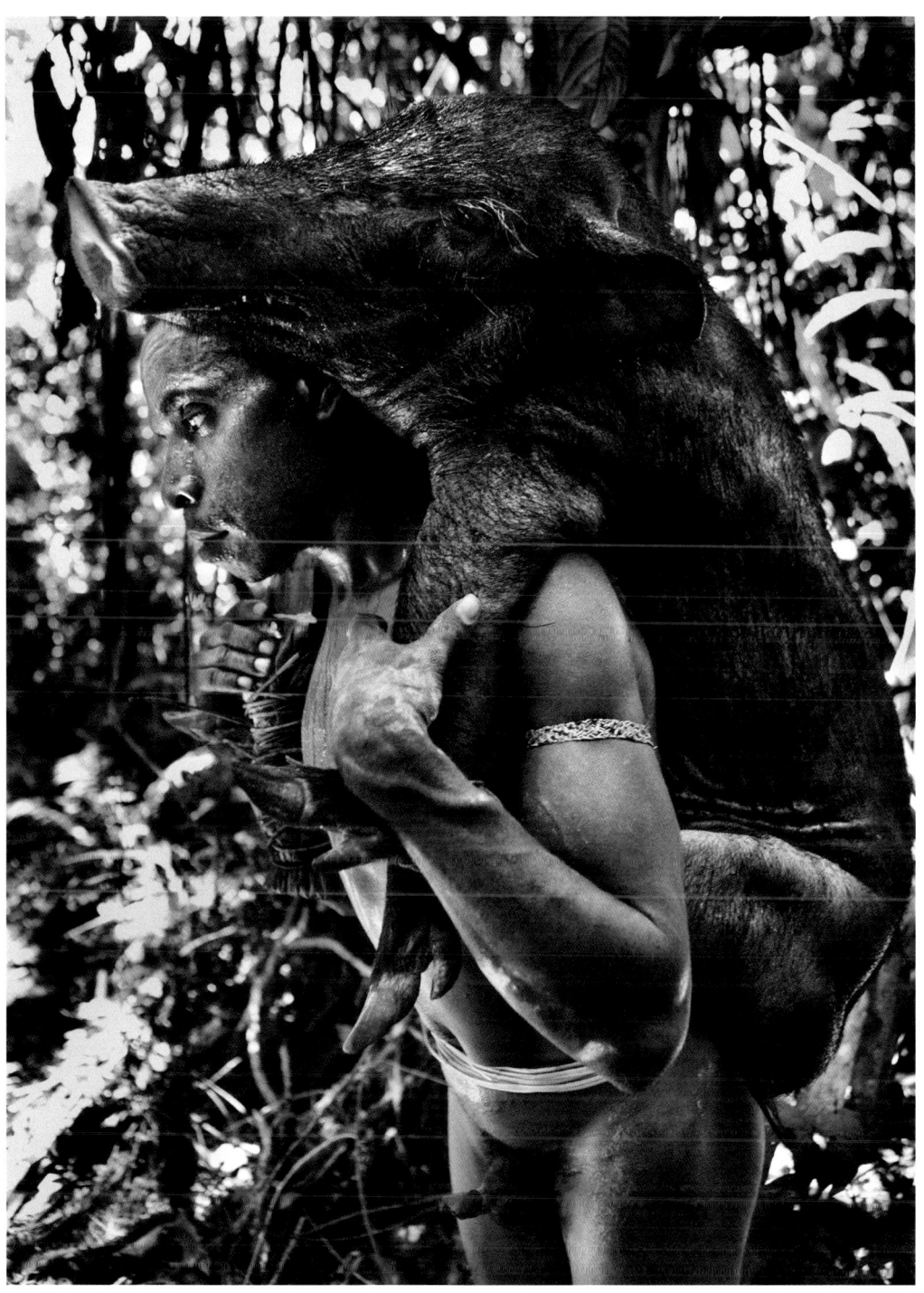

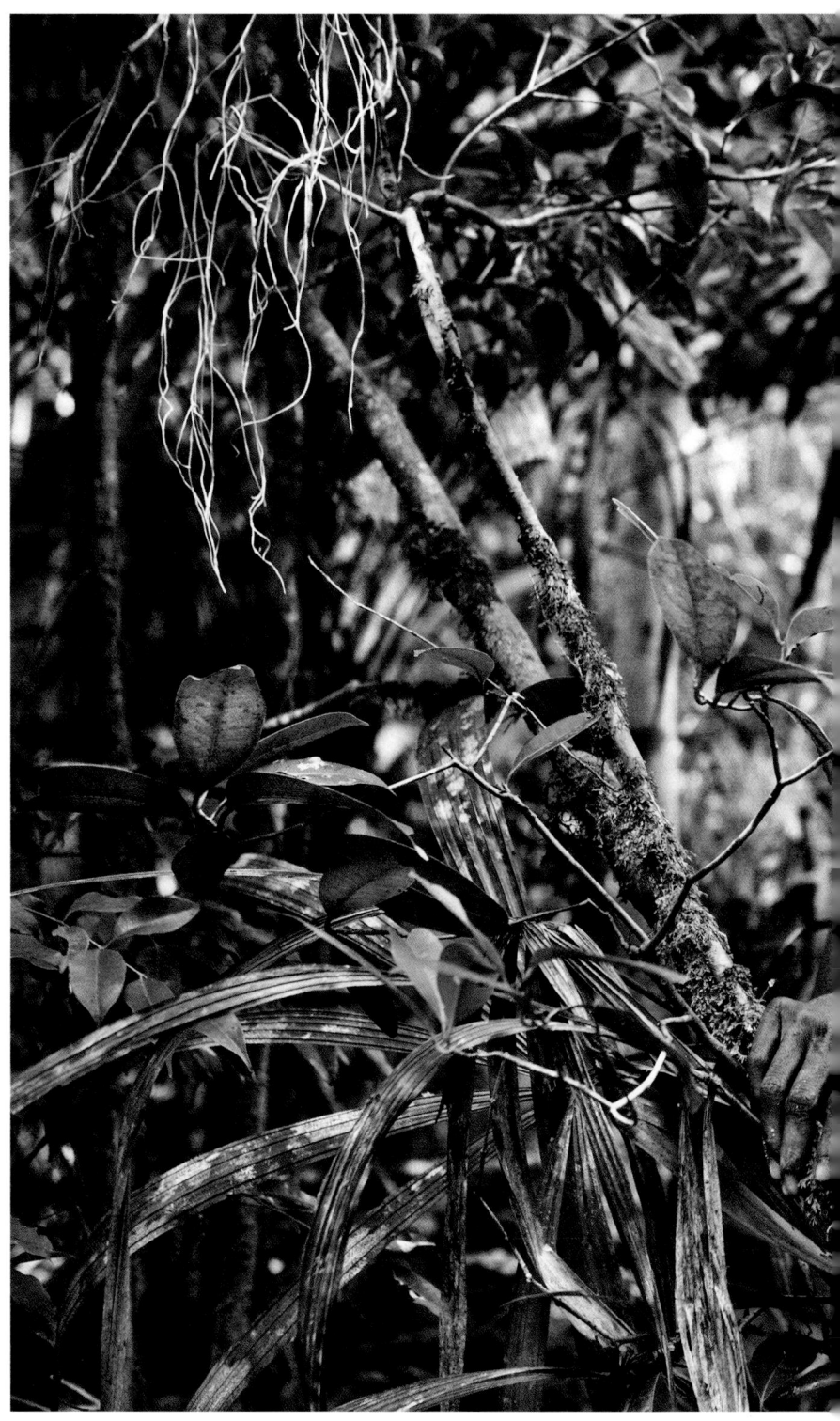

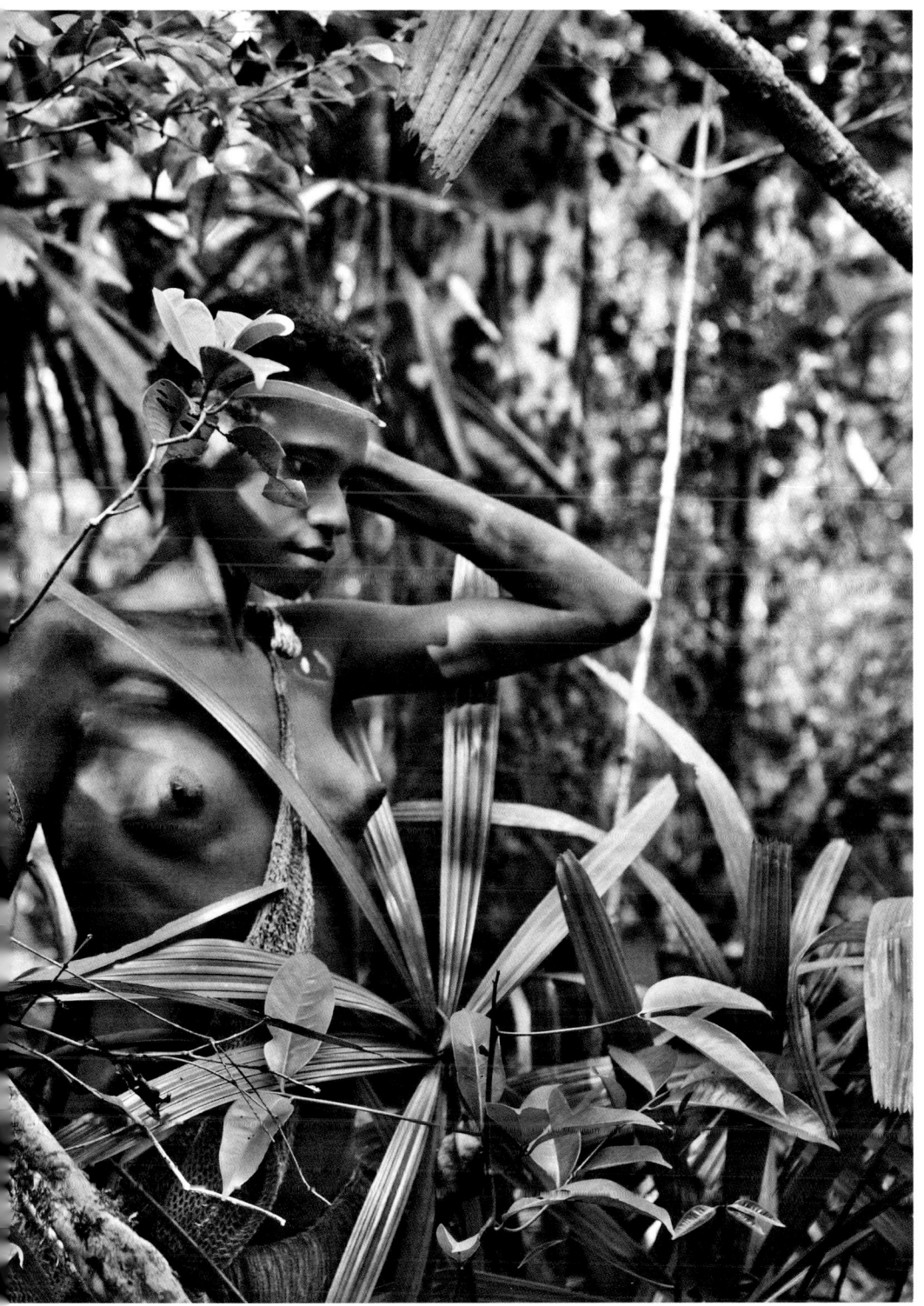

Opposite The Yali people live in West Papua's Jayawijaya mountain range, a stunningly rugged terrain, with rivers carving narrow gorges and steep-sided valleys. This remote and spectacular landscape shielded the Yali from contact with the modern world until Christian missionaries penetrated the area in the 1970s. But even now, like many isolated peoples, the Yali have what to outsiders seems like a charmingly simple life. Yali men wear traditional "skirts" composed of long strips of rattan, roughly a fifth of an inch (five millimeters) in width, which are wrapped around the mid-riff and then open out into a rustic skirt. The front is held up by a *koteka*, a penis cover made from a dried-out gourd. Ethnic groups can often be identified by the shape of the men's *koteka*. West Papua. Indonesia. September 2010.

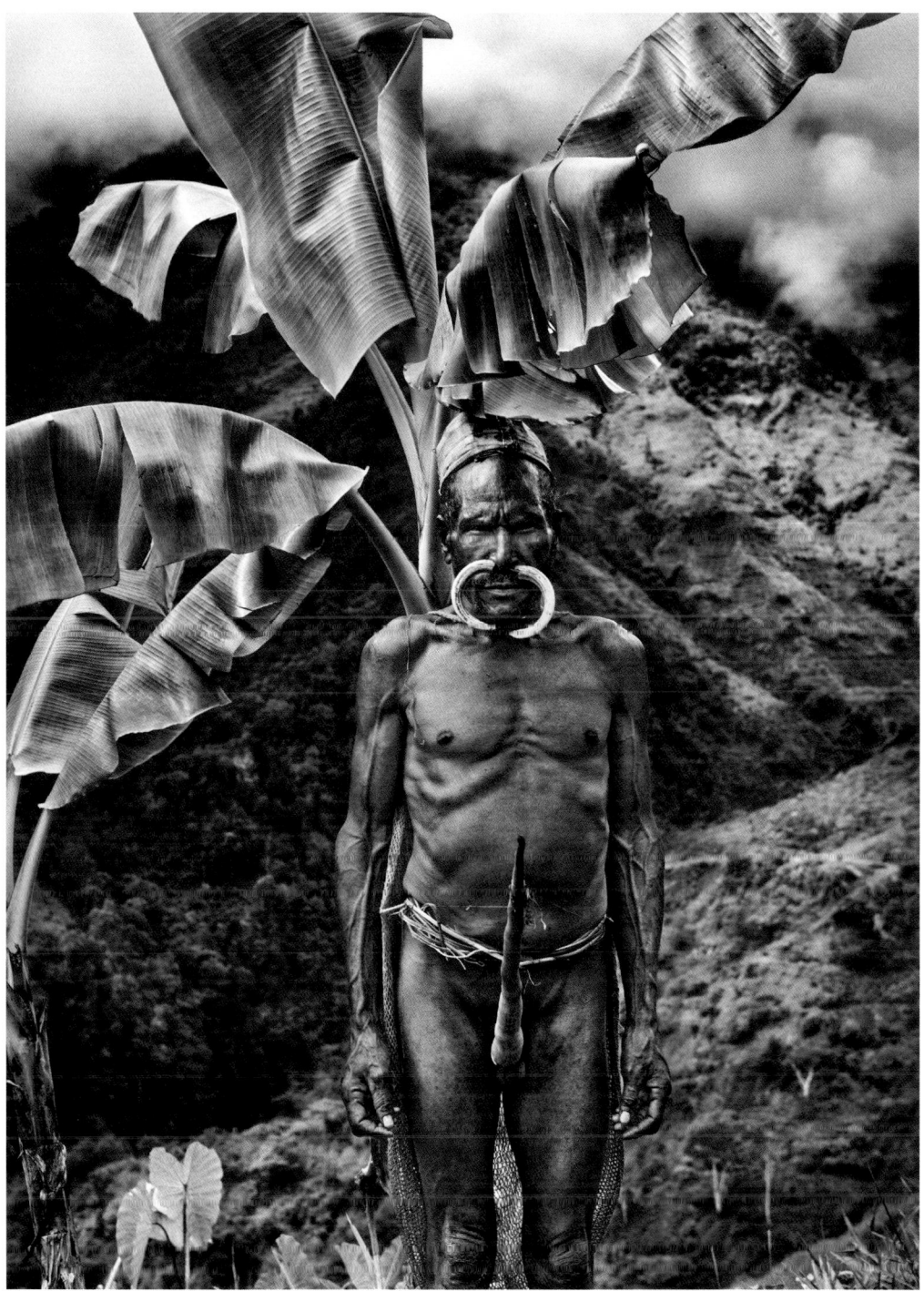

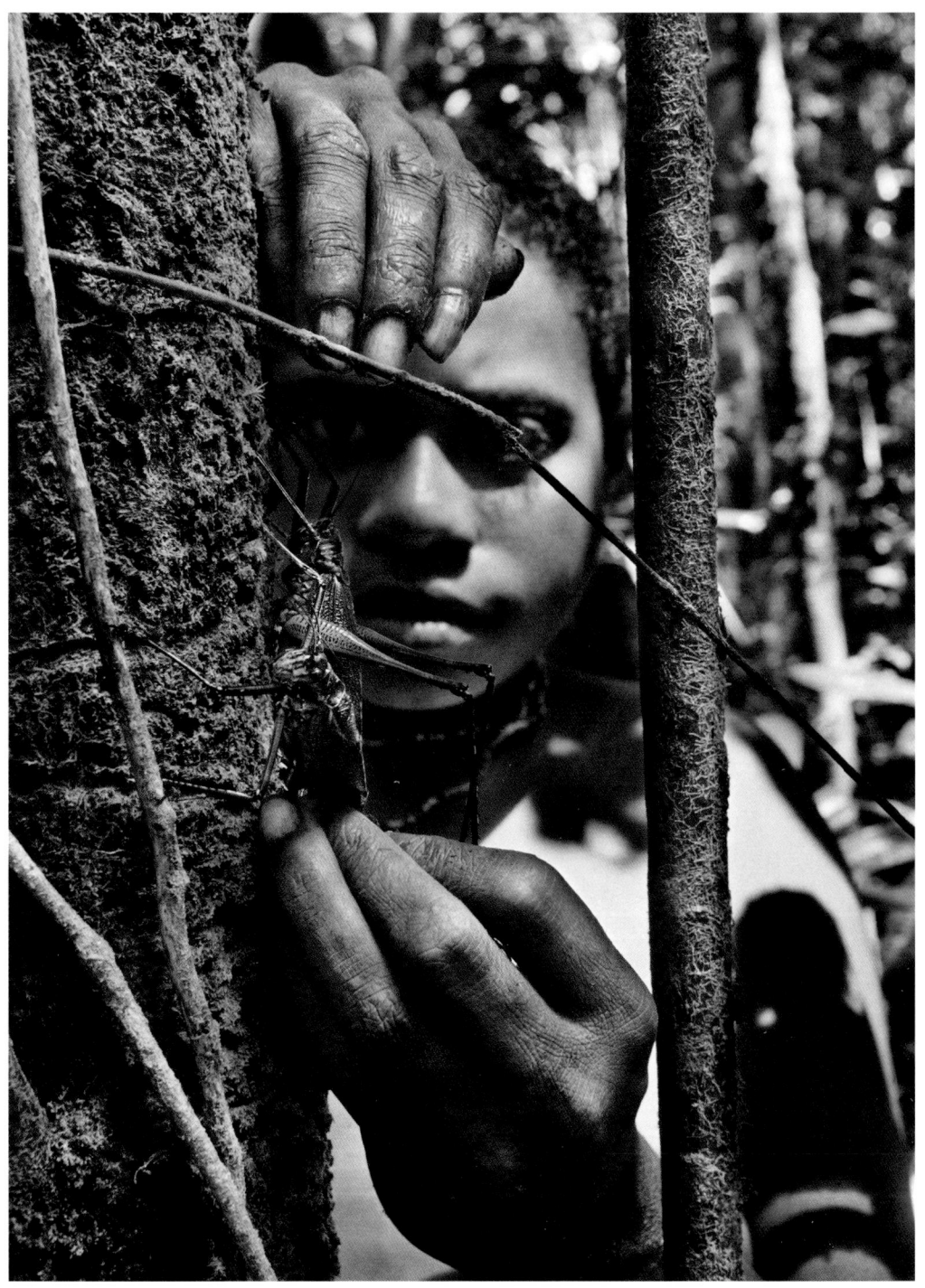

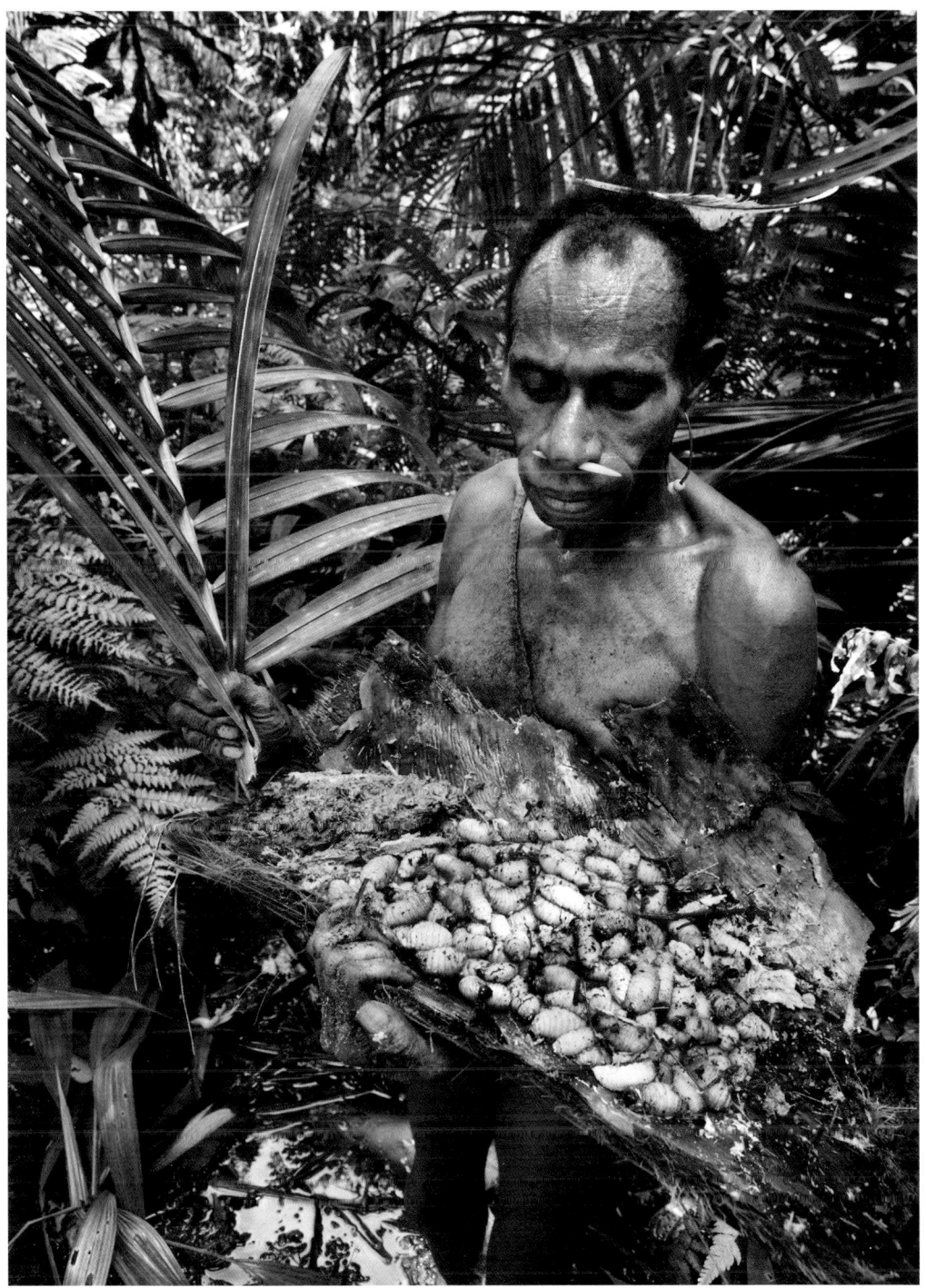

145

Page 144 The Korowai spend their days in the forest collecting all they need to survive. Since wild pigs are a delicacy difficult to find, they eat almost any animal as well as insects and fruit. West Papua. Indonesia. February and March 2010.

Page 145 Once cut down, part of the sago tree is immediately used to grind flour, while the rest becomes a nest where capricorn beetles lay their eggs; several months later, the Korowai return to collect the larvae, which they consider a delicacy. West Papua. Indonesia. February and March 2010.

Opposite Korowai homes are usually built between 20 and 80 feet (6 and 25 meters) above the ground. They can house families of up to eight members, with men and women sleeping separately. Their few belongings include instruments for decorating their bodies. West Papua. Indonesia. February and March 2010.

Pages 148/149 The Korowai live in small family groups in tree houses. However, when there is a dispute with neighbors or a nearby community, security demands that tree houses are built at heights of up to 130 feet (40 meters). West Papua. Indonesia. February and March 2010.

Pages 150/151 The Yali people live in West Papua's Jayawijaya mountain range, a stunningly rugged terrain, with rivers carving narrow gorges and steep-sided valleys. This remote and spectacular landscape shielded the Yali from contact with the modern world until Christian missionaries penetrated the area in the 1970s. West Papua. Indonesia. September 2010.

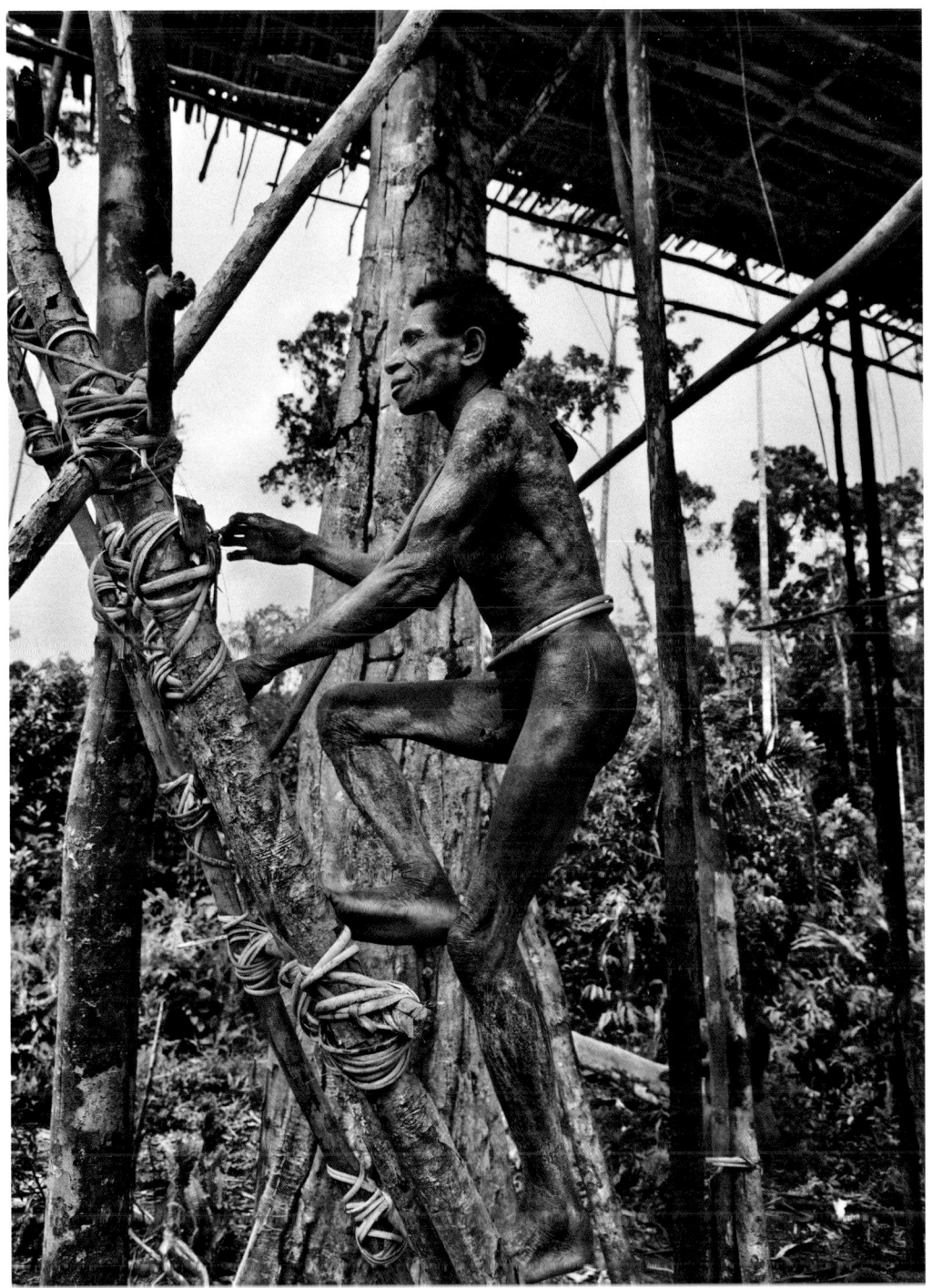

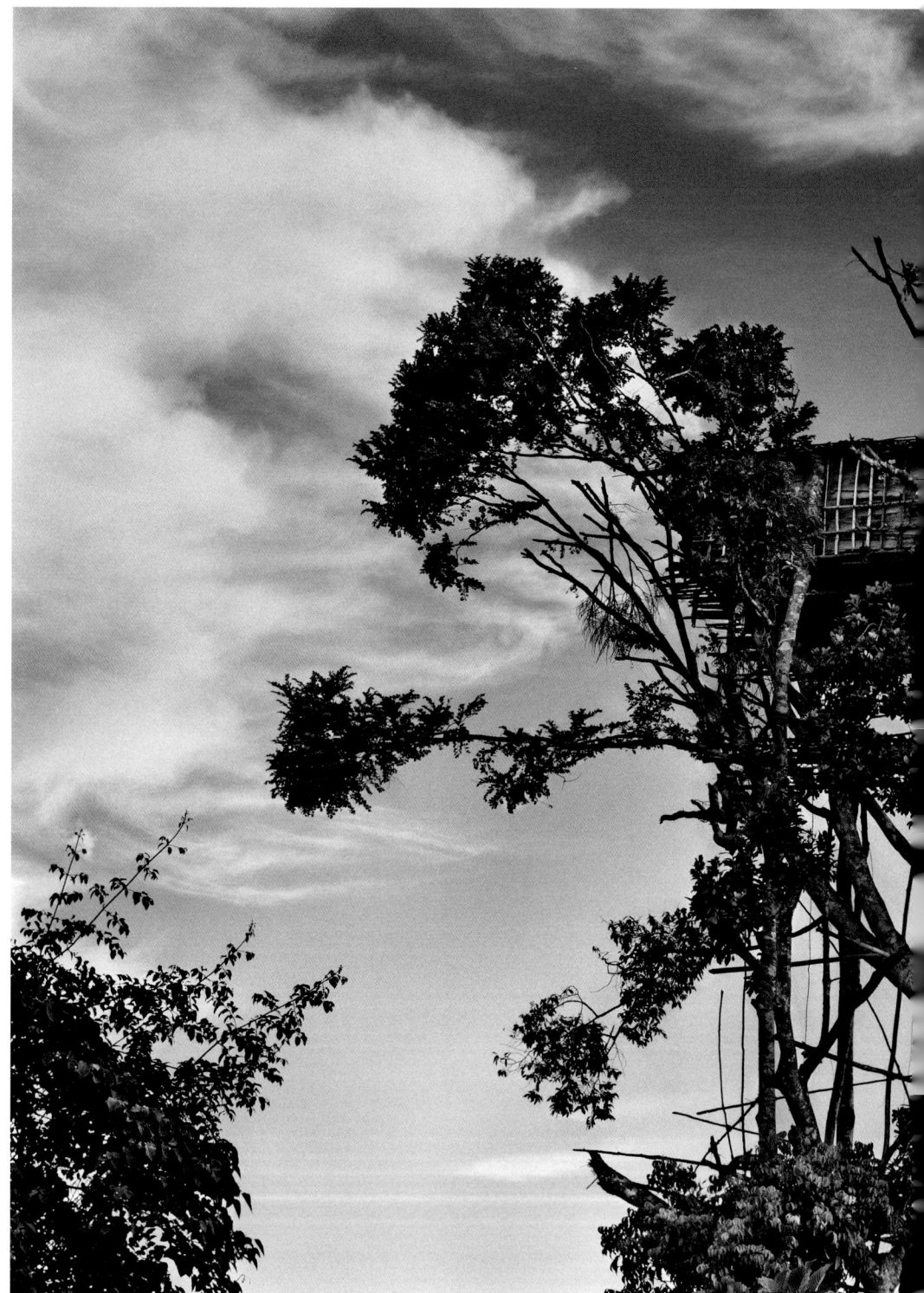

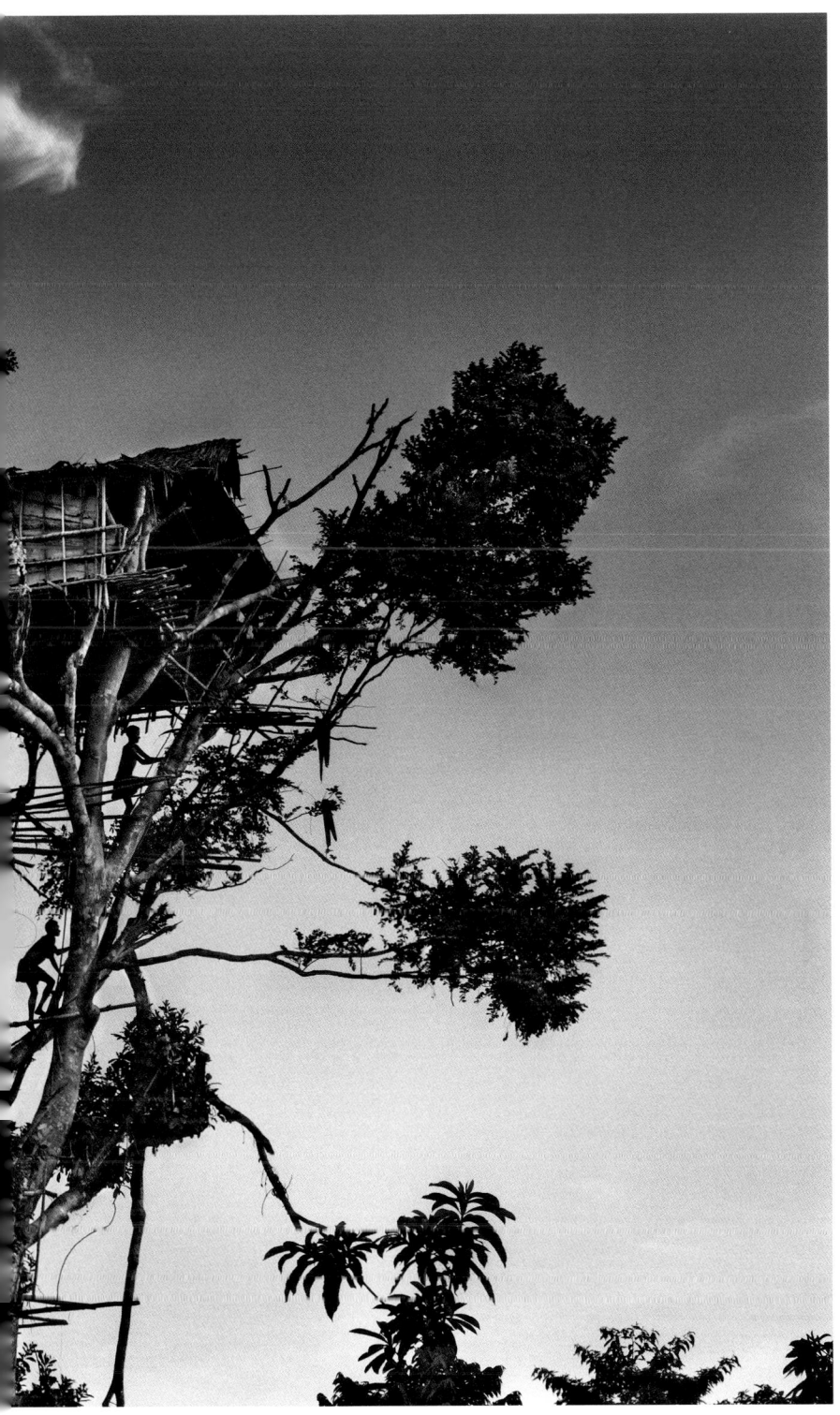

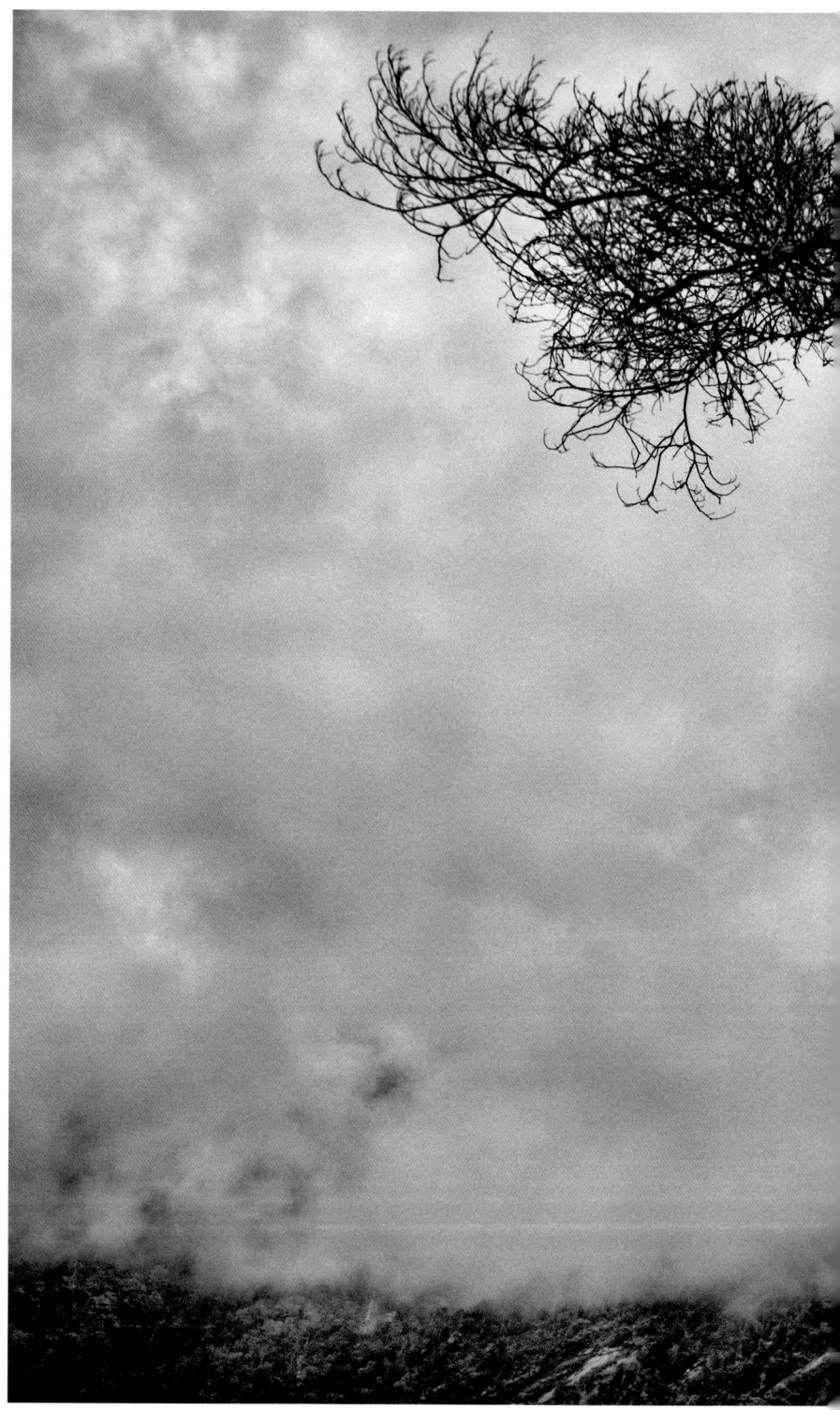

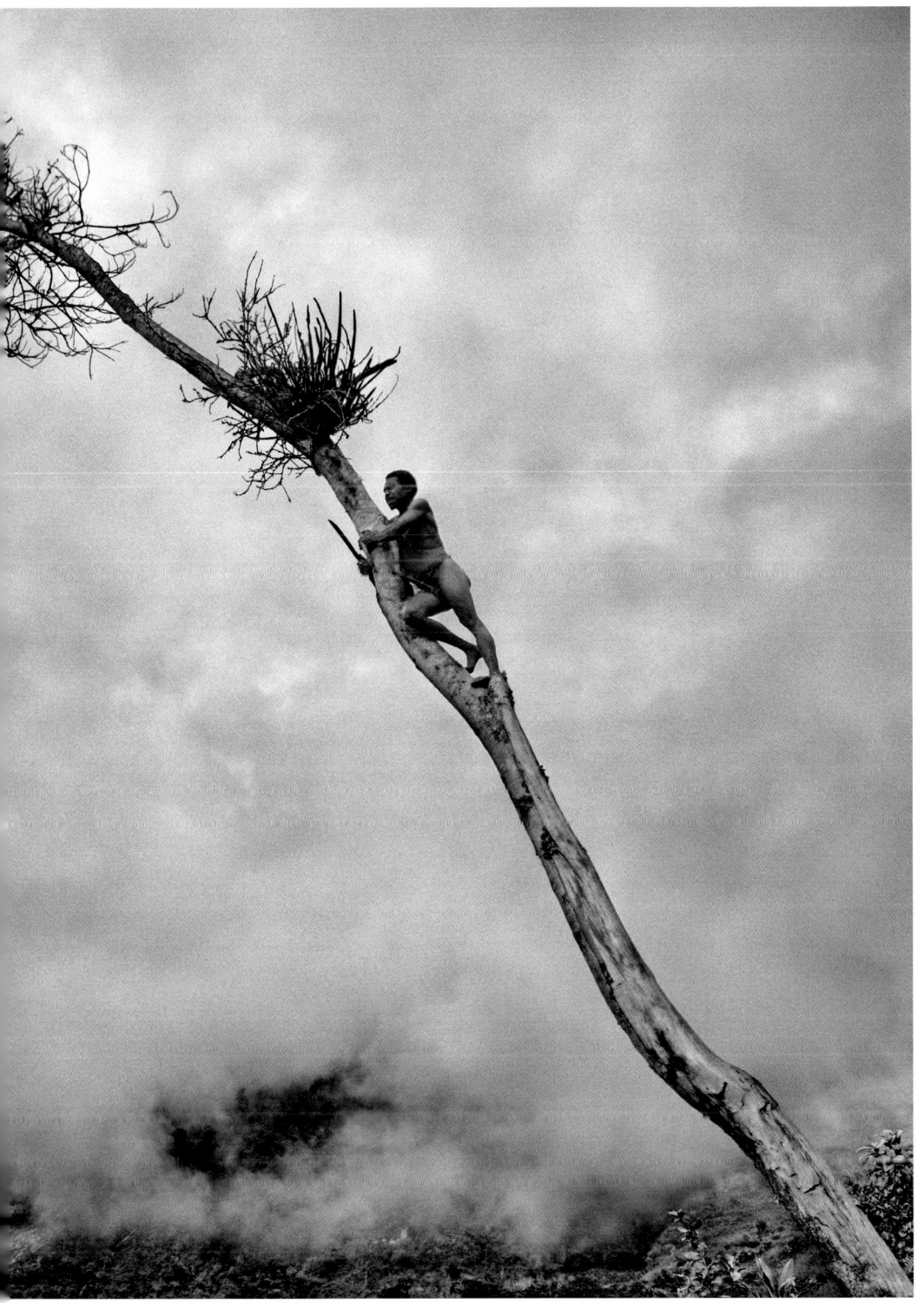

Opposite For most indigenous peoples across New Guinea, pigs' teeth are key elements of decoration. Among the Yali, the men put one through their nose and the women wear them as necklaces. West Papua. Indonesia. September 2010.

Pages 154/155 The Yali usually eat only the wild pigs they hunt, but they may occasionally kill one they have raised for special ceremonies. These semi-domesticated pigs are usually caught as piglets when their parents are hunted in the forest. During these convivial ceremonies, while the men prepare the meat, the women collect leaves to add savor to the food. The "oven" comprises stones heated by firewood for hours and placed in a pit. West Papua. Indonesia. September 2010.

Pages 156/157 As this father and daughter demonstrate, the most important items of clothing for the Yali are skirts for the women and *kotekas*, or penis gourds, for the men. The skirts consist of four layers.

The first layer is given to a girl when she is around four, with an extra layer added every four years. With four layers in place around the age of 16, the girl is ready to be married. As to the *koteka*, stone weights are tied to the bottom of the dried gourd to stretch it. String is also used to give it different shapes. It is sometimes waxed with beeswax or native resins and can be painted and decorated with shells and feathers. West Papua. Indonesia. September 2010.

Pages 158/159 The diet of the Yali people is composed of a large variety of vegetables. The most important is sweet potato, which is cultivated everywhere. There are individual and collective plantations of sweet potato. They also grow tarot, cassava, banana and pandanus and collect insects and leaves from many different trees. The women carry large bags woven from orchid fibers, in which they put all they collect during the day. West Papua. Indonesia. September 2010.

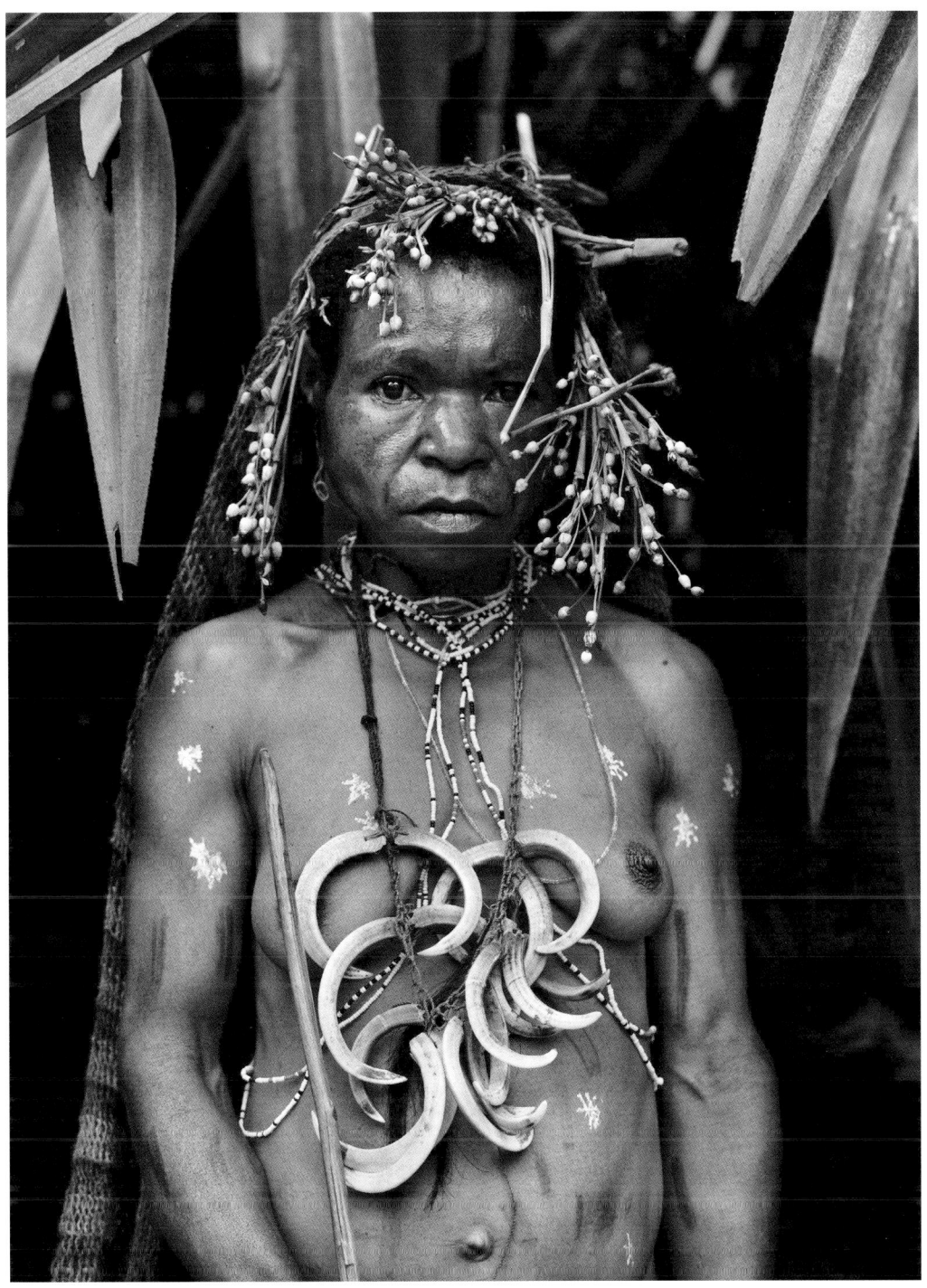

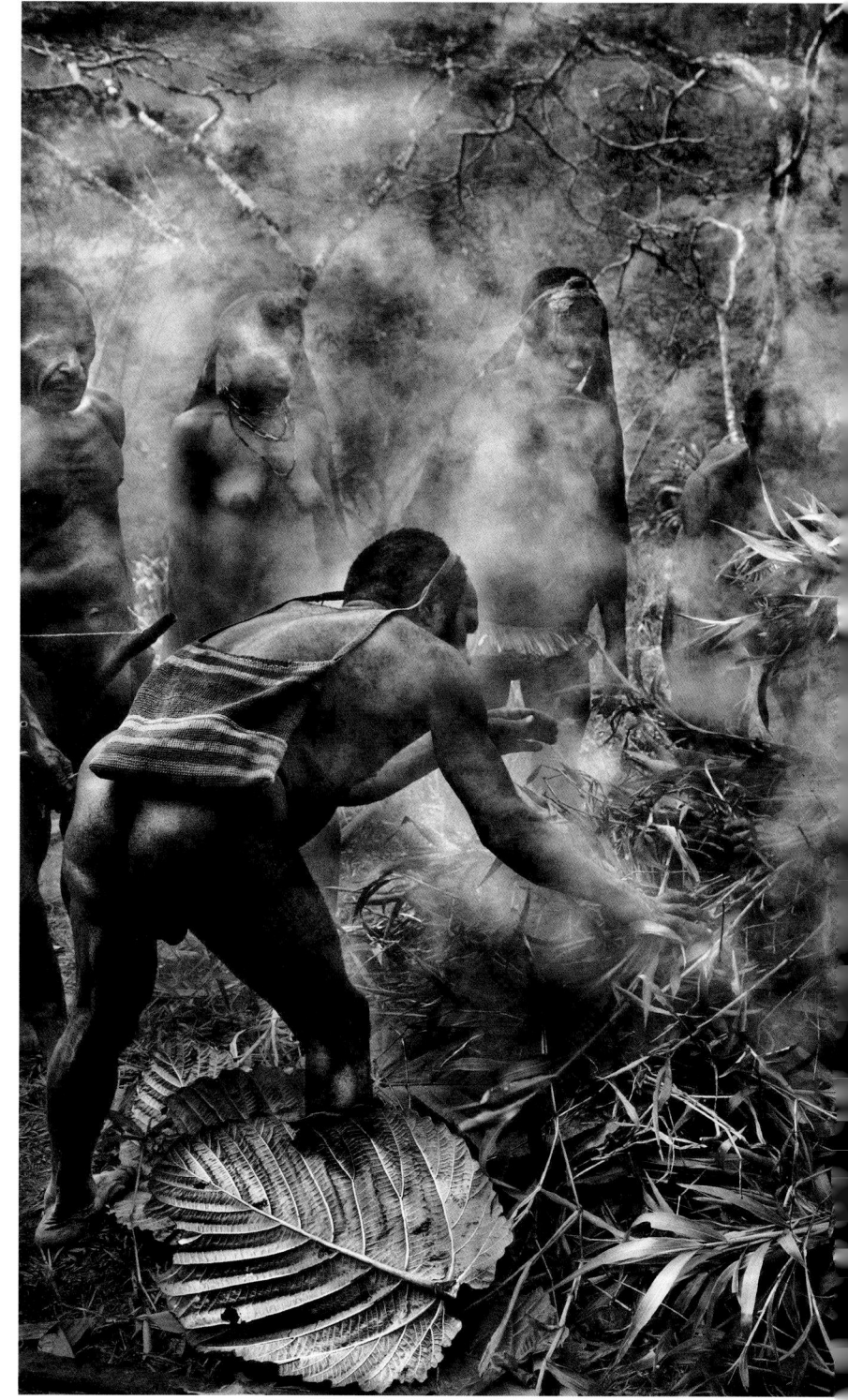

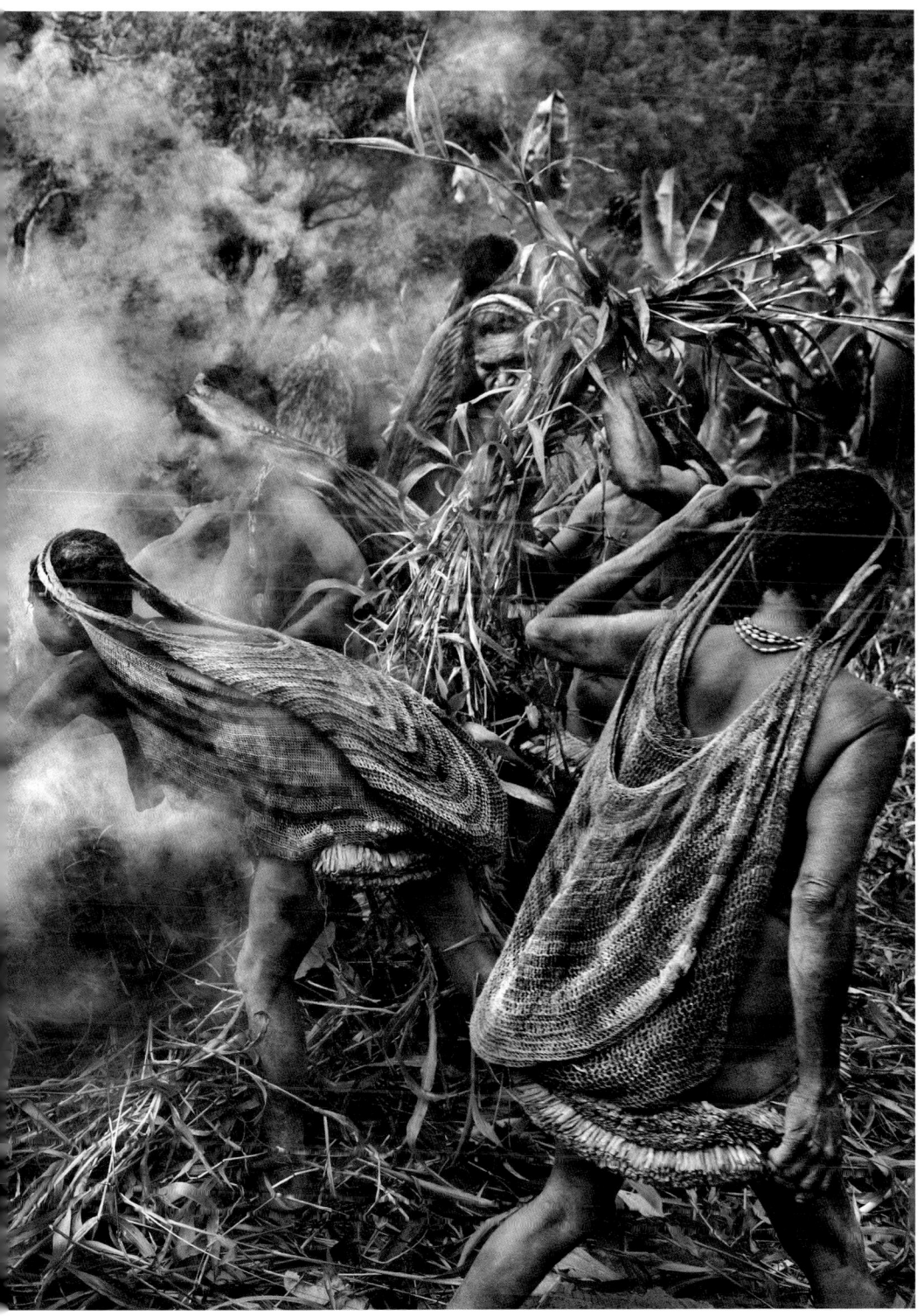

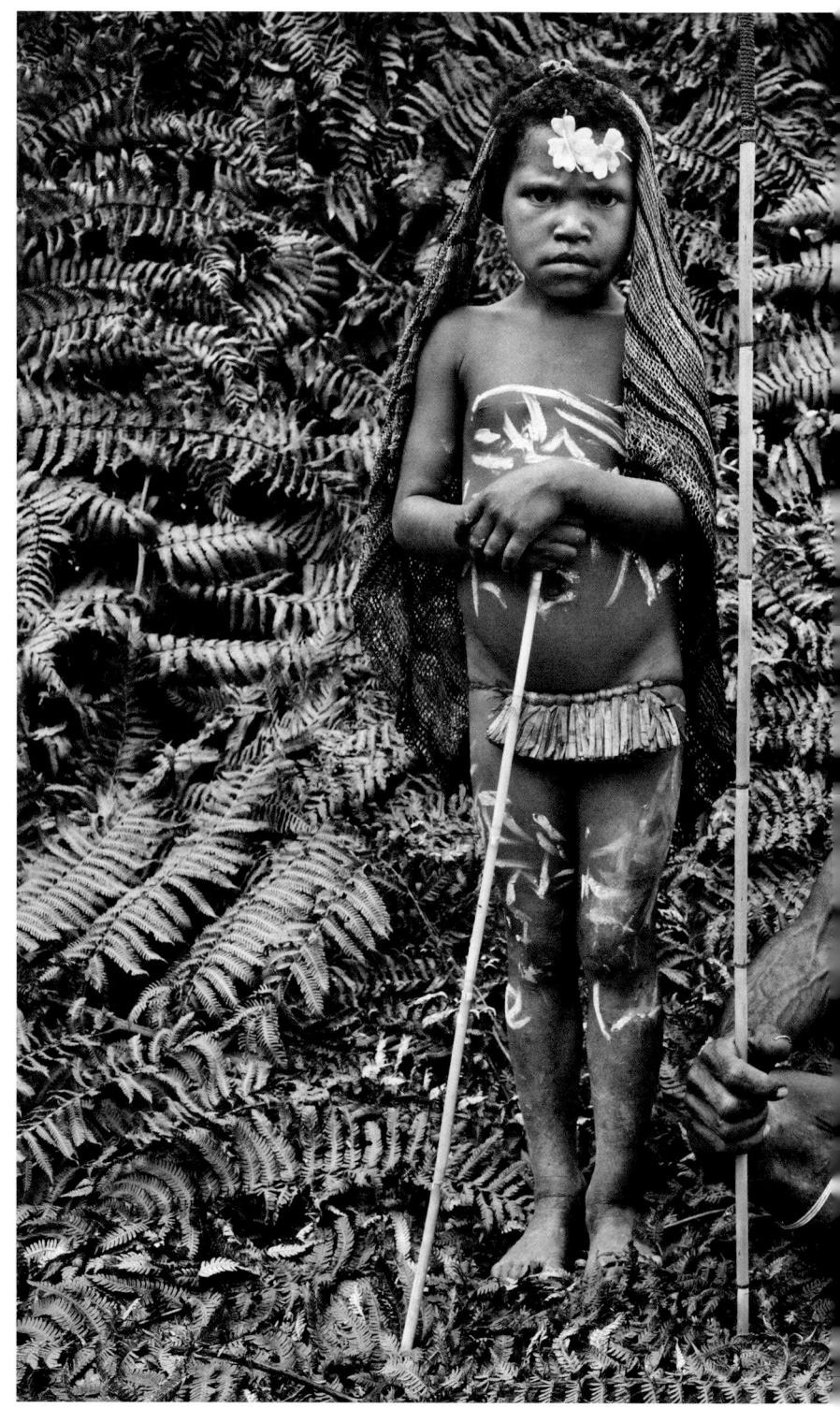

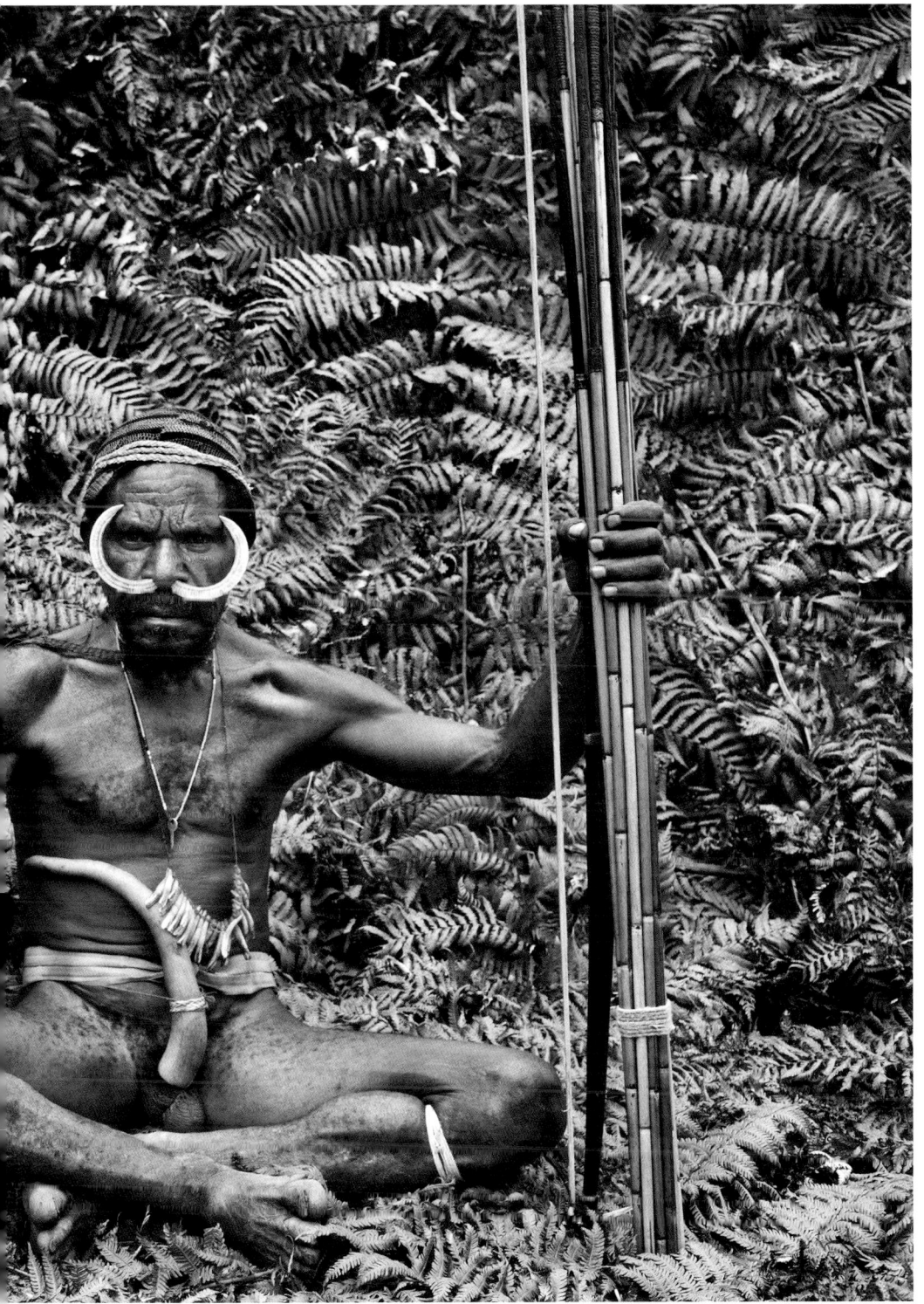

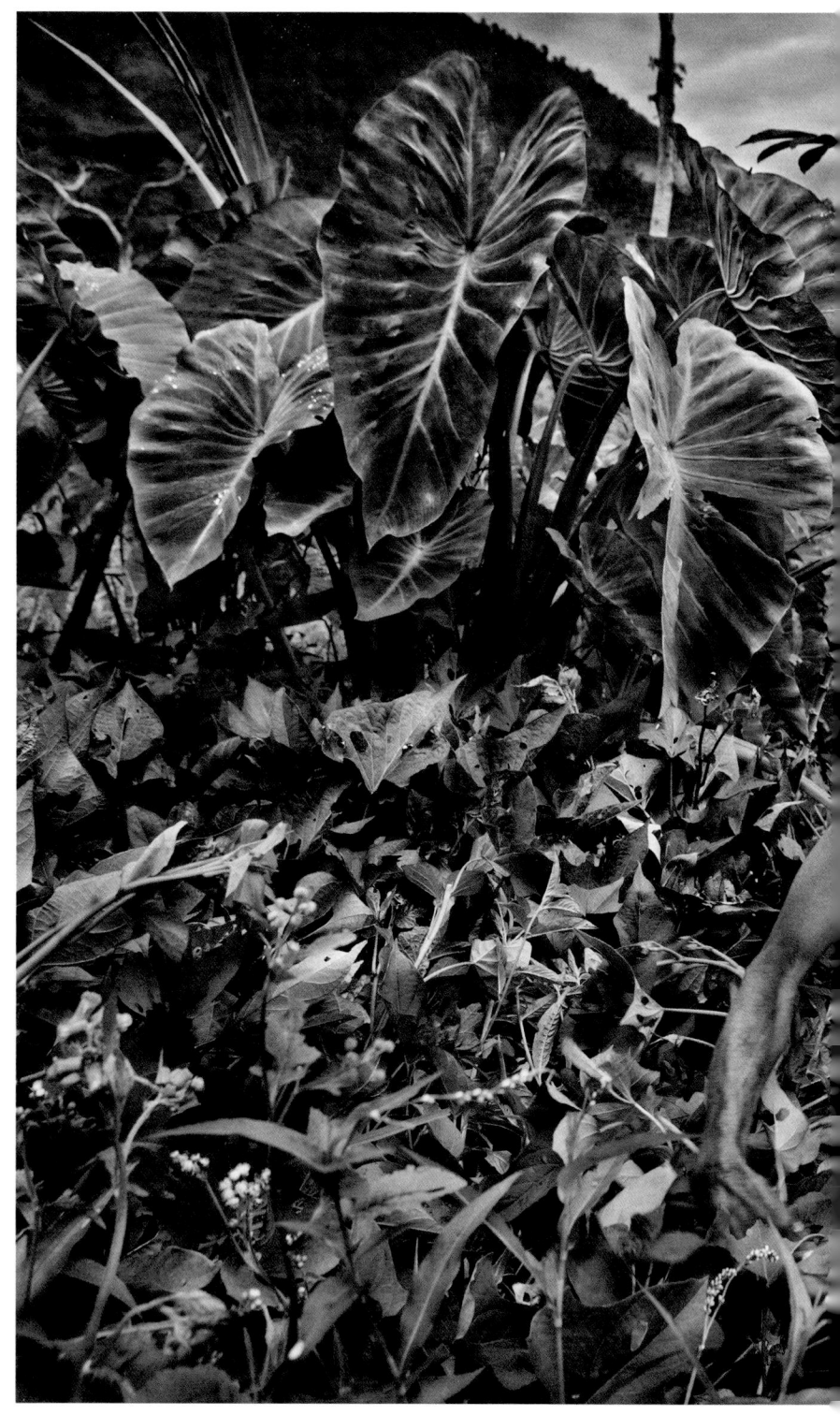

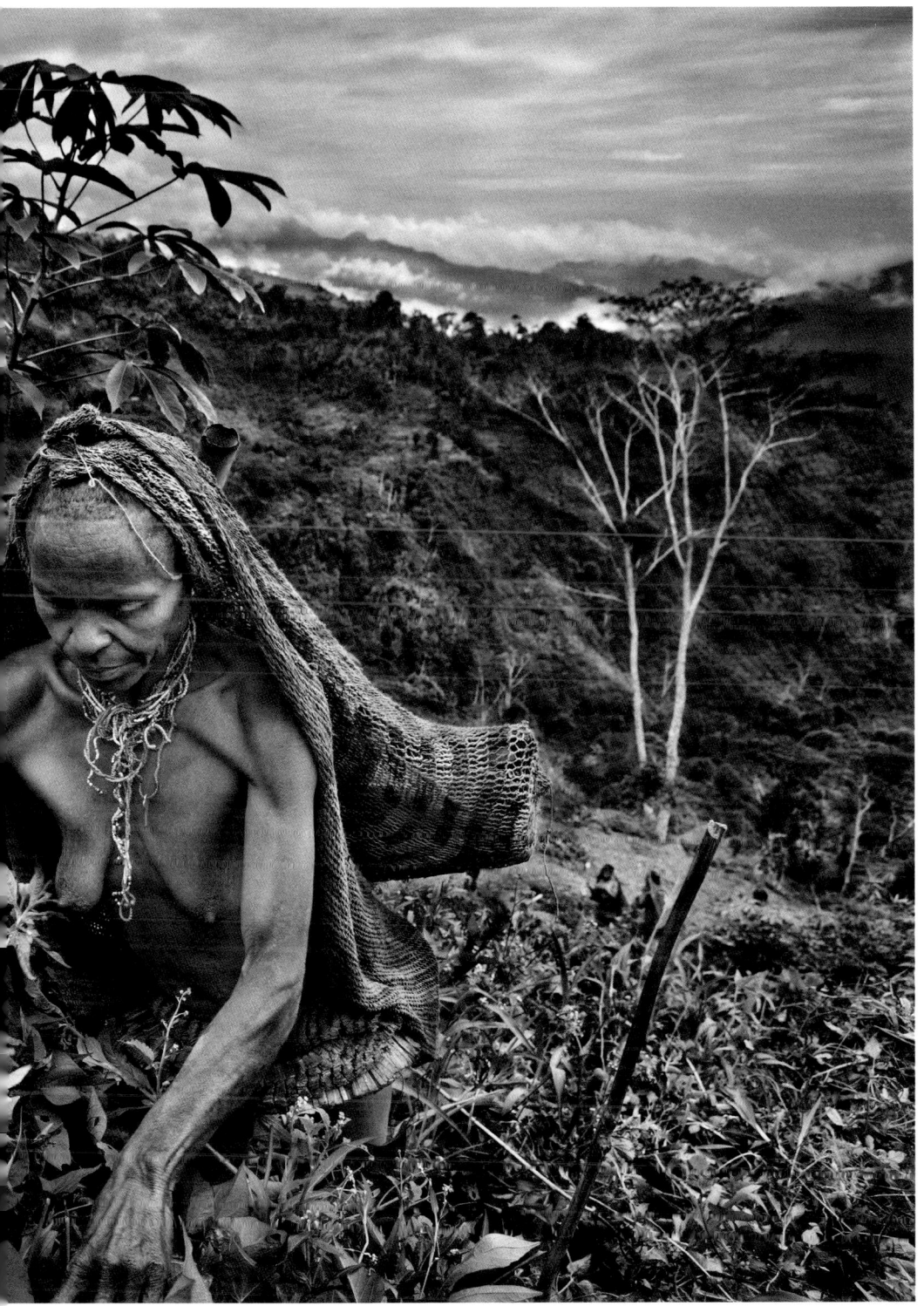

Opposite Men from several of New Guinea's ethnic groups, in the main those living in the highlands, cover and protect their genitals with the *koteka*, or penis gourd, usually made from a dried fruit, such as a calabash (*Lagenaria siceraria*) or a common swamp pitcher-plant (*Nepenthes mirabilis*). This is held in place by a small loop of fiber attached to the base of the *koteka* and placed around the scrotum. Another fiber wrapped around the chest or abdomen is attached to the main body of the *koteka*. The men in one group will usually wear similar *kotekas*: for example, the Yali favor a long, thin *koteka*, which holds up the rattan hoops worn around their waist. Other groups opt for different shapes and angles: pointed, straight out, straight up, at an angle or in other directions. In practice, though, there is no correlation between the size or length of the *koteka* and the man's social status. West Papua. Indonesia. September 2010.

Pages 162/163 During the Yali ceremonies, women are isolated from the men, who cook the pigs and distribute the cooked meat by groups. West Papua. Indonesia. September 2010.

Pages 164/165 In the mountains of West Papua, the Yali build round wooden huts, with roofs covered with pandan leaves. Women live separately in their own houses, while men live in community houses, known as *honai*. Yali settlements are traditionally located on ridgetops because, in the past, this offered some protection from enemies. This remote and spectacular landscape shielded the Yali from contact with the modern world until Christian missionaries penetrated the area in the 1970s. But even now, like many isolated peoples, the Yali have what to outsiders seems like a charmingly simple life. West Papua. Indonesia. September 2010.

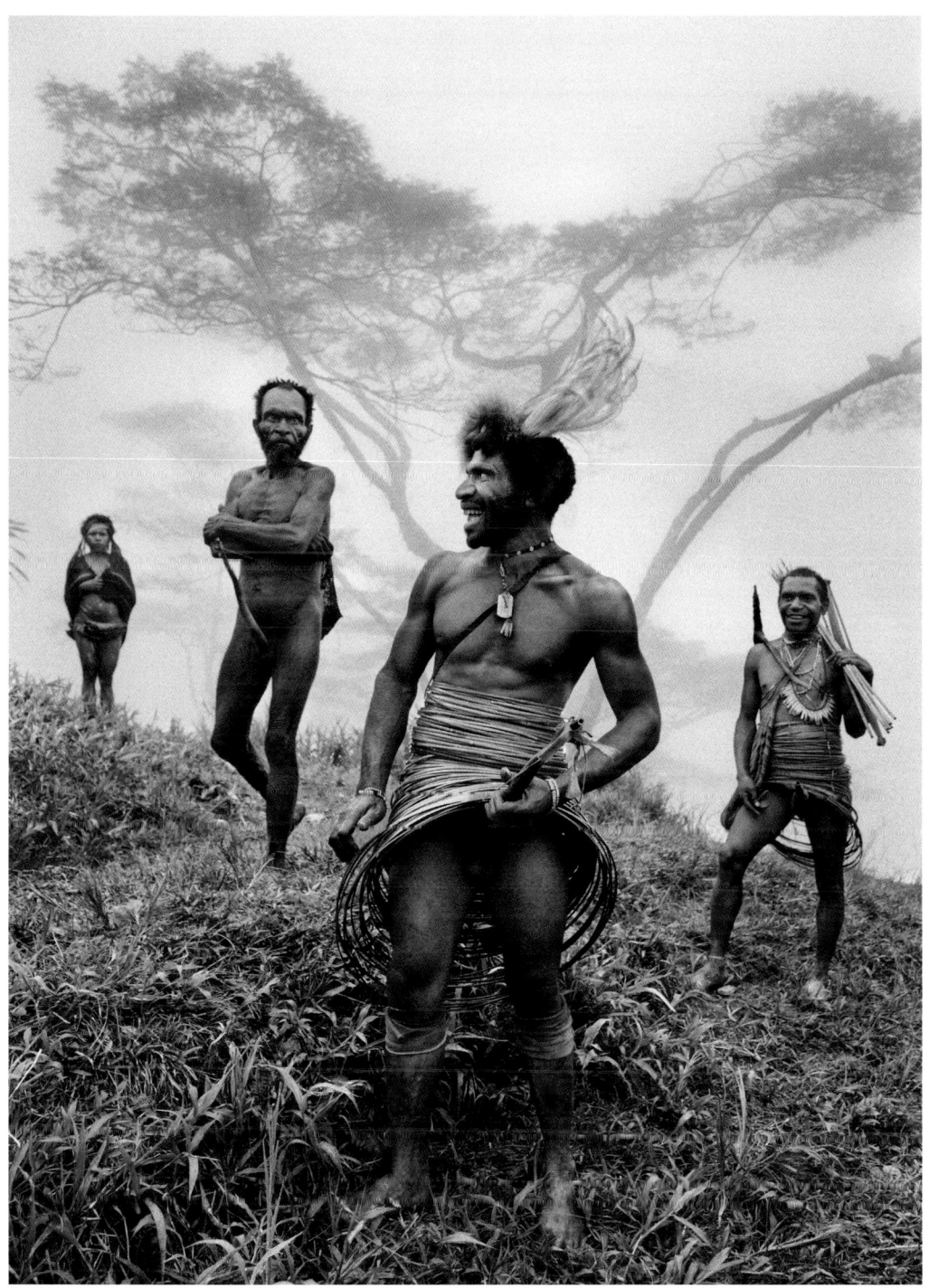

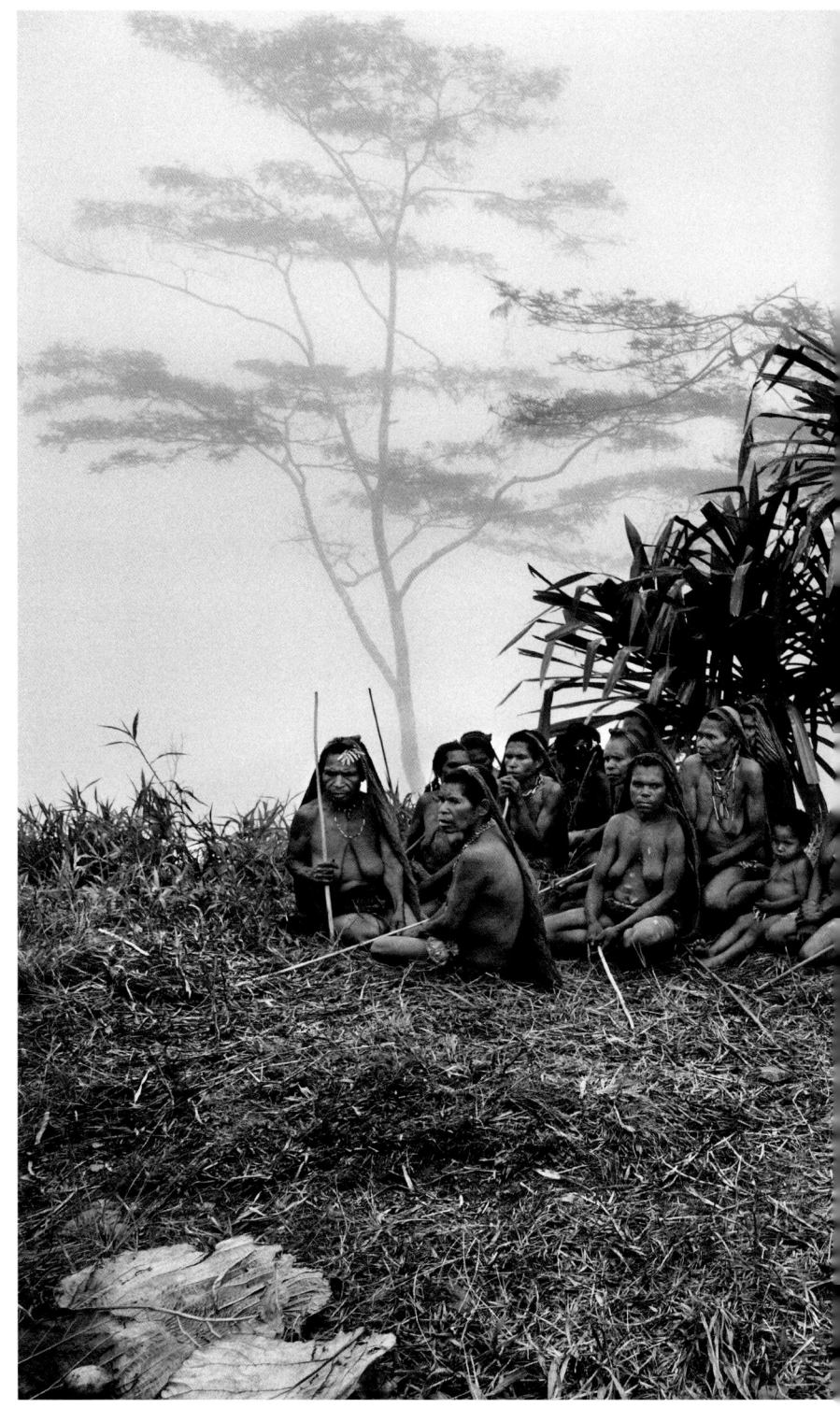

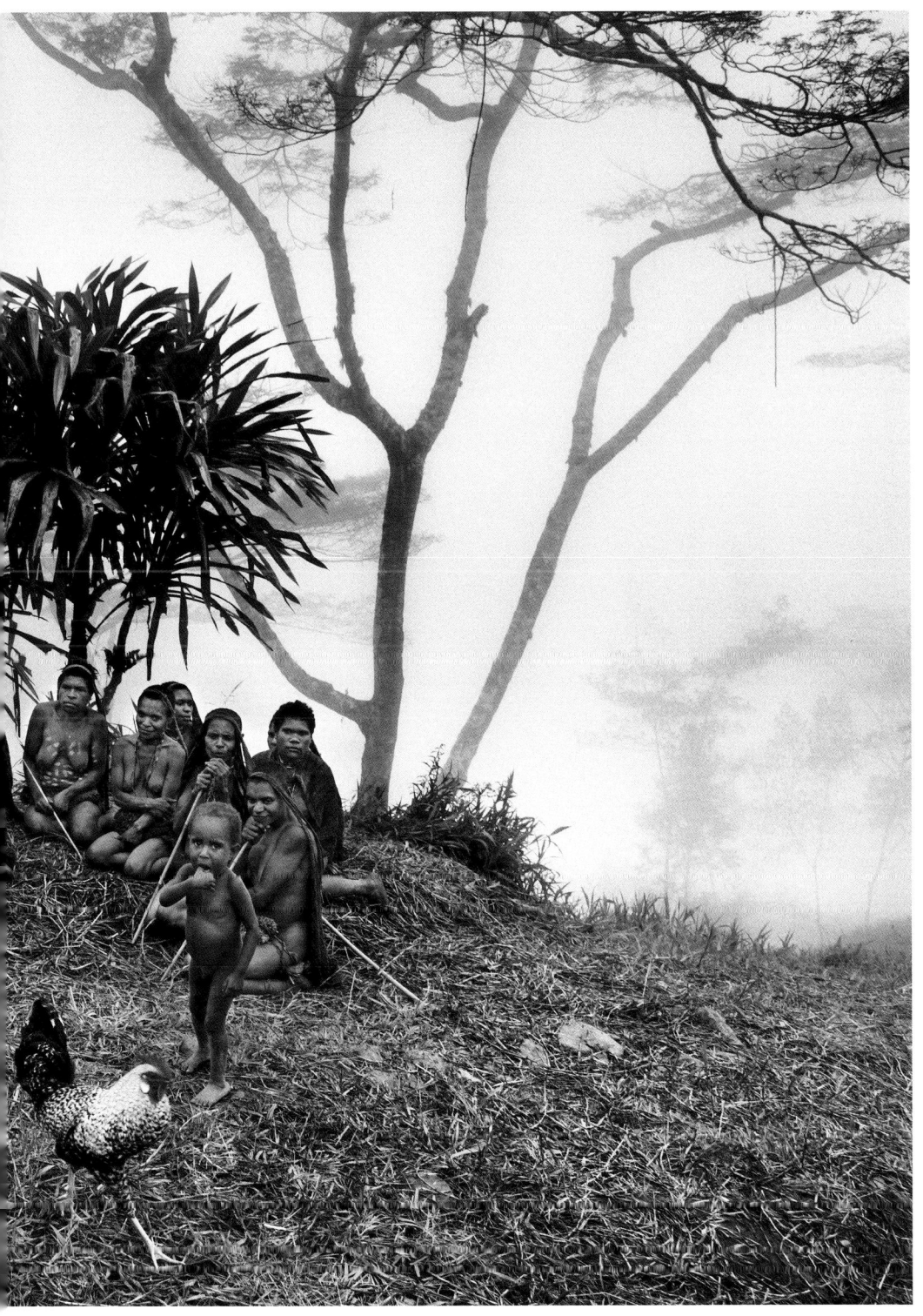

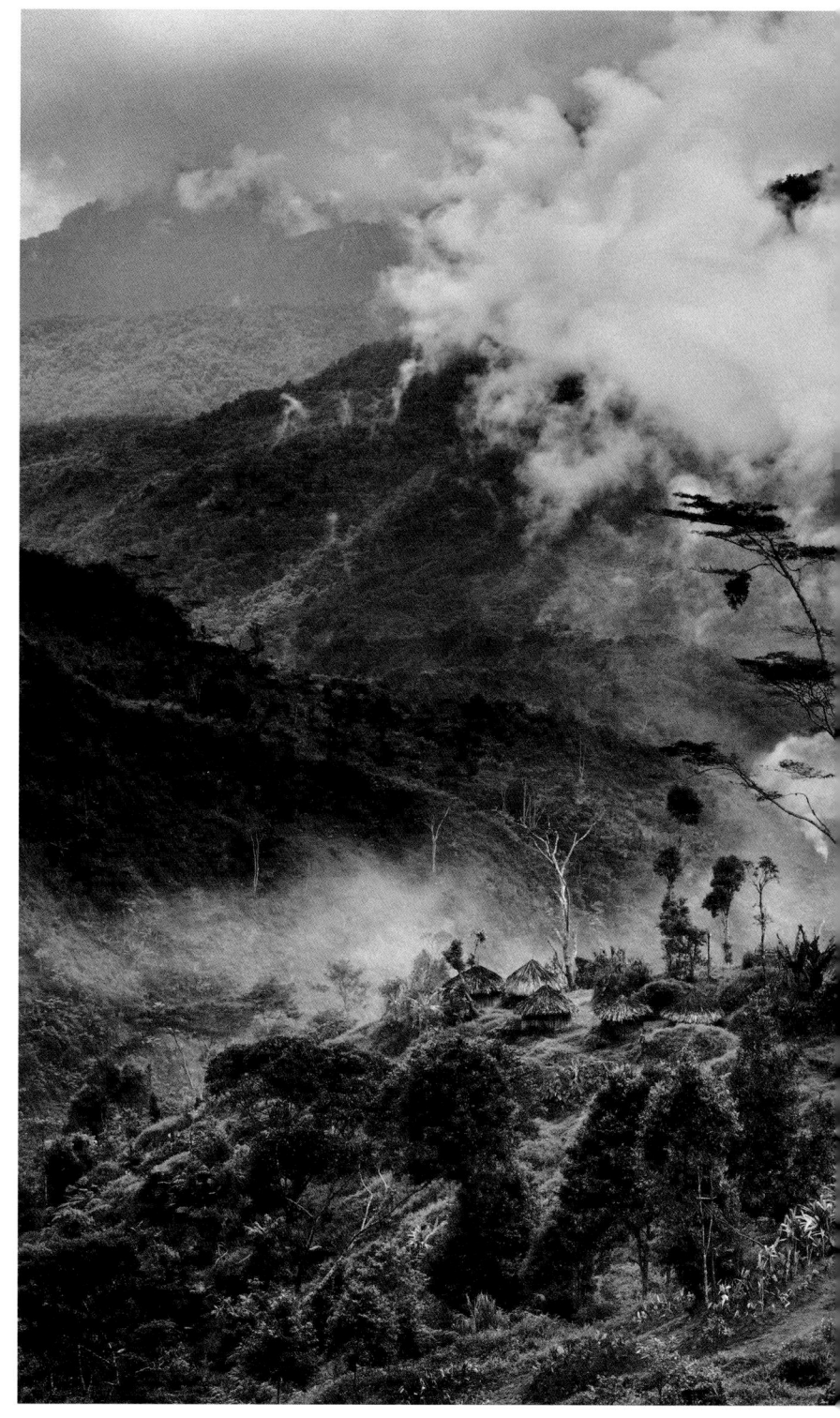

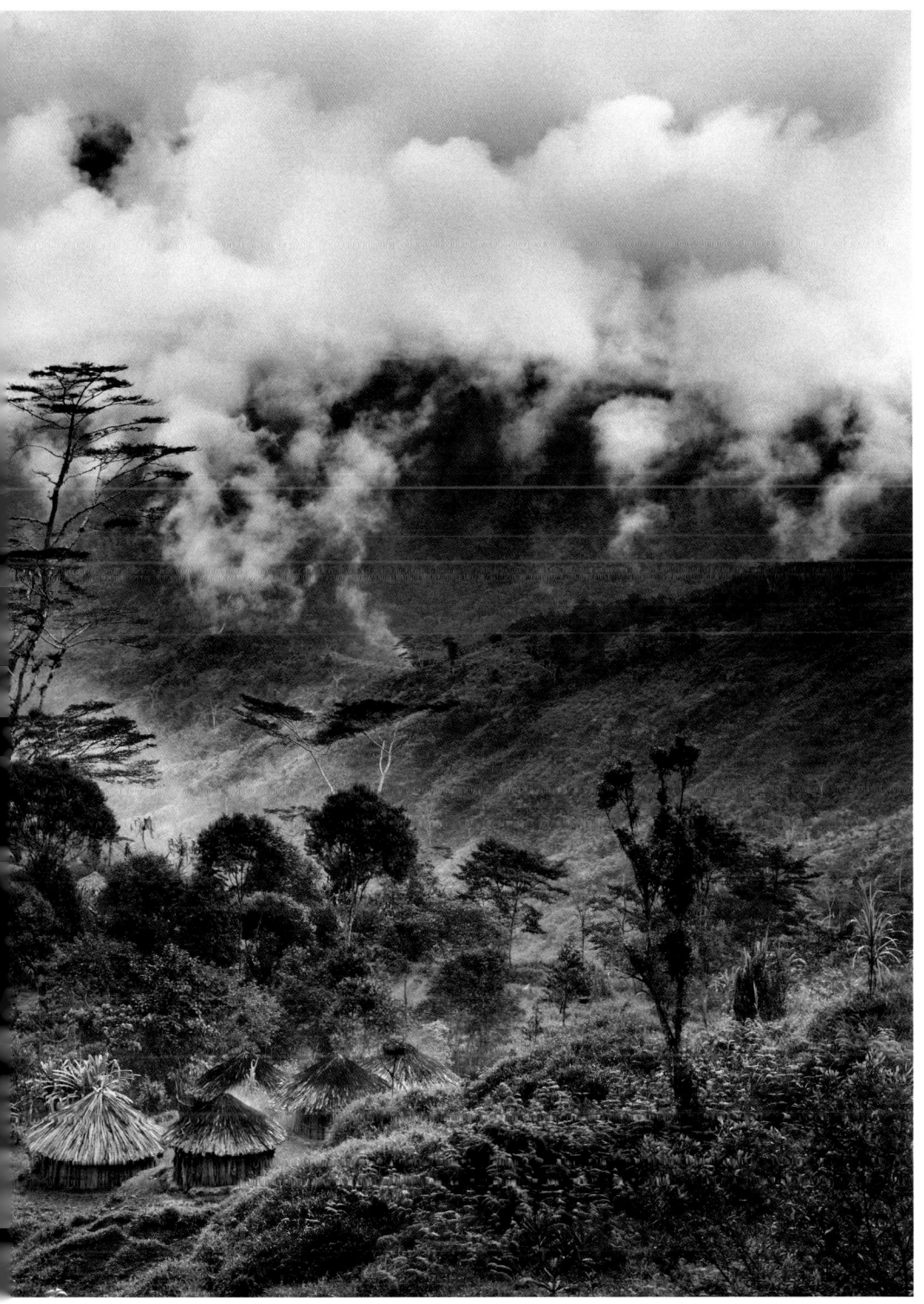

MADAGASCAR

Pages 167 through 195

Located in the Indian Ocean off the southern coast of Africa, Madagascar is the world's fourth-largest island. This isolation explains its privileged place in nature, comparable in its endemic species and diversity with a small continent. Scientists have defined it as a biological "hotspot" of great importance since most of its plant and animal species are endemic to the island. This endemism is accompanied by what experts define as a megadiversity of natural life. Lemurs are Madagascar's most famous flagship species, with 50 different kinds found only here.

The island has three broad geographic zones. These are the highlands, a plateau region in the center of the island ranging in altitude from 2,200 to 4,500 feet (762 to 1,372 meters) above sea level; a narrow and steep escarpment that runs the length of the eastern coast and contains much of the island's remaining tropical rainforest; and a wide, dry plain that slopes gently from the western boundaries of the highlands toward the Mozambique Channel.

Today, Madagascar's rich ecosystems are highly endangered, due largely to incessant and numerous fires, for which a fast-growing population is largely responsible. But widespread agriculture, rice-growing and cattle-raising are also damaging the island's delicate ecosystems. Furthermore, large forested areas are regularly cut to provide firewood and charcoal for cooking. The central plateau region, for instance, is now almost entirely deforested. Surviving natural habitats are now to be found mainly in coastal areas to the east, west and south. It is probable that 90 percent of Madagascar's natural forest has already been lost.

Opposite Crowned lemurs (*Eulemur fulvus coronatus*) in Ankarana National Park. Madagascar. November and December 2010.

Pages 168/169 A crater lake in the rainforest of Amber Mountain National Park. Madagascar. November and December 2010.

Pages 170/171 Sandbars formed by the Manambolo River on the west coast. Accumulation of sand and soil along the coast and in river estuaries testifies to the high level of erosion across the country. Madagascar. November and December 2010.

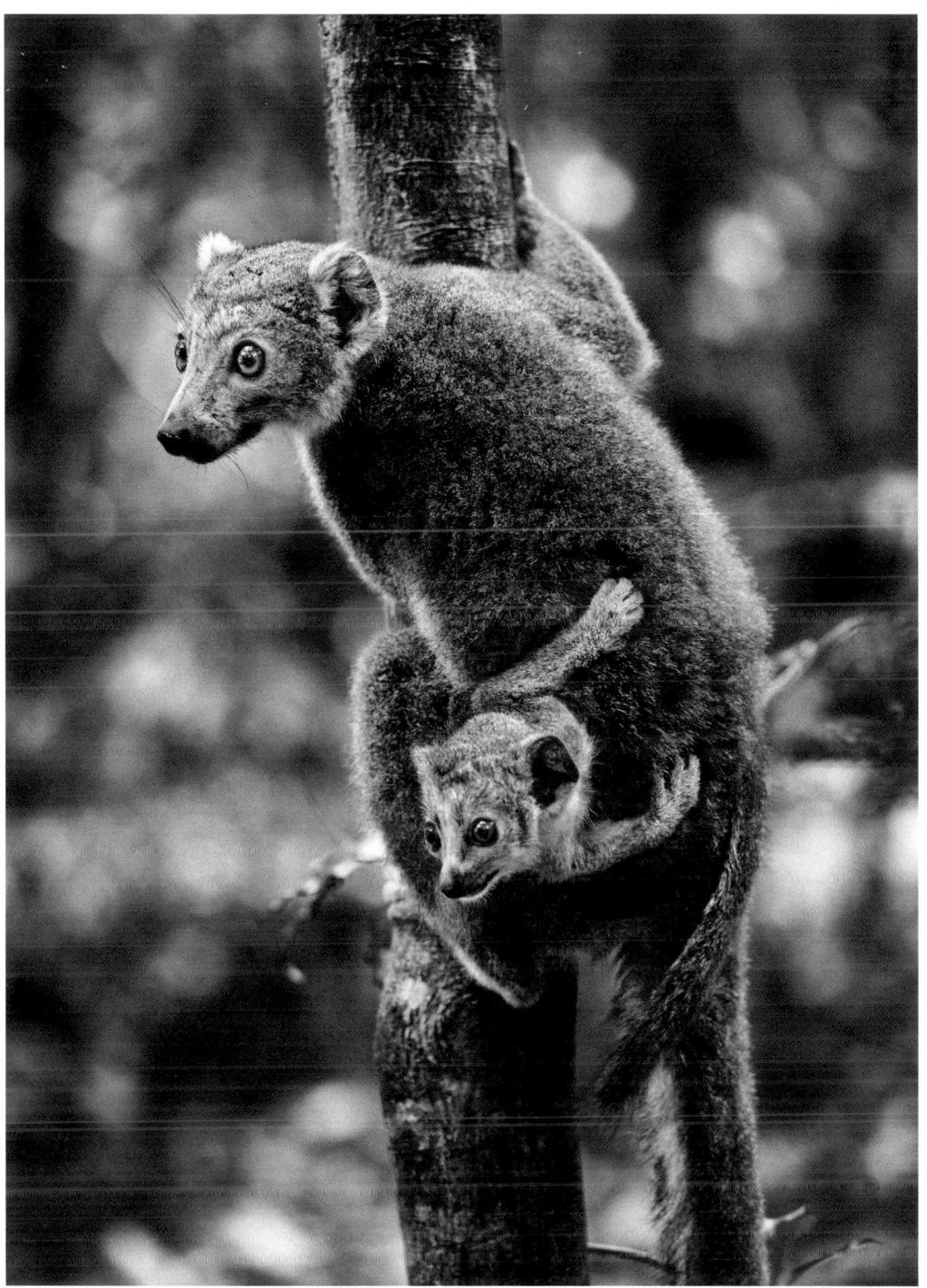

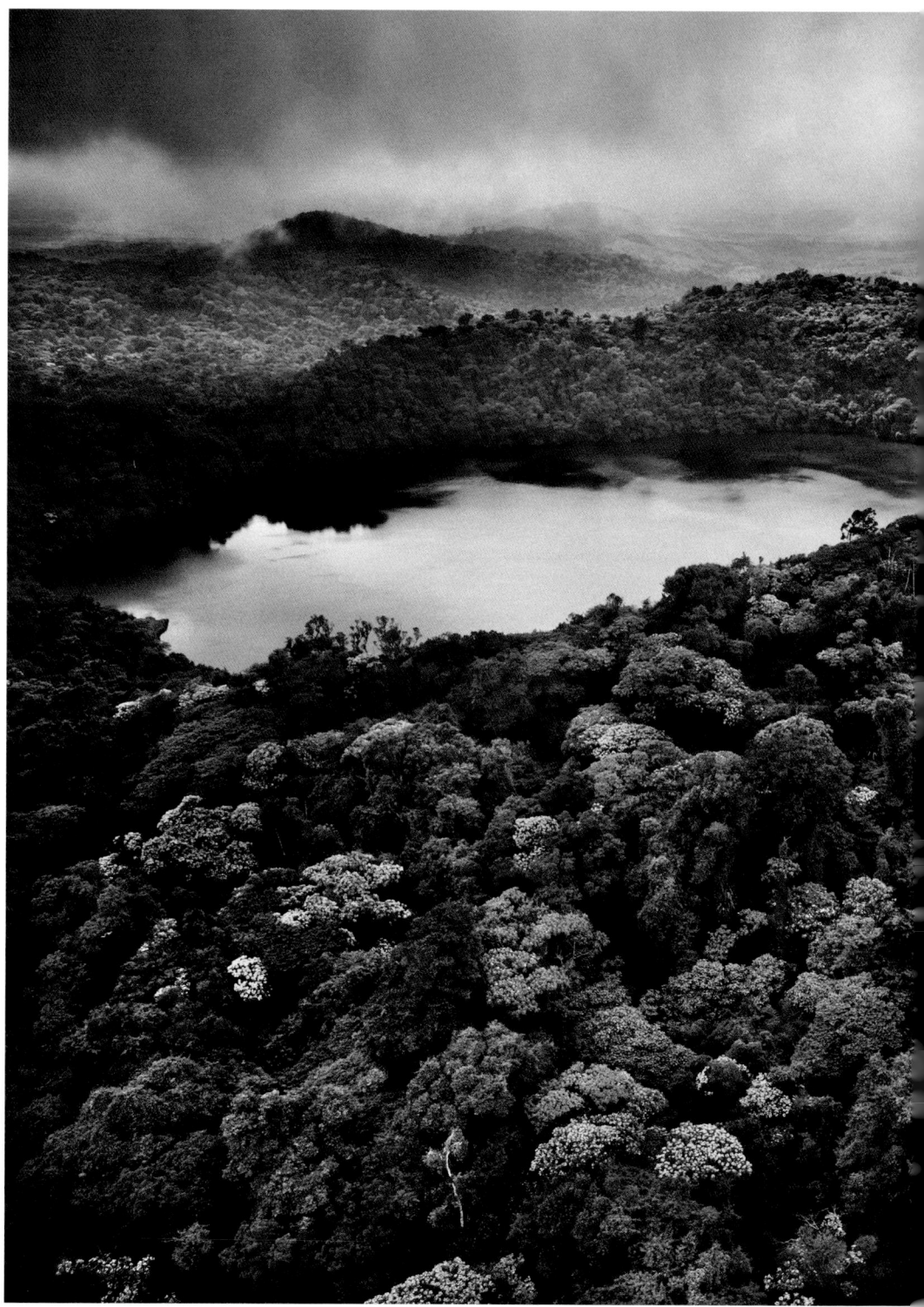

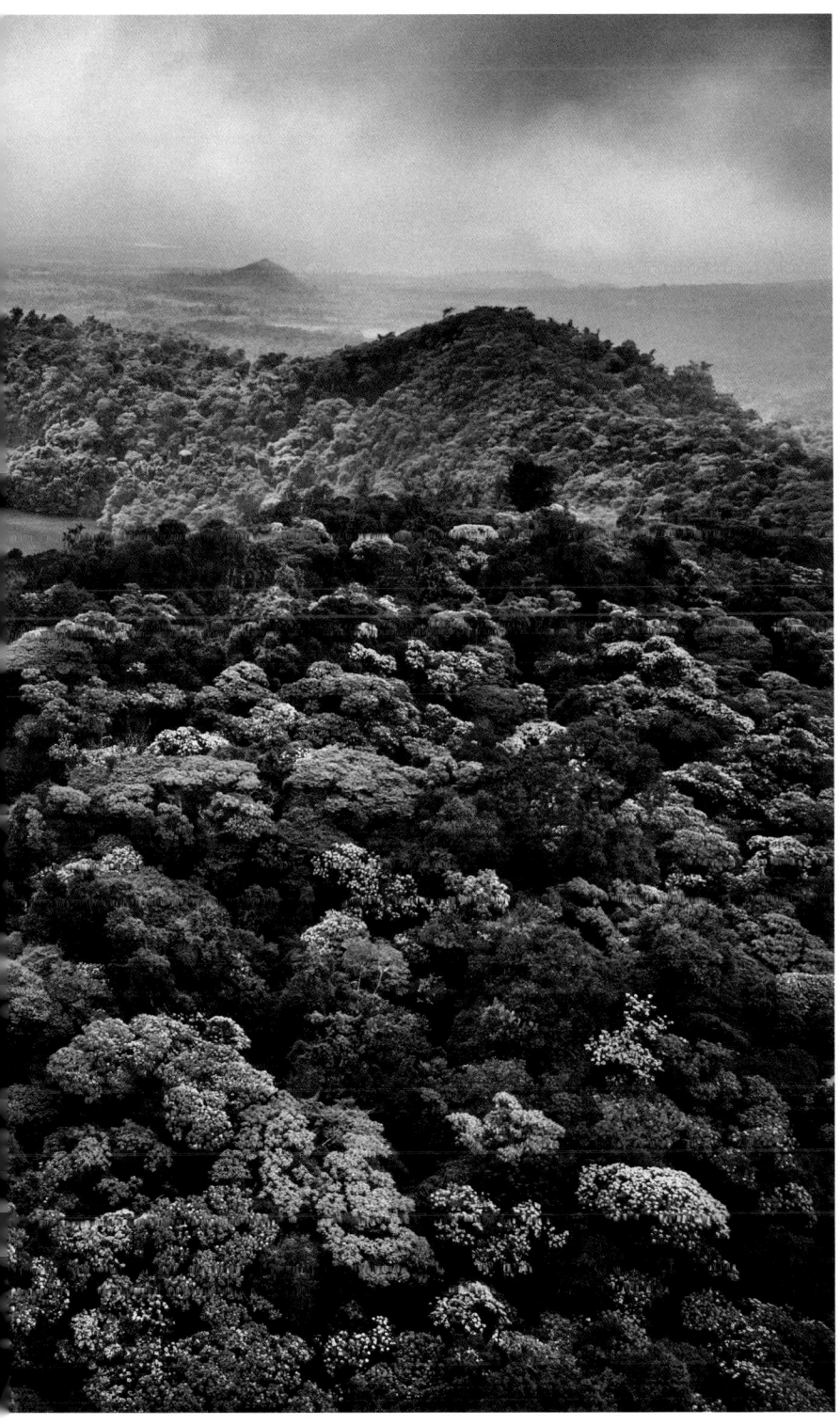

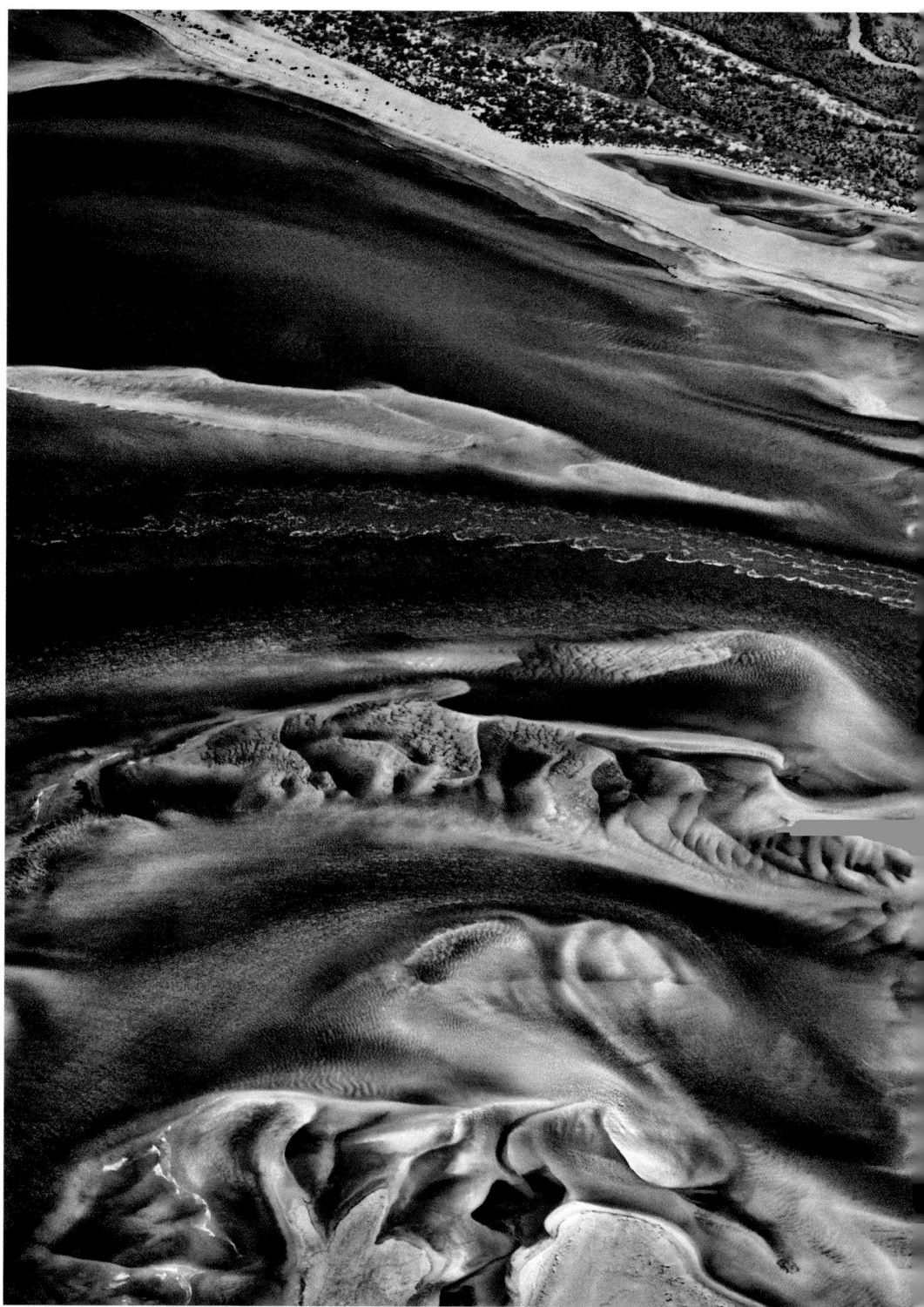

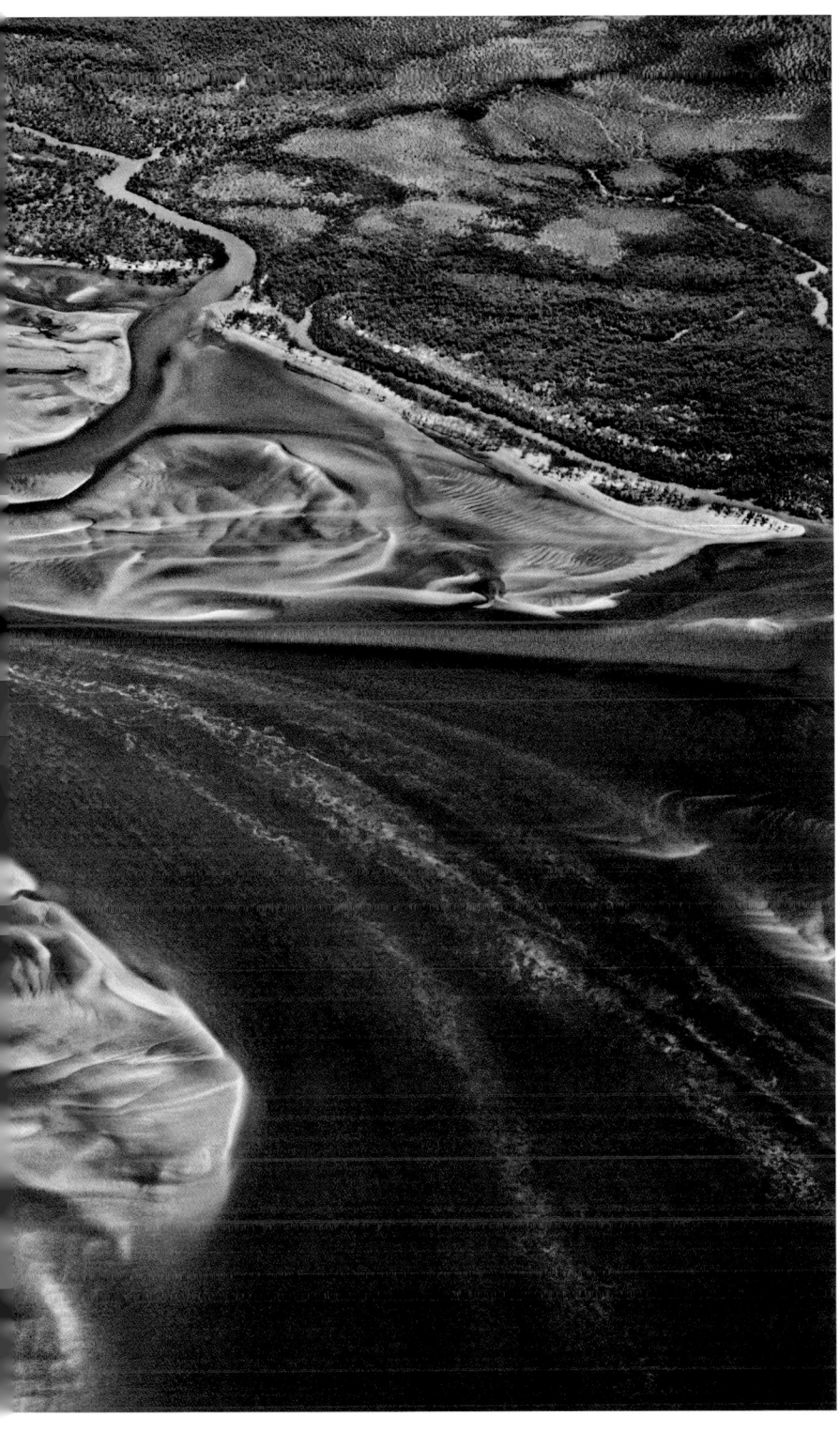

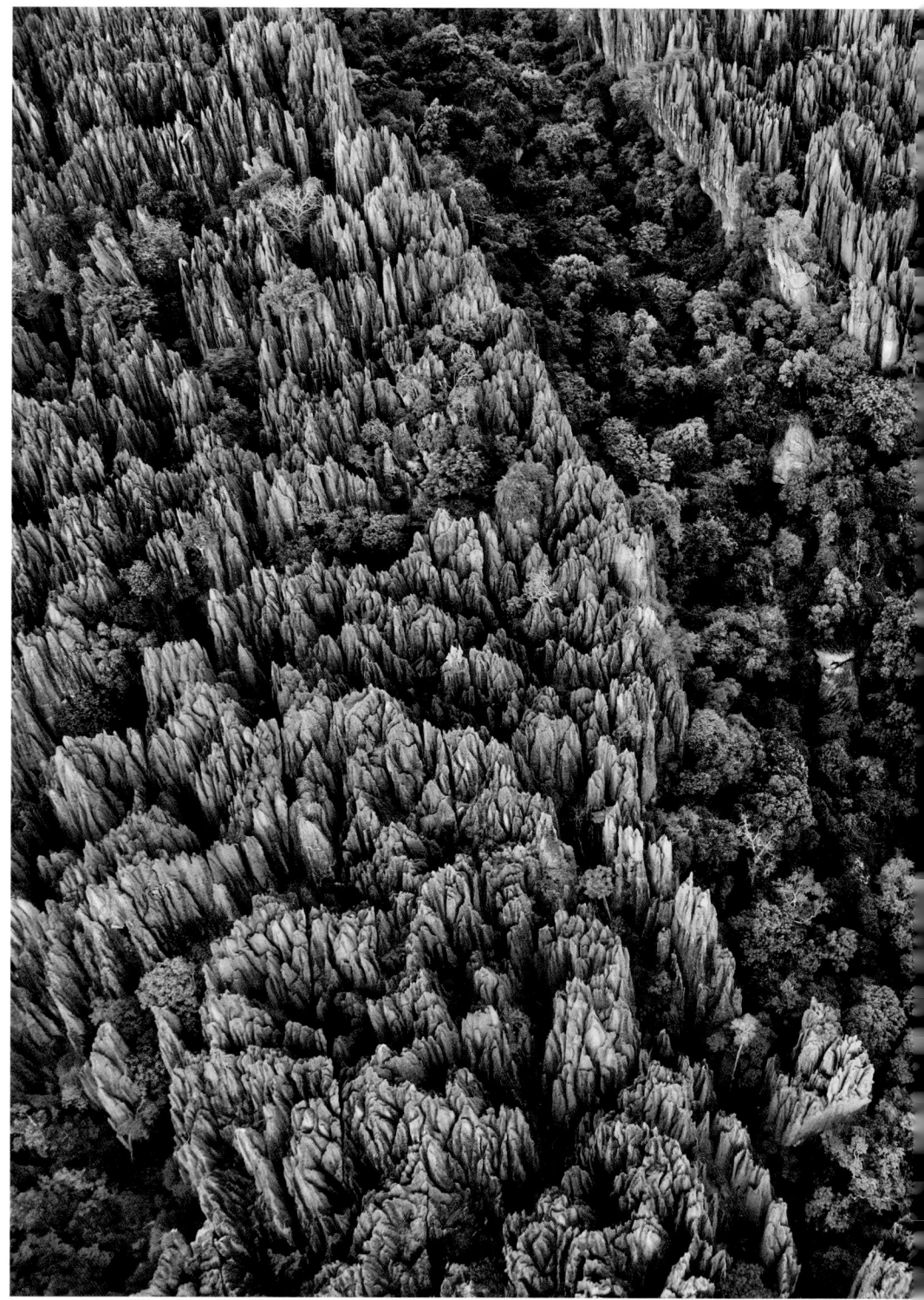

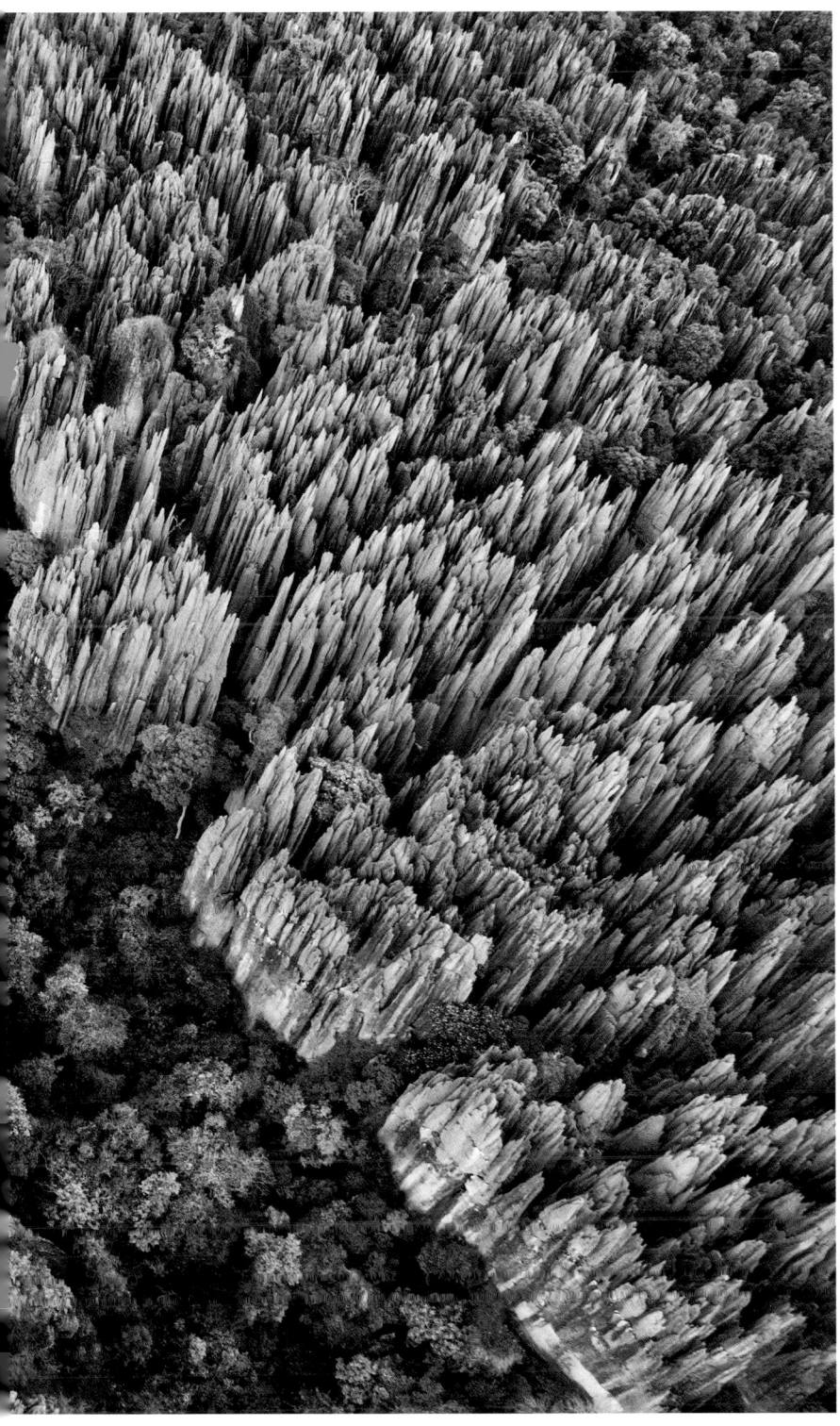

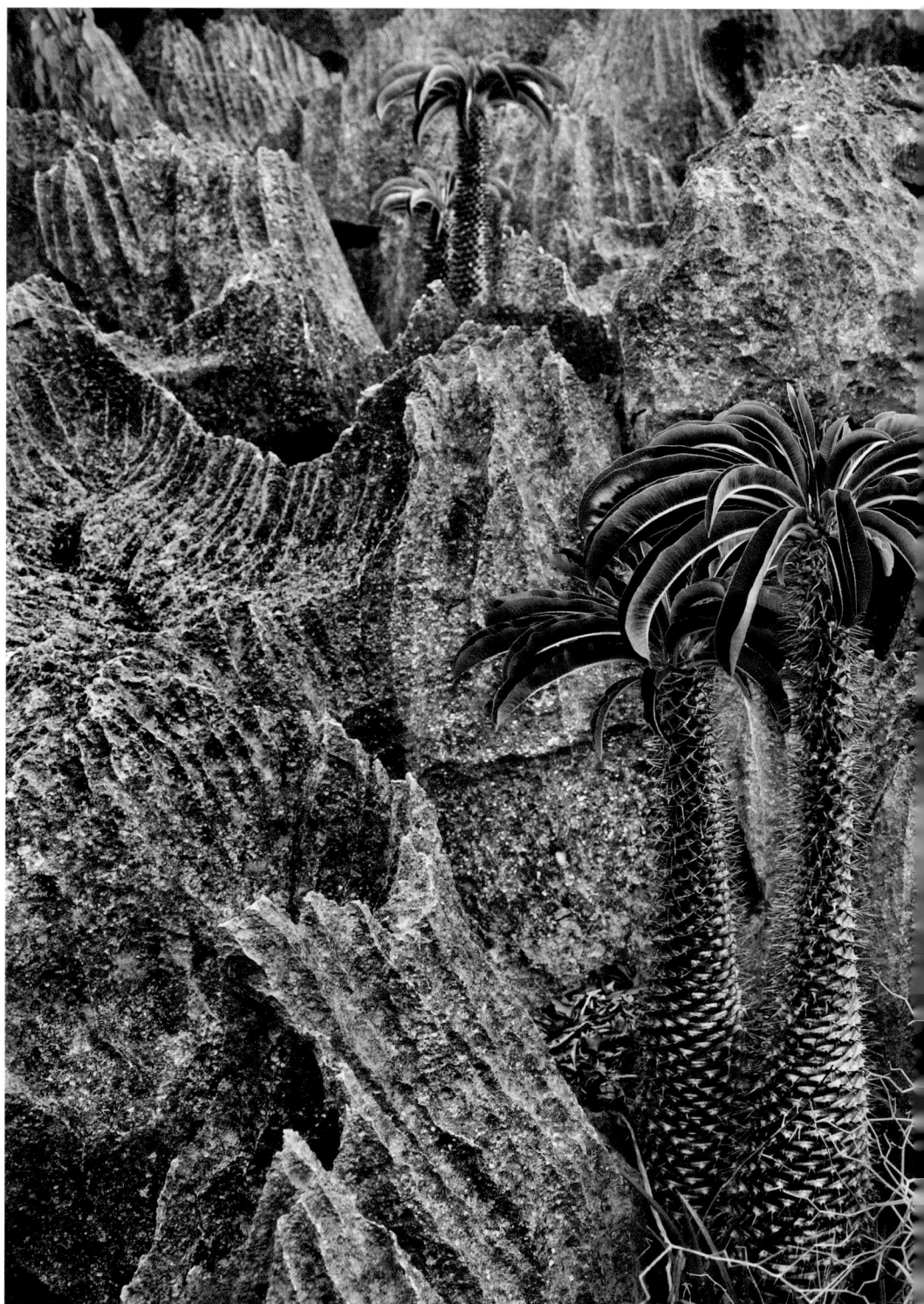

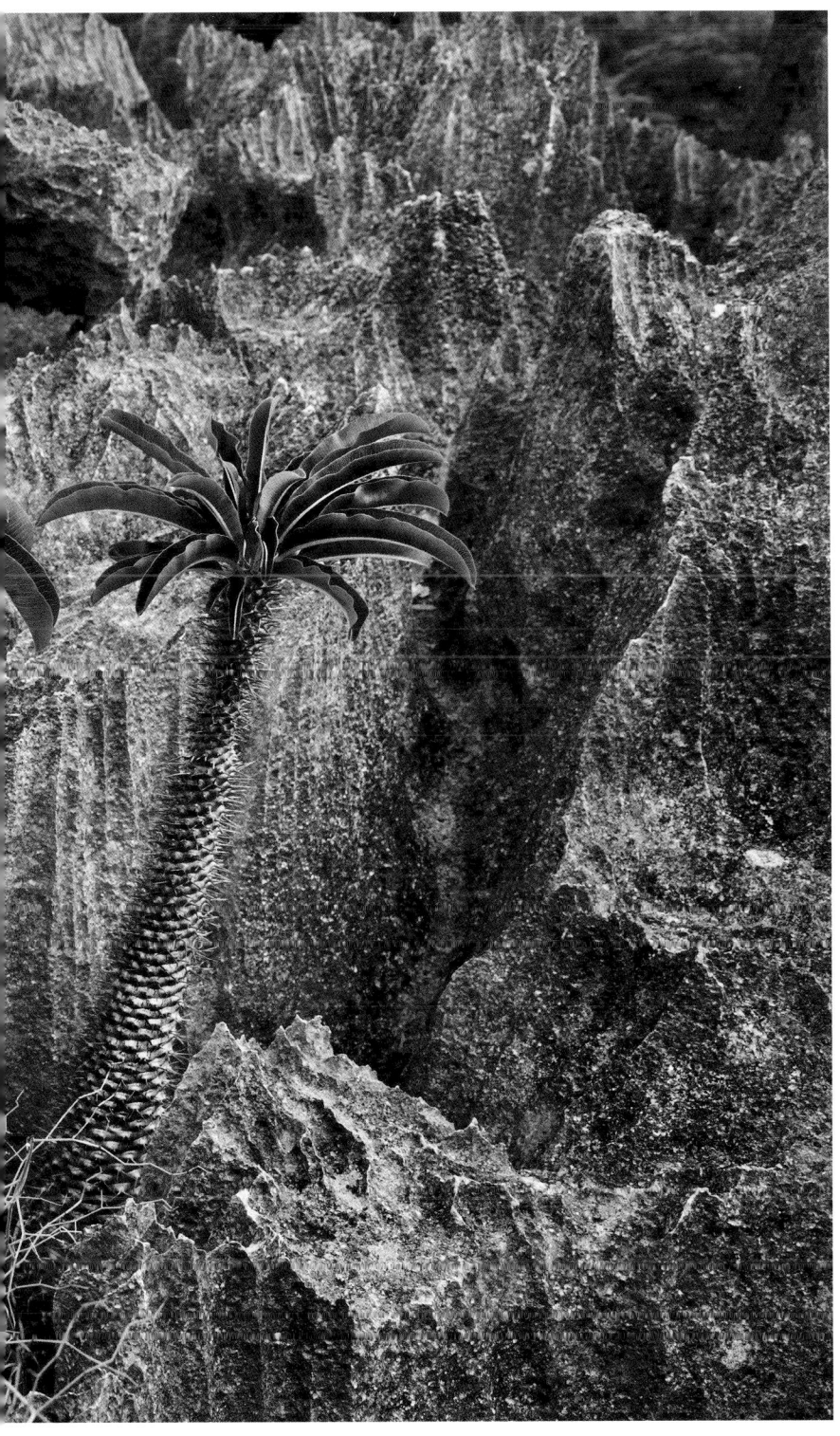

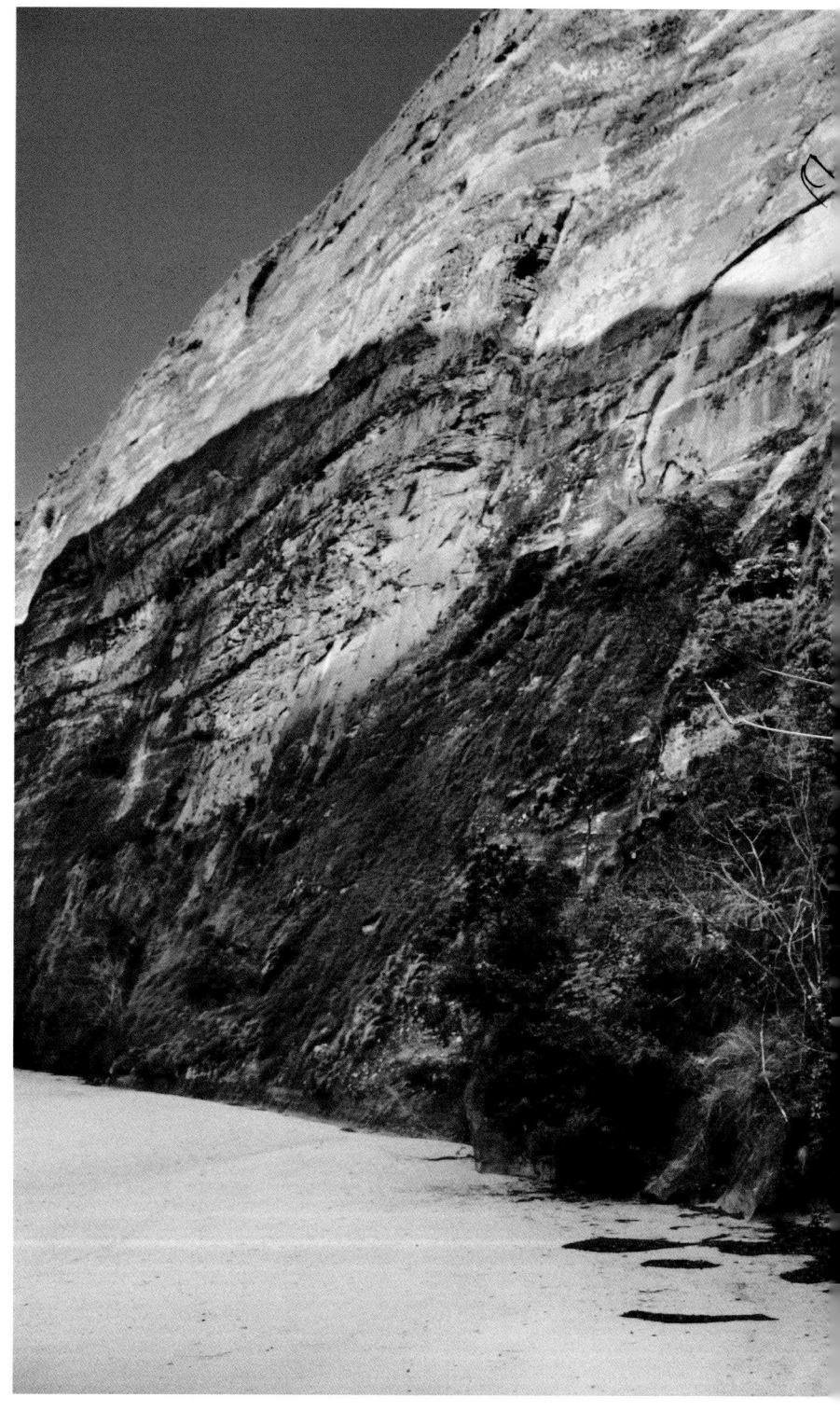

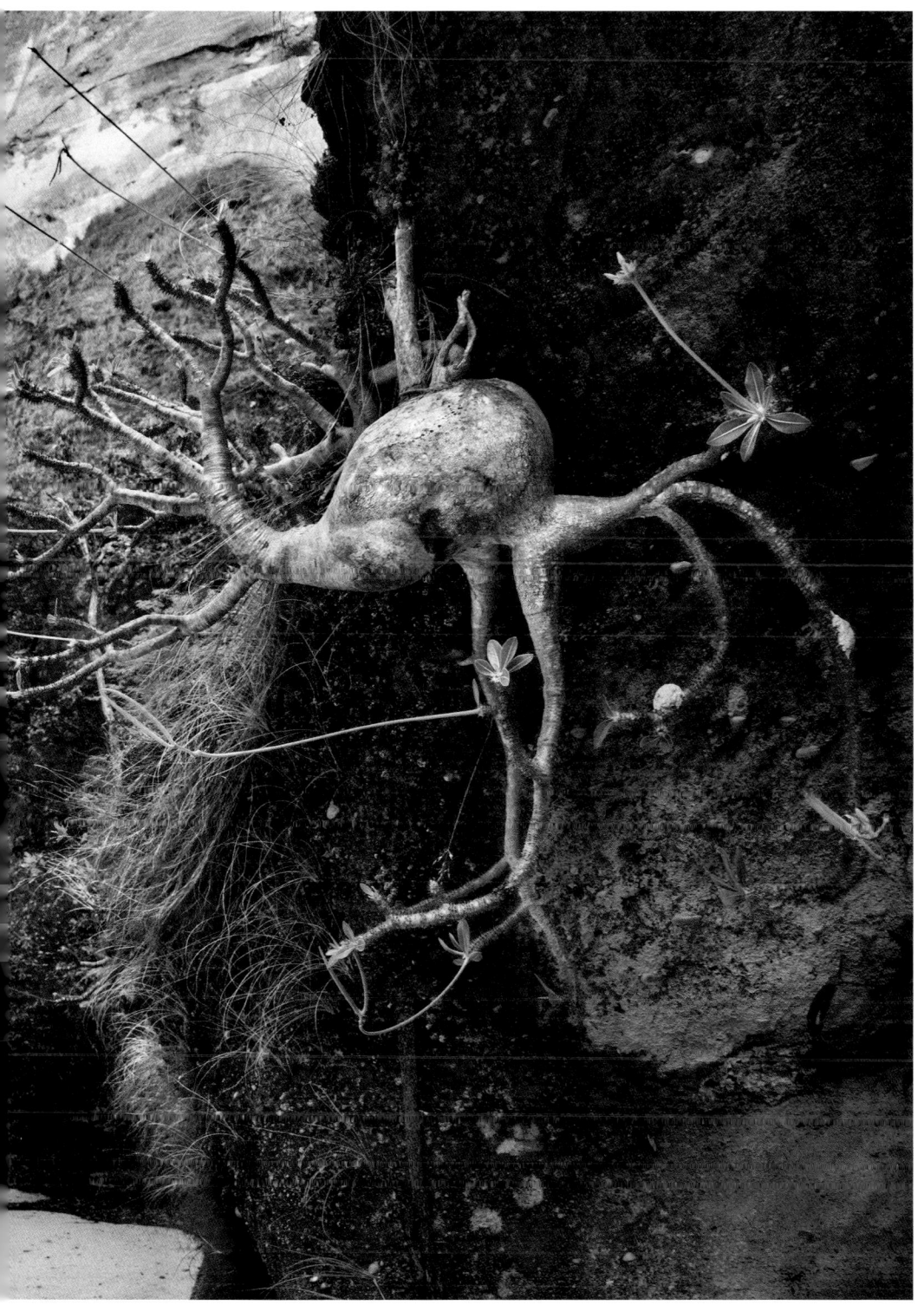

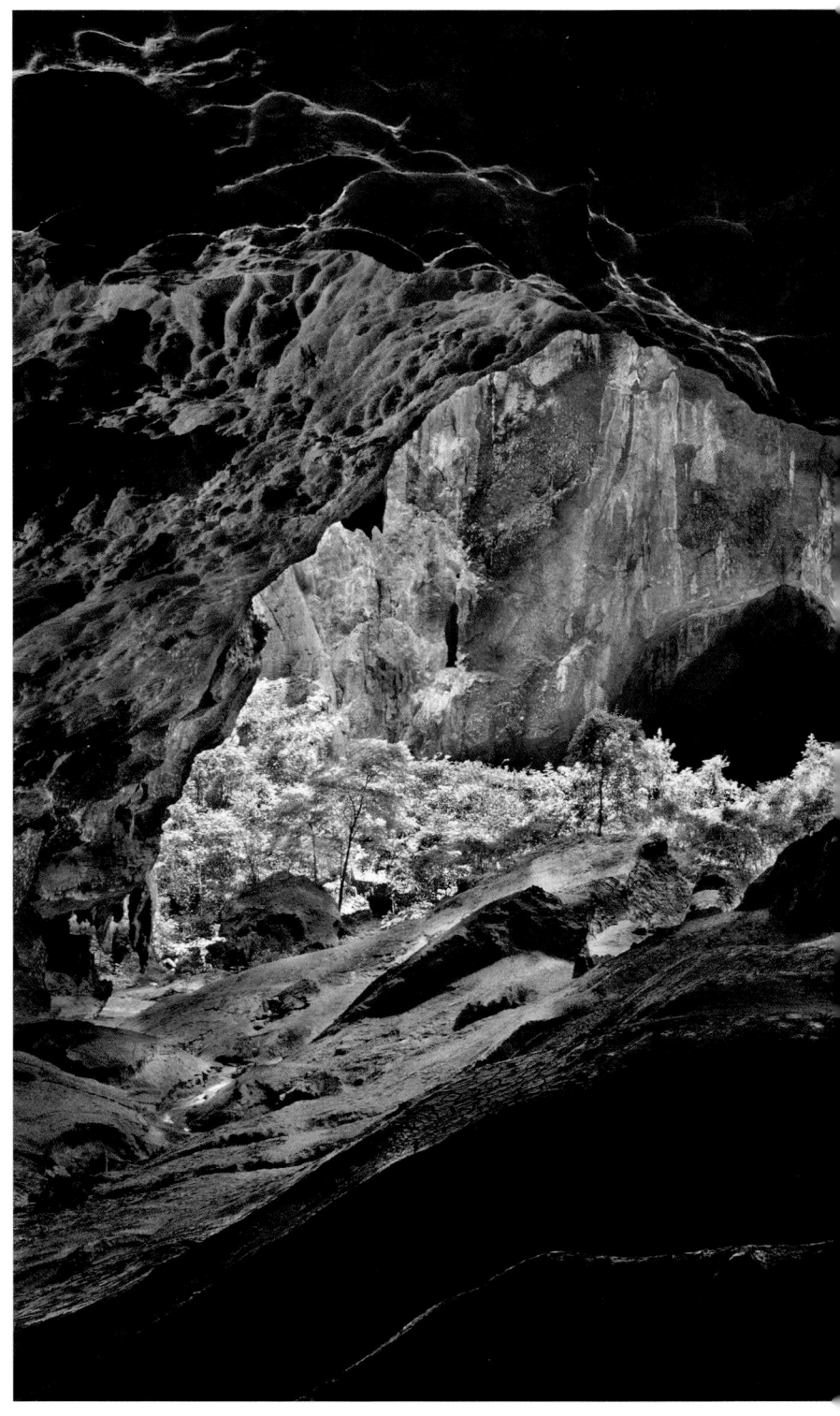

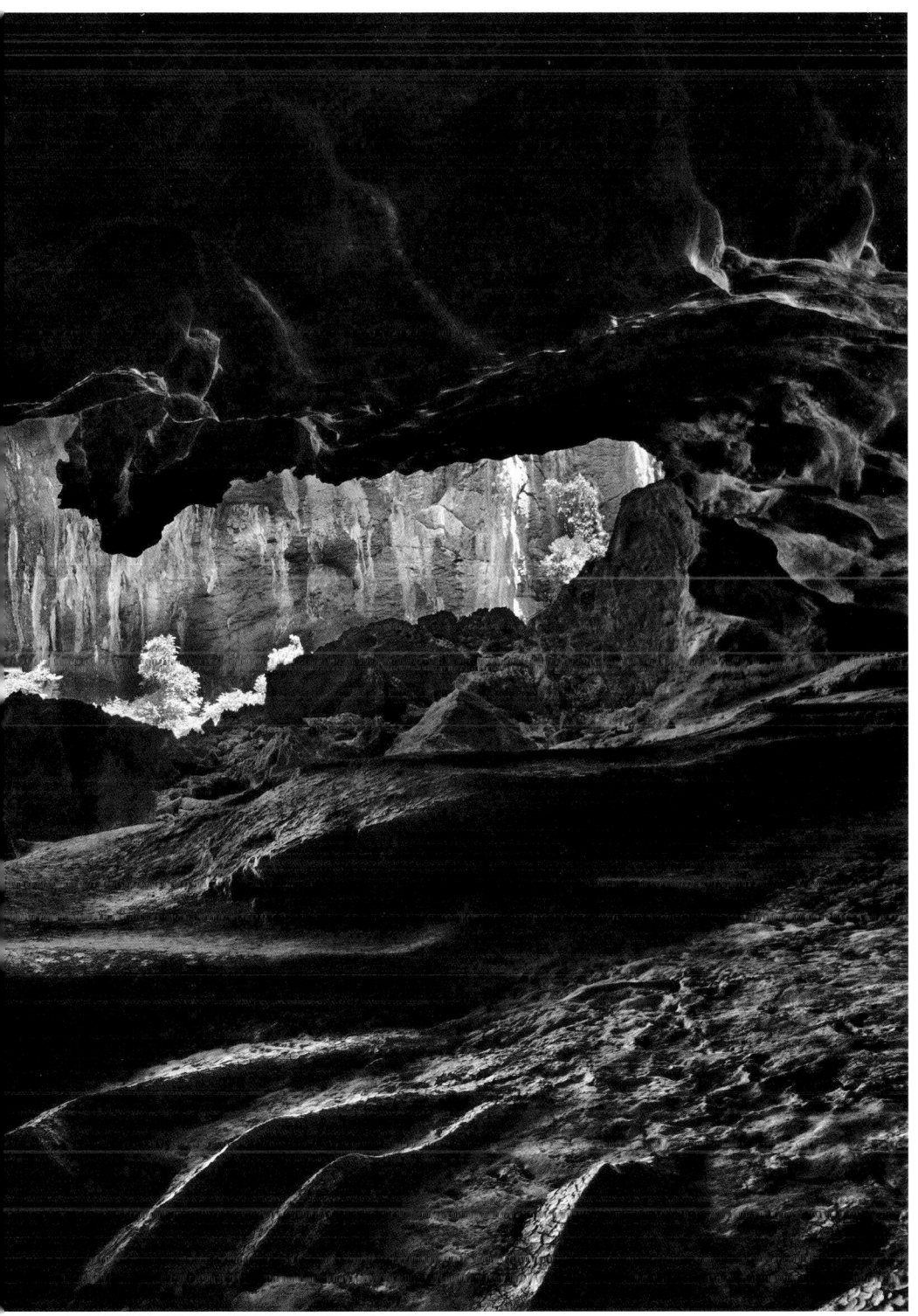

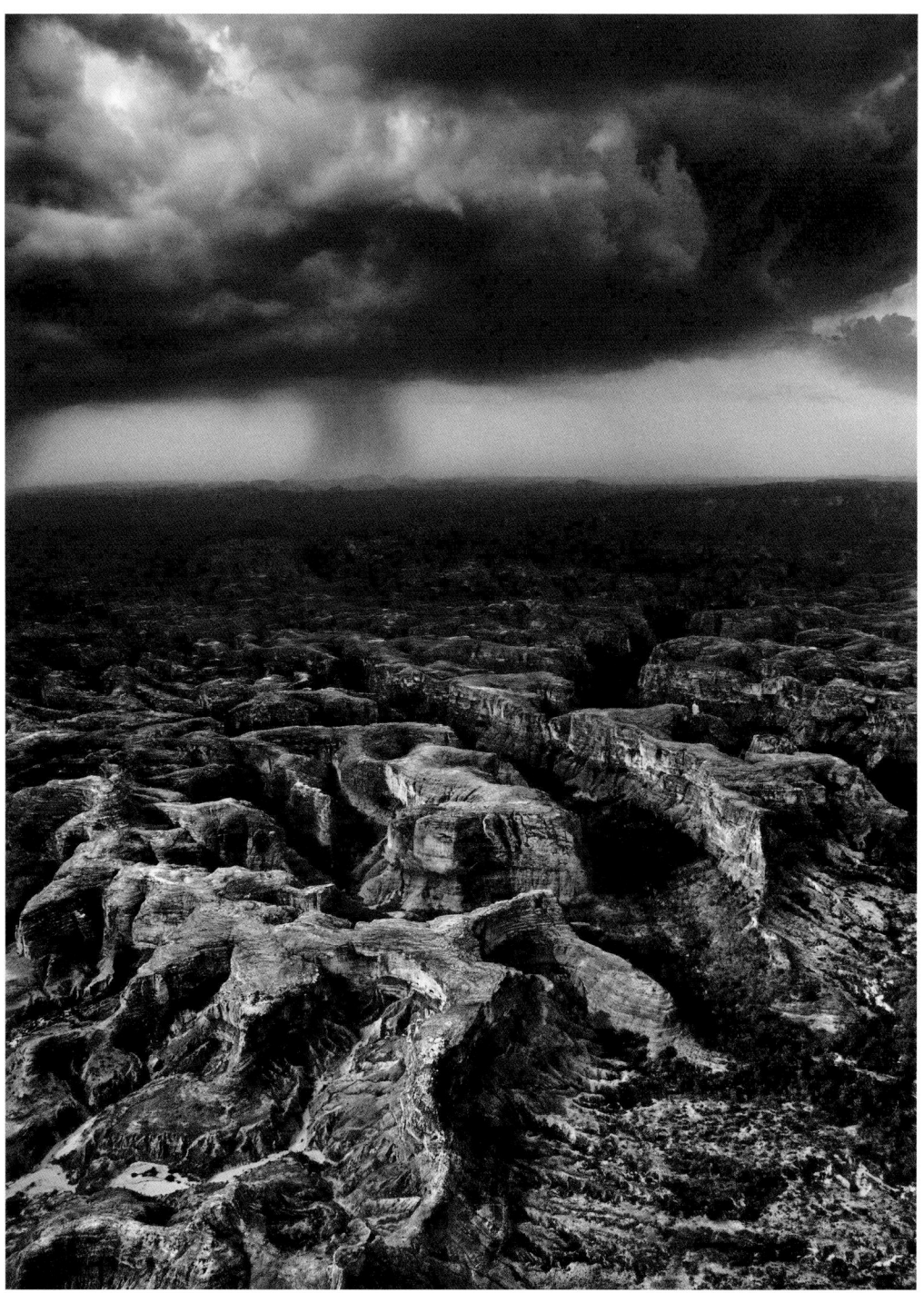

Pages 172/173 Tsingy of Bemaraha National Park. *Tsingy* are among the strangest geological formations to be seen anywhere. Subterranean drainage has dissolved part of a plateau, gouging caverns and fissures into the limestone. Because of local conditions, the erosion is patterned vertically as well as horizontally, creating veritable "forests" of limestone needles. The *tsingy* are to be found in the Melaky Region of western Madagascar, where the Tsingy of Bemaraha National Park has been a UNESCO World Heritage site since 1990. The nature reserve also boasts ancient mangrove forests as well as large populations of birds and lemurs. Madagascar. November and December 2010.

Pages 174/175 Tsingy of Bemaraha National Park. The pachypodium plant (*Pachypodium lamerei*) is a popular decorative plant, normally seen outside Madagascar no taller than 15 inches (40 centimeters). However, as shown here, in its homeland it can grow up to 20 feet (6 meters) in height. Madagascar. November and December 2010.

Pages 176/177 Pachypodium plant (*Pachypodium rosulatum*) in the Makay range. Madagascar. November and December 2010.

Pages 178/179 Cathedral cave. Tsingy of Ankarana National Park. In the far north of Madagascar, the Ankarana National Park and Reserve features landscapes where, as in the Tsingy of Bemaraha National Park, groundwater has transformed an ancient limestone plateau into a striking topographic spectacle. Madagascar. November and December 2010.

Opposite Thunderstorm in the Makay range. As a result of erosion over millions of years, this magnificent sandstone mountain range in the southern part of Madagascar harbors innumerable inaccessible canyons that have provided a unique refuge for biodiversity. Madagascar. November and December 2010.

Opposite Basaltic organ pipes on Mitsio Island. The archipelago of Mitsio Island is situated off the northwest coast. Madagascar. November and December 2010.

Pages 184/185 *Adansonia grandidieri*, sometimes known as Grandidier's baobab, is a very strange-looking tree because its thick trunk seems out of all proportion with its toupee of branches, leaves and fruit. This bloated trunk, though, can store a large amount of water, assuring the tree's good health in drought conditions. The baobab can also be found on the African mainland, although the Grandidier's is native to Madagascar and is the most widely exploited of the island's six kinds of baobab. Its seeds and fruit pulp, rich in vitamin C, can be eaten literally off the tree, while its seeds can be pressed into cooking oil. Using wooden pegs hammered into the trunk, local men climb the tree to collect its fruit.

Fibers extracted from the tree's bark can also be made into strong rope without harming the tree. The trunk of a fallen tree can in turn be pressed into sheets of fiber for use as roof covering.

Fortunately, most of these activities pose little danger to the baobab's survival, but it is nonetheless now considered an endangered species because of encroachment by farming land. No less alarming is that fires, seed predation, competition from weeds and an altered physical environment have increasingly diminished the baobab's ability to reproduce.

This photograph was taken about 62 miles (100 kilometers) northeast of the Makay range. Madagascar. November and December 2010.

Pages 186/187 Baobab trees (*Adansonia rubrostipa*) on a mushroom island in Bay of Moramba. Madagascar. November and December 2010.

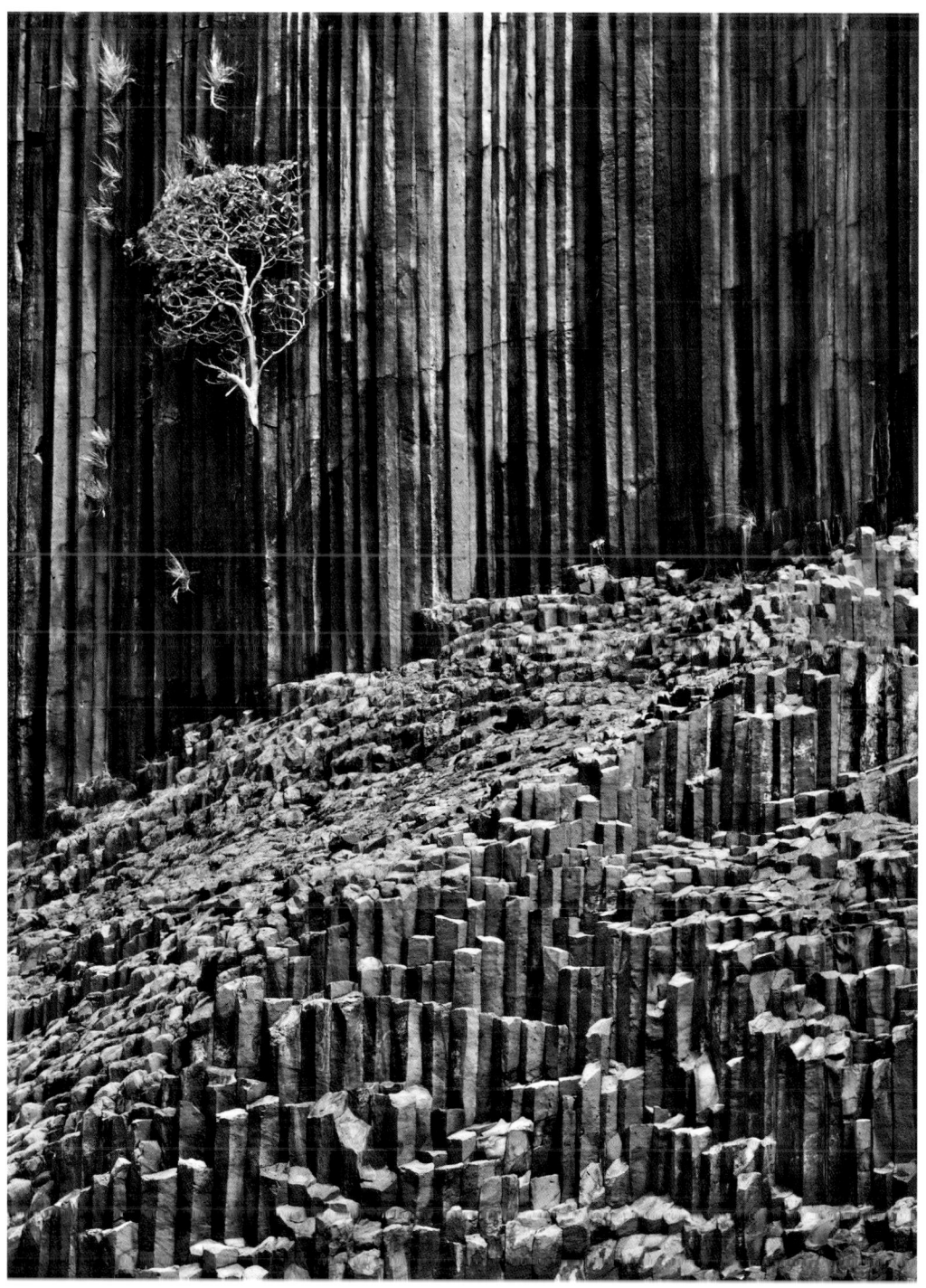

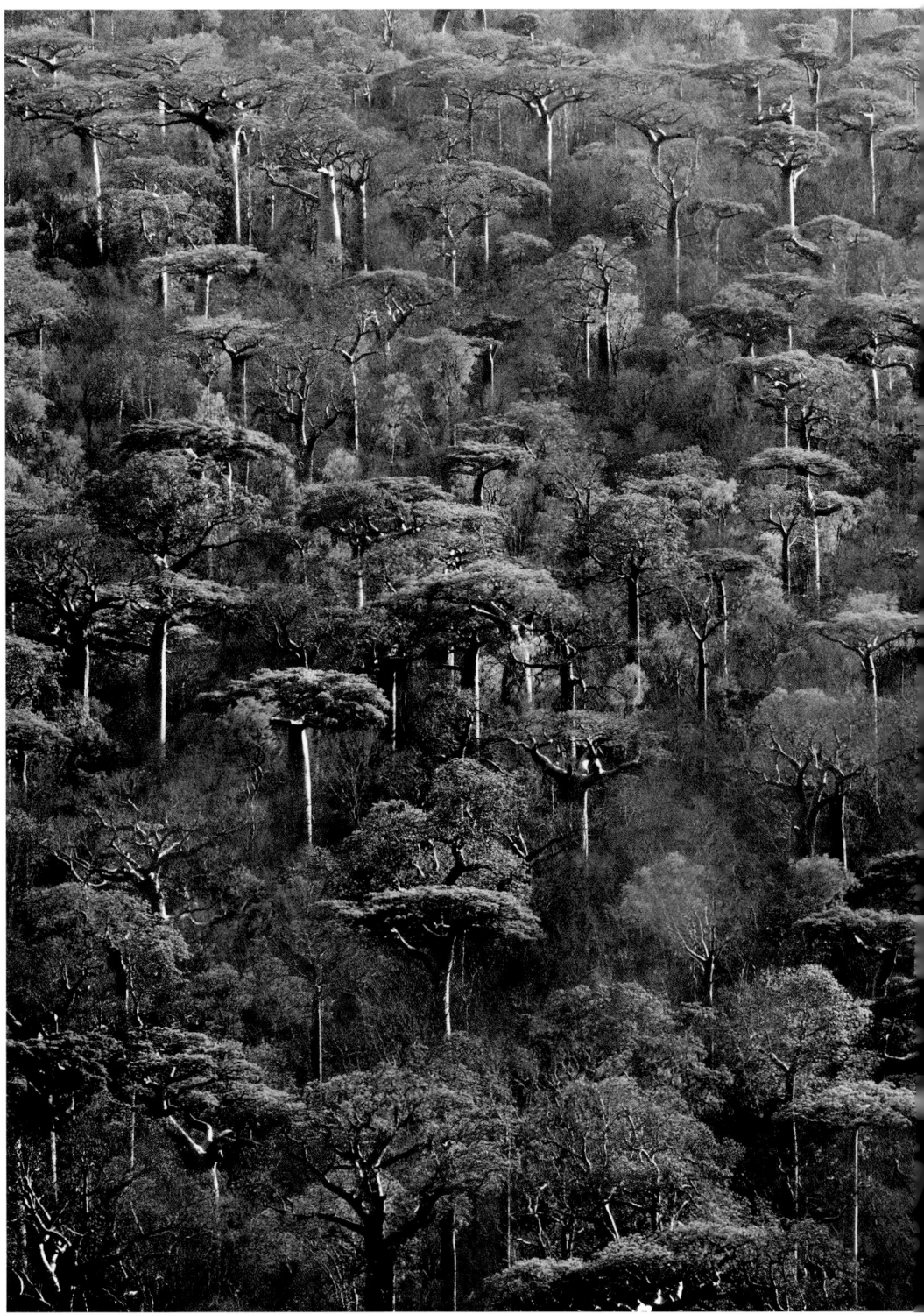

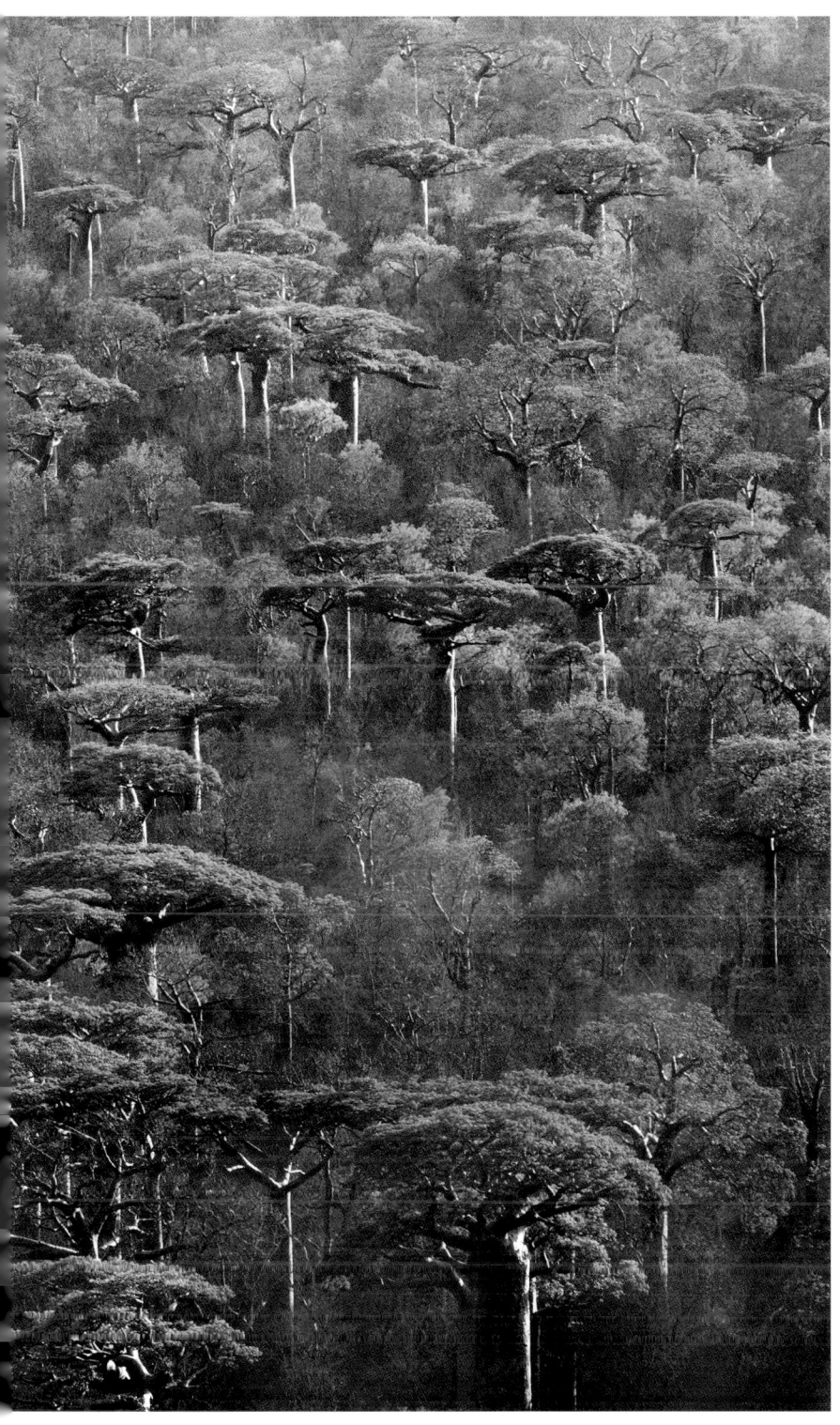

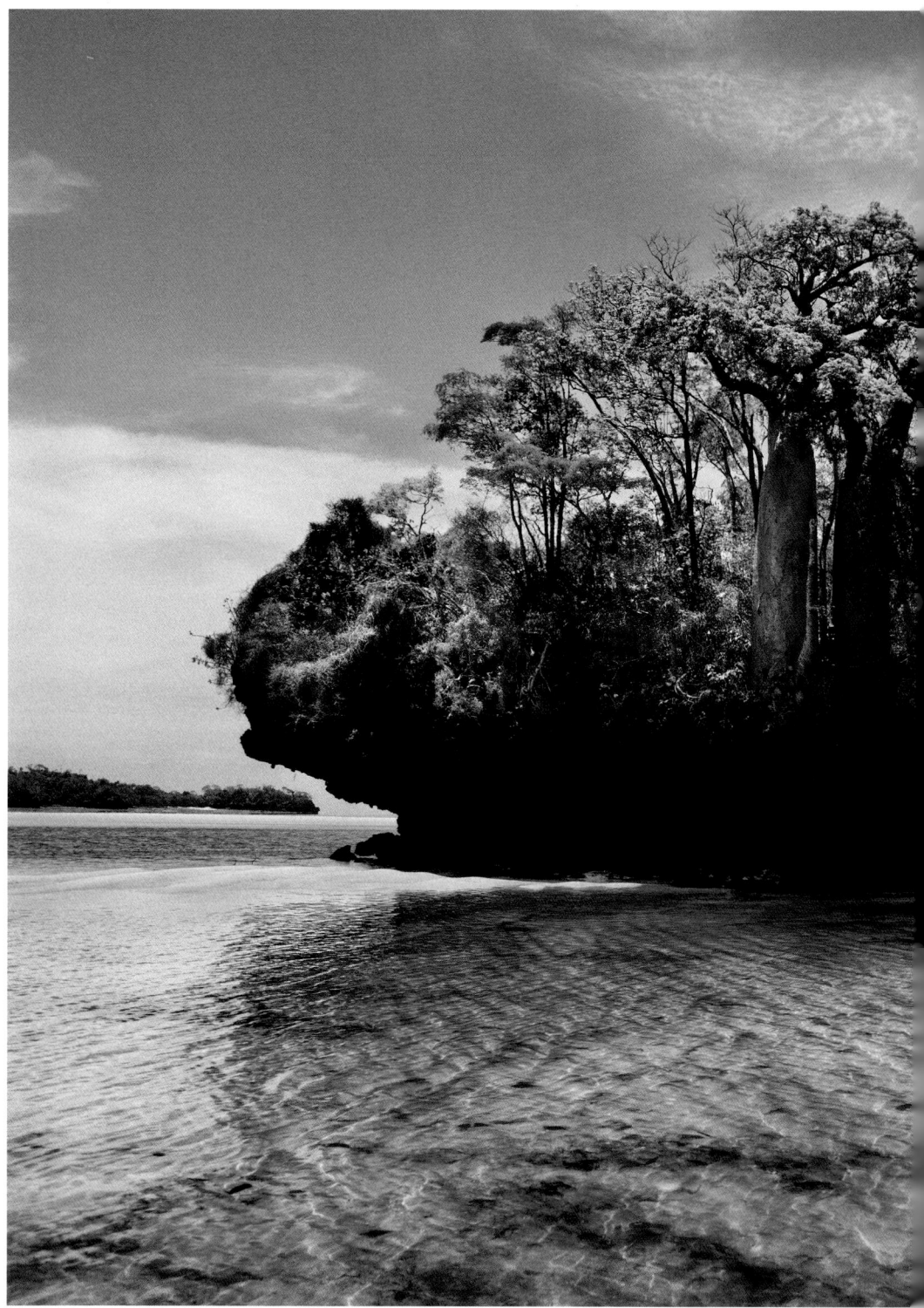

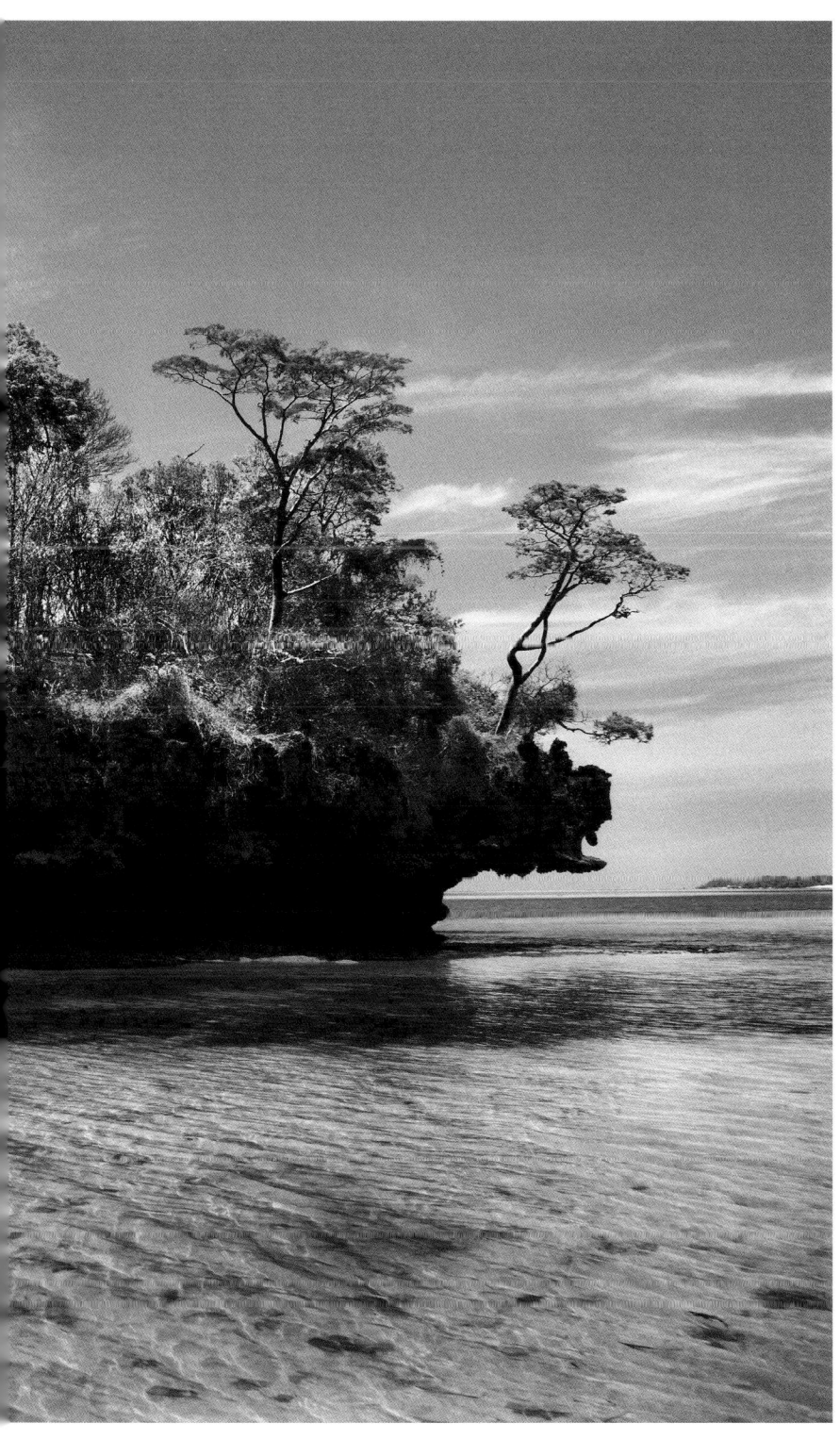

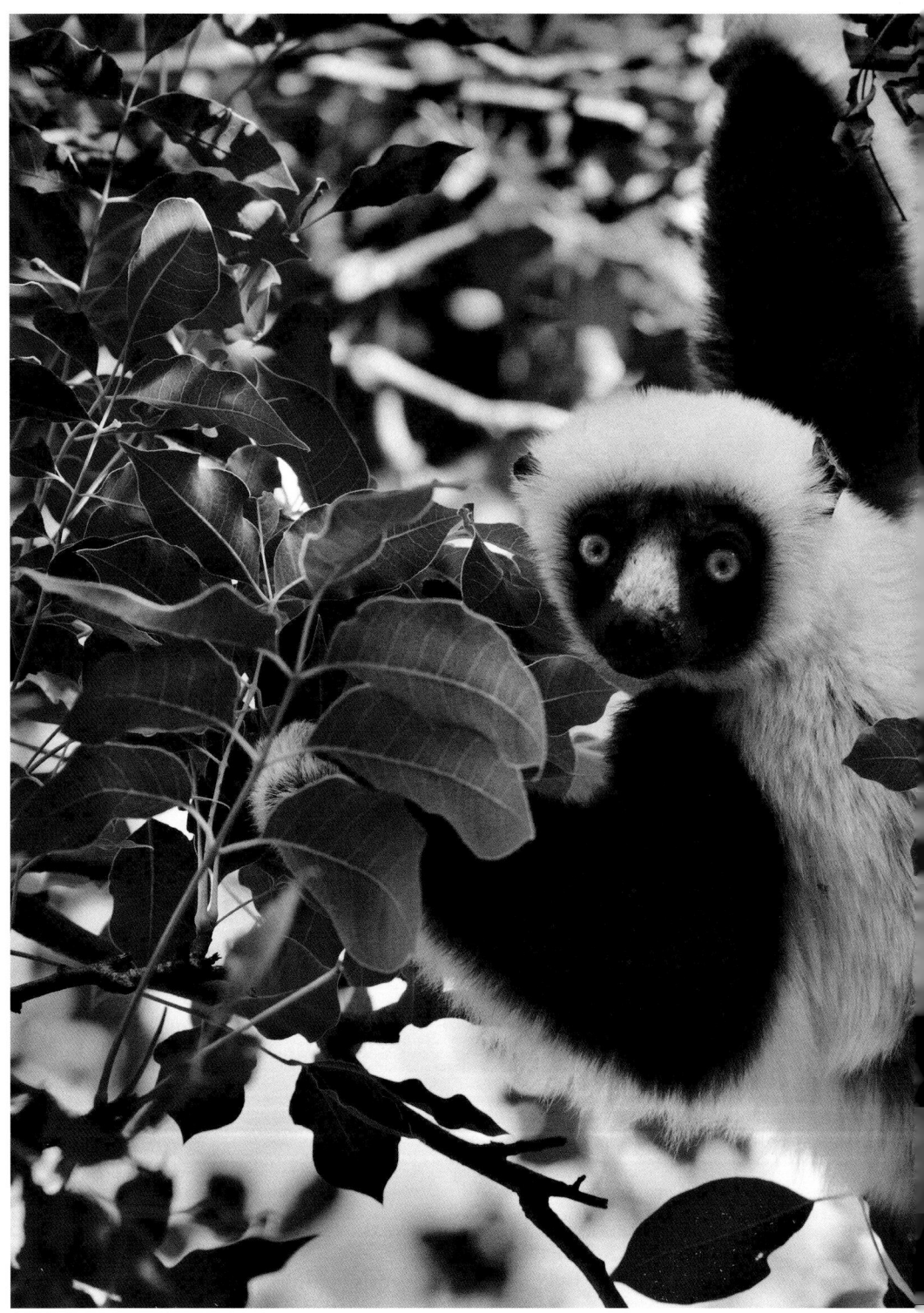

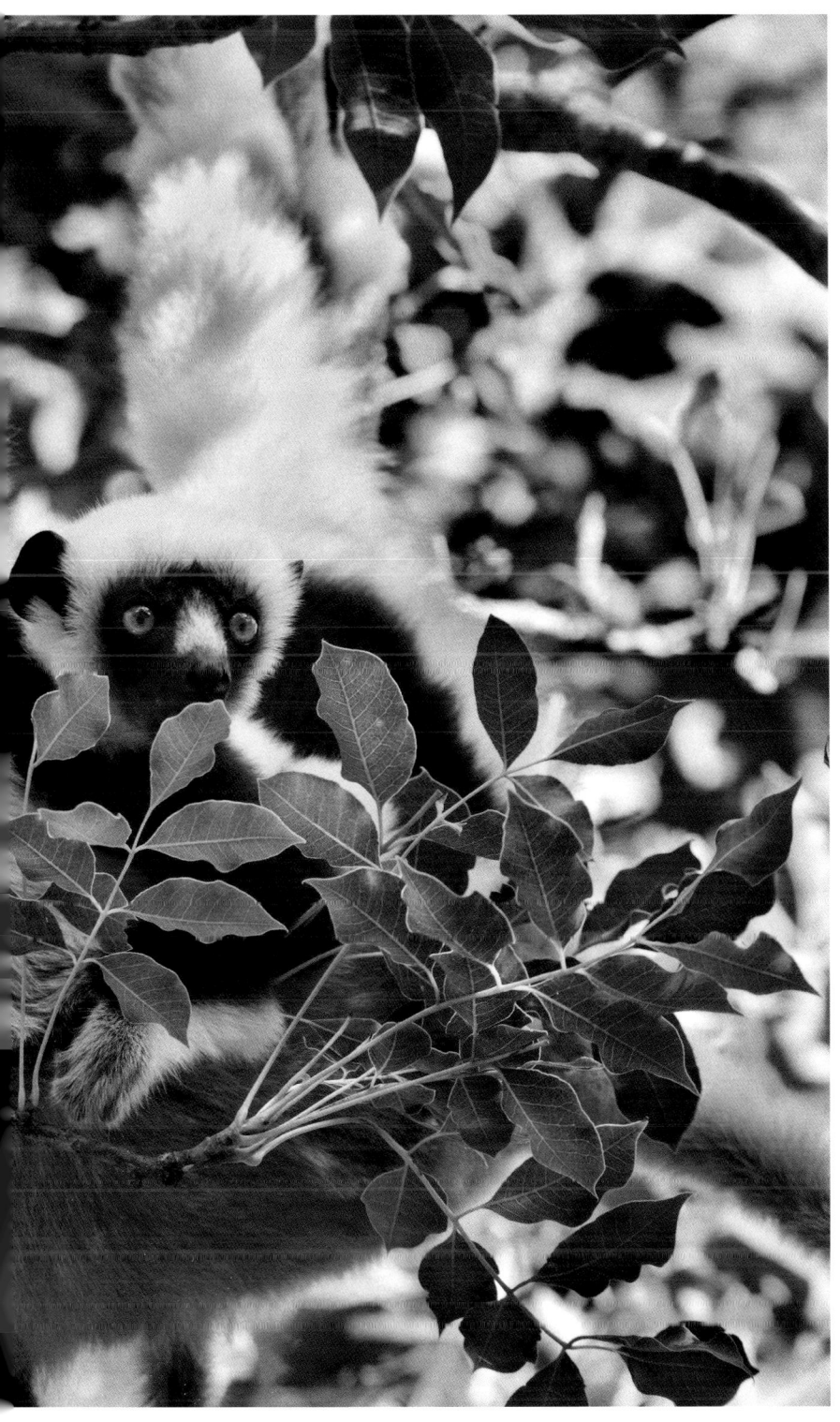

Pages 188/189 Coquerel's sifaka lemur (*Propithecus coquereli*) in the Anjajavy area on the northwest coast. Madagascar. November and December 2010.

Opposite Von der Decken's sifaka lemurs (*Propithecus deckenii*), in Tsingy of Bemaraha, Strict Nature Reserve. Madagascar. November and December 2010.

Pages 192/193 Pachypodium plant (*Pachypodium lameri*) in Andohahela National Park, situated in southeast Madagascar, is remarkable for its variety of habitats. The park covers 293 square miles (760 square kilometers) of the Anosy mountain range, the southernmost spur of the Malagasy Highlands. Madagascar. November and December 2010.

Pages 194/195 Bats (*Pteropus rufus*) on tamarind tree (*Tamarindus indica*) in the Berenty Reserve. It is a small private reserve of gallery forest along the Mandrake River, set in a semiarid spiny forest ecoregion of the far south of Madagascar.

The Madagascan flying fox (*Pteropus rufus*) is native to Madagascar. Its other common names include the Madagascar fruit bat and the Madagascar flying fox. It is one of many species of megabat and the largest bat that can be found on the island of Madagascar. With a wingspan of 40 to 50 inches (100 to 125 centimeters), it can weigh between 1 and 1 ½ pounds (500 and 750 grams). Its diet consists of flowers, fig leaves and, of course, fruit. Because of the loss of its habitat, it is now considered a vulnerable species. Madagascar. November and December 2010.

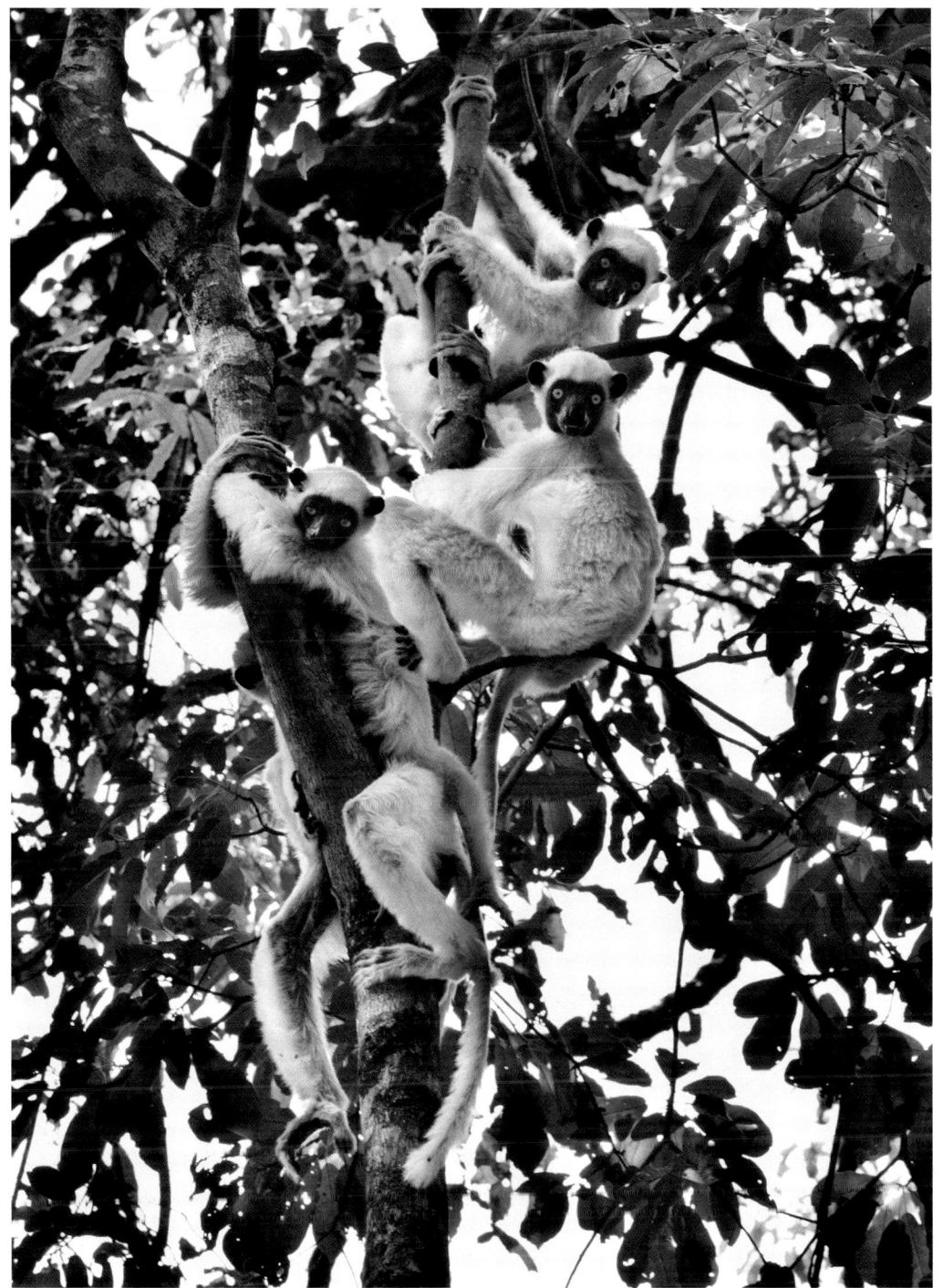

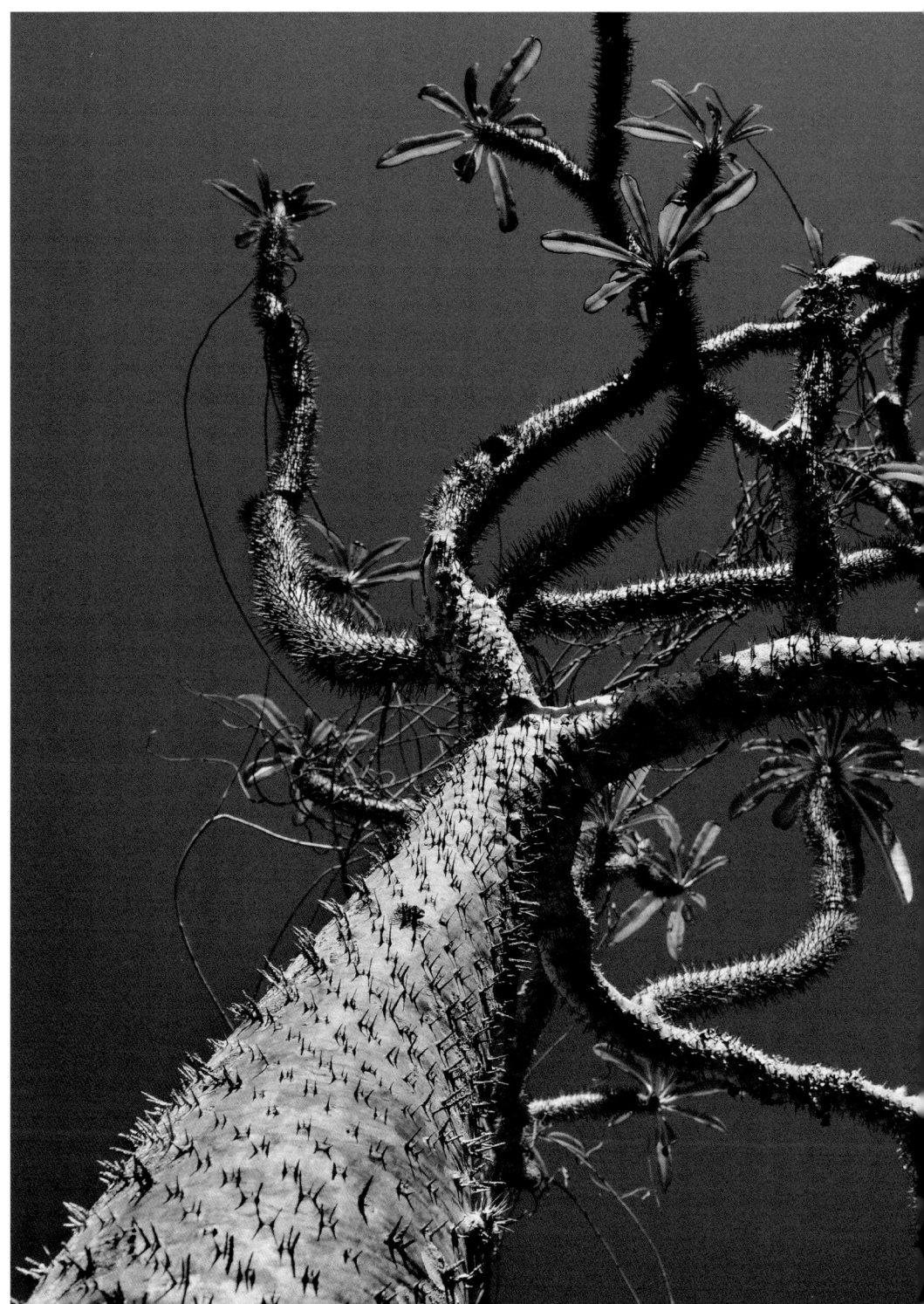

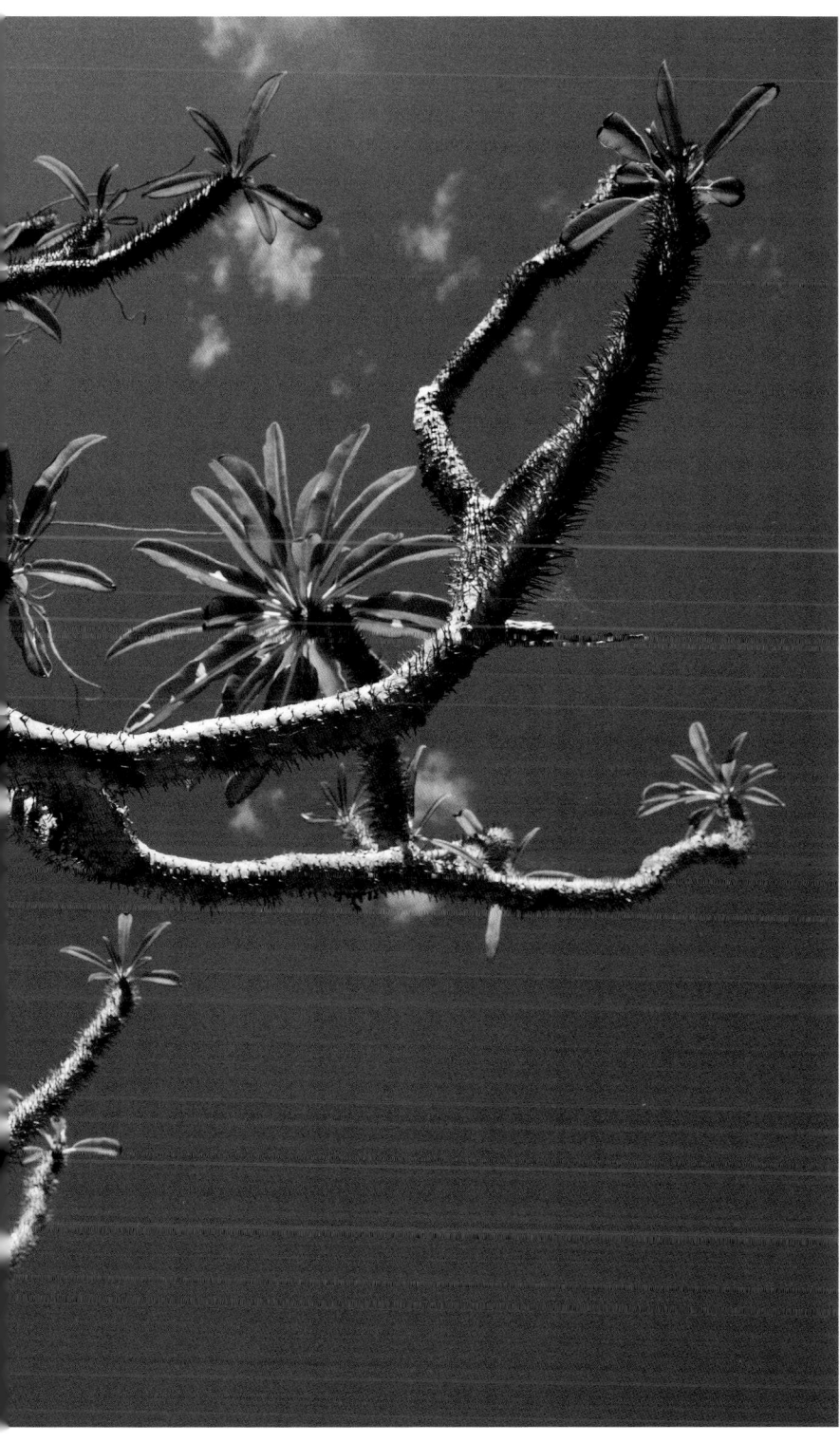

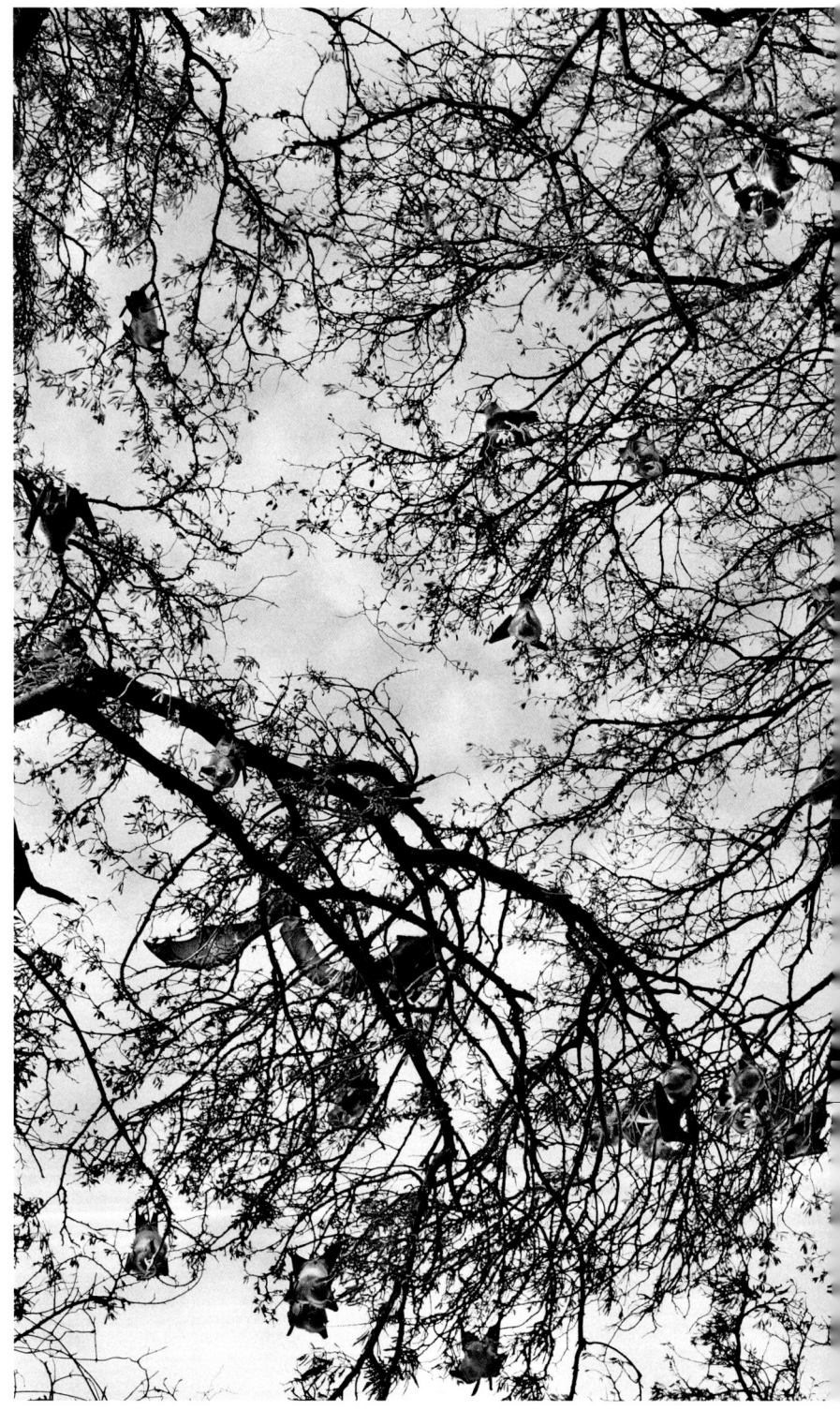

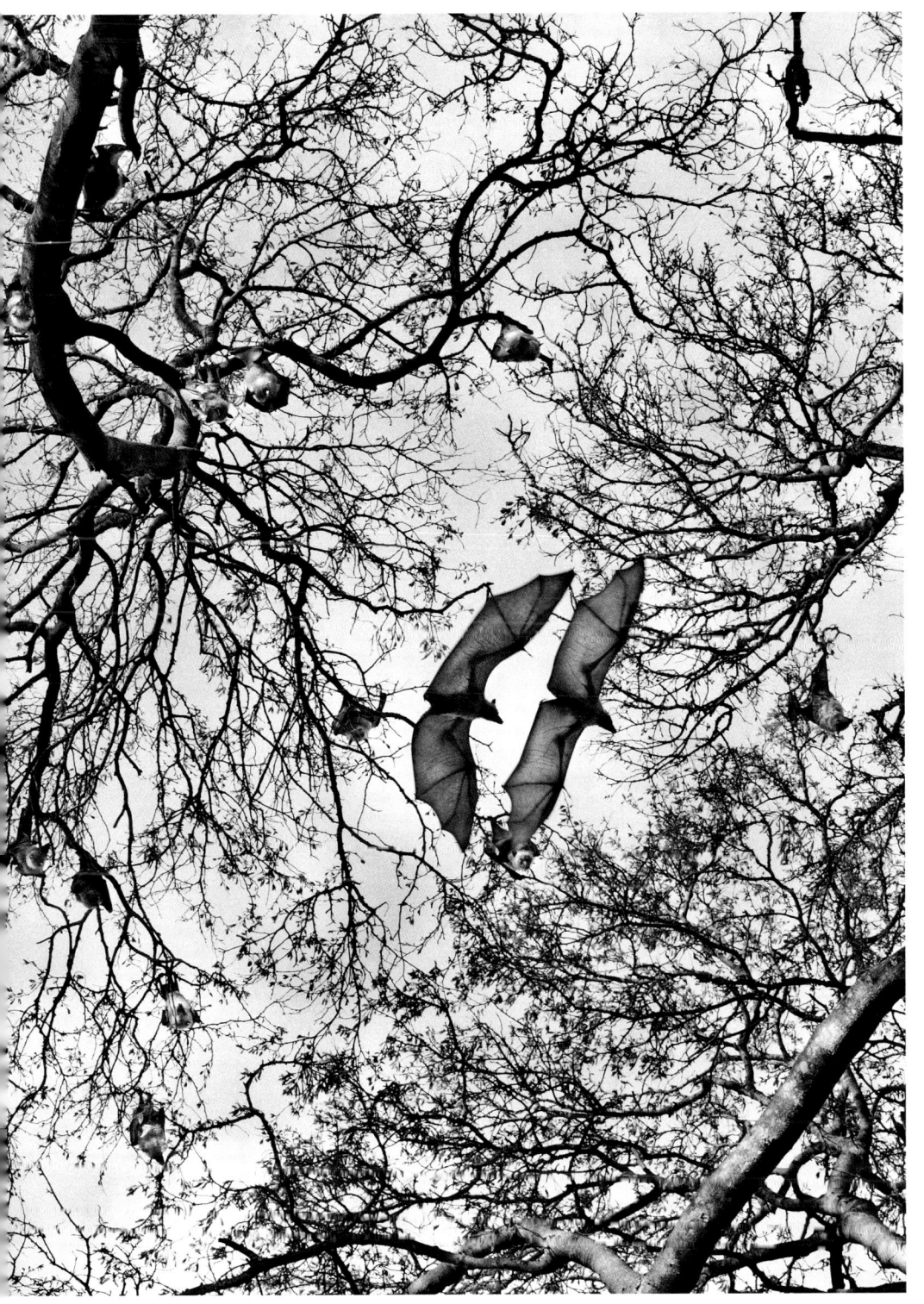

PAPUA NEW GUINEA'S HIGHLANDS

Pages 197 through 203

The highlands of Papua New Guinea are dramatic and beautiful, with fertile valleys, turbulent rivers and seemingly endless saw-toothed mountains. But they are also the country's most densely populated and productive region. It is therefore all the more surprising that it was only in the 1930s that the outside world first came face-to-face with the diverse and artistically inventive indigenous peoples that live here.

The first European explorers to enter this rugged interior had expected to find an unbroken tangle of mountains. Instead, they came across broad, heavily cultivated valleys and a population of more than one million. They were still more surprised by the cultural chasm that separated them from these newly contacted peoples.

Since then, much has changed. The region's five provinces—Eastern Highlands (around Goroka), Simbu (around Kundiawa), Western Highlands (around Mount Hagen), Enga (around Wabag) and Southern Highlands (around Mendi)—now have the country's most extensive road system and a healthy economy based on coffee, tea, gold and copper. All the photographs presented here are about the *singsing* festivals in the highlands. The *singsing*, a celebratory festival or dance, can happen for all sorts of reasons and it is always spectacular, with highlanders in traditional costume and face paint dancing in formation and playing their *kundus* (an hourglass-shaped drum with lizard skin). The Enga Show, the Hagen Show and the Paya Show are annual events that bring together thousands of performers. Body art and personal decoration, called *bilas*, are particularly sophisticated. While the Sepik people and other Papua New Guineans create beautiful carvings and artifacts, the highlanders use themselves as rustic canvases: they paint their bodies and dress up in feathers, pearls and animal skins to represent birds, trees or mountain spirits. On occasions, an important event, such as legendary battle, is reenacted at a *singsing*.

Opposite and pages 198/199 Performers of the *singsing* festival of Mount Hagen. Western Highlands Province. Papua New Guinea. July and August 2008.

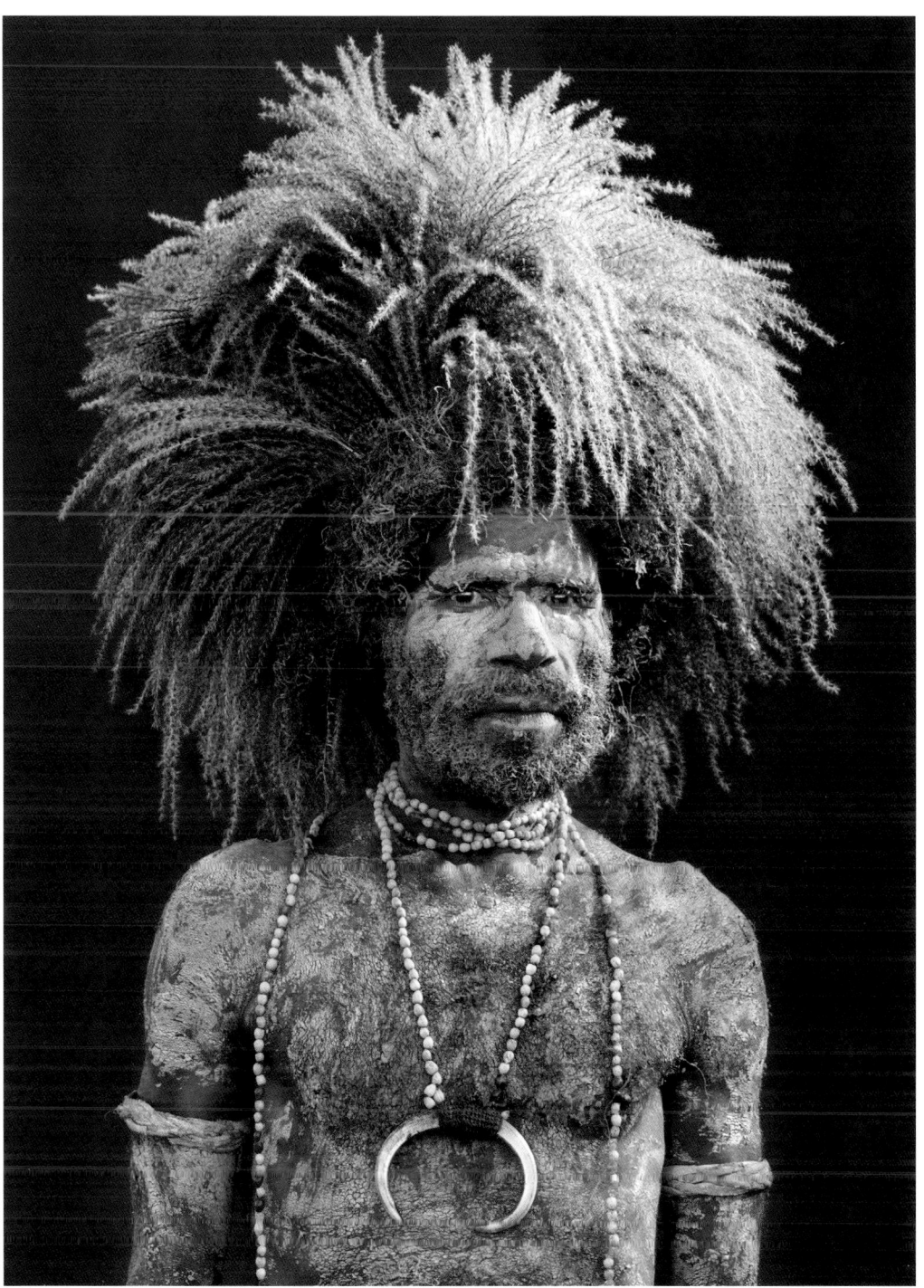

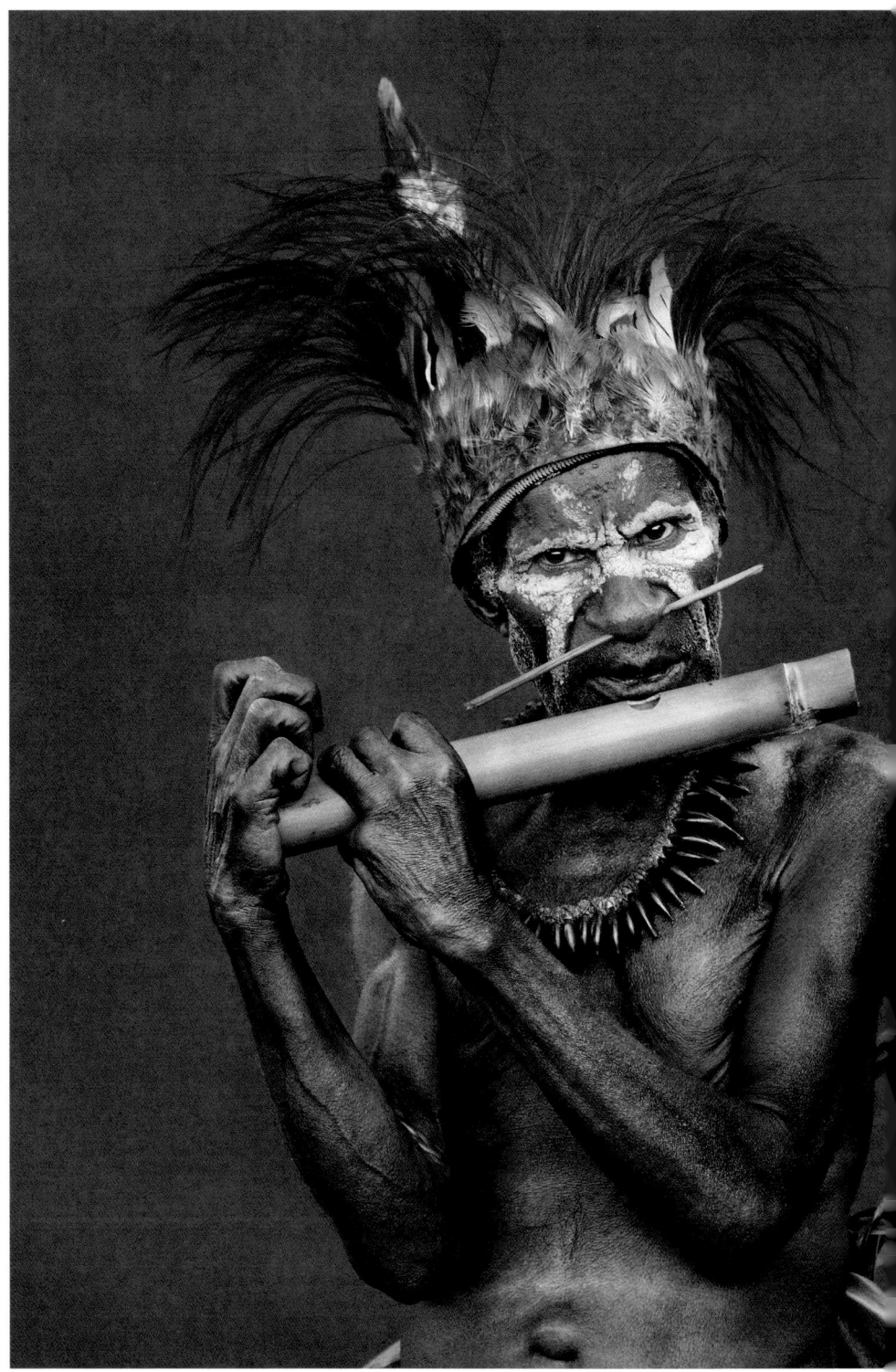

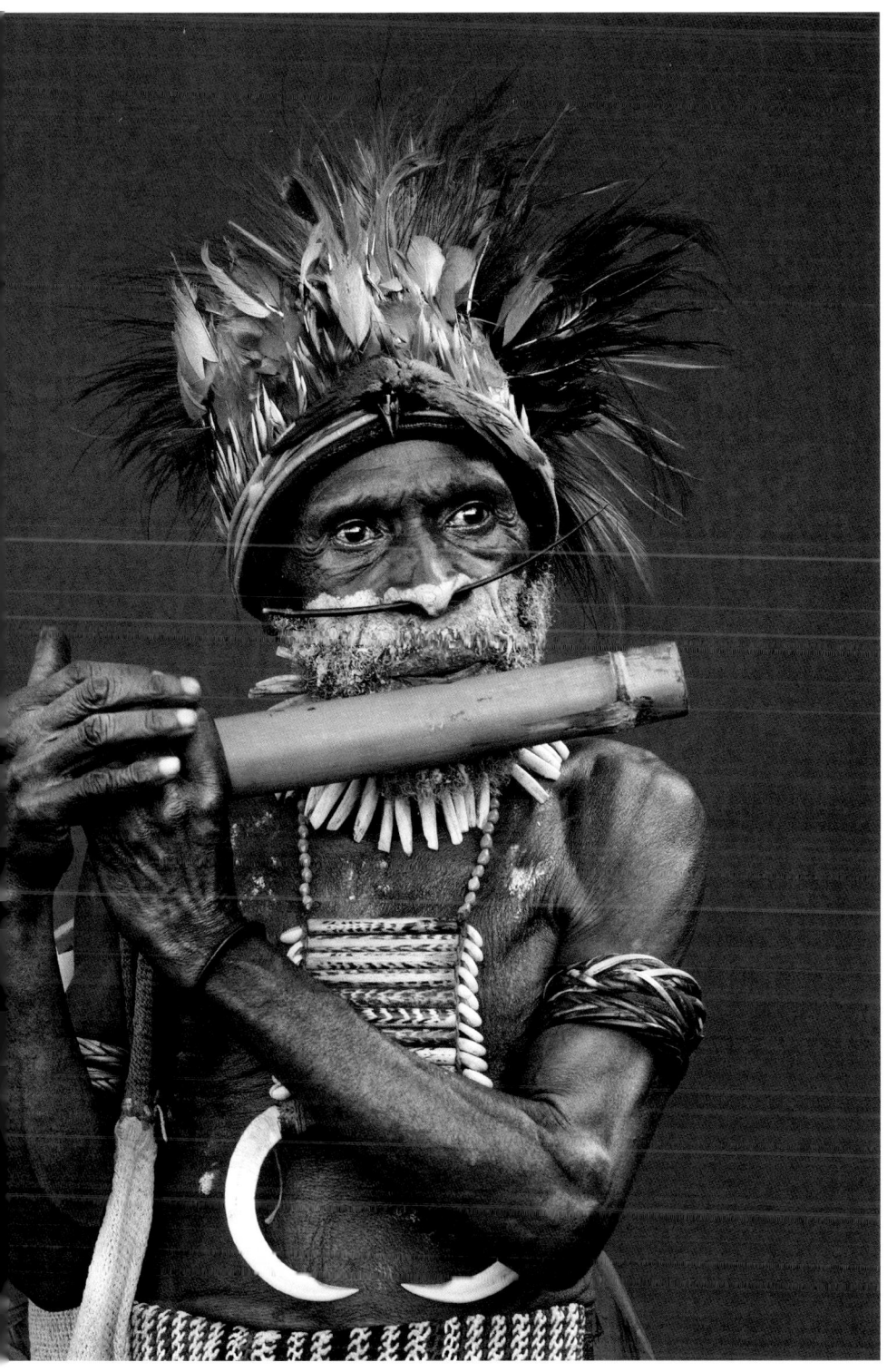

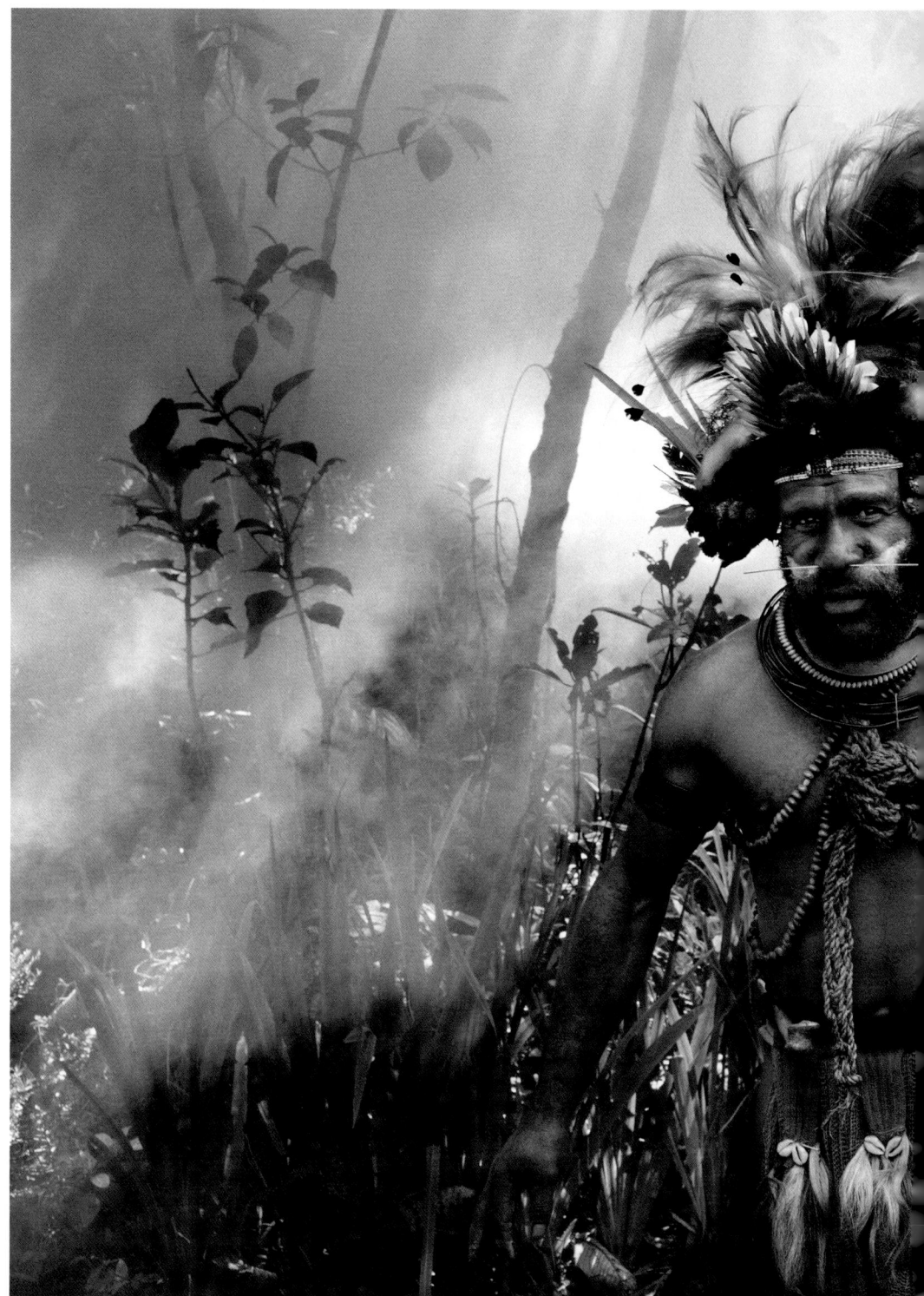

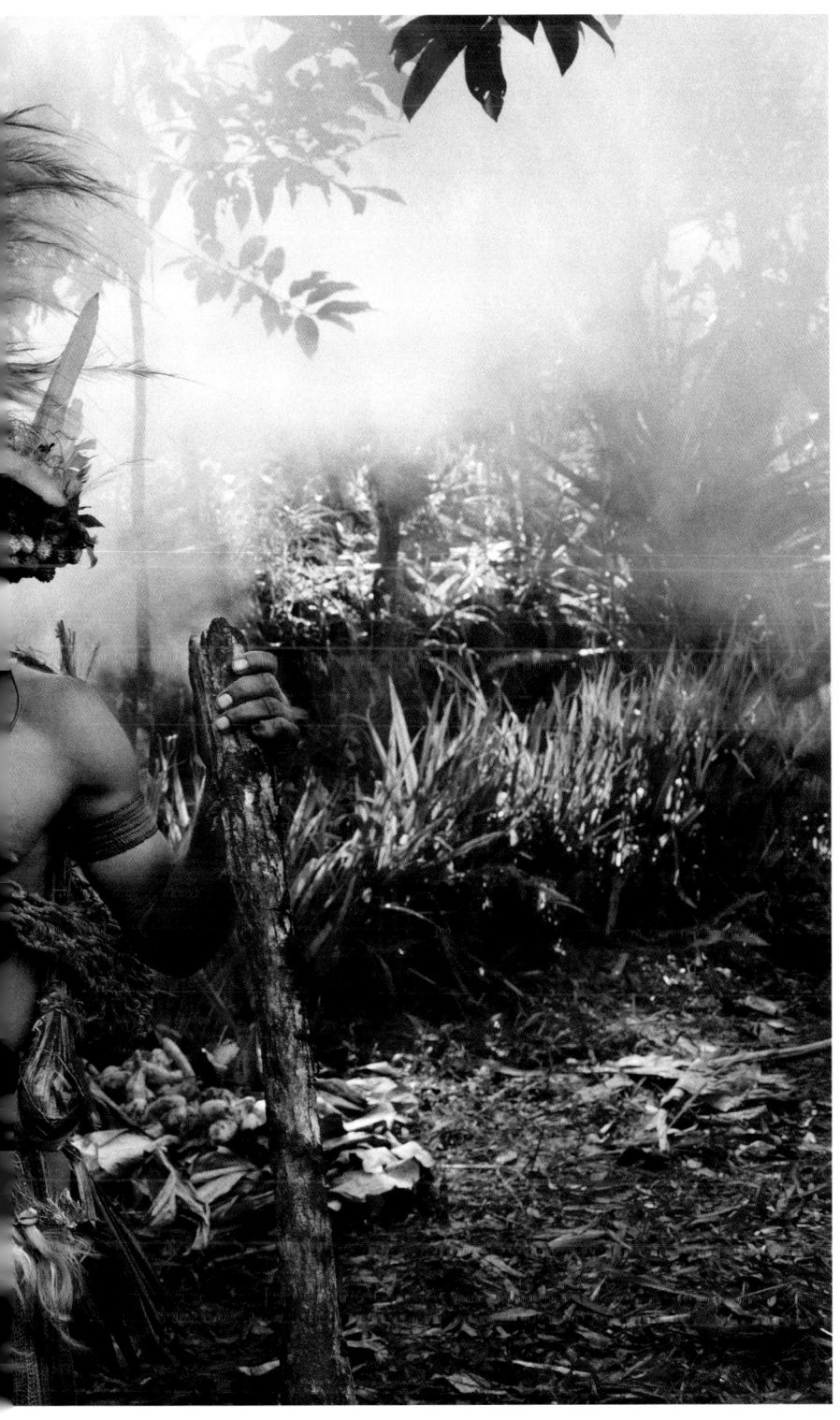

Pages 200/201 Huli men wear decorative wigs woven with human hair. The hair is the wigman's own, grown over many months by unmarried men living in isolation from the rest of their community. Under the tutelage of a master wigman, spells are cast, diets are prescribed and rituals adhered to—all to ensure a healthy head of hair. Many Huli wigmen have more than one wig, but all must be made with hair grown before the men marry. Village of Hademari. Southern Highlands Province. Papua New Guinea. July and August 2008.

Opposite Performer at the *singsing* festival of Paya. Western Highlands Province. Papua New Guinea. July and August 2008.

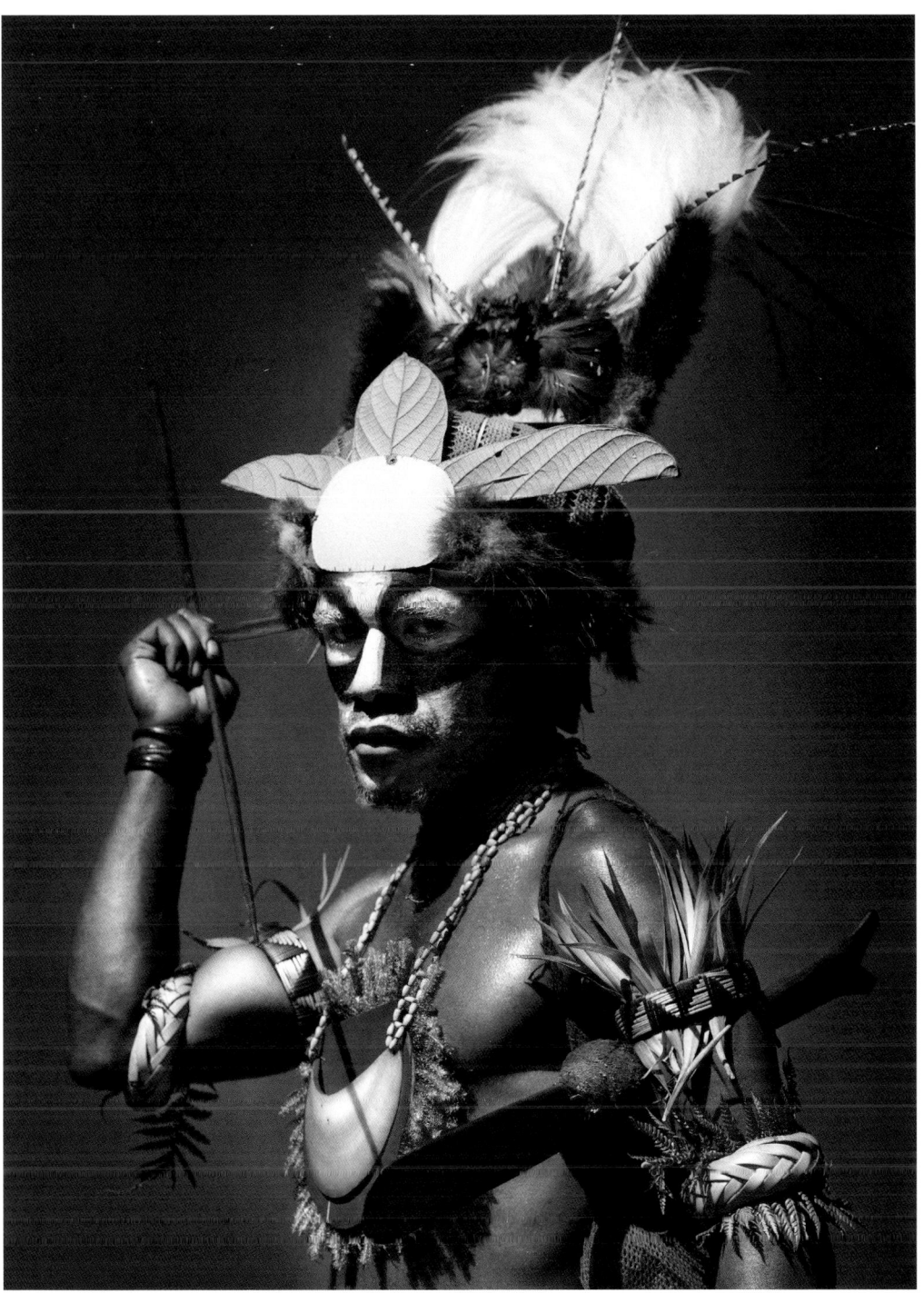

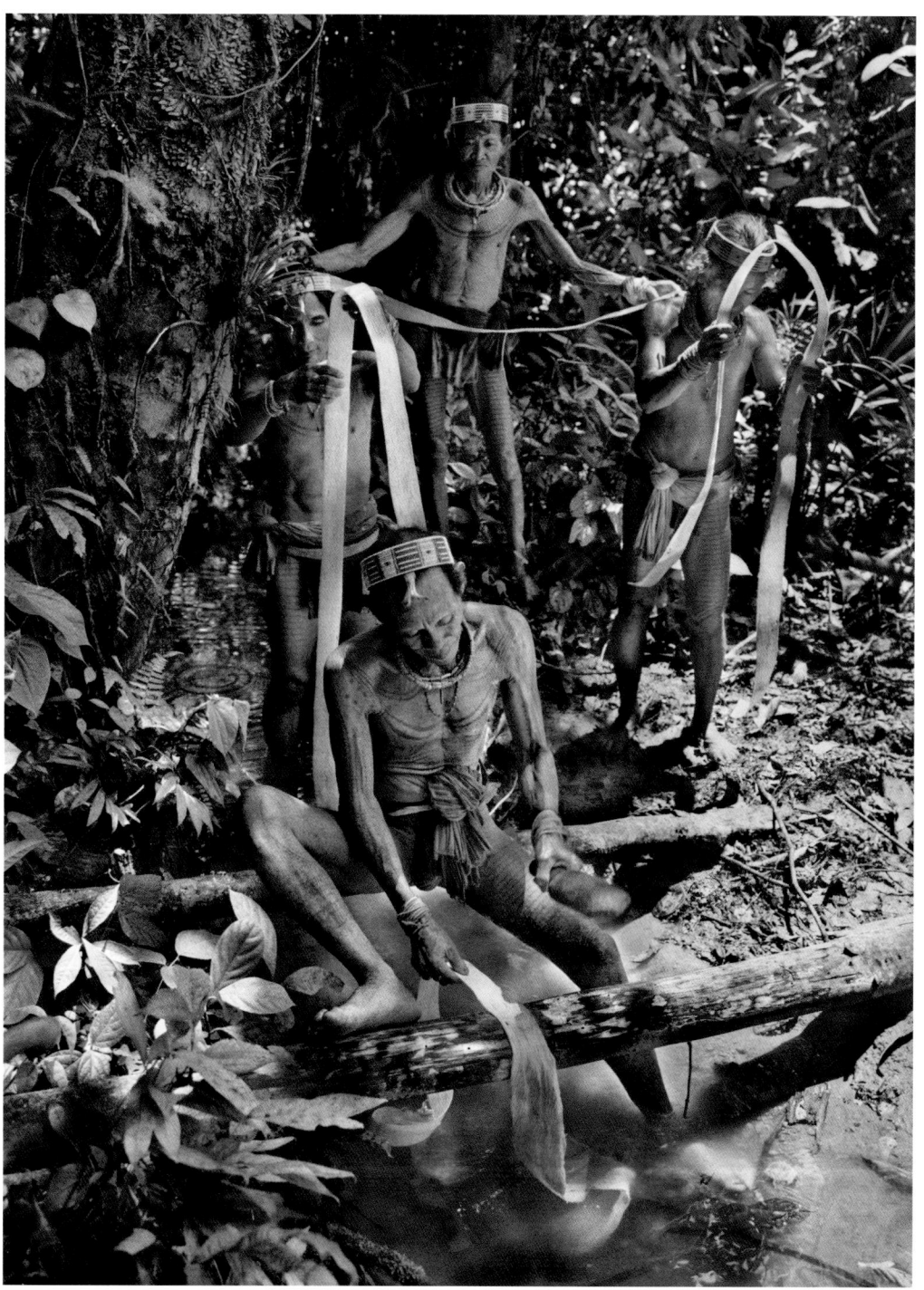

THE MENTAWAI, INDONESIA

Pages 204 through 213

The Mentawai (also known as the Mentawei and Mentawi) are the native people of the Mentawai Islands, some 80 miles (130 kilometers) west of Sumatra. They live a semi-nomadic hunter-gatherer lifestyle in the coastal and rainforest environments of the islands. The people are renowned for their spirituality, body art and their practice of sharpening their teeth, which they feel adds to their beauty. The Mentawai are among the very few traditional indigenous groups remaining in Asia. They still build almost everything out of natural products from the rainforests, and their lifestyle and rituals have changed little in thousands of years. The Mentawai language belongs to the Austronesian language family. The largest and northernmost island is Siberut. Here, most Mentawai live in small settlements dotted along major rivers or close to the coast. They commute between their settlements and smaller dwellings some distance away on ancestral land. There, they raise pigs in the jungle and harvest seasonal fruits, such as durian, jackfruit and other wild species. Chickens are usually raised close to the settlement, while sago palms are tended in low-lying swampy areas, usually beside a river. Flour ground from the sago palm heart and from the taro tuber is an important part of their diet. The Indonesian government has worked for decades to assimilate the Mentawai by luring them into government controlled villages, today, only a handful of unassimilated clans live in the jungle. Led by *sikeireis* (Mentawai shamans), they live according to tradition in long communal houses called *umas*. While the modern world is moving ever closer, traditional clans take from it only what they need. All use metal objects such as axes and cauldrons, and some have started using plastic cups and pitchers. The government and various religious groups have forced assimilated Mentawai to wear modern clothes, but in the traditional *umas*, the men usually wear only tree bark loincloths and the women traditional dresses. They love to wear colorful necklaces and bracelets and tropical flowers in their hair. Shamans and their wives have their bodies entirely tattooed.

Opposite The bark of a felled *baiko* tree is cut into strips, then plunged into water and pounded at length with a mallet without tearing it. The objective is to crush the fibers and to soften the bark. After drying in the sun, it is dyed red with sap from another tree, and worn by men around their hips; this loincloth is called the *kabit*. Siberut Island, West Sumatra. Indonesia. March and April 2008.

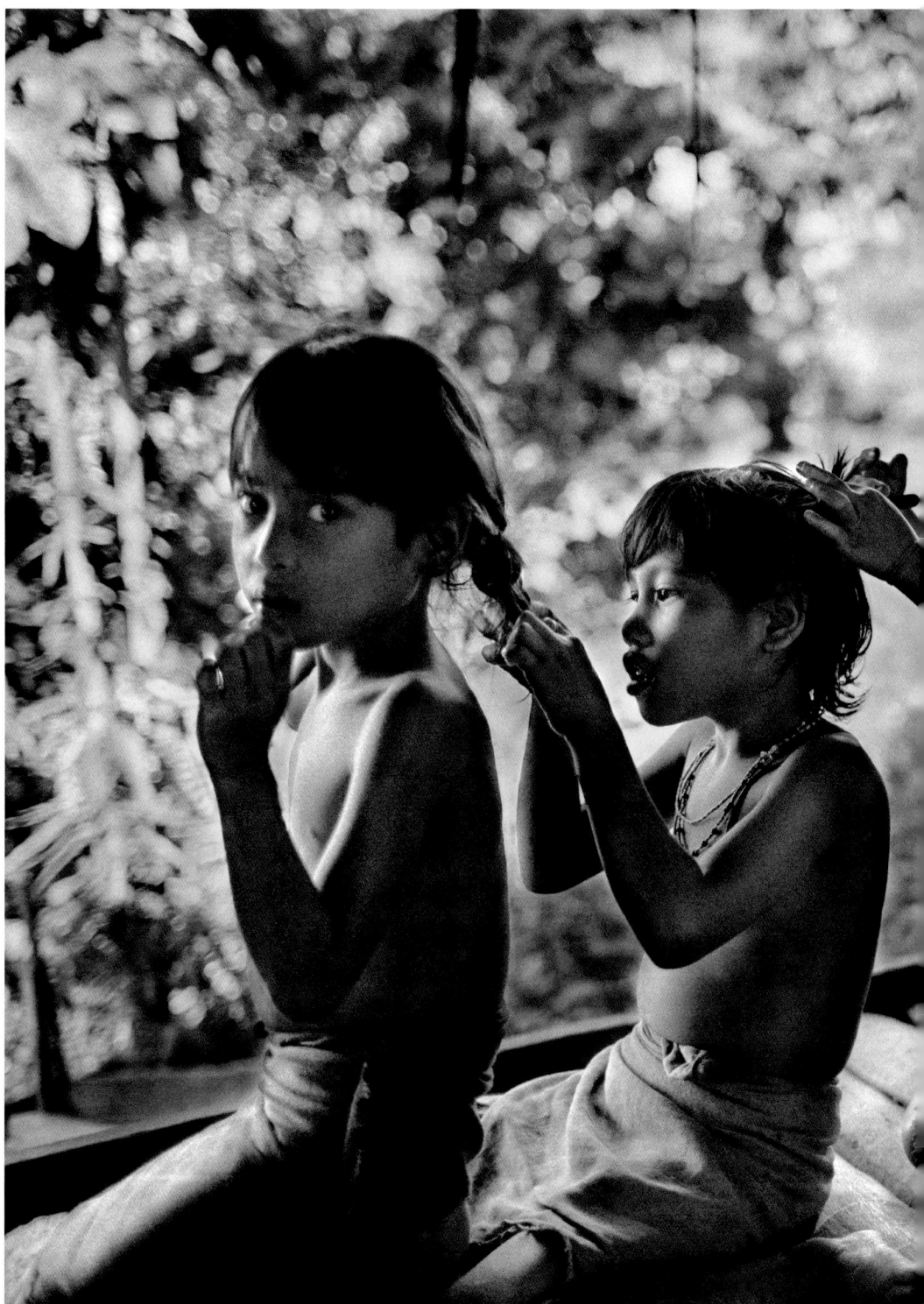

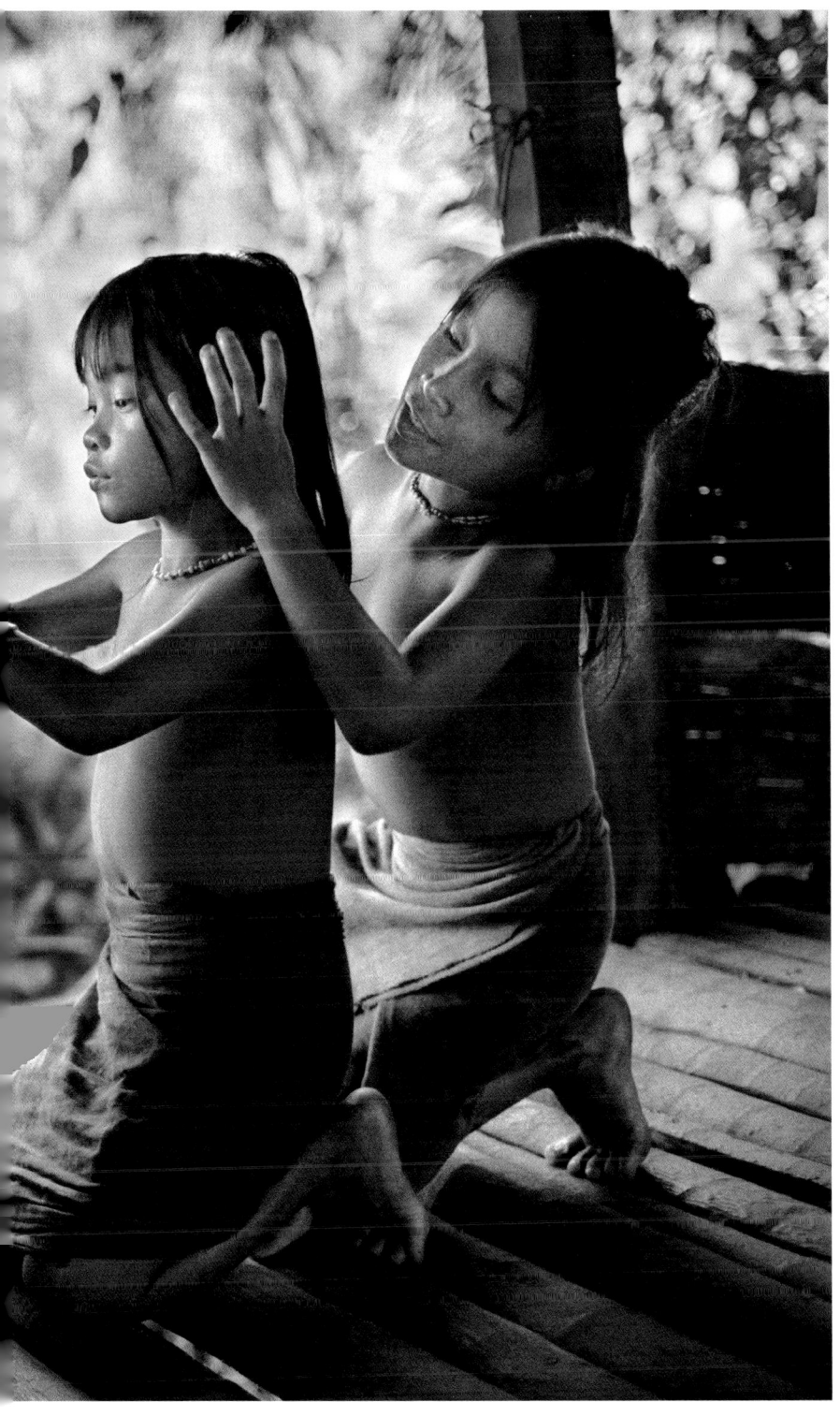

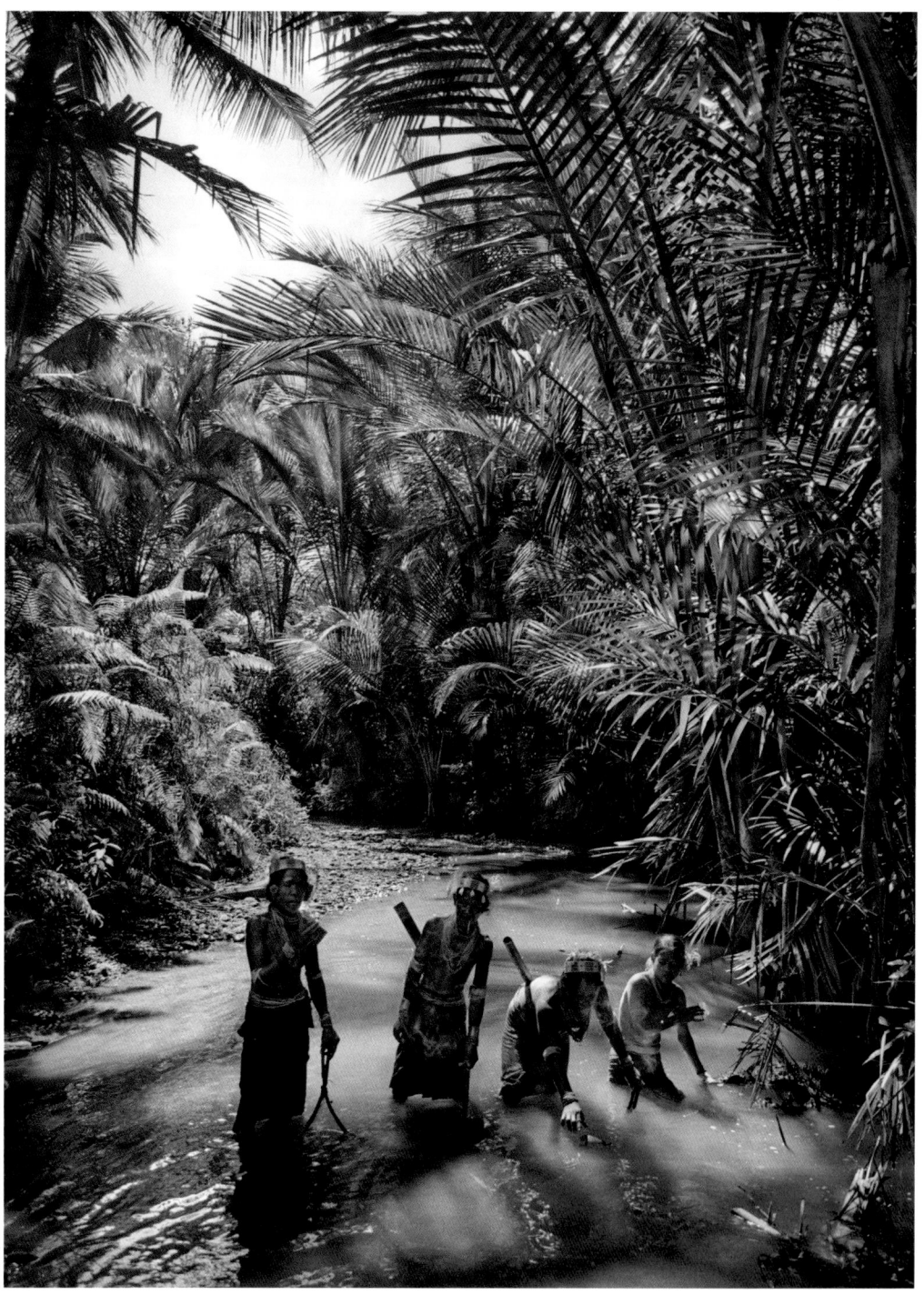

Pages 206/207 Scene inside the *uma*. The uma is a large, long wooden communal house in which the clan lives, although at night men sleep on one side and women on the other. There are many taboos in Mentawai society, taboos that must be respected. For instance, intimacy between couples cannot take place in front of the rest of the family. Each couple owns a *sapo*, a small individual house, which offers them privacy. Siberut Island. West Sumatra. Indonesia. March and April 2008.

Opposite Fishing, usually the responsibility of women, provides Mentawai families with their daily requirement of protein. Siberut Island. West Sumatra. Indonesia. March and April 2008,

Pages 210/211 These baskets carry, among other things, chickens sacrificed during religious rites. Siberut Island. West Sumatra. Indonesia. March and April 2008.

Pages 212/213 Agile young men climb gigantic trees, some 40 meters (130 feet) high, to collect *durian*, an excellent fruit and a favorite of the Mentawai clan. Some of those fruits are also sold to finance the purchase of modern products, such as machetes and tobacco. Siberut Island. West Sumatra. Indonesia. March and April 2008.

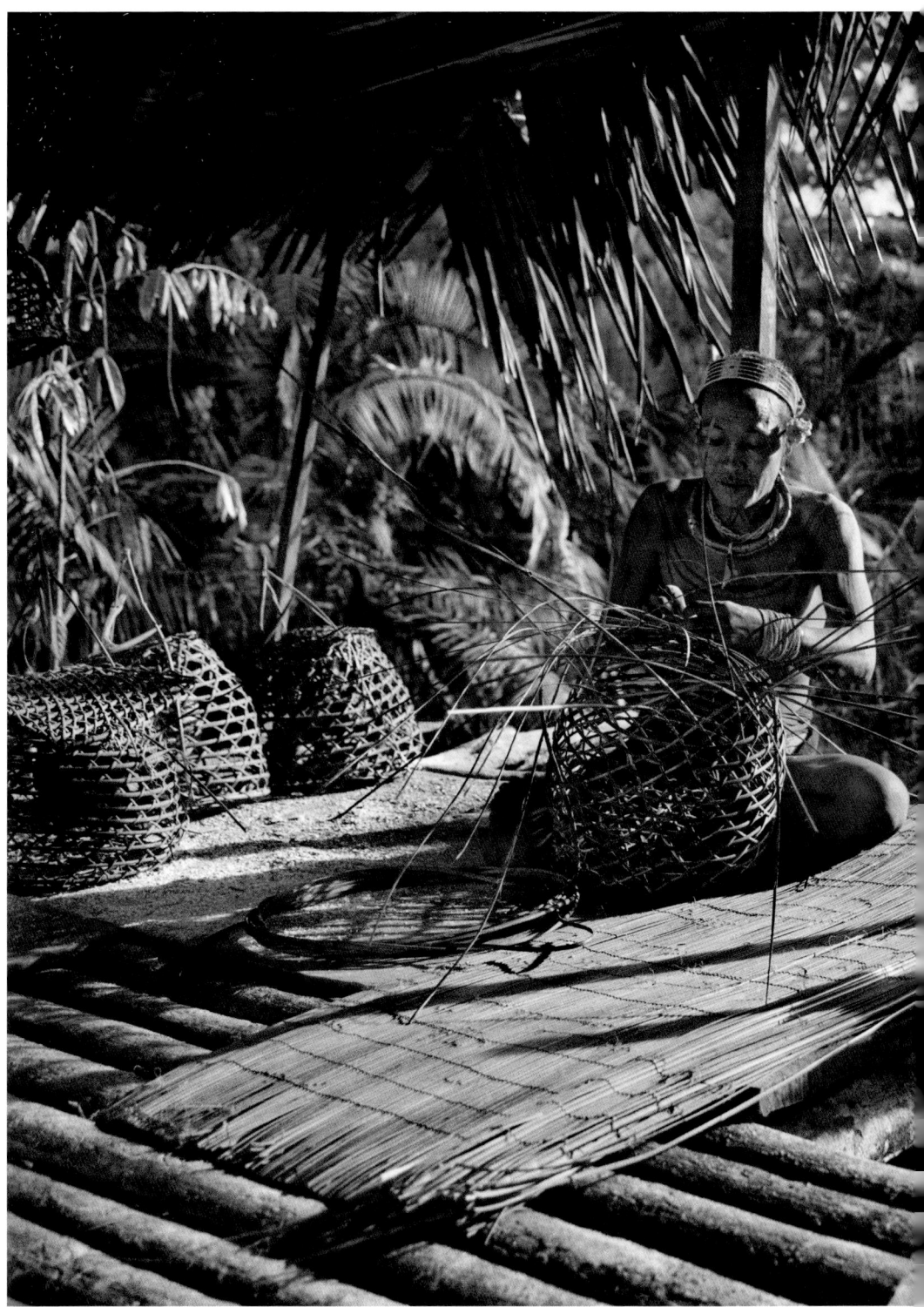

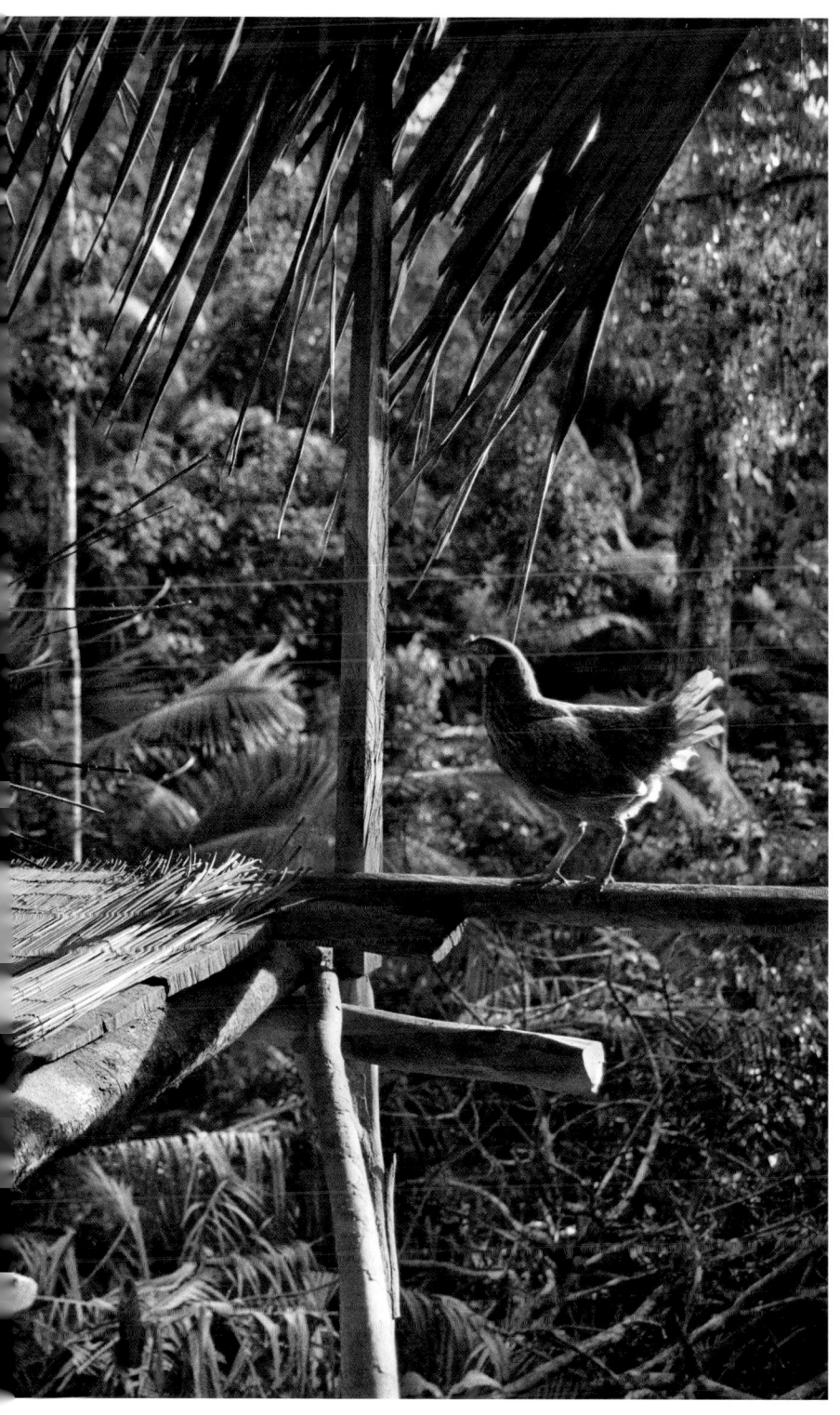

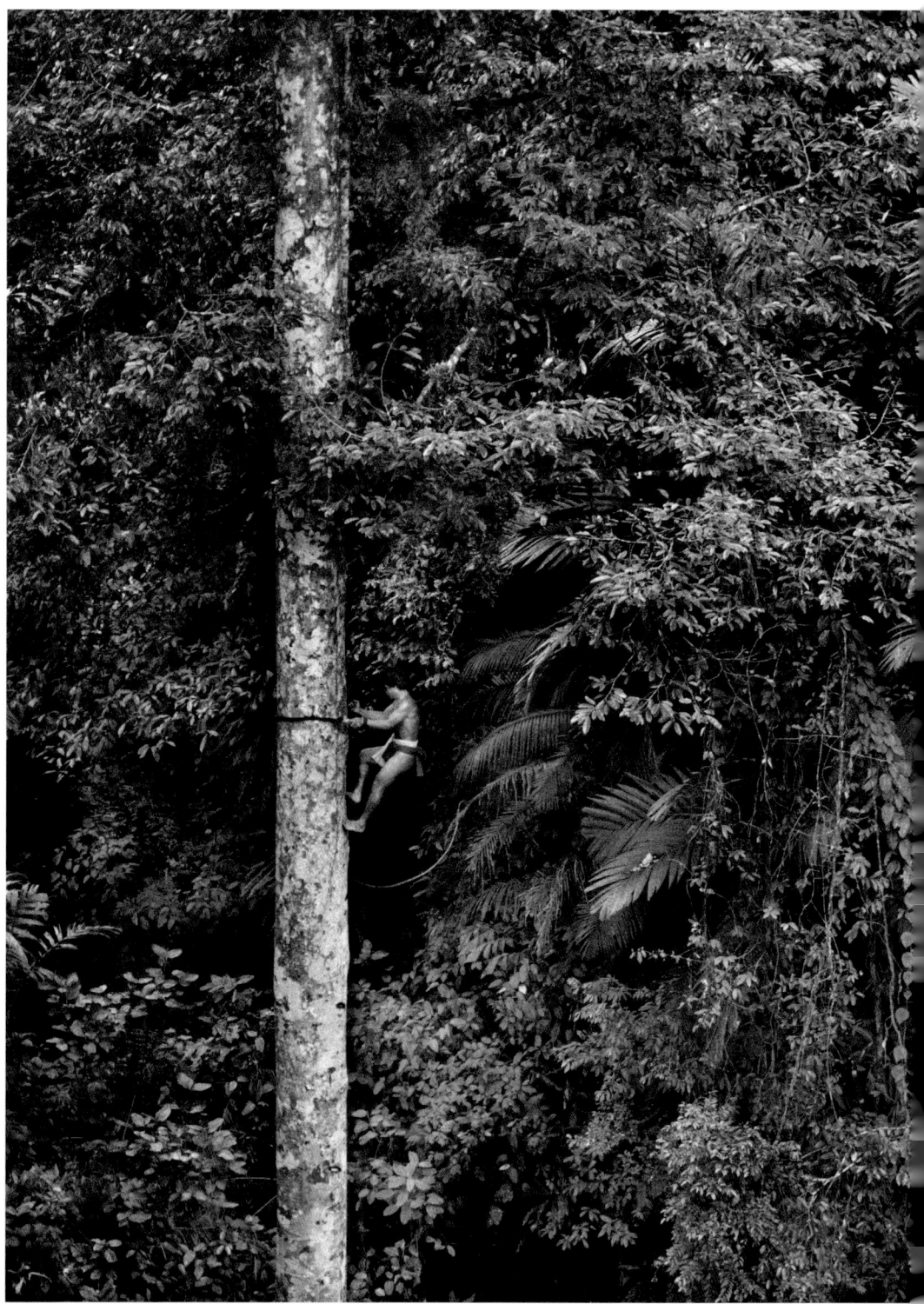

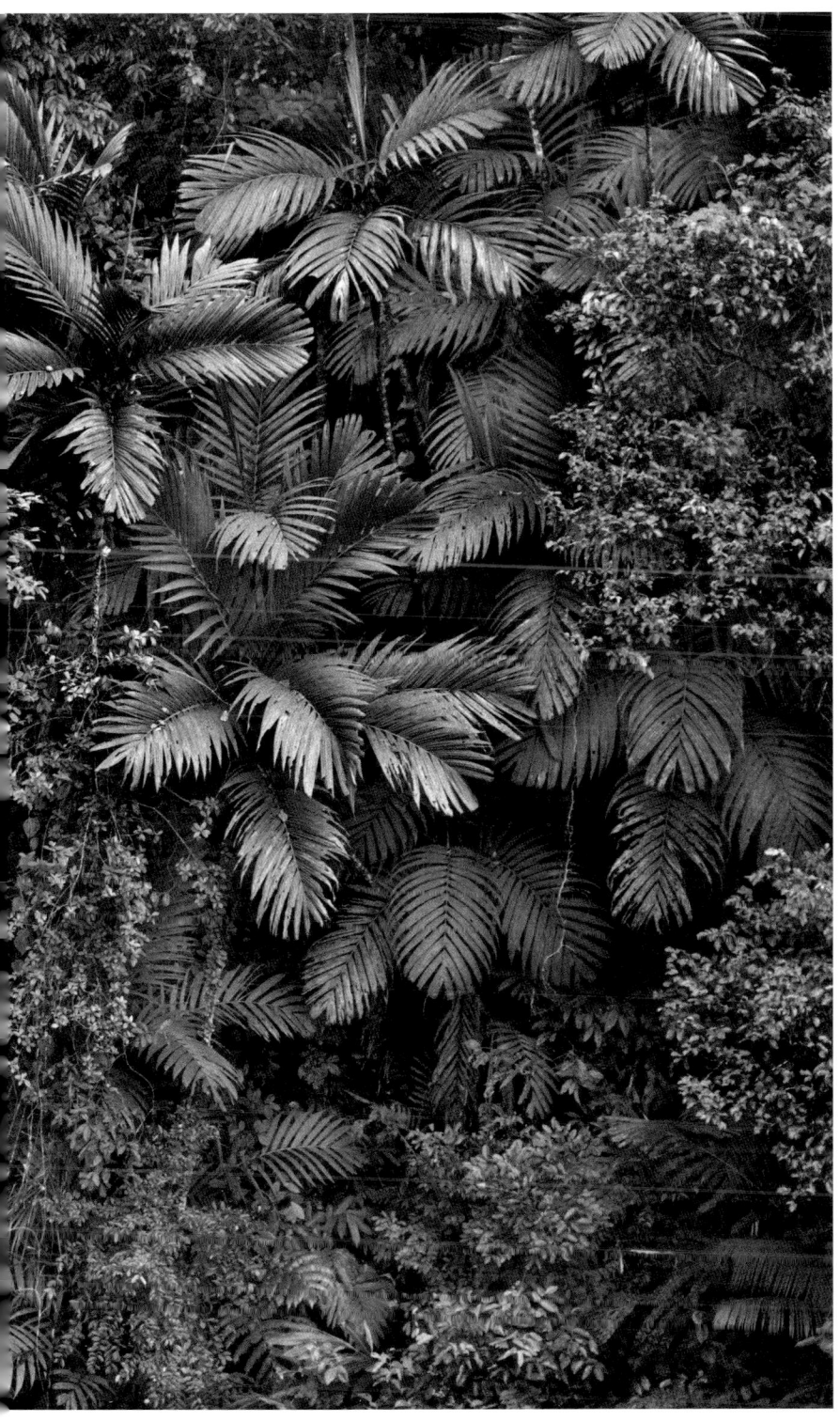

AFRICA

Since my first visit to Niger, in 1973, I have always felt a deep attachment to Africa. Even when assignments meant confronting crises of famine, drought or war, I jumped at the chance to return. With *Genesis*, however, I had an altogether happier experience—that of recording a seemingly eternal Africa, one of ancestral tribes, majestic landscapes and breathtaking wildlife. The continent may be vast and varied, yet its many ecosystems remain uniquely African.

The Sahara, which embraces ten countries and covers one-third of the entire continent, serves as an impressive gateway to Africa. Images of endless expanses of sand dunes may be familiar, yet every dust storm moves and reshapes their contours, much like a child playing in a giant sandbox. My trips to the deserts of southwest Libya and south-east Algeria were also full of surprises. I came across stunning oases and deep ravines where rivers once flowed. And we found evidence of human settlements dating back 16,000 years in rock art depicting the wildlife of the time, including elephants, rhinoceroses, antelopes, giraffes and crocodiles.

At the other end of the continent, the Namib Desert, said to be the world's oldest desert, covers much of Namibia, with sand dunes up to 990 feet (300 meters) high stretching along the entire coastline. Heading north into Damaraland, we tracked down rare black rhinoceros, but found them too threatening to photograph at close quarters. Even elephants have their moods, as we discovered the day an agitated male charged us. Still farther north, we came across the Himba, a large nomadic group of cattle and goat herders. The men wear few clothes, but the women cover themselves with a mixture of butter, ash and an ocher iron-ore powder that gives their skin a distinct reddish glow.

Cattle are a distinctive feature of many African savannas. For the Dinka of South Sudan, they are a symbol of wealth and power. In the rainy season, these seminomadic tribesmen grow maize, sorghum and other cereals, and set up cattle camps for their herds. This is the time when the Nile floods and creates small lakes, which become rich pastures during the dry season. The Dinka then lead their cattle for hundreds of miles along these feeding grounds and build little villages and corrals where the herds shelter at night. They also burn cow dung and spread the ash on their bodies and on their cattle as protection from insects. One tradition has not survived: because of frequent warfare in the region, automatic rifles have now replaced bows and arrows. The cattle-herding tribes of southern Ethiopia are more isolated. Usually naked, they decorate their bodies and hair for ceremonies, while many women wear ceramic plates in their lower lips.

Some traditional peoples have suffered at the hands of traders, missionaries and government officials. To make room for diamond miners, Botswana's government has driven the San people of the Kalahari Desert from their ancestral lands. We spent time in the Ghanzi District with a small, resettled community that keeps alive its age-old culture thanks to tourist groups. For a modest fee, they demonstrate how they hunt small animals, draw water from sand through a straw and make fire by rubbing sticks. But, unable to return home, growing numbers of San people now live in poverty in urban areas.

We came across hardier traditions during a 55-day long hike across northern Ethiopia. We set off from Lalibela, an ancient Christian town famous for its churches carved out of red volcanic rock in the 12th century. On the mountain of Abune Yosef, 14,0000 feet (4,200 meters) above sea-level, Christian services are held in cave churches built into hillsides, while centuries-old Bibles written on animal skins are still in use. These mountain people are skilled farmers, growing grains on ancient terraces and raising dairy cattle on high slopes. Beyond them lay the region long inhabited by Ethiopian Jews, the Falusha, although most have now migrated to Israel. Finally, in the Simien National Park, we found species I had never seen before, including the gelada baboon, the simien fox and the walia ibex.

Even on a continent synonymous with wildlife, perhaps no African animal is viewed with greater awe than the mountain gorilla. Only some 800 survive in a small area straddling Congo, Uganda and Rwanda. Three groups live on the forested slopes of Virunga Volcanoes National Park, a safe distance from the park's two lava-spewing volcanoes. I came close enough to several family groups to identify the dominant males by the silver fur on their back. These gentle animals, some weighing up to 550 pounds (250 kilos), pay little attention to humans and spend most of their time looking after their families and feeding themselves.

For sheer variety of wildlife, few places match the Okavango Delta in Botswana, where the Okavango River—"the river that never finds the sea"—literally spills its water onto the land. When the delta floods and vegetation blooms, it draws some 400 species of birds as well as the great beasts of Africa, from elephants, hippopotamuses, rhinoceroses and buffalos to lions, leopards, cheetahs, zebras and hyenas. Later, in Zambia, we saw the same spectacular display from the quiet of a balloon. And here, nature barely noticed we were watching.

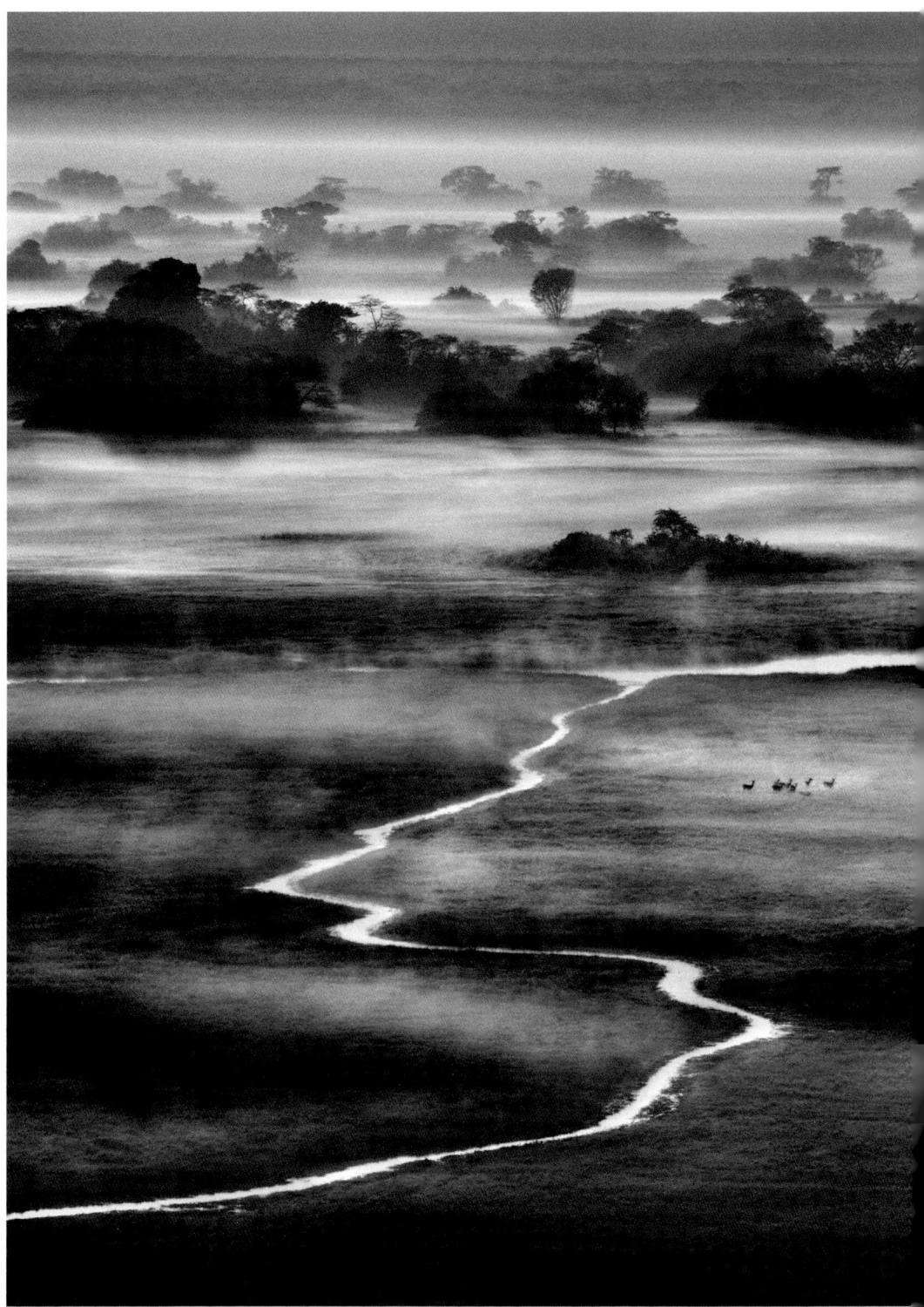

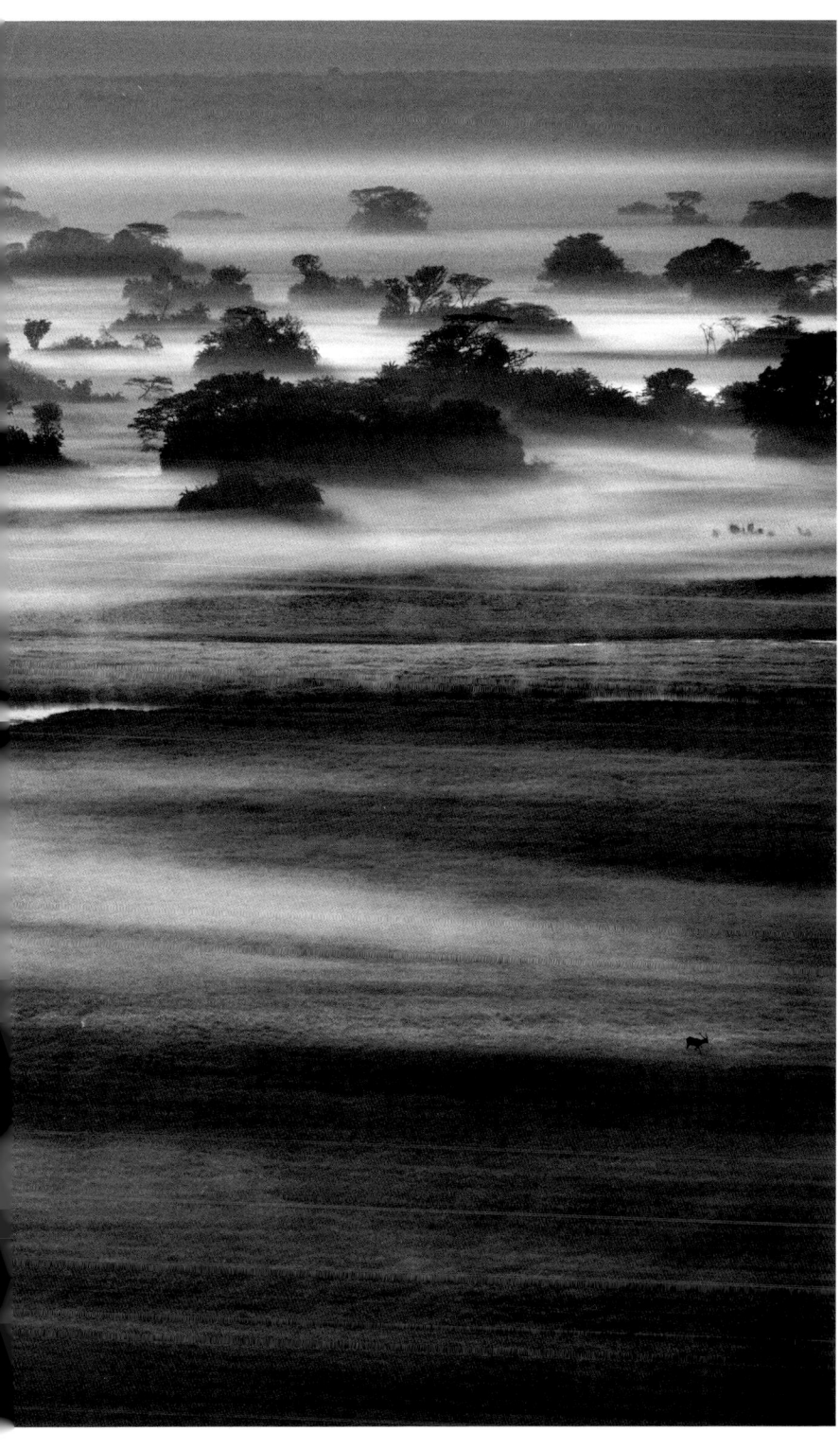

Pages 216/217 Nights can be chilly during the Zambian winter. At dawn, the water in lakes and small rivers, still warm from the previous day's sun, vaporizes and condenses to form strange and beautiful fog banks. Seen here from a balloon in the Kafue National Park, Zambia, at 5:30 a.m. July and August 2010.

Opposite At first impression, the Sahara seems lifeless. With golden sand dunes stretching as far as the eye can see, it suggests a hostile landscape unchanged since time immemorial. Yet this desert has had many lives. In fact, during my travels, it is one of the places where I felt closest to the distant past of wildlife and humanity. The Sahara experienced its most recent major transformation some 10,000 to 20,000 years ago, when the last Ice Age brought rain, rivers and lakes as well as animals and vegetation to most of North Africa. And where there is sand and rock today, savannah-like conditions once sustained human settlements. Proof of this is rock art dating back some 10,000 years, which depicts buffalos, elephants, rhinoceroses, ostriches, antelopes, giraffes and crocodiles. Northwest area of Djanet, Algeria. January and February 2009.

Pages 220/221 View of the inside of the crater of Nyiragongo at the moment of an explosion at the level of the lava lake, 2,600 feet (800 meters) below.

The Virunga region is defined by eight volcanoes, ranging in age between 100,000 and 500,000 years and rising to heights of 14,800 feet (4,500 meters). They stand as an imposing barrier across the western branch of the great African Rift Valley.

Two of these volcanoes, both located in Congo, are still active. In January 2002, the Nyiragongo destroyed a large part of the town of Goma, on the shores of Lake Kivu. The other, the Nyamulagira, erupted in May 2004. Democratic Republic of Congo. May and June 2004.

Pages 222/223 Fiery lava flows out of the crater through an underground break. The surrounding lava fields are fresh, with a temperature inside the lava flow of 2,300° Fahrenheit (1,260° Celsius), too hot to approach at close quarters. Flowing at a high speed, the lava resembles a furious orange river. Volcanic eruption of Mount Nyamulagira in May 2004. Democratic Republic of Congo. May and June 2004.

Pages 224/225 The lake in the crater of the 12,200-foot (3,711-meter)-high Bisoke volcano straddles the border between Rwanda and the Democratic Republic of Congo. Giant senecio plants (*Dendrosenecio erici-rosenii*), visible in the foreground, cover almost the entire top of this mountain. Rwanda. May and June 2004.

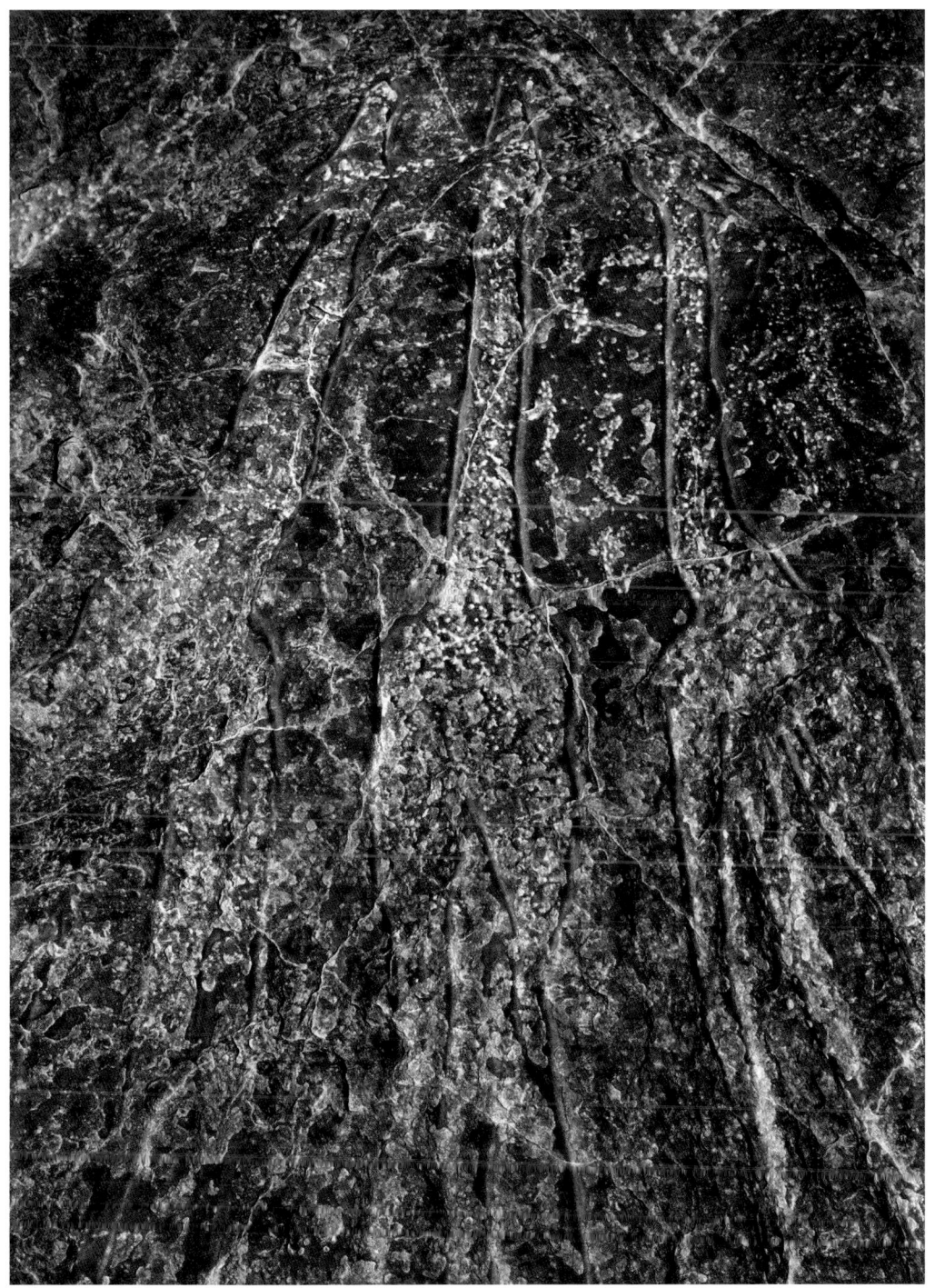

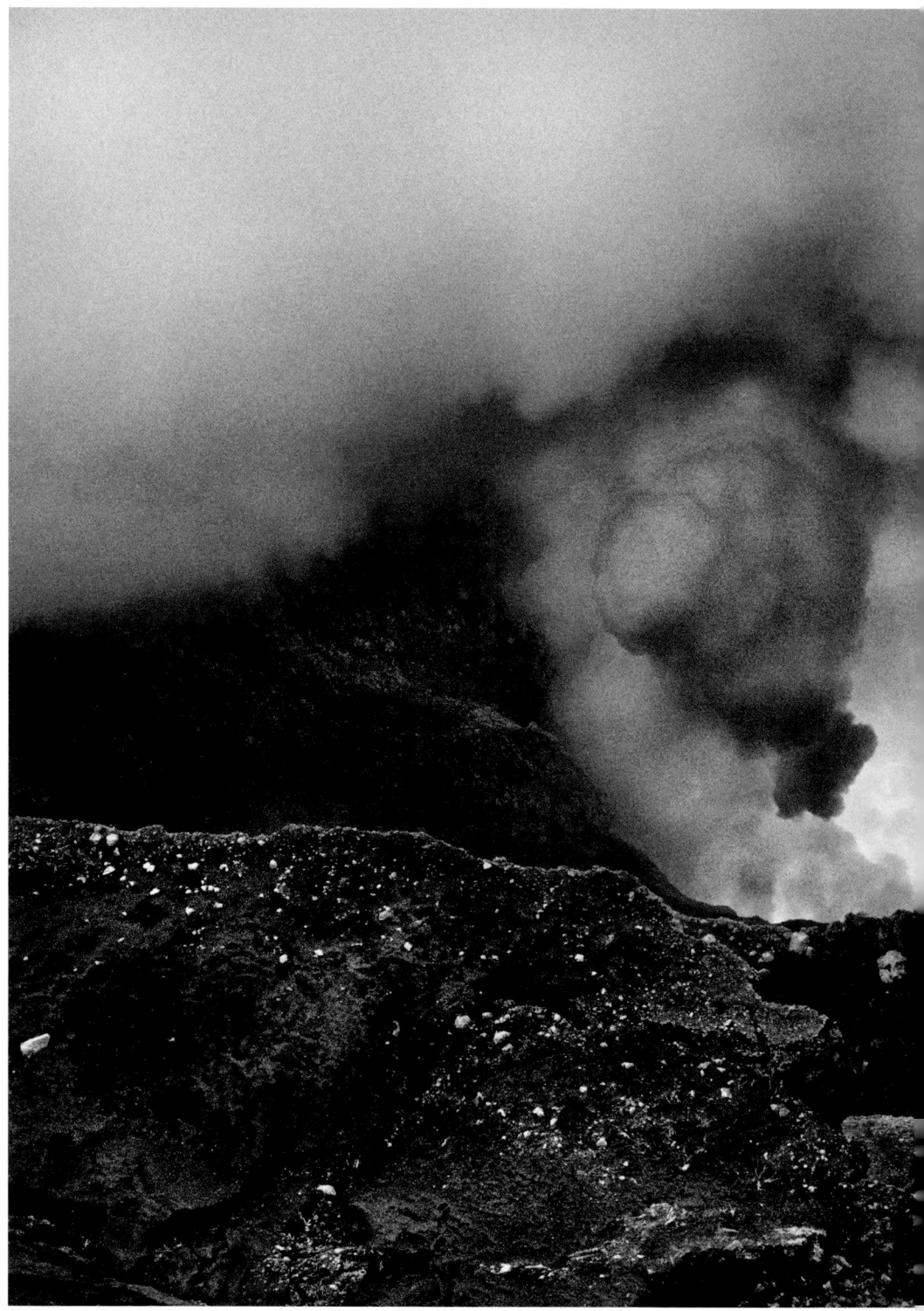

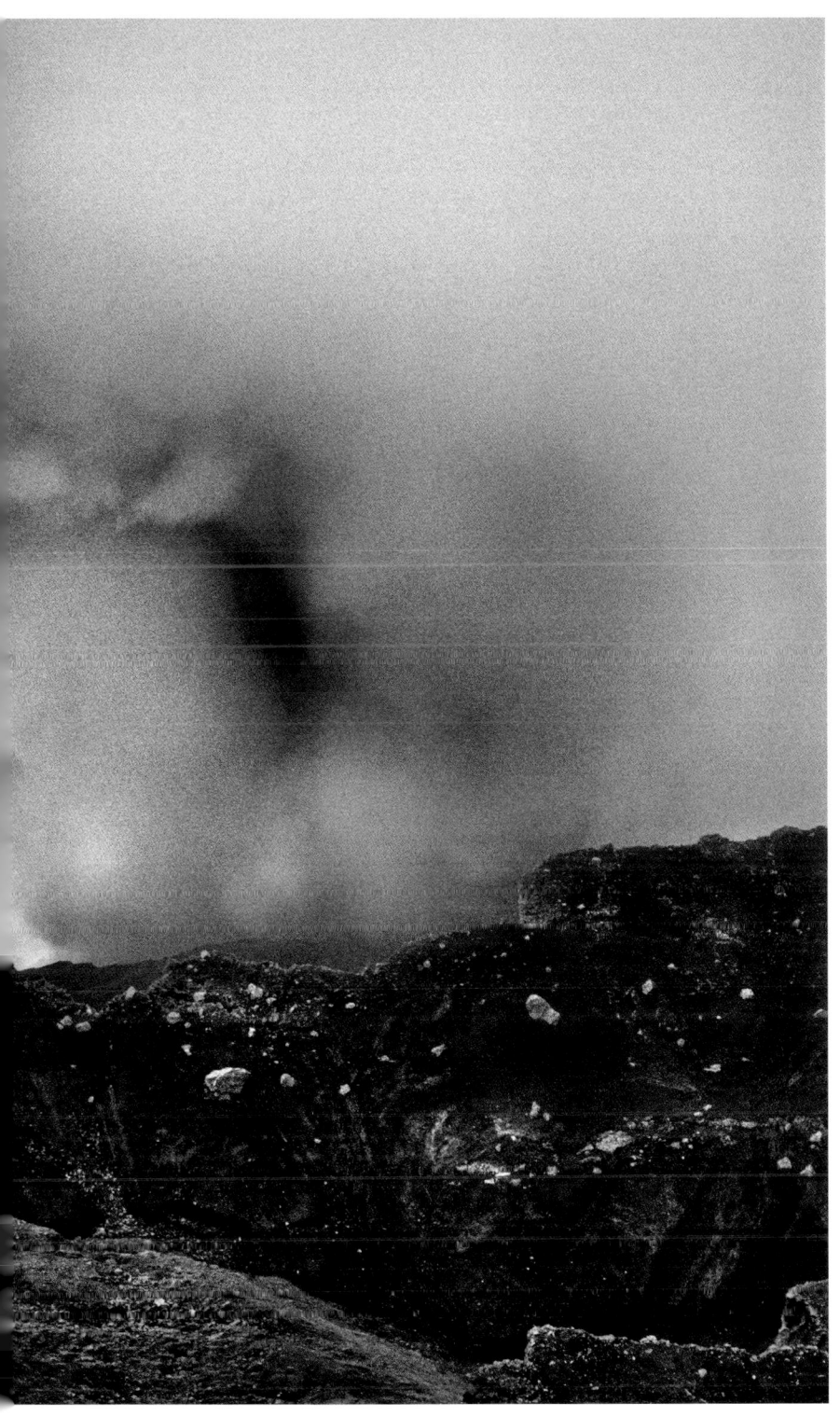

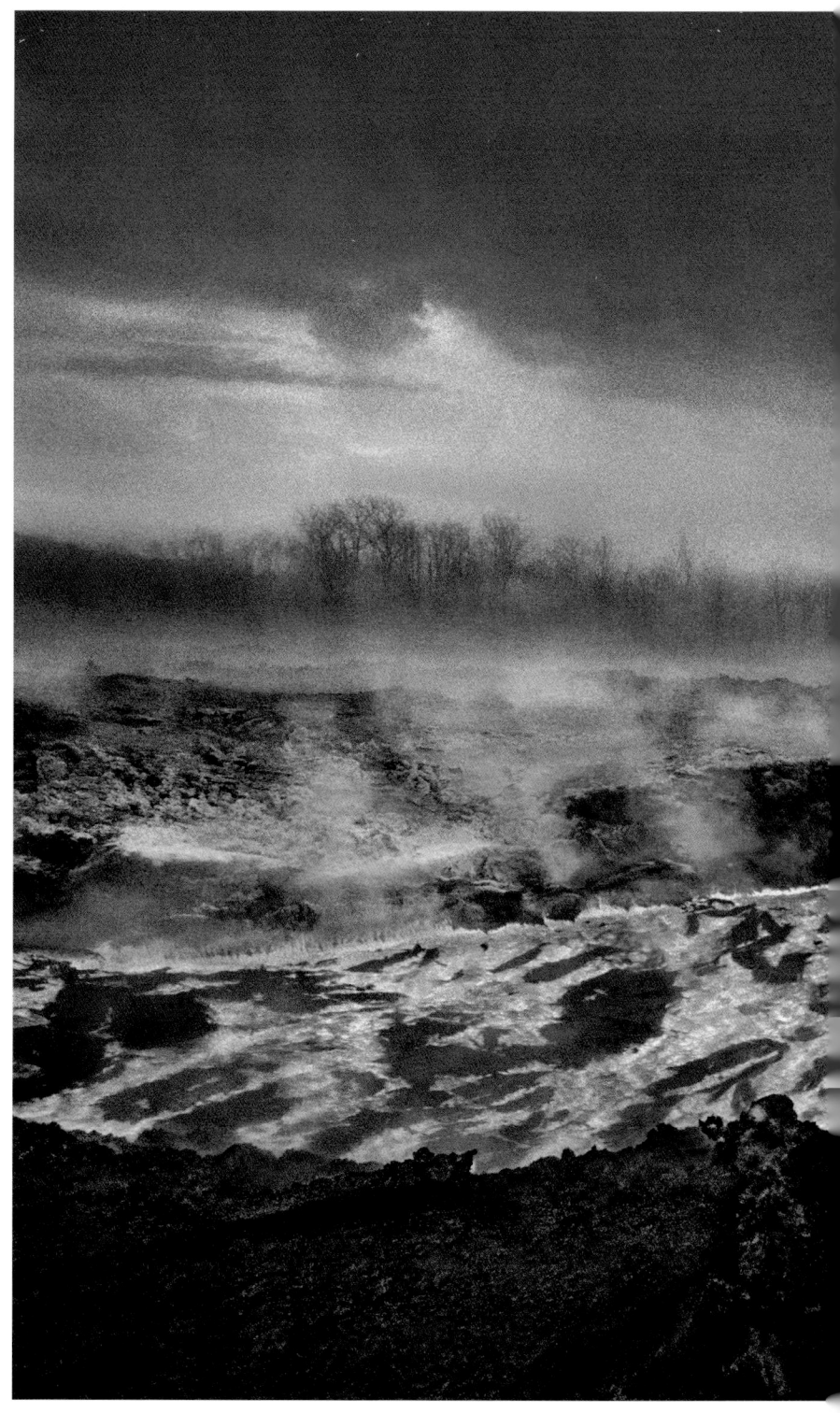

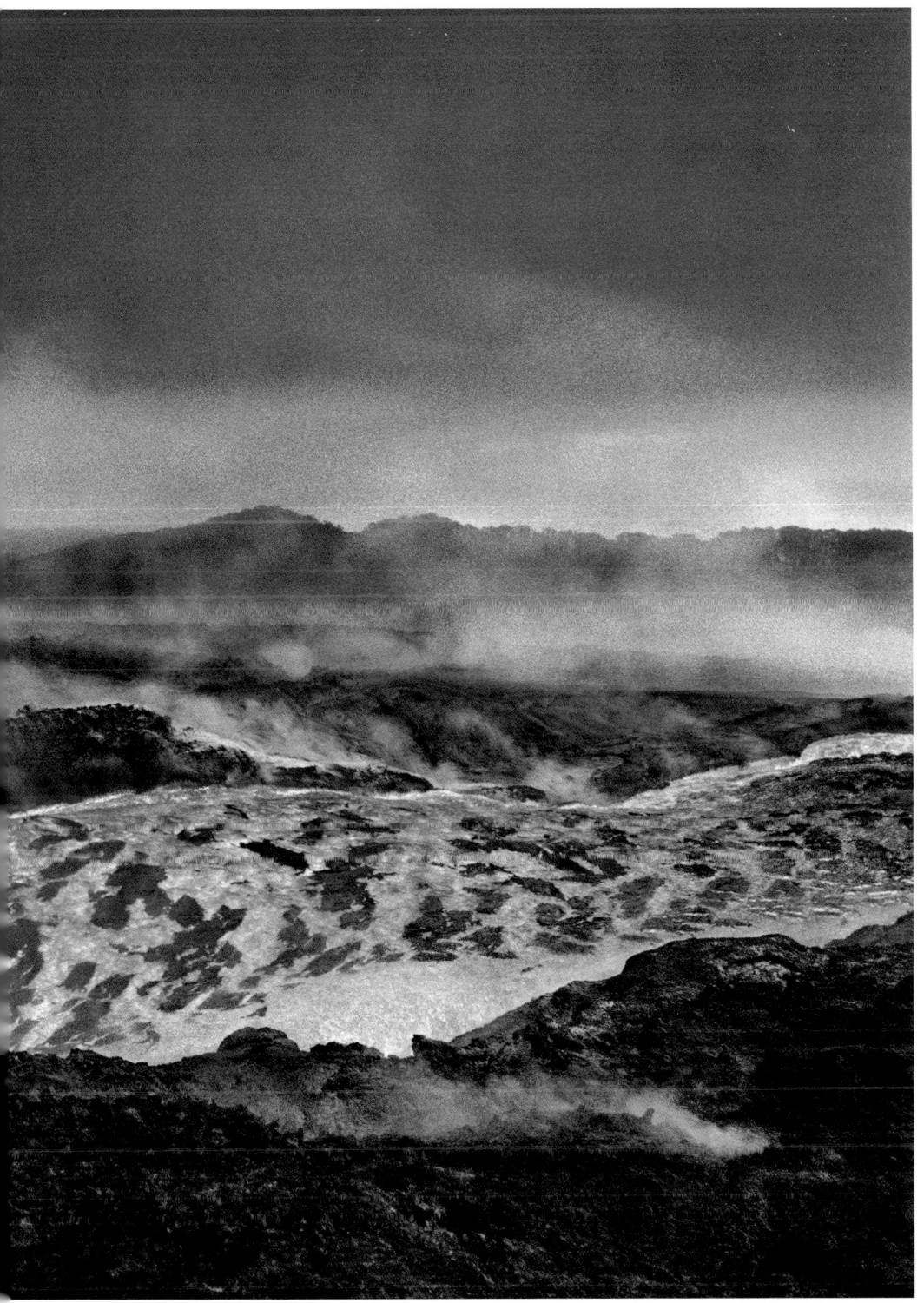

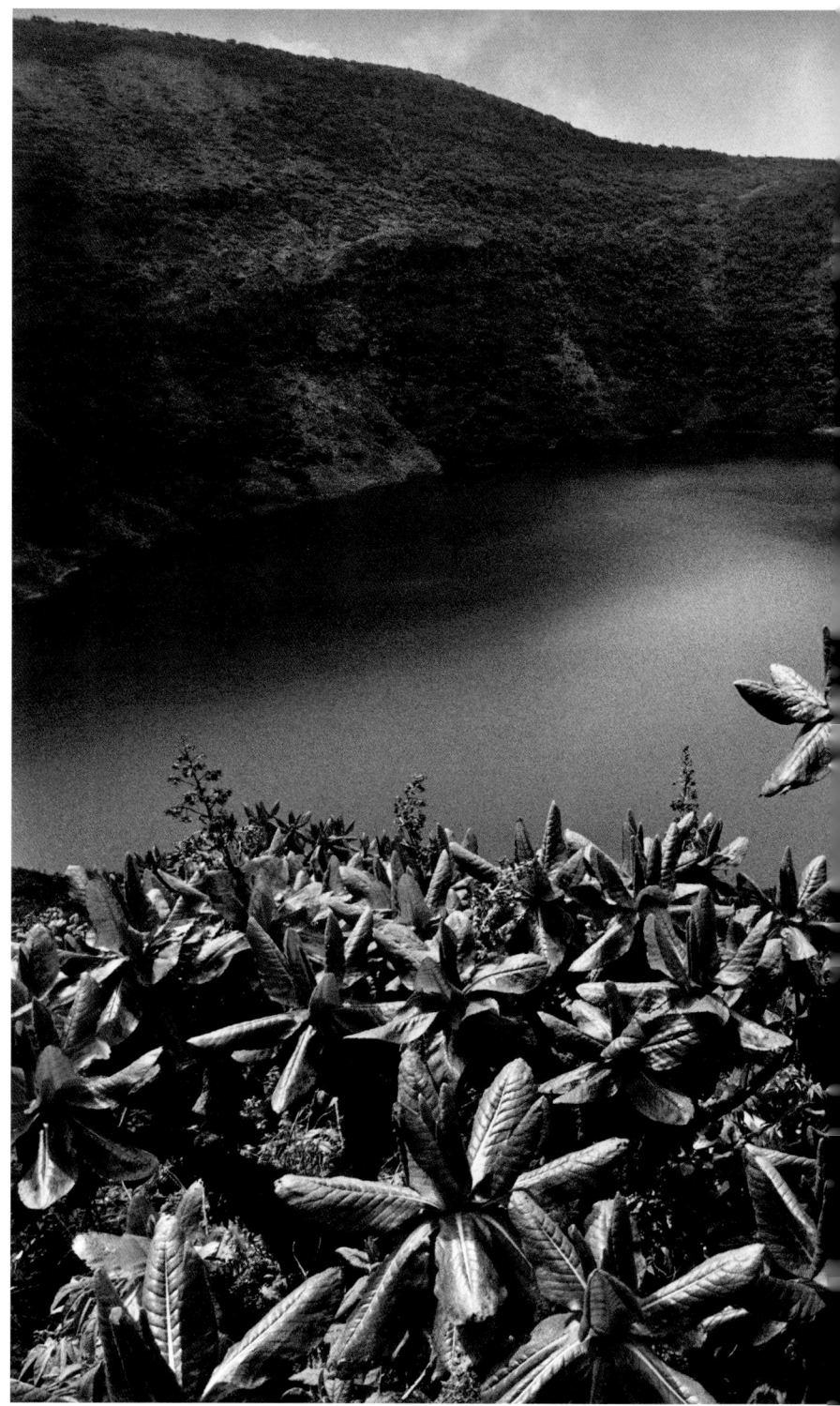

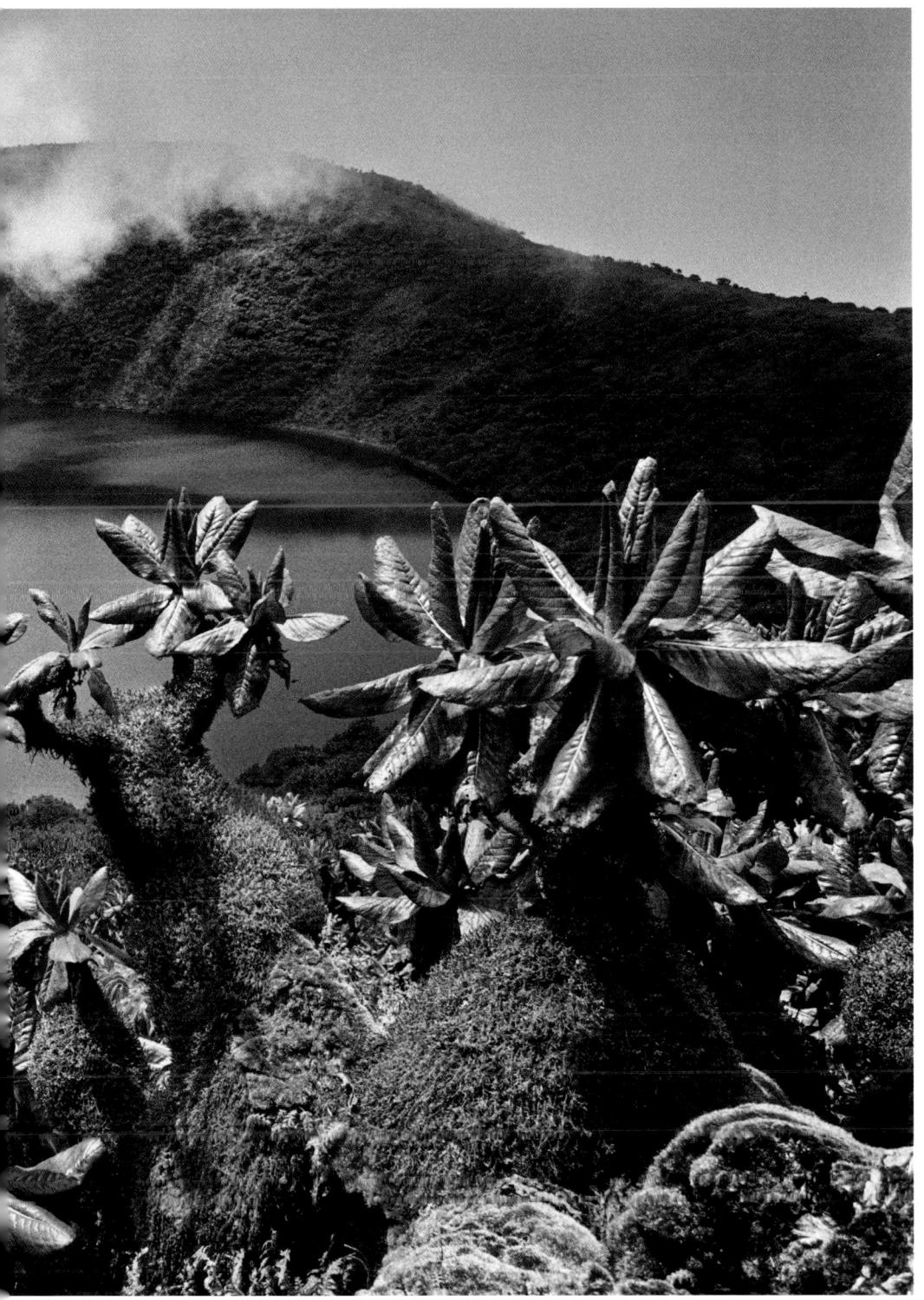

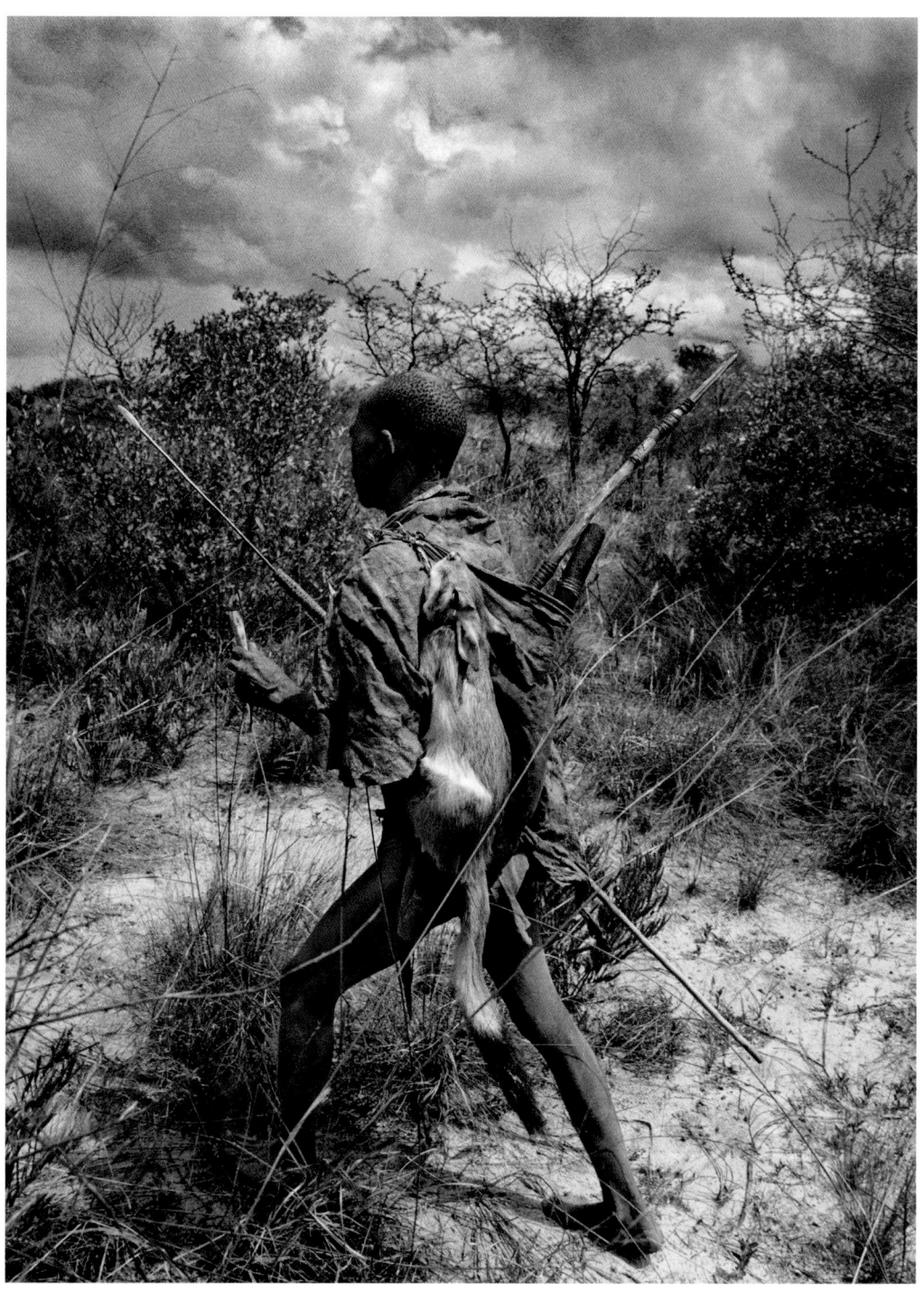

THE SAN PEOPLE

Pages 226 through 235

The Kalahari Desert in Botswana may look arid and hostile, but it is paradise to the San people (or Bushmen or Bochimans), among the earliest inhabitants of Africa. Over a period of 40,000 years, they have proven to be masters of survival. With its vast horizons, the Kalahari presents spectacular daytime cloud formations, particularly during the rainy season. And at night, the sky glitters with the most fabulous constellations, all of which have a name in the San language.

Unfortunately this immense natural cradle, home to one of just 14 "ancestral population clusters" from which modern man evolved, is no longer the exclusive territory of the San people. In several waves of evictions, from 1997 through 2002, Botswana's government has driven them from their ancestral land into overcrowded resettlement camps. These are truly sad places. Since there is almost no nearby wildlife, they are dependent on the government for food and water. Cut off from meaningful lives, San men grow depressed through tedium. The Botswana government claims that they moved the San in order to bring them development. The San are not persuaded. Why was development not brought to them where they had always lived? San lawyers have challenged their eviction, but so far, no court has authorized their return. In the meantime, the San people need permission just to enter their former game reserves and, even then, they risk detention and torture.

The reality is that the government wanted to clear them out of the way so that Kalahari's important diamond reserves could be exploited without the bother of having to negotiate with traditional San communities.

Nonetheless, a few small San groups still maintain their traditional way of life: encouraged by some nonprofit groups, several large, privately owned farms have allowed the San people to resume their hunter-gatherer practices; in exchange, the San people invite outsiders to observe how they hunt, build fires, cook and construct their huts.

These photos were taken during time spent with some 20 San men in the region of Ghanzi, Botswana, on the land of Trail Blazer Farm. They show how, despite the loss of their land, with their culture intact, they are ready to pick up where they left off in their beloved Kalahari.

Opposite A hunter carrying a native hare, a springhaas (*Pedetes capensis*). To capture his prey, the San people introduced a long stick into the hole where the hare was hiding; while the animal was pinned down by the stick, a large hole was dug around it until it could be pulled from its refuge. Botswana, January 2008.

Pages 228/229 A hunter is shown holding a korhaan (*Eupodotis melanogaster*), a bird native to southern Africa. It can be captured relatively easily by using its own eggs as bait and a snare made of twigs. A thin string is woven from palm tree fiber and, when the korhaan tries to take the egg with its beak, its neck gets trapped in the noose. Botswana, January 2008.

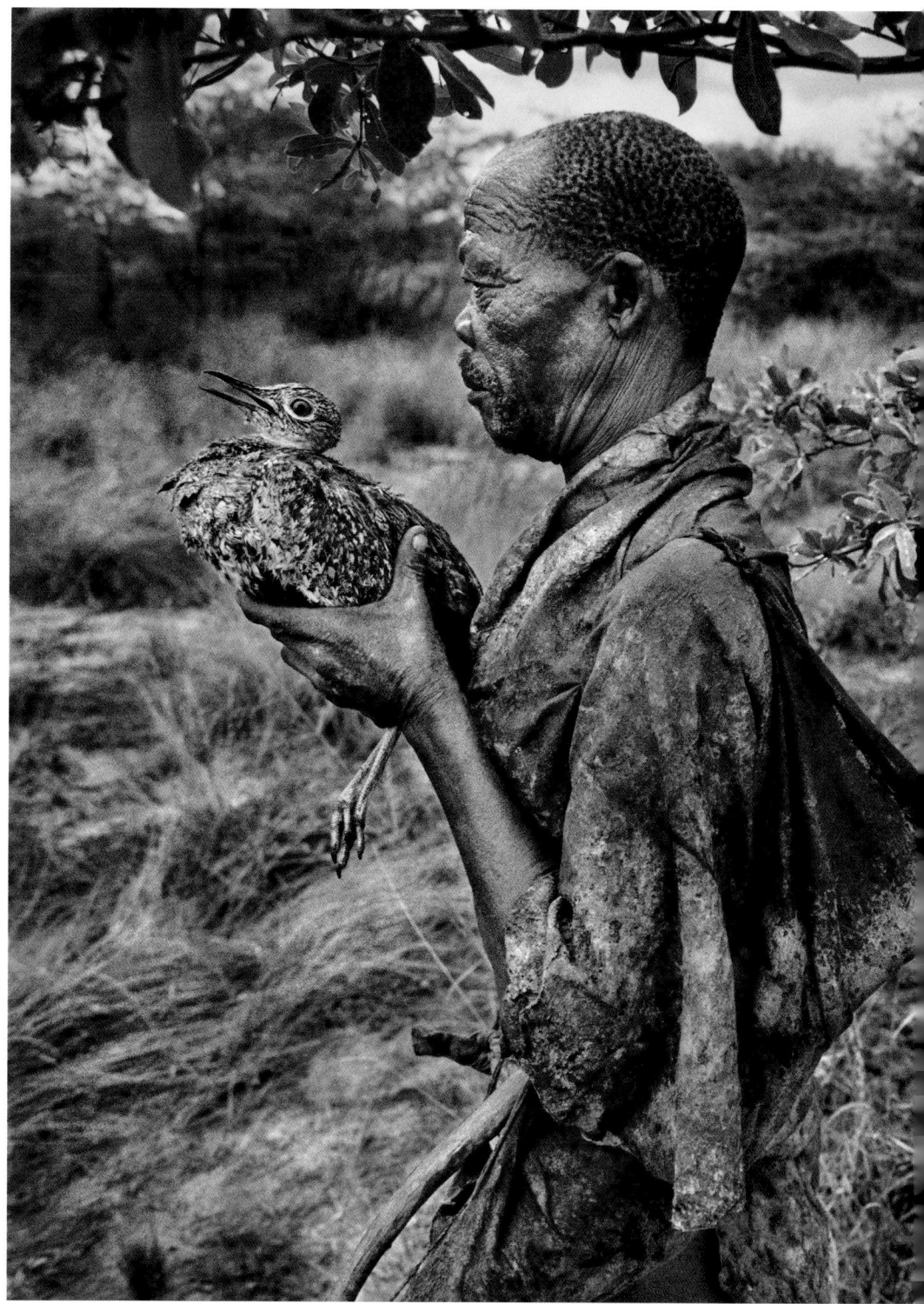

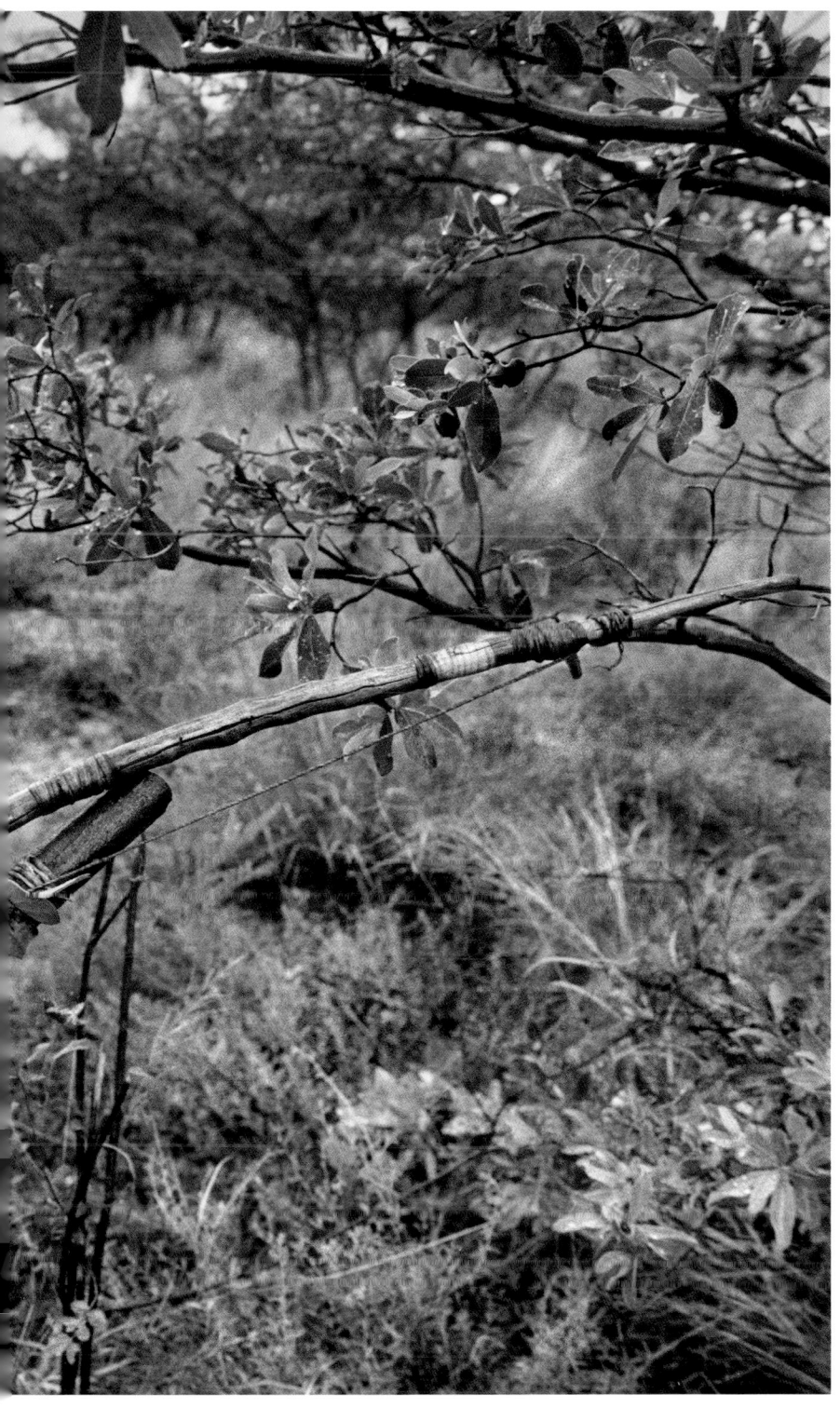

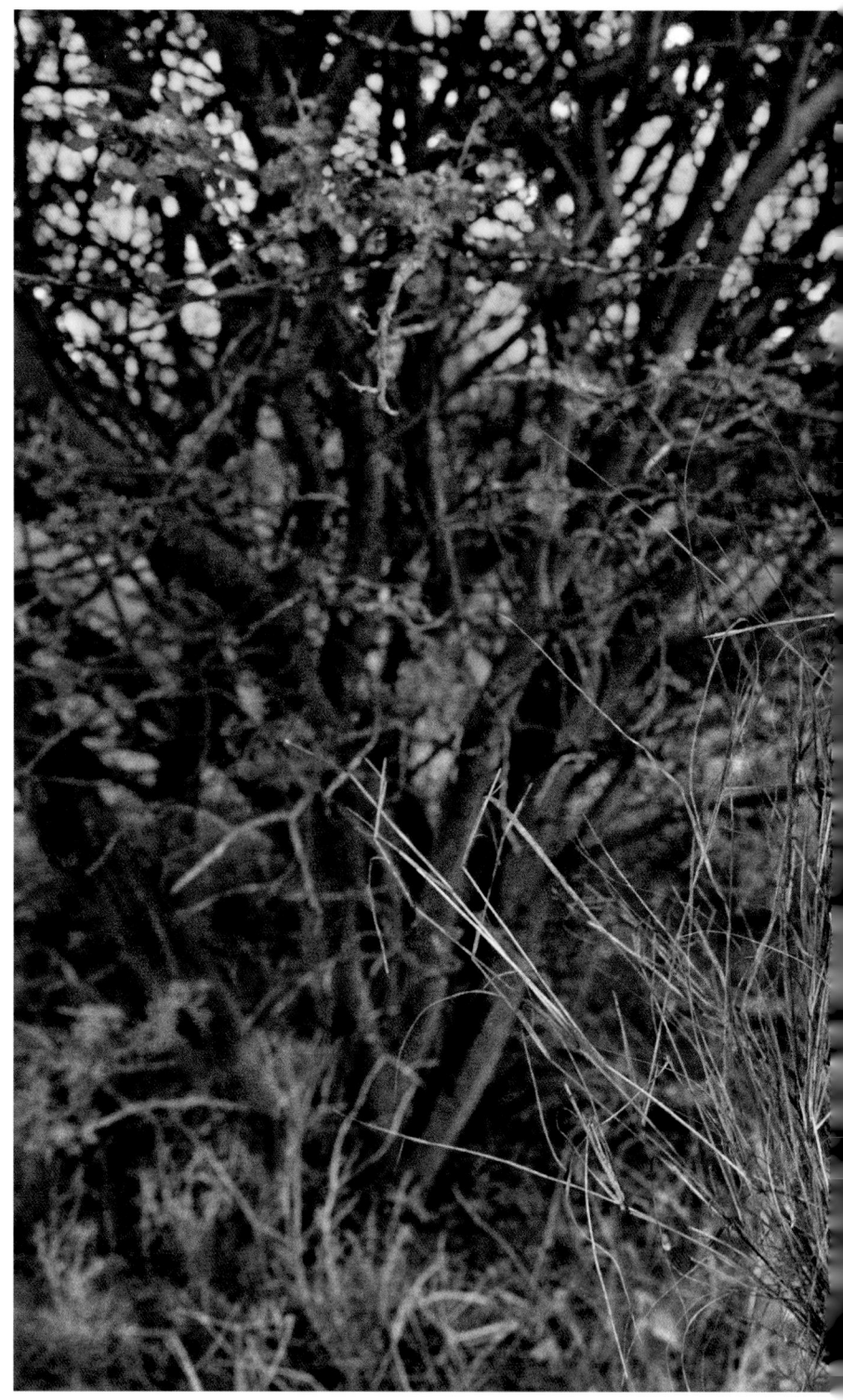

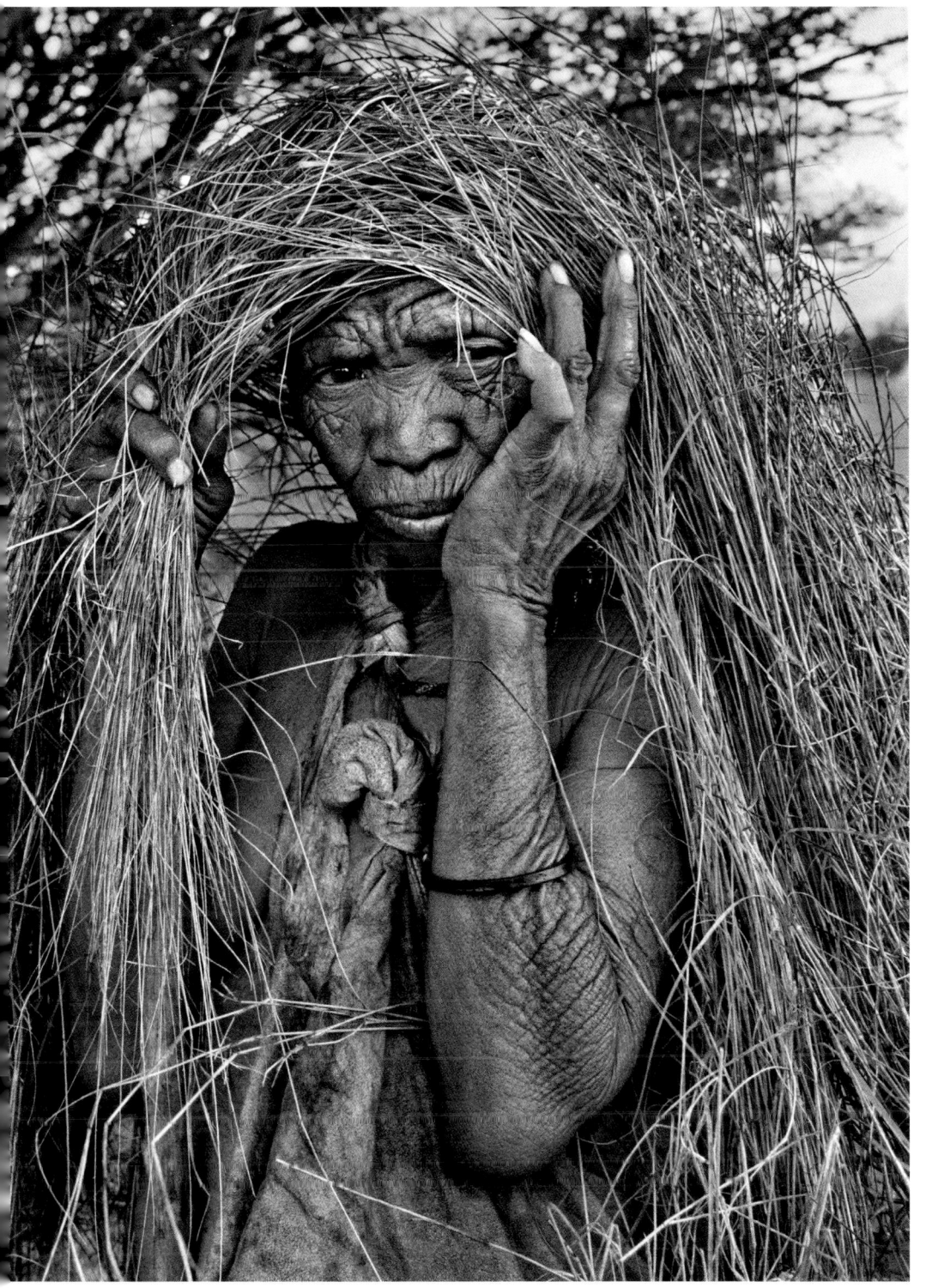

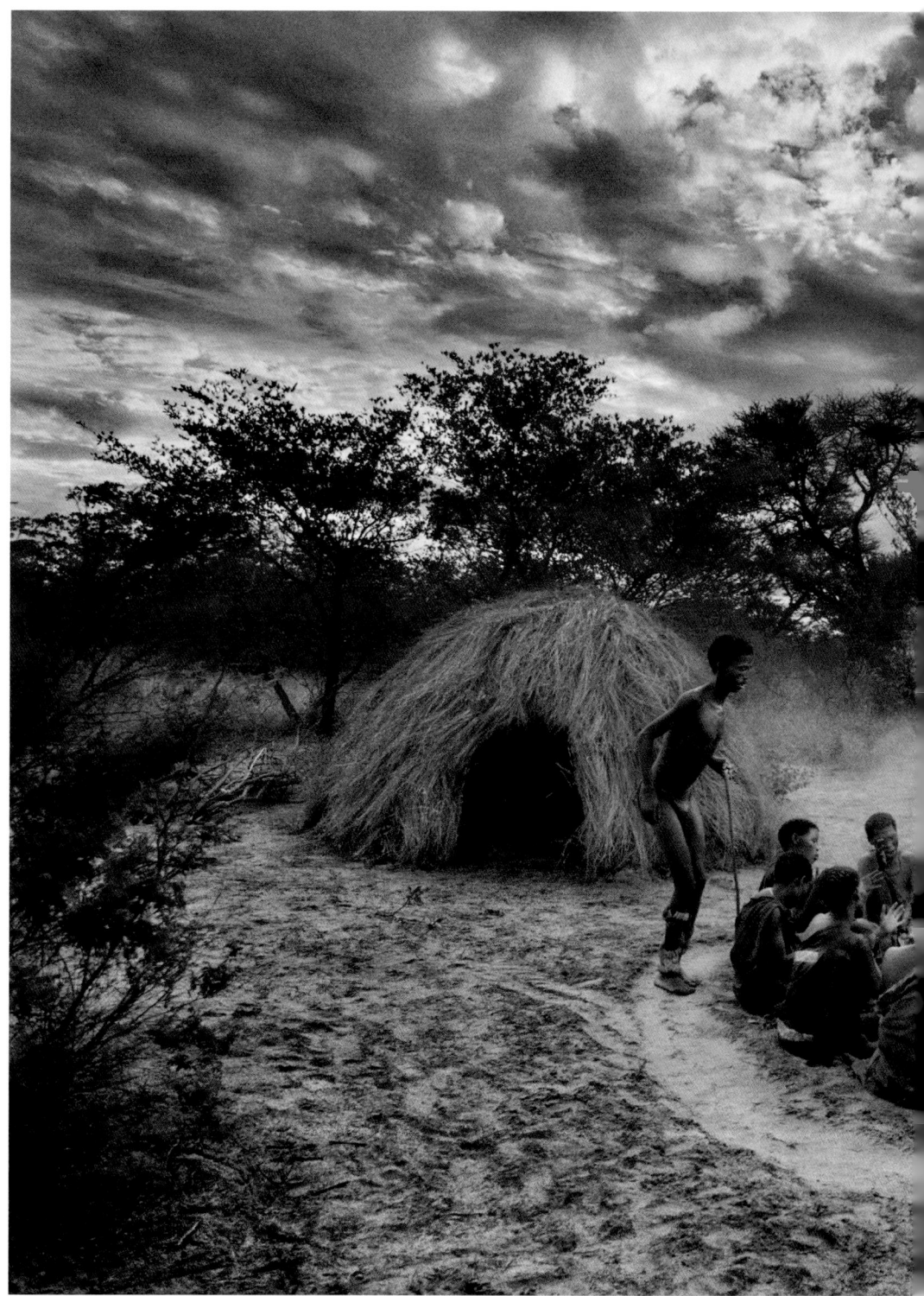

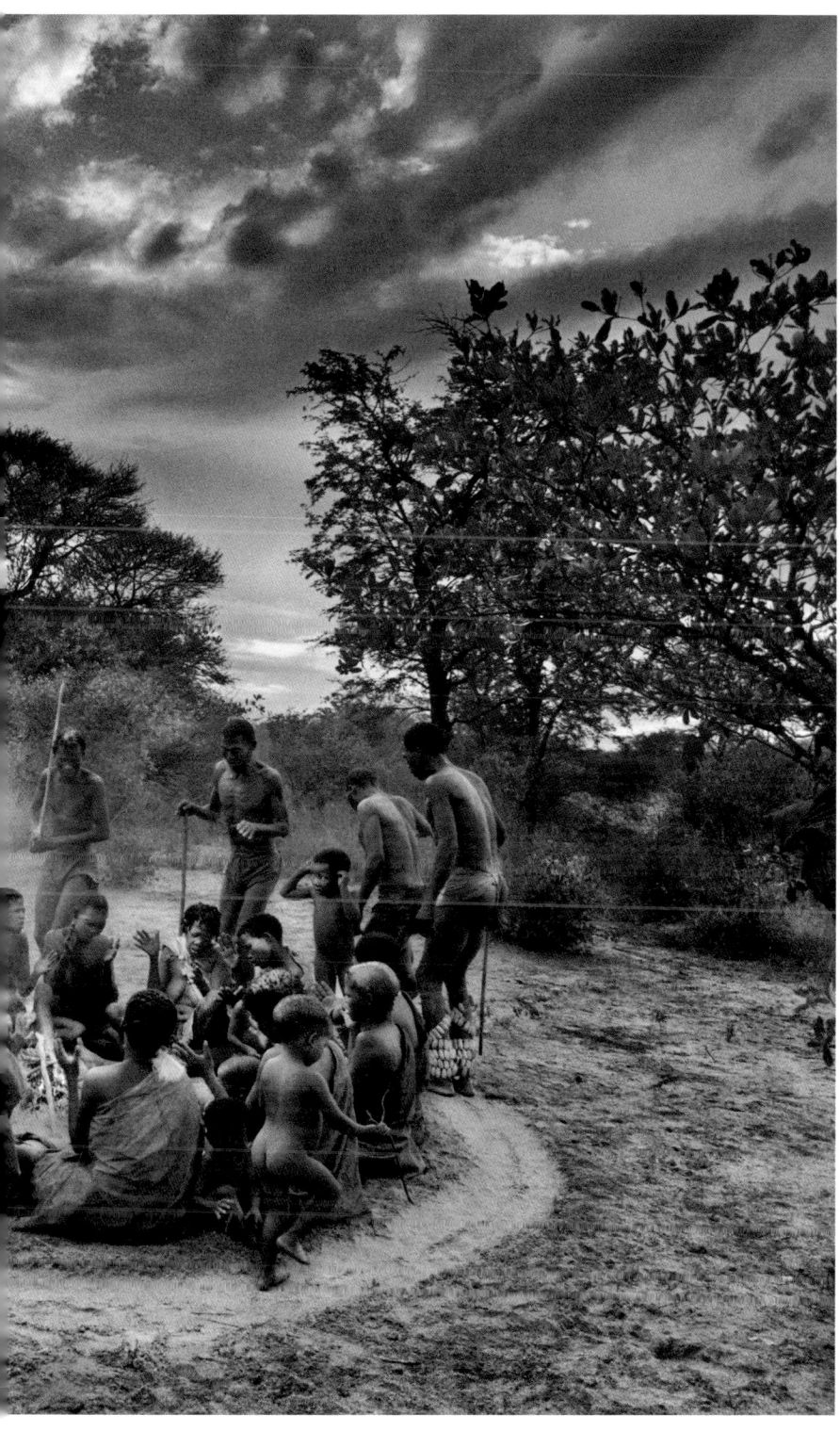

Pages 230/231 The ability of the San people to respond quickly and efficiently to the elements is impressive. For instance, in light rain, they cover themselves with grass. But when the rain is heavy, they build a hut within a few seconds, using whatever is within reach, whether leaves, grass or branches. Conversely, as protection against the fierce sun, they cover themselves with large leaves. Botswana. January 2008.

Pages 232/233 The healing or trance dance is the San's most important mystical ritual. As the women sing and clap in rhythm, the men dance in a circle around them. During this dance, medicine men lay their hands on everyone present to draw out the "arrows of sickness." Dried seed pods are filled with small stones and, when tied to the legs of medicine men, rattle loudly as they dance. The frenzy of their trance, the San people believe, marks their entry into the world of spirits. Botswana. January 2008.

Opposite The Kalahari Desert in Botswana may look arid and hostile, but it is paradise to the San people (or Bushmen or Bochimans), among the earliest inhabitants of Africa. Botswana. January 2008.

Pages 236/237 The Erg Ubari is a vast expanse of sand dunes covering about 31,000 square miles (80,000 square kilometers). It has no fresh water, but it contains a number of salt lakes concentrated in an area known in Arabic as the "Ramla d'El Daouda," meaning the Dune of the Worm-Eaters. There are more than 20 of these lakes, although most have dried up after intense extraction of underground water for new agricultural projects. Libya. January and February 2009.

Pages 238/239 Sand dunes in Ili Dama, Tadrart. South of Djanet, Algeria. January and February 2009.

Pages 240/241 Large sand dunes in Maor, Tadrart. South of Djanet, Algeria. January and February 2009.

Pages 242/243 Baboon (*Papio hamadryas ursinus*). This species of baboon is found across the Namib Desert, although it is most populous in central and northern regions. This photograph was taken in dunes beside the Kunene River, which marks Namibia's border with Angola. Namibia. October and November 2005.

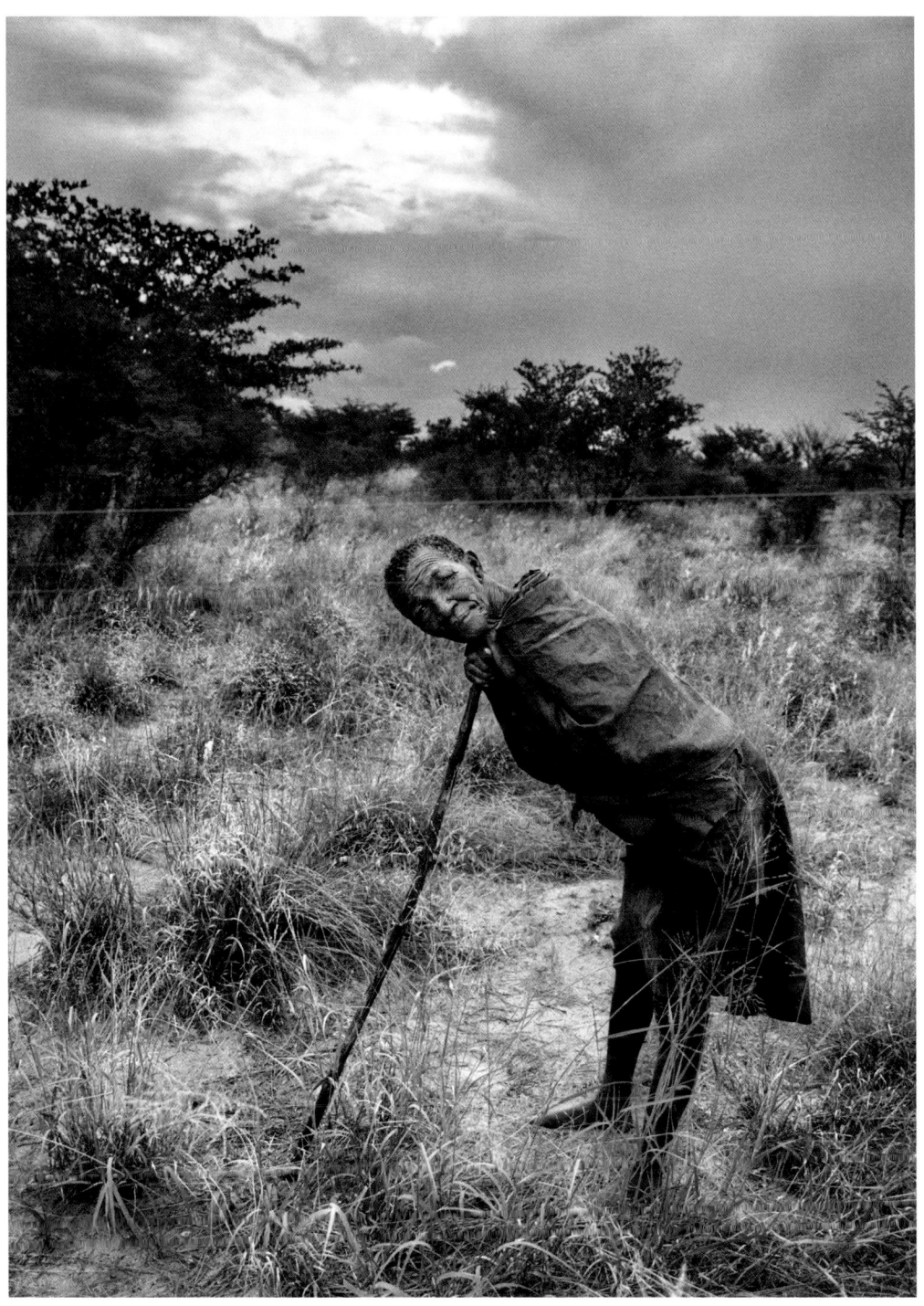

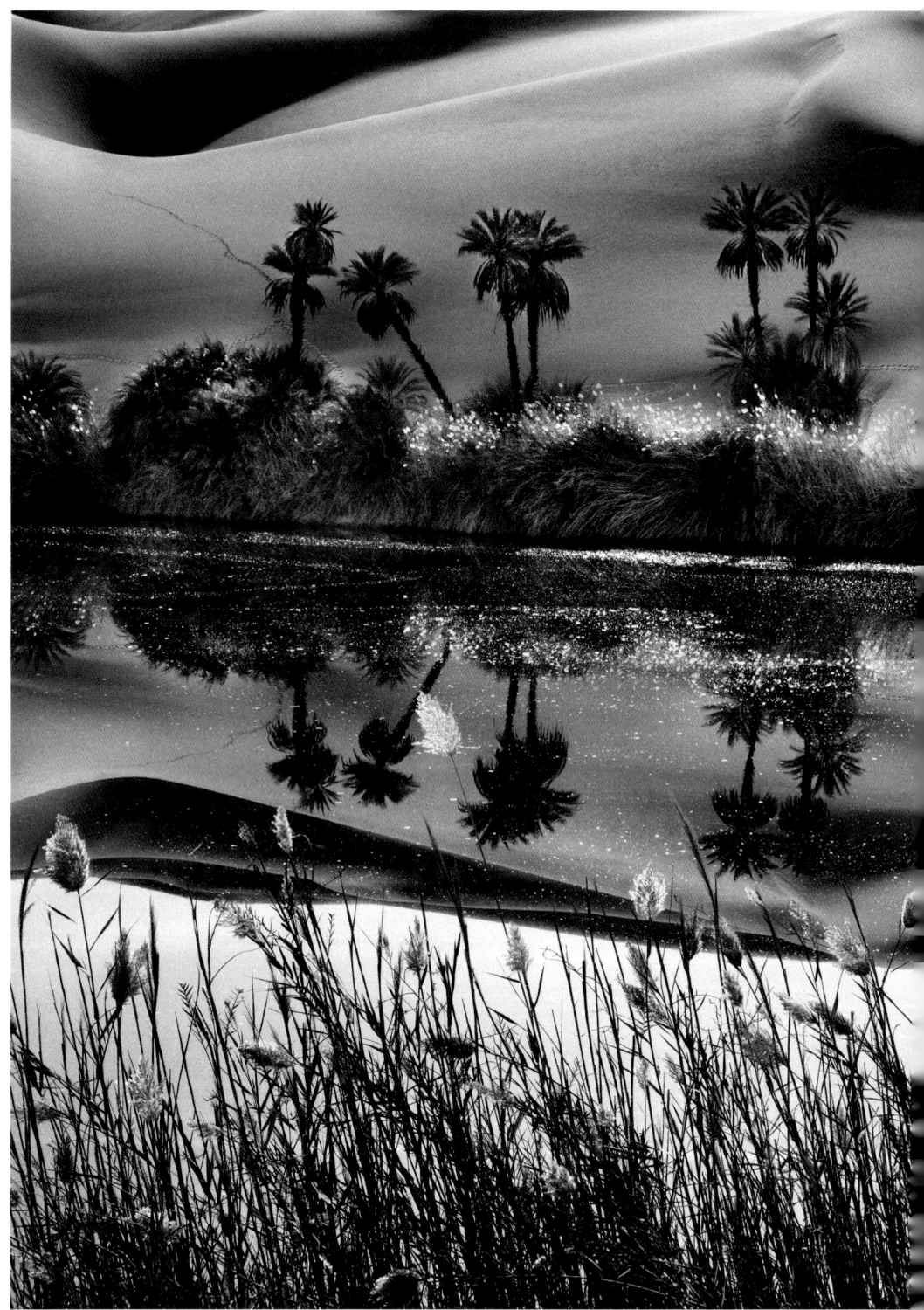

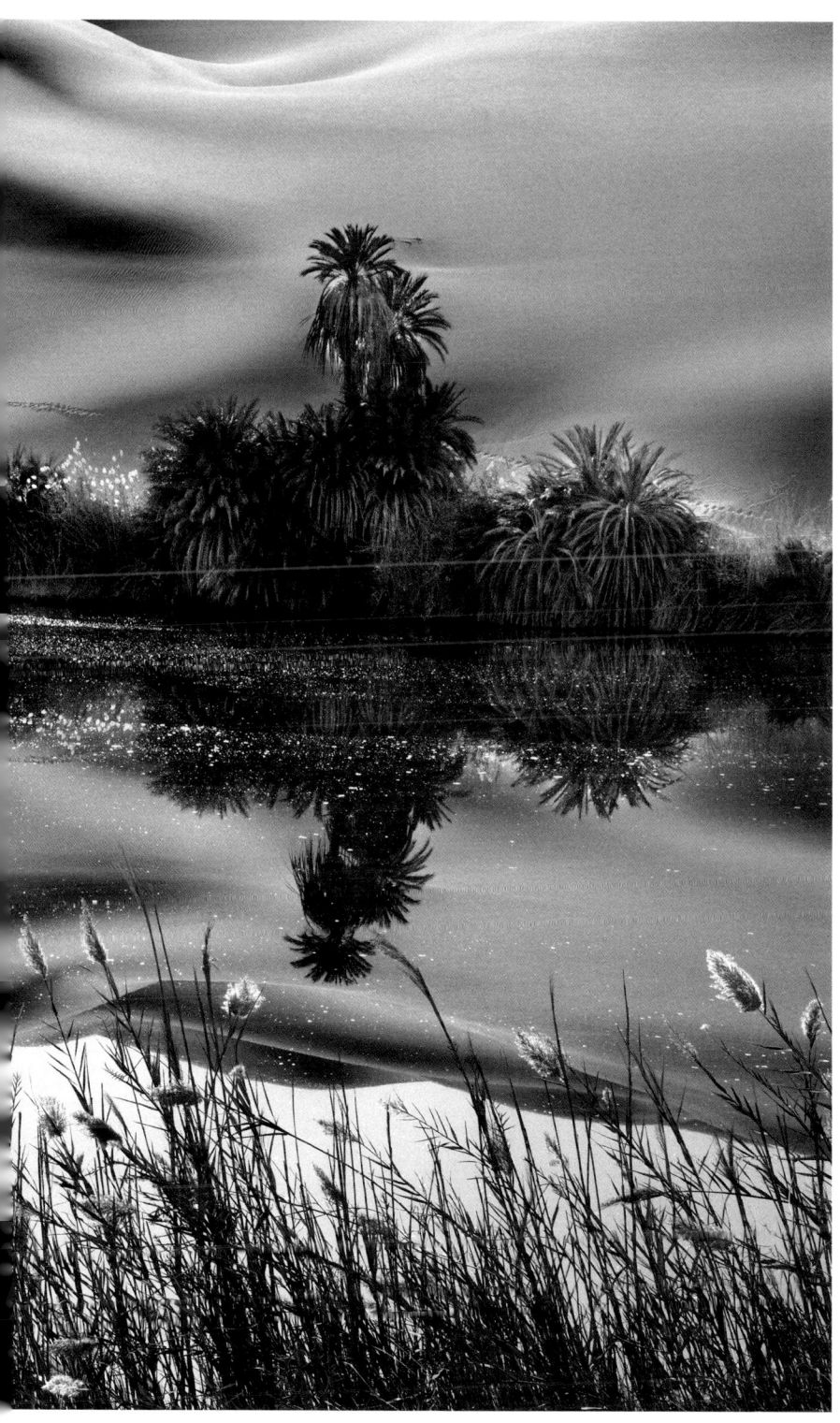

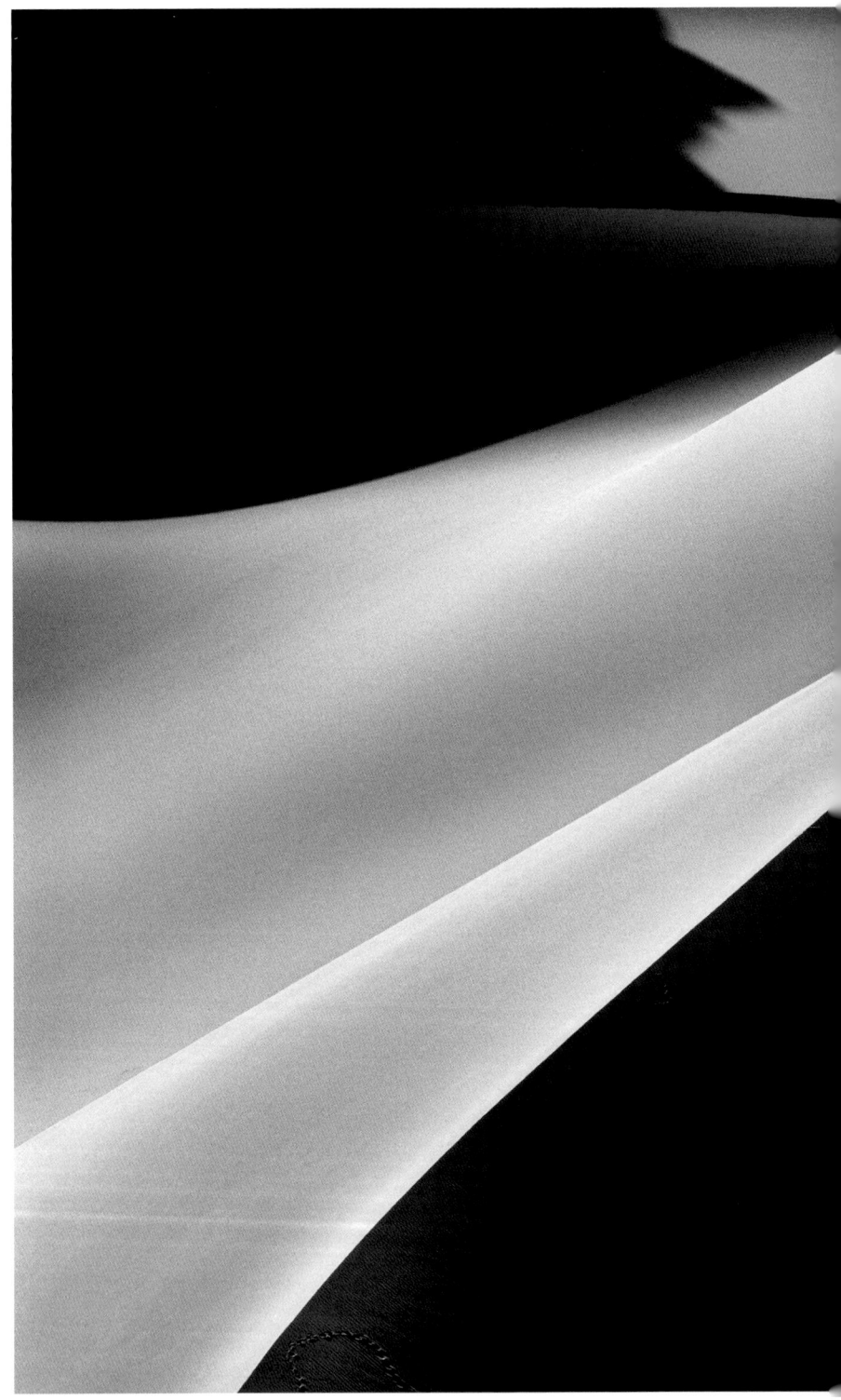

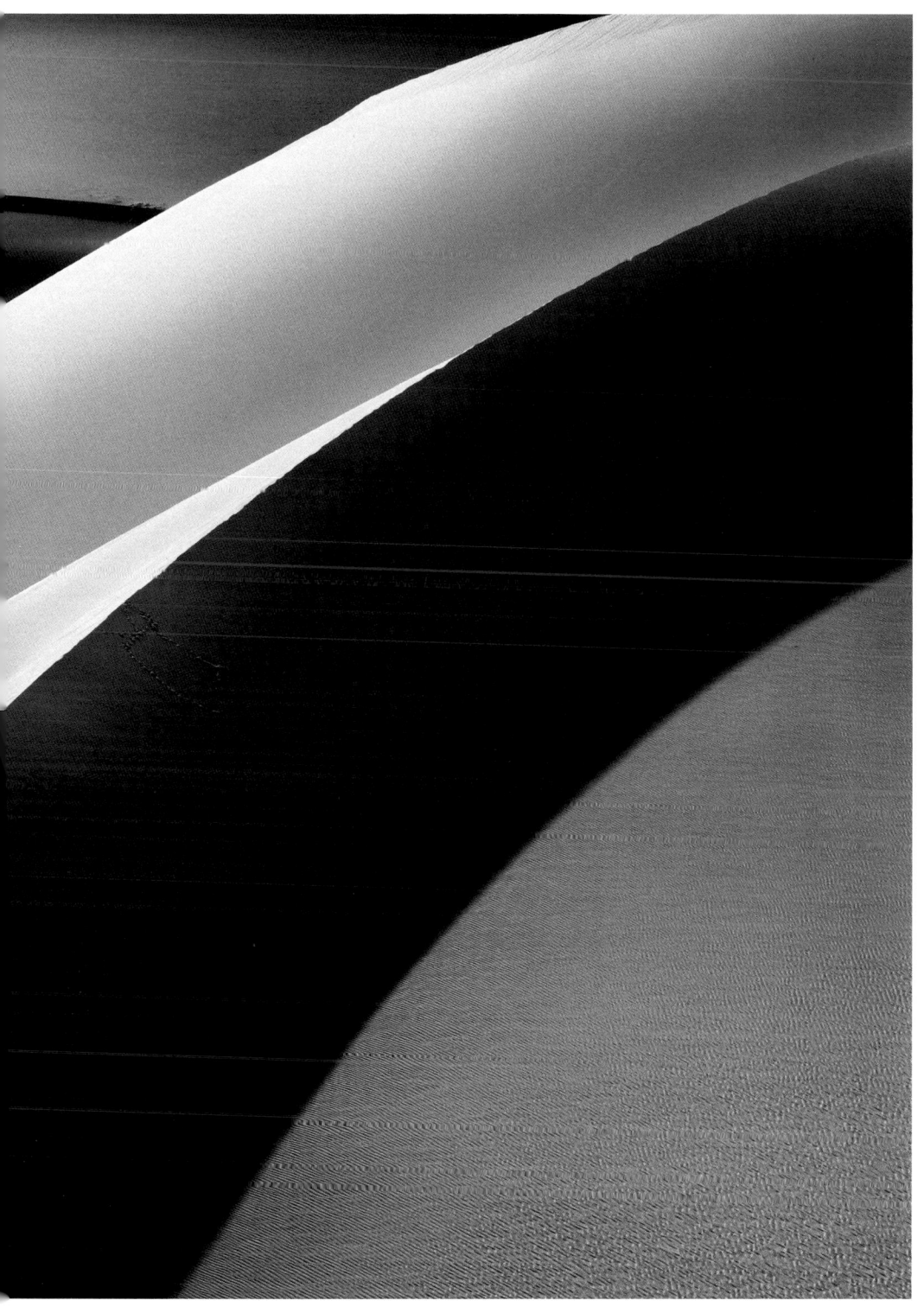

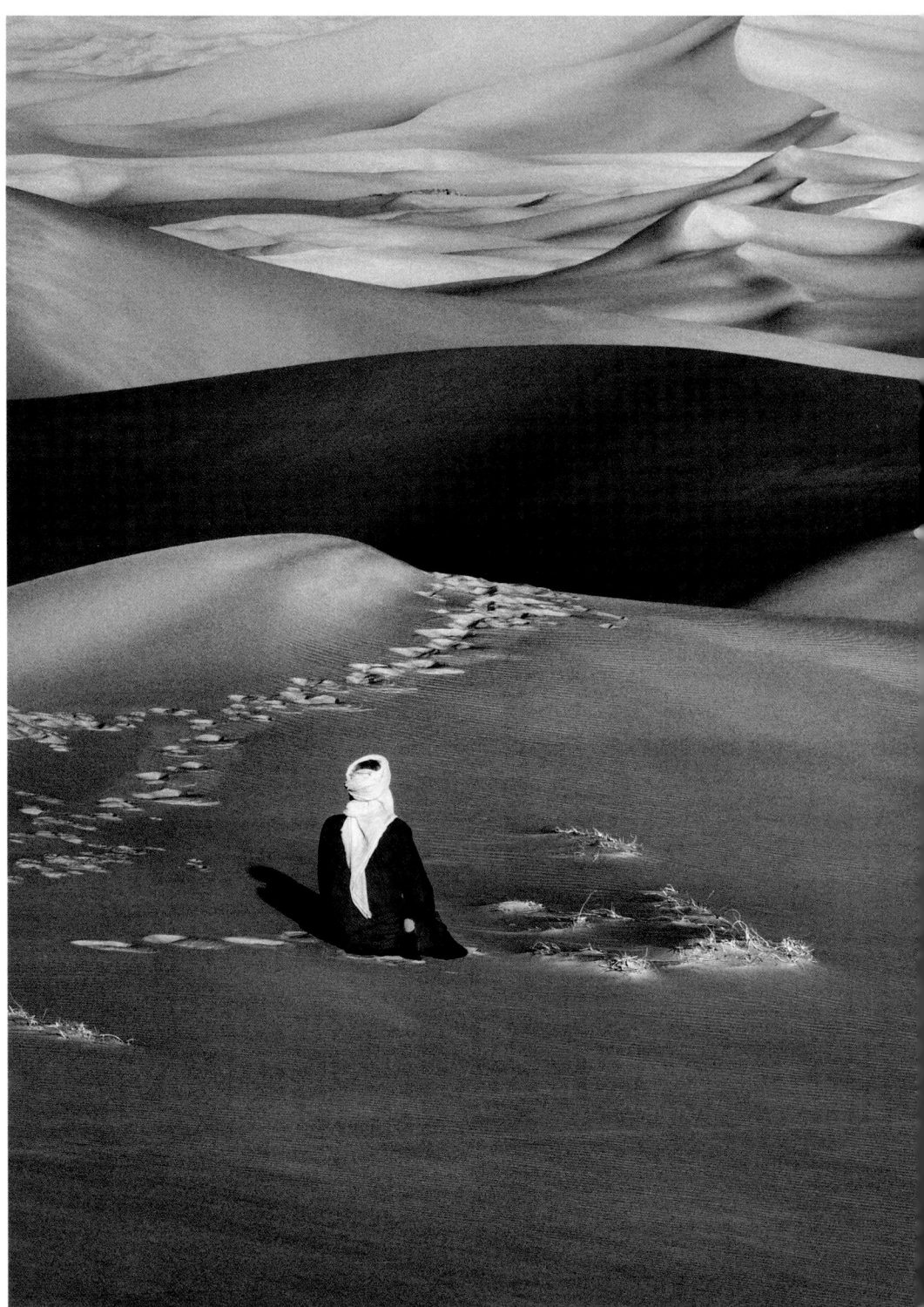

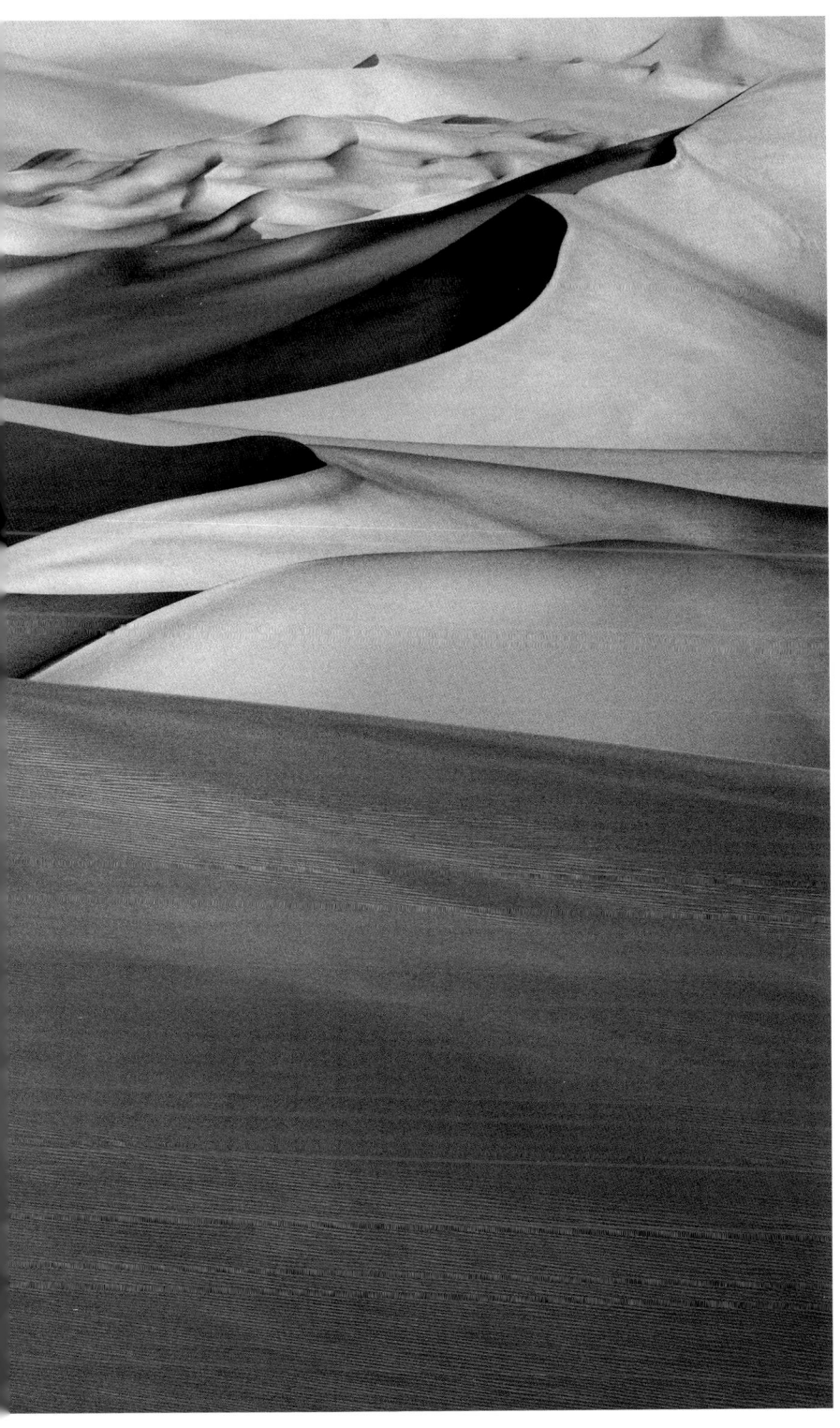

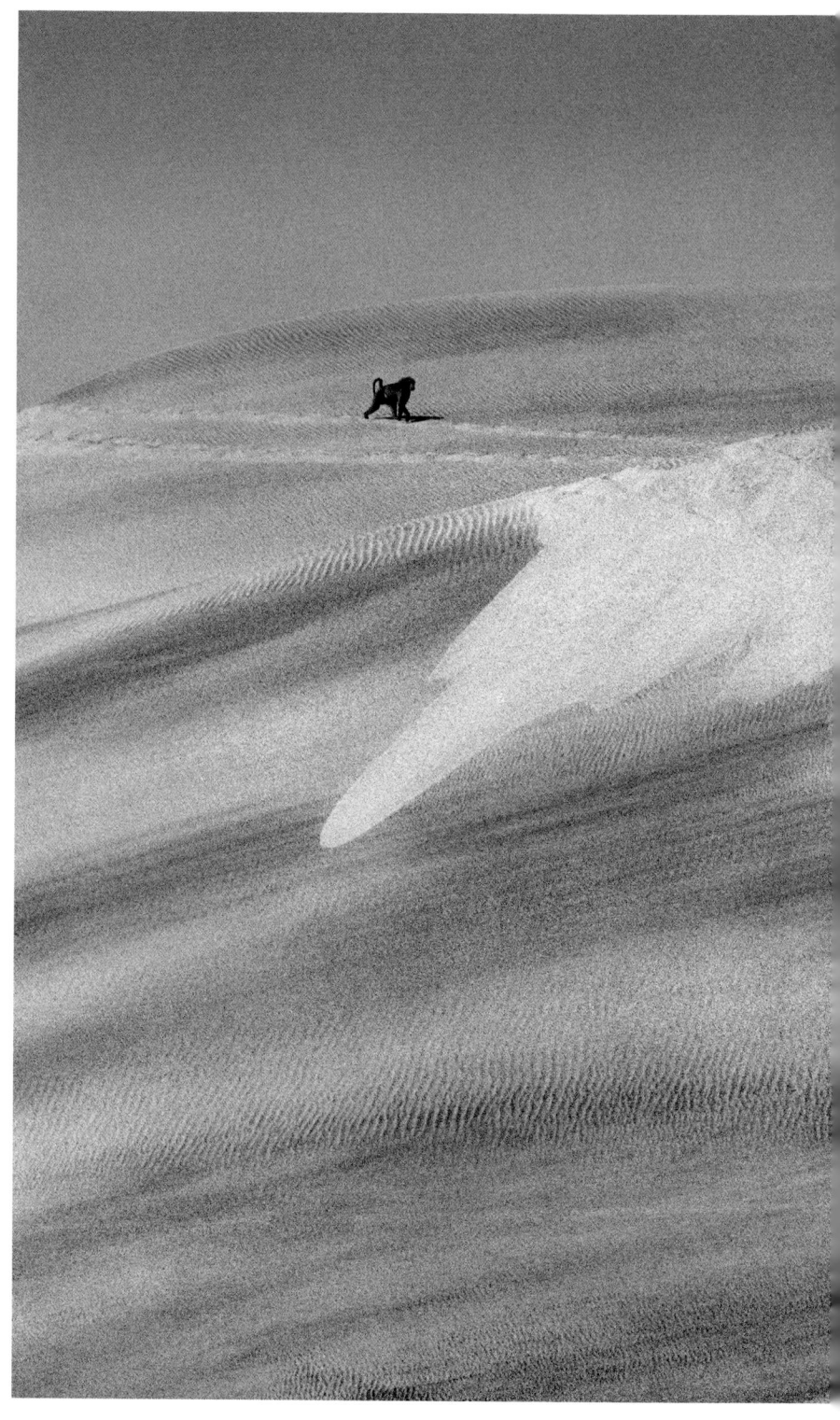

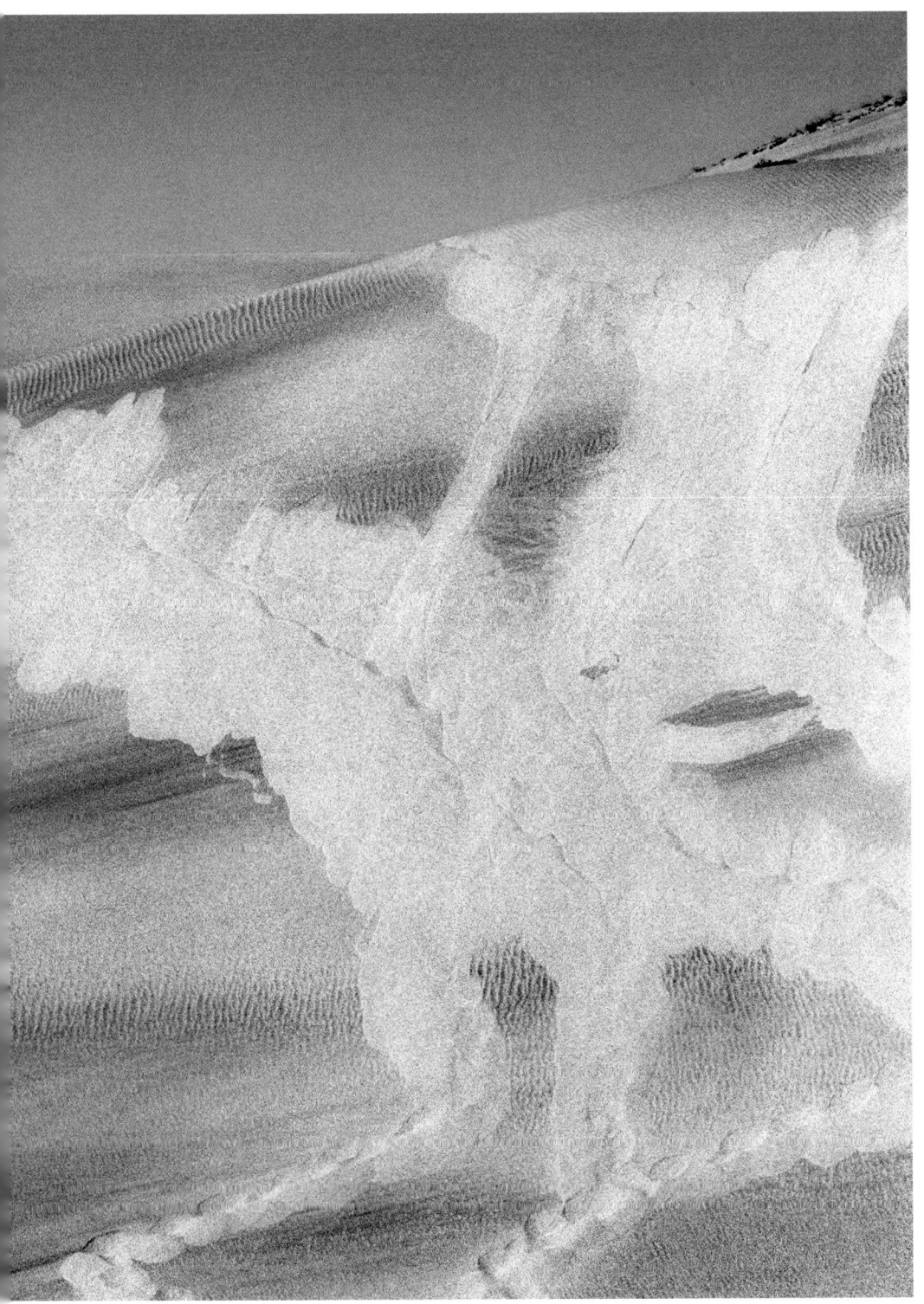

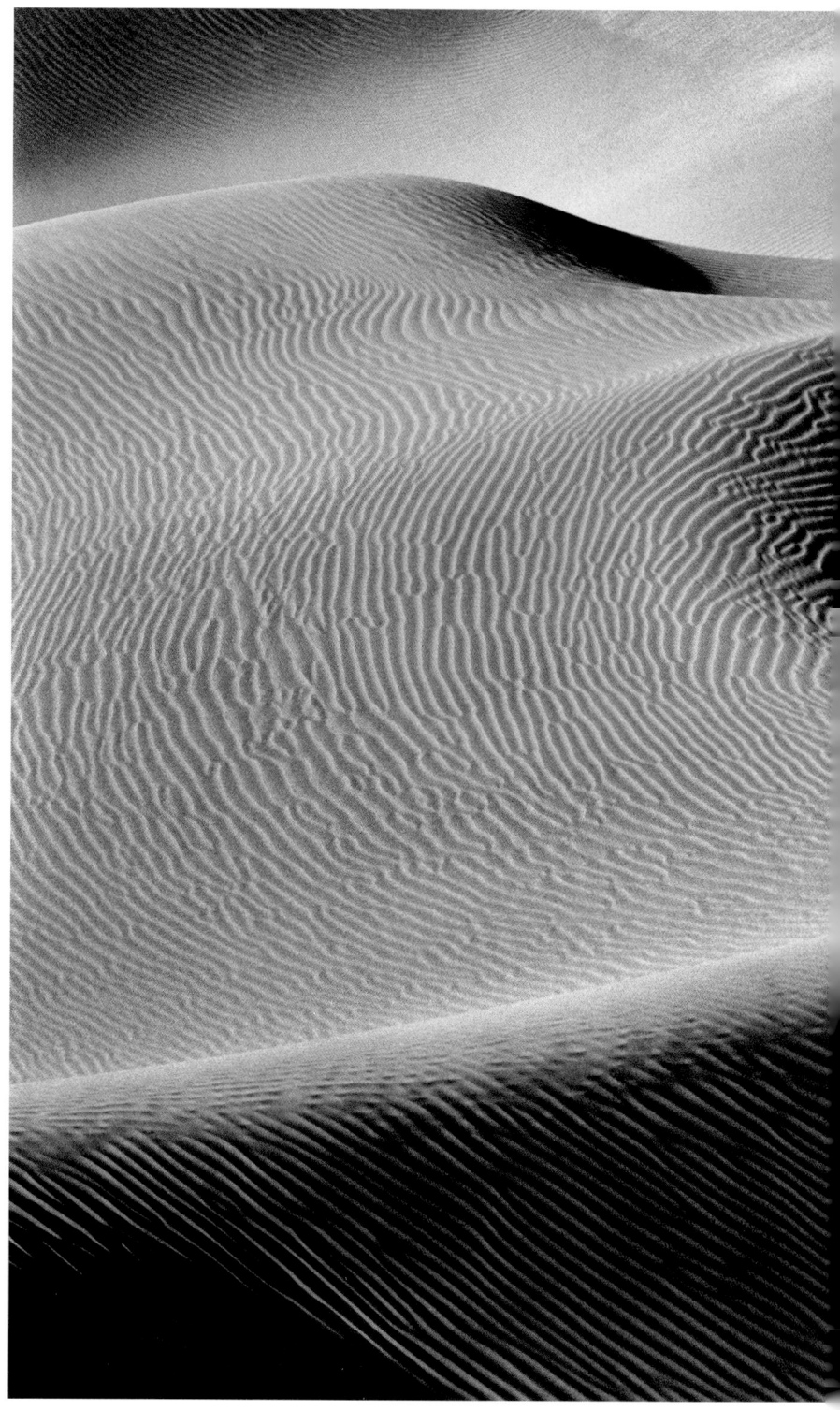

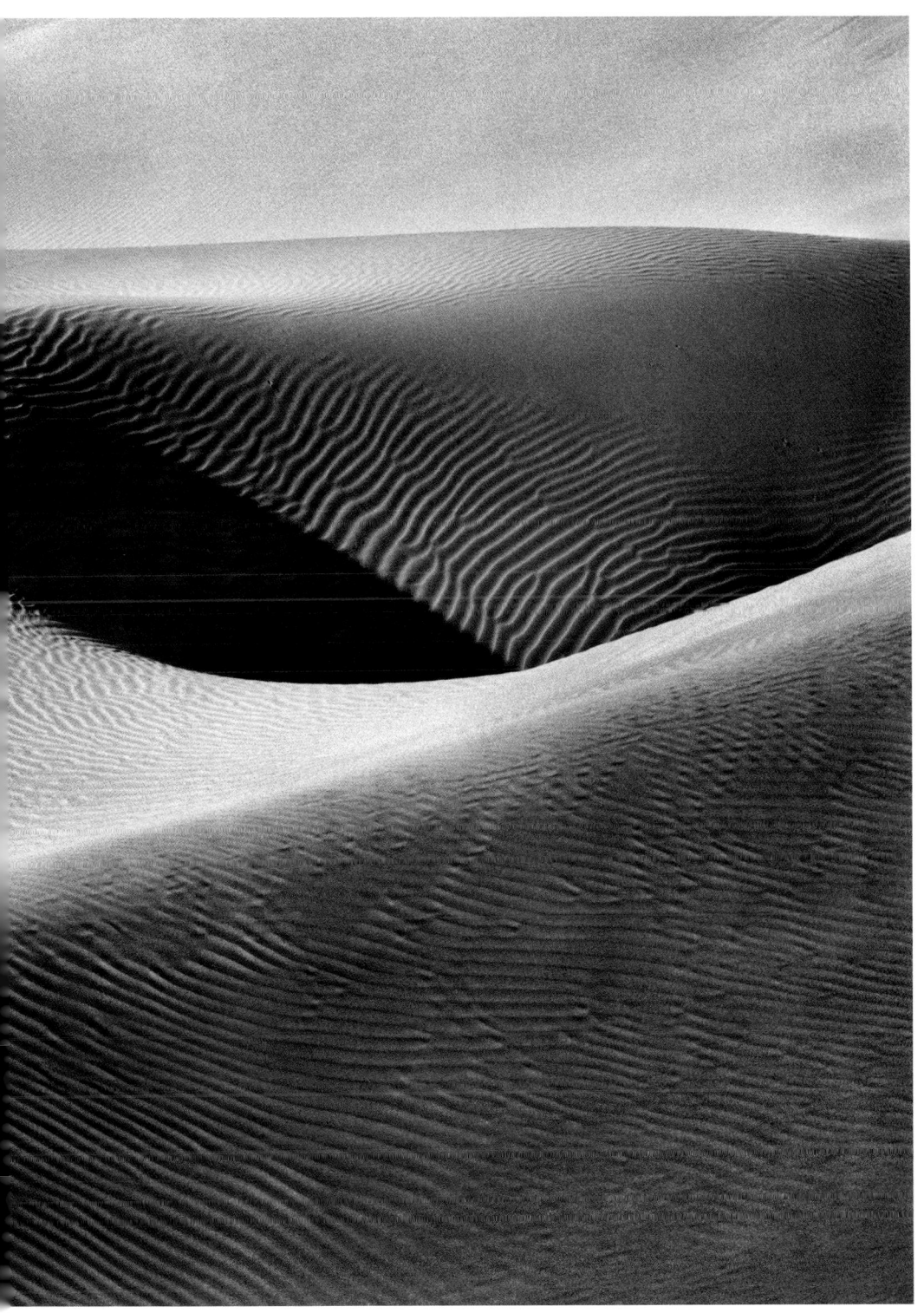

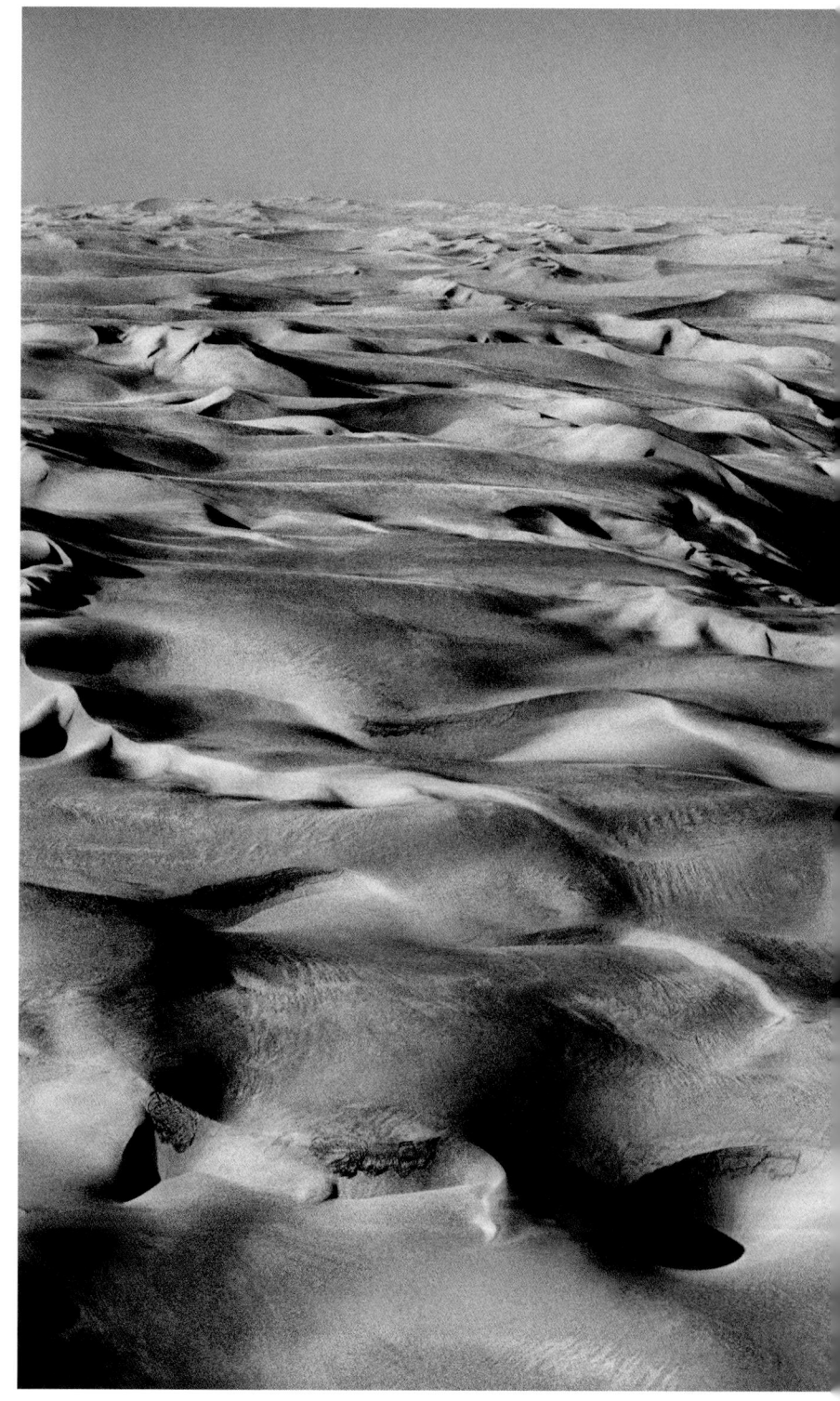

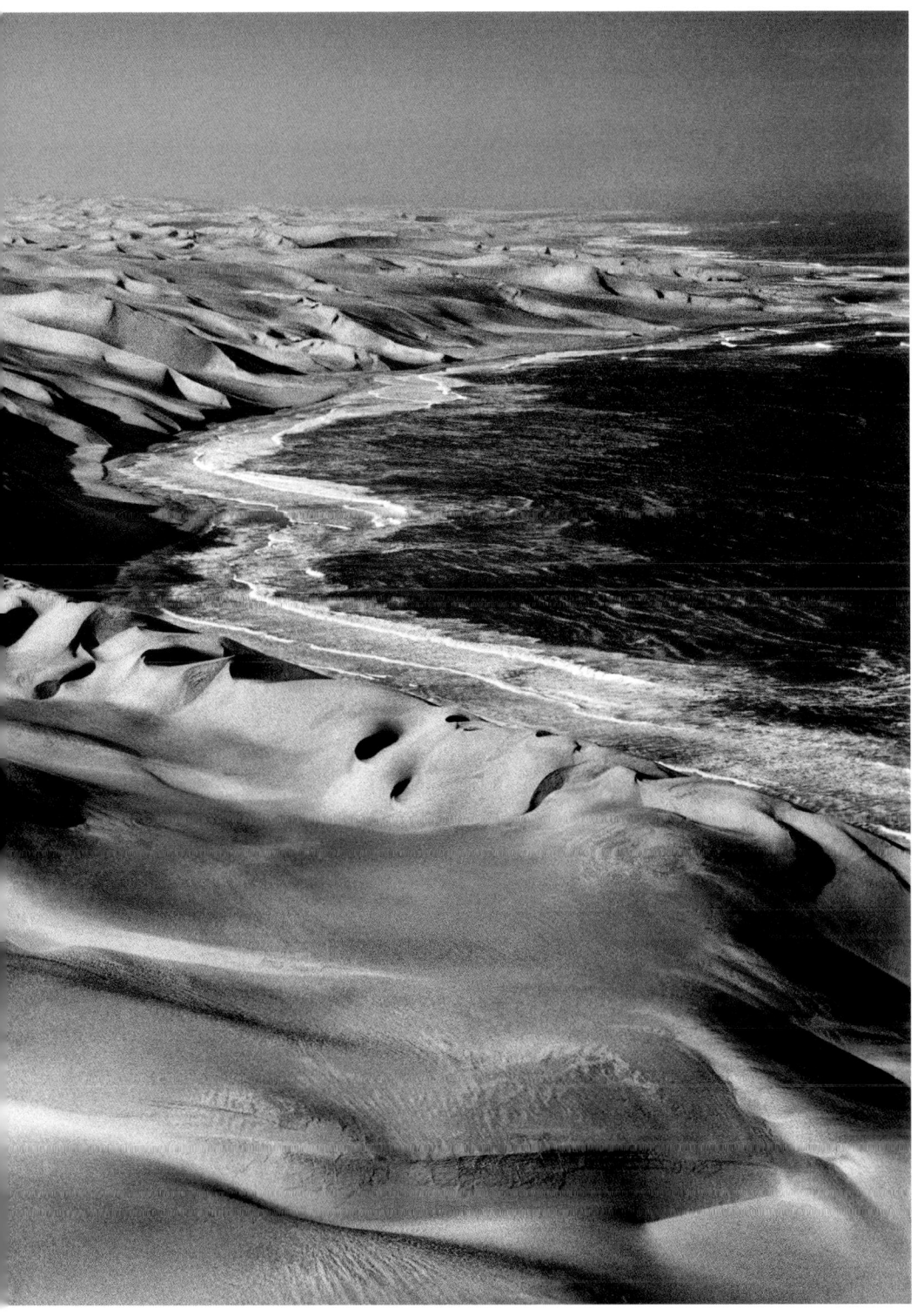

THE DINKA OF SOUTHERN SUDAN

Pages 249 through 255
Southern Sudan is far more ethnically diverse than northern Sudan. Three tribal groups account for around 30 percent of the region's inhabitants: the Dinka, with a population of over one million, followed by the Nuer and the Shilluk. But other groups are also important, including the Hamar, the Toposa, the Anuak, the Murle, the Bari, the Moros-Madi, the Lotuko, the Luo, the Acholi, the Lango, the Didinga, the Ber and the Mundari. Most of these are known as Nilotic peoples because their languages are rooted in ancient Nilo-Saharan languages and because they live in the Upper Nile region. However, some groups have gone south to find pasture for their cattle and have assumed different identities, such as the Massai in Kenya and the Tutsi in Rwanda and Burundi.

These photos show Dinka in their cattle camps, in the region situated between Rumbek and Bor. During the rainy season, they live in villages and grow grain, such as millet, sorghum and maize, while their cattle graze on plentiful grass. But during the dry season, when grass disappears from this semiarid region, the villages are abandoned and the Dinka set off in search of fresh pastures with their entire cattle herd, sometimes more than 5,000 strong. They bring few belongings but carry all the cereal they will need during the long months of drought. When they find an area with water and grass, they establish cattle camps. During the day, the animals may walk several kilometers to graze and drink and at night they are driven back to the camps. The lives of the Dinka are inseparable from those of their cattle. Every morning, they use the urine of the cows to wash their faces but also to add to fresh milk as a preservative. They further collect cow dung, which, once dried in the sun, is burned at night and helps to chase away mosquitoes drawn by the cattle.

They then cover themselves and their animals with the ash, which protects the skin against the stings of insects and parasites.

Pages 244/245 Covering some 14,000 square miles (36,000 square kilometers), vast sand dunes stretch inland from much of Namibia's coast, embracing the Namib-Naukluft National Park and reaching as far north as Walvis Bay. Namibia. October and November 2005.

Pages 246/247 The Namib Desert boasts an extraordinary variety of dune types. The most unusual are known as parabolic or multicyclic dunes, which are the result of winds of almost equal strength blowing from a number of different directions during the year. These winds produce sand hills of exceptional beauty. This sand originates from the high hinterland of Namibia through the Fish River and from South Africa, where it is washed into the Orange River drainage system. This is then deposited on the banks and islands of the Orange River and then washed through the river's mouth at Oranjemund. Most of this sand is washed ashore approximately 62 miles (100 kilometers) north of Oranjemund, while the rest is swept farther north along the southern Namibian coast. Here, the wind shapes it into distinctive dunes that form the vast Namib Desert. Sand Sea, south of Walvis Bay, Namibia. October and November 2005.

Opposite In the village of Ger, a symbolic representation of horns is molded on the inside wall of a traditional home. Southern Sudan. February and March 2006.

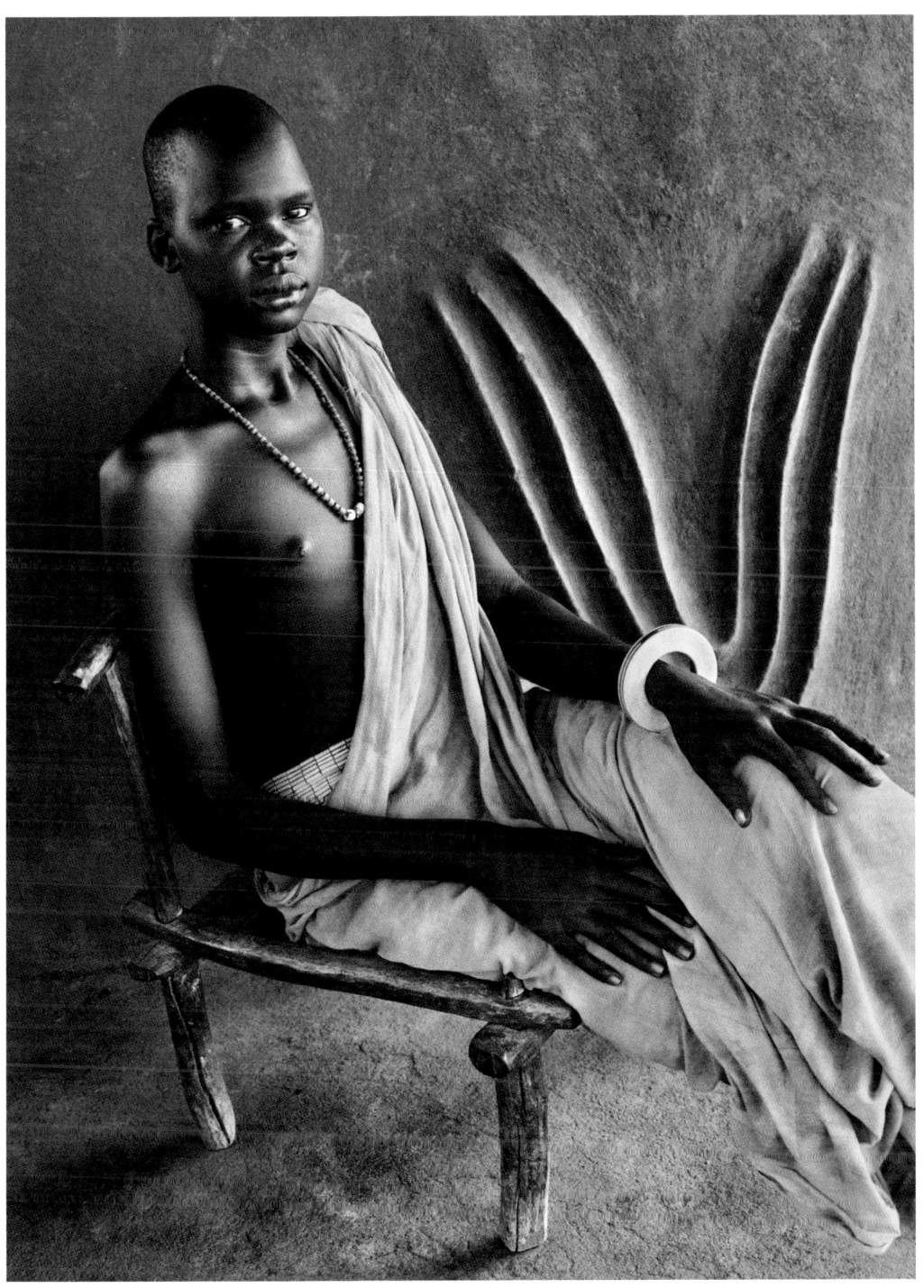

Opposite In a cattle camp at Kolkuei. Southern Sudan. February and March 2006.

Pages 252/253 Cattle camp of Amak at the end of the day, when the herd has returned to the camp for the night. This is the most active time at the camp. Several piles of burning cow pats can be seen here; the smoke keeps the insects away from the camp. Southern Sudan. February and March 2006.

Pages 254/255 Cattle camp of Kei. The Dinka choose the best bulls for mating and identify them by giving a distinct shape to the animals' horns as they grow. Southern Sudan. February and March 2006.

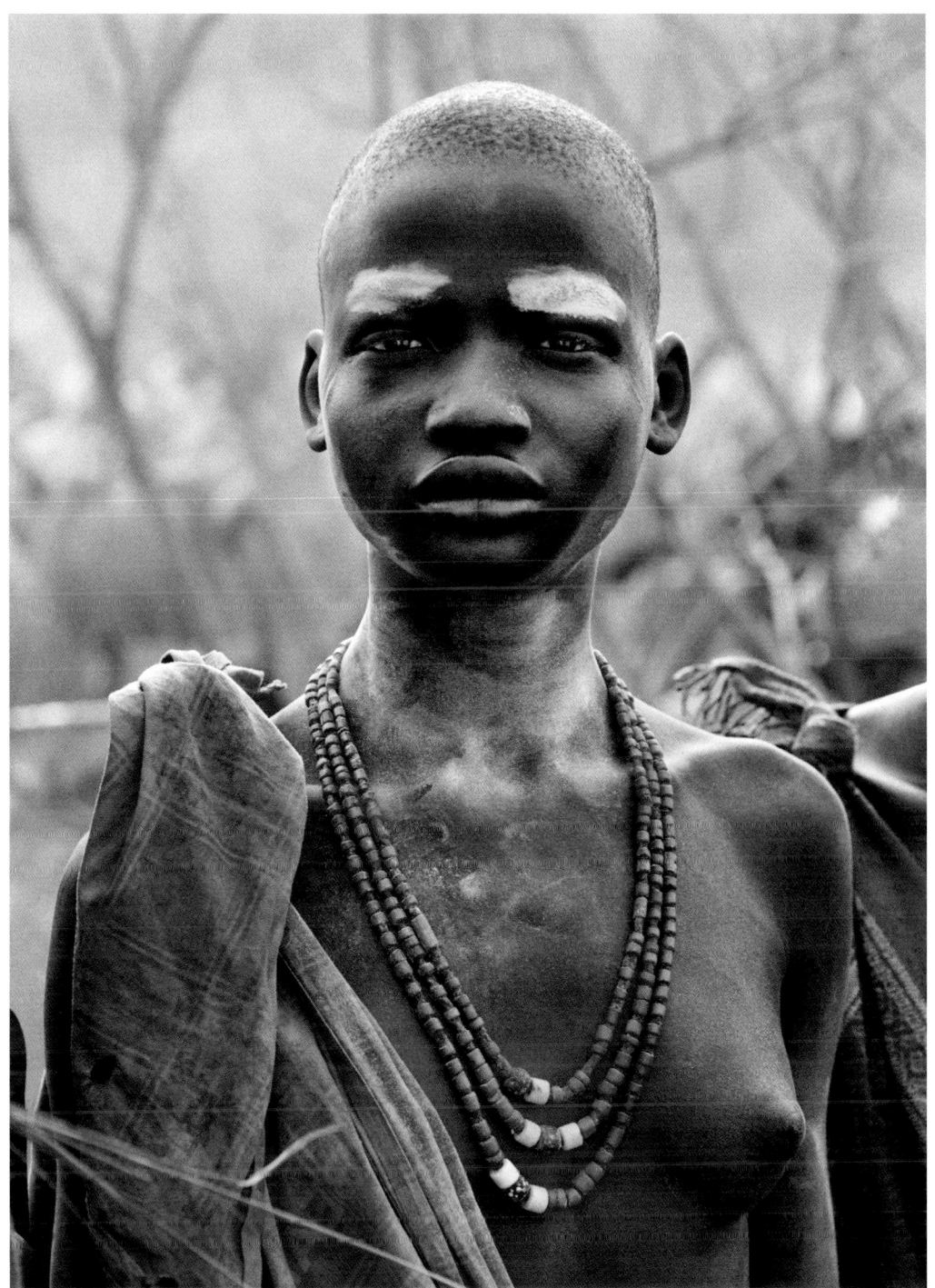

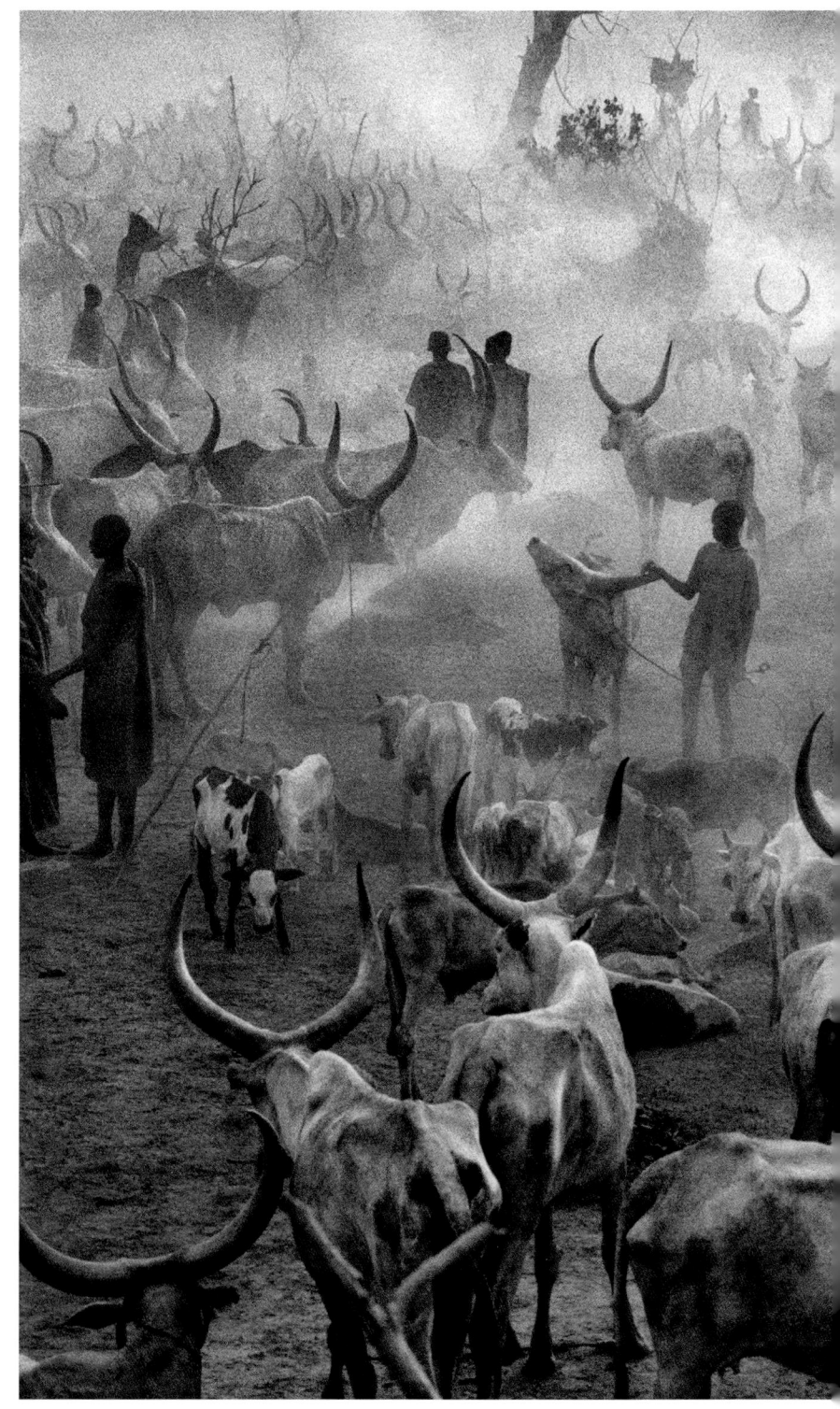

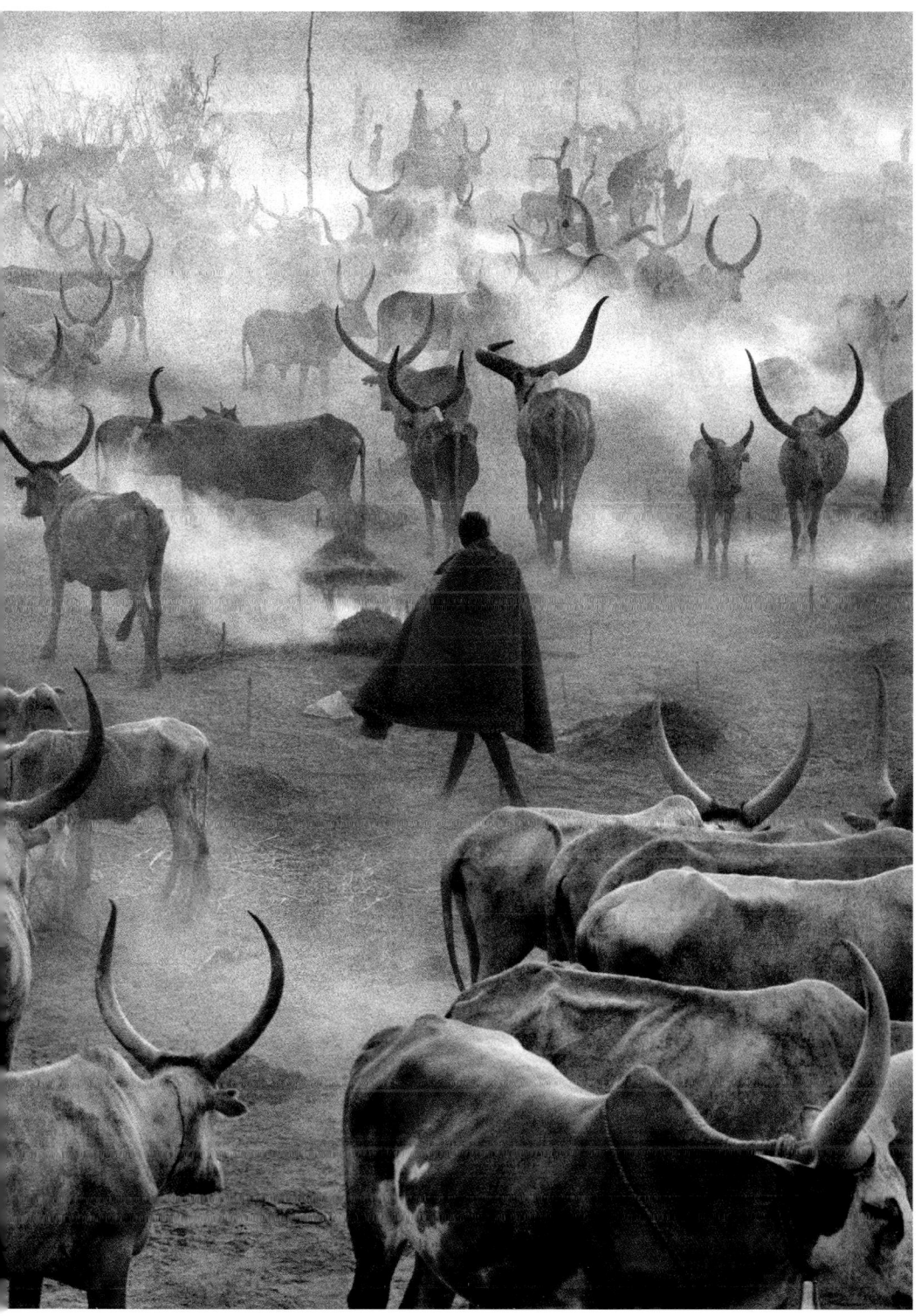

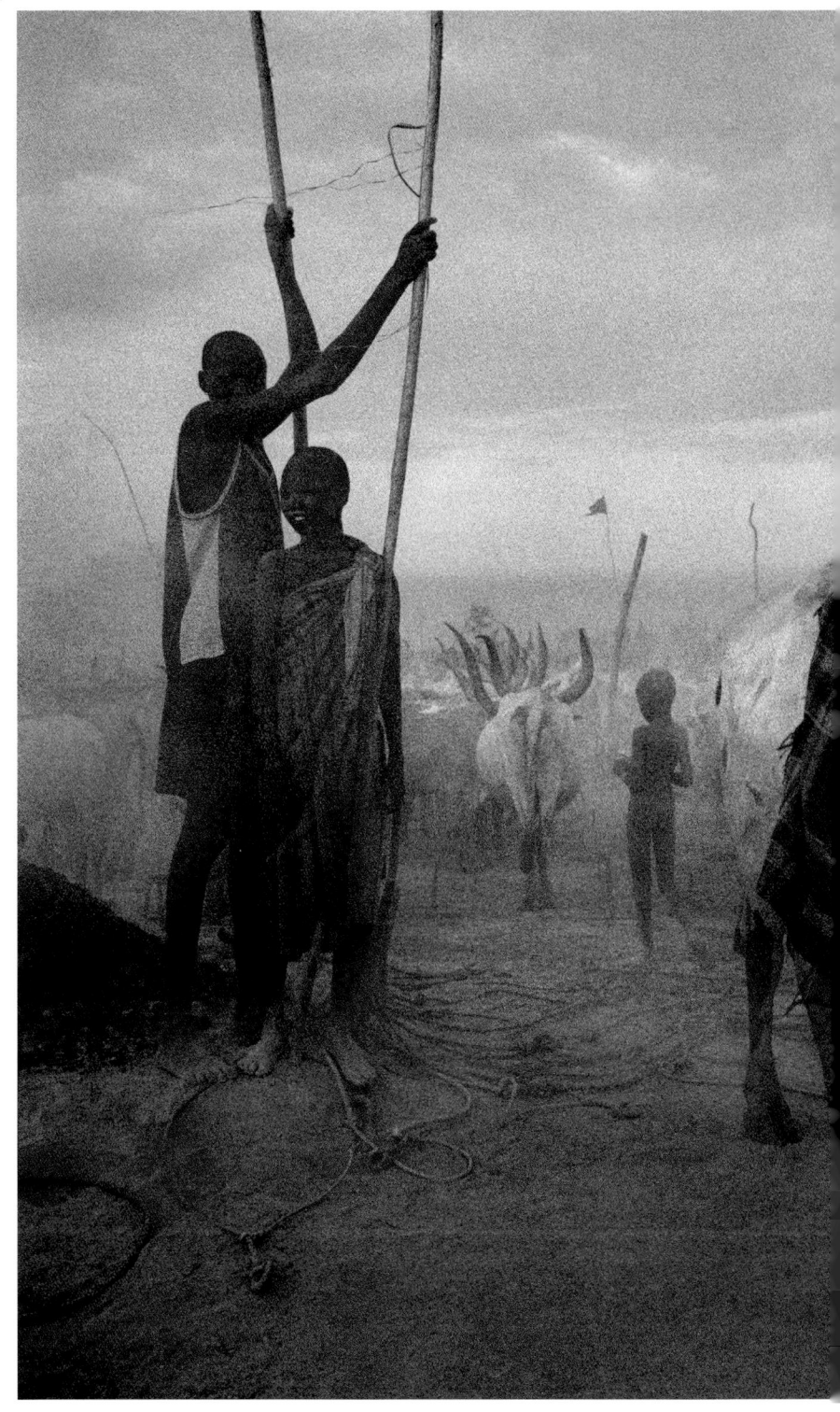

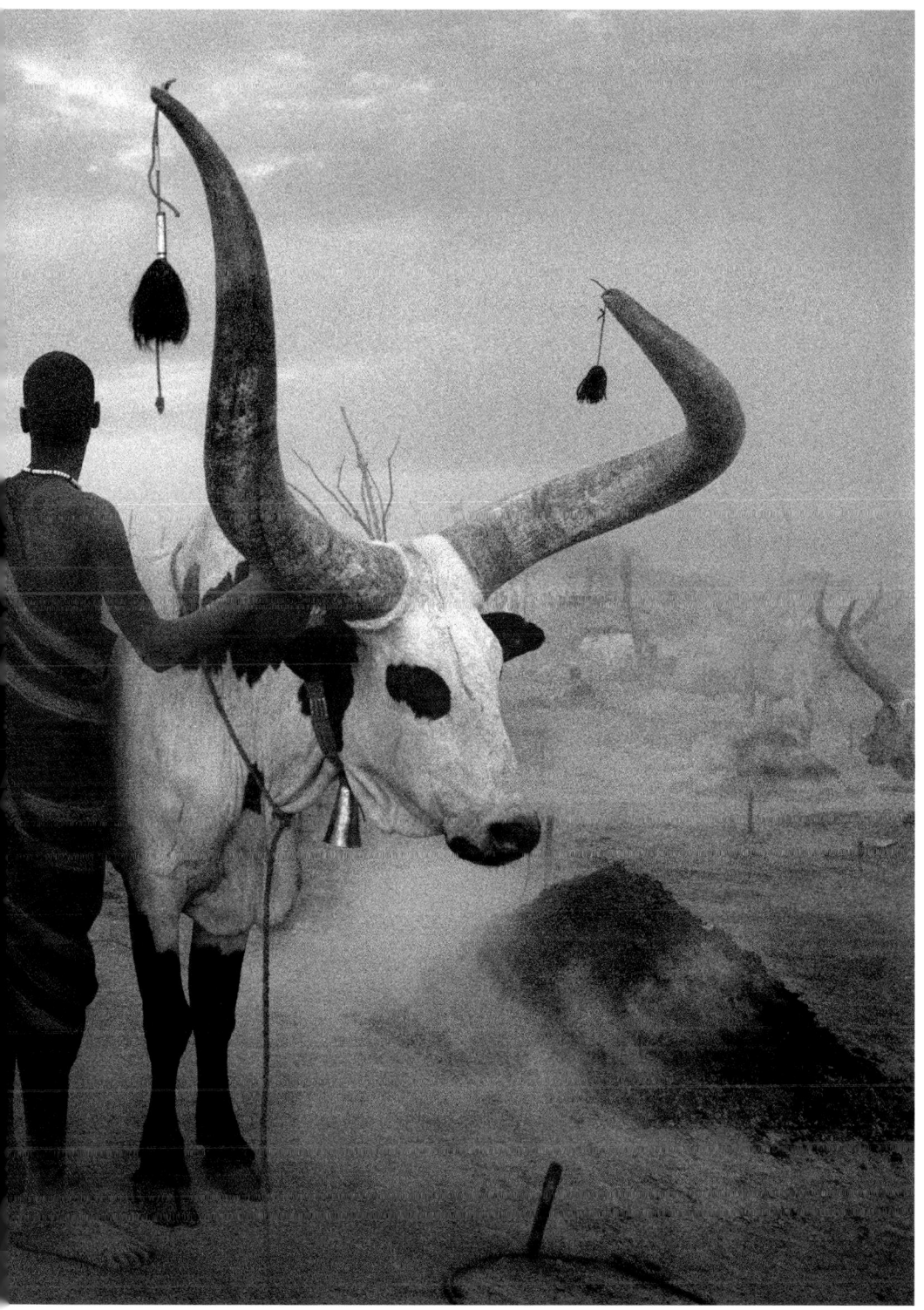

THE HIMBA

Pages 257 through 262
The Himba of Kaokoland in Namibia are semi-nomadic cattle herders who live in small groups, dependent on finding water and grass for their cattle. They are scattered across northern Kaokoland, where the proximity of the Kunene River makes living conditions adequate for both humans and livestock. The Himba have had a complicated history.

Known as the Herero in the 16th century, they migrated from the Moçâmedes Province of Angola towards the Kunene River. They called the land to their left "okaoko," from which Kaokoveld and, later, Kaokoland, were derived.

Later, when the main Herero group migrated to central and eastern Namibia, a smaller group remained in the arid and mountainous Kaokoland. In the mid-19th century, these Herero fell victim to marauding bands of cattle thieves and slid into deep poverty. The Herero to the south began to call them "Tjimba-Herero," meaning "very poor Herero." Many "Tjimba" fled back across the Kunene River to Angola to seek refuge with the Ngambwe people, who called them "ovaHimba" ("beggars"). Over time, they rebuilt their cattle herds and, when they finally returned to Kaokoland, they retained the name of Himba.

Opposite and page 262 This Himba group in Orutanda was made up almost entirely of women since their men had gone in search of water and pastures with their cattle. Kaokoland, Namibia. October and November 2005.

Pages 258/259 A Himba group near the Katapati River in Marienfluss, Kaokoland. Namibia. October and November 2005.

Page 260/261 A Himba group in Omuramba, near the Zebra Mountains in Kaokoland. Namibia. October and November 2005.

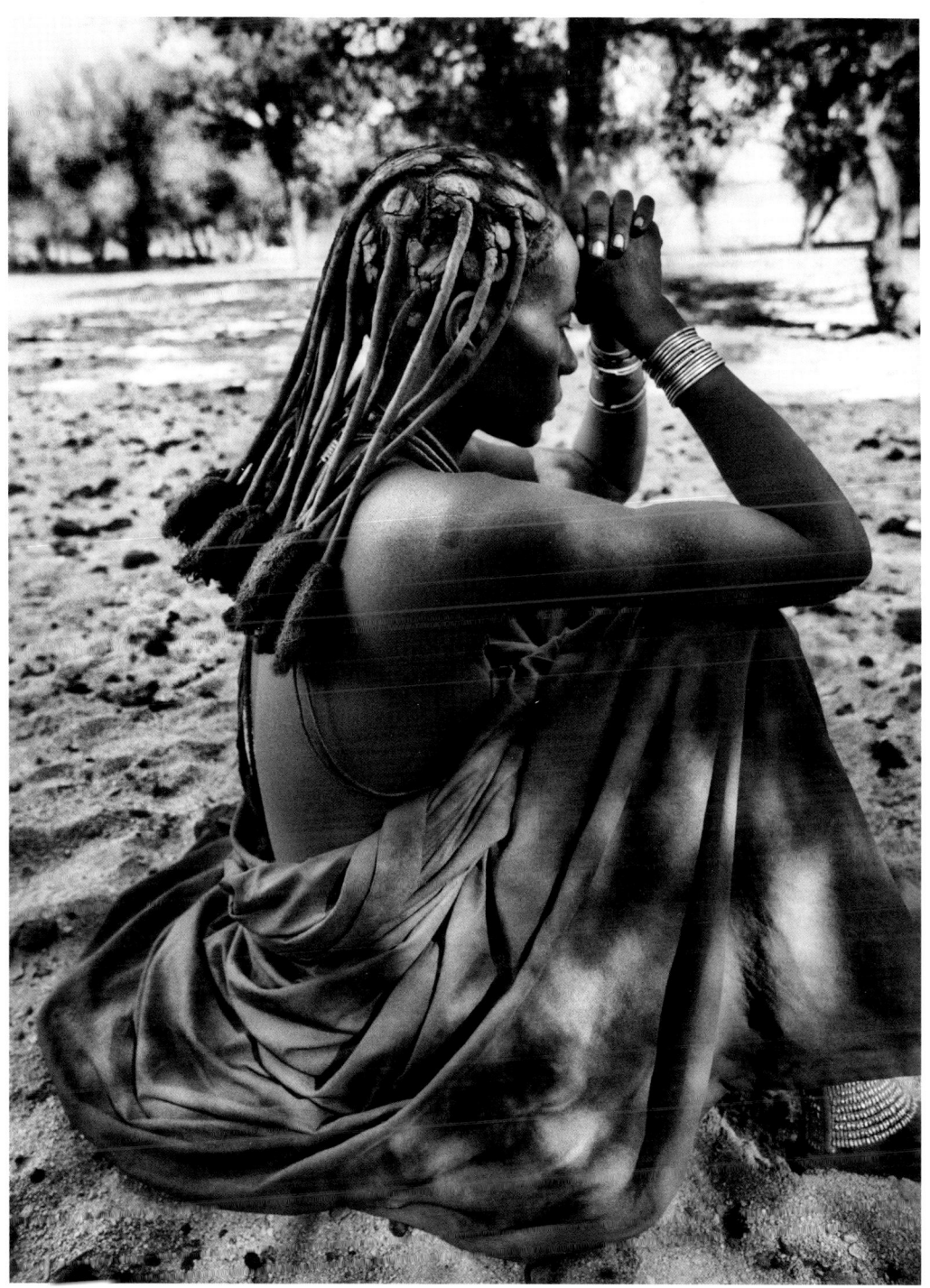

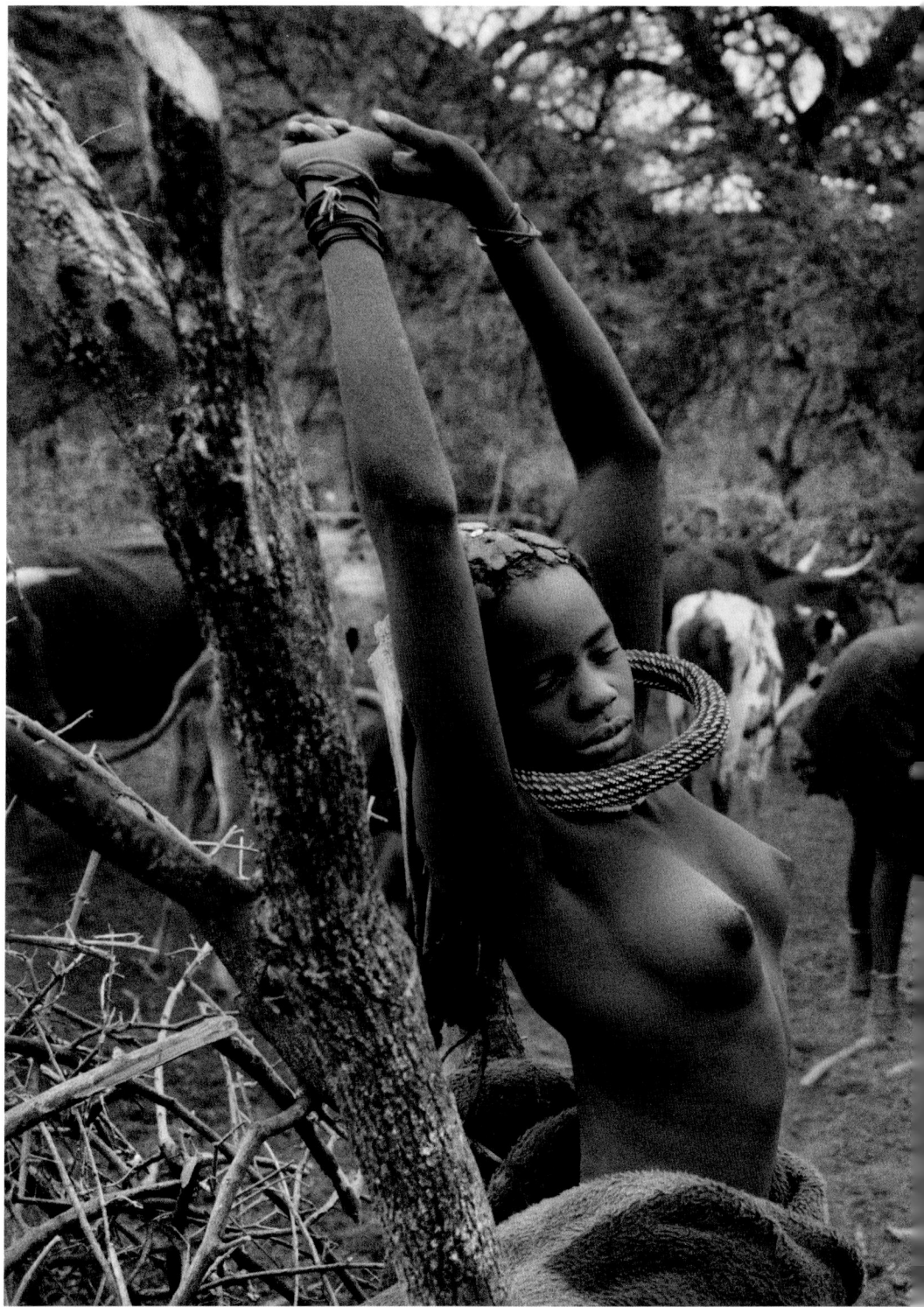

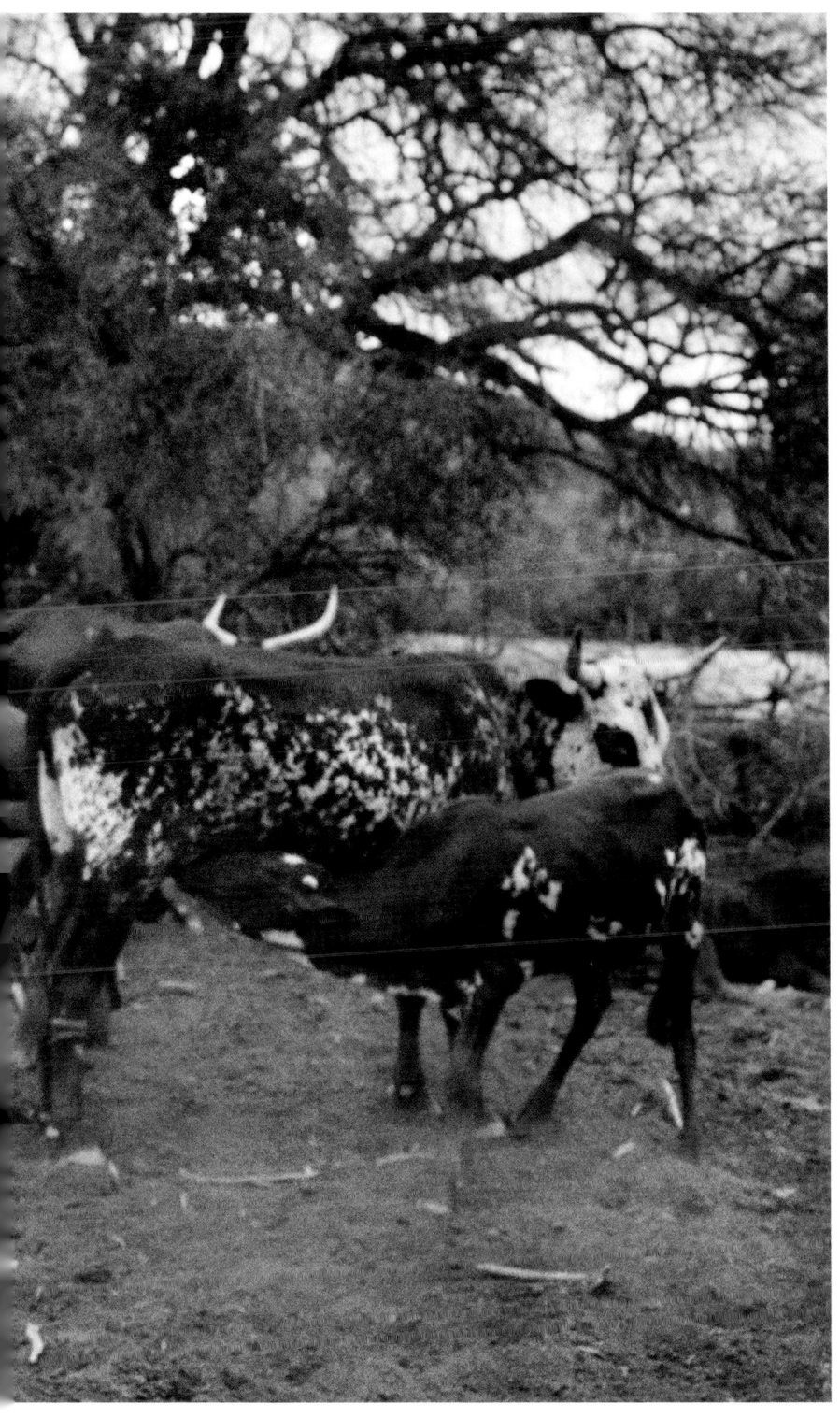

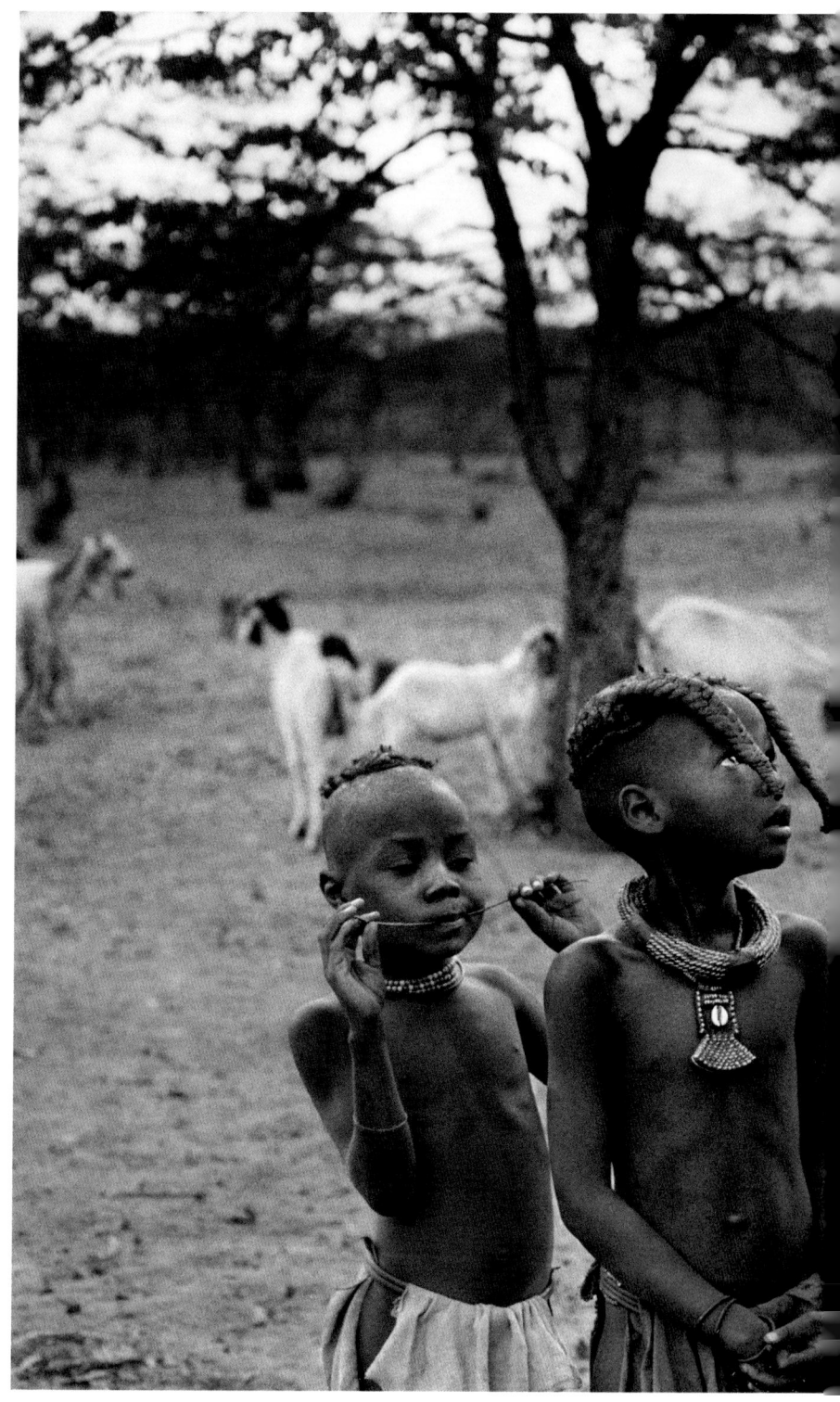

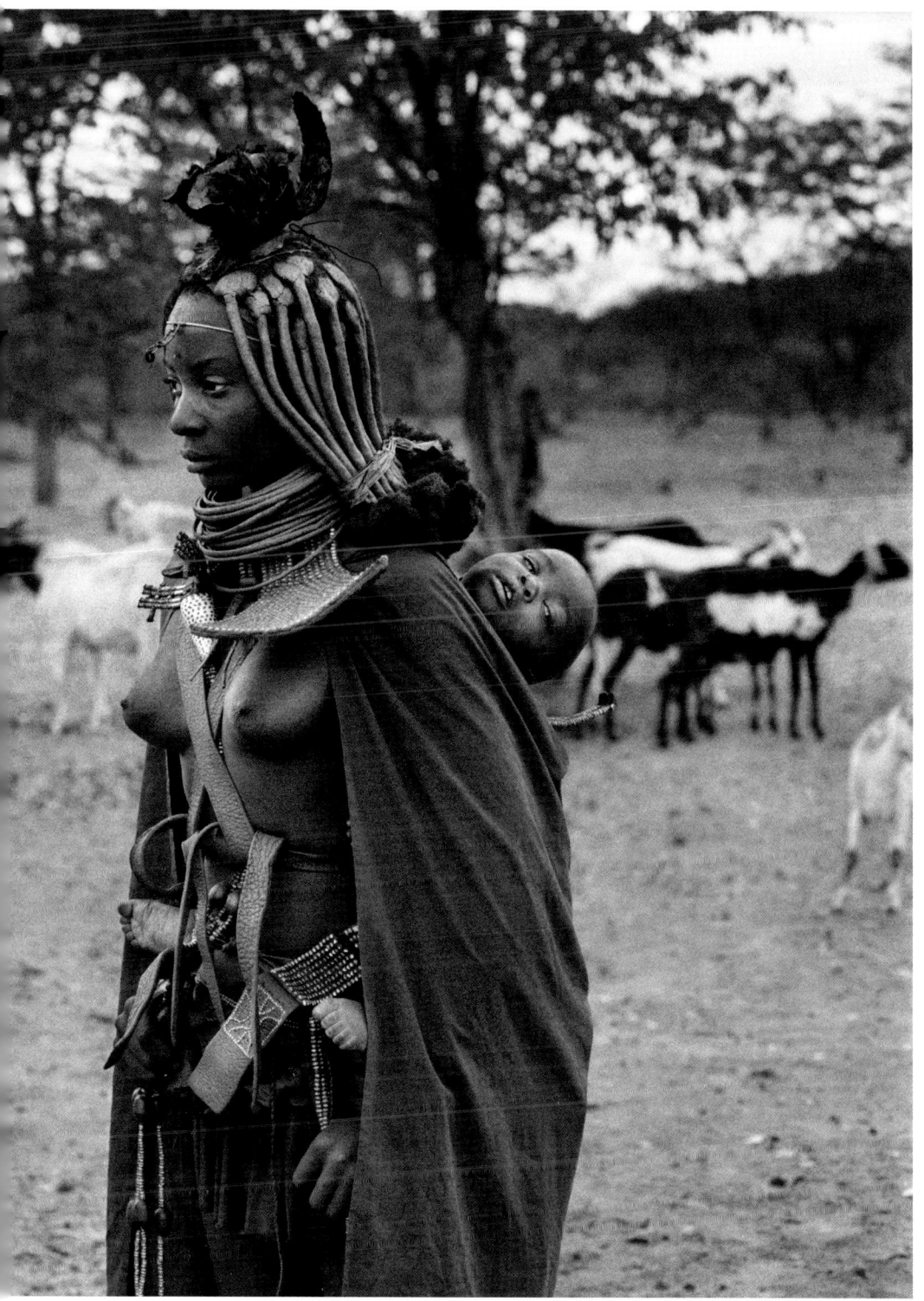

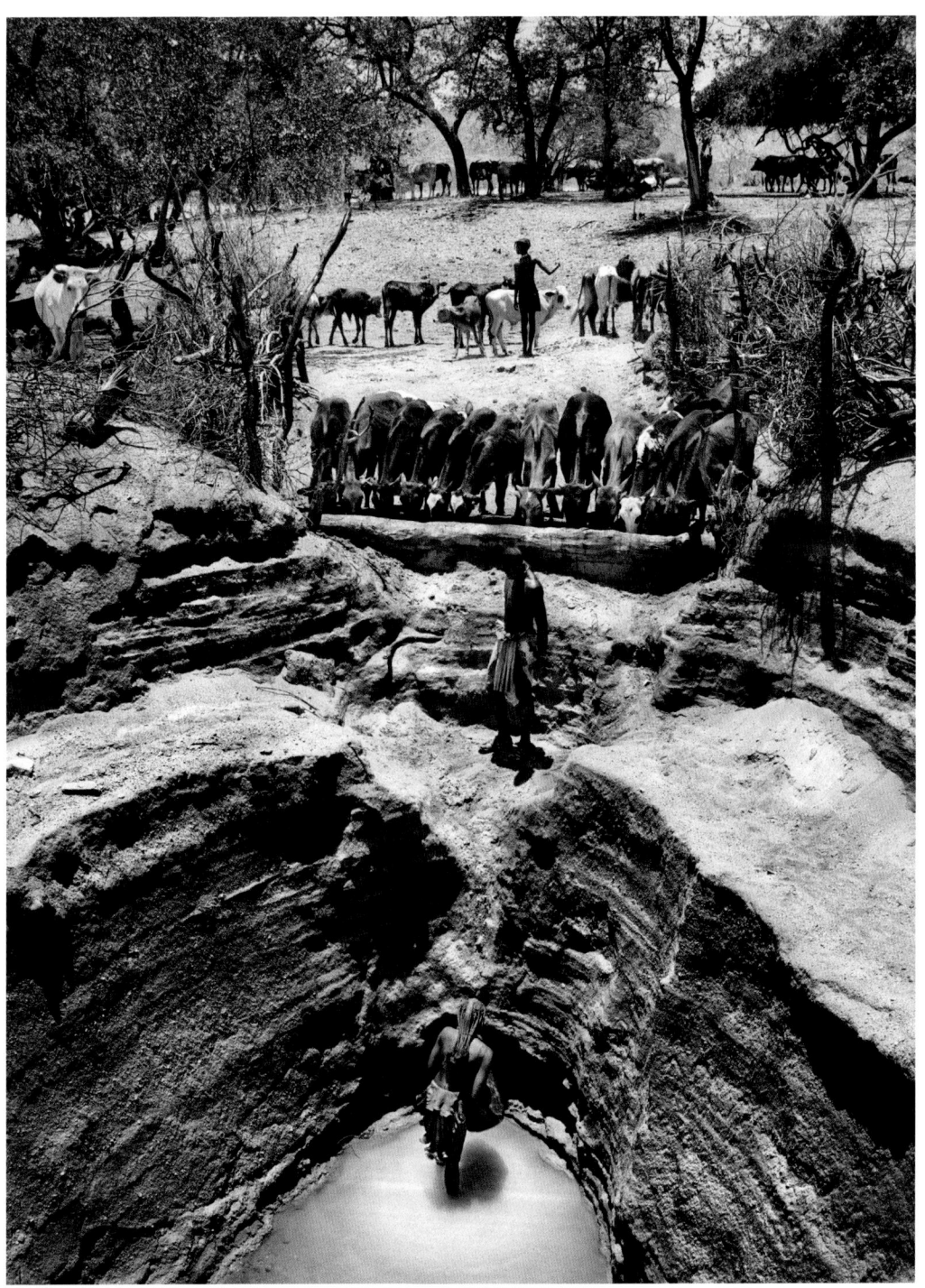

Pages 264/265 Animals are understandably frightened when they hear a helicopter flying overhead, but in a balloon it was possible to come close to this herd of buffalos (*Syncerus caffer*) without disturbing them. Balloons, however, pose other problems. It is crucial to fly very early in the morning before spirals of hot air rising from the ground cause dangerous turbulence. There is also the risk that wind can send the balloon way off course. Kafue National Park, Zambia. July and August 2010.

Pages 266/267 Since elephants (*Loxodonta africana*) are hunted by poachers in Zambia, they are scared of humans and vehicles. Alarmed when they see an approaching car, they usually run quickly into the bush. Kafue National Park, Zambia. July and August 2010.

Pages 268/269 Leopard (*Panthera pardus*). Although leopards usually hunt at night, occasionally they can be sighted in the early morning or late afternoon, as seen here shortly after a leopard had killed a large male impala (*Aepyceros melampus melampus*). Okavango Delta, Botswana. June and July 2007.

Pages 270/271 Giraffes (*Giraffa camelopardalis*). With their spindly legs and long necks, giraffes may appear clumsy, but they can run surprisingly quickly. Females will also fiercely defend themselves and their calves with violent blows from their rear hooves; they have even been known to kill lions. Okavango Delta, Botswana. June and July 2007.

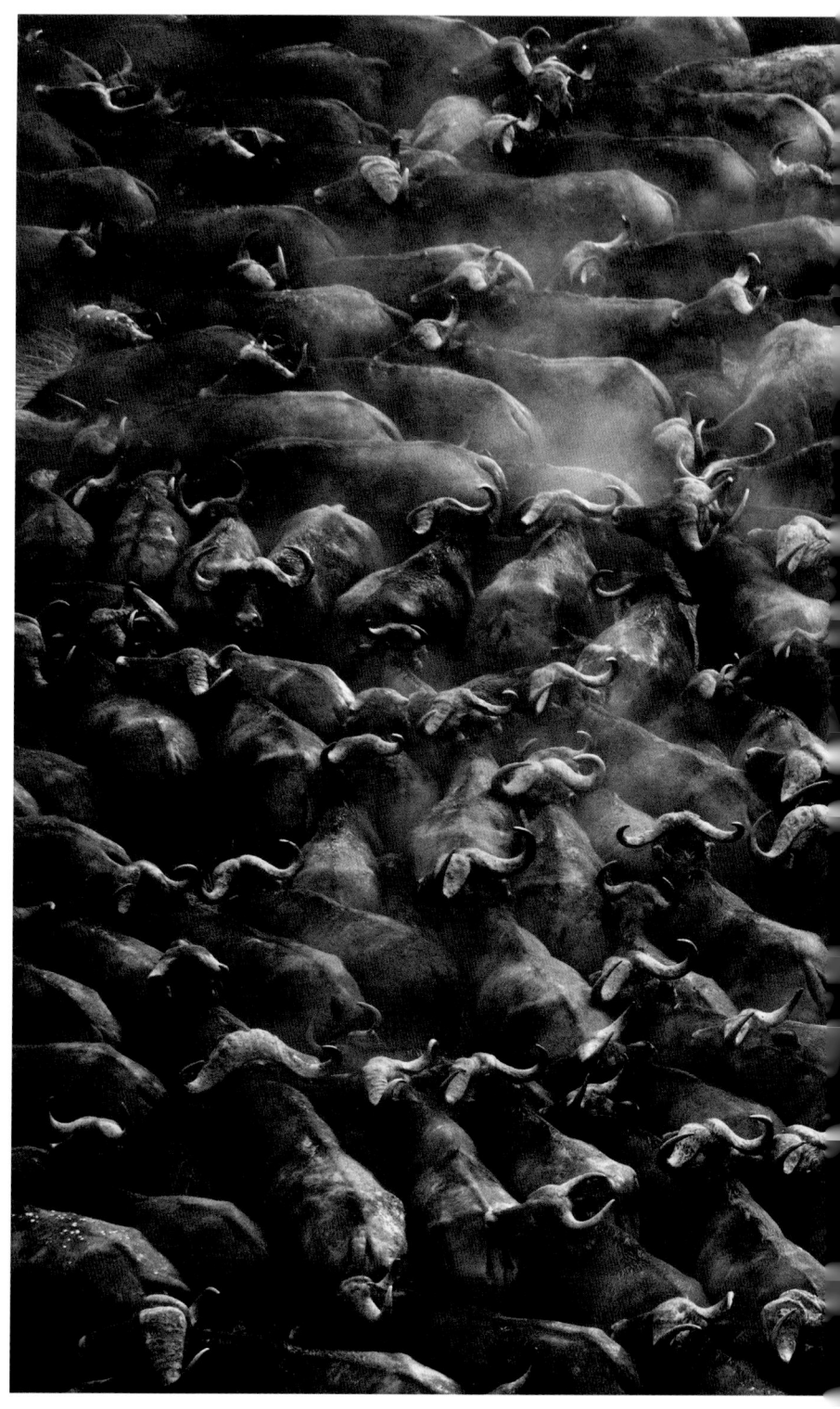

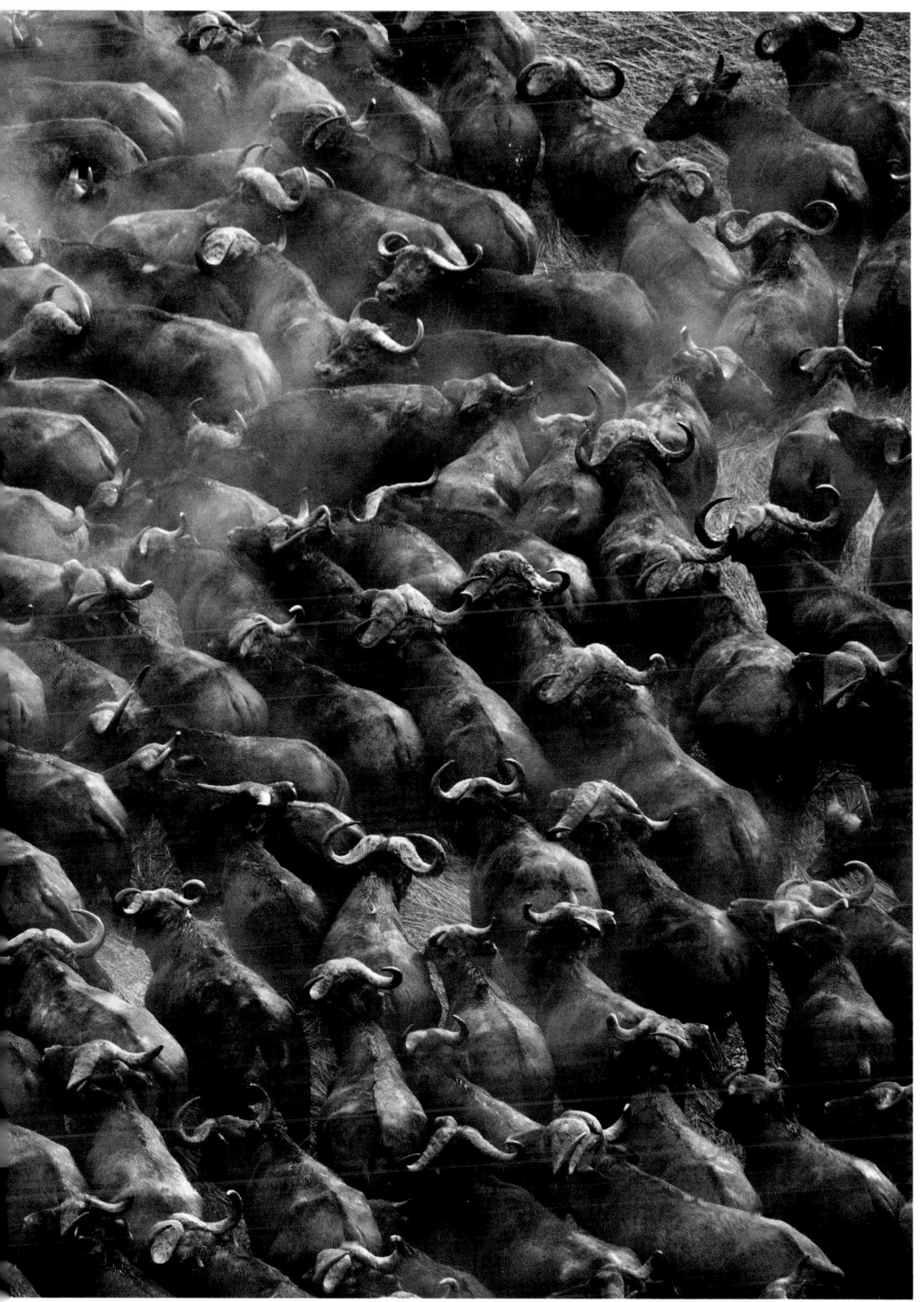

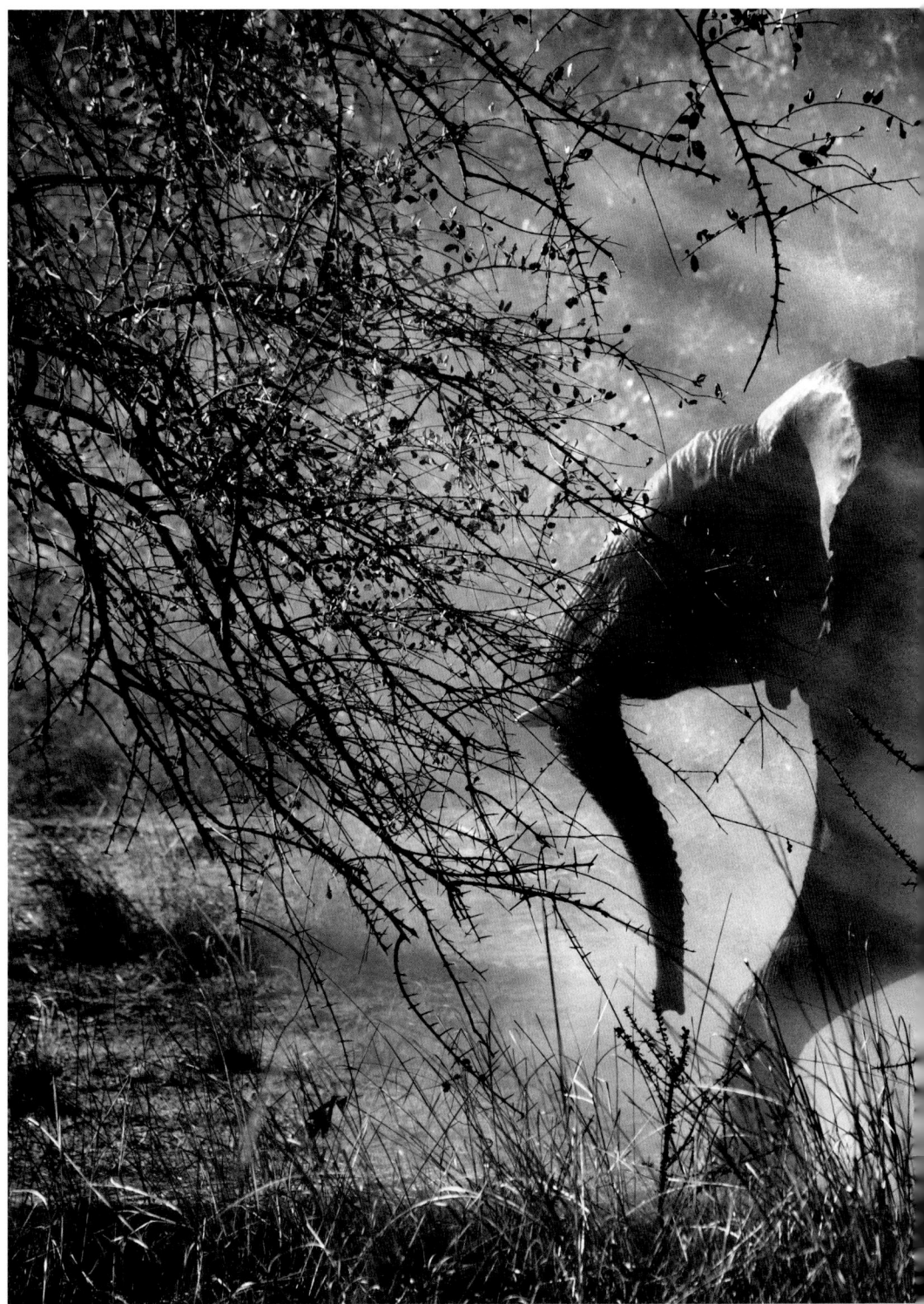

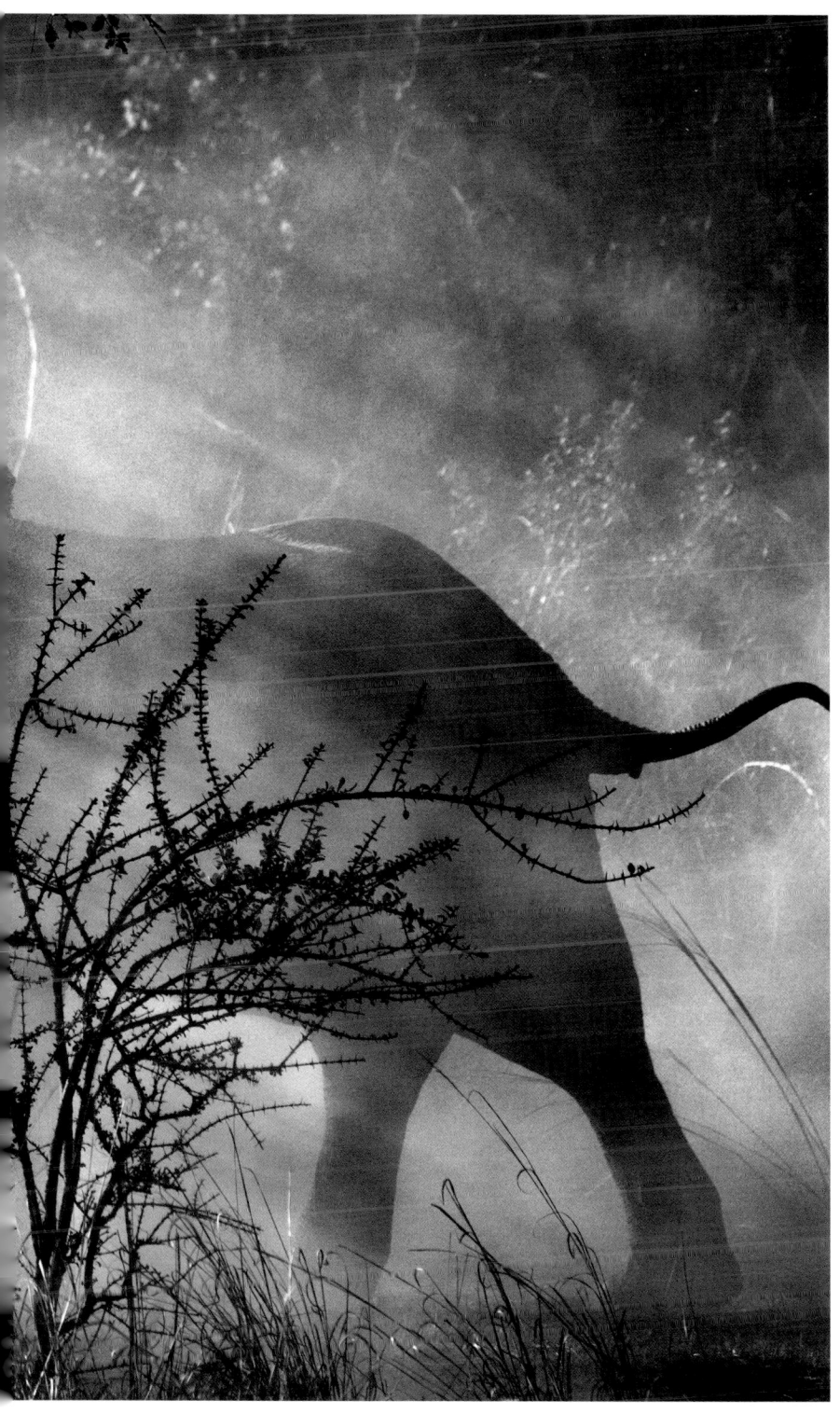

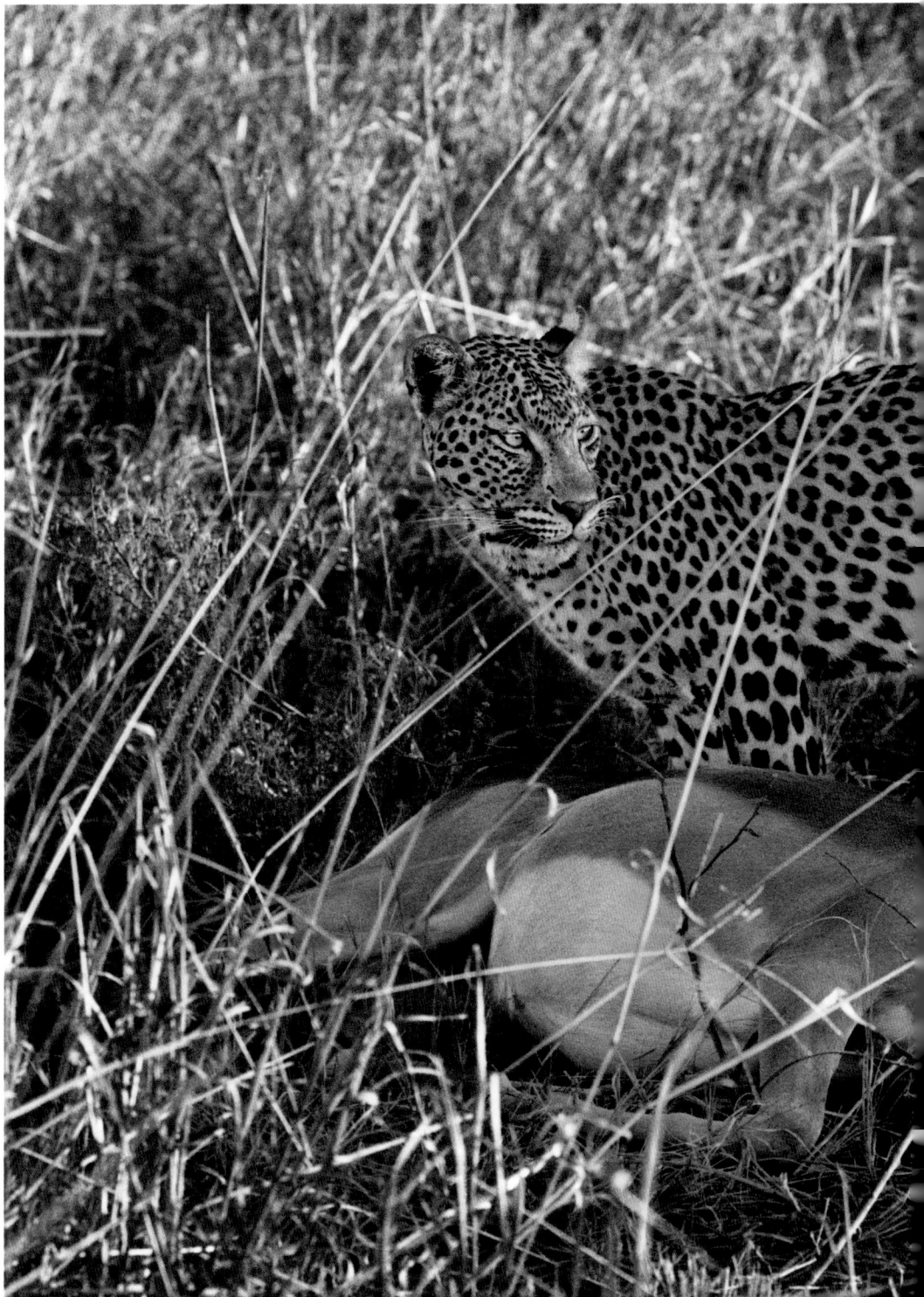

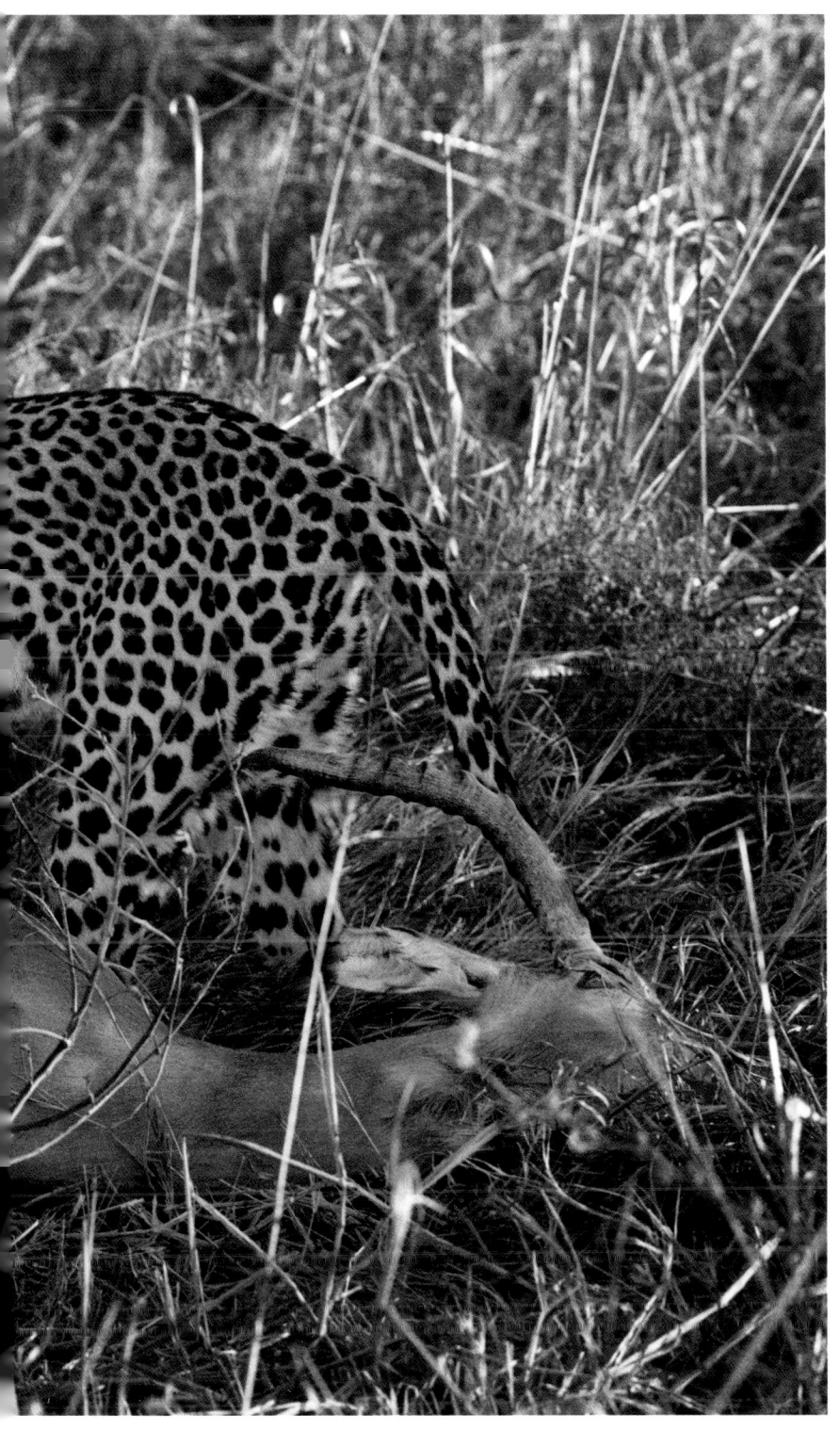

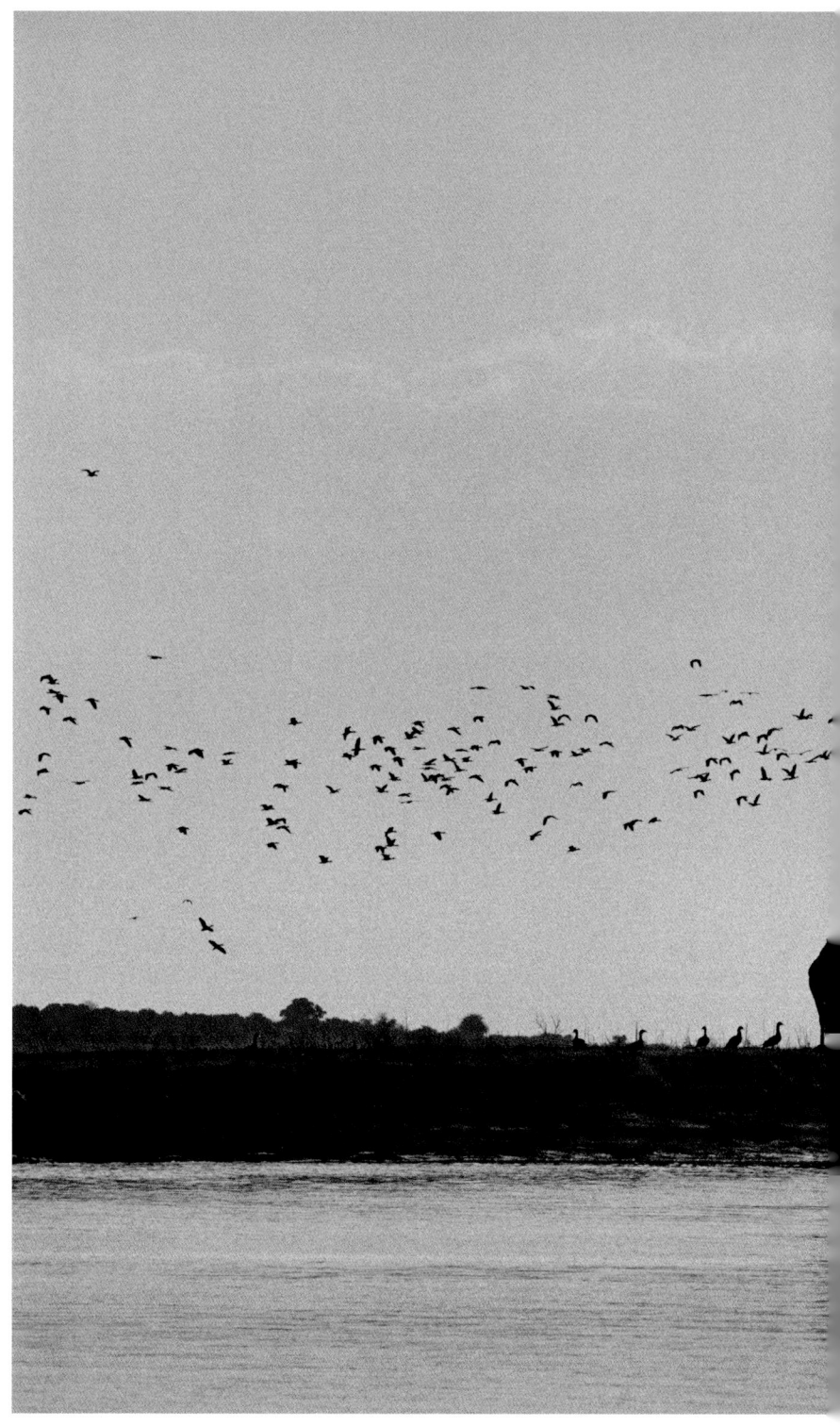

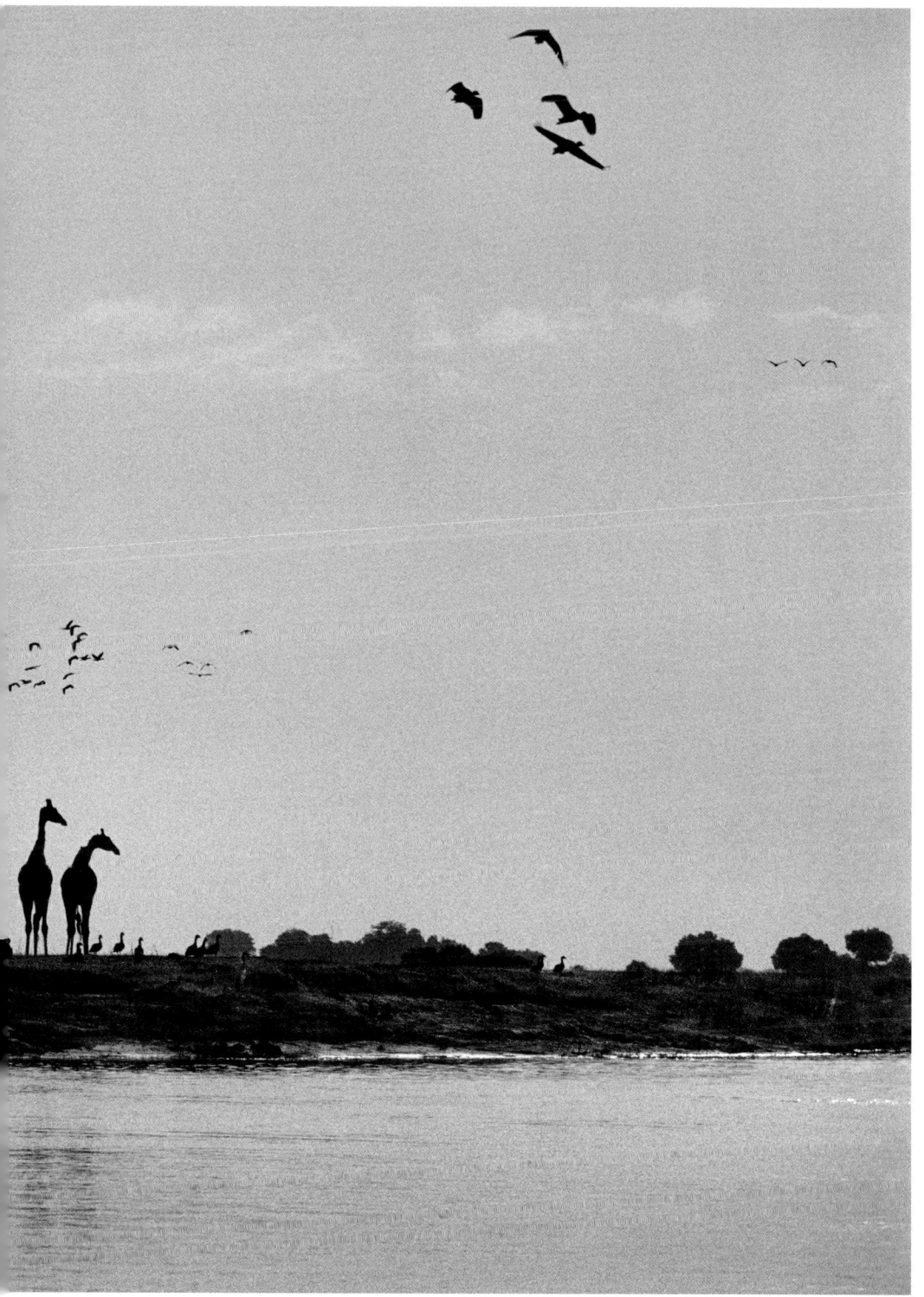

Opposite Animals are understandably frightened when they hear a helicopter flying overhead, but in a balloon it was possible to come close to this herd of buffalos (*Syncerus caffer*) without disturbing them. Balloons, however, pose other problems. It is necessary to fly very early in the morning before spirals of hot air rising from the ground cause dangerous turbulence. There is also the risk that wind can send the balloon way off course. Kafue National Park, Zambia. July and August 2010.

Pages 274/275 Plains zebra (*Equus quagga*) in areas surrounding the Okavango Delta, gather in small groups of four to nine. But on the grassy plains of the delta's wetlands, herds can number over 50 animals. Okavango Delta, Botswana. June and July 2007.

Pages 276/277 A leopard (*Panthera pardus*) in the Barab River Valley, Damaraland. Namibia. October and November 2005.

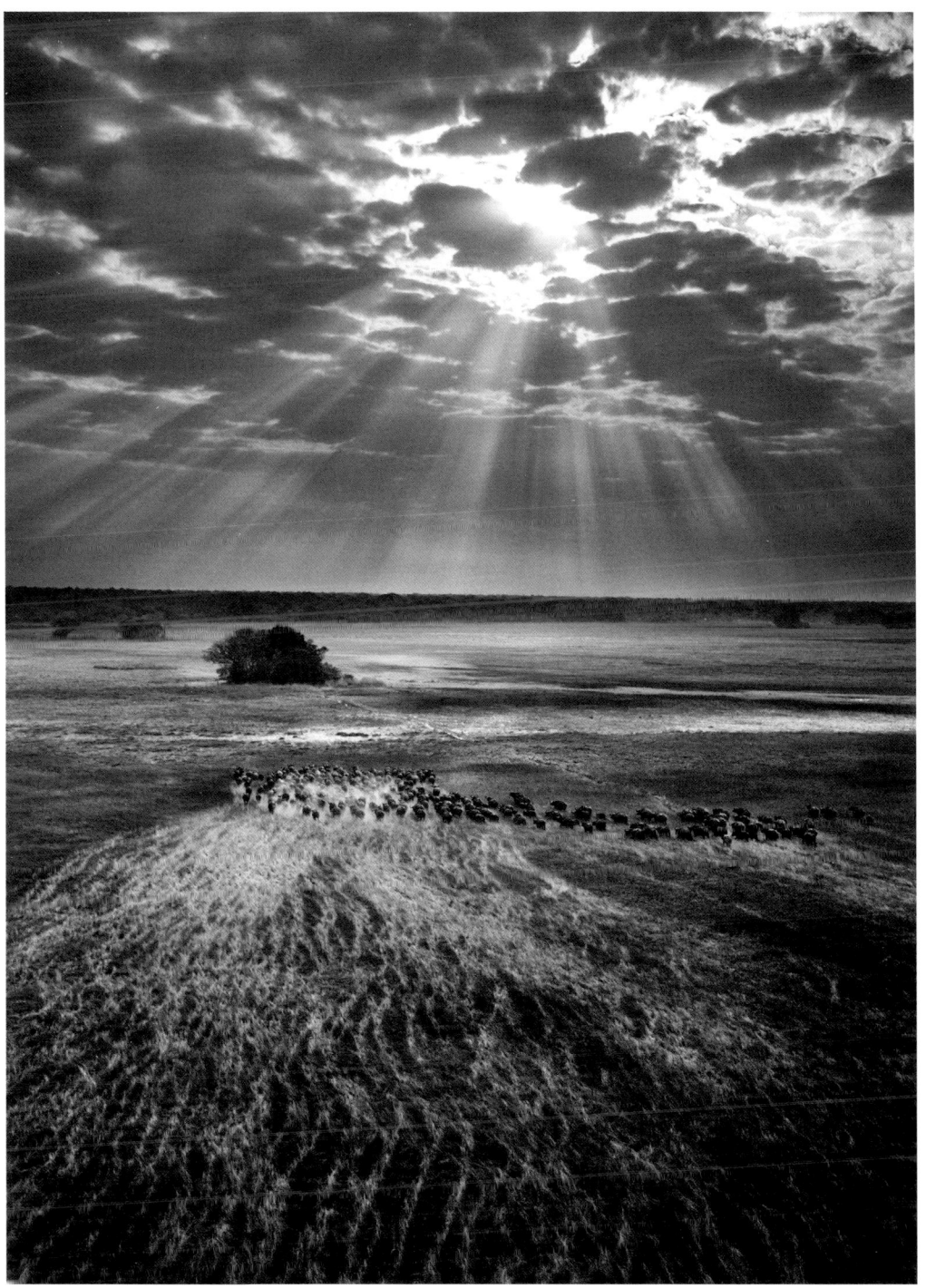

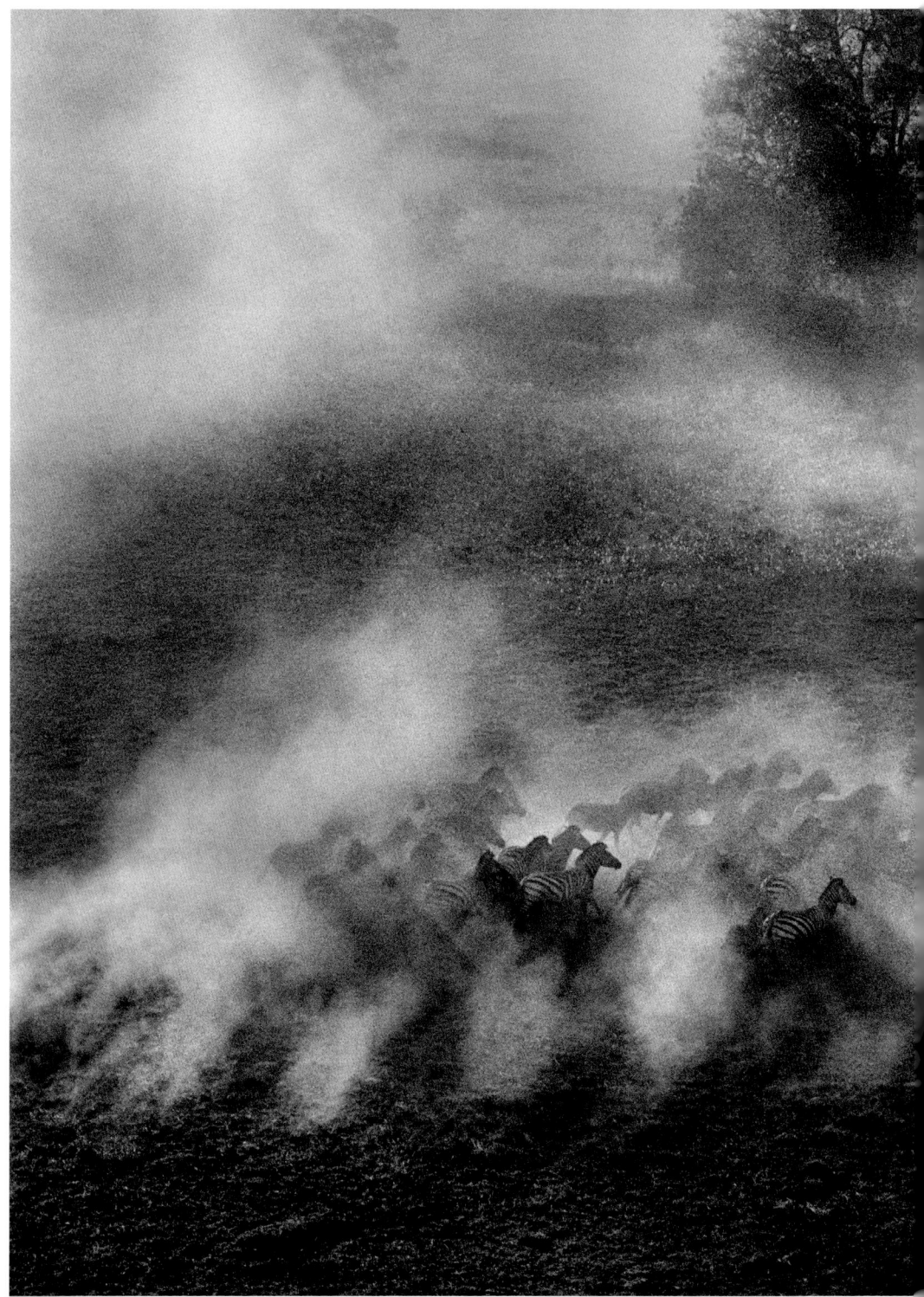

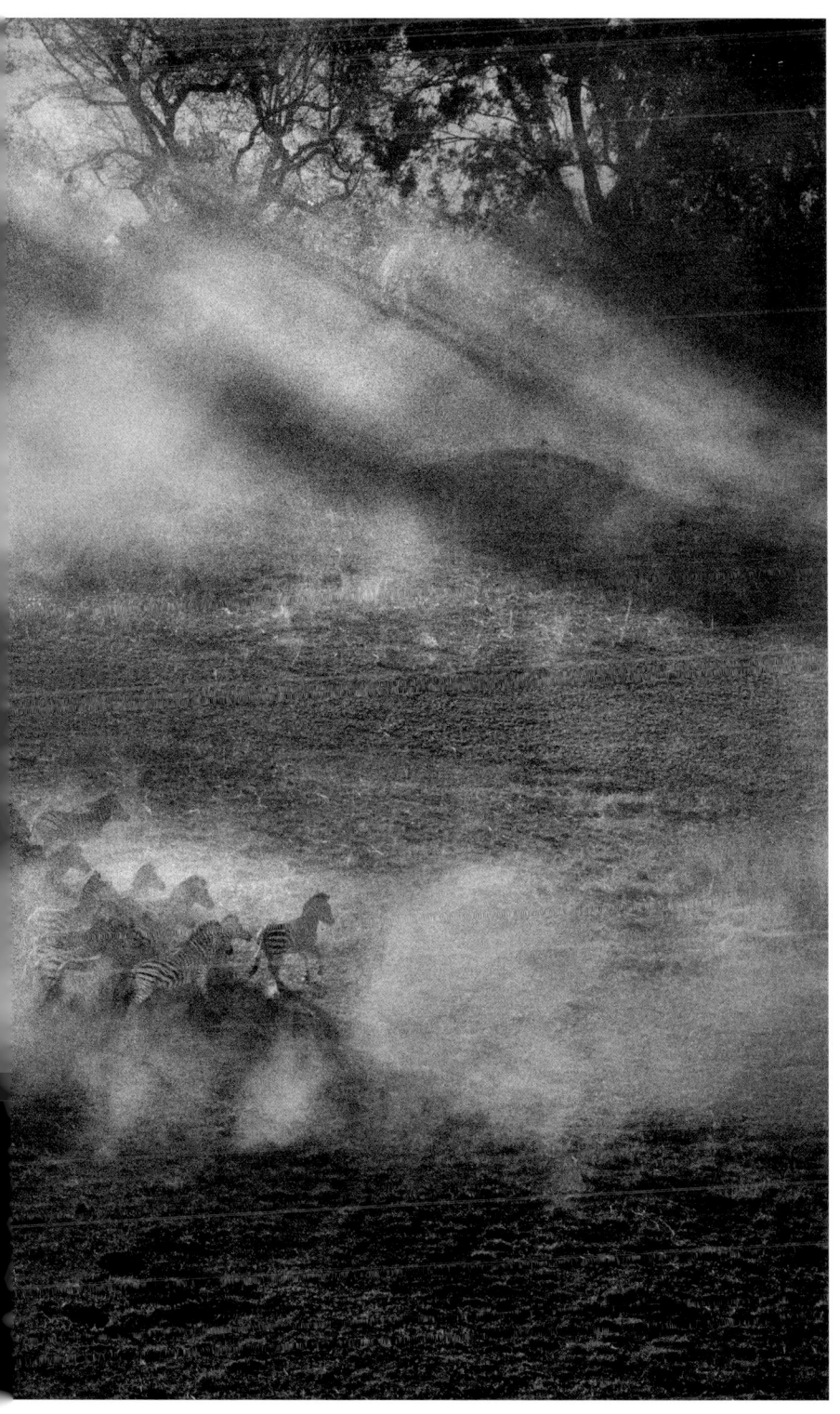

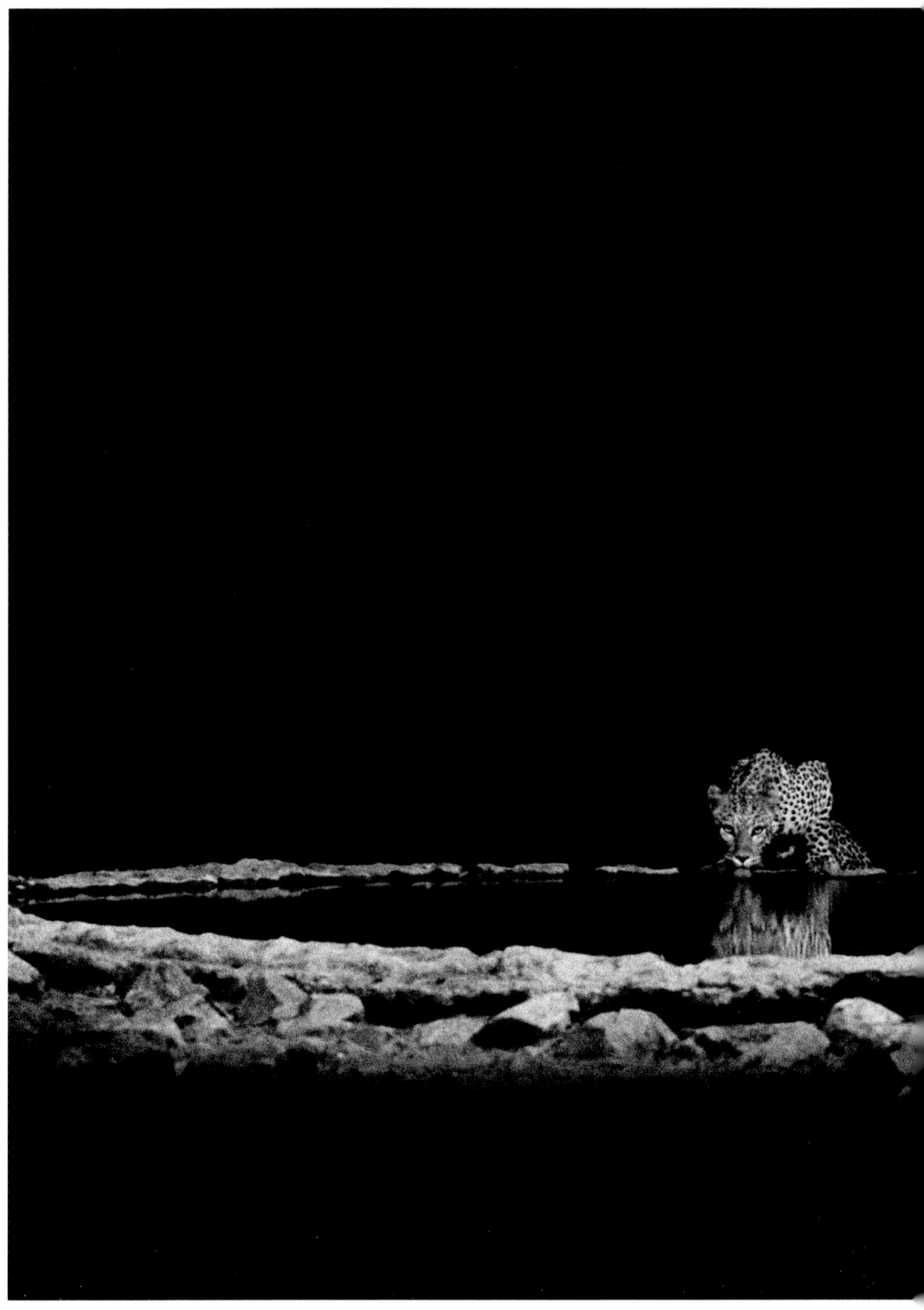

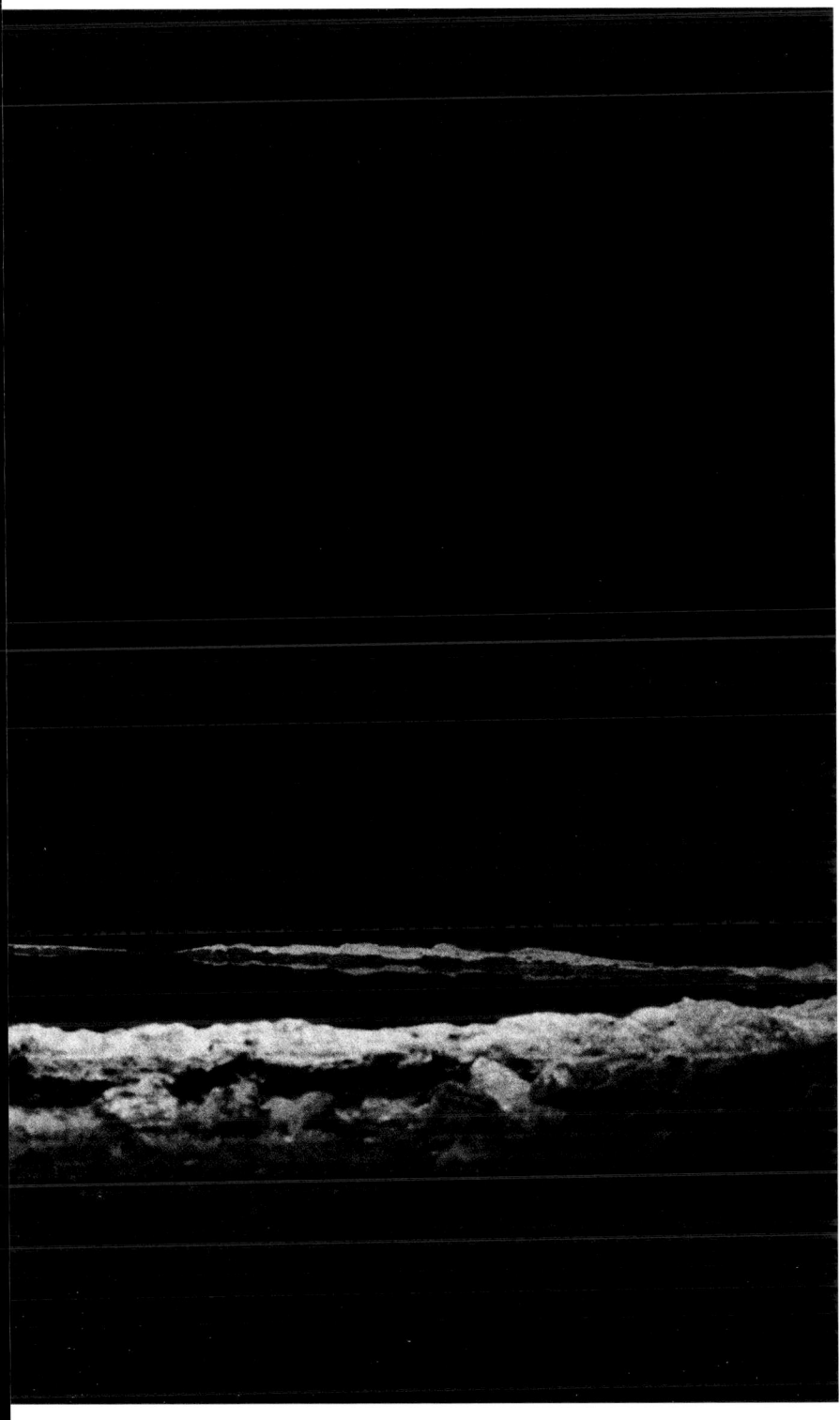

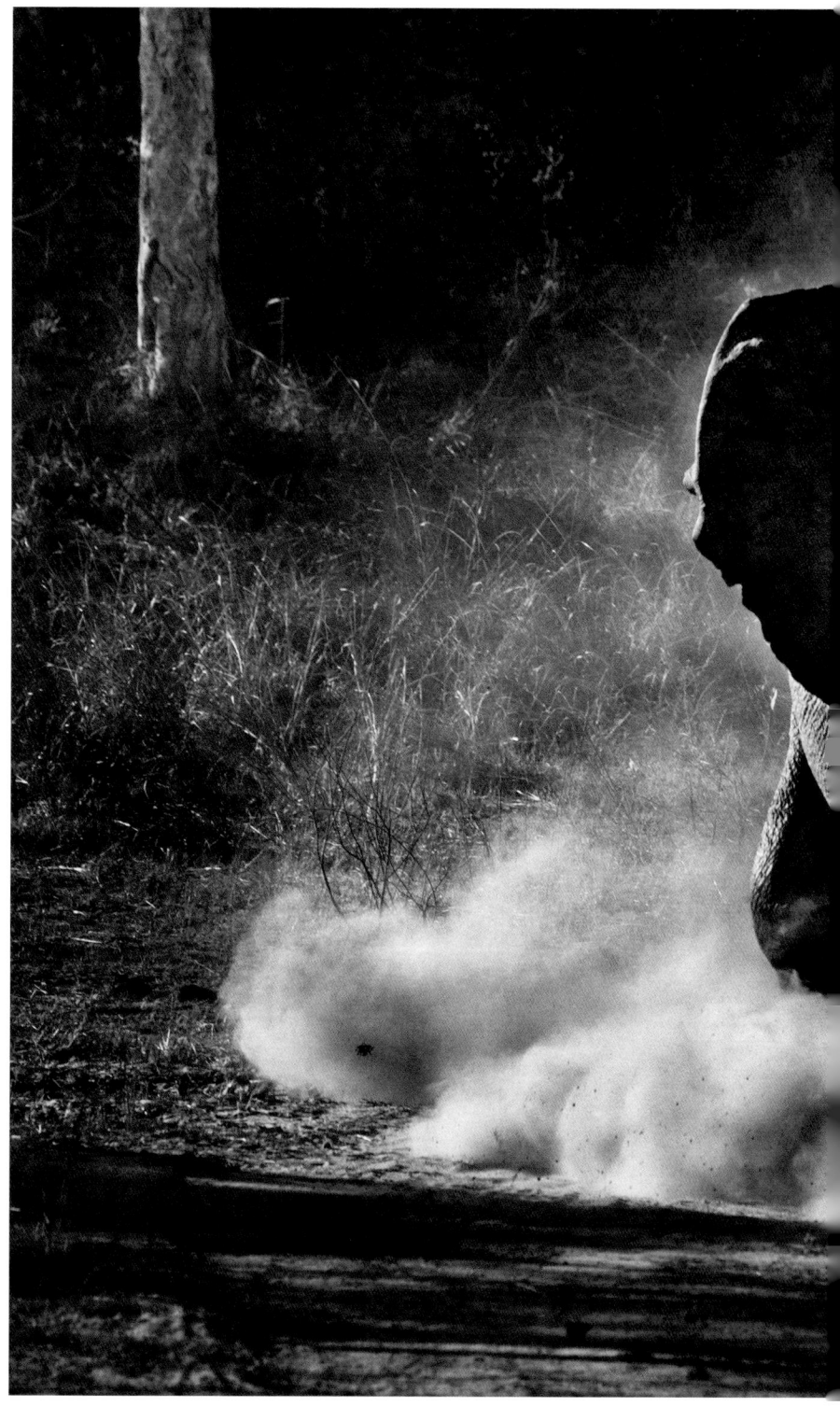

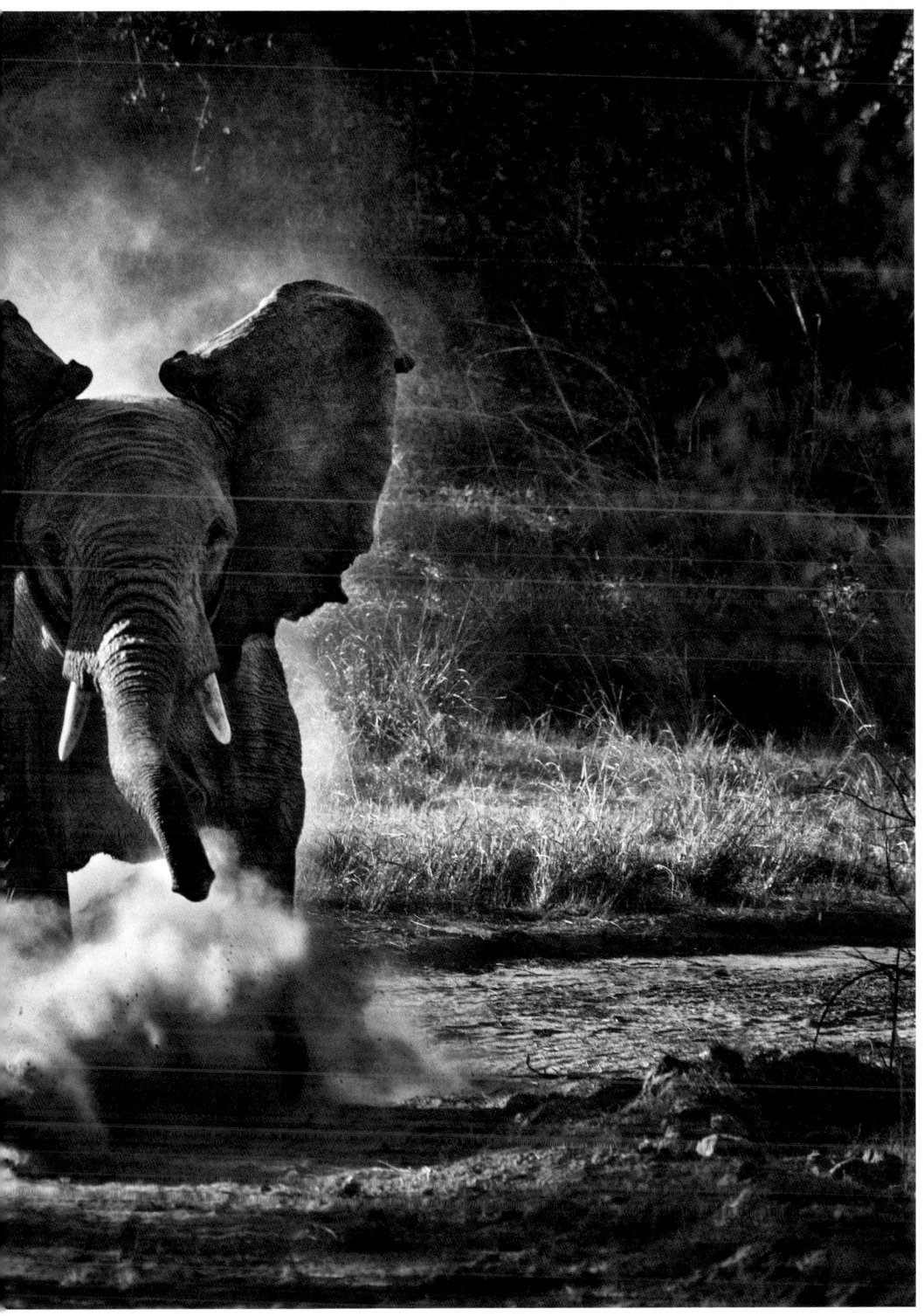

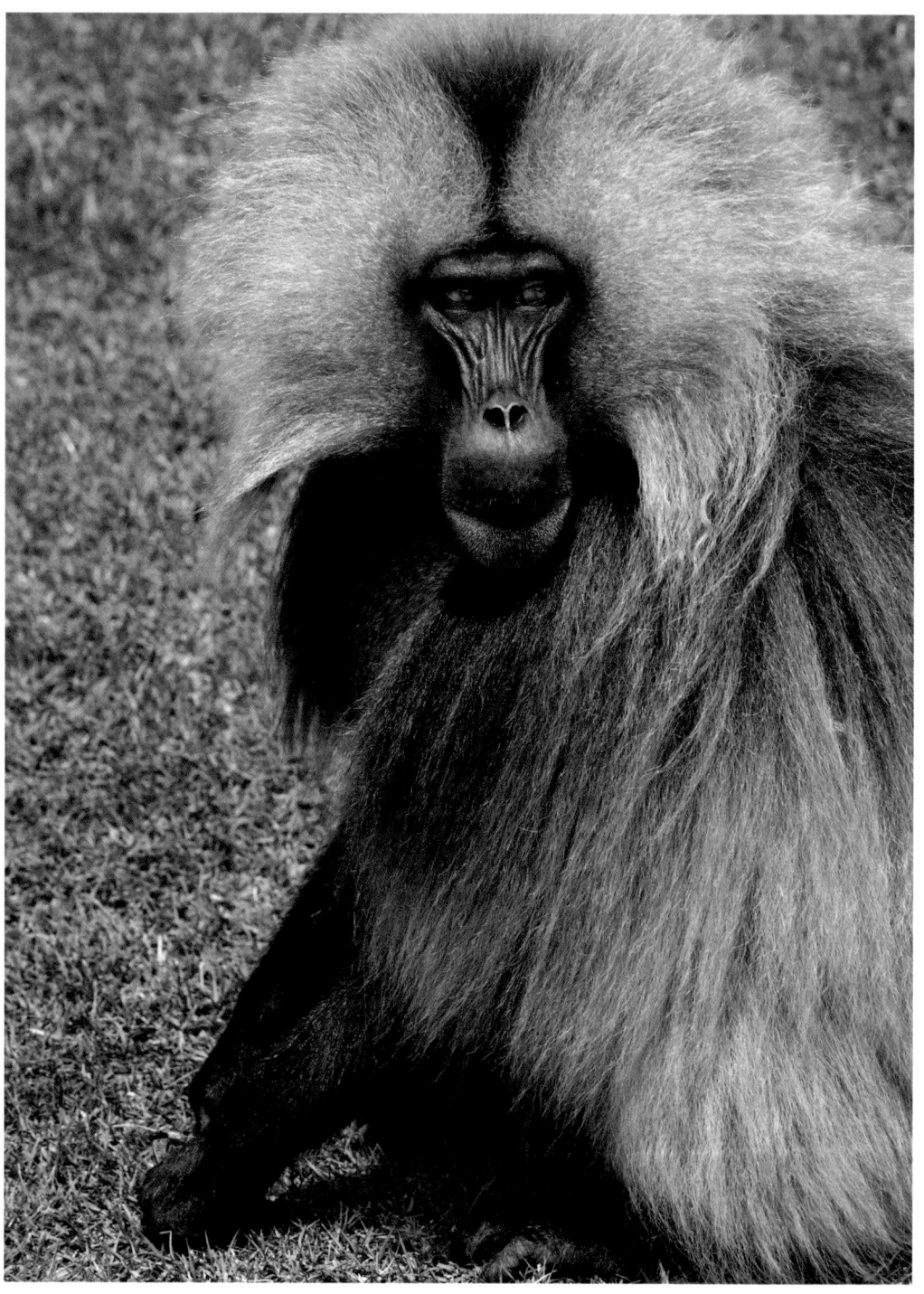

Pages 278/279 Since elephants (*Loxodonta africana*) are hunted by poachers in Zambia, they are scared of humans and vehicles. Alarmed when they see a car approaching, they usually run quickly into the bush. However, in this case, instead of fleeing the elephant charged our vehicle. We quickly drove away. Kafue National Park, Zambia. July and August 2010.

Opposite The Simien National Park in northern Ethiopia is home to some extremely rare animals such as the Walia ibex (*Capra walie*), a goat found nowhere else in the world, and the gelada baboon (*Theropithecus gelada*). This tall monkey, which resembles a baboon yet belongs to a different species, is best suited to high altitudes. Near the village of Ginche. Altitude 11,834 feet (3,607 meters). Ethiopia. October and November 2008.

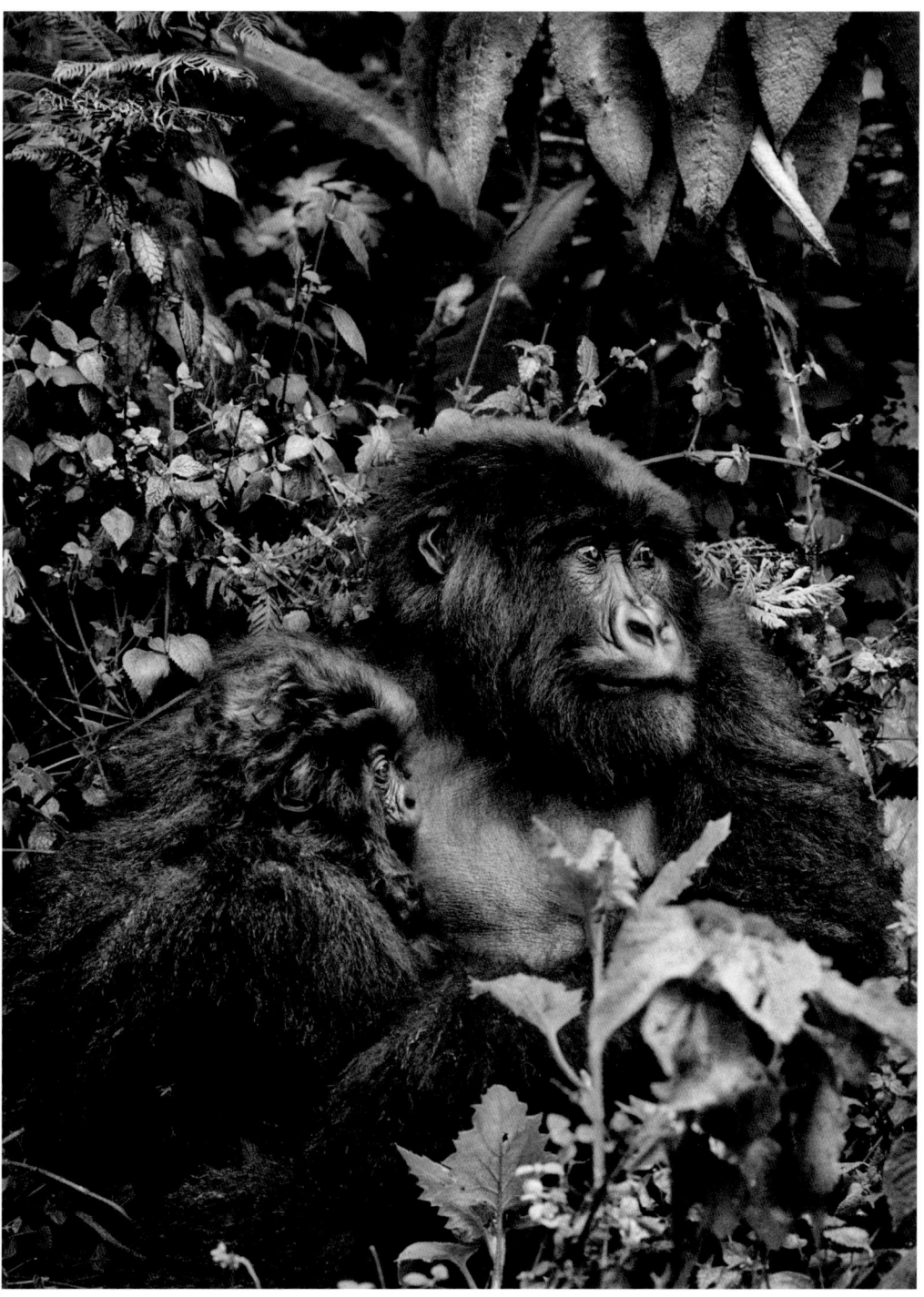

Opposite The mountain gorilla (*Gorilla beringei beringei*) is the rarest of the three species of gorilla, numbering only about 800, with roughly half in the volcanic region of Virungas and the rest in the Bwindi Impenetrable National Park in Uganda. For all their formidable size, with adult males weighing up to 550 pounds (250 kilos), gorillas are peaceful animals, preferring family life to anything more adventurous. Here, a female gorilla displays typical tenderness towards her infant. Family groups of young males, females and their infants are led by a dominant silverback male, whose name derives from the saddle of gray hairs that develops across his back once he reaches full maturity. Young silverbacks often leave the group, opting for a solitary life until they can attract a female from a different group to form a family. Females sometimes transfer between groups and, in this way, inbreeding is avoided. Gorillas are vegetarians, with a diet that includes bamboo shoots, wild celery, thistles, nettles, galium, a leafy vegetable called *vernonia* and various roots and vines.

Unless a zoo succeeds in breeding these gorillas, every one seen in captivity is there as the result of a tragedy. Since adult gorillas are difficult to capture,

their young are targeted. But they can only be taken if their parents are first killed. When the slain father is the silverback leader of the group, the entire family often falls apart and many gorillas end up dying from solitude. Virunga National Park. Rwanda. May and June 2004.

Pages 284/285 African elephants (*Loxodonta africana*) are both diurnal and nocturnal, forming herds of as few as six and as many as 200 animals, with a cow as leader. Chobe River. Botswana. June and July 2007.

Pages 286/287 The lion (*Panthera leo*) is the largest of Africa's cat family, with males weighing between 400 and 530 pounds (180 and 240 kilos) and females between 265 and 400 pounds (120 and 180 kilos). Cubs are born at any time of the year after a gestation period of around 110 days. Here two brothers rest after a night of hunting in preparation for the following night's hunt. Young males are pushed out of the group by the male leader when they are strong enough to create their own group. Kafue National Park. Zambia. July and August 2010.

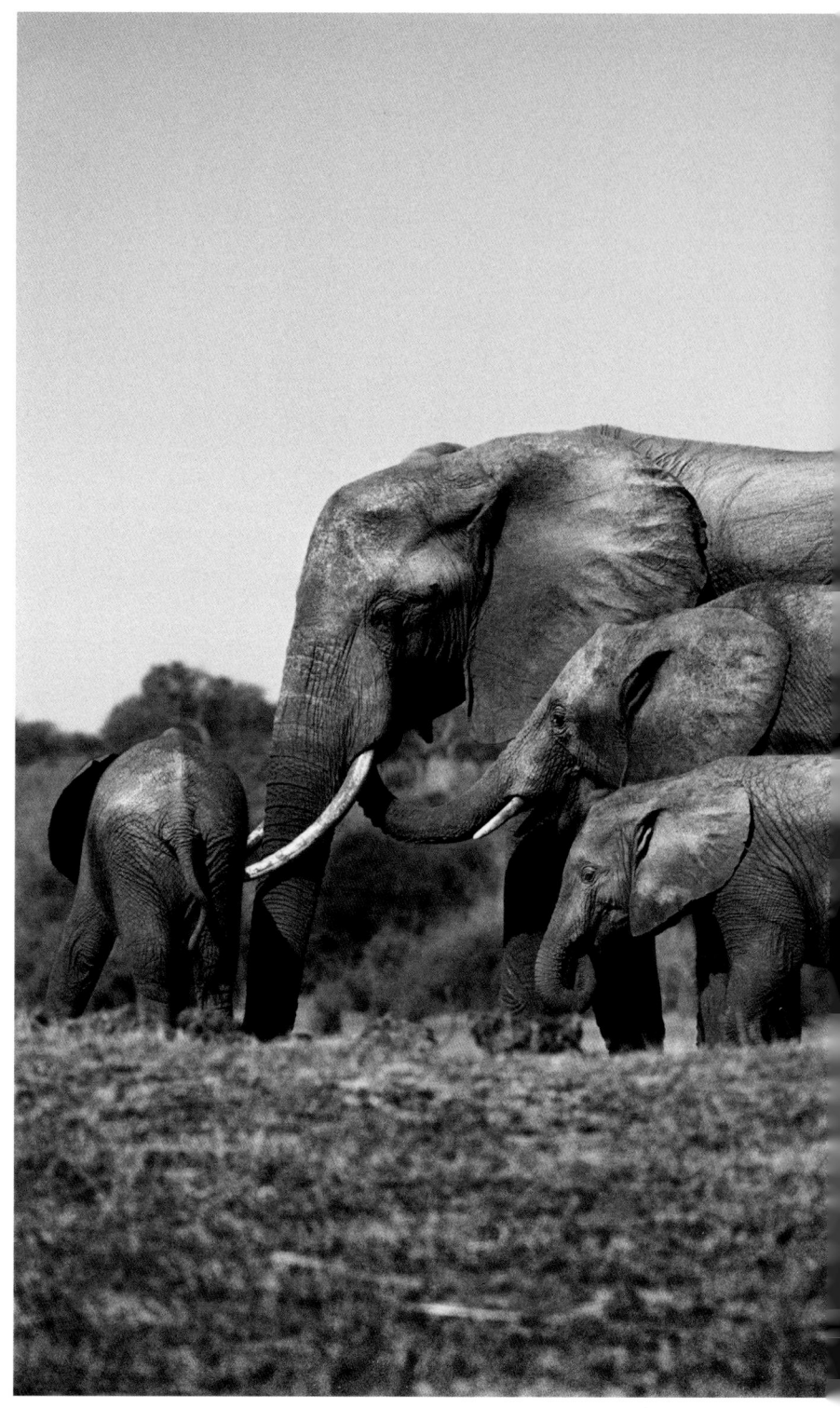

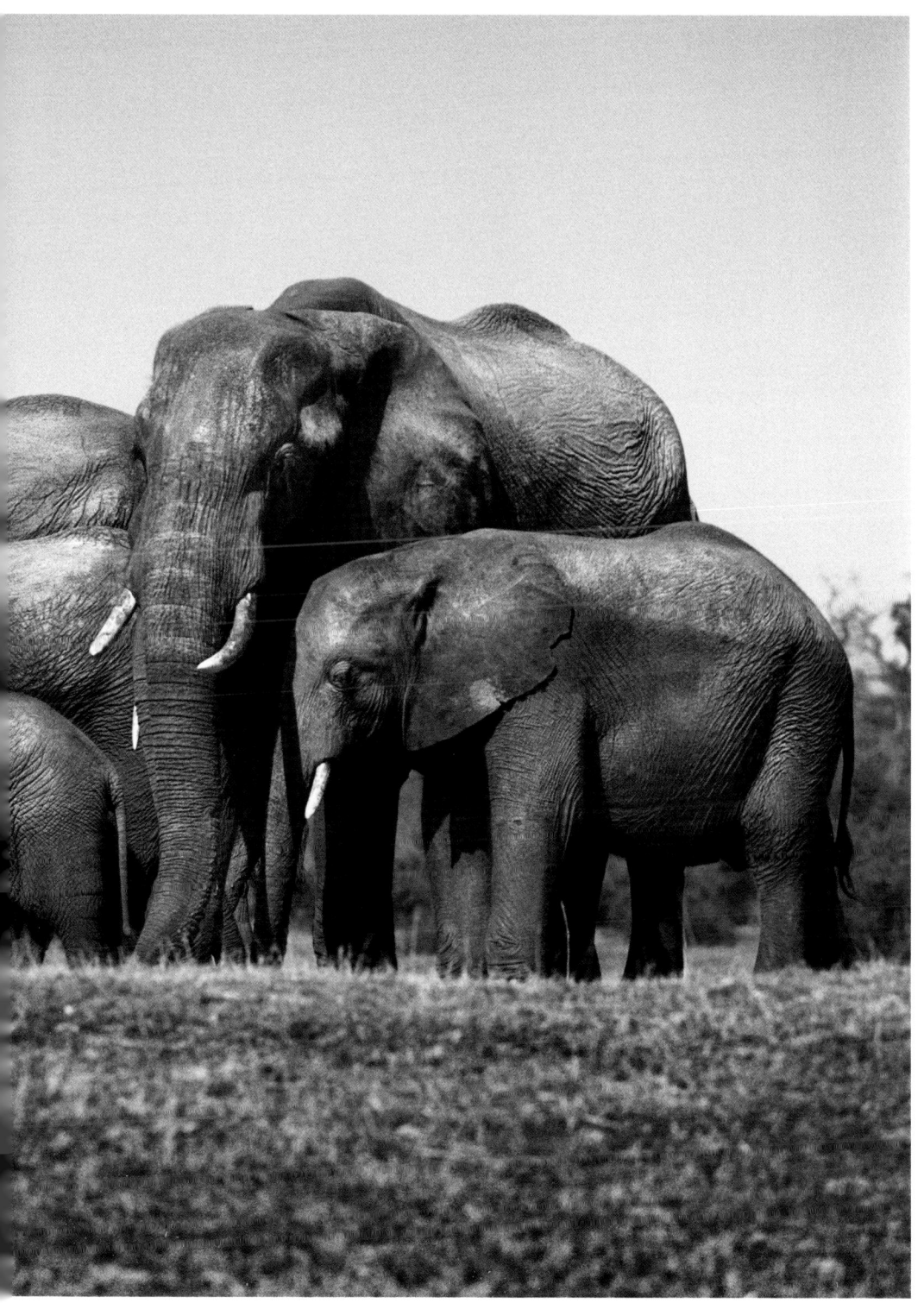

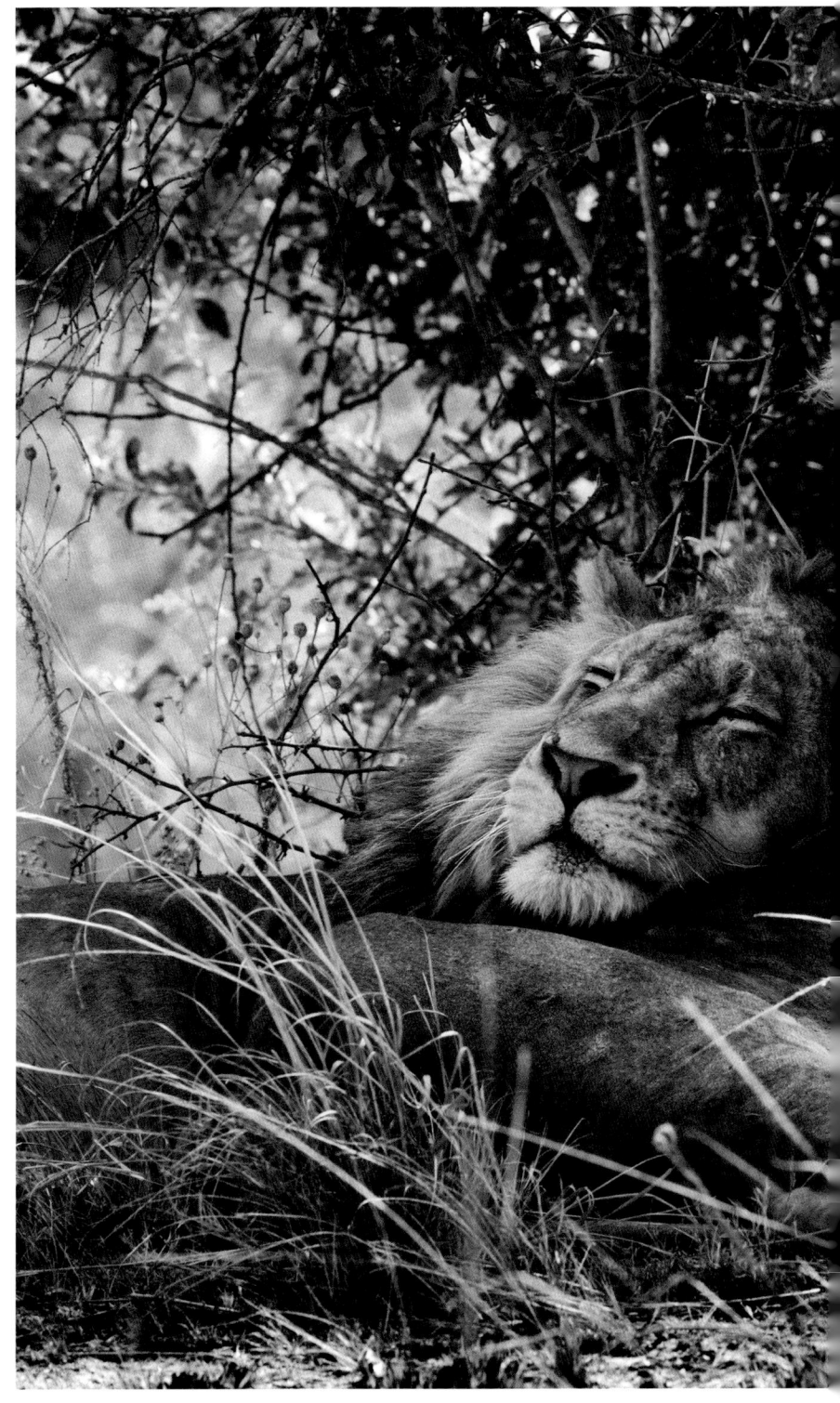

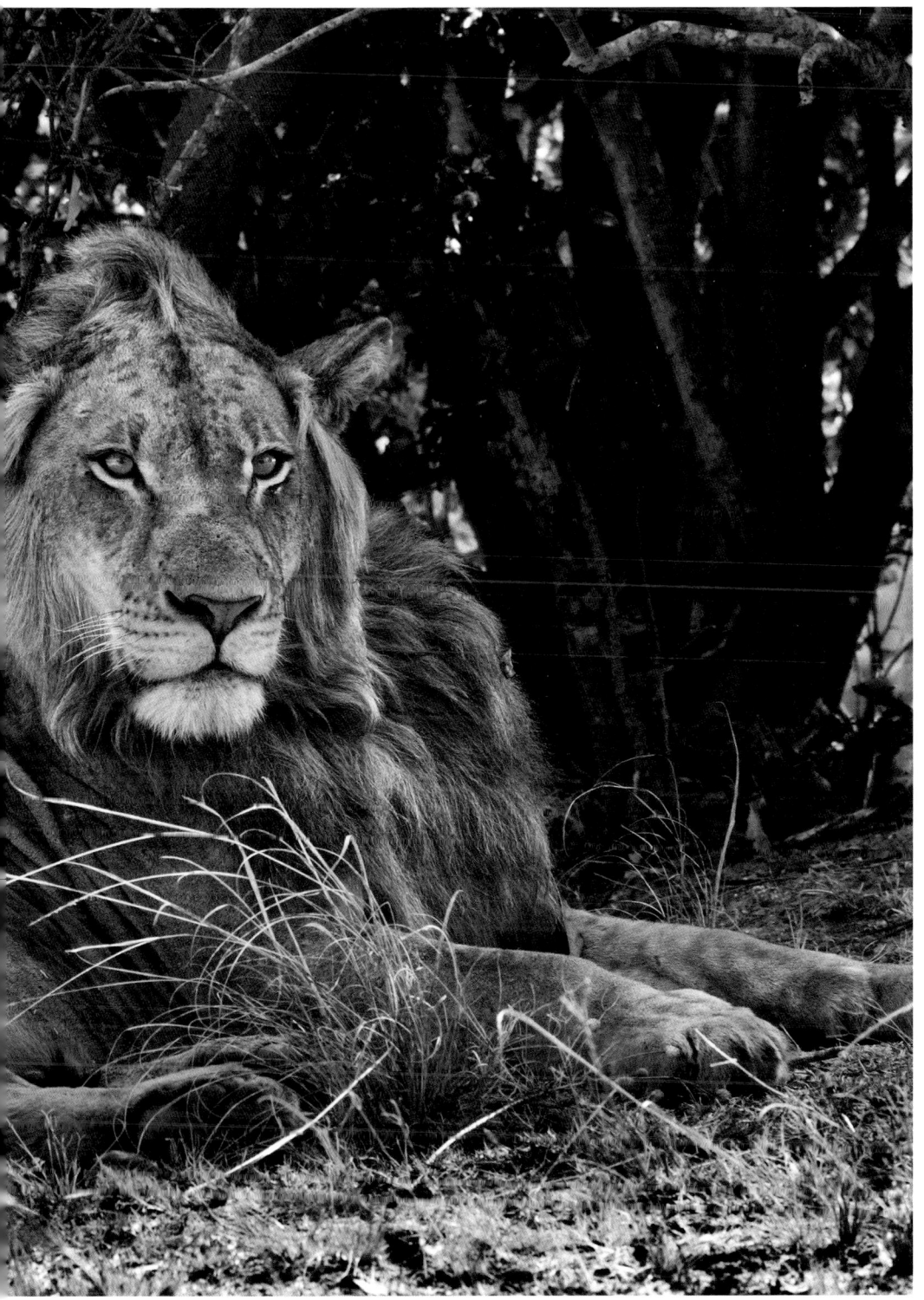

Opposite Hippopotamus (*Hippopotamus amphibius*). Led by a female, these gregarious animals form groups of six to 15 members. Although generally placid, if they feel threatened they can become aggressive and even very dangerous. This is especially true of cows with calves. Okavango Delta, Botswana. June and July 2007.

Pages 290/291 Victoria Falls, viewed from Zimbabwe. January 2008.

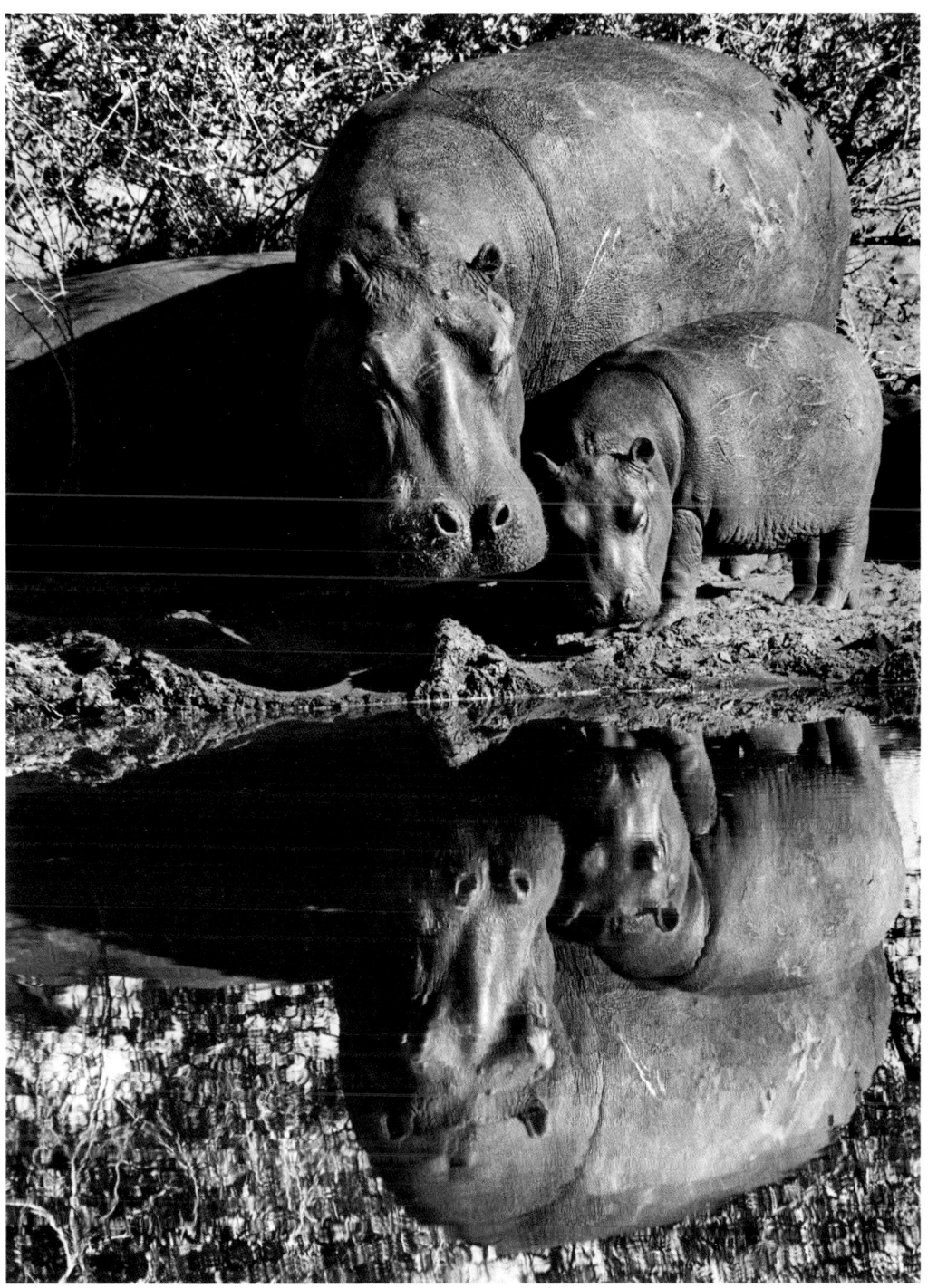

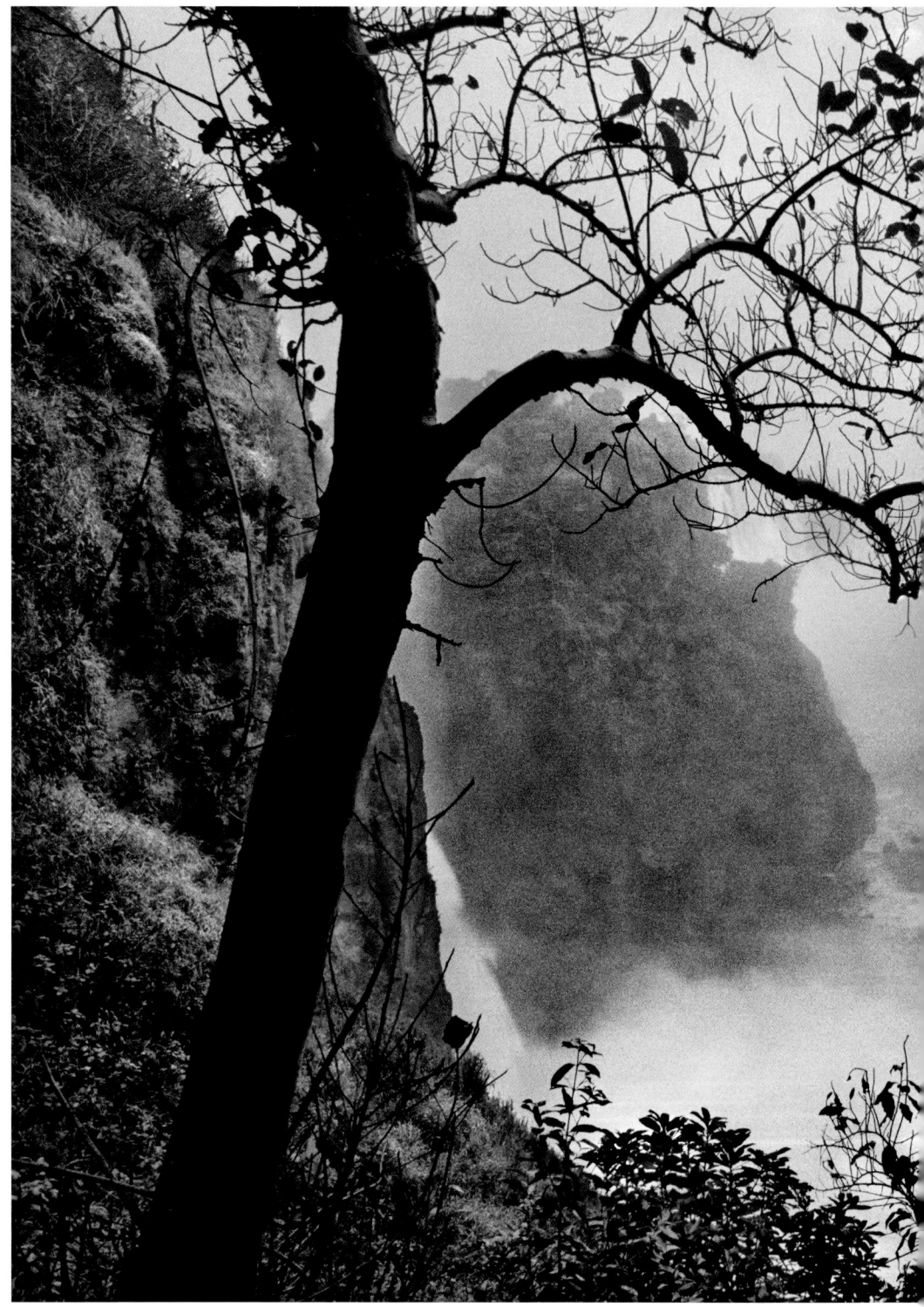

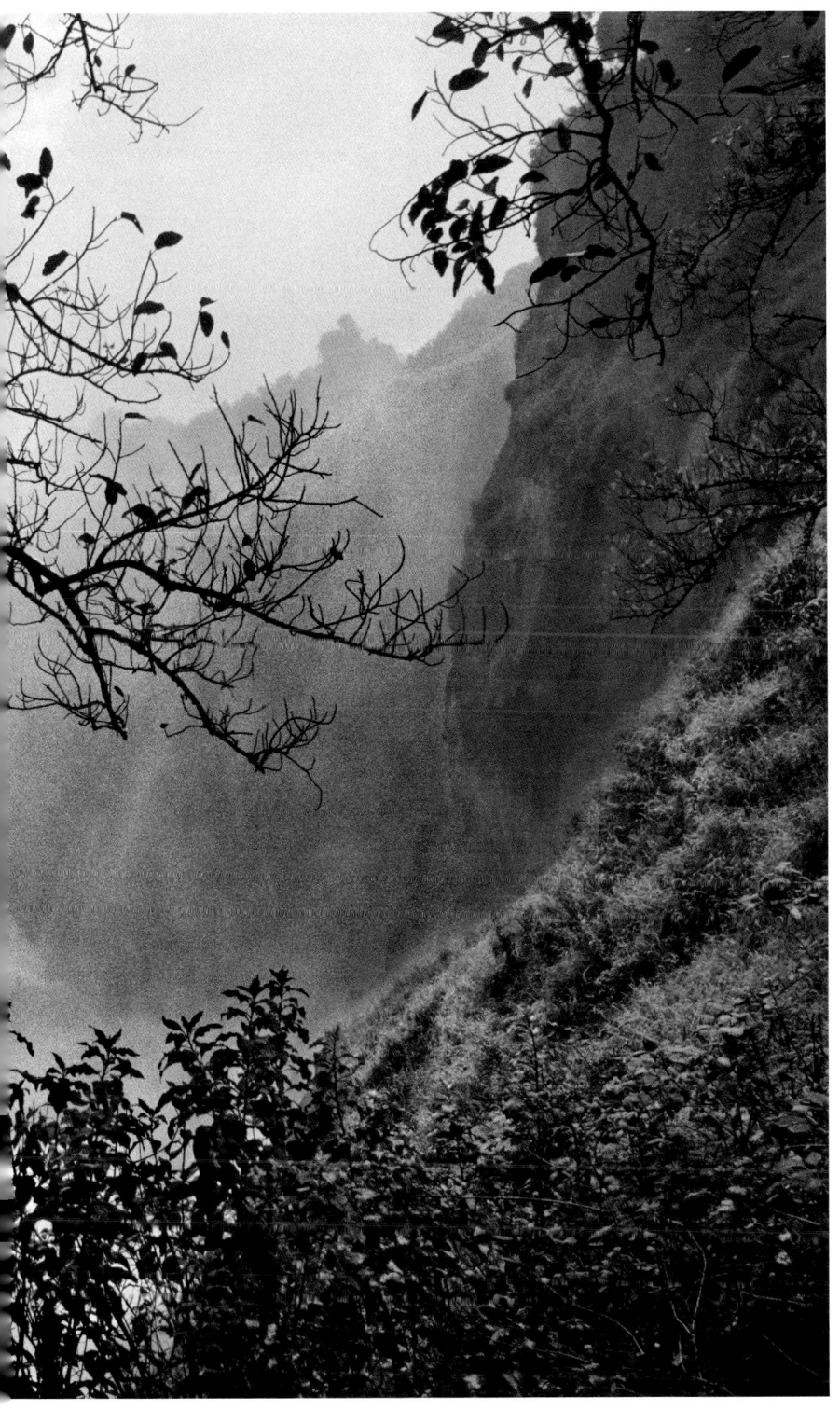

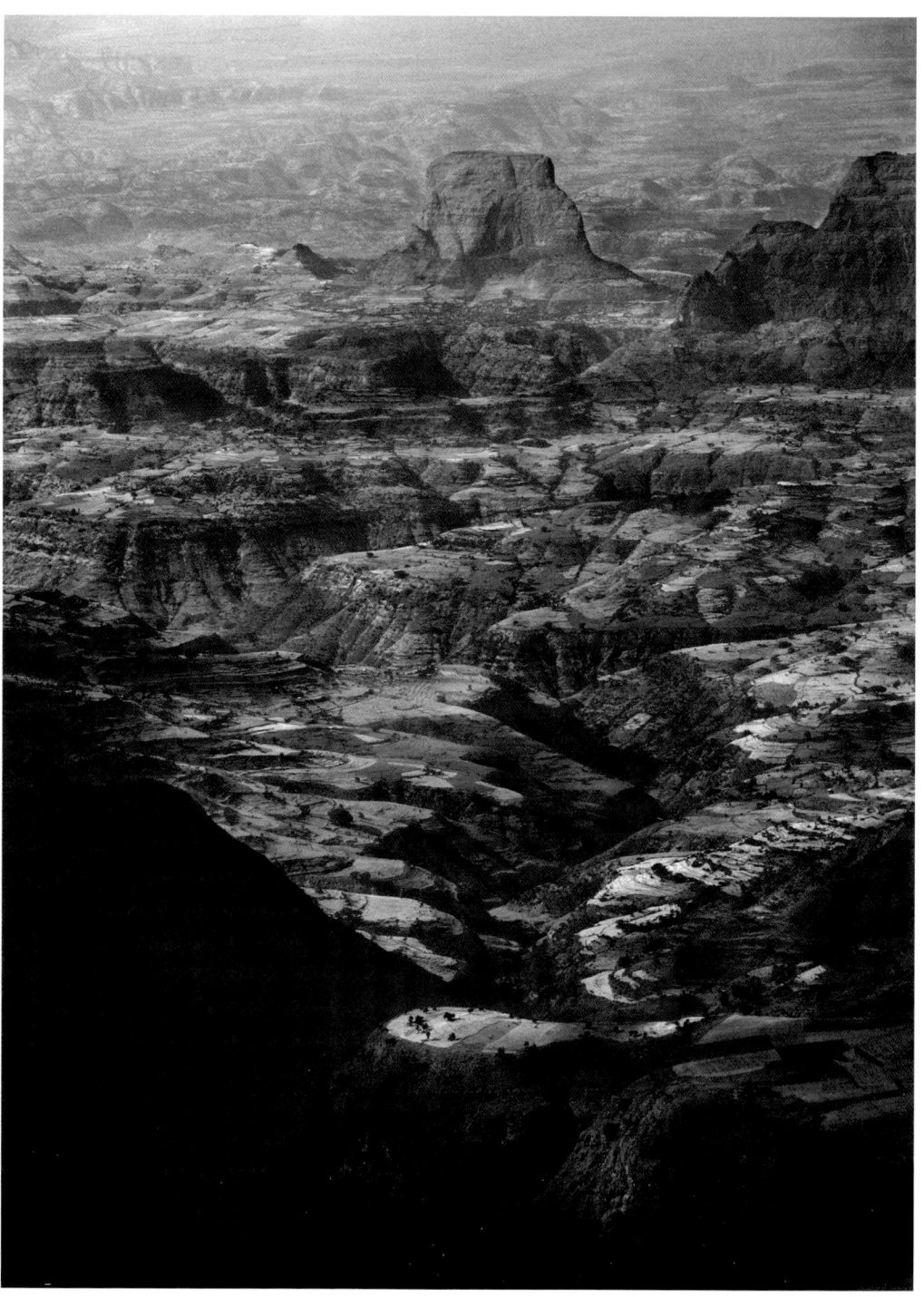

A JOURNEY THROUGH THE OLD TESTAMENT

Pages 292 through 305

Modern Ethiopia has been beset by political instability, war and famine spawned by drought, but it is also a country that retains remnants of one of the world's oldest civilizations. This trip took me across an extraordinarily remote region of northern Ethiopia where, in many senses, time has stood still. It is here that you can find some of the world's oldest Christian communities, whose lives, farming practices and ways of worship have changed little for centuries. It is also a rugged, mountainous area sliced into imposing canyons by rivers, which have carried away the soil to bring fertility to the Nile Valley far to the north. The region is so inaccessible that it can only be reached on foot. Unsurprisingly, the logistics involved in what turned out to be a 55-day-long hike of more than 500 miles (800 kilometers) were immensely complicated. To carry everything needed to work, eat and sleep, I hired 15 donkeys, with each donkey accompanied by its owner. During the most difficult climbs, the owners would even carry some of the donkeys' burden in order to protect their most valuable possession. Even so, five donkeys died of exhaustion and, naturally, we compensated the owners for their loss.

Our journey began in Lalibela, one of Ethiopia's oldest Christian towns, famous above all for its 11 Orthodox churches carved out of red volcanic rock in the 12th century. From there, we headed northeast, taking a week to reach the high plane of Abune Yosef, 14,000 feet (4,200 meters) above sea level. On our way, we passed through Christian villages where a hole in a hillside announced the entrance to a cave church. Some ancient Christian traditions survive: for example, on Wednesdays and Fridays, they refuse to consume any product of animal extraction, such as milk or meat. Their Bibles and church documents are written on animal skins. Local priests are allowed to marry and they work in the fields like other farmers, but they enjoy the special status of being elders of the church.

As we traveled west, the mountains slowed our progress, requiring long hikes up and down steep slopes in order to advance just a few kilometers on the map. But we kept coming across farming communities that grow grains on ancient terraces and raise cattle that provide milk for yoghurt and cheese; here, at least, we saw no evidence of hunger. In some areas, the patchwork patterns of cultivated fields stretch as far as the eye can see. Because many languages and dialects survive in a relatively small area, a product of the isolation imposed by the mountainous terrain, we had to change guides every two or three villages. When we could, we also often spent two or three days in villages to give us time to explore nearby areas and to be accepted by villagers. And since on some days we walked as many as 22 miles (35 kilometers), we were glad for the rest. For the most part, families live in round huts, with walls made of wood and mud. Their sleeping quarters are on a wooden mezzanine, directly above their animals, whose body heat brings welcome warmth at over 9,800 feet (3,000 meters) above sea level. Our journey eventually led us into the region long inhabited by Ethiopian Jews, known as the Falusha or, more formally, as Beta Israel. The roots of this community remain mysterious, although legend has it that its members descended from Menelik I, said to be the son of King Solomon and the Queen of Sheba. In the 1980s and 1990s, about 85 percent of the 140,000 Falusha emigrated to Israel, but Judeo-Christian traditions and values continue in the home and in schools. Local Ethiopians also watch over the Jewish cemeteries. Finally, we reached the Simien National Park, a wonderfully unspoiled area that is home to many rare species, including the gelada baboon, the Simien fox and the Walia ibex, unique to this area. Here, as during much of the journey, the developed world belonged to another age.

Opposite and page 292 The Simien National Park. Massive erosion over the years on the Ethiopian plateau has created one of the most spectacular landscapes in the world, with jagged mountain peaks, deep valleys and sharp precipices of some 4,900 feet (1,500 meters). The average altitude here is 13,000 feet (4,000 meters). Ethiopia. October and November 2008.

Pages 296/297 While crossing the Tekezé River, the largest tributary of the Blue Nile, the Simien mountains can be seen in the background. The altitude here is 3,630 feet (1,106 meters). From here, we could see how, over millions of years, eroded soil from this region has been carried by the Tekezé River into the Nile to create the fertile banks of the Nile in Egypt. Ethiopia. October and November 2008.

Pages 298/299 A Christian worshiper leaves the church of Makina Lideta Maryan. This church is inside a grotto, at an altitude of 9,646 feet (2,940 meters). Ethiopia. October and November 2008.

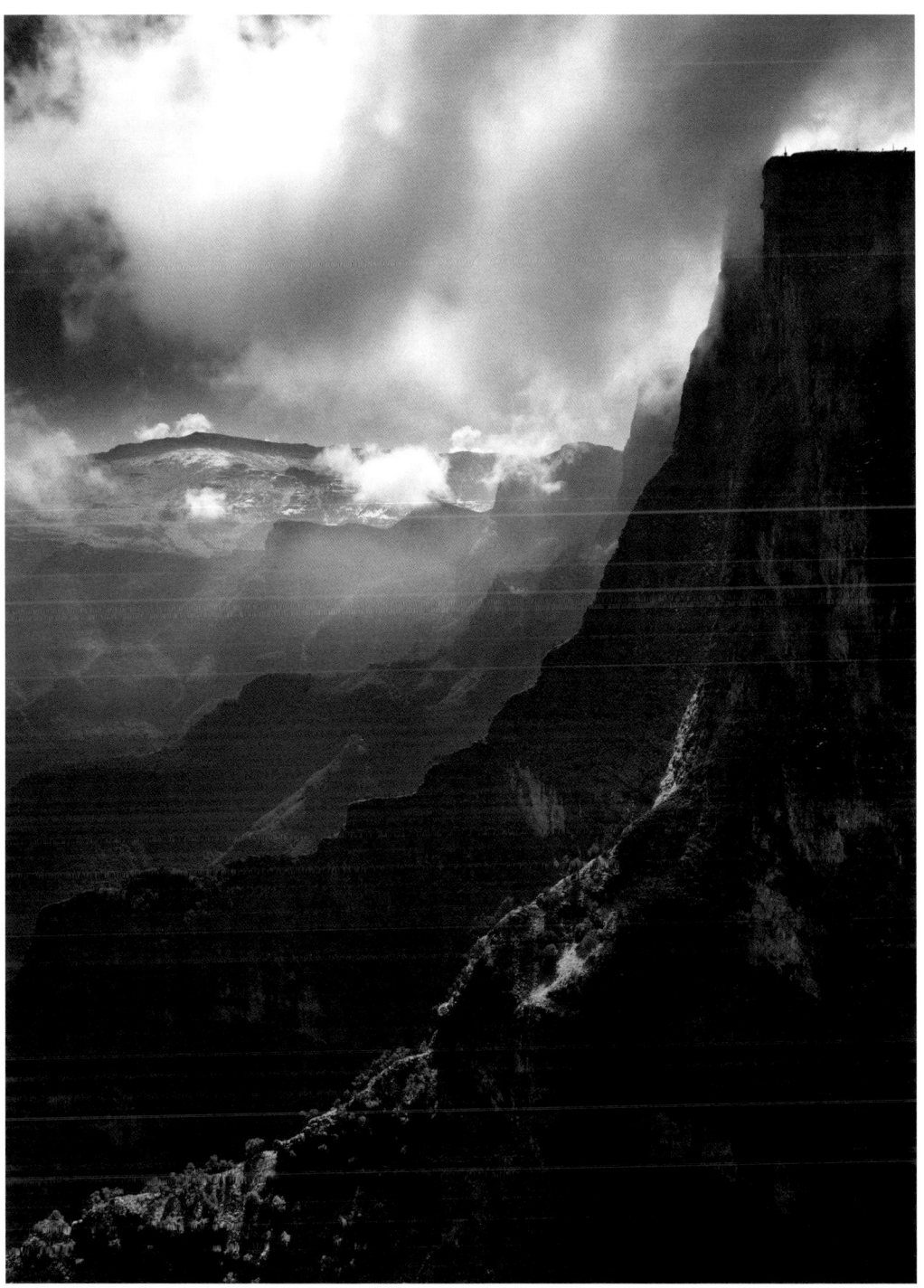

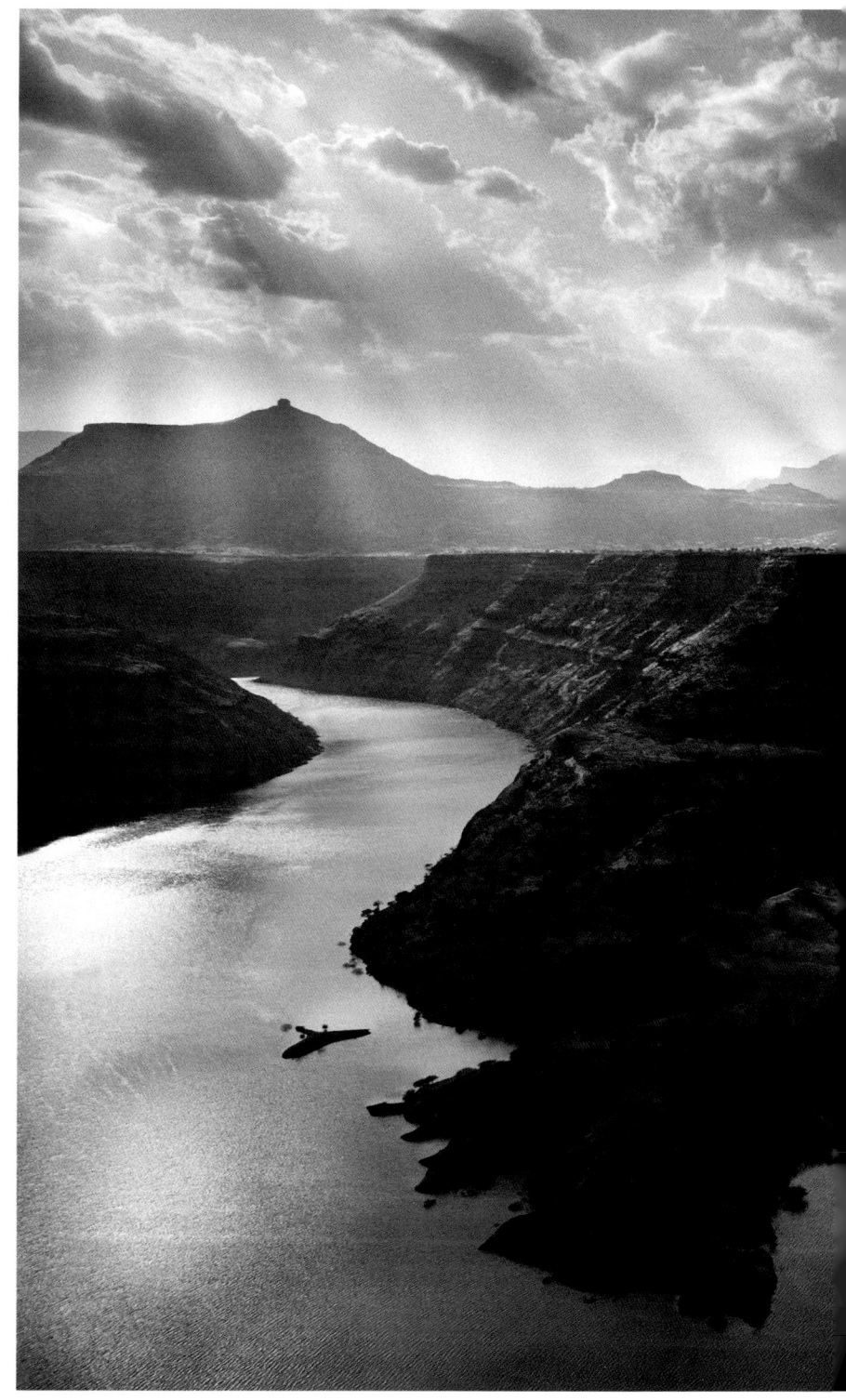

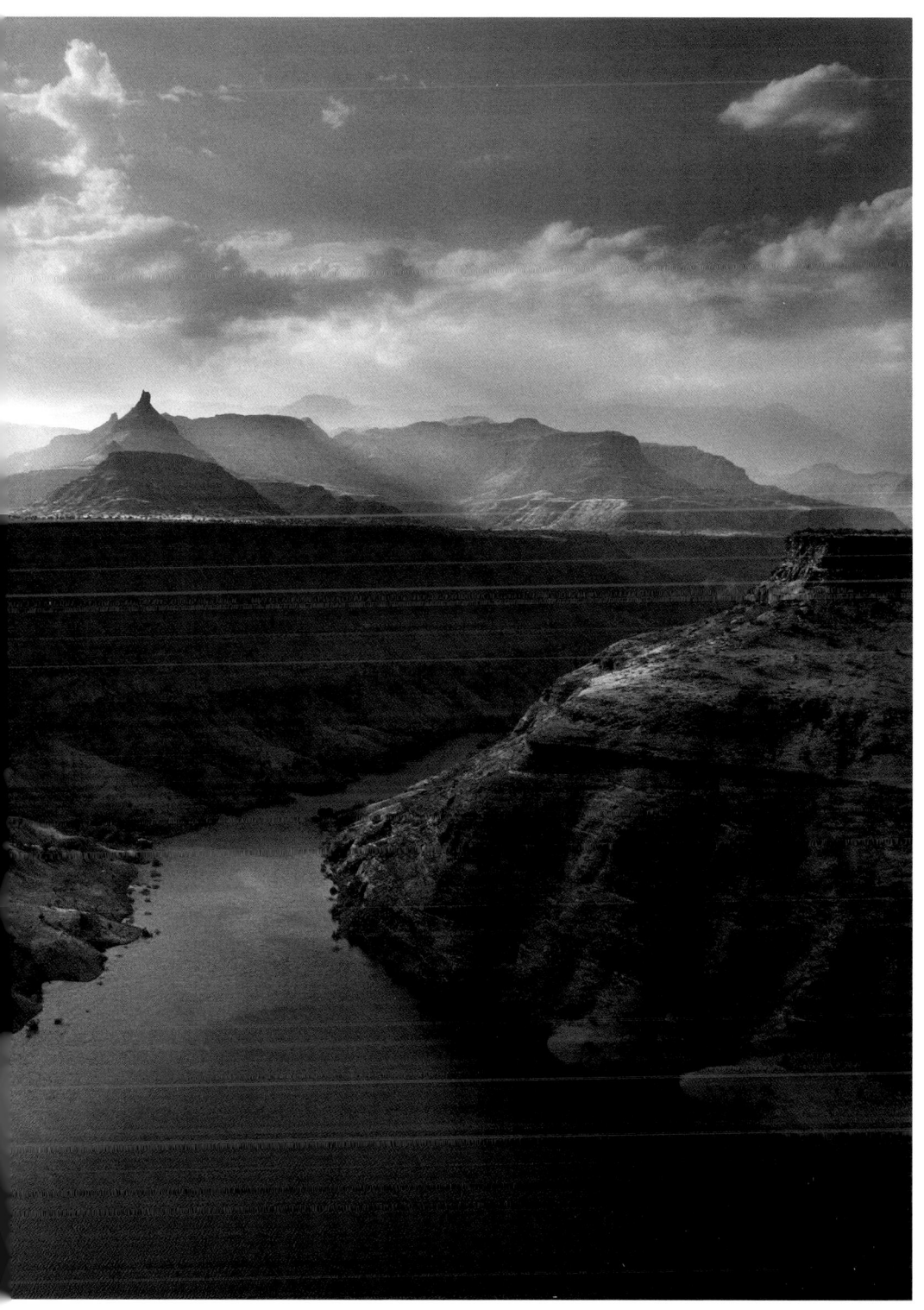

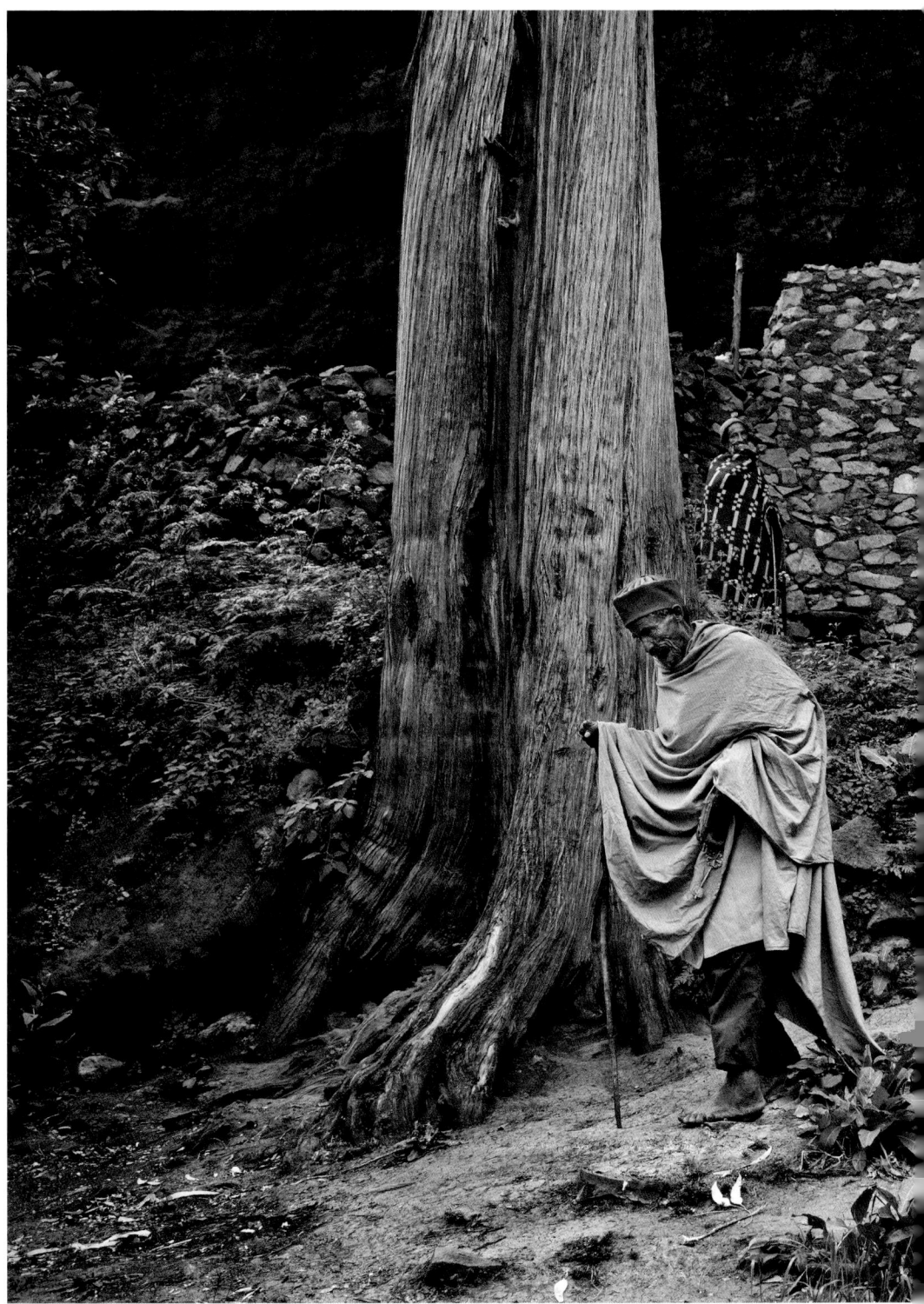

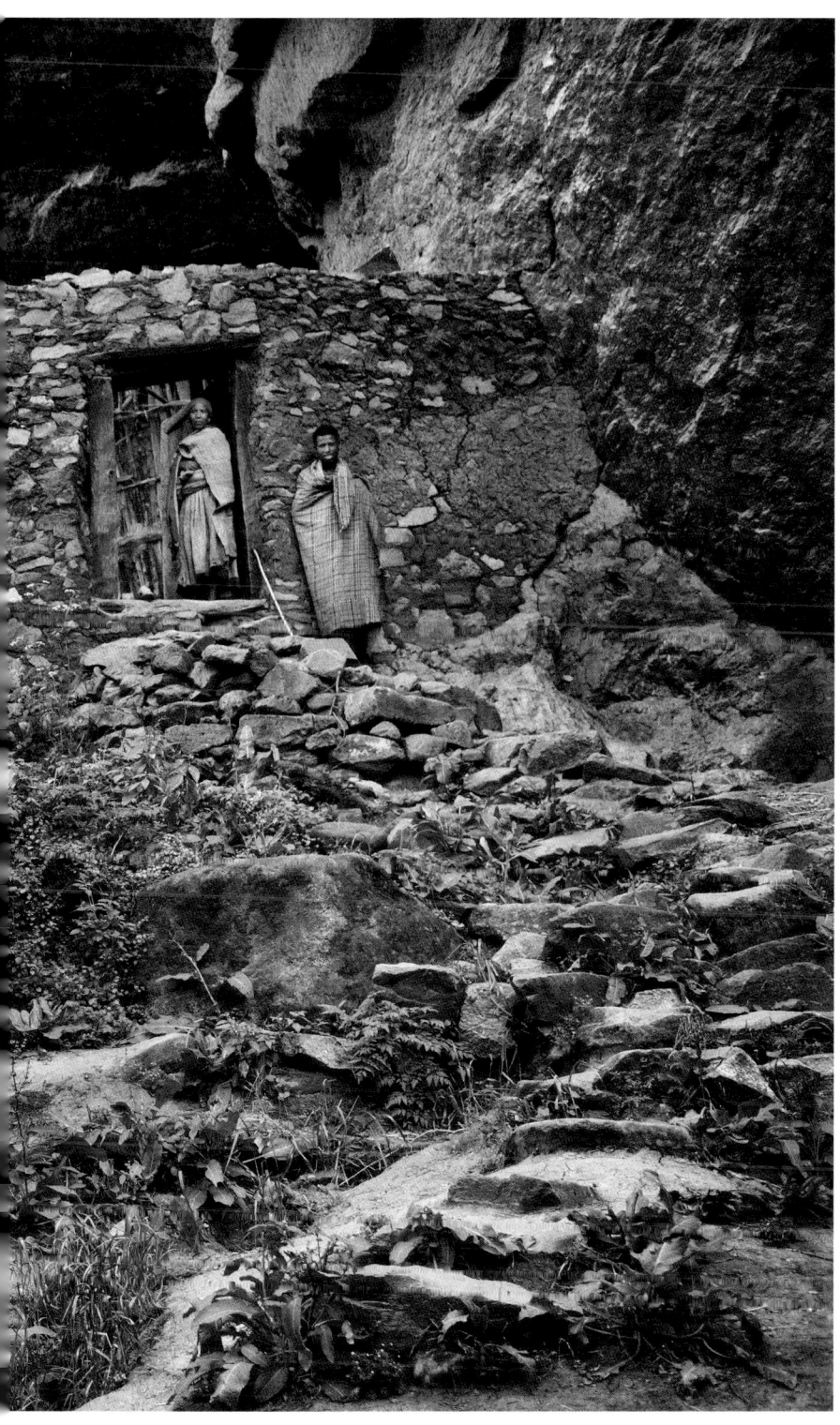

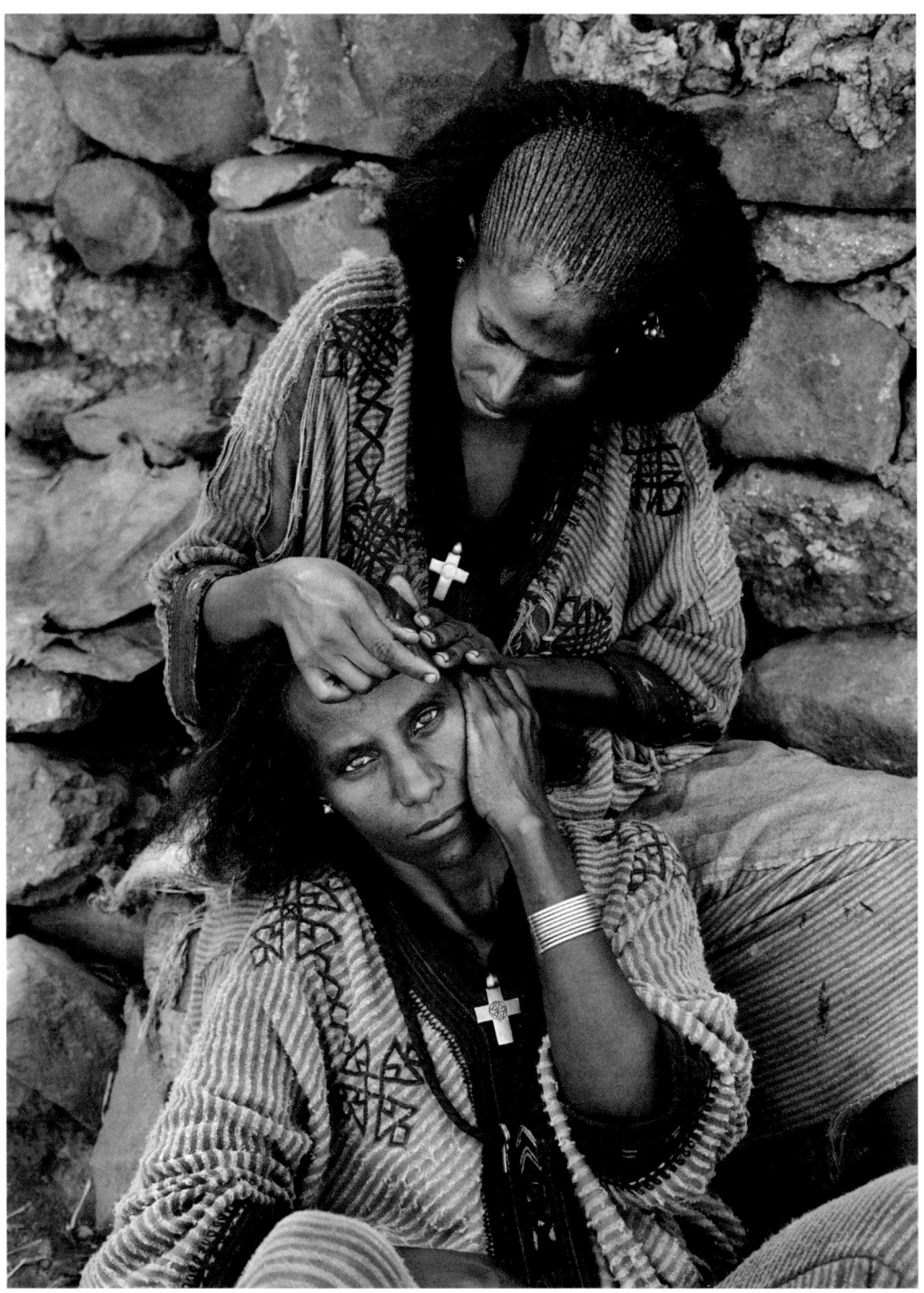

Opposite The village of Yetku at an altitude of 4,530 feet (1,380 meters). Several weeks before reaching Yetku, we were told that it boasted the most beautiful women of these mountains. Ethiopia. October and November 2008.

Pages 302/303 View of the valley that stretches from Lalibela to Makina Lideta Maryan. From this location, more than 9,800 feet (3,000 meters) above sea level, thousands of cultivated fields in the valley below resemble patchwork quilts. With no roads connecting them to the modern world, the people in this area live much as their ancestors did in biblical times. Ethiopia. October and November 2008.

Pages 304/305 This village situated at the base of Abune Yosef is at an altitude of 12,970 feet (3,953 meters). Nights are very cold. People keep their cattle inside their houses at night to protect them from temperatures below freezing. Ethiopia. October and November 2008.

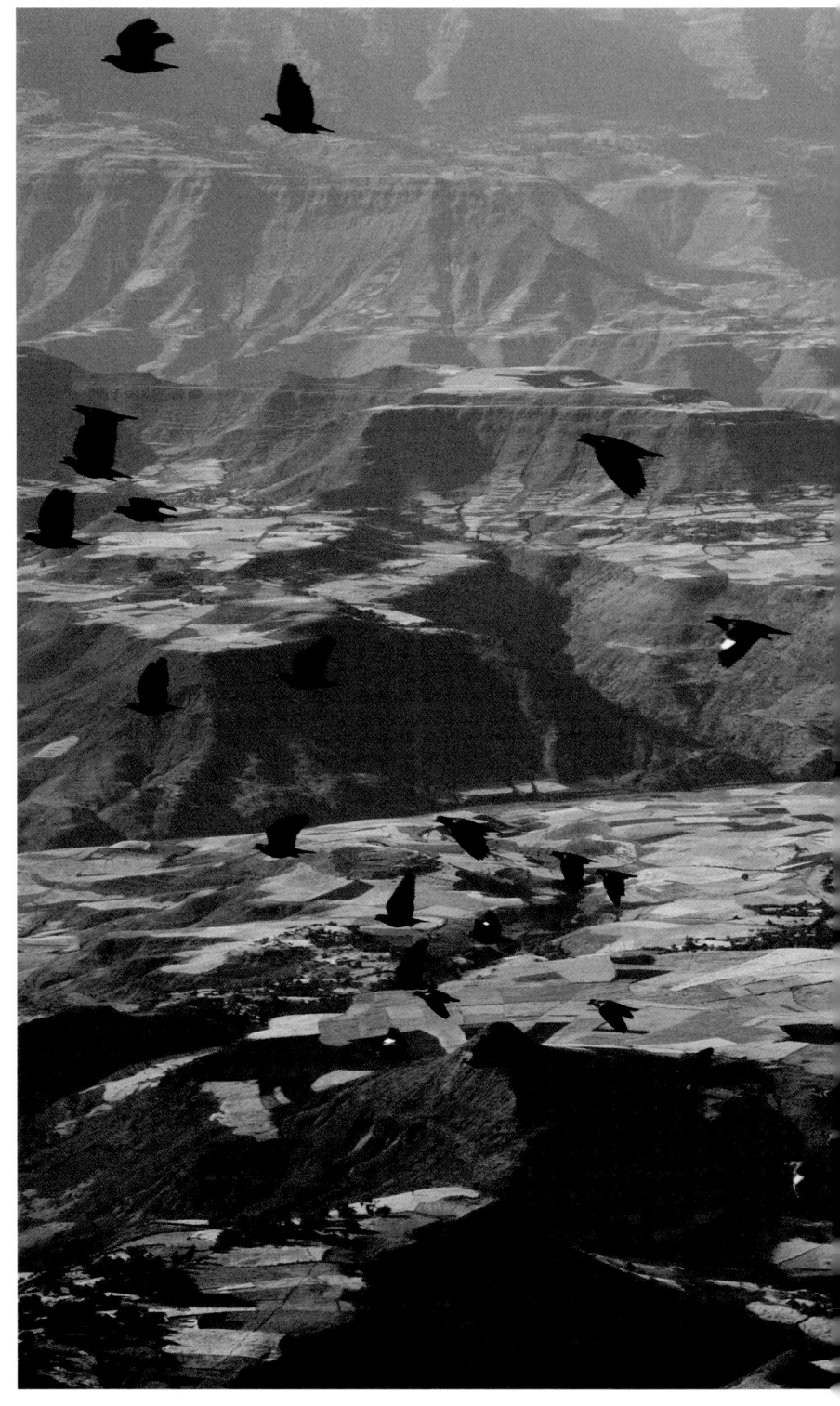

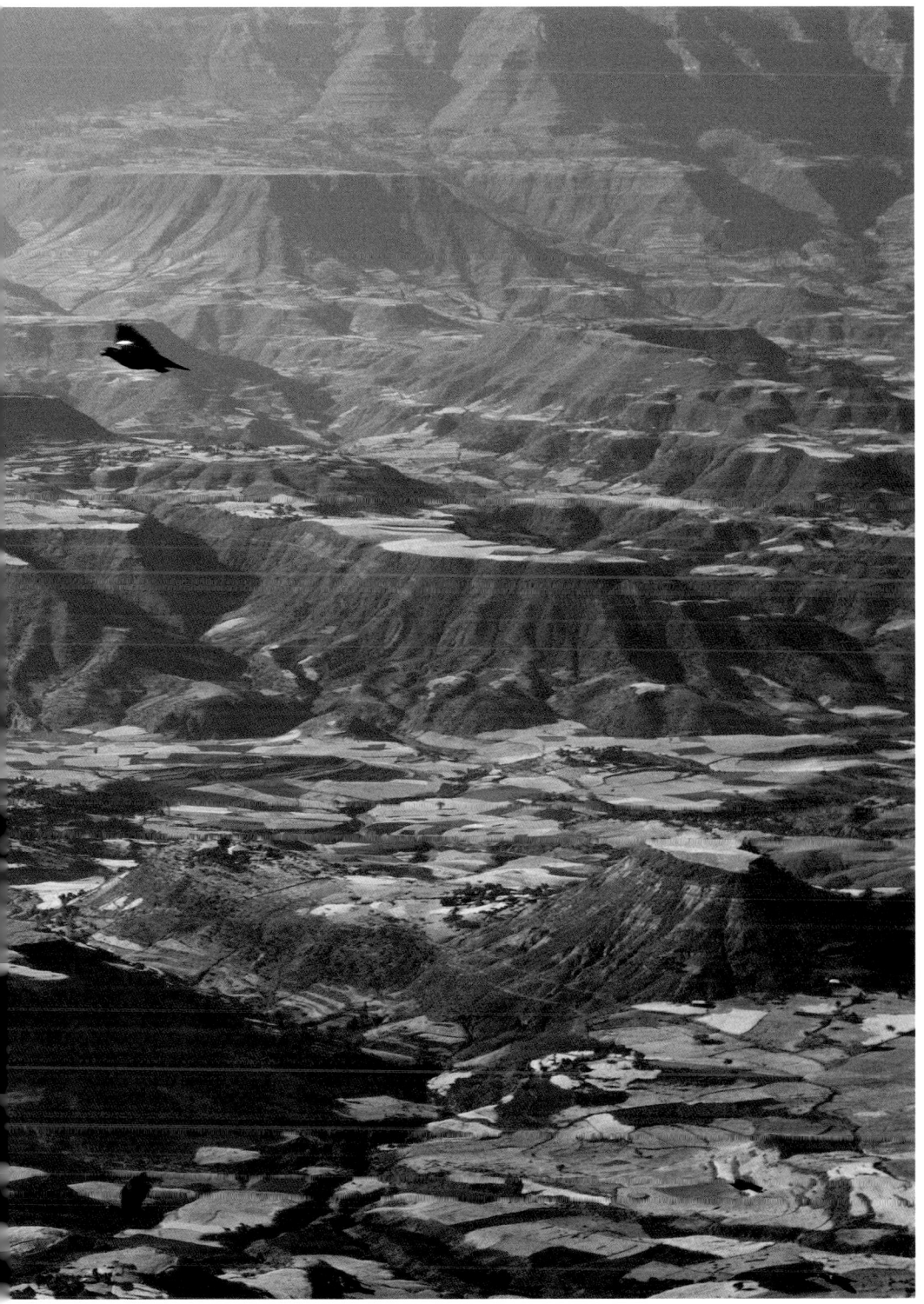

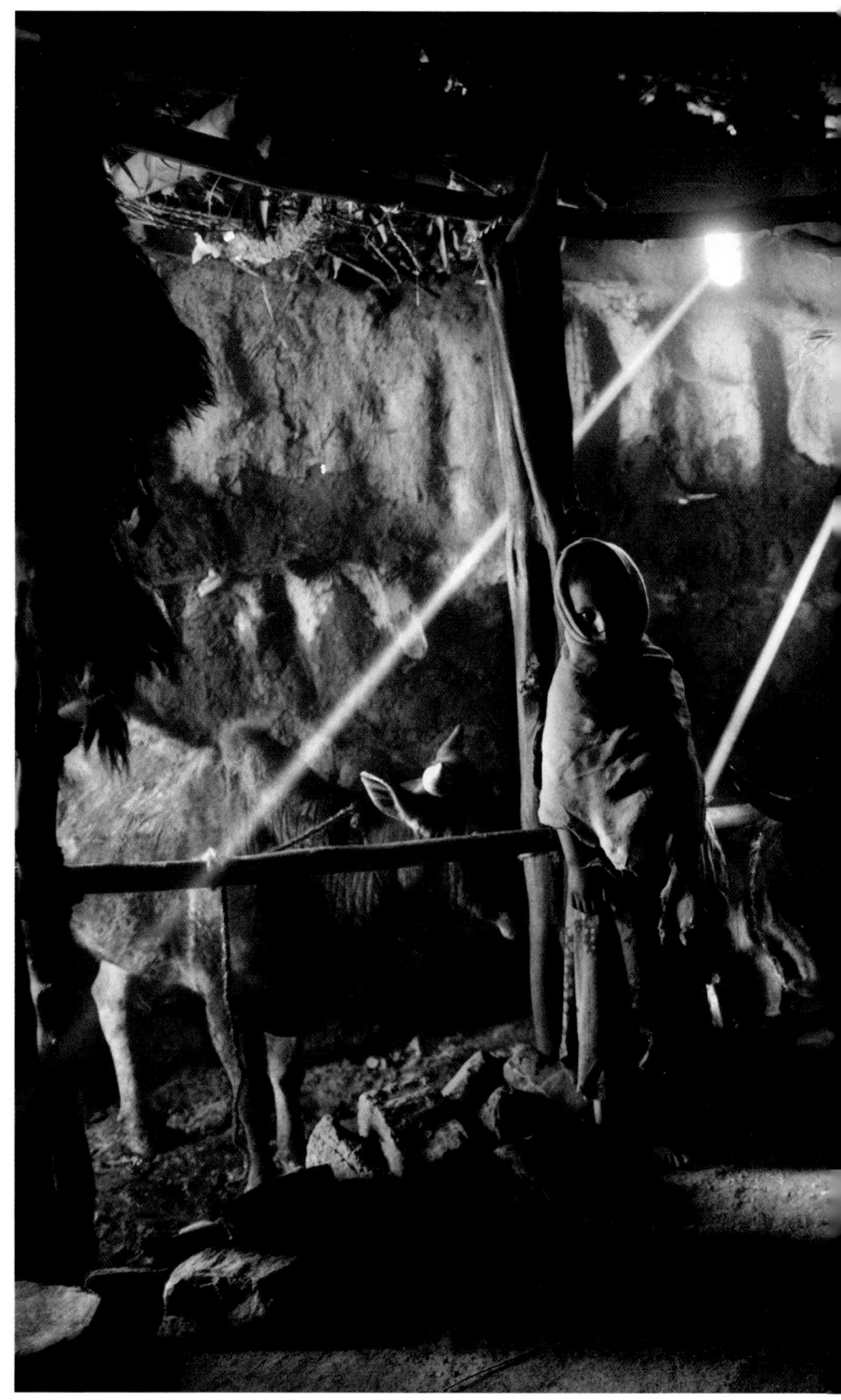

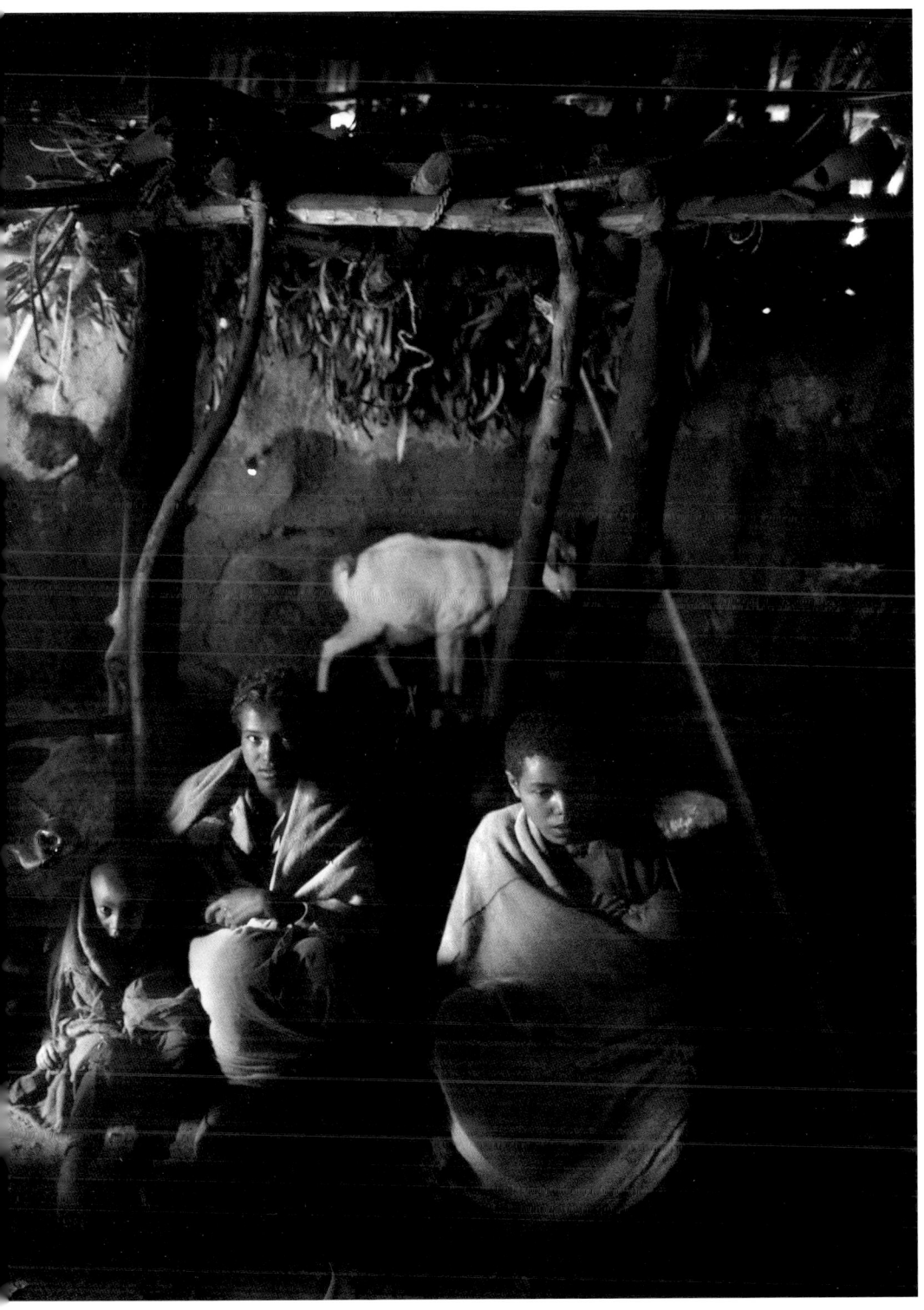

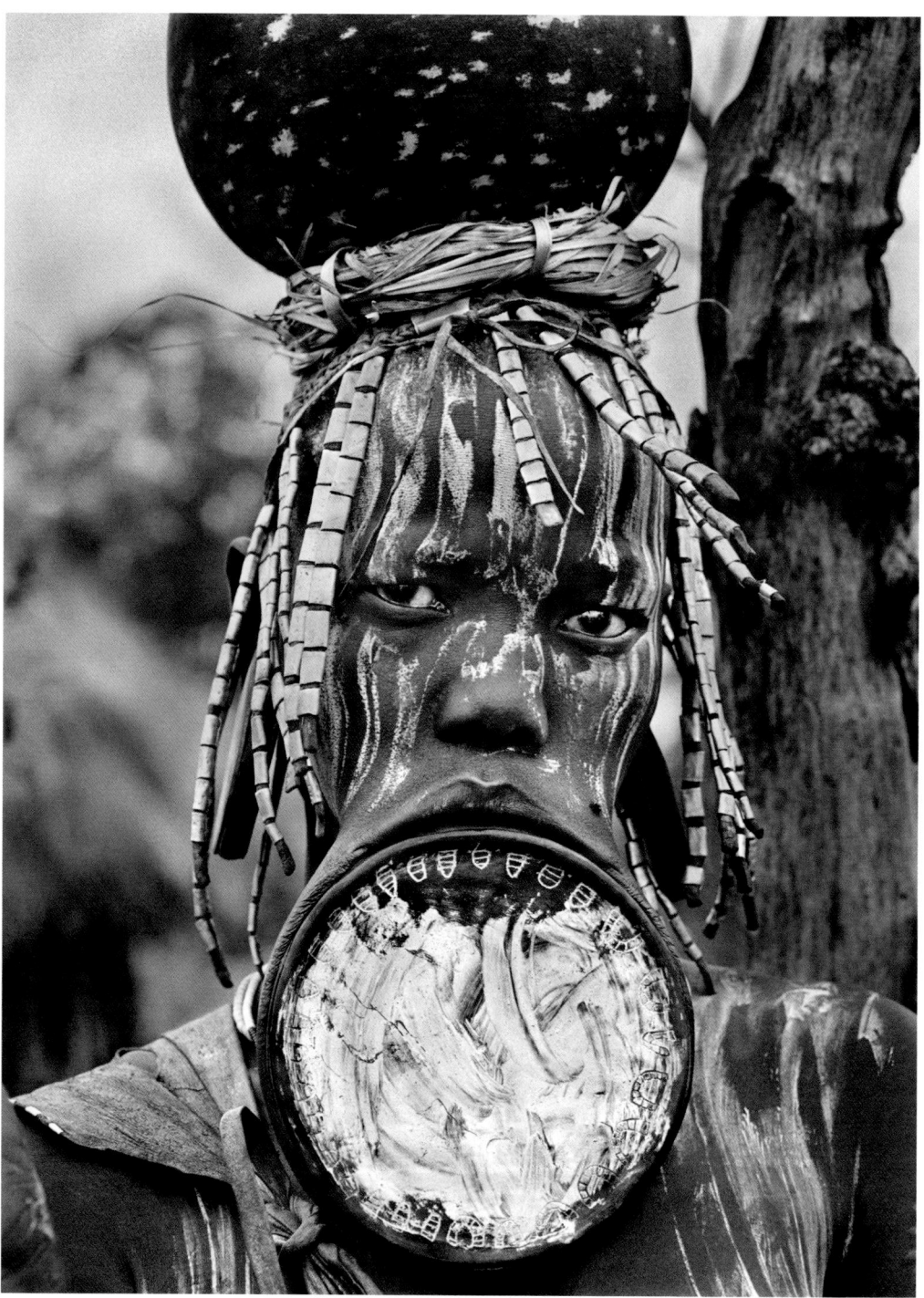

THE ETHNIC GROUPS OF OMO VALLEY, SOUTH ETHIOPIA

Pages 306 through 315

The plains of South Omo, which lie between the mountainous center of Ethiopia and the highlands of Kenya, are home to some of Africa's most culturally diverse and traditional ethnic groups. For the most part agropastoralists, their lives are little different from those of their ancestors. To spend time among them is to feel transported to another age.

As many as two dozen ethnic groups occupy South Omo, some numbering tens of thousands, others no more than 500, each culturally unique. These photographs were taken during visits to four different groups: the Hamer, the Nyangatom, the Mursi and the Surma.

The Hamer are famous for the elaborate hairstyles of their women. After rubbing their hair with a mixture of ocher, water and a binding resin, they create copper-colored tresses known as *goscha*, which are considered a sign of health and welfare. The Hamer, who number around 50,000, are typical agropastoralists, cultivating sorghum, vegetables, millet, tobacco and cotton as well as rearing cattle and goats.

The Nyangatom, whose semiarid territory spills into South Sudan, are famous for their warrior tradition and are often in conflict with neighboring groups, principally because of cattle rustling and competition for water and pastureland. They raise zebu cattle and grow cereals and tobacco.

The Mursi are a small ethnic group, numbering some 6,500, who live in the Mago National Park in southwest Ethiopia. Moving with the seasons between the plains and the Mursi Hills, they grow crops and rear cattle, with honey being a favorite delicacy.

The Surma, also known as the Suri, with a population of some 45,000, live in a territory covering southwest Ethiopia and South Sudan. Their most famous traditions are fierce stick fighting between the men and lip plates worn by the women. Once nomadic, the Surma now live in permanent settlements and cultivate their land, although males usually own some 30 to 40 head of cattle as proof of their wealth and importance. Occasionally, wars are fought with their traditional enemy, the Nyangatom, with automatic weapons increasingly used on both sides.

Opposite Mursi and Surma women are the last women in the world to wear lip plates. No anthropologist has been able to explain with certainty the origin or the function of this practice. Some say that this mutilation, unaesthetic to the eyes of the slavers, was imposed by men to protect their women from slavers' raids. Only women belonging to a high caste have the right to wear lip plates, which they display proudly when they walk around the village in the company of their husband and sons. Mursi village of Dargui in Mago National Park, near Jinka. Ethiopia. September and October 2007.

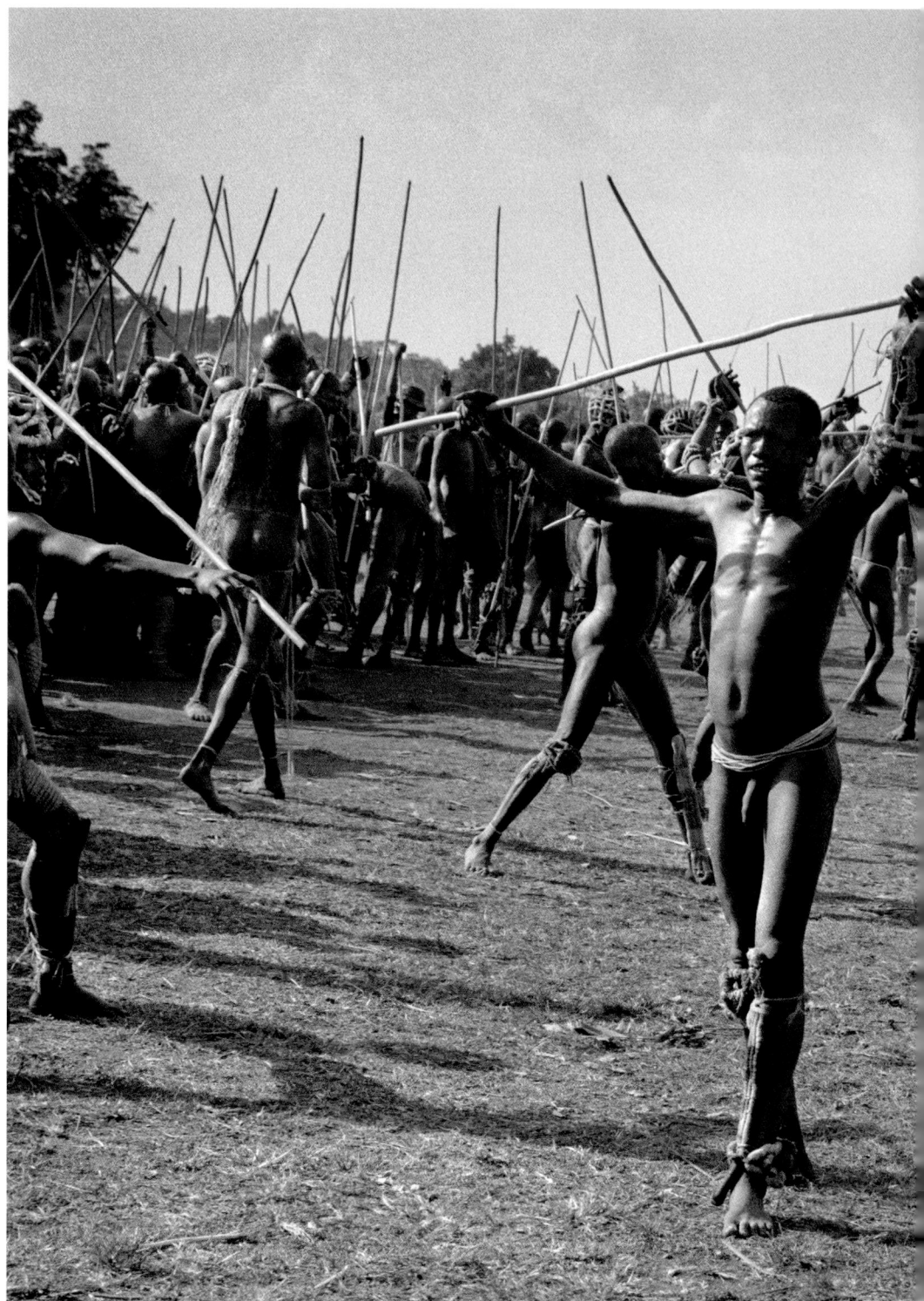

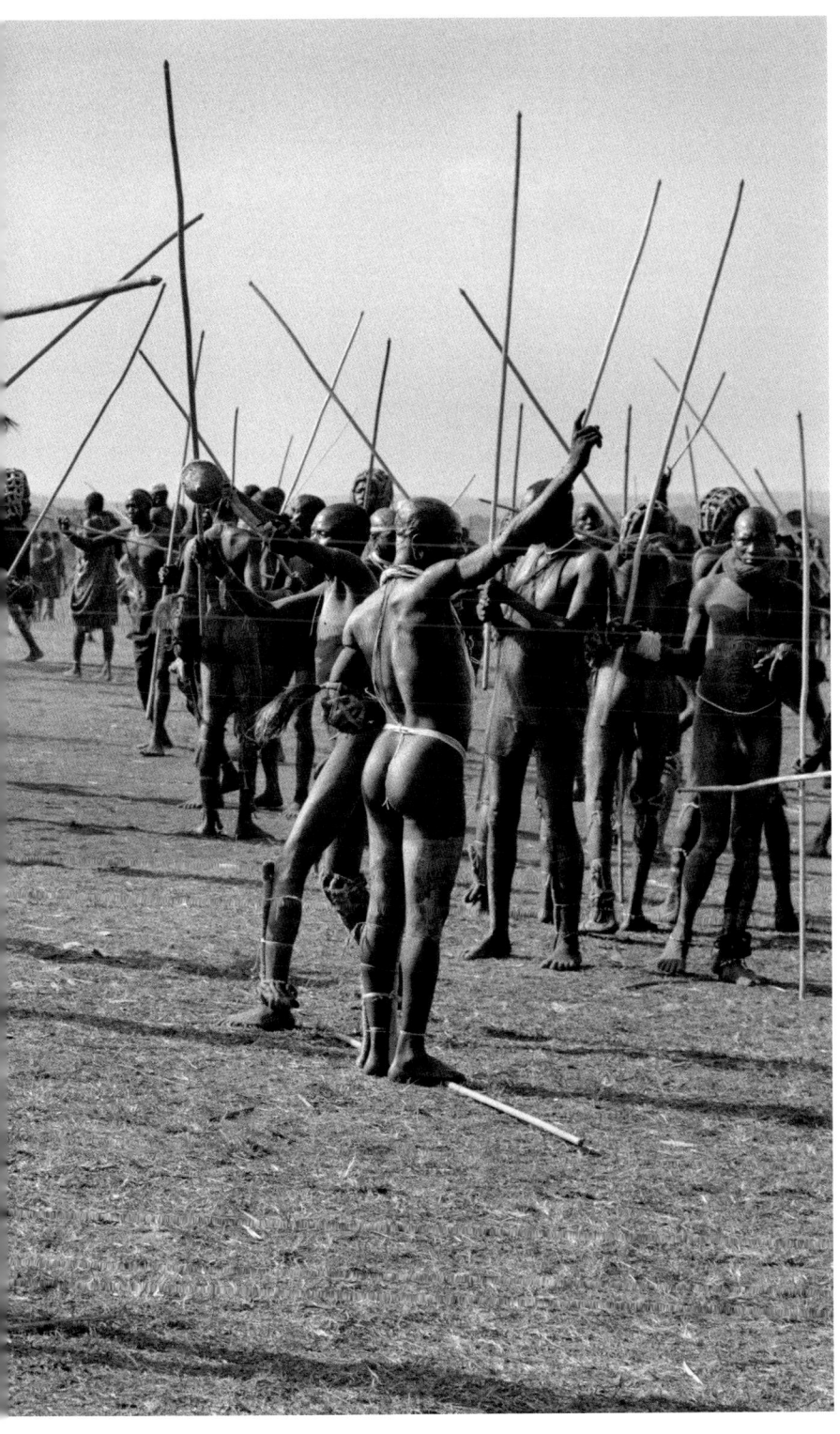

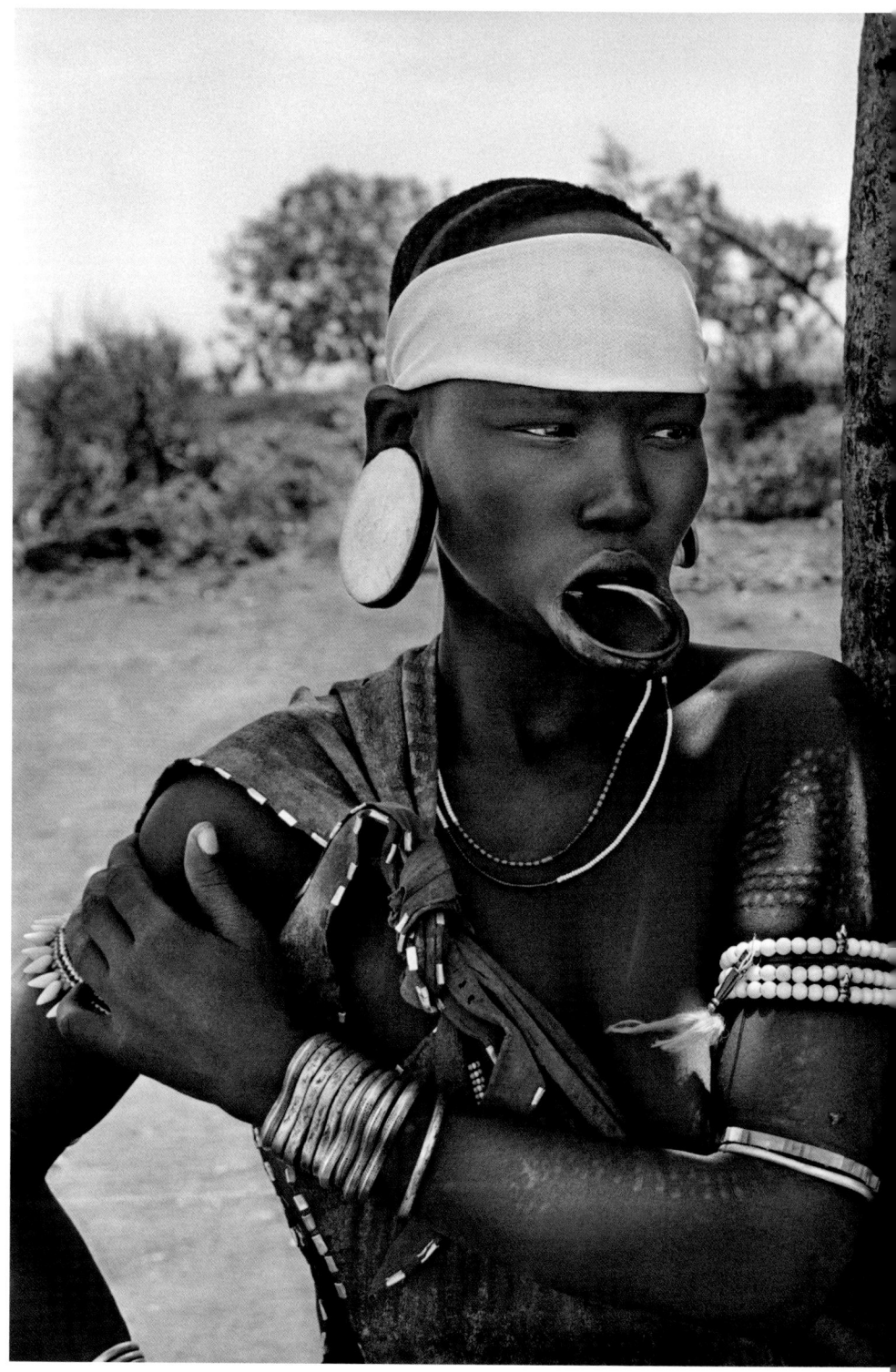

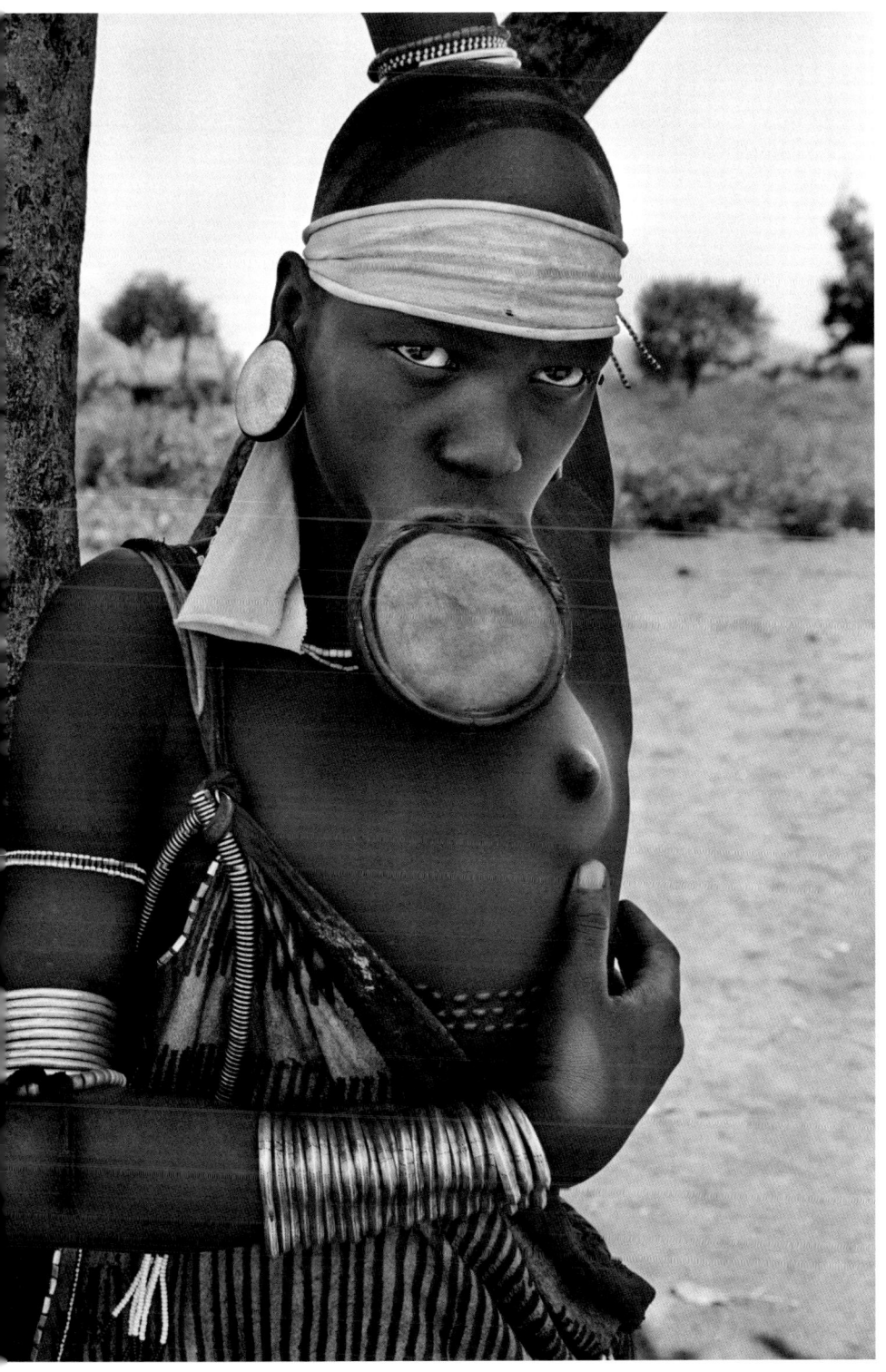

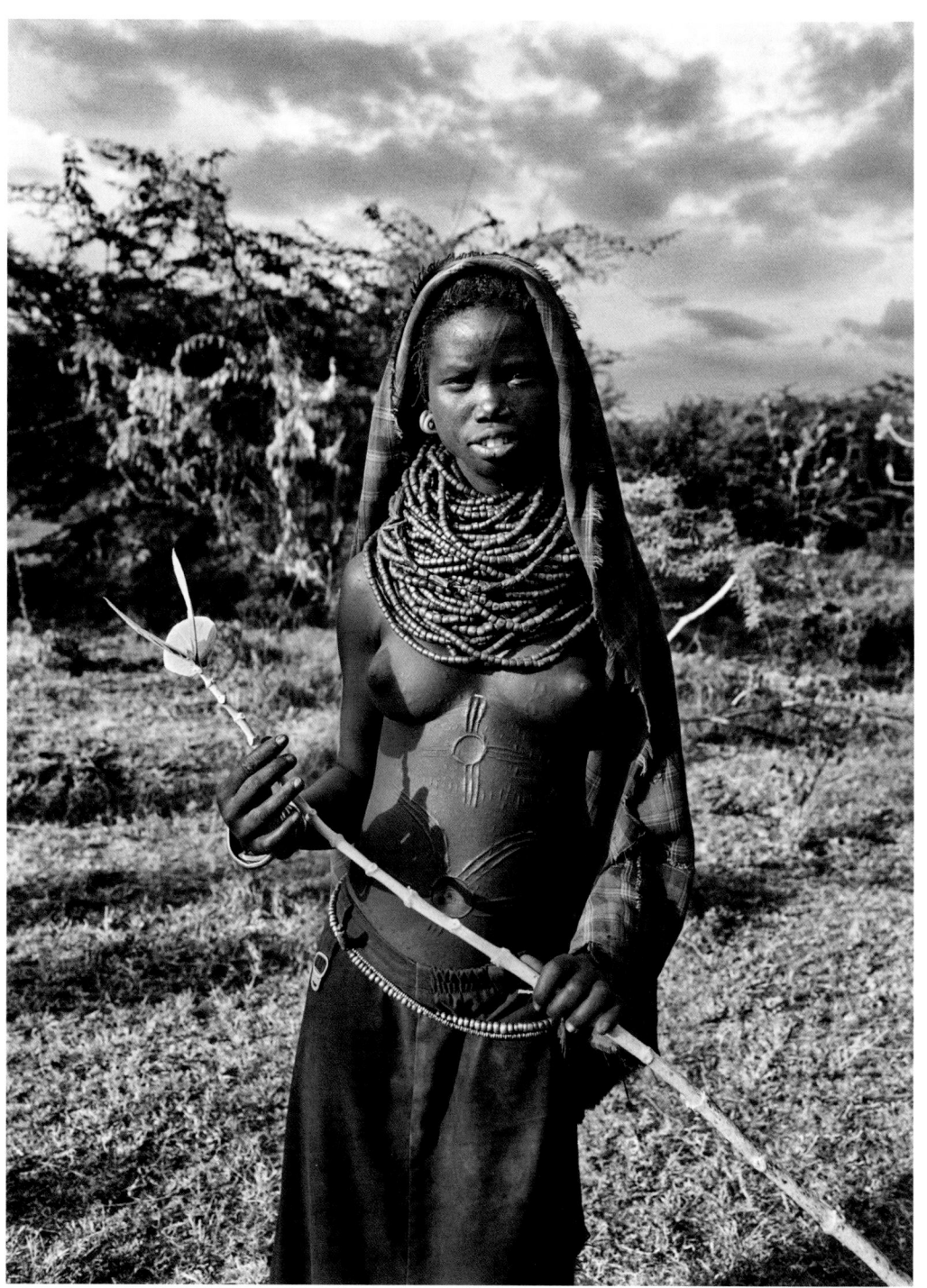

Pages 308/309 Surma men practice stick fighting known as *donga* in order to develop an aggressive spirit, to learn agility and endurance and to display their virility as future warriors. For this, the fighters paint their bodies with white symbolic figures designed to protect them from supernatural forces. Using long sticks as weapons, their aim is to dominate and neutralize their adversary, with winners celebrated by the women. Although *donga* is only one of several rites of passage from adolescence to manhood, it is the most violent: blood is spilled, heads and ribs are cracked and occasional deaths are reported. Surma village of Tulgit. Omo National Park. Near Maji. Ethiopia. September and October 2007.

Pages 310/311 Mursi and Surma women are the last women in the world to wear lip plates. No anthropologist has been able to explain with certainty the origin or the function of this practice. Some say that this mutilation, unaesthetic to the eyes of the slavers, was imposed by men to protect their women from slavers' raids. Only women belonging to a high caste have the right to wear lip plates, which they display proudly when they walk around the village in the company of their husband and sons. Mursi village of Dargui in Mago National Park, near Jinka. Ethiopia. September and October 2007.

Opposite A young Nyangatom wears necklaces that are rolled hundreds of times around her neck. The necklaces are lubricated with butter to prevent their weight and friction from irritating the skin. Group of 15 villages named Lorognettes, near Kibbish. Ethiopia. September and October 2007.

Opposite The Surma village of Regia during festiv-
ities at which young girls are presented as ready for
marriage. Omo National Park, near Maji. Ethiopia.
September and October 2007.

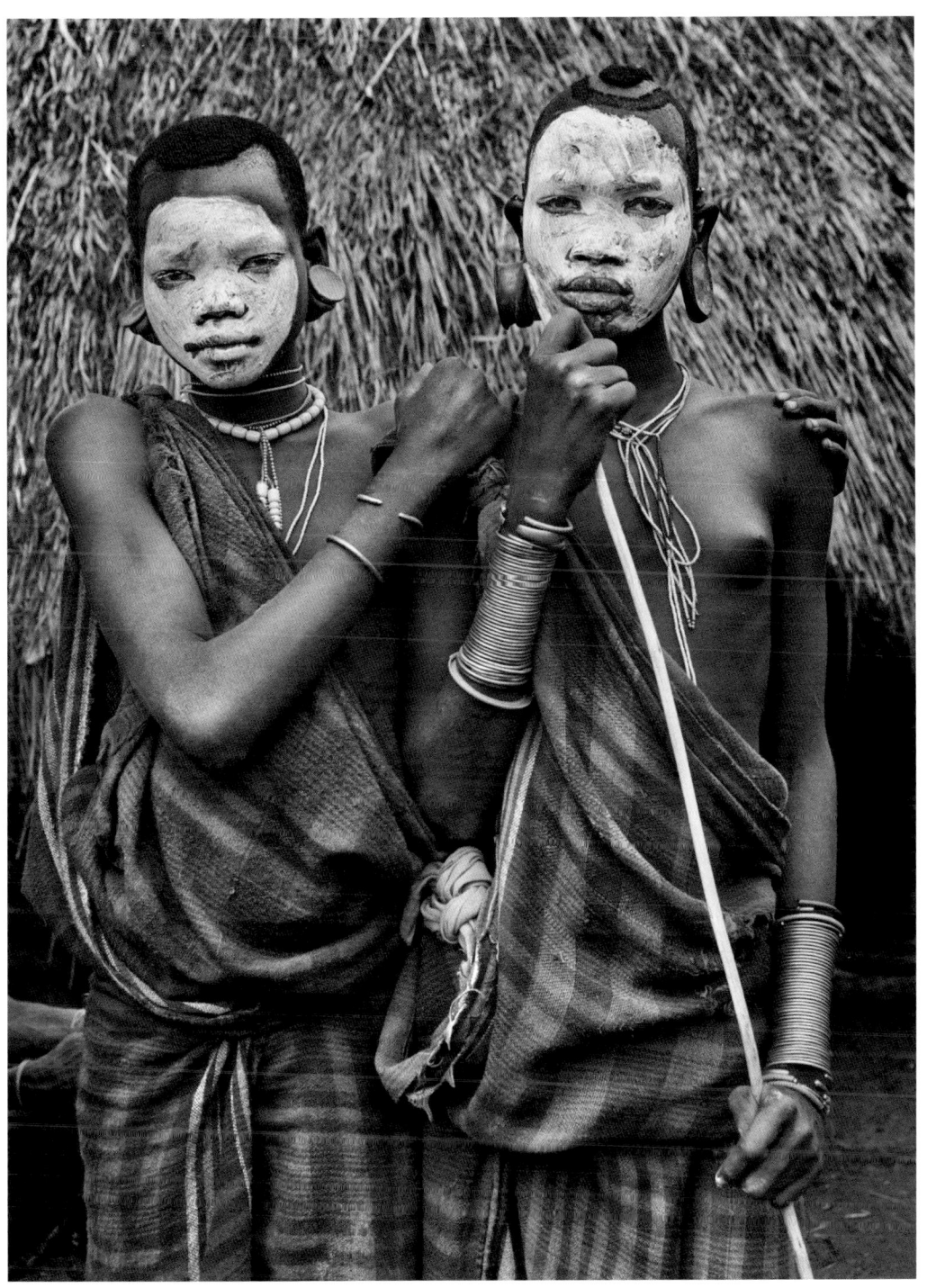

NORTHERN SPACES

The North Pole stands on ice, surrounded by hundreds of kilometers of frozen ocean, but the Arctic Circle itself is ringed by the northernmost regions of the Americas, Europe and Asia. As a result, the Arctic ecosystem reaches well into Alaska, Canada, Greenland, Scandinavia and Russia. In some areas, the ice gives way to permafrost and tundra; in others, volcanoes, glaciers and canyons recall the geological convulsions that marked the formation of the Earth. Yet, for all this, tenacious animals and peoples have chosen to live there.

The Kamchatka Peninsula in eastern Russia has always intrigued me, not least because, as the home base of the Soviet nuclear submarine fleet, it was off-limits to foreigners (and most Russians) throughout the Cold War. Its 780-mile (1,250-kilometer)-long coastline faces the Bering Sea, but I was most drawn to its wild interior, with its 160 volcanoes, 29 of them still active. It was thrilling to fly above and around them as their cone shapes and white peaks came in and out of view amid ever-changing cloud formations. Above the ice-covered summit of the Kronotsky volcano, I peered down from 13,000 feet (4,000 meters) into its smoking crater. Later, we trekked through lava-filled valleys with hot springs and dark lakes. It was there that we came across awesome brown bears, the monarchs of the peninsula's rich fauna.

Some 1,200 miles (2,000 kilometers) to the northeast, the Arctic National Wildlife Refuge in Alaska seems almost as rugged from the air as Kamchatka, with snow-capped mountains and valleys etched by glaciers and rivers. Photographing on the ground, however, proved difficult because the terrain is steep and rivers are too fast and cold to cross on foot. Even in midsummer, the temperature was well below zero. The porcupine caribou, the area's most emblematic animal, usually flees when it smells approaching human beings. But in the end, we were able to follow tens of thousands of these elegant creatures during their annual migration to the coastal plains to breed.

Adjacent to southeast Alaska is Canada's Kluane National Park and Reserve, which is dominated by the Saint Elias Mountains and includes Mount Logan, Canada's highest peak. Its huge icefield, glaciers and rivers make it virtually inaccessible on foot. Our good fortune was that, during the month we worked there, we had two weeks of good weather for aerial photography. It meant that, on long summer days, we could work until 11:00 p.m. One of many unforgettable sights was that of glaciers spreading like the fingers of a hand then darkening as they gather up rocks and stones in their steady slide down steep valleys.

To gain an understanding of how human life survives inside the Arctic Circle, we sought out the Nenets, a nomadic people in northern Siberia numbering some 42,000. They spend the winter within reach of towns where some of their families now live. But from mid-March, they set off with their large herds of reindeer into the Yamal Peninsula where by the summer the animals can feed off shrubs, grasses and lichens which they find by burrowing into the tundra. We accompanied one group with some 6,000 reindeer in temperatures far below zero. It was an extraordinary adventure. While some reindeer pulled sleds loaded with food and the poles and fur needed to build overnight shelters, dogs kept the main herd on track. On the day we crossed the Ob River onto the peninsula, we traveled 32 miles (52 kilometers), no fewer than 47 of them across the frozen river; on other days, we were trapped by snow storms and struggled to stay warm.

Still inside the Arctic Circle but 2,400 miles (4,000 kilometers) to the east is Wrangel Island, which we reached after a 30-hour-long boat ride from the town of Pevek on the eastern Siberian coast. I had been told it was a treasure trove of biodiversity and, above all, a favorite breeding ground for polar bears. Instead, our first encounter was with the detritus of what had once been a Soviet air base, including abandoned fuel barrels and wrecks of cars and planes. Fortunately, a large part of Wrangel remains unspoiled and even the unpleasant Soviet legacy is slowly being cleaned up. However, our visit proved frustrating. The island is home to large numbers of musk oxen, but they were hard to photograph because they fear humans. Walruses also once came in their tens of thousands to Wrangel, but they have apparently been disoriented by warming oceans and we found only a few hundred of them. The scarcity of polar bears was still another disappointment: in the end, we saw only a handful.

But we were amply rewarded by our trip to the national parks of the American Southwest, truly among the most beautiful places I have ever seen. The parks are spread across the Colorado Plateau, but we decided to explore Utah and Arizona. Naturally, this included the Grand Canyon. We worked first from the air, then from the water, taking an 8-day-long boat ride down 280 miles (450 kilometers) of the Colorado River. We were there in the late spring, but snow was still falling at the top of the canyon. Bryce Canyon in Utah is, in turn, memorable for the elaborate spires formed there by millennia of erosion of its limestone rock. As we watched nature's Gothic city change colors with the path of the sun, condors and eagles observed us from the skies.

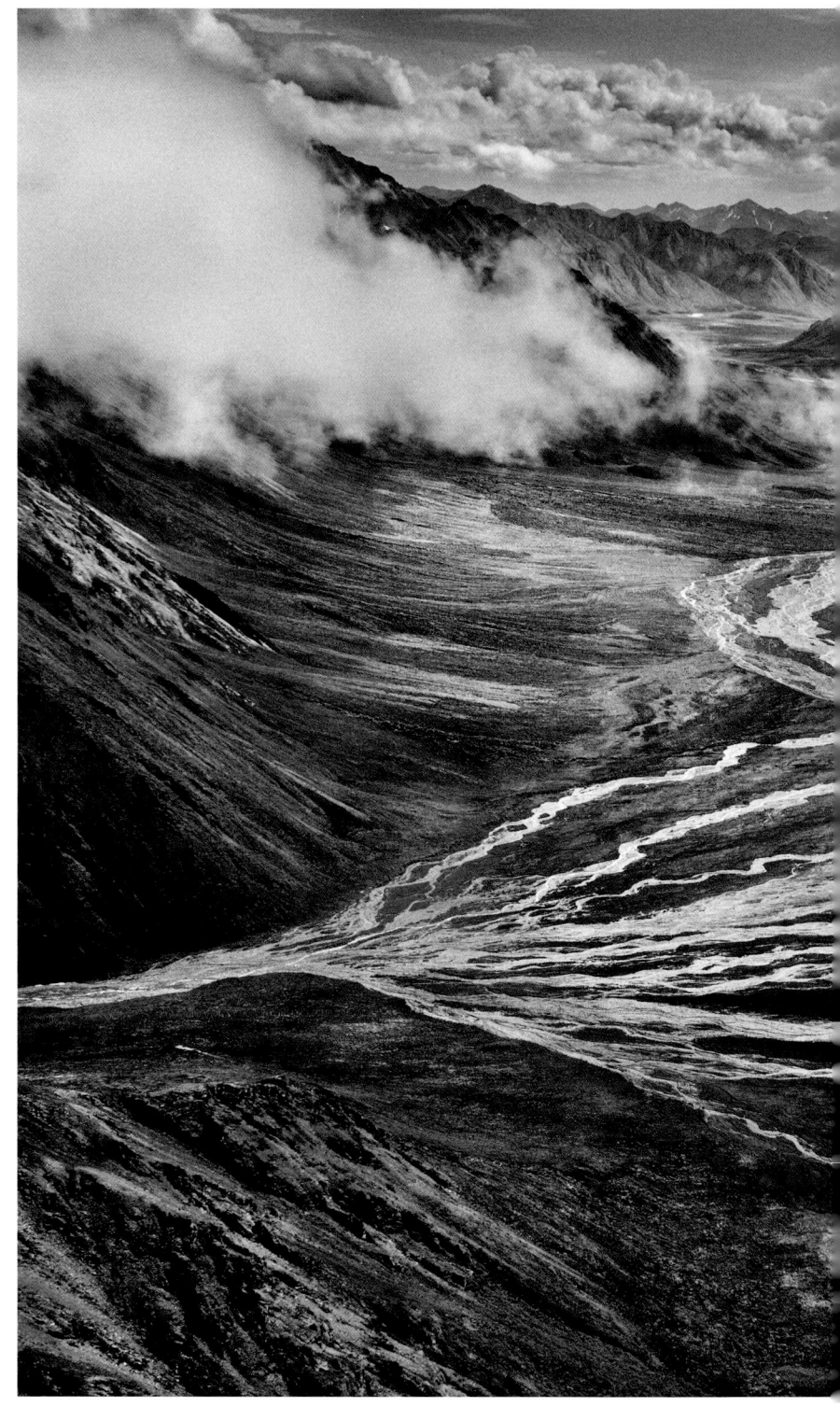

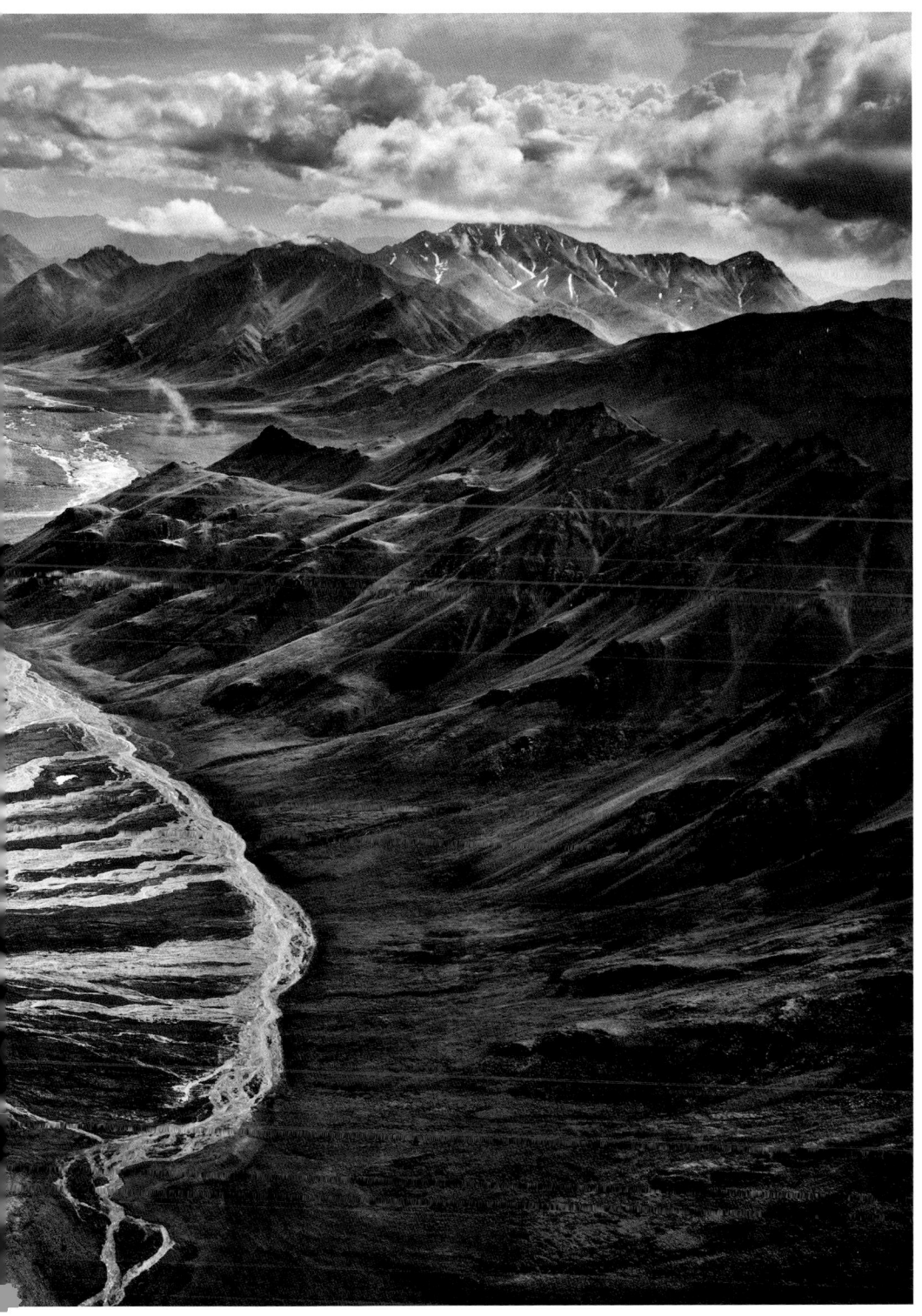

Pages 318/319 The southern boundaries of the Brooks Range, close to the Gwich'in settlement of Arctic Village in northern Alaska. The waters of these rivers flow south, joining the great Yukon River and eventually entering the Bering Sea. Alaska. USA. June and July 2009.

Opposite The Arctic National Wildlife Refuge (ANWR) in northeastern Alaska is the largest wildlife refuge in the United States, covering no fewer than six ecozones and stretching some 200 miles (300 kilometers) from north to south. Along its northern coast, barrier islands, coastal lagoons, salt marshes and river deltas of the Arctic coastal tundra provide a marvelous habitat for migratory water birds. Coastal land and sea ice are sought by caribou seeking relief from insects during the summer and by Arctic bears for hunting seals and breeding during winter.

This photograph was taken in the eastern part of the Brooks Range, which rises to over 9,800 feet (3,000 meters); the rugged stretch of mountains is sliced by deep river valleys and numerous glaciers. The immense variety of microclimates results from the collision of cold air from the Arctic and hot air coming from the Yukon River region of central Alaska. Alaska. USA. June and July 2009.

Pages 322/323 and 324/325 The Kamchatka Peninsula is a strange and mysterious land, almost lost in the far east of Russia and long isolated from the world: during the Cold War, it was home to the Soviet Union's principal nuclear submarine fleet as well as to a large air force base and a strategic missile base. Until the 1990s, no foreigner and few Russians were allowed onto the peninsula. Its strategic location is self-evident: separated from Alaska by the Bering Sea, it is far closer to the United States than to, say, Moscow. The peninsula stretches 780 miles (1,250 kilometers) south of the Russian mainland, with ocean on either side. But what truly distinguishes it is the extraordinary number of volcanoes, both dormant and active, that run down its spine.

The photograph on pages 324/325 shows the Karimsky Volcano, which currently rises to a height of 4,800 feet (1,468 meters) and is quite the most active on the Kamchatka Peninsula. Kluchevskoy Volcano is in fact more powerful and, in the course of a year, ejects far more material, but Karimsky is in a permanent state of rumbling unrest. More than 100 times per day, it expels a plume of gas and ash several hundred meters into the air and sends boulders careening down its steep slopes. Karimsky's last big eruption was in 2003. Kamchatka. Russia. September and October 2006.

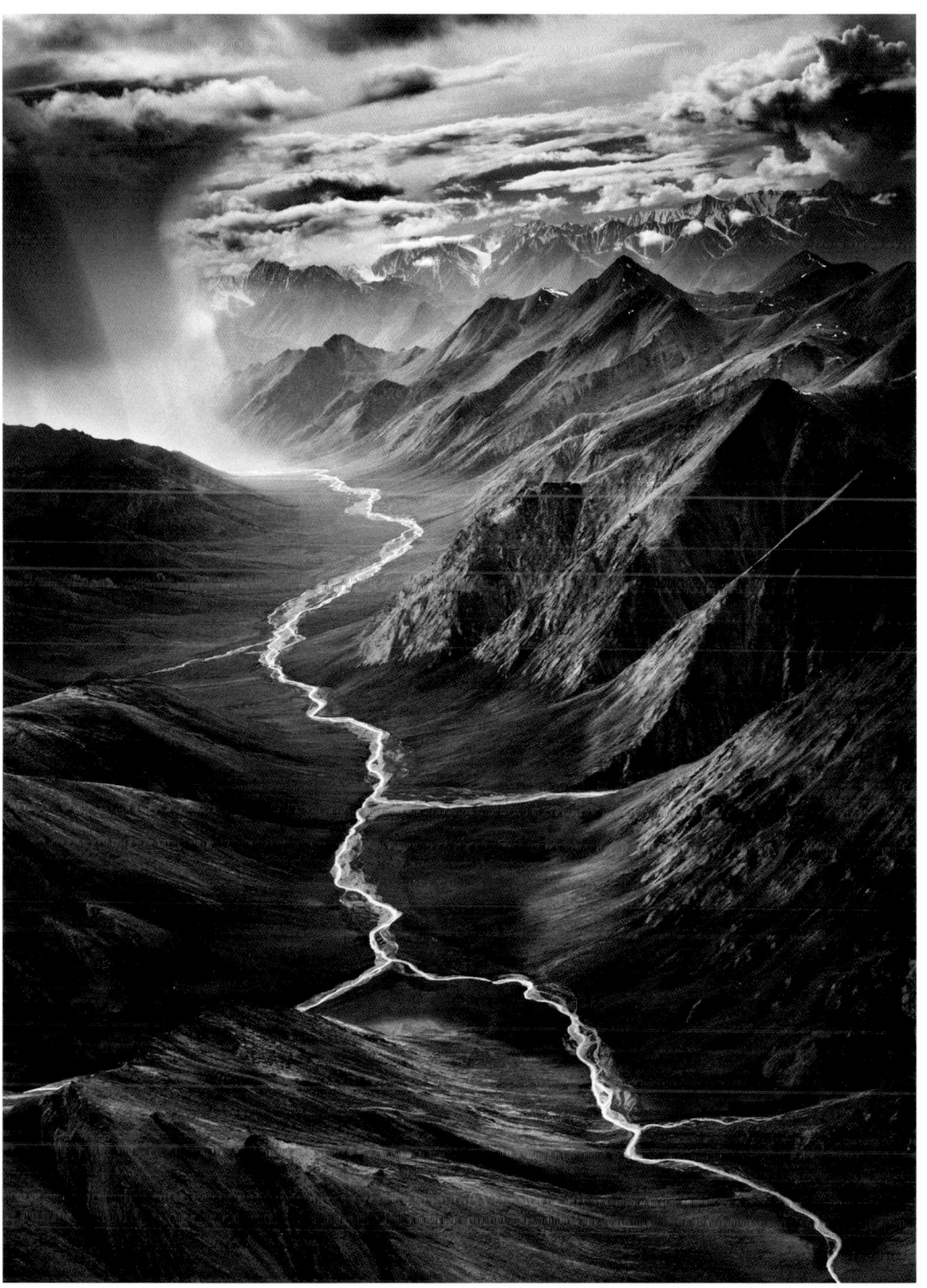

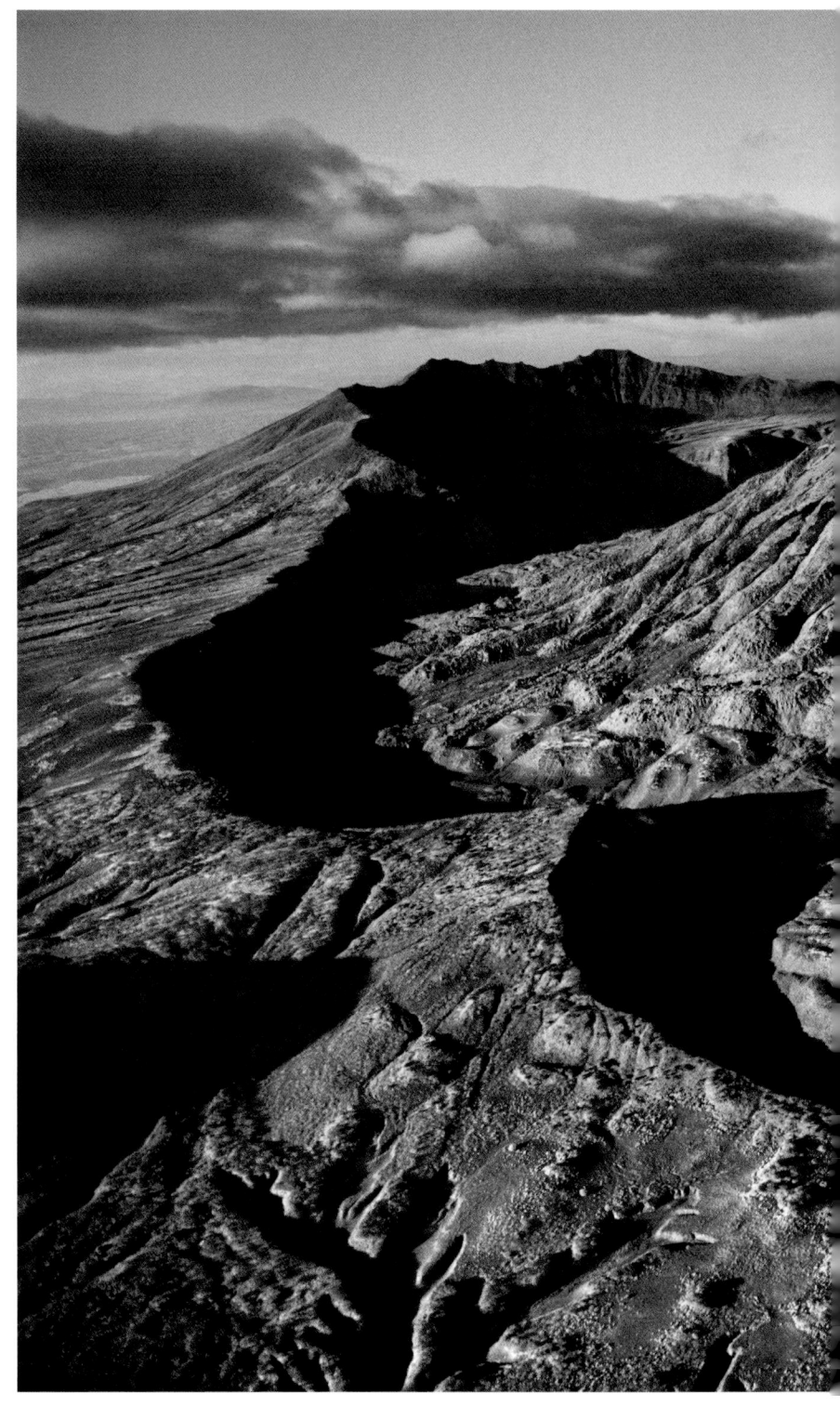

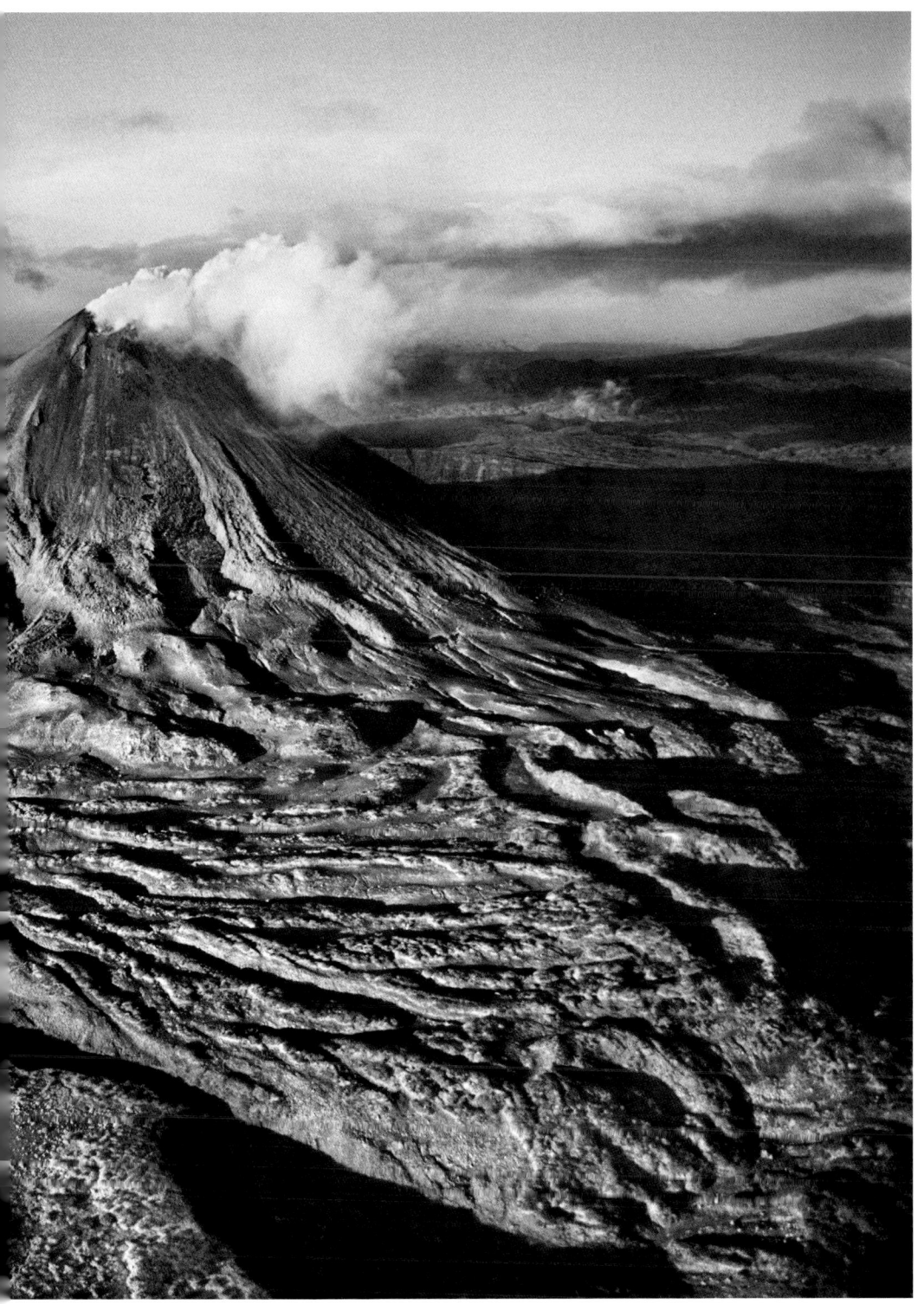

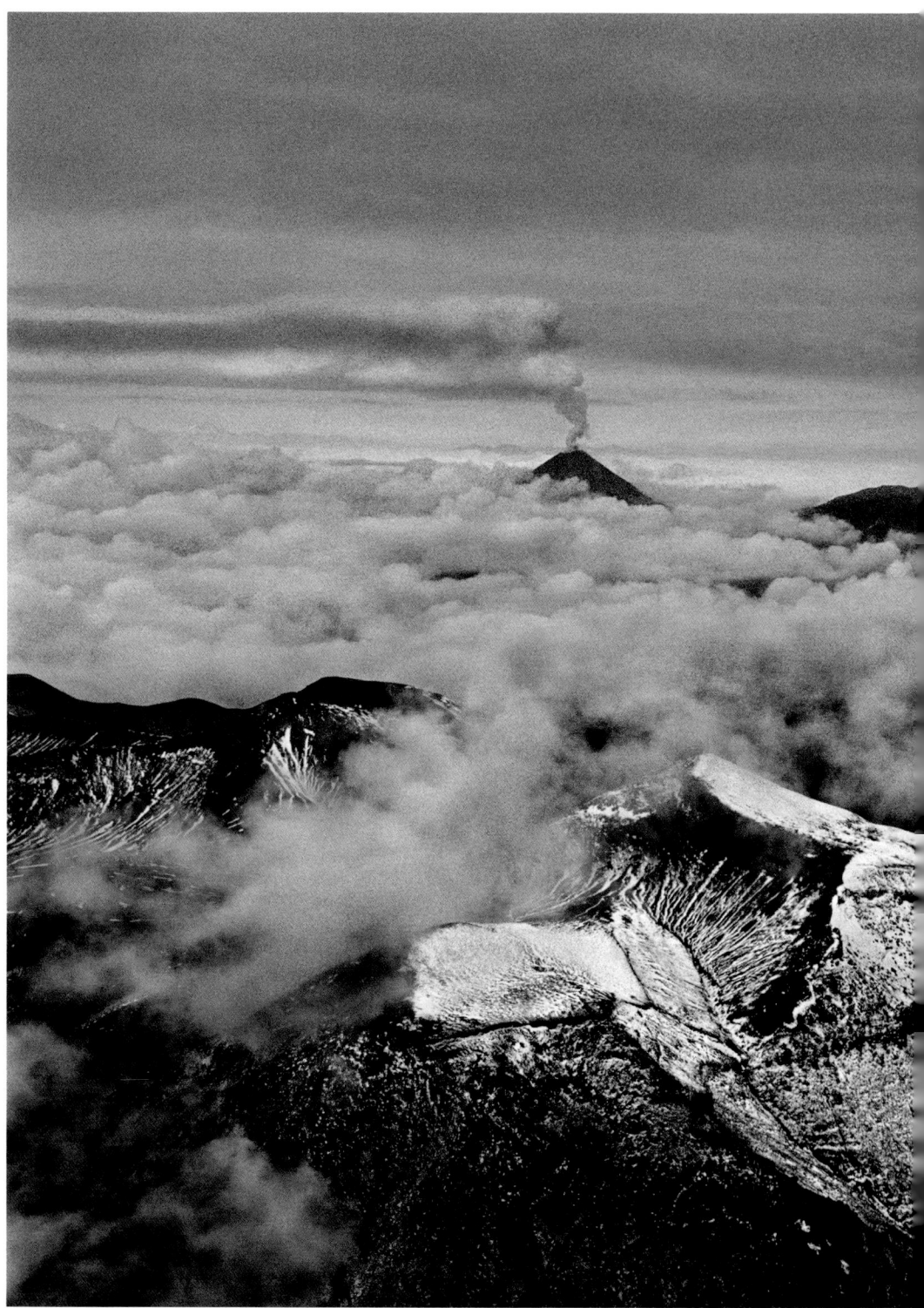

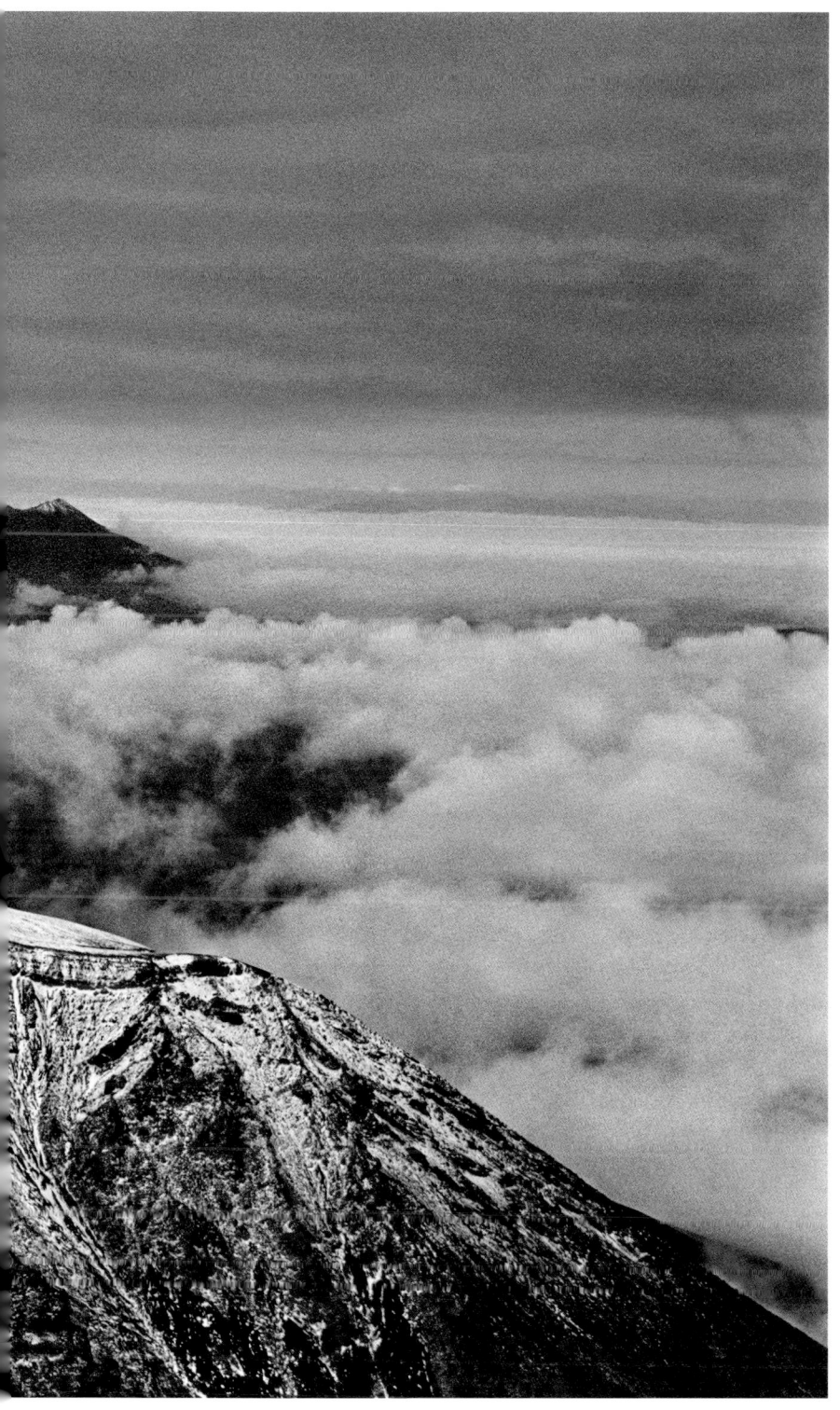

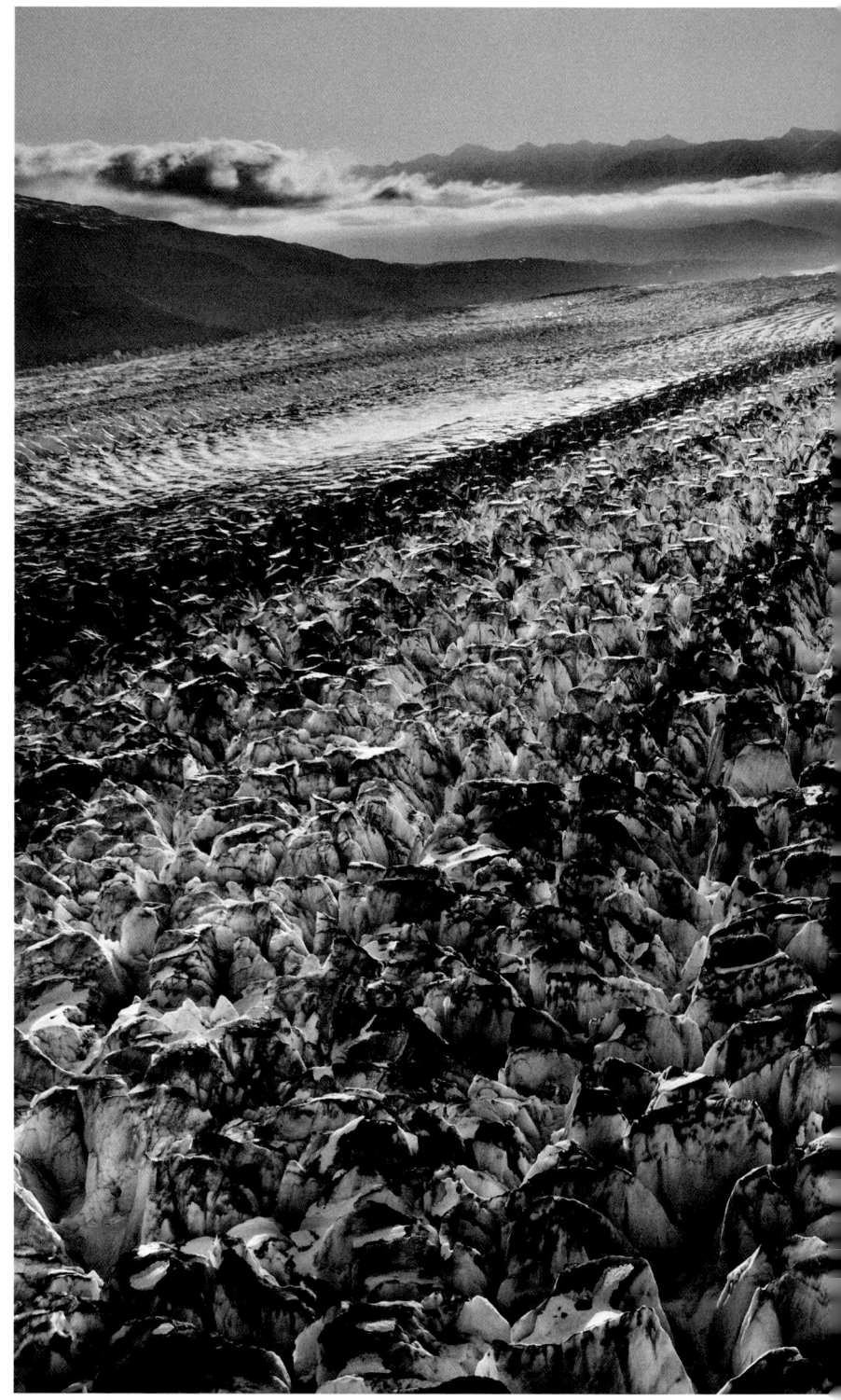

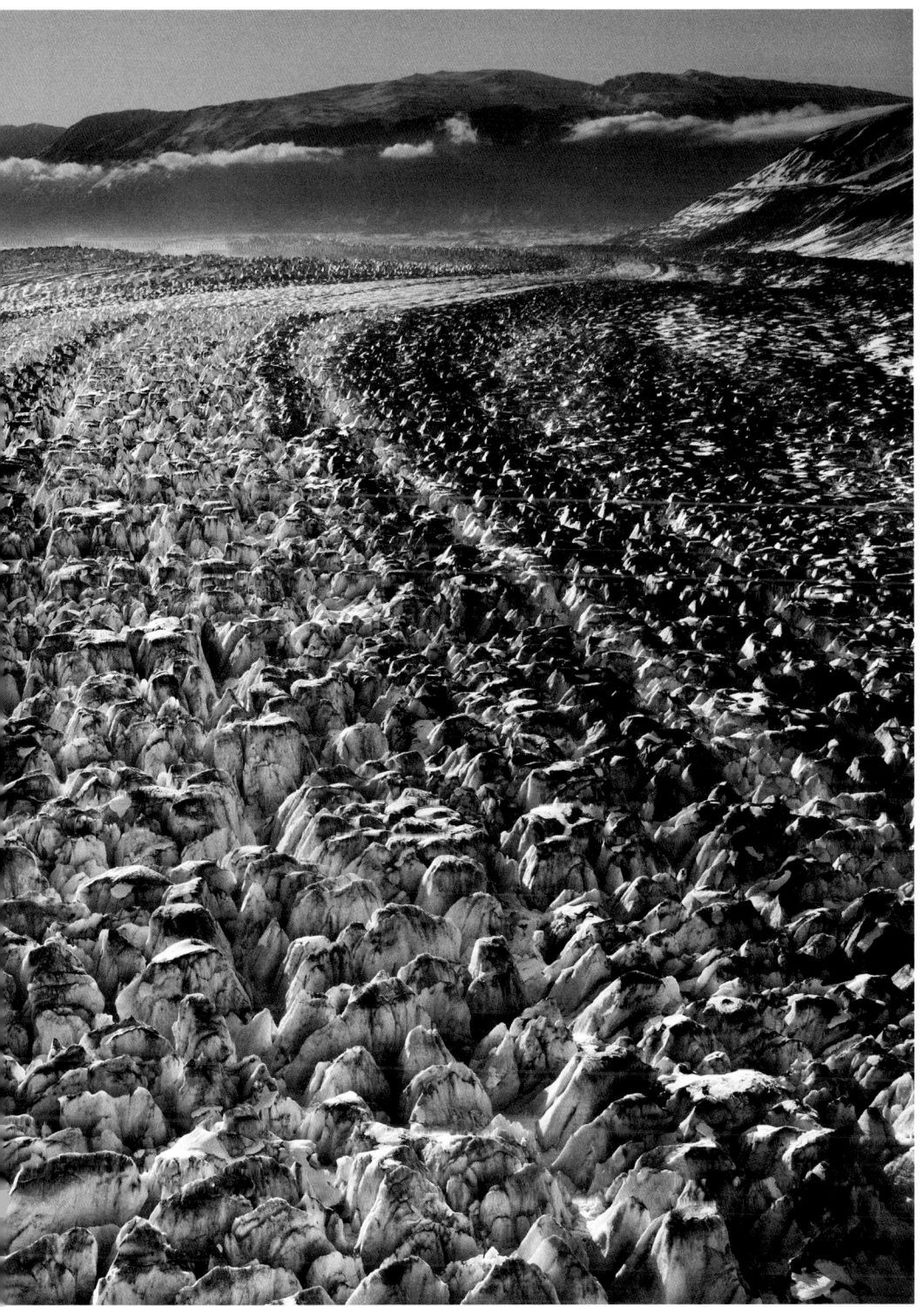

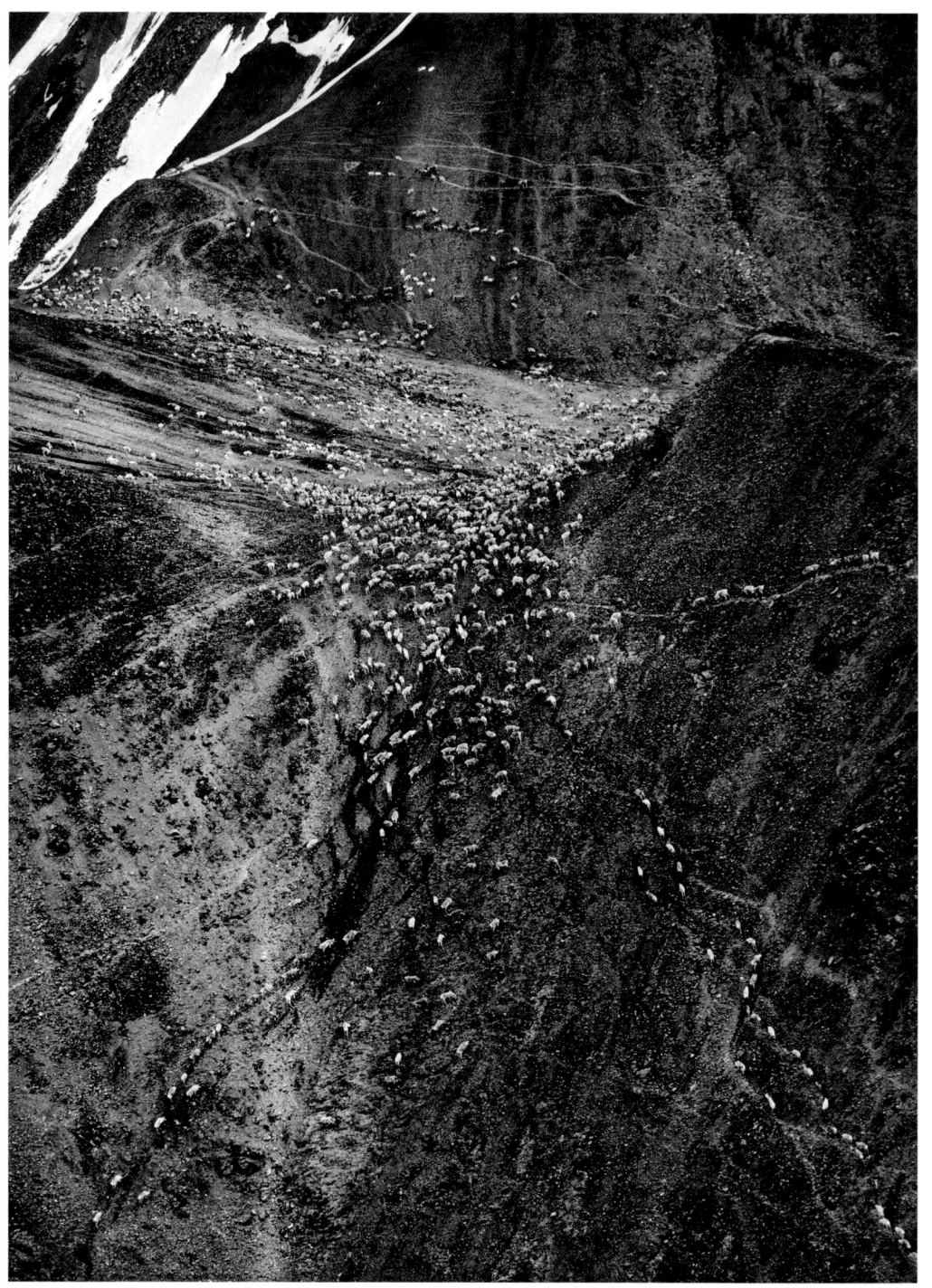

THE CARIBOU IN THE ARCTIC
NATIONAL WILDLIFE REFUGE

Pages 328 through 333

The caribou is the emblematic animal of the far northwest of the American continent. In the summer, they number some 200,000 in Alaska, with over 60 percent belonging to the Porcupine caribou or Grant's caribou (*Rangifer tarandus granti*) species. They winter in Canada's Yukon Territory and south of Alaska's Brooks Range. They then move northwards in the spring into the Arctic National Wildlife Refuge, where their calves are born and they can feed on the tundra vegetation, although they keep on the move to avoid overgrazing. In total, they migrate some 1,500 miles (2,500 kilometers) each year, but the paths they take often depend on climatic conditions.

Wild caribous are still hunted in North America. For the Inuit, the northern First Nations people and Alaska's natives, the caribou has always been an important source of food, clothing, shelter and tools. Many who depend on the *Porcupine caribou*, named after the Porcupine River that cuts through Alaska, follow traditional management practices, such as prohibiting the sale of caribou meat and controlling overhunting. Alaska. USA. June and July 2009.

Pages 326/327 The Kluane National Park and Reserve is located in the southwestern corner of Yukon Territory, almost bordering on Alaska. Towering over this extraordinary park is Mount Logan, at 19,550 feet (5,959 meters), Canada's highest peak. Kluane also includes one of the largest non-Arctic ice fields in the world, with glaciers dominating much of its landscape. Valley glaciers, such as the Lowell and the Kaskawulsh, connect the ice fields with the rest of the park. Meltwater from these glaciers, in turn, feeds rivers and lakes and helps to sustain an abundance of animal and plant life. The meeting of Pacific and Arctic air masses adds to the diversity of flora and fauna in northern Canada.

The vegetation, which includes forested areas, provides a habitat for many species of wildlife, such as grizzly bears, black bears, moose, wolves, lynx, mountain goats and Dall sheep. It is also home to a great variety of birds, with over 180 species reported, among them trumpeter swans, falcons, and golden and bald eagles. The lakes and streams are rich in fish, notably lake trout and landlocked salmon.

This photograph shows the Lowell Glacier, which is some 45 miles (70 kilometers) long and is on average 3 miles (5 kilometers) wide. The Alsek River flows into Lowell Lake from the north and exits at the south end of the lake. Canada. May and June 2011.

Opposite The caribou (*Rangifer tarandus granti*) population in the Arctic National Wildlife Refuge is estimated at around 200,000 animals. The largest herd, with some 125,000 animals, enters this area of northern Alaska in the early summer. When warmer days permit the hatching of mosquitoes on the permafrost of the lowlands, the herd seeks out the cool and breezy higher ground to escape the mosquito onslaught. Alaska. USA. June and July 2009.

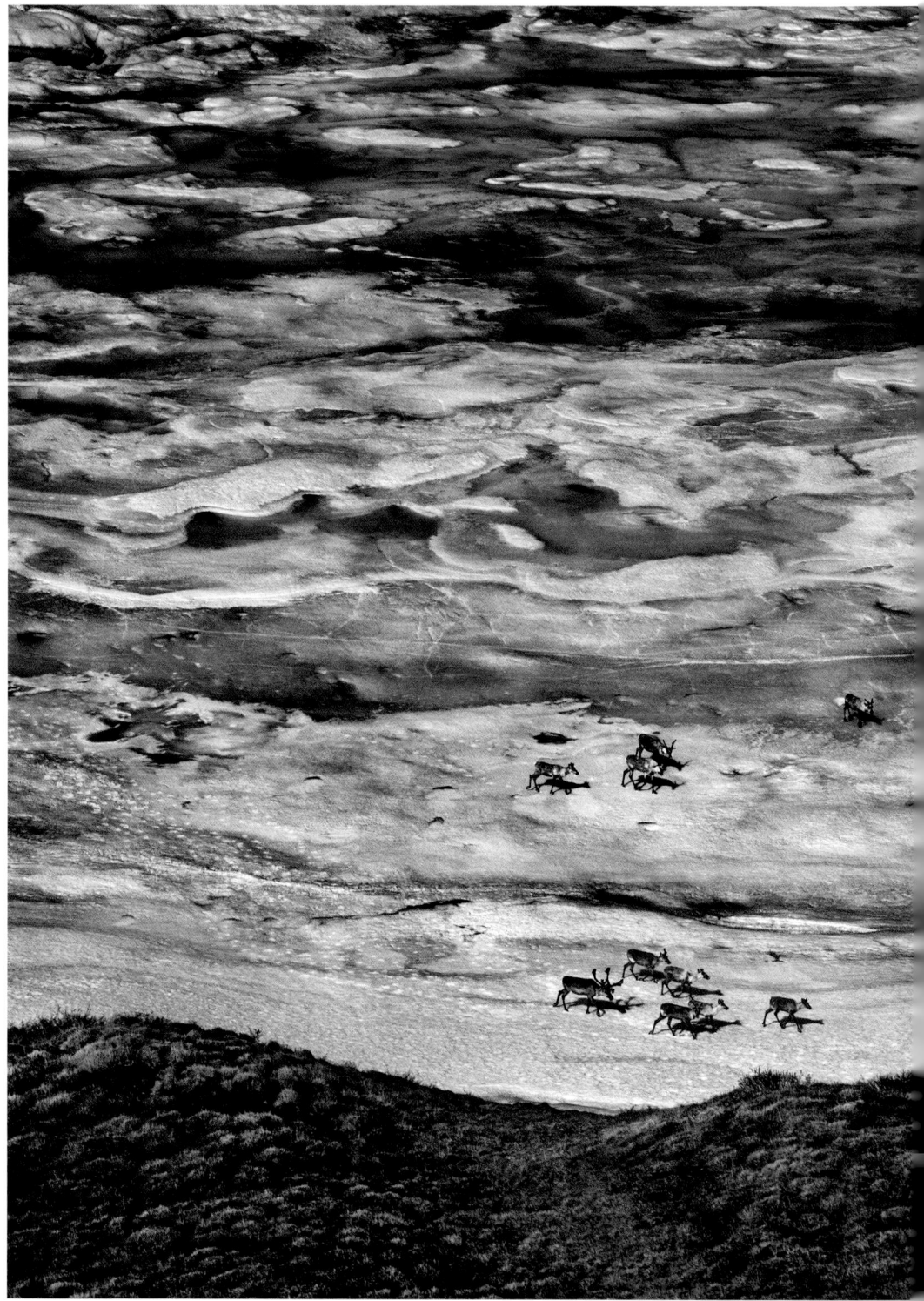

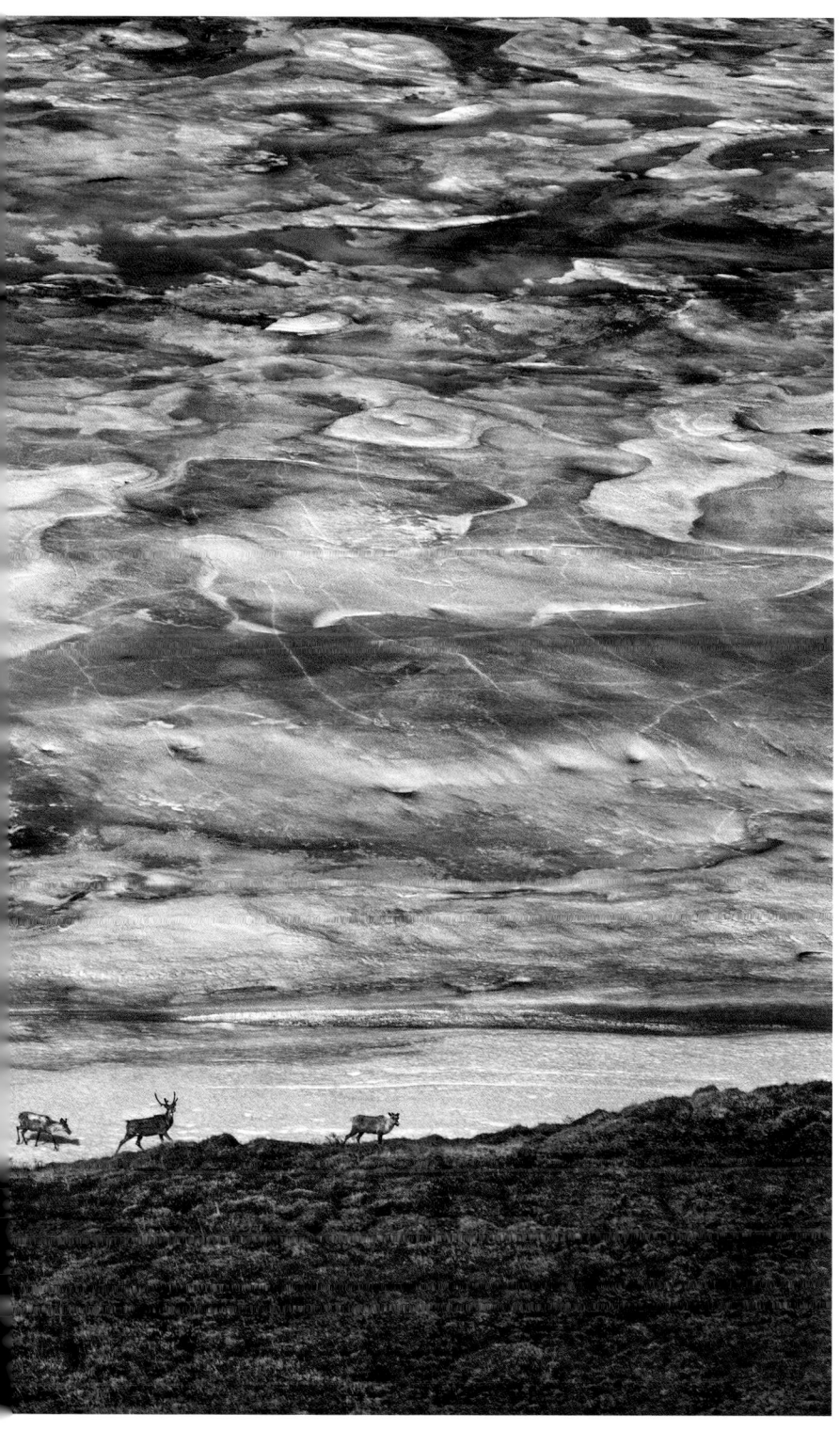

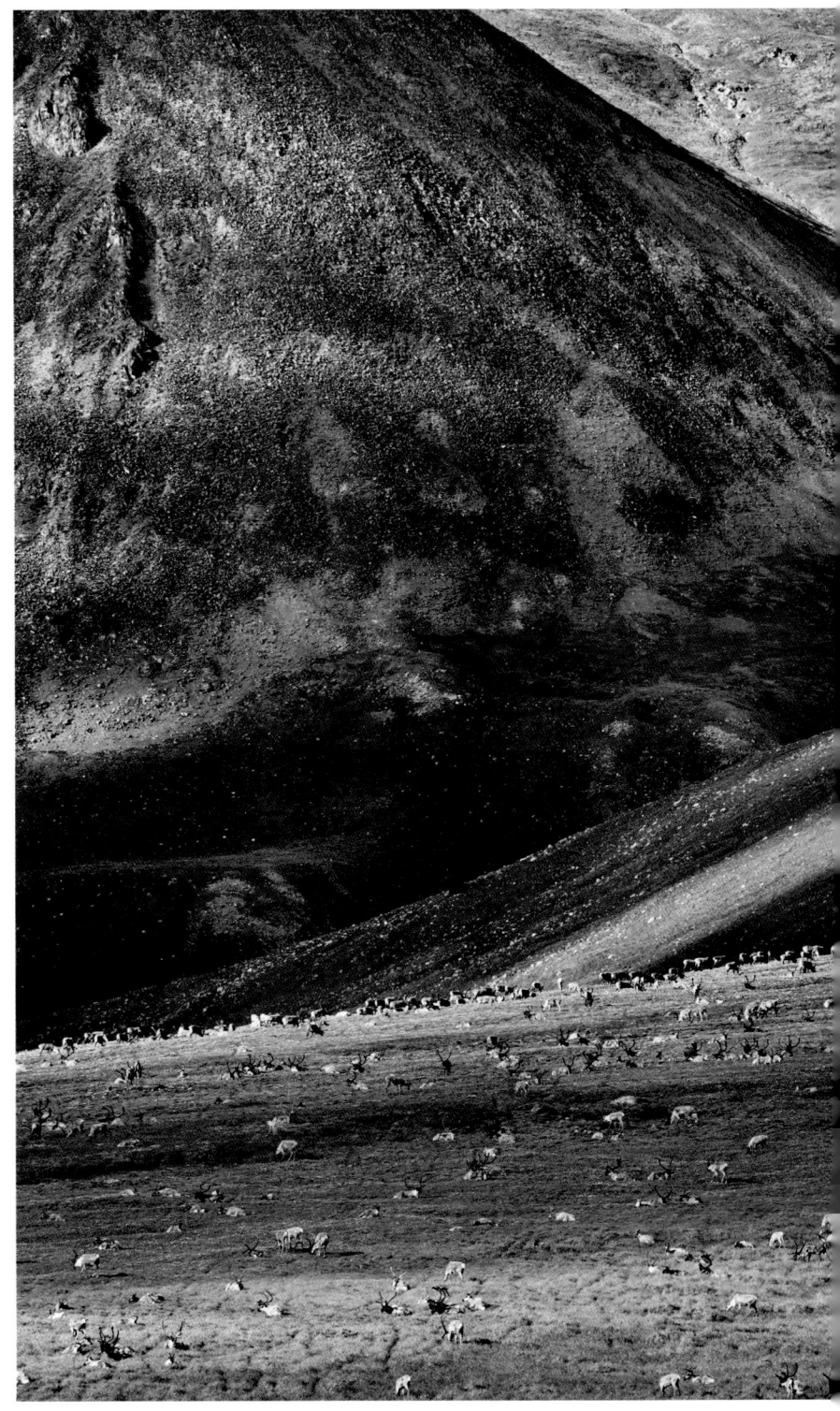

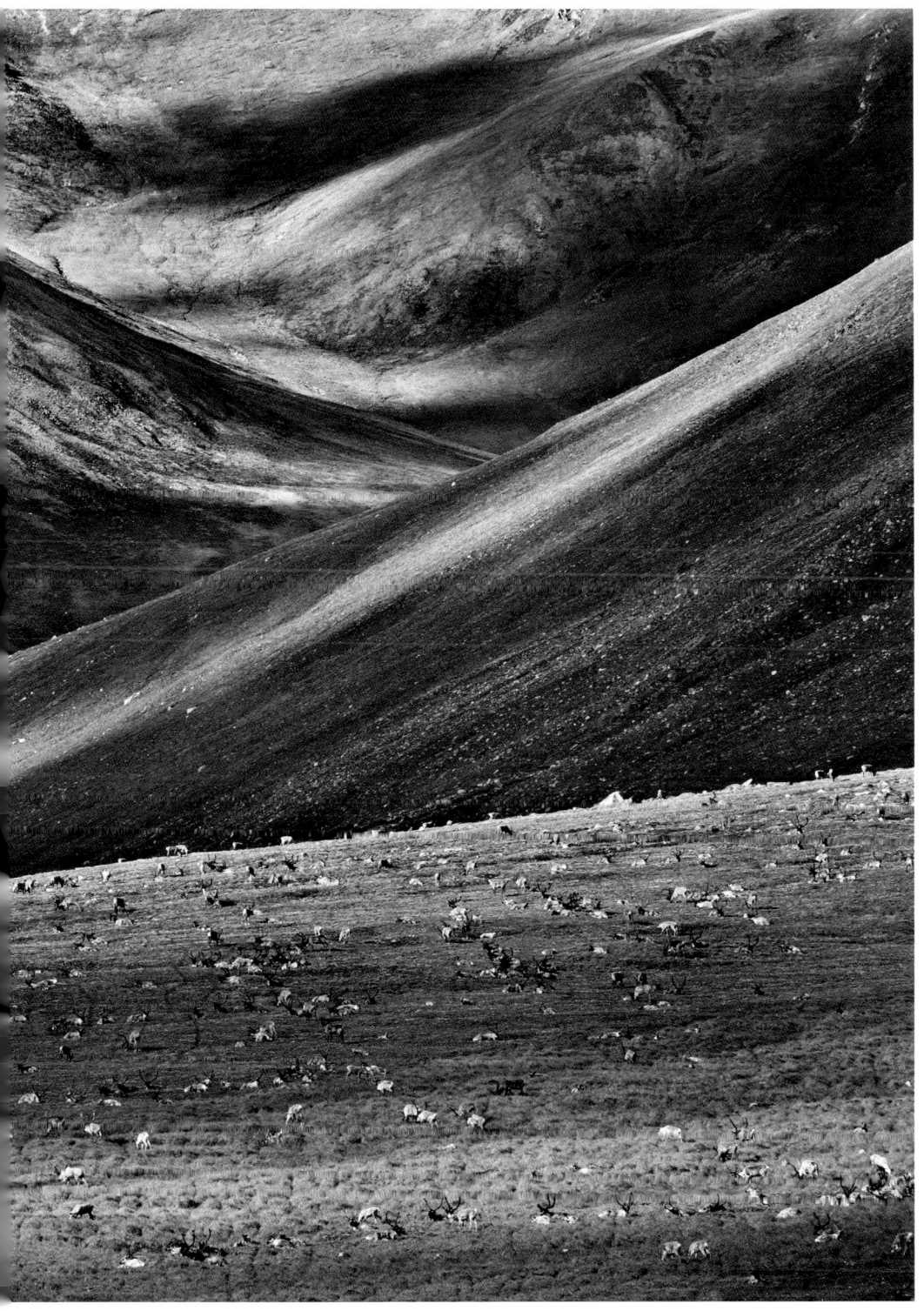

Pages 330/331 The Arctic coastal plain stretches southward from the ocean to the foothills of the Brooks Range. In this undulating region of small lakes and north-flowing rivers, low shrubs, sedges and mosses push through the tundra in the summer. In June and July, caribous also move to the coastal plain to give birth to and raise their young. These Porcupine caribous (*Rangifer tarandus granti*) are on the plain between the village of Kaktovik on the Arctic Ocean coast and the foothills of the Brooks Range. Alaska. USA. June and July 2009.

Pages 332/333 A large number of Porcupine caribous (*Rangifer tarandus granti*) are drawn to the Jago area in the central part of Brooks Range because of the abundance of grass and altitudes less plagued by mosquitoes. Alaska. USA. June and July 2009.

Opposite Ksudach Caldera (3,540 feet/1,079 meters). The last major eruption at the northern end of Ksudach Caldera, in 1907, left a clearly defined cinder field that reaches northward from the caldera. Such was the power of this eruption that, at the time, as far away as Europe, ash in the atmosphere darkened days and was the cause of abnormally red sunrises and sunsets. Ksudach Caldera was formed between 2,000 and 8,000 years ago when the slopes of Ksudach Volcano collapsed following a series of massive pyroclastic blasts, so named when hot gas and rocks move at great speed away from the volcano. Today, the impact of the 1907 eruption can still be felt in hot sands warmed by the 176° Fahrenheit (80° Celsius) water of lakeside hot springs. Kamchatka. Russia. September and October 2006.

Pages 336/337 Kamen Volcano (foreground) and Kluchevskoy Volcano (background). Kamchatka's two highest peaks are Kamen at 15,000 feet (4,579 meters) and Kluchevskoy at 15,600 feet (4,750 meters). Kamen is dormant, with no record of its last eruption. But Kluchevskoy, a young volcano formed only 7,000 years ago, is not only Kamchatka's highest peak and Eurasia's highest active volcano, but it is also the peninsula's most powerful volcano. During the past half century, it has spewed out an average of 60 million tons of volcanic material per year. Its last major eruption was in 2003. Kamchatka. Russia. September and October 2006.

Pages 338/339 This photograph was taken in the eastern part of the Brooks Range, which rises to over 9,800 feet (3,000 meters); the rugged stretch of mountains is sliced by deep river valleys and numerous glaciers. The immense variety of microclimates results from the collision of cold air from the Arctic and hot air coming from the Yukon River region of central Alaska. Alaska. USA. June and July 2009.

Pages 340/341 A tundra valley extends between Tolbachik and Kamen Volcanoes. In the background, a line of clouds separates a "small" crater some 2,600 feet (800 meters) high from the huge base of Kamen Volcano, which rises 15,000 feet (4,579 meters) above sea level. Kamchatka. Russia. September and October 2006.

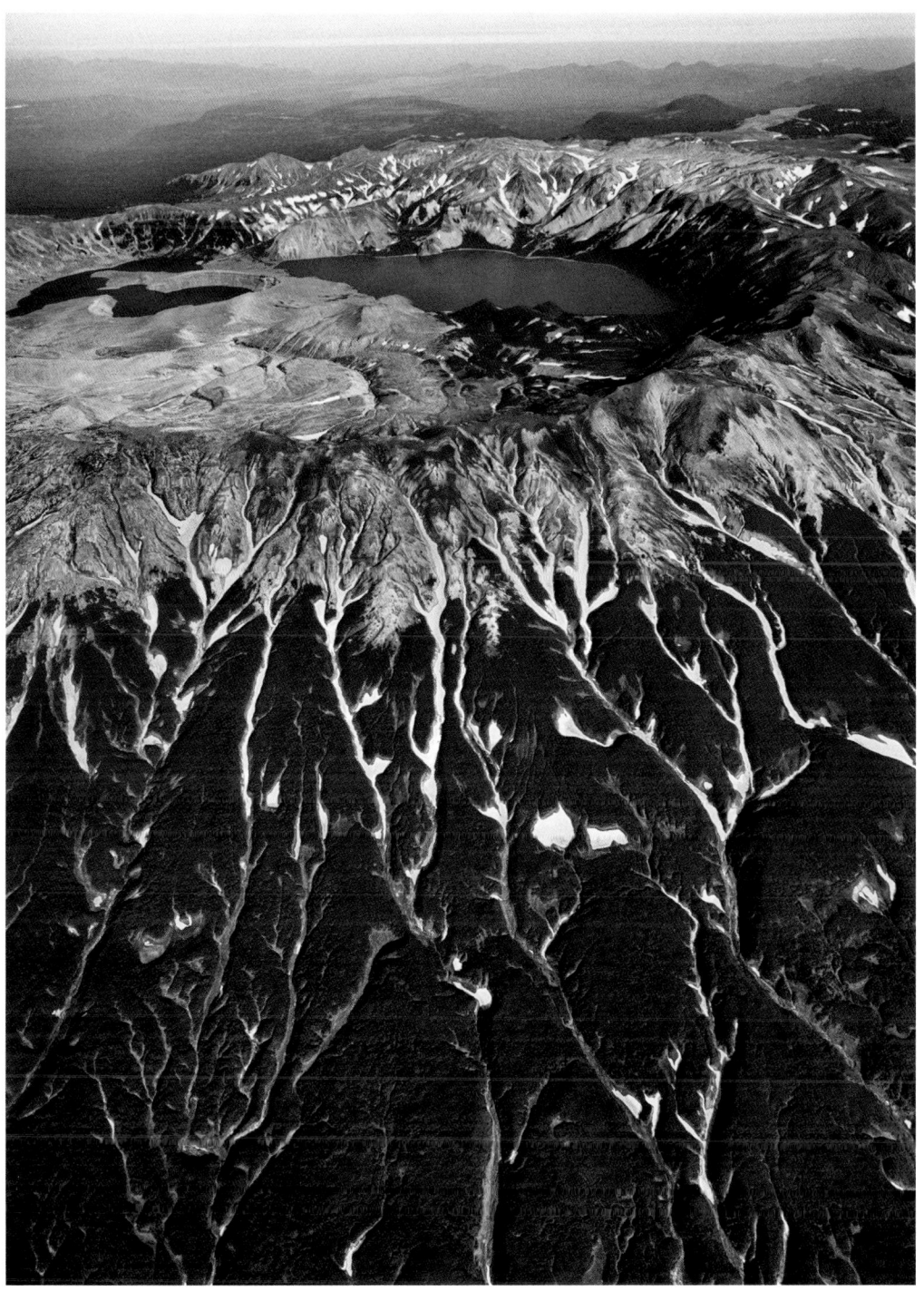

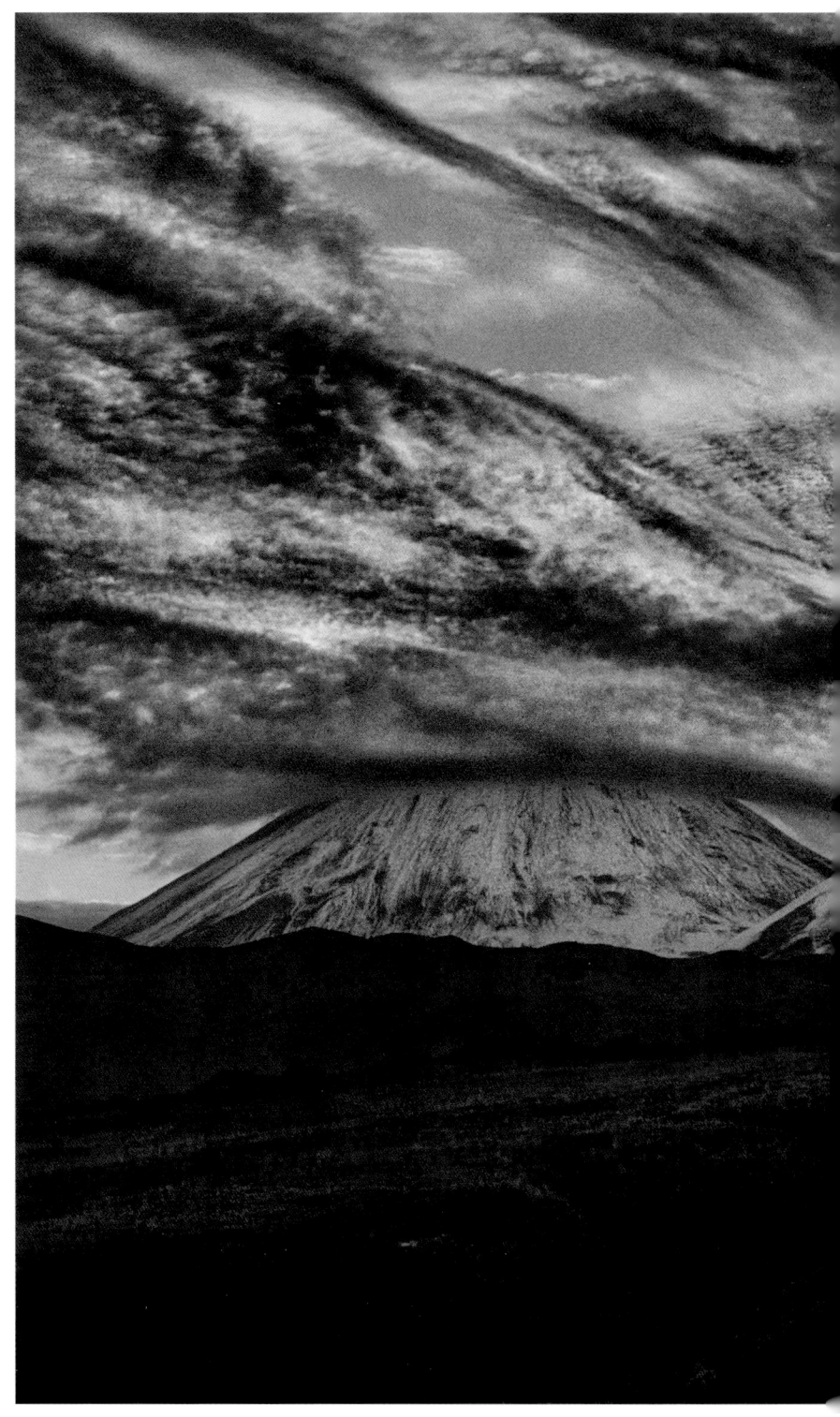

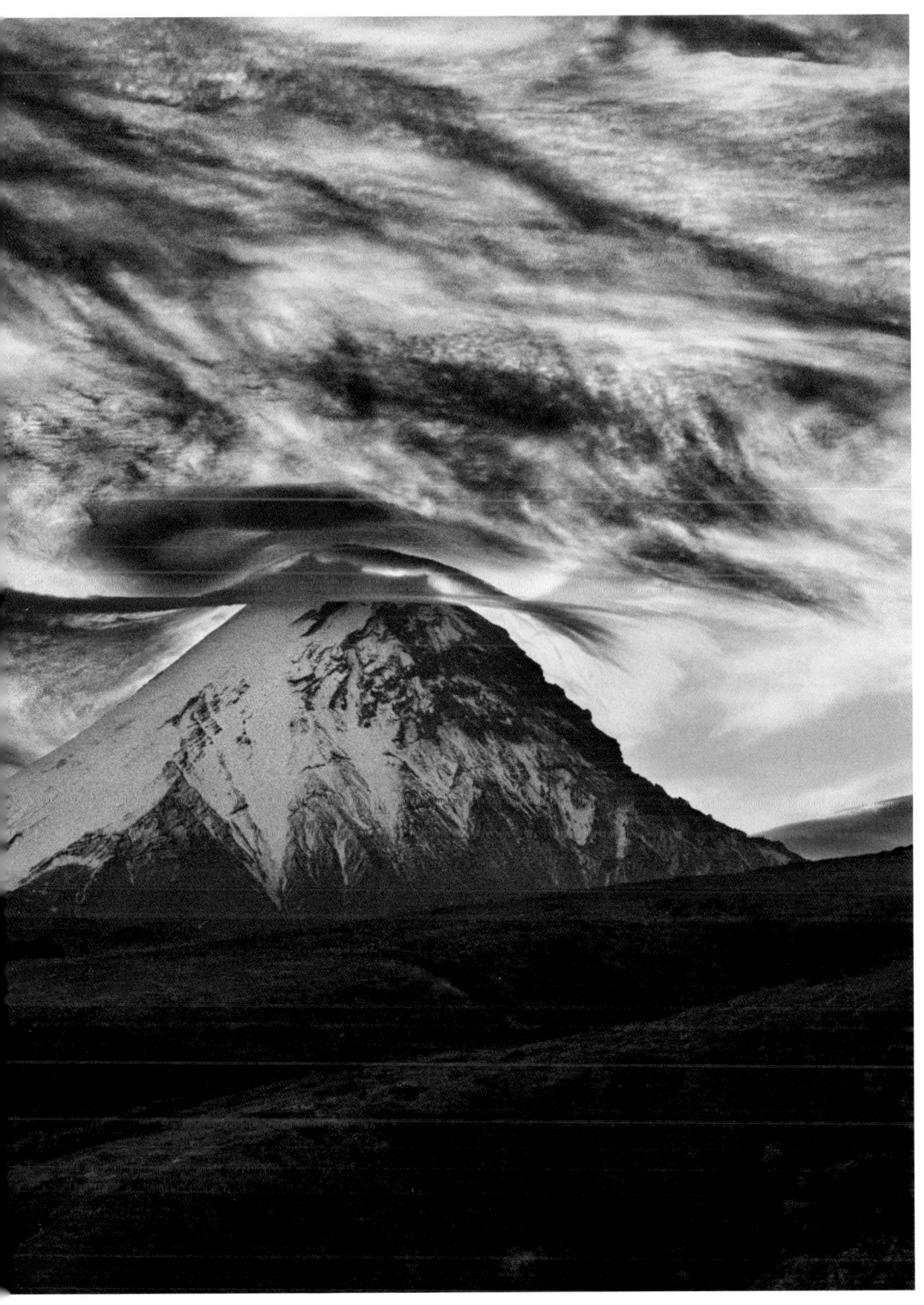

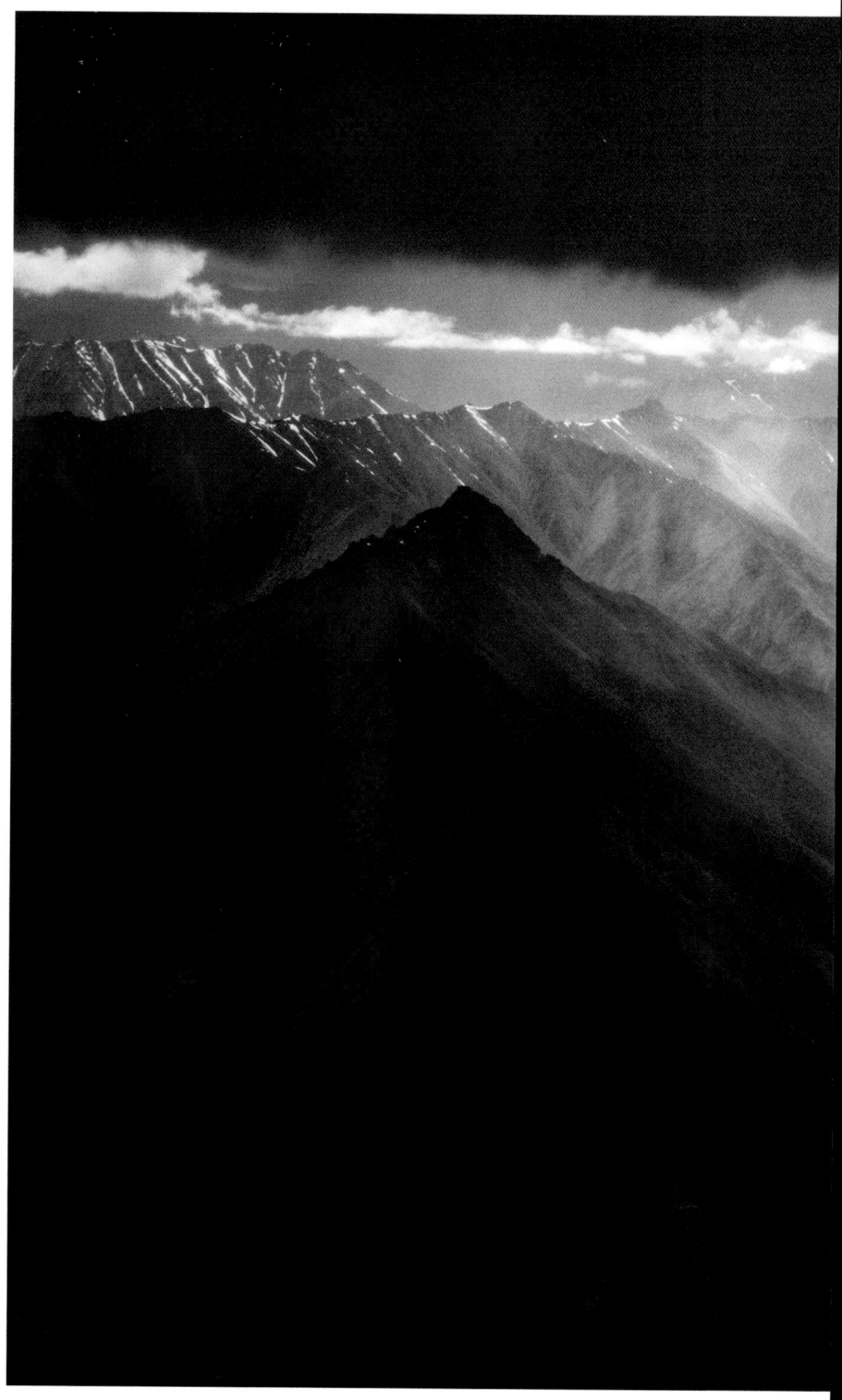

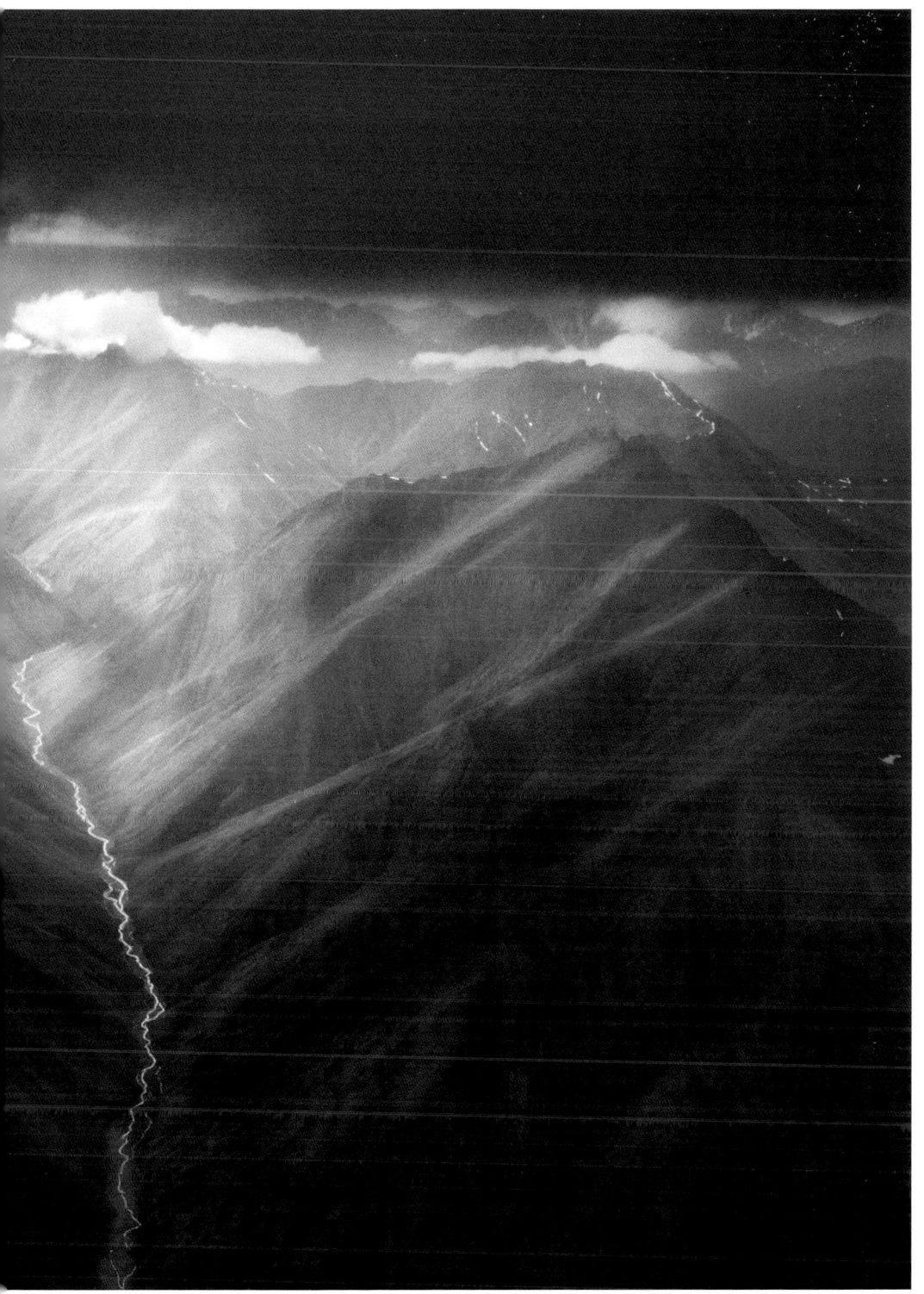

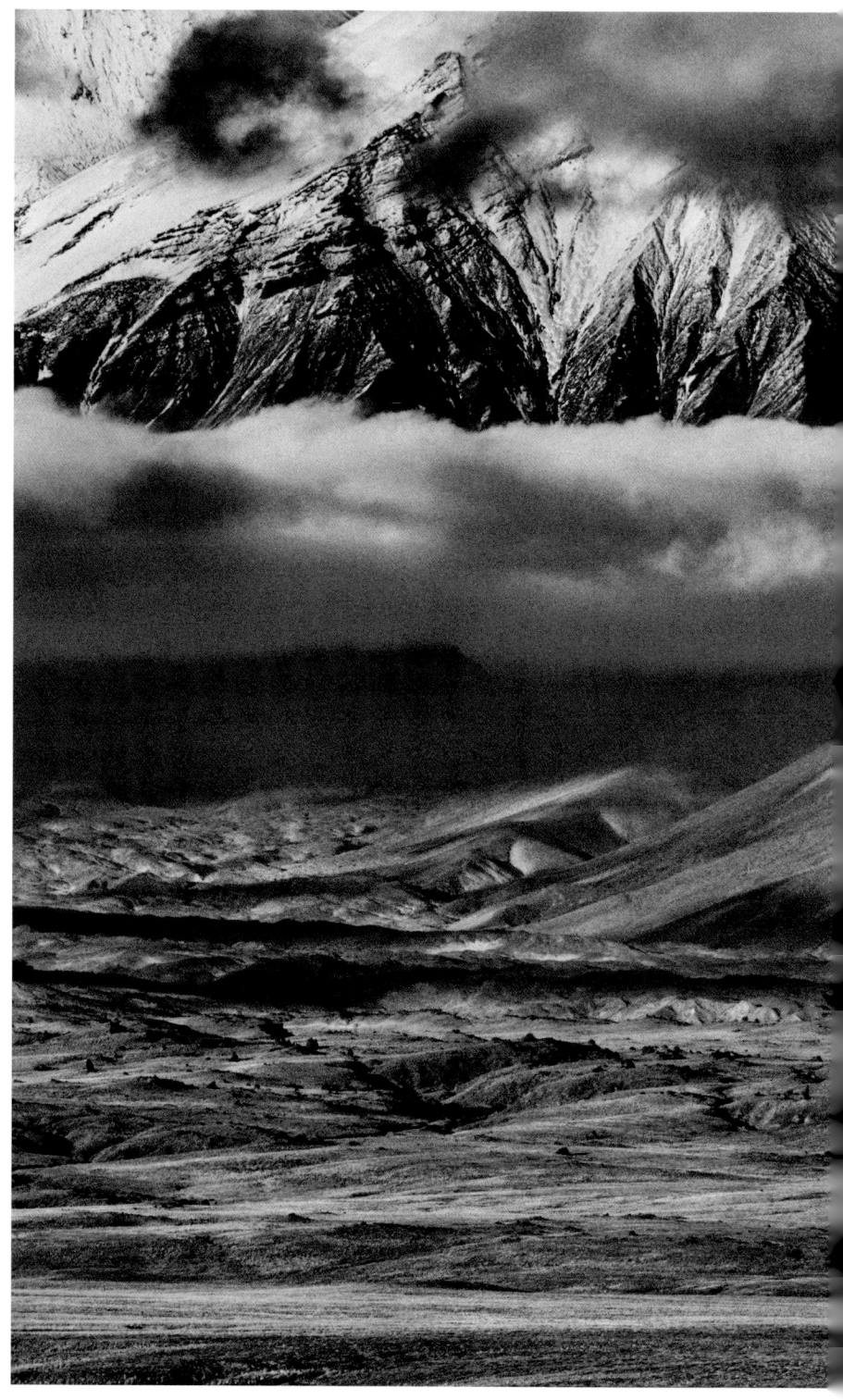

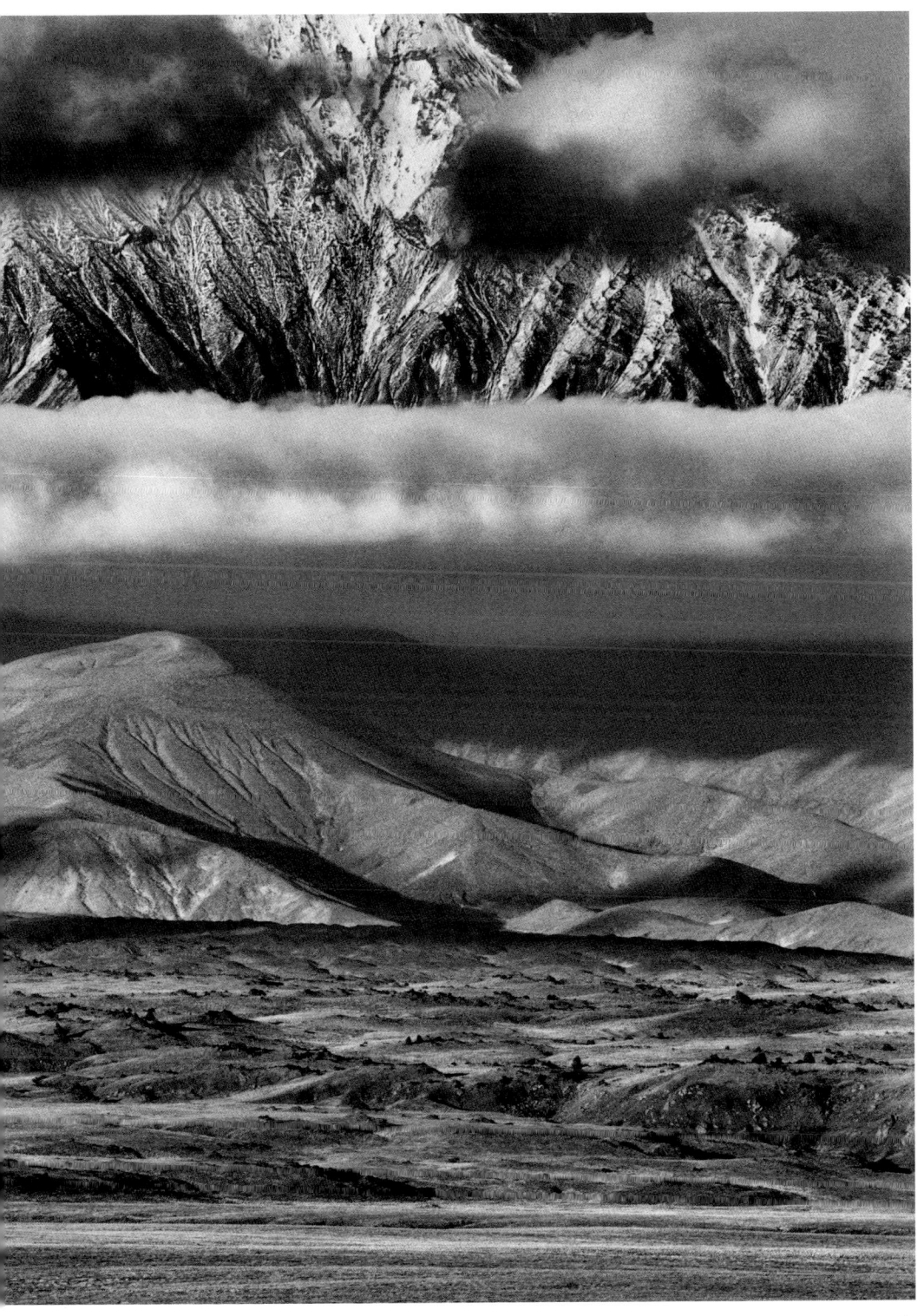

Opposite Krasheninnikov Volcano (6,089 feet / 1,856 meters). This distinctive-looking volcano is named after Stepan Krasheninnikov, a famous Russian naturalist and ethnographer who came to Kamchatka with Vitus Bering's second Alaska expedition in 1740. Its two adjoining cones rise from the center of an enormous ancient caldera, visible here as a dark circle. There is no record of Krasheninnikov's last eruption. Kamchatka. Russia. September and October 2006.

Pages 344/345 The southern portion of the Arctic National Wildlife Refuge lies within the Interior Alaska-Yukon lowland taiga, or boreal forest, ecoregion. This photograph shows the southern boundaries of the Brooks Range, close to the Gwich'in settlement of Arctic Village in northern Alaska. The waters of these rivers flow south, joining the great Yukon River before entering the Bering Sea. Alaska. USA. June and July 2009.

Pages 346/347 The Ancient Bristlecone Pine Forest in the White Mountains. Bristlecone pinewood that has fallen to the ground can remain intact for thousands of years in the cold, dry climate of the White Mountains. Using a cross-dating technique that overlaps tree-ring patterns of living trees with the still intact patterns of deadwood, scientists have assembled a continuous tree-ring chronology extending back nearly 10,000 years. This bristlecone pine chronology is the longest in the world and provides an unrivaled look into past climatic and environmental conditions. California. USA. April, May and June 2010.

Pages 348/349 The Colorado Plateau, which embraces parts of Colorado, New Mexico, Utah and Arizona, offers some of the world's most stunning geophysical spectacles. Covering an area of 130,000 square miles (337,000 square kilometers), it boasts the greatest concentration of national parks in the United States, many of which appear in these images: Grand Canyon National Park, Zion National Park, Bryce Canyon National Park, Canyonlands National Park, Arches National Park and Monument Valley Navajo Tribal Park.

The Colorado Plateau comprises mainly desert, with scattered areas of forest. Its most dramatic natural feature is the Grand Canyon of the Colorado River, which sets the tone for much of the area's jagged and disrupted landscape. Brightly colored rock stripped of all vegetation by drought and erosion has given the area the nickname of "Red Rock Country." Here, the Colorado River in the Grand Canyon is viewed from Navajo territory. Arizona. USA. April, May and June 2010.

Pages 350/351 In the rapids of the Colorado River in the Grand Canyon. Arizona. USA. April, May and June 2010.

Pages 352/353 View of the confluence of the Colorado and the Little Colorado from the Navajo territory. The Grand Canyon National Park begins after this junction. Arizona. USA. April, May and June 2010.

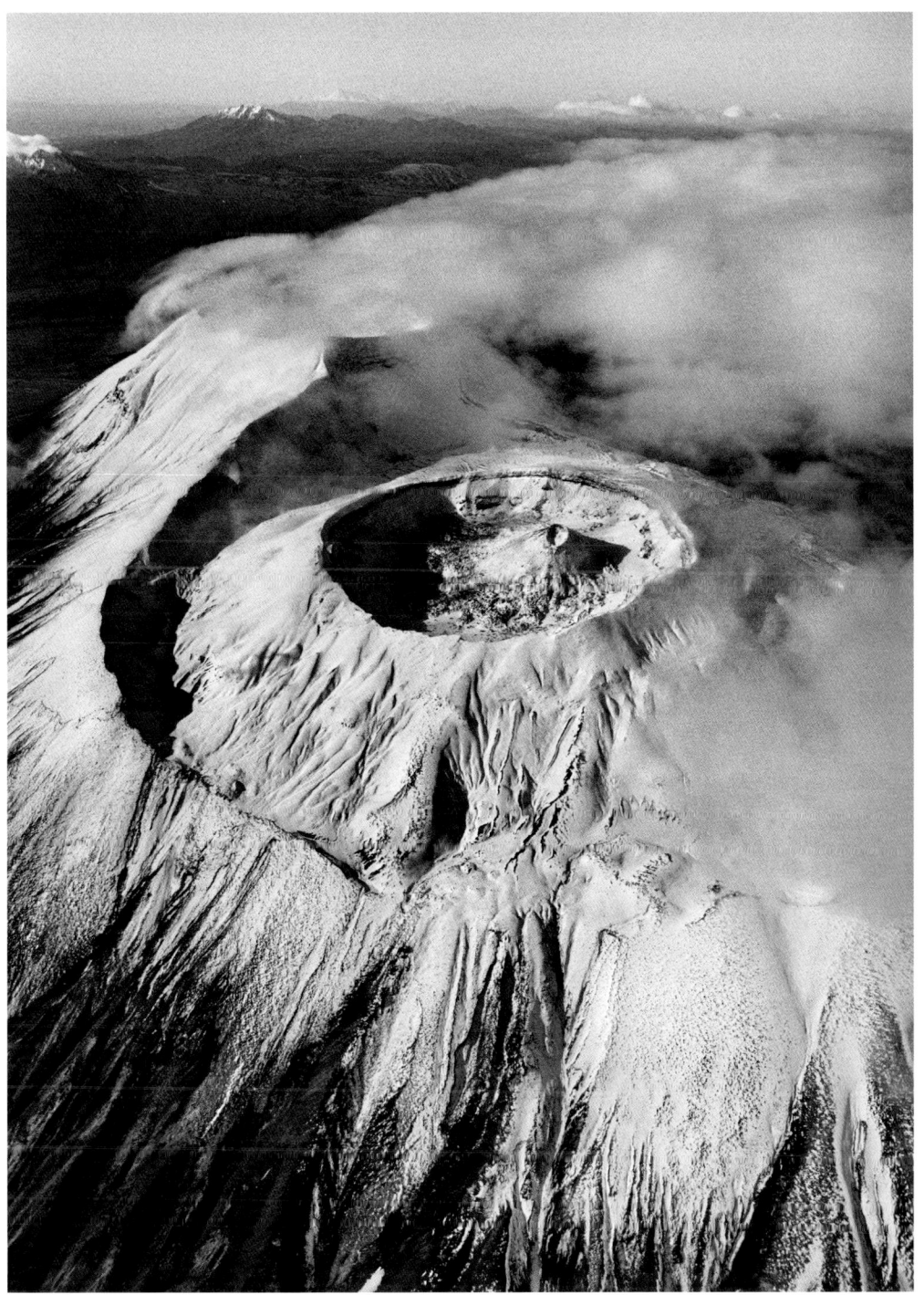

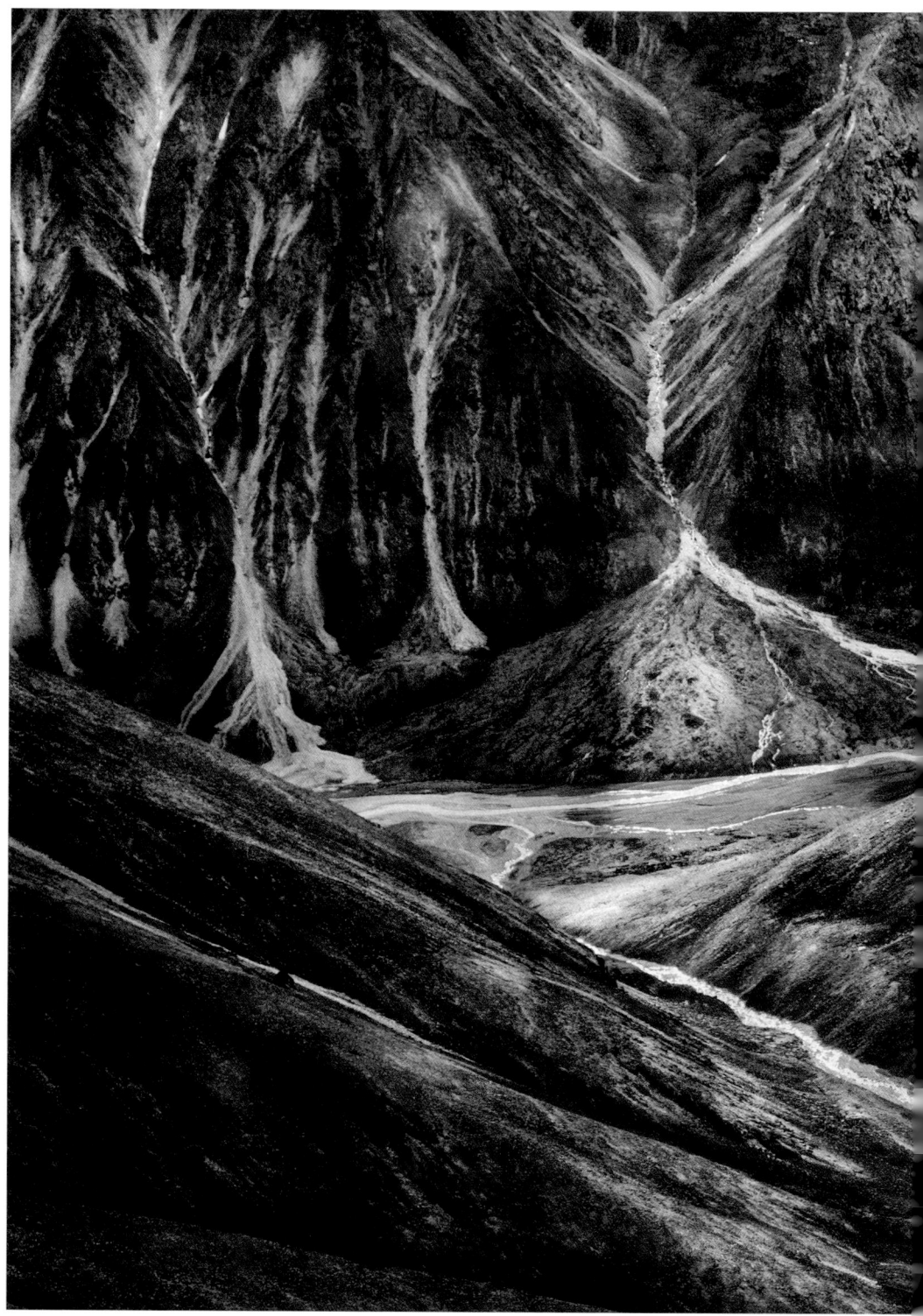

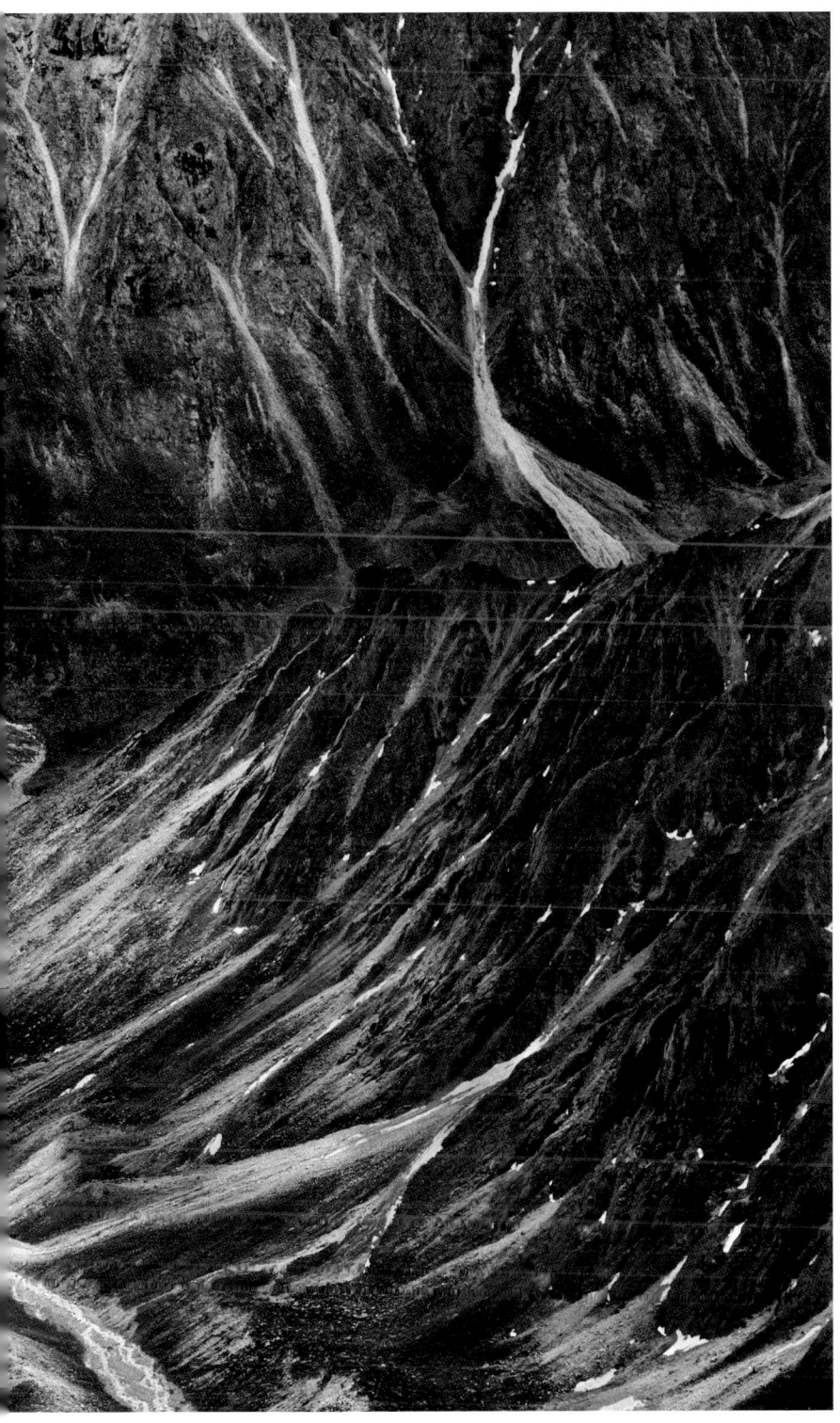

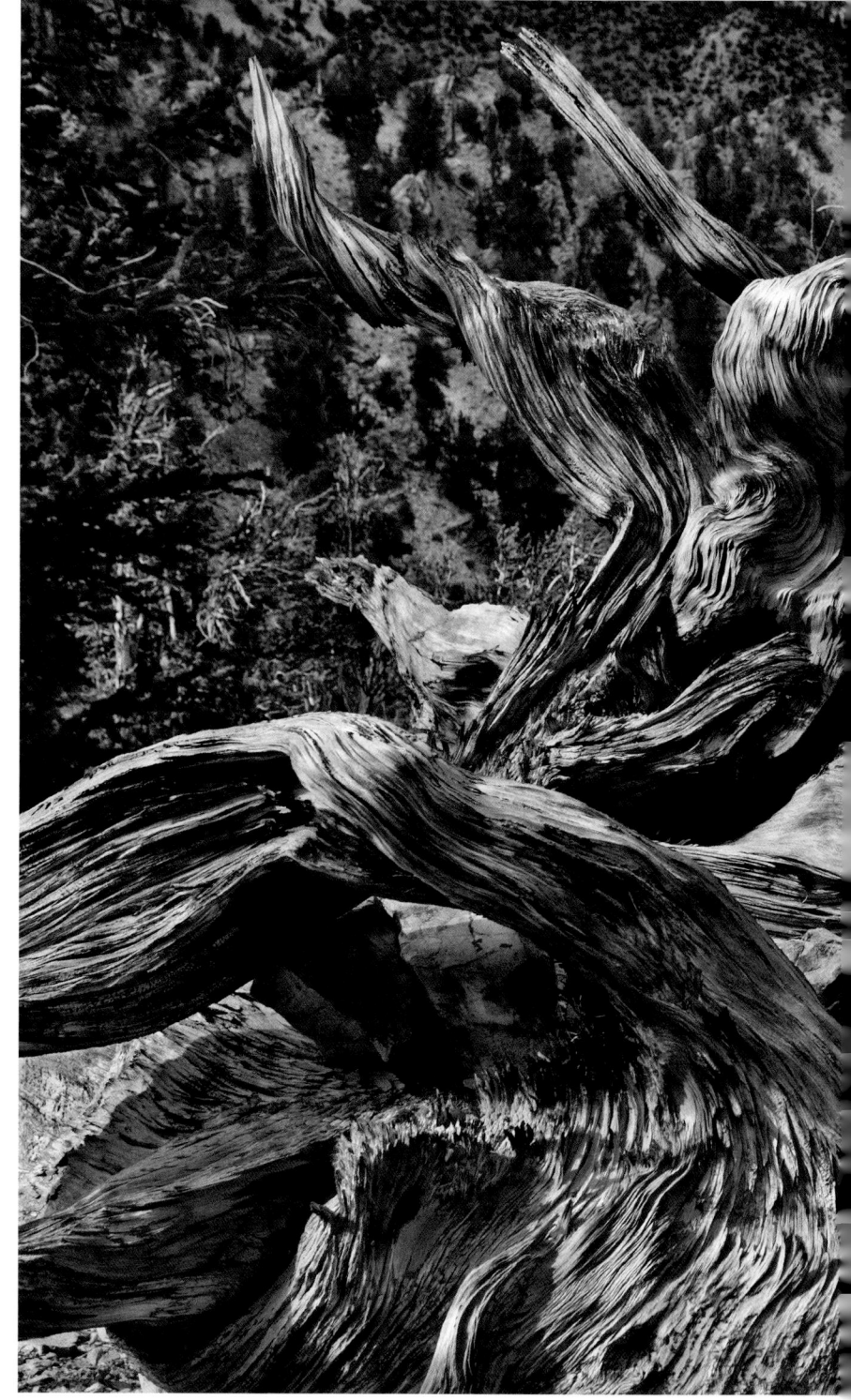

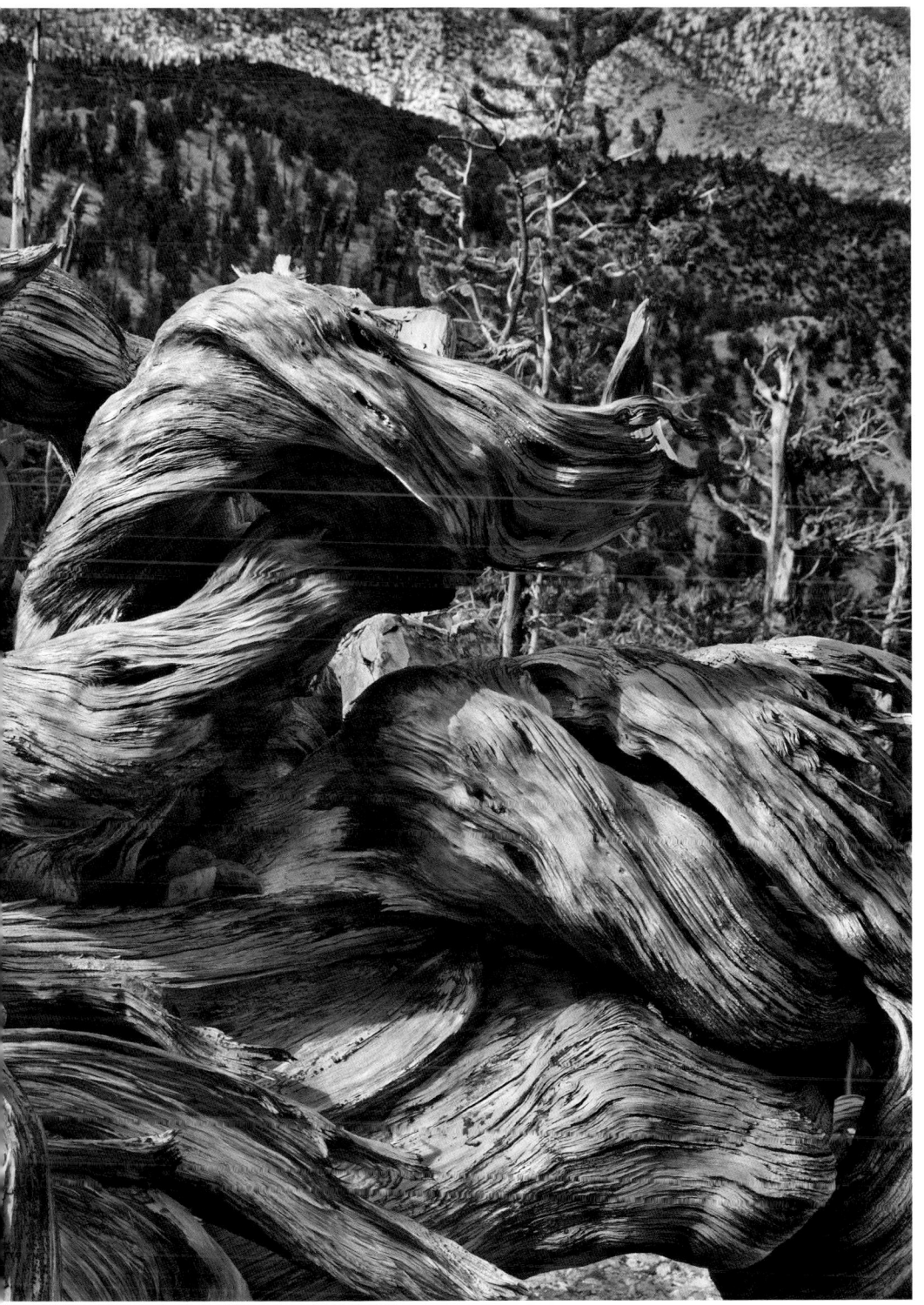

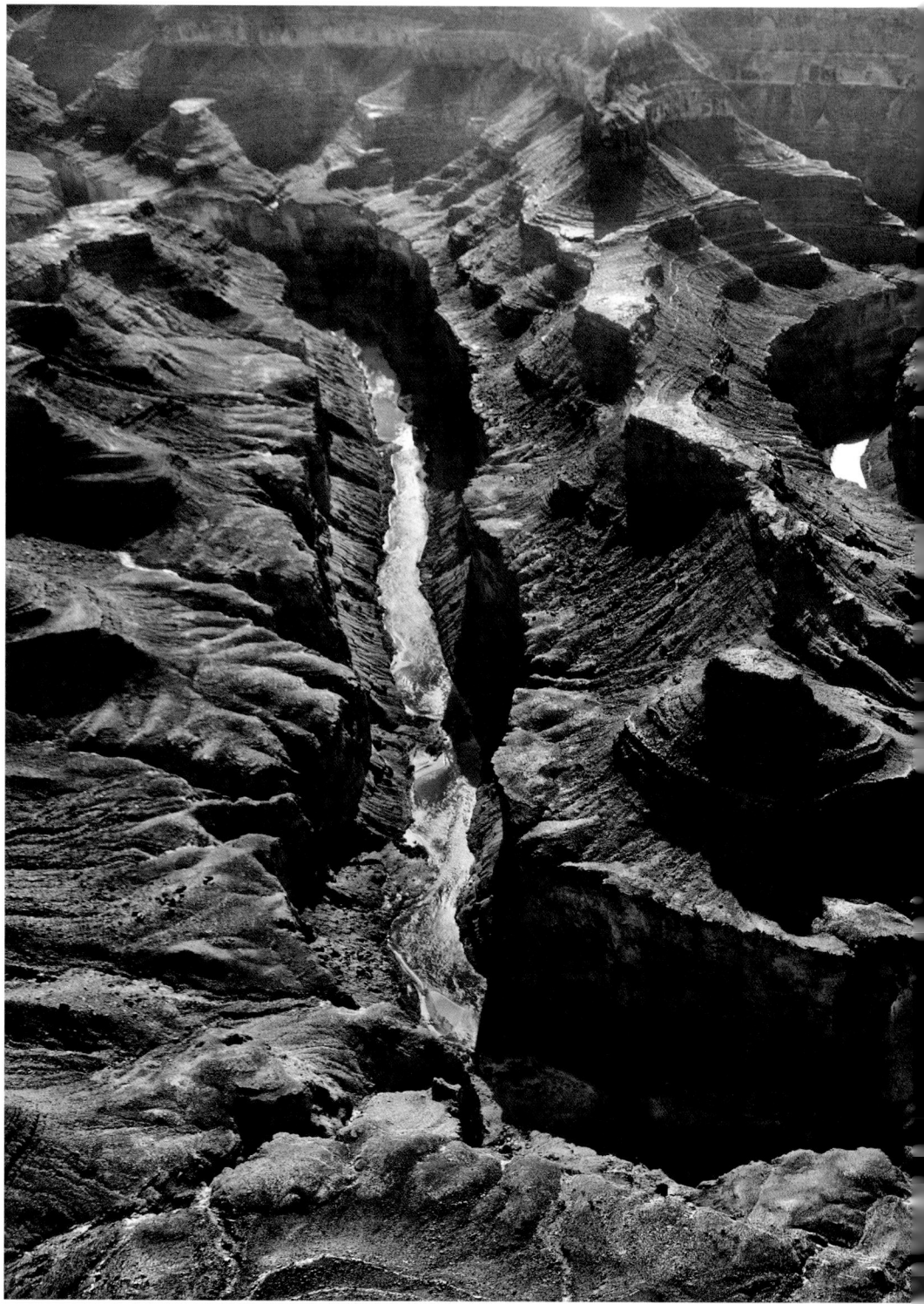

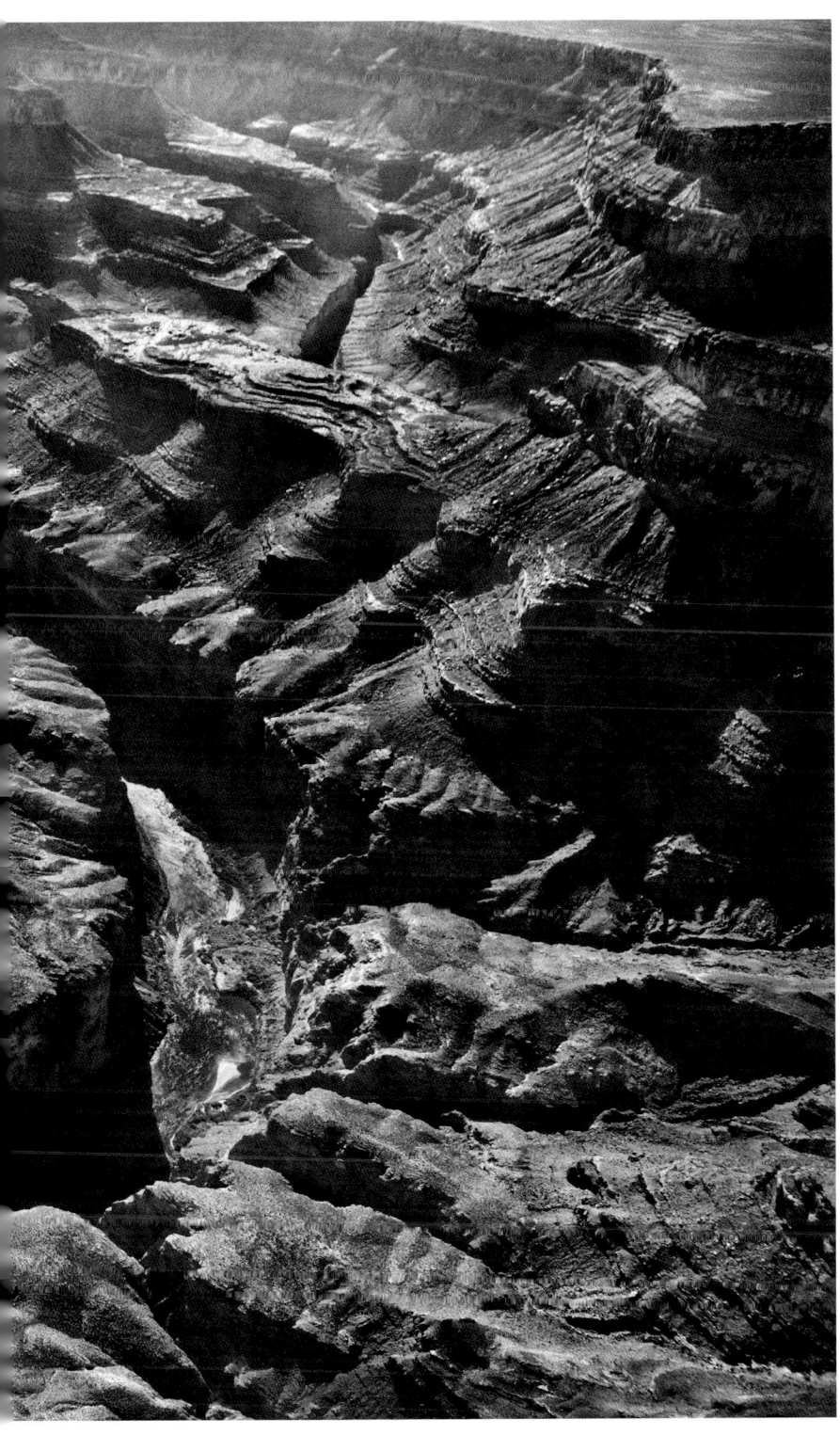

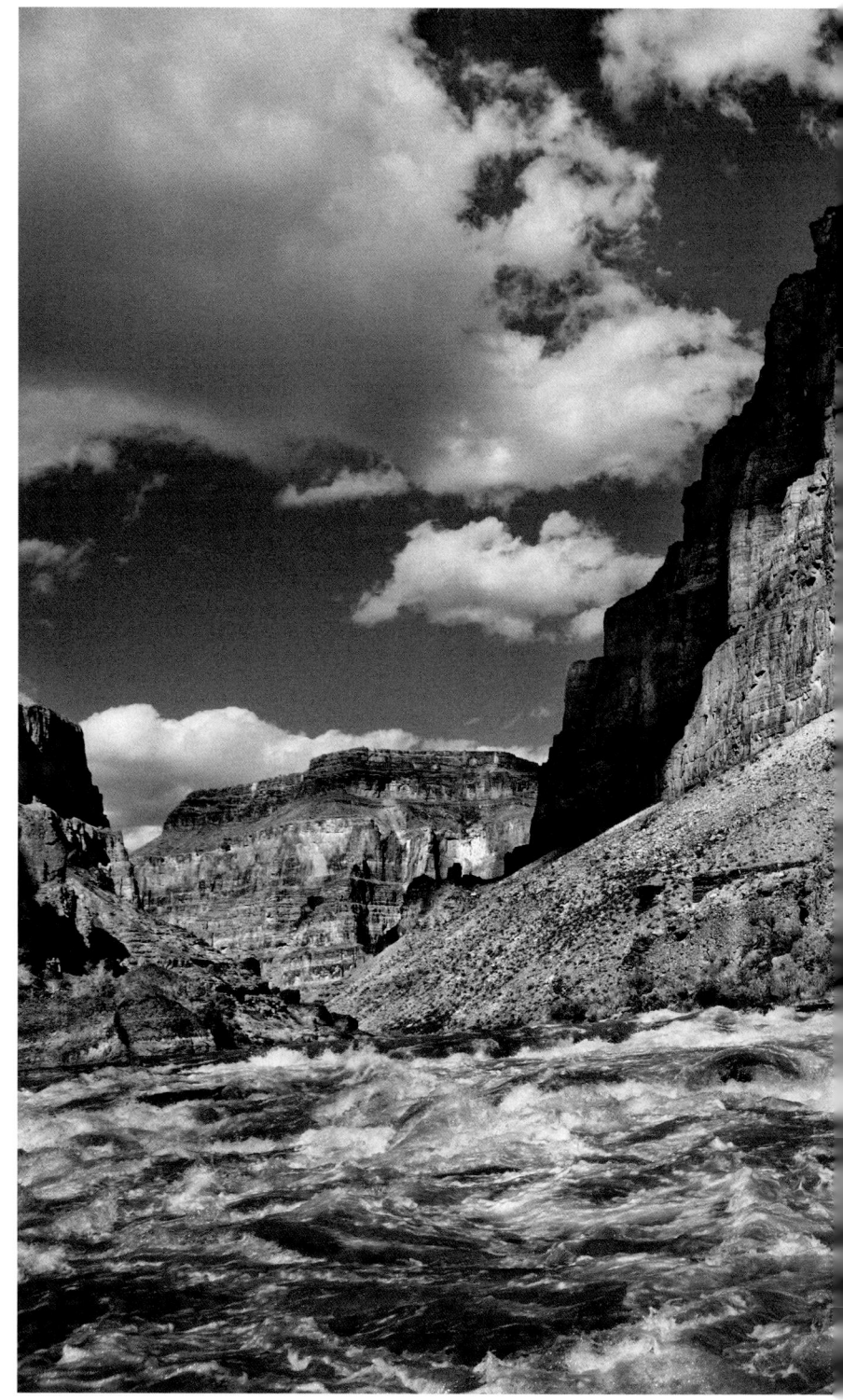

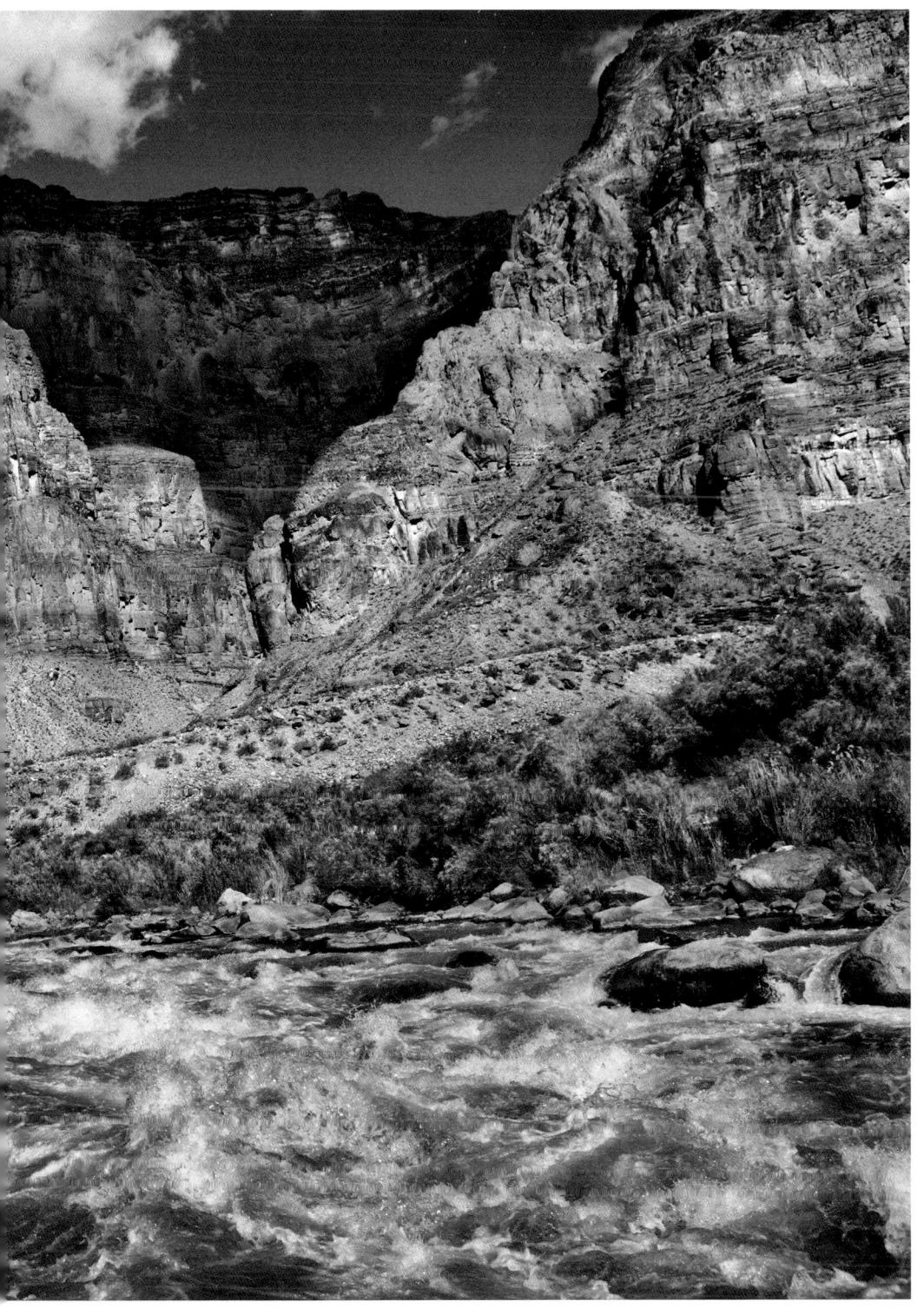

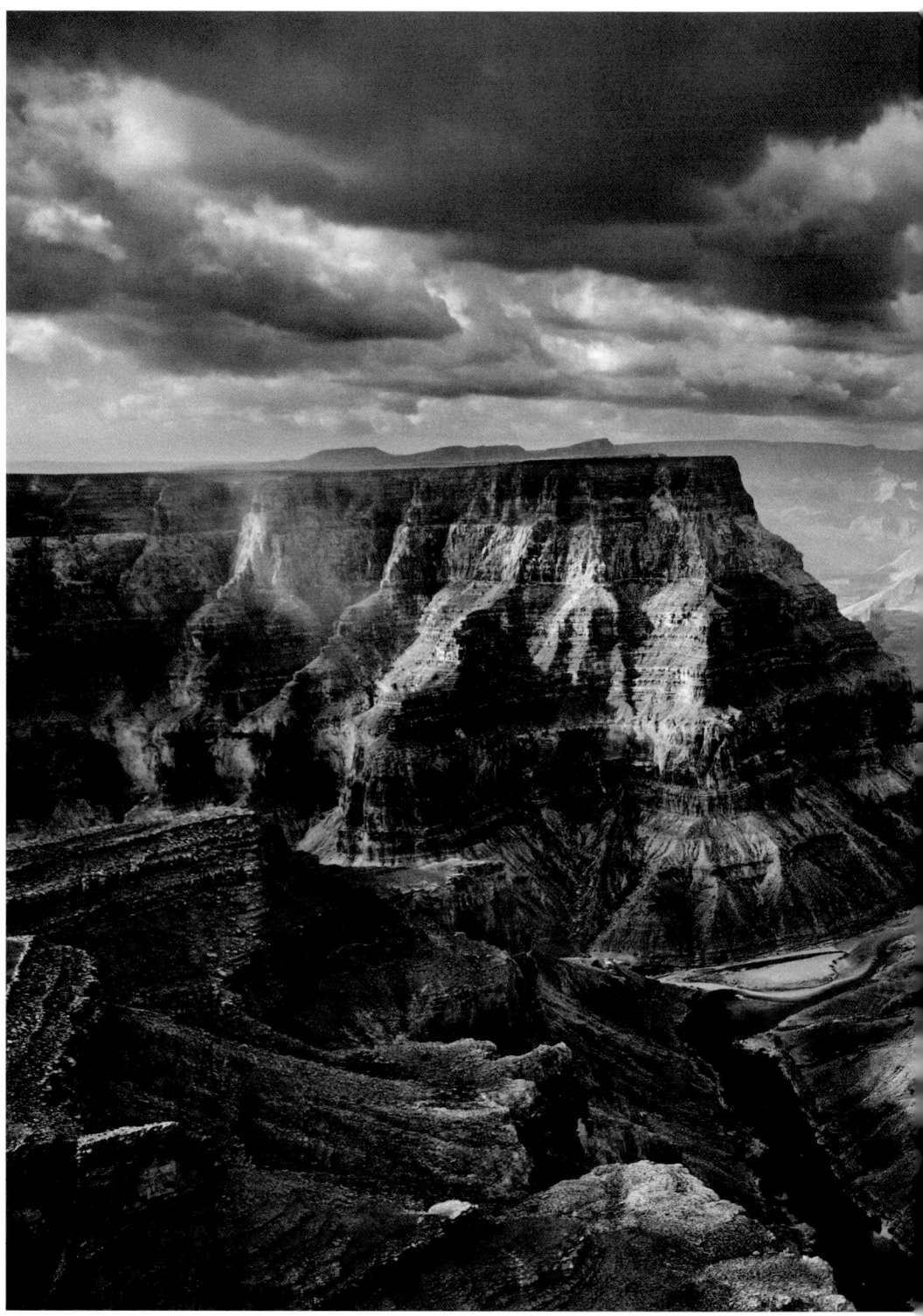

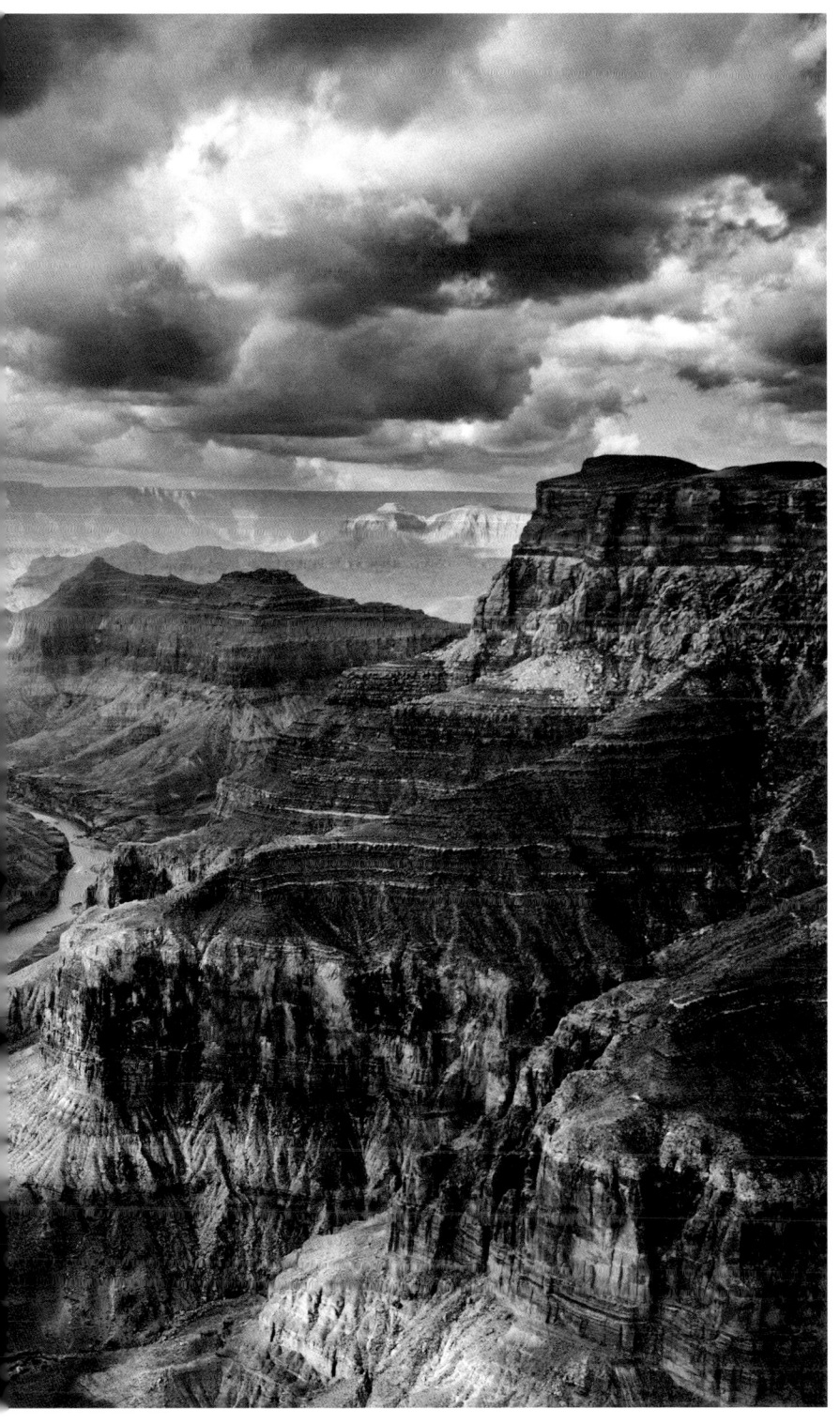

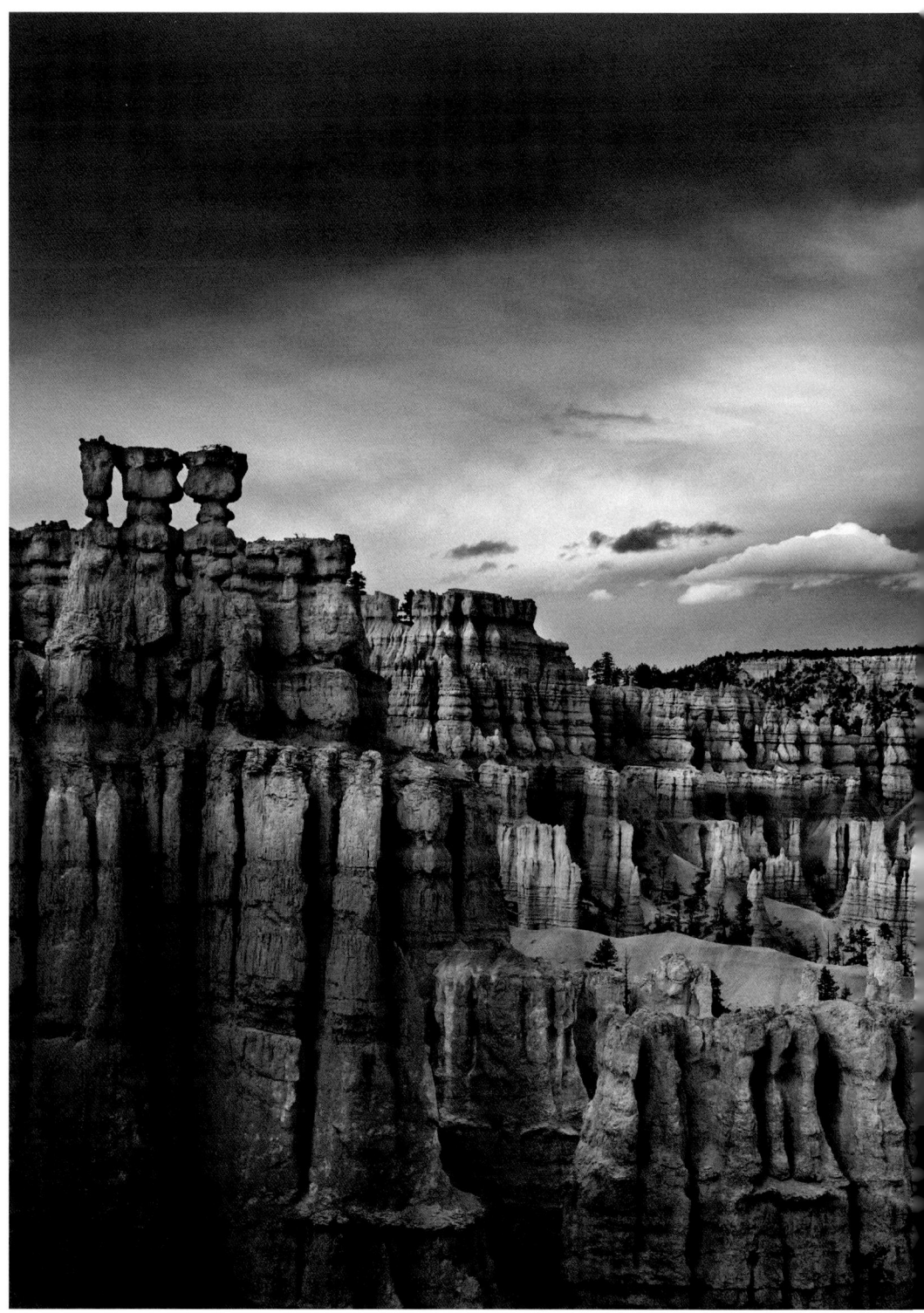

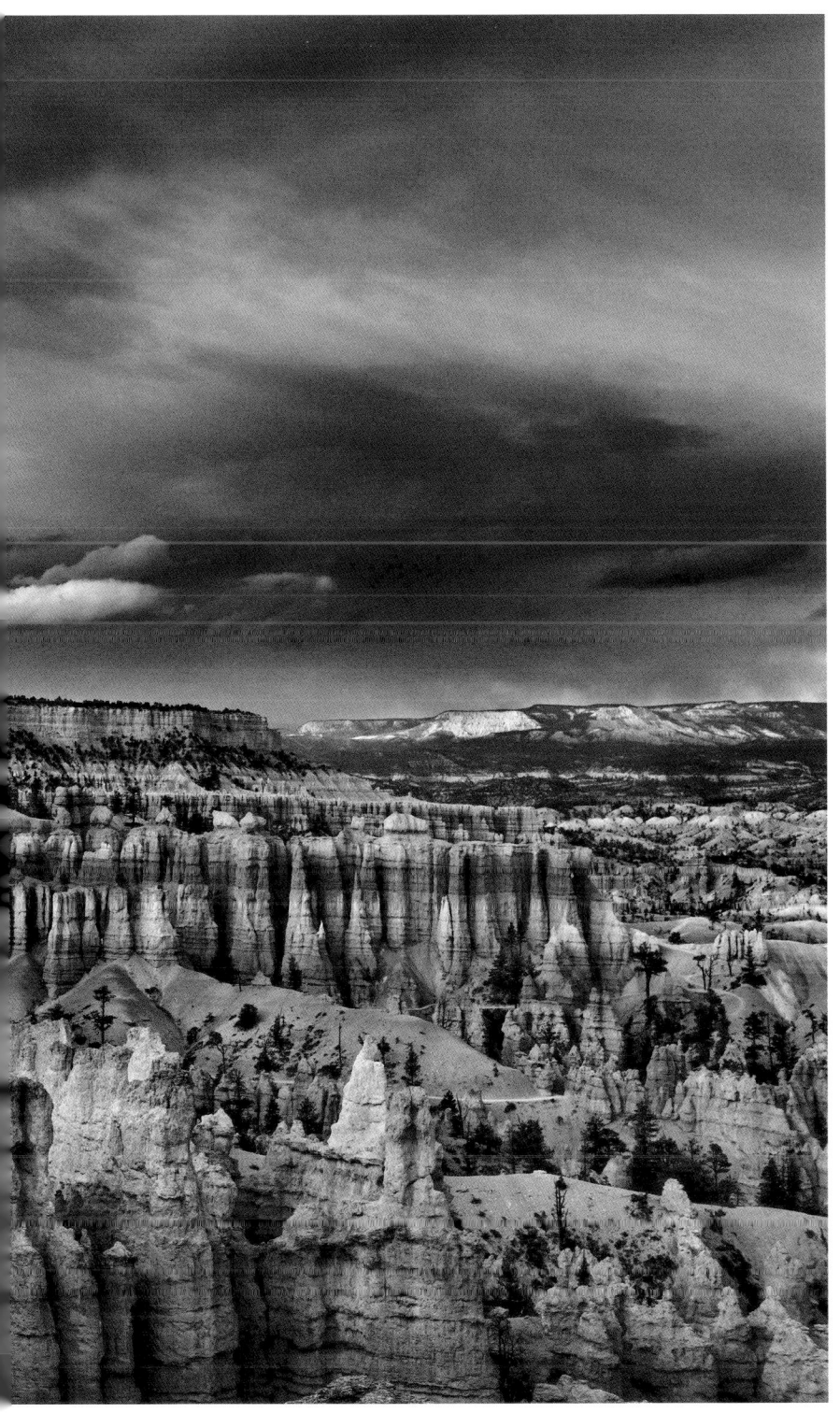

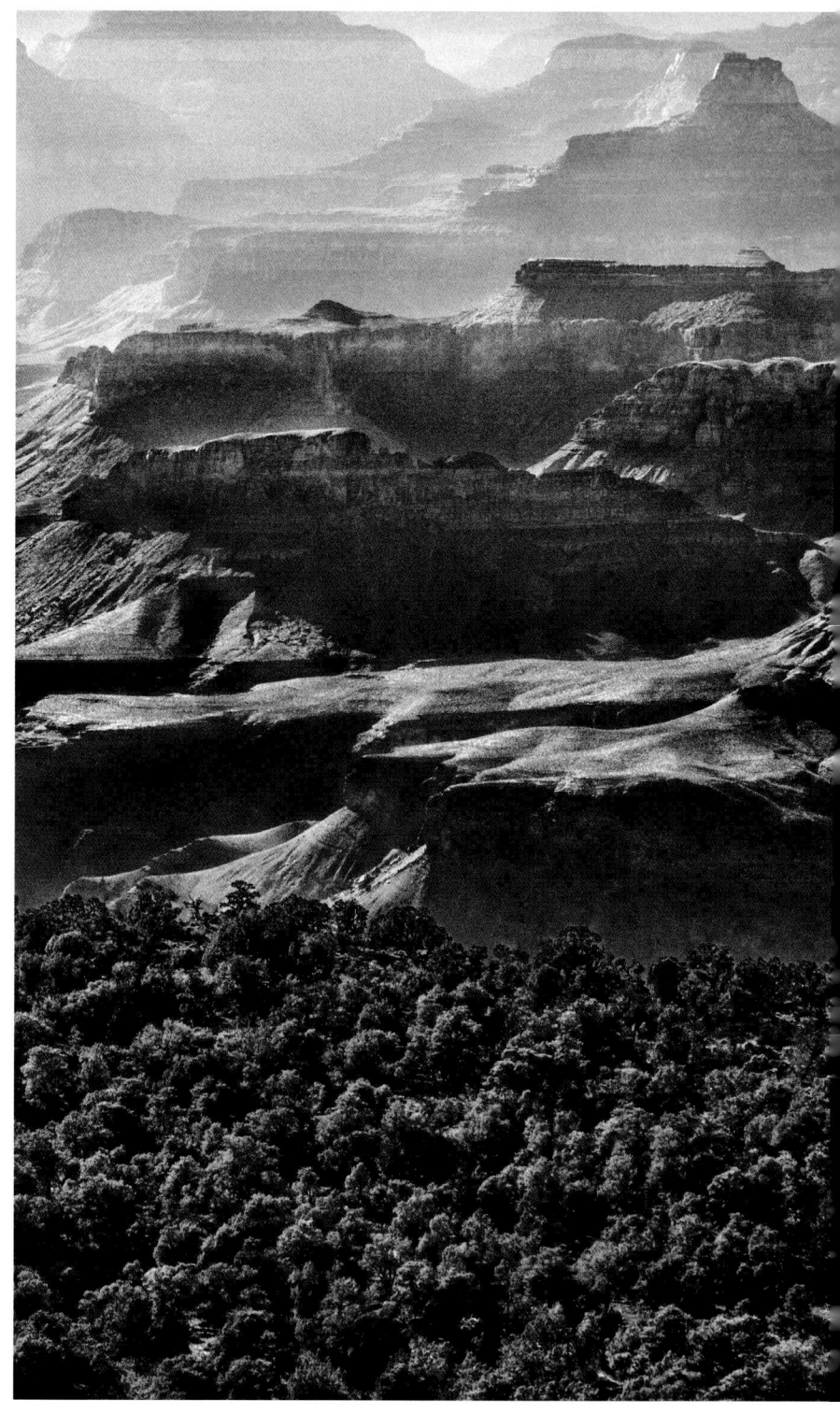

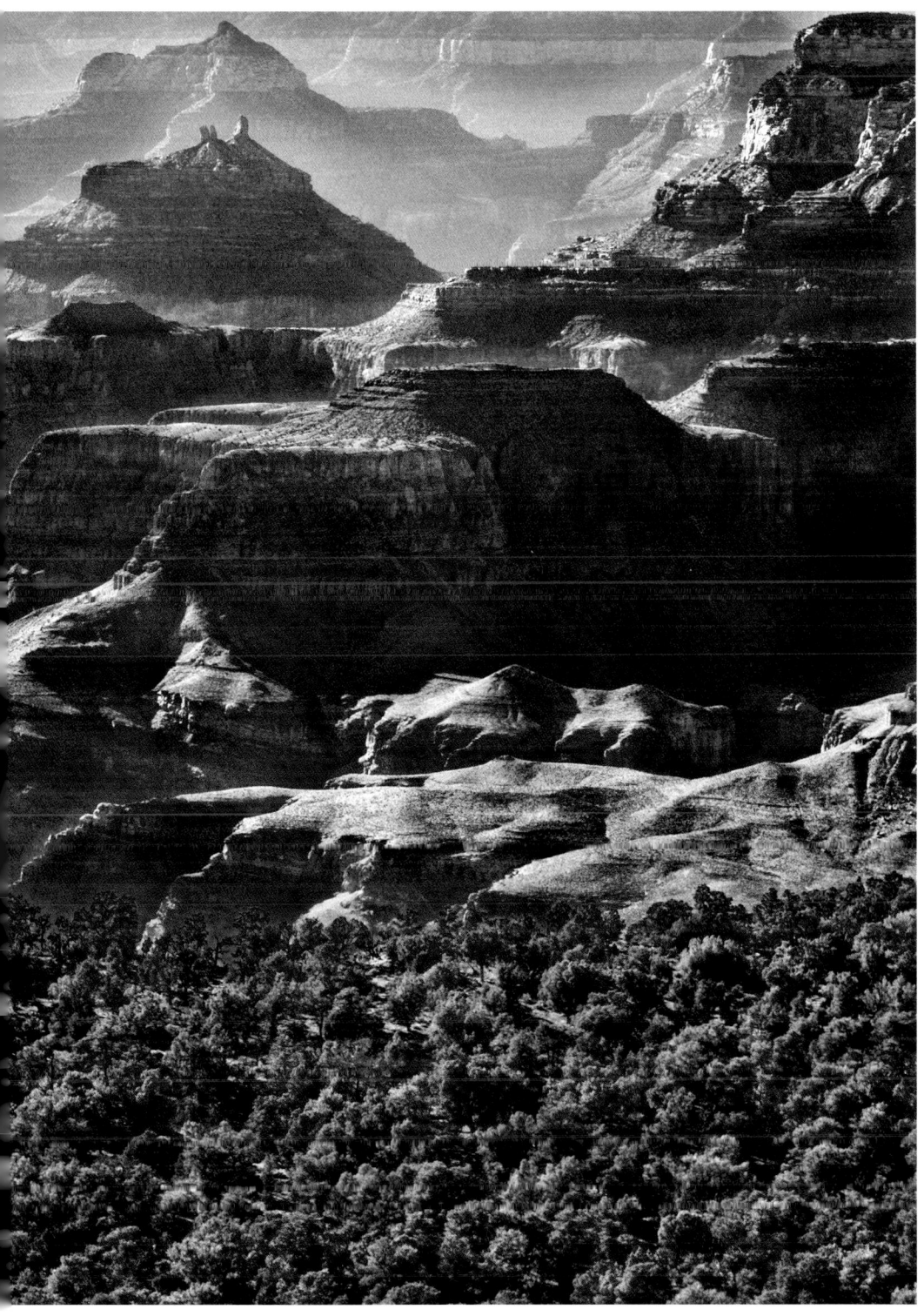

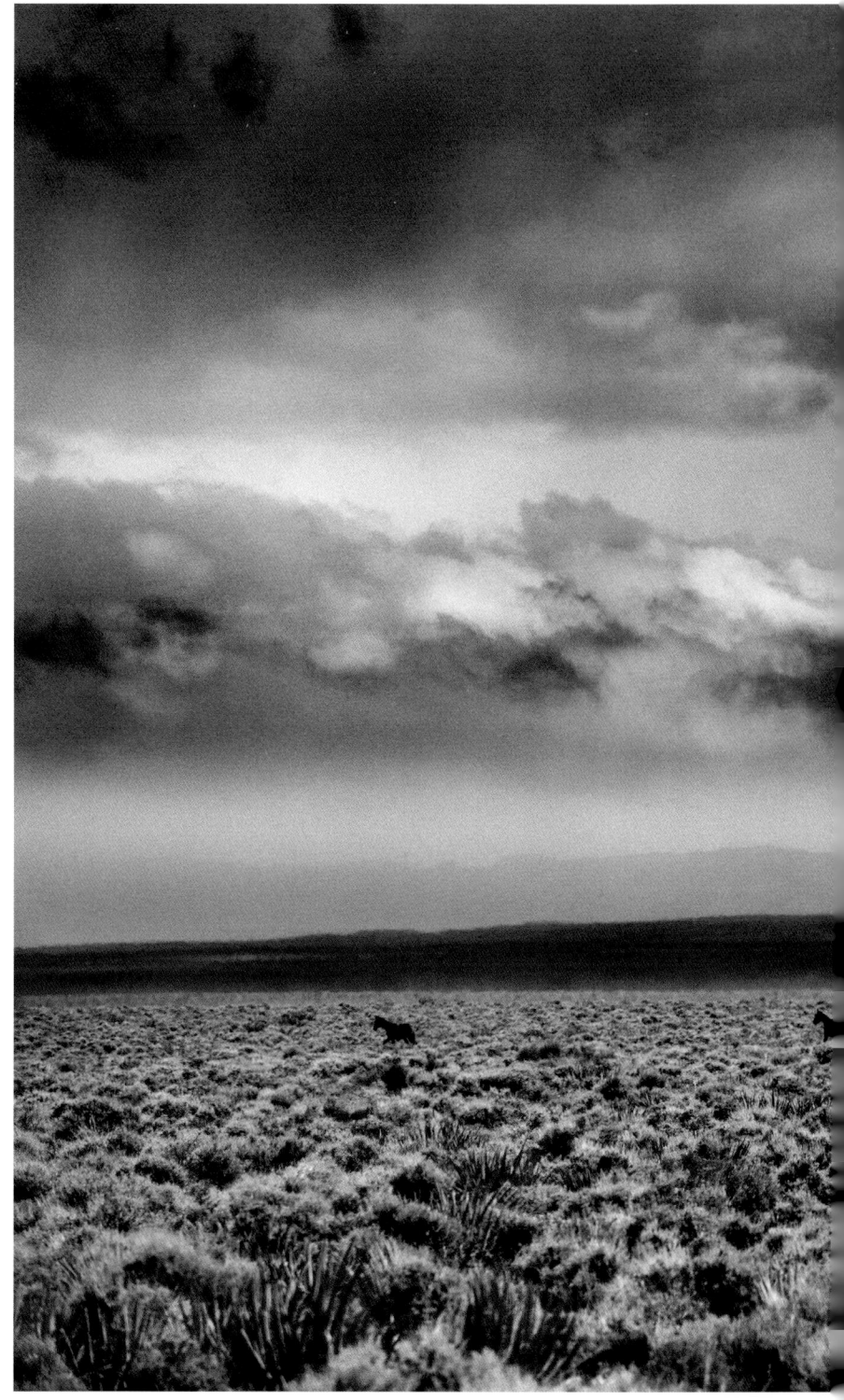

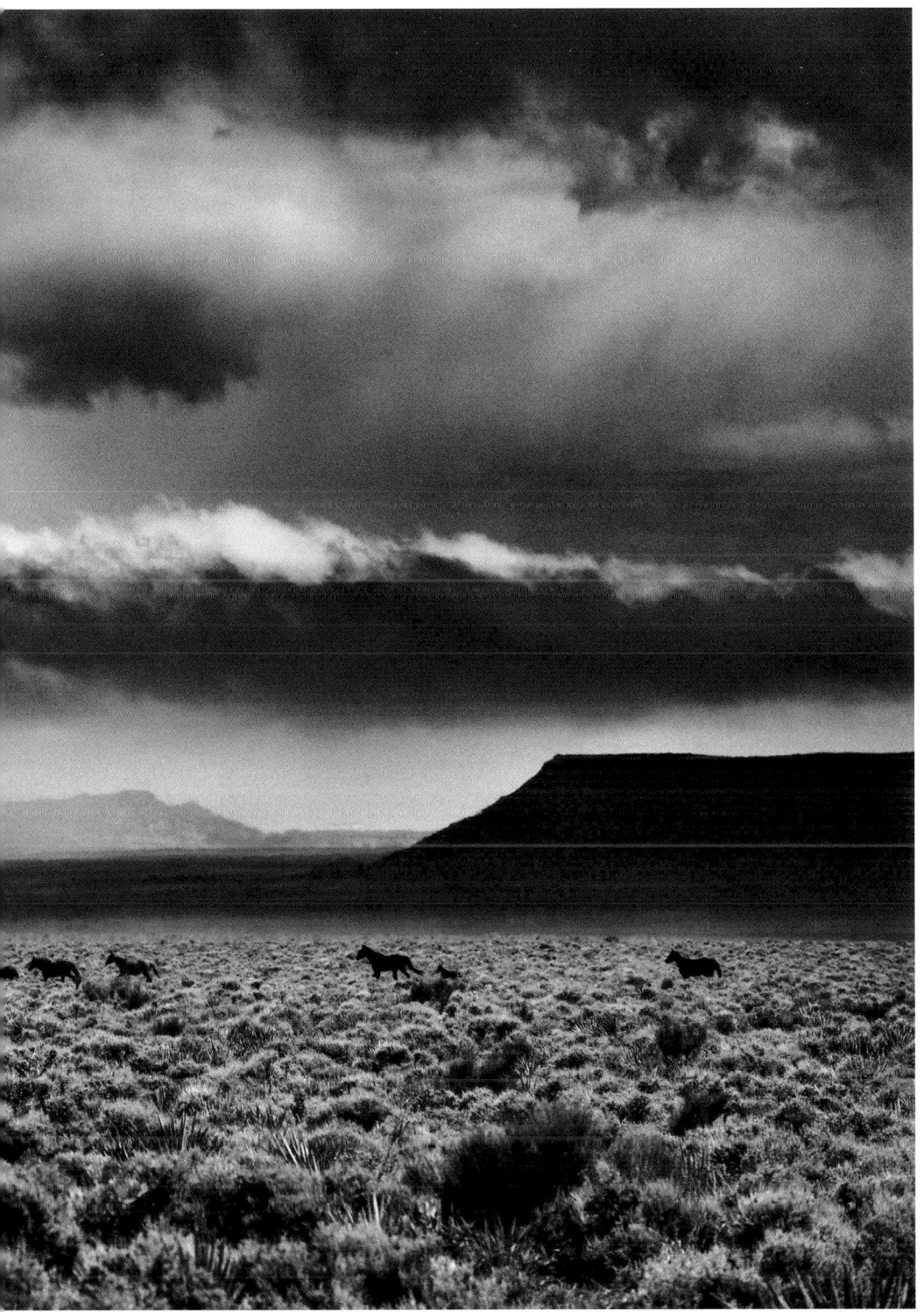

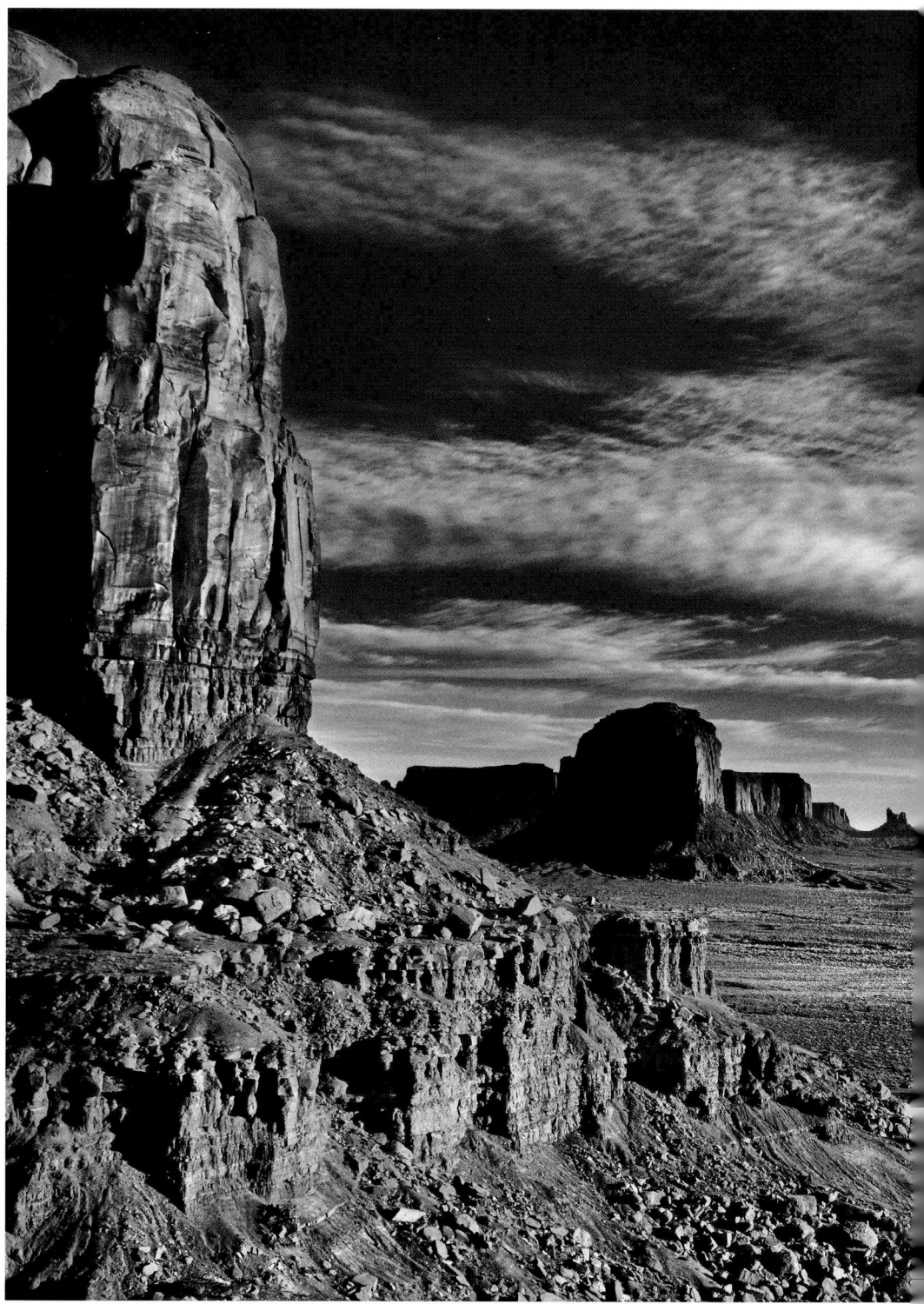

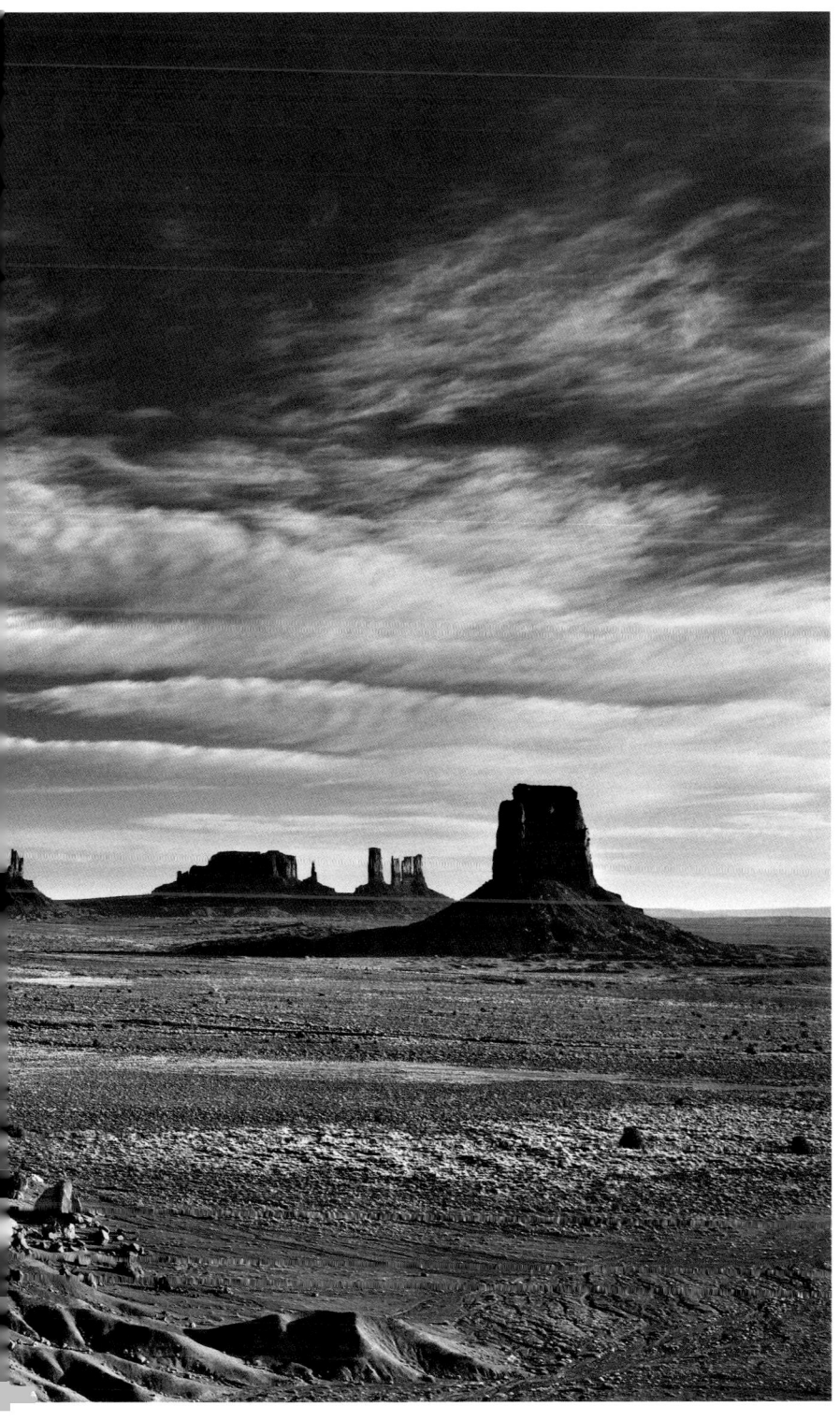

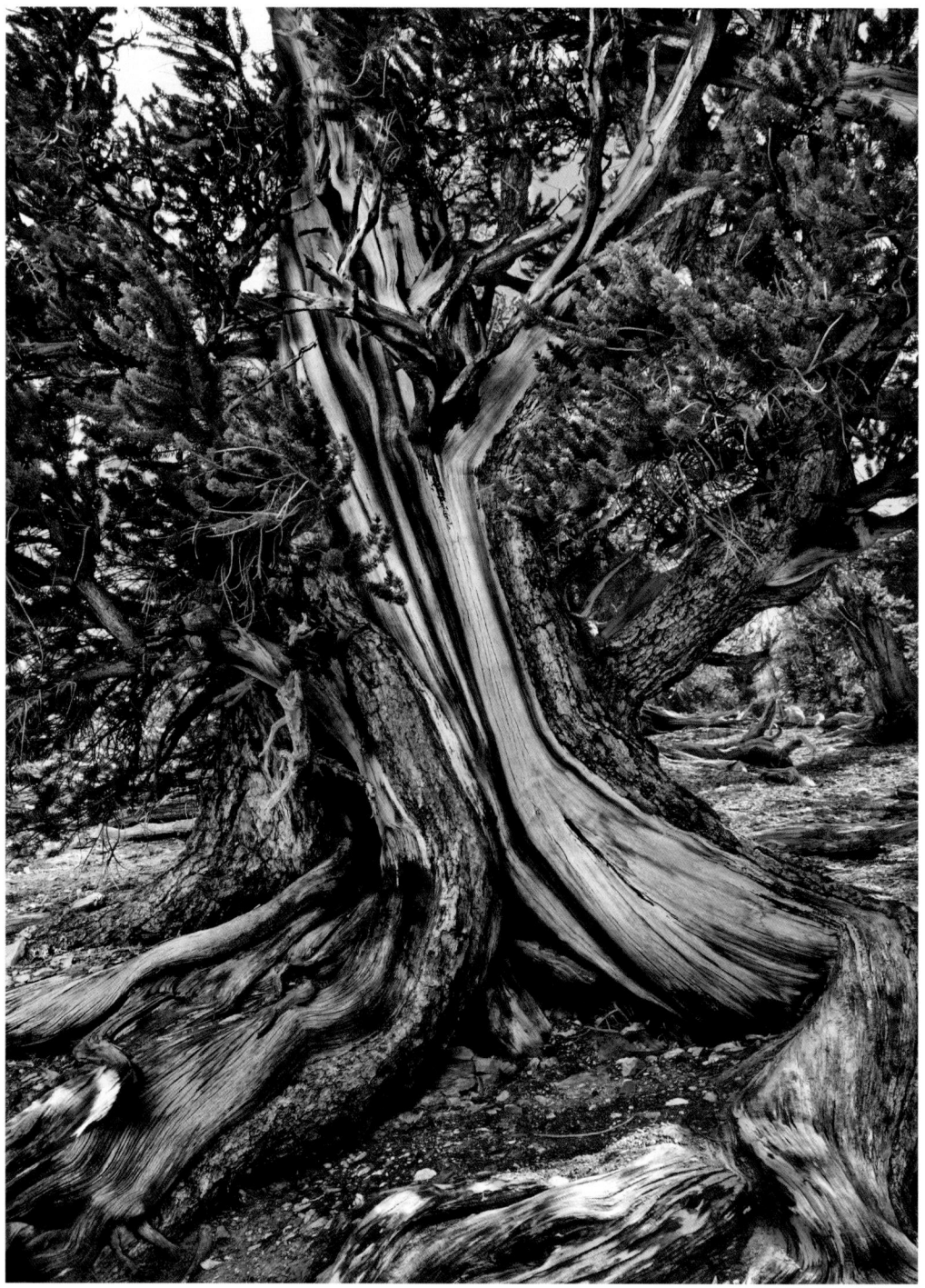

Pages 354/355 Bryce Canyon National Park. Bryce Canyon is not, in fact, a canyon but a giant natural amphitheater created by erosion along the eastern side of the Paunsaugunt Plateau. Bryce is famous for its extraordinary geological structures, known as *hoodoos*, formed by frost weathering and water erosion of the river and lakebed sedimentary rocks. Utah. USA. April, May and June 2010.

Pages 356/357 Grand Canyon National Park. Arizona. USA. April, May and June 2010.

Pages 358/359 Wild horses in Navajo territory, bordering on the Grand Canyon. Arizona. USA. April, May and June 2010.

Pages 360/361 and 366/367 Monument Valley Navajo Tribal Park. This is a breathtaking part of the Colorado Plateau. The fragile pinnacles of rock are surrounded by kilometers of mesas and buttes, shrubs, trees and windblown sand. The floor is largely siltstone, or sand derived from it, deposited by the meandering rivers that carved the valley. The valley's vivid red color comes from iron oxide exposed in the weathered siltstone. The darker, blue-gray rocks in the valley are in turn colored by manganese oxide. Utah and Arizona. USA. April, May and June 2010.

Opposite The Ancient Bristlecone Pine Forest in the White Mountains. Bristlecone pinewood that has fallen to the ground can remain intact for thousands of years in the cold dry climate of the White Mountains. Using a cross-dating technique that overlaps tree-ring patterns of living trees with the still intact patterns of deadwood, scientists have assembled a continuous tree-ring chronology extending back nearly 10,000 years. This bristlecone pine chronology is the longest in the world and provides an unrivaled look into past climatic and environmental conditions. California. USA. April, May and June 2010.

Pages 364/365 The Grand Canyon viewed from National Forest, Arizona. The big mesa visible on the far side of the canyon is in Navajo territory. This photograph was taken during a localized snowstorm. Utah. USA. April, May and June 2010.

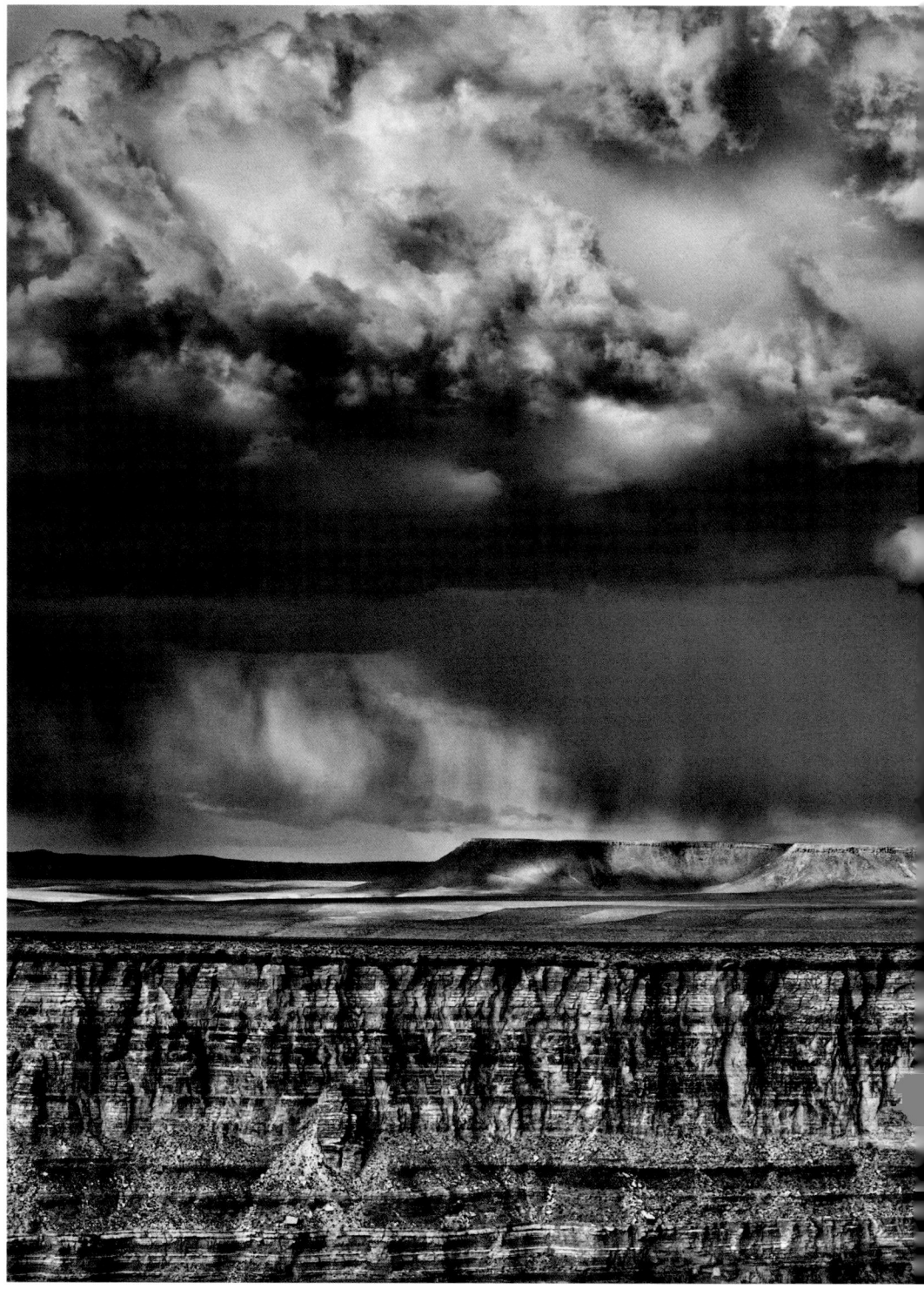

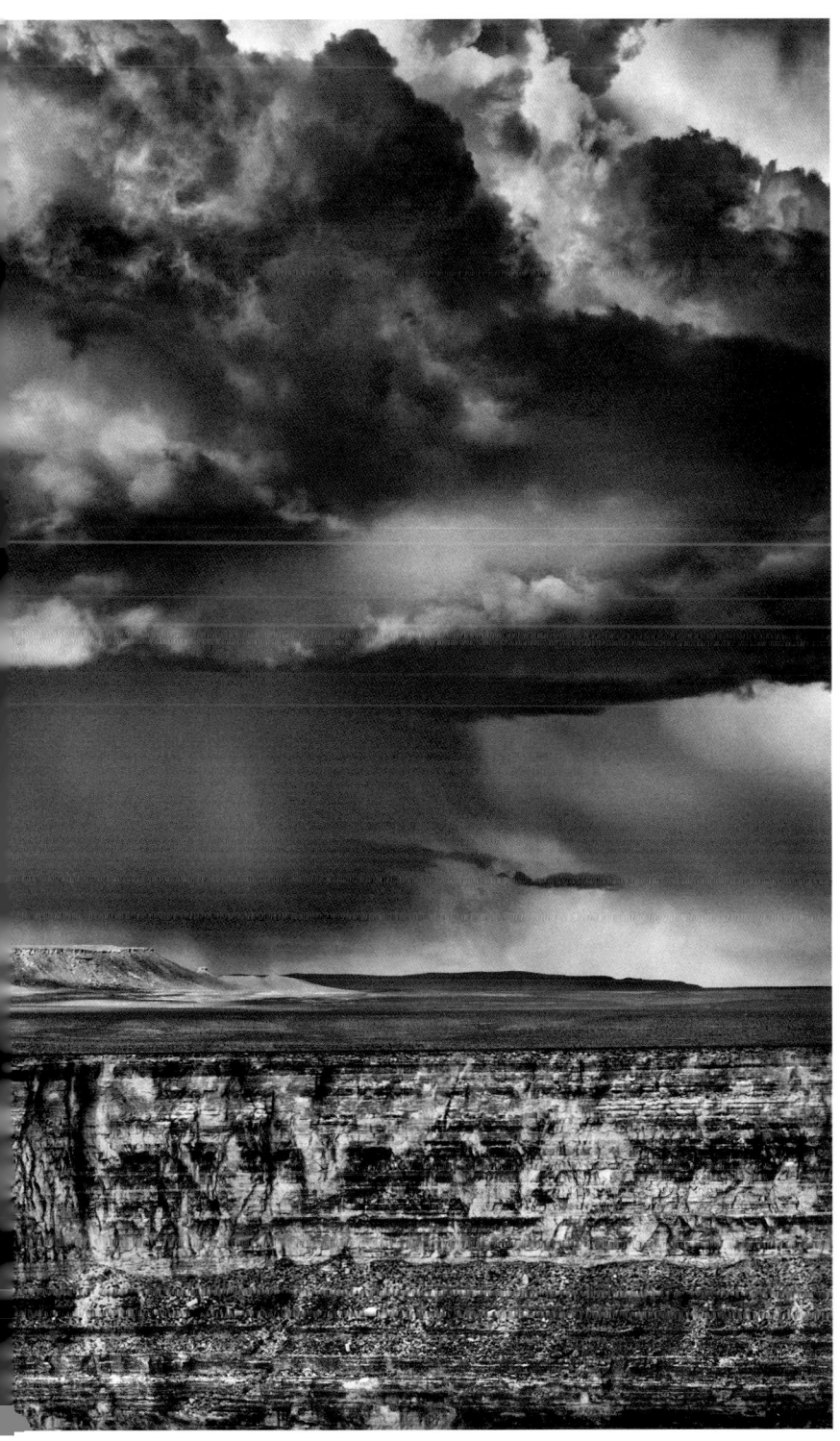

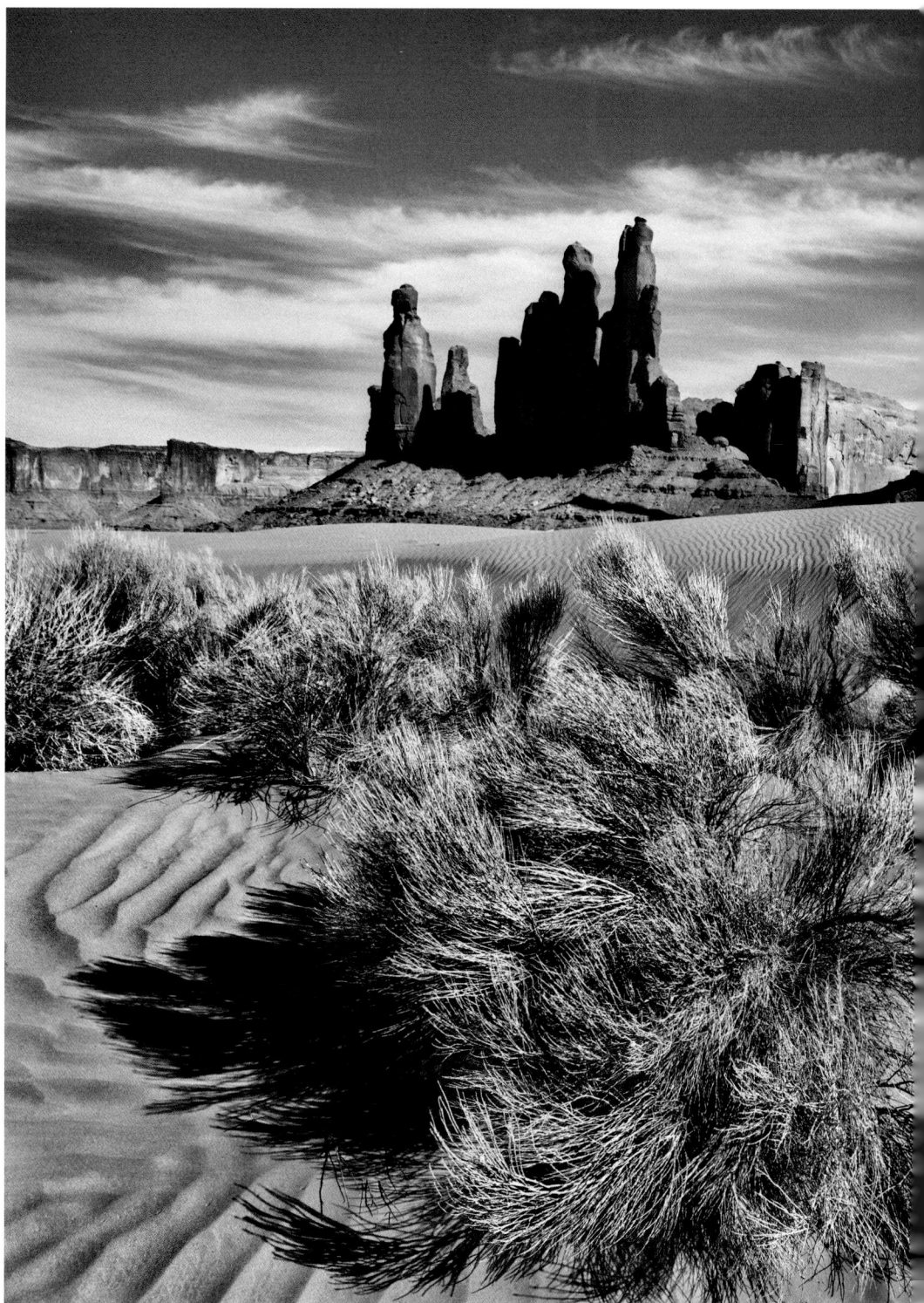

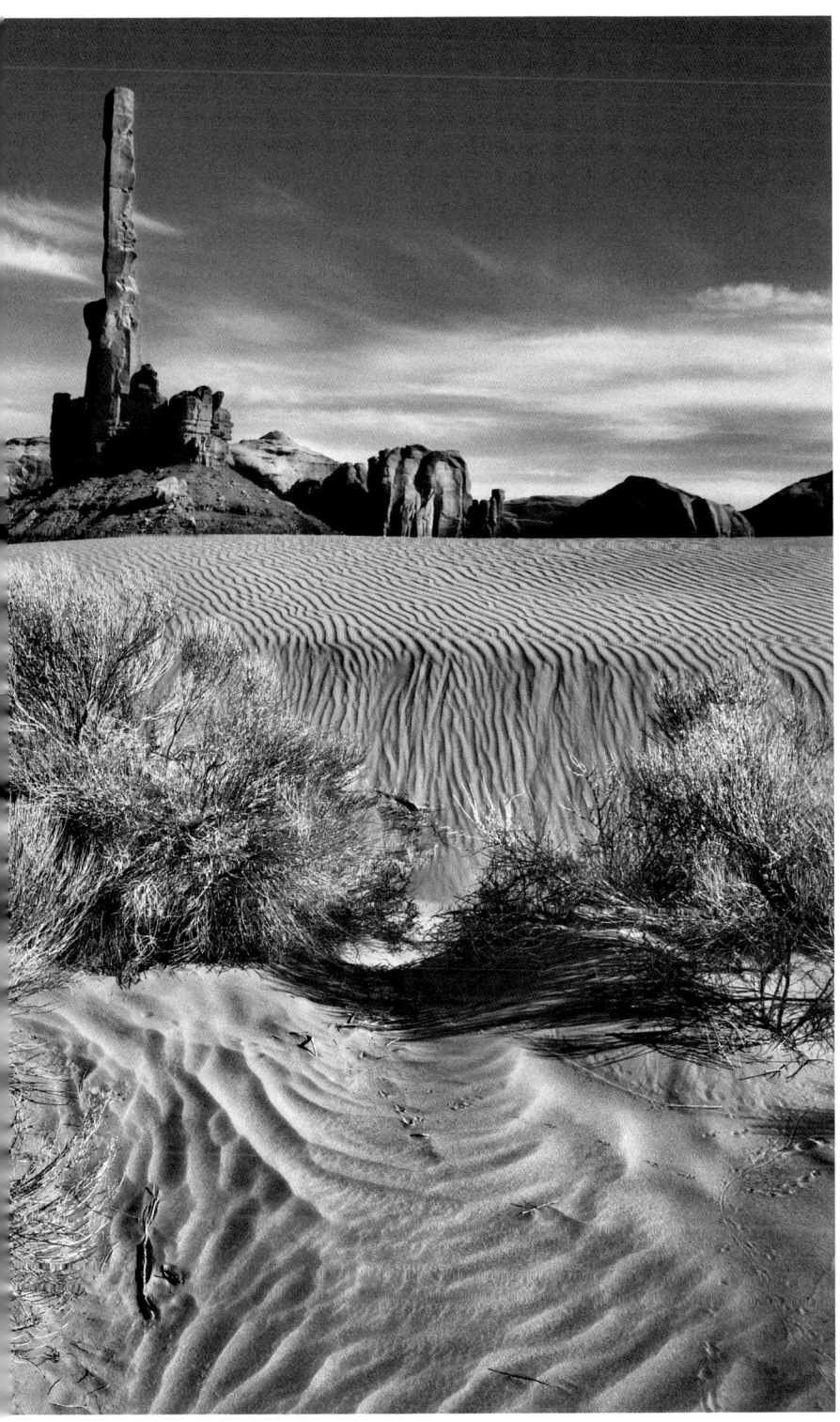

Opposite Bryce Canyon National Park. Bryce Canyon is not in fact a canyon but a giant natural amphitheater created by erosion along the eastern side of the Paunsaugunt Plateau. Bryce is famous for its extraordinary geological structures, known as *hoodoos*, formed by frost weathering and water erosion of the river and lake bed sedimentary rocks. Utah. USA. April, May and June 2010.

Pages 370/371 Bryce Canyon National Park during a snowstorm. Utah. USA. April, May and June 2010.

Pages 372/373 The divide of an ice field marks where, in this case, the ice field from Mount Logan (19,550 feet / 5,959 meters) meets that coming from Saint Elias Mountains (9,550 feet / 2,911 meters). Kluane National Park. Canada. May and June 2011.

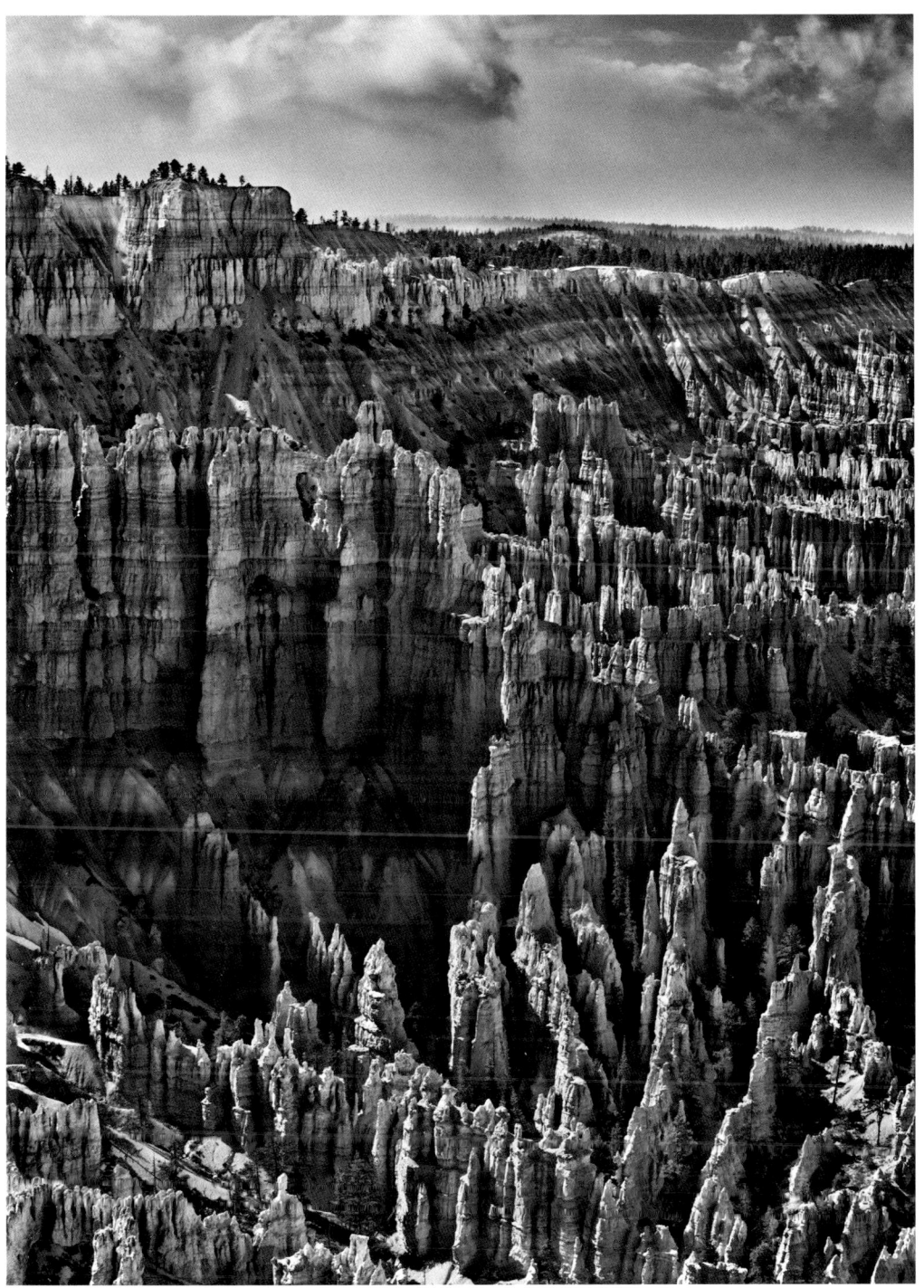

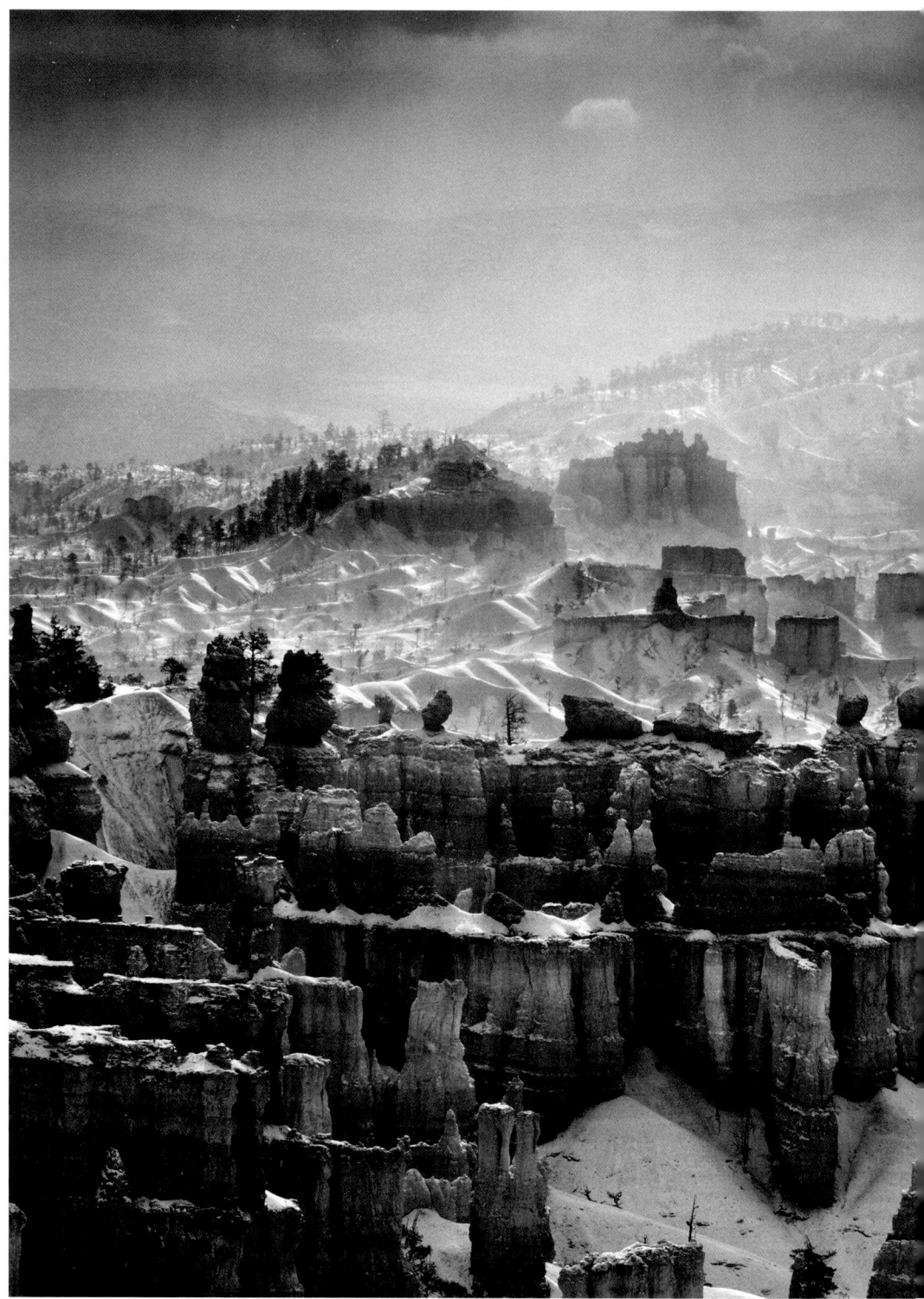

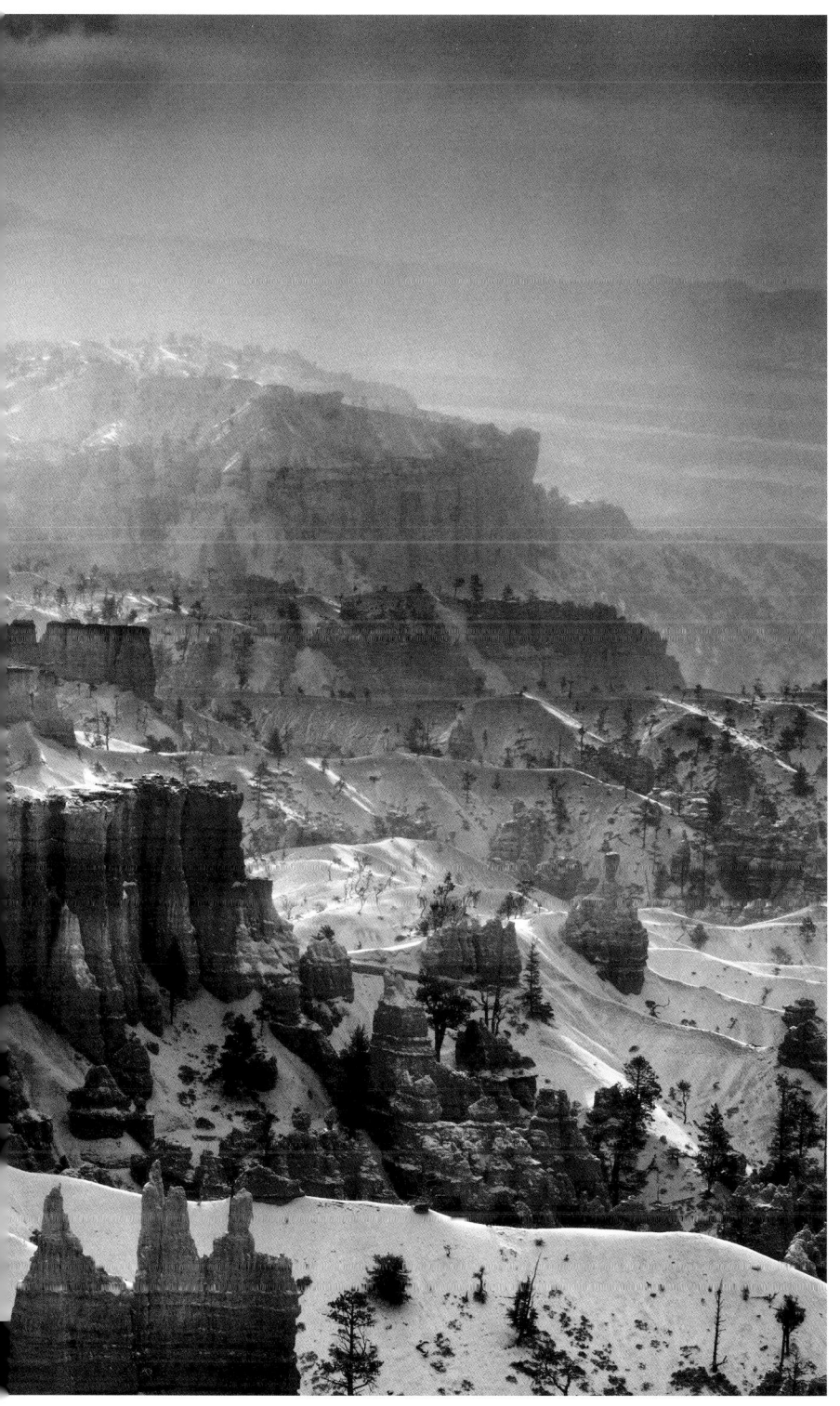

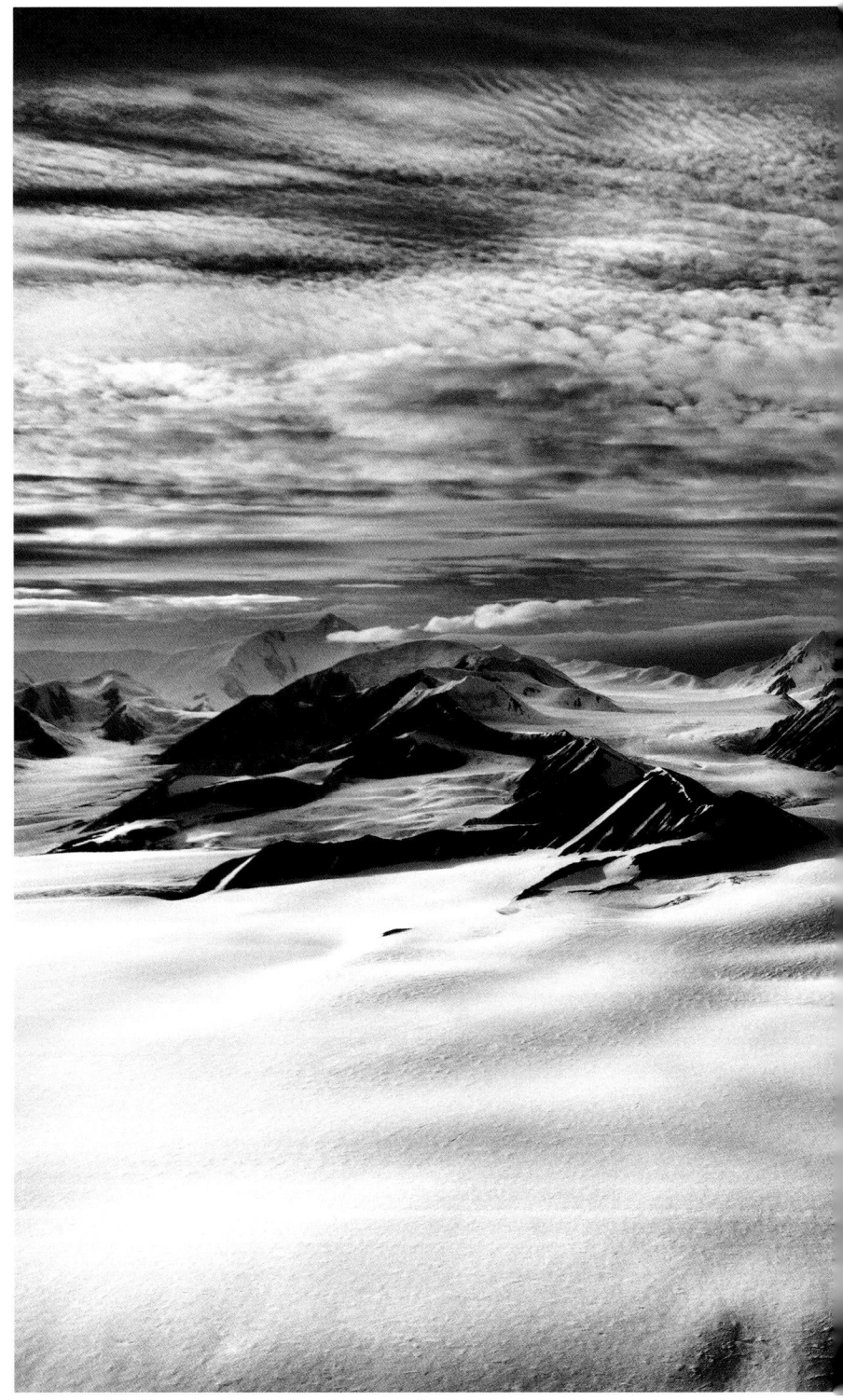

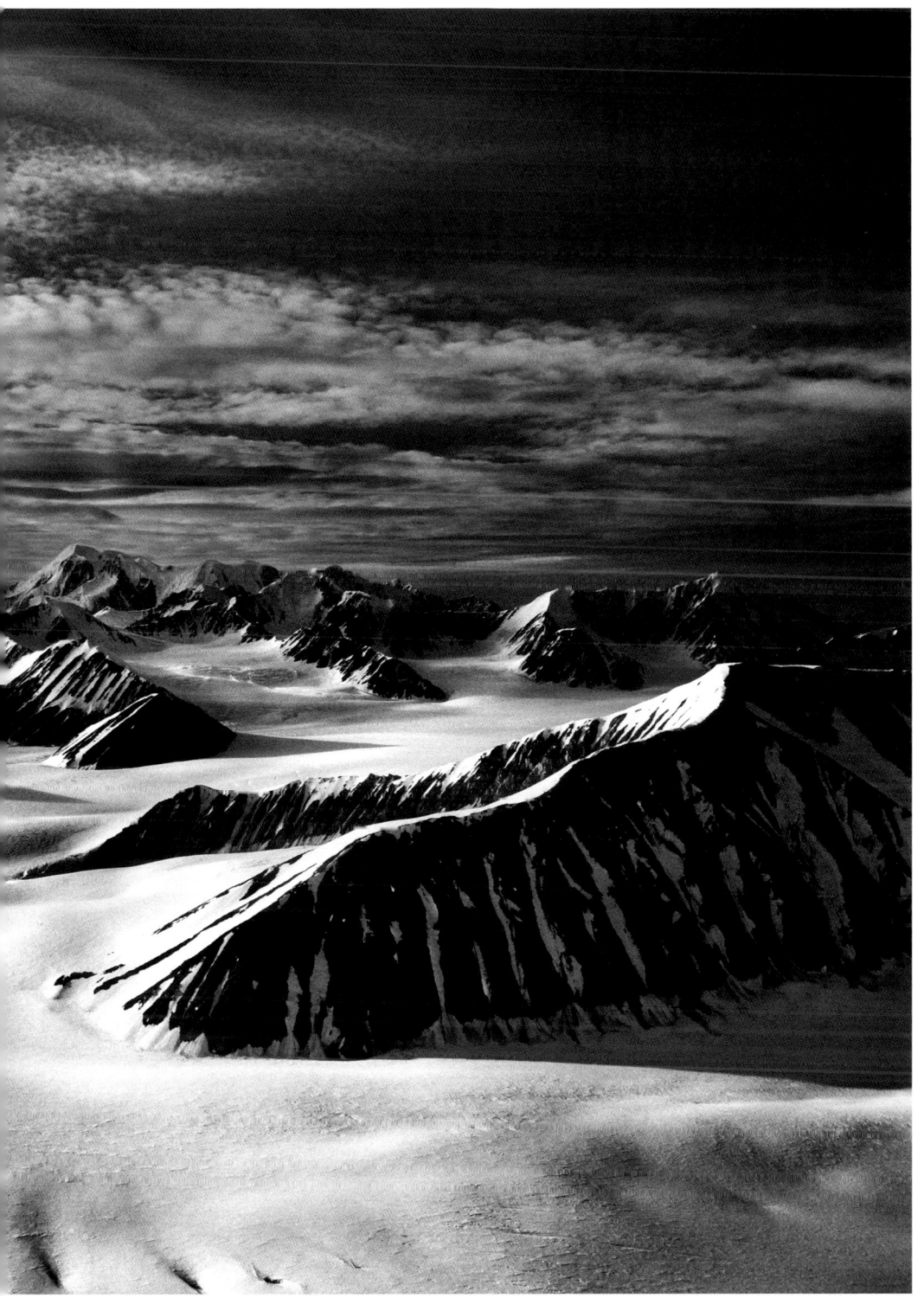

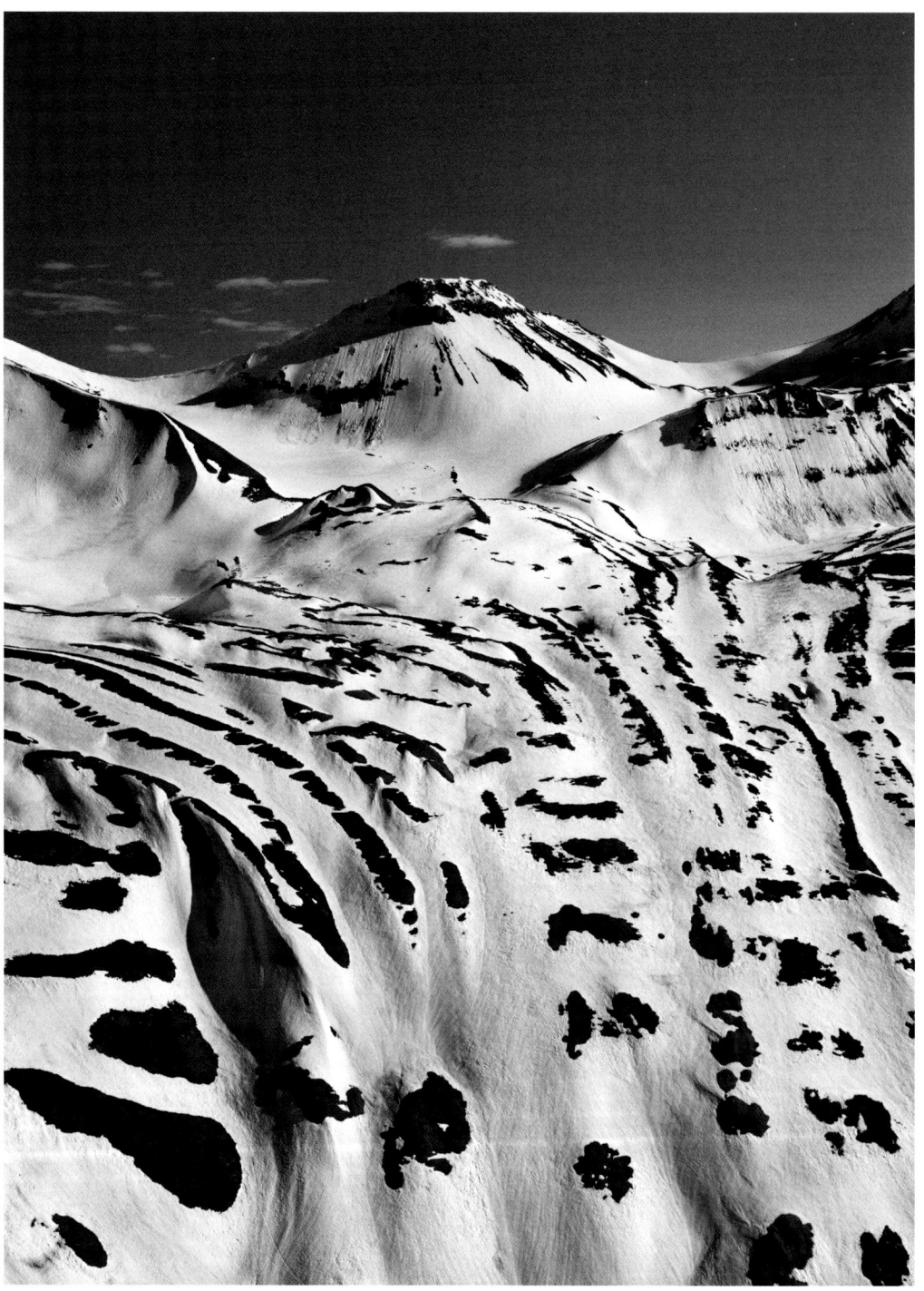

Opposite The Felsite Peak measuring 8,300 feet (2,530 meters) stands at the beginning of the Felsite Glacier. Kluane National Park. Canada. May and June 2011.

Pages 376/377 Saint Clare Creek. This stream rises from the base of Mount Constantine, Teapot Mountain and Saint Elias Peak, all around 9,842 feet (3,000 meters) high and bordering on Kluane National Park boundary. Canada. May and June 2011.

Pages 378/379 A lake on Wolverine Plateau in northwest Canada, outside Kluane National Park. Canada. May and June 2011.

Page 380 The upper part of the Kaskawulsh Glacier where the ice floe coming from Saint Elias Moun-tains to the right meets the ice floe descending from Mount Queen Mary. Kluane National Park. Canada. May and June 2011.

Page 381 The lower part of the Kaskawulsh Glacier. Kluane National Park. Canada. May and June 2011.

Pages 382/383 Bighorn Creek in the western part of the Kluane National Park. Canada. May and June 2011.

Pages 384/385 Disappointment River is fed by Disappointment Glacier. Kluane National Park. Canada. May and June 2011.

Pages 386/387 Dusty River in the lower part of the Kluane National Park. Canada. May and June 2011.

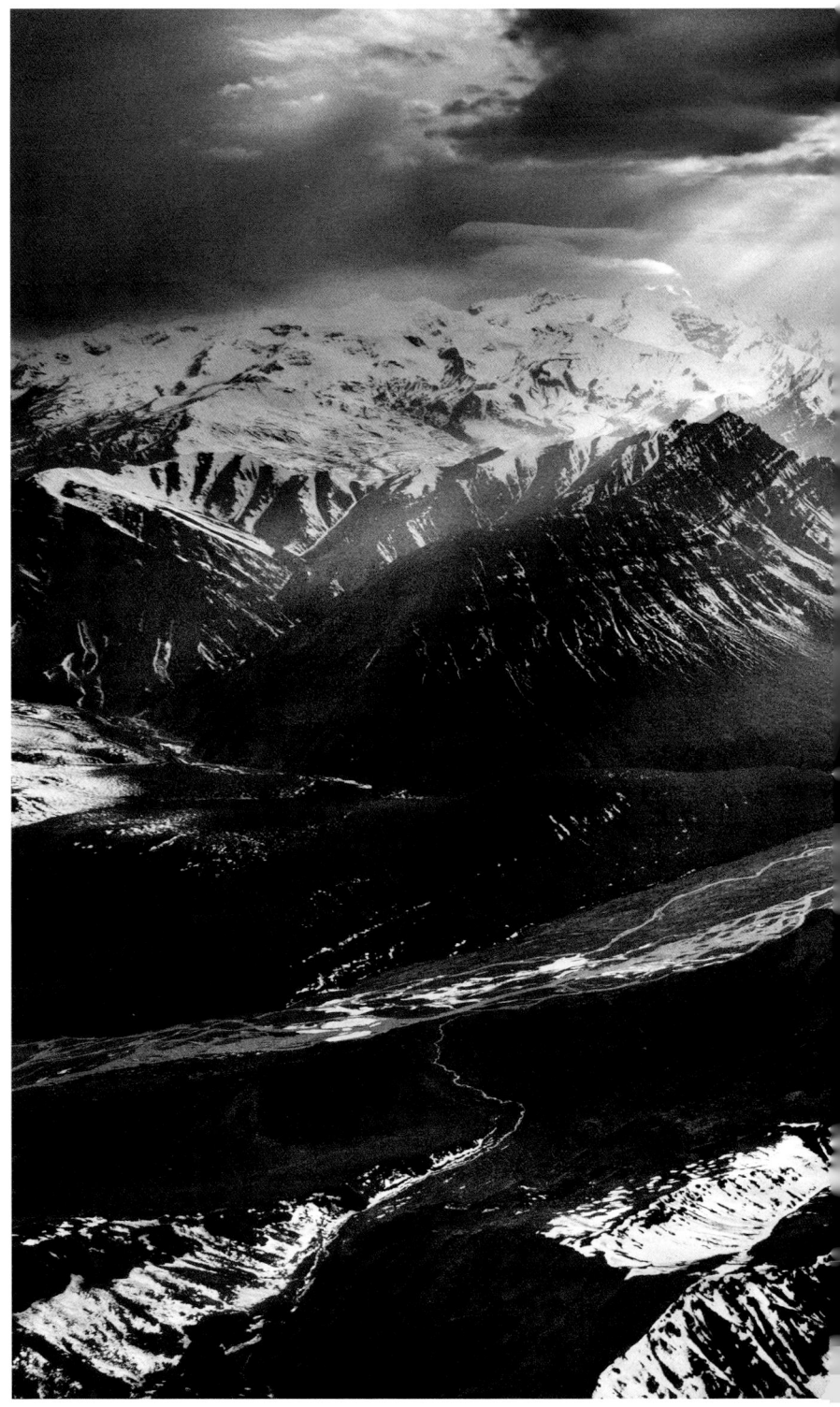

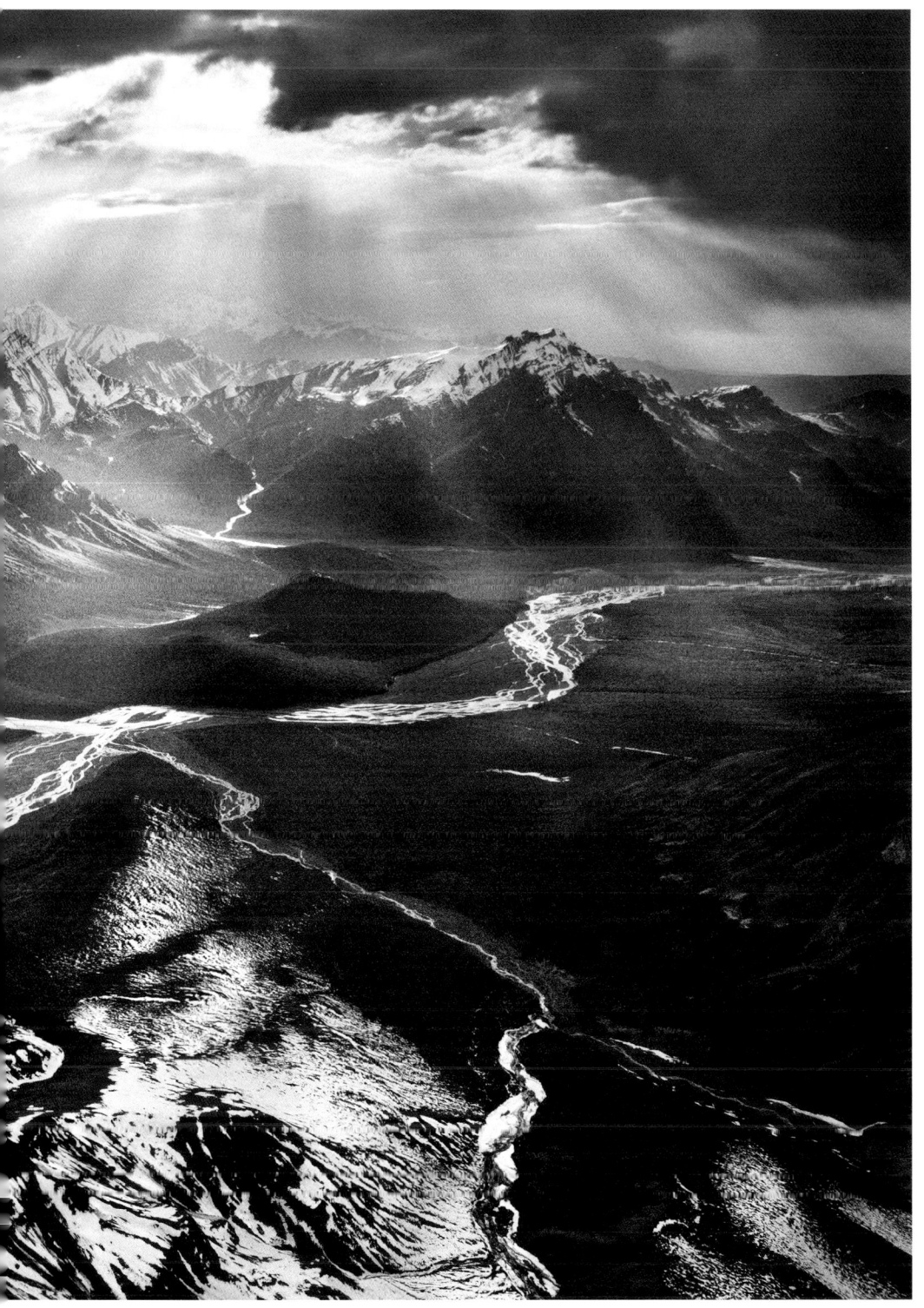

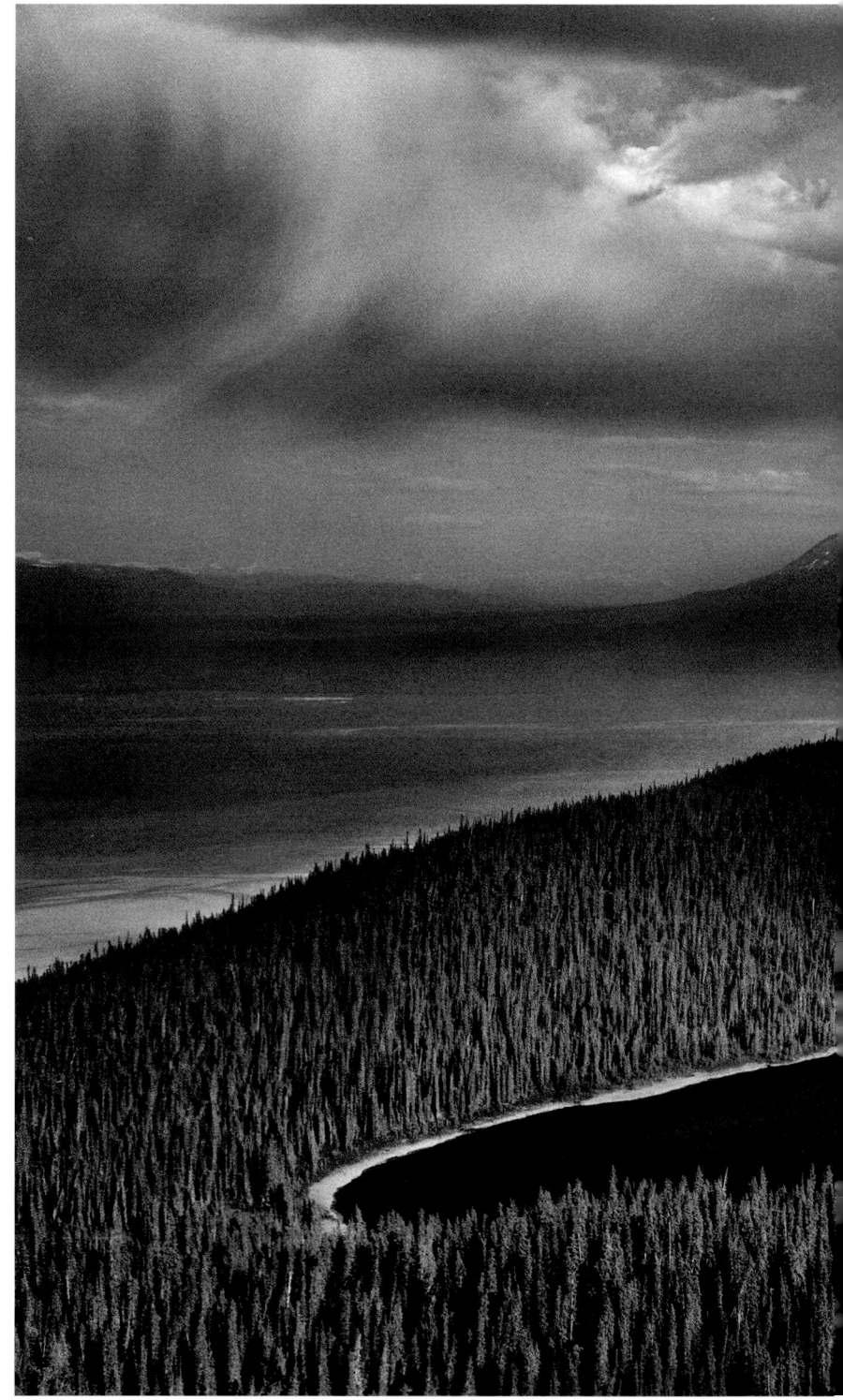

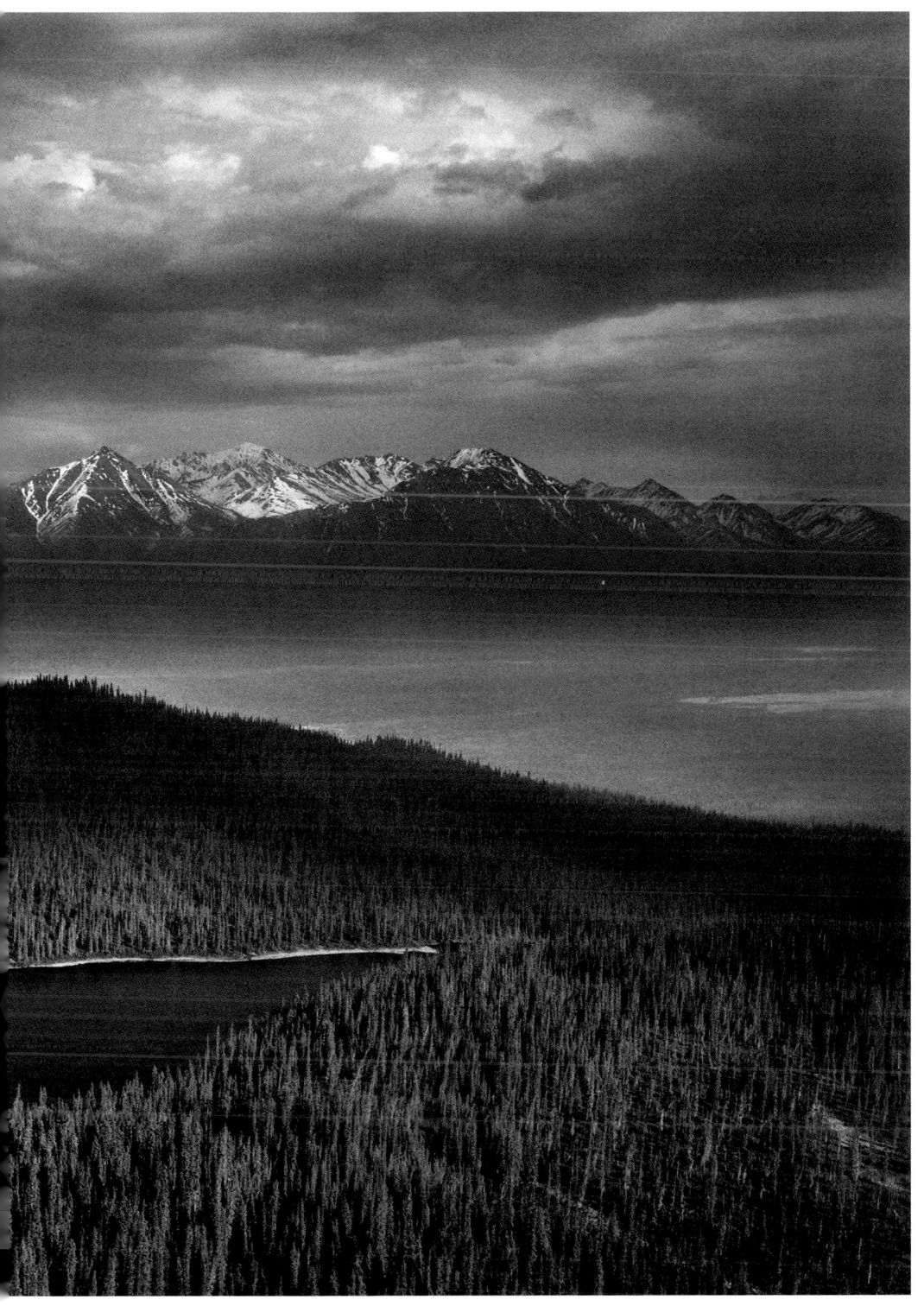

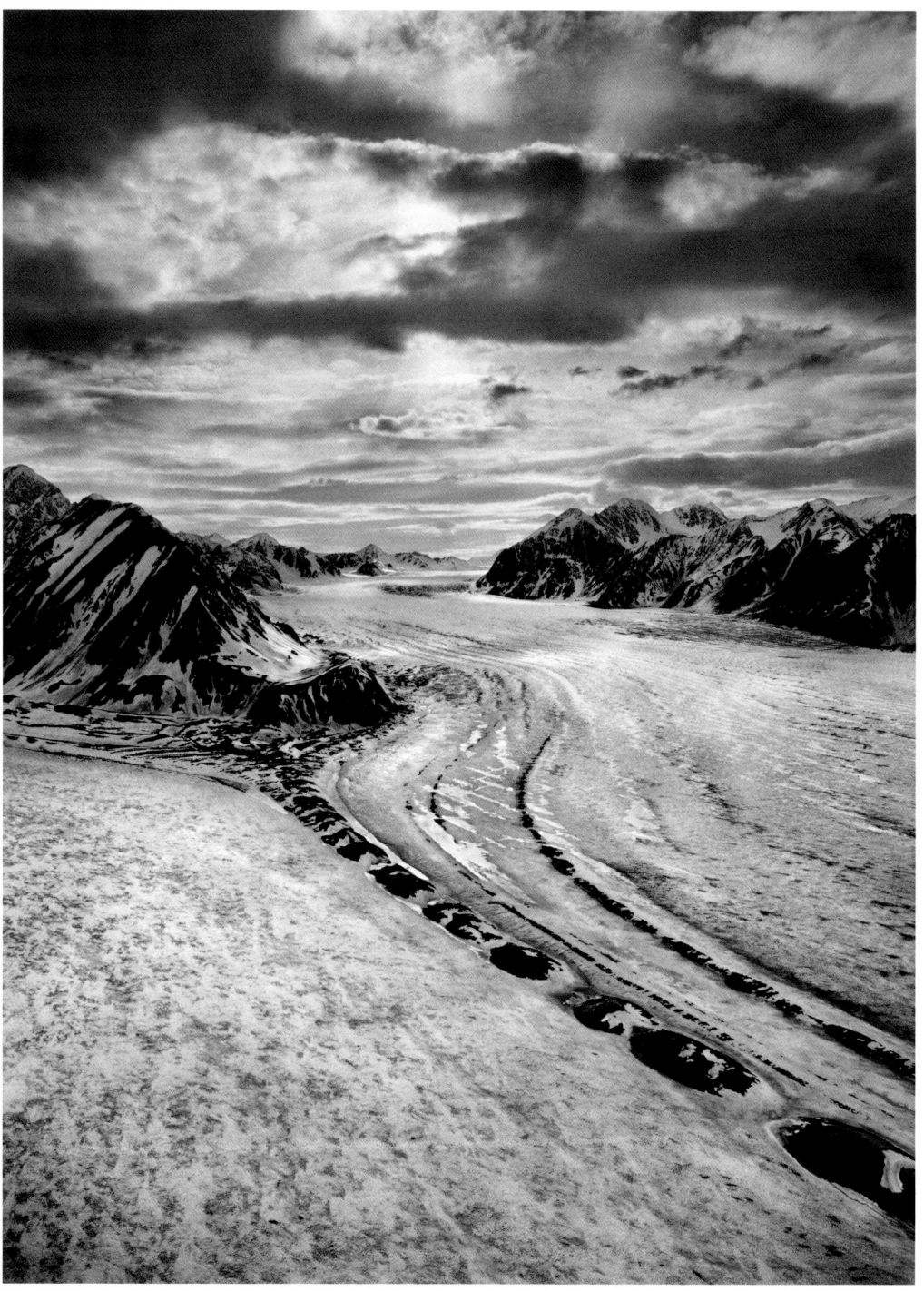

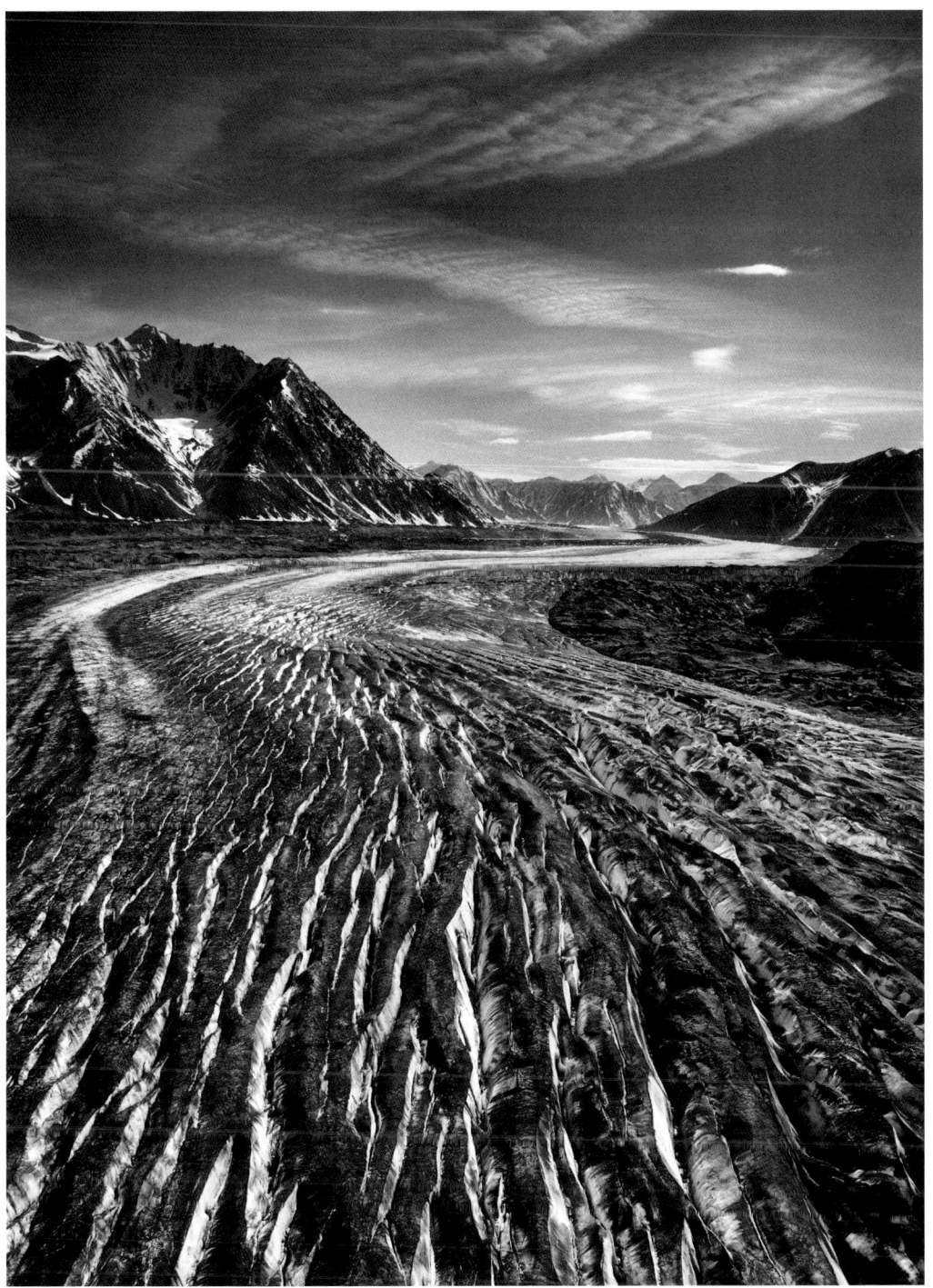

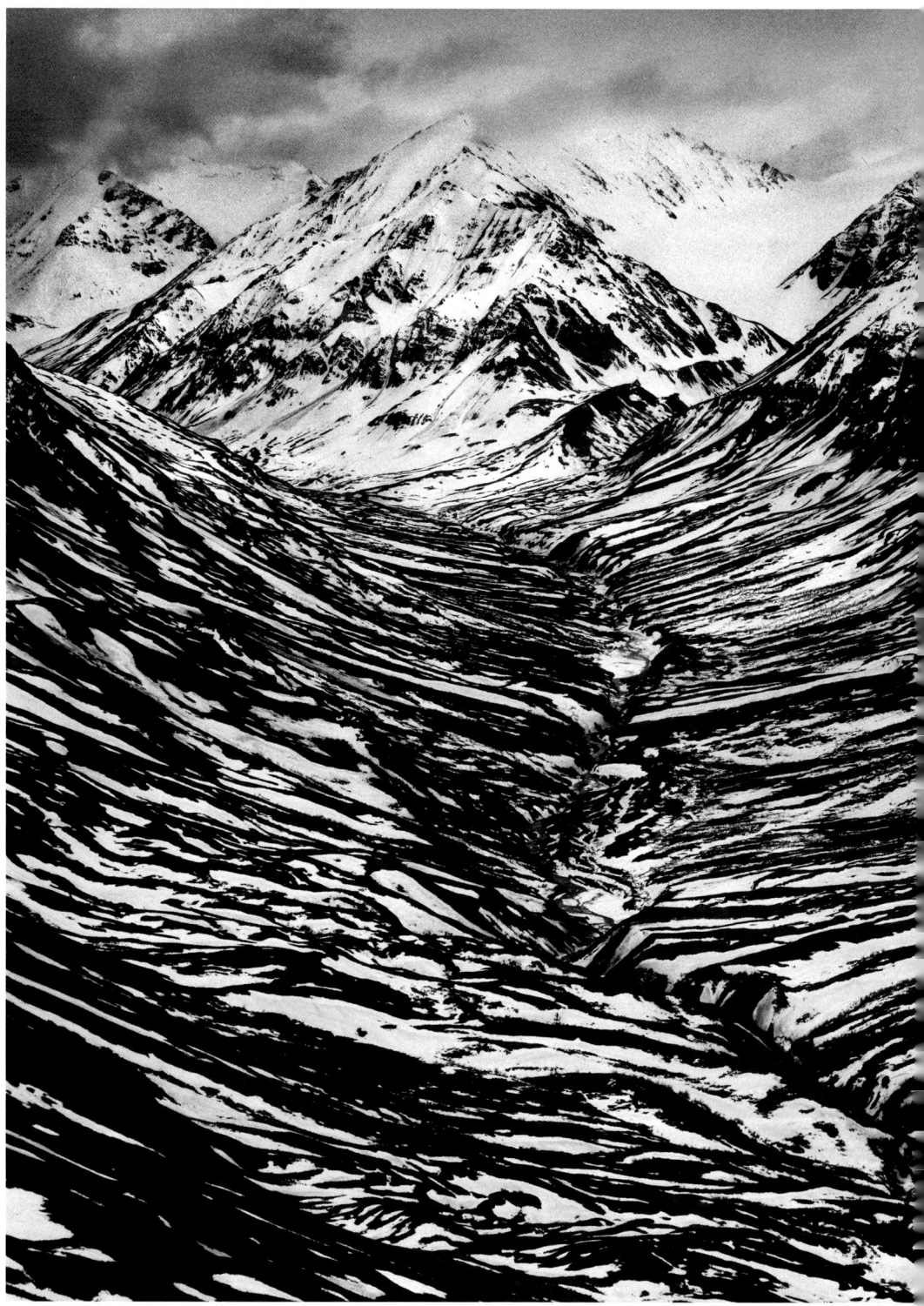

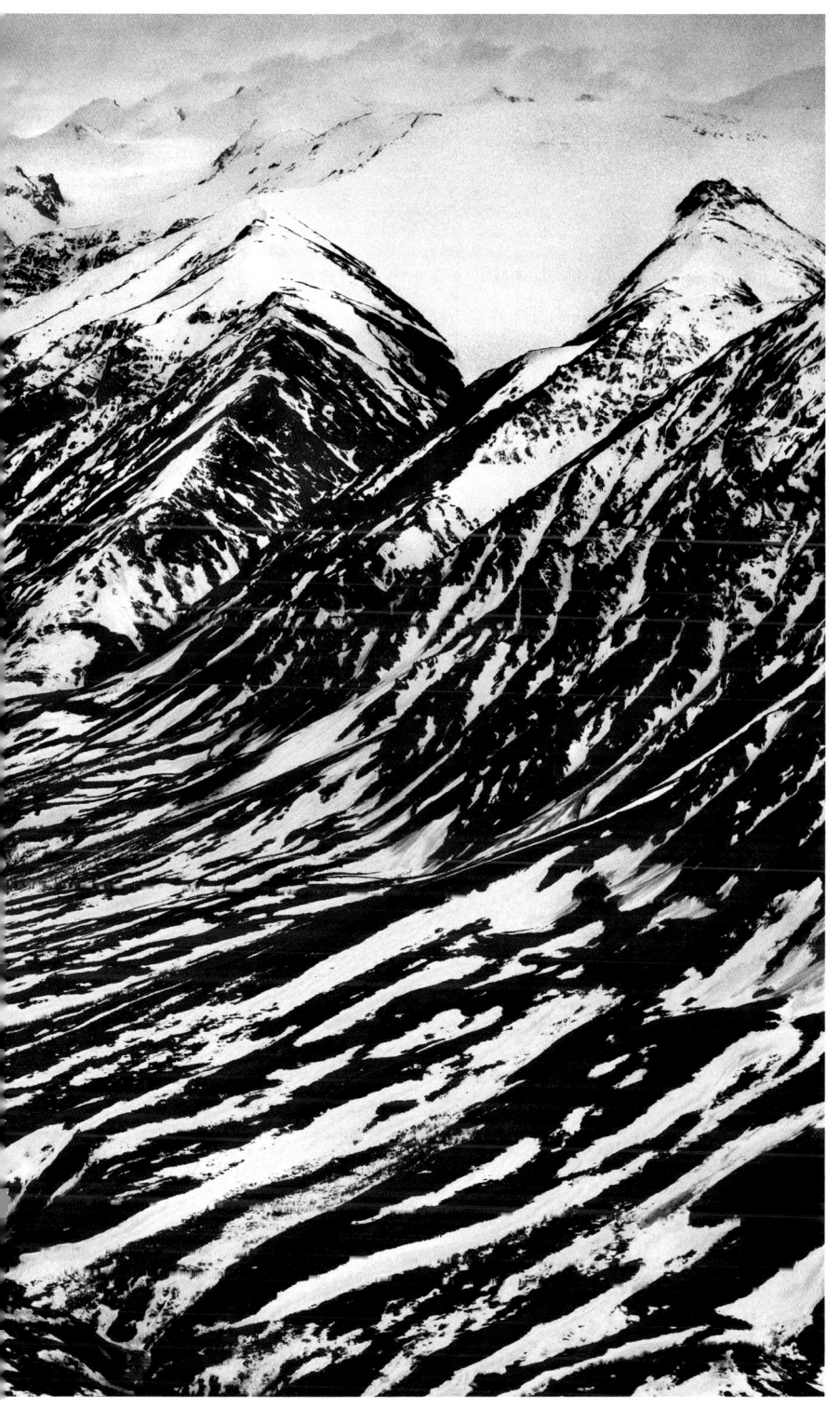

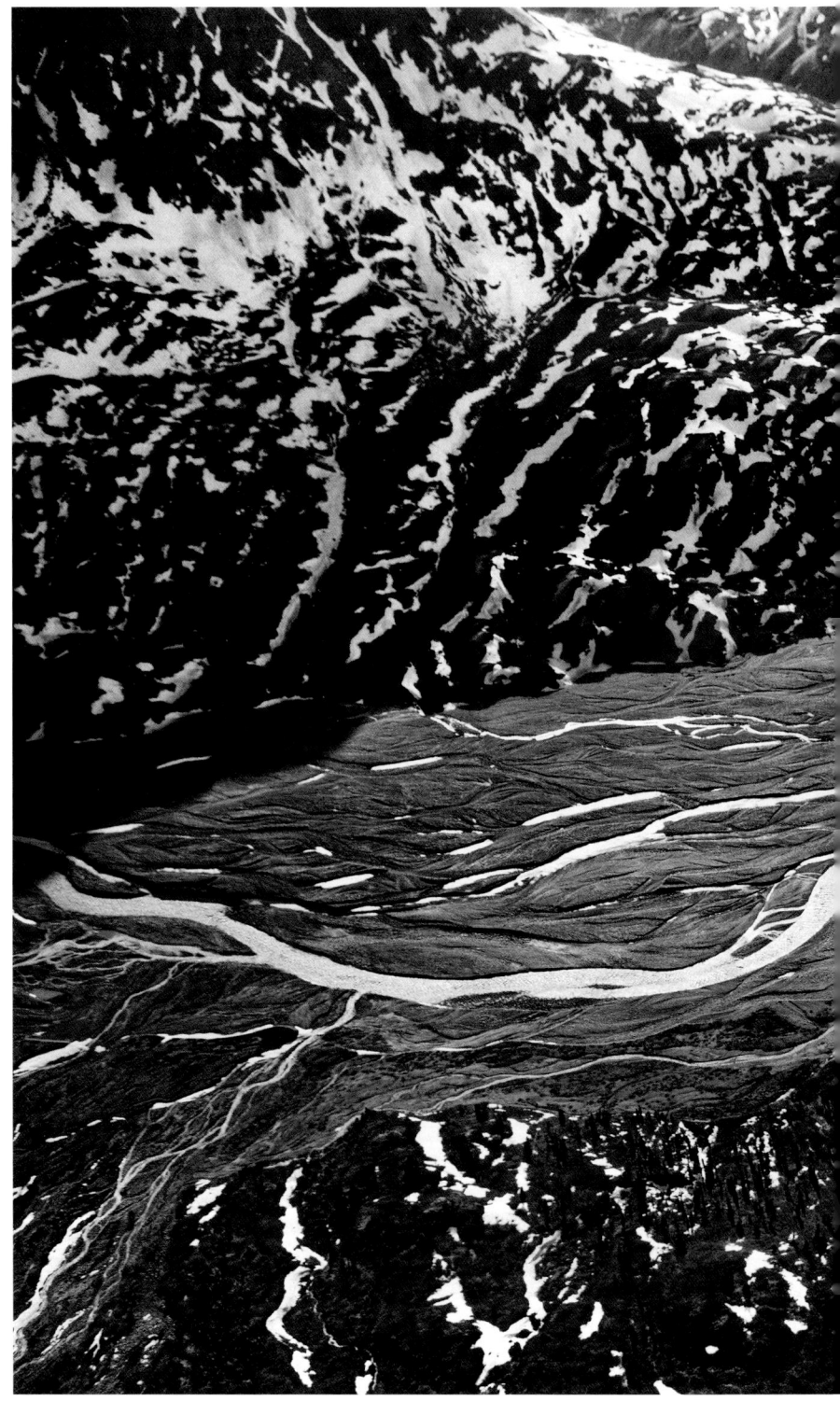

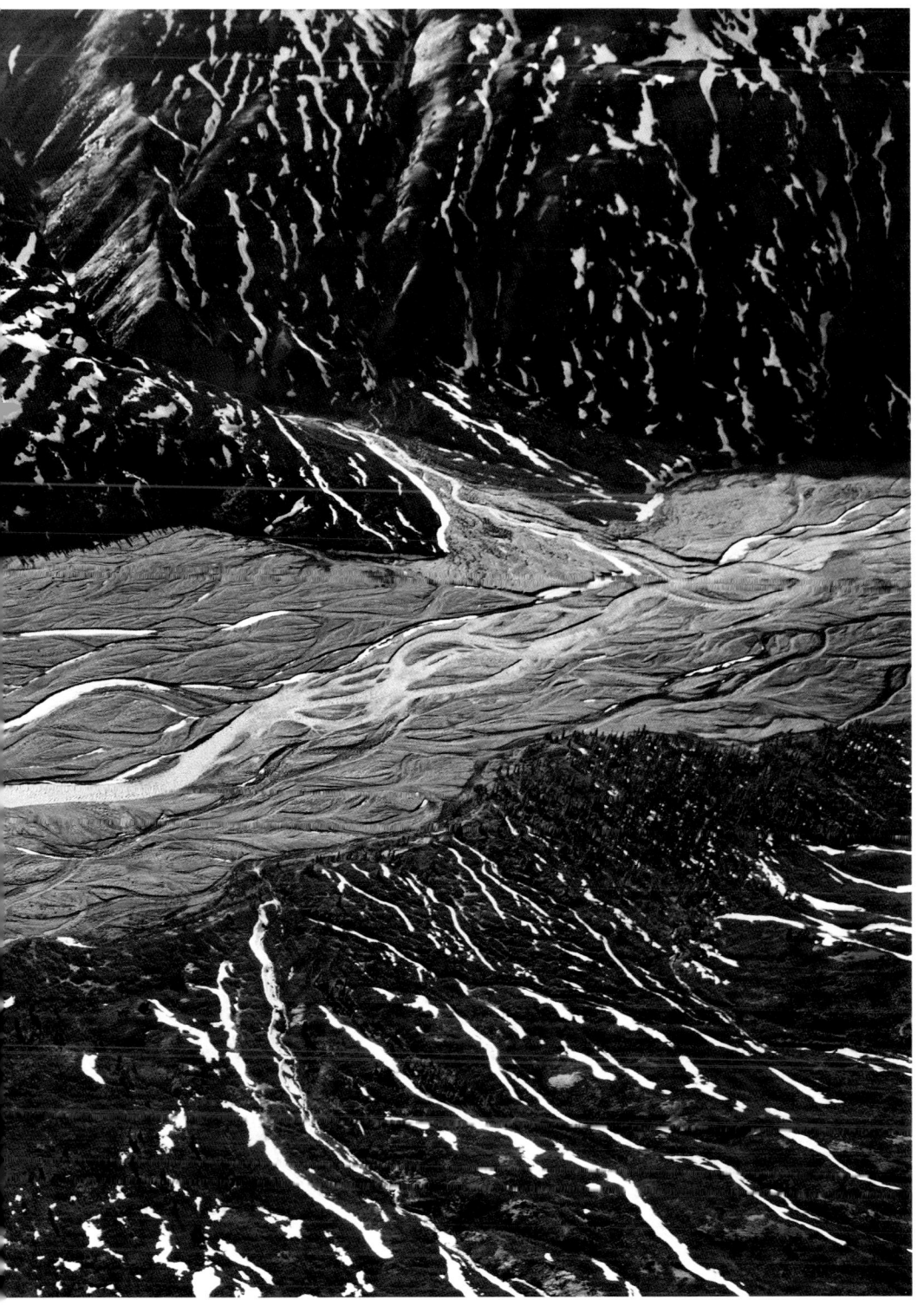

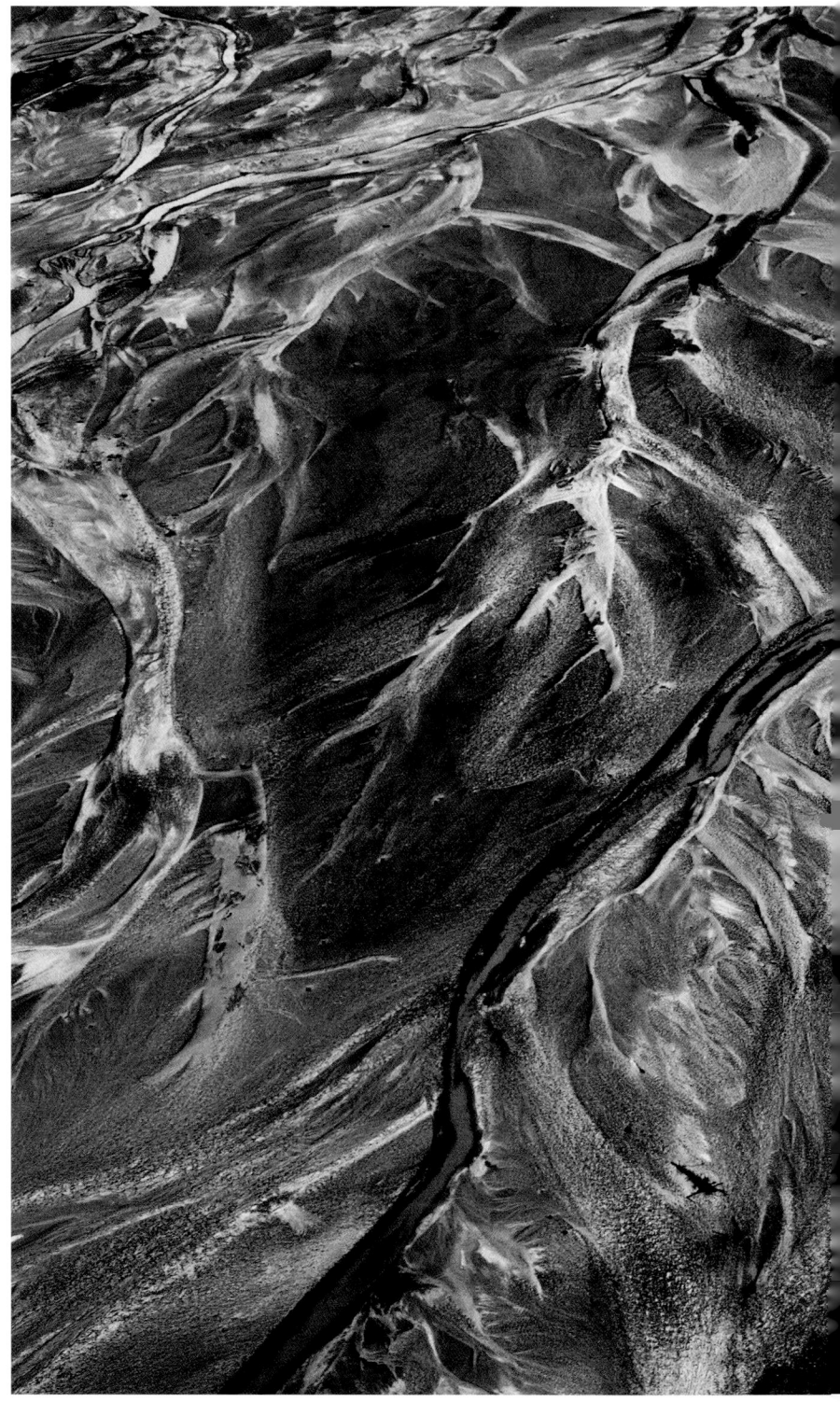

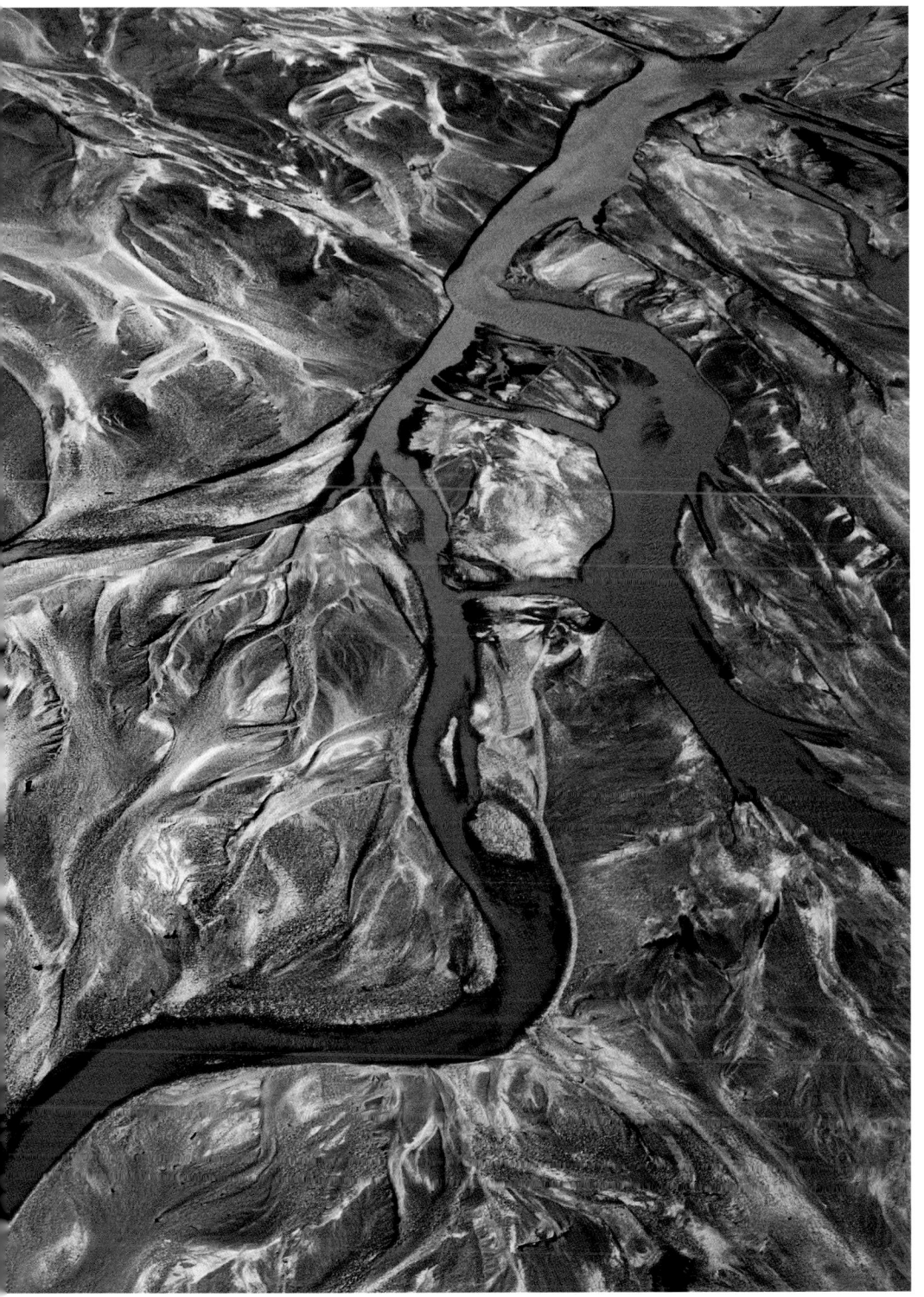

THE NENETS

Pages 389 through 411

The Nenets are an indigenous people number-ing some 42,000 who live in the Yamalo-Nenets Autonomous District of Russia's northern Siberian region. Their culture and way of life are defined by the reindeer (*Rangifer tarandus sibiricus*). They spend winters in their own communities near the Kanin and Taymyr Peninsulas, around the Ob and Yenisey Rivers, with a few now settled in small towns like Kolva. Then, in the summer, they lead their rein-deer herds northwards into the Arctic Circle, where the animals are skilled at digging under the tundra for grasses and other hardy vegetation. The Nenets travel on sledges drawn by reindeer, while they breed the Samoyed dog to help them herd their reindeer (this dog has also been used by Europeans during Arctic expeditions). Even in the summer, they live with the danger posed by tundra wolves, which prey on reindeer herds. During their migration north, the Nenets fish through holes in the ice. Their ability to live in such conditions is bolstered by a shamanistic and animis-tic belief system that stresses respect for the land and its resources.

But they have not been shielded from political and environmental change. As part of its nationwide collectivization program, the Soviet government tried to force this nomadic population to become sedentary. Many had to settle in villages and place their children in state boarding schools, weakening their cultural identity and, in some cases, even strip-ping them of their native tongue. Today they face a different threat. In some areas, such as the Yamal Peninsula, development of oil and gas fields is dam-aging reindeer grazing land. Climate change is also affecting the Nenets since they can only cross some areas of the Arctic Circle when they are frozen—and melting ice is shrinking the effective length of winter.

Opposite This portrait of a young girl illustrates both the beauty of and the importance given by the Nenets to their clothes. Her main coat is made of the inside of reindeer skins, while her hood is made with the fur of blue fox. Yamal Peninsula. Siberia. Russia. March and April 2011.

Pages 390/391 Reindeer move in large herds. This one, numbering some 6,000 animals, is starting its move north after the winter. At this point, about 62 miles (100 kilometers) south of the Ob River and still some way from the Yamal Peninsula, trees are still plentiful. Siberia. Russia. March and April 2011.

Pages 392/393 At the end of the day, after leading the herd north across the Yamal Peninsula towards the Kara Sea on the Arctic Ocean, the Nenets set up their tent, or *tchoum*. They first put all their belong-ings in a circle on the ground, around which they place wooden supports covered with reindeer skins. North of Ob River. Yamal Peninsula. Siberia. Russia. March and April 2011.

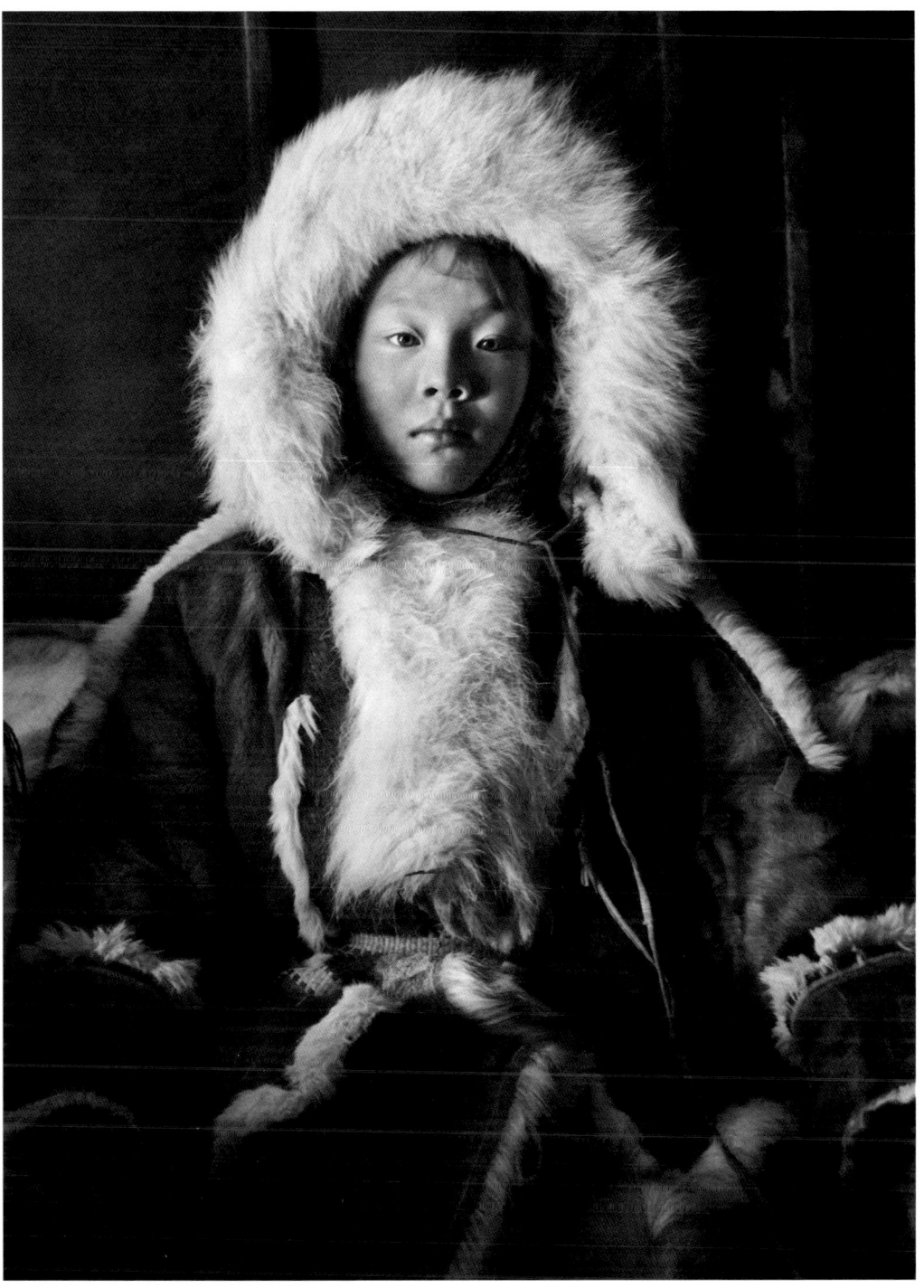

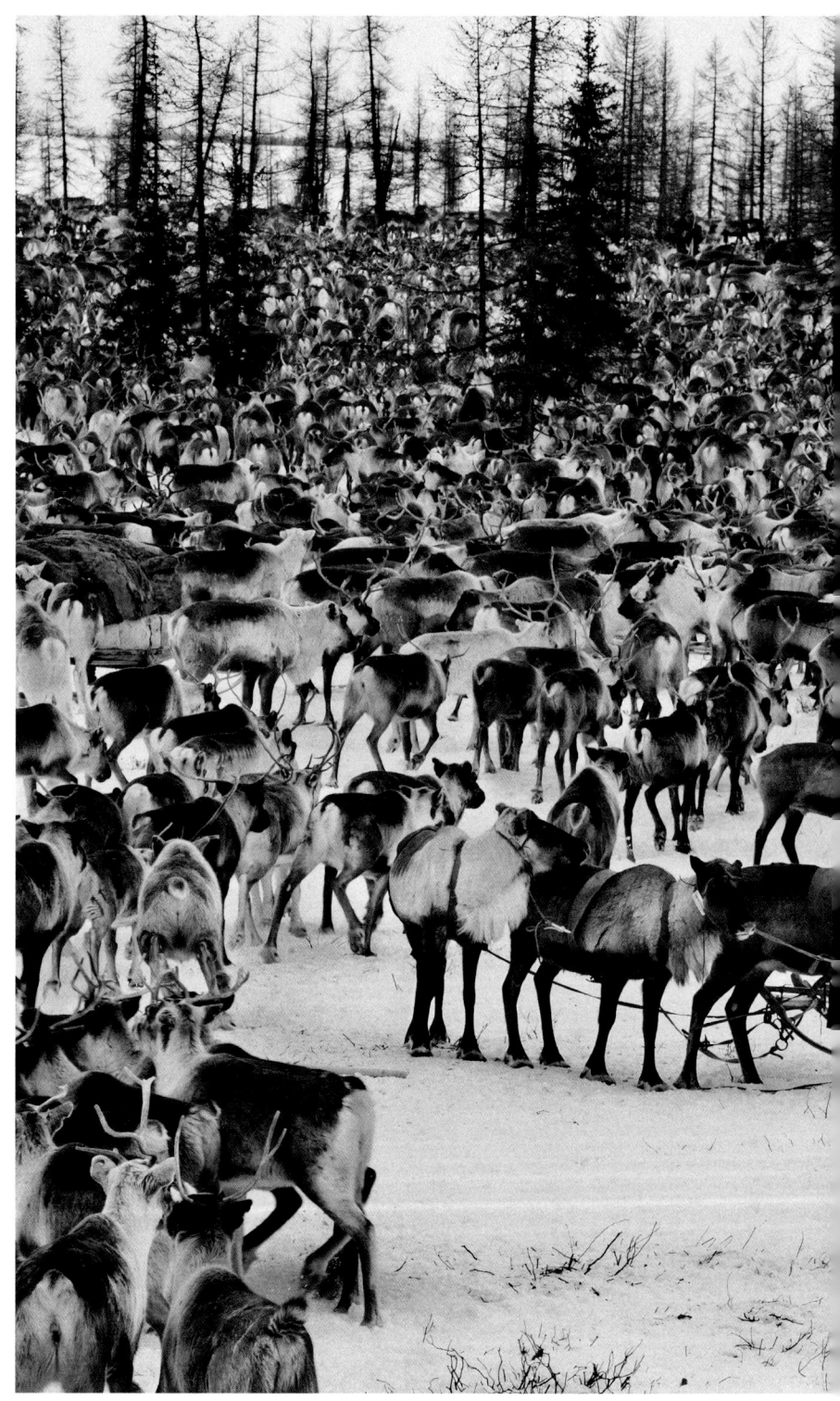

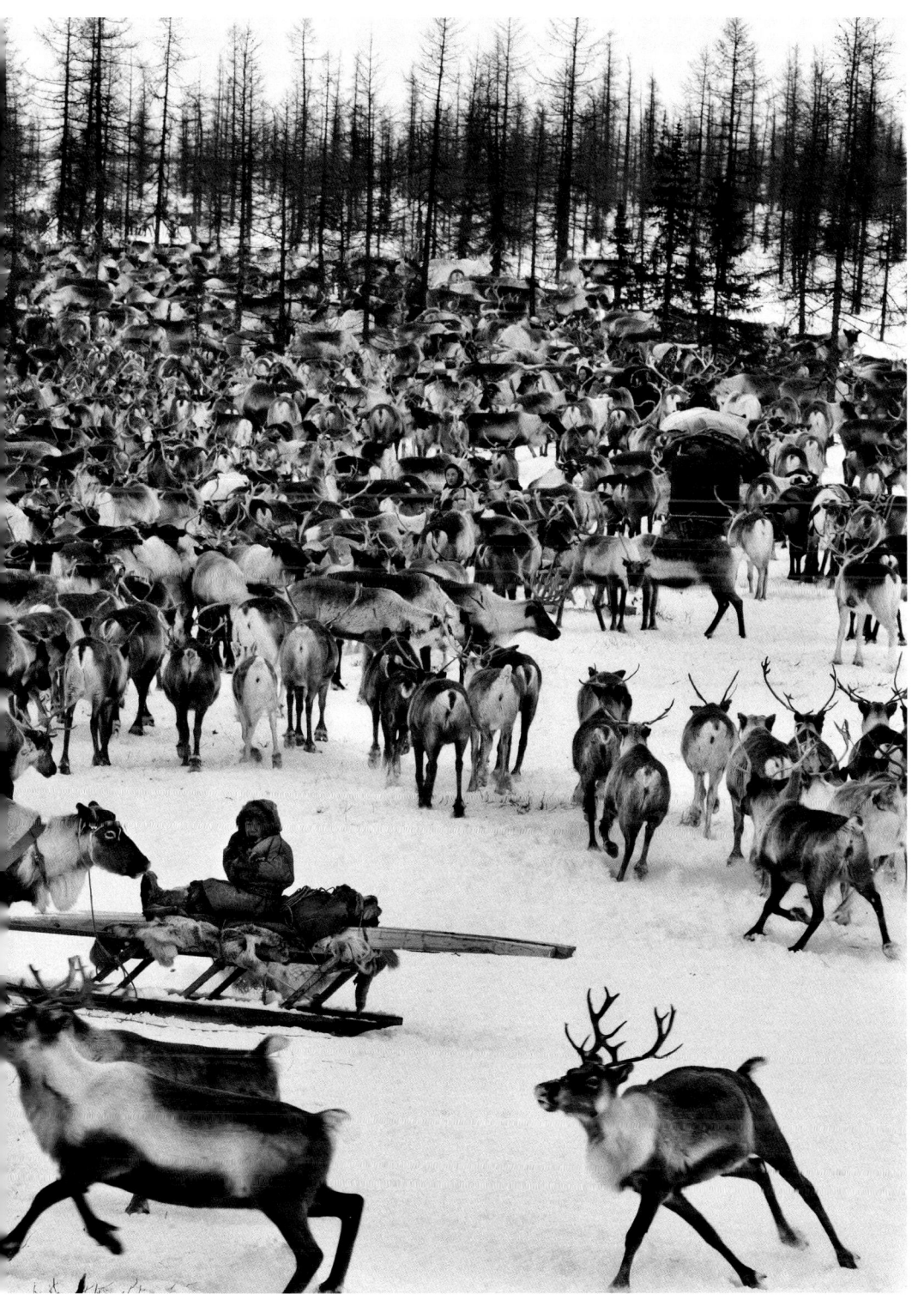

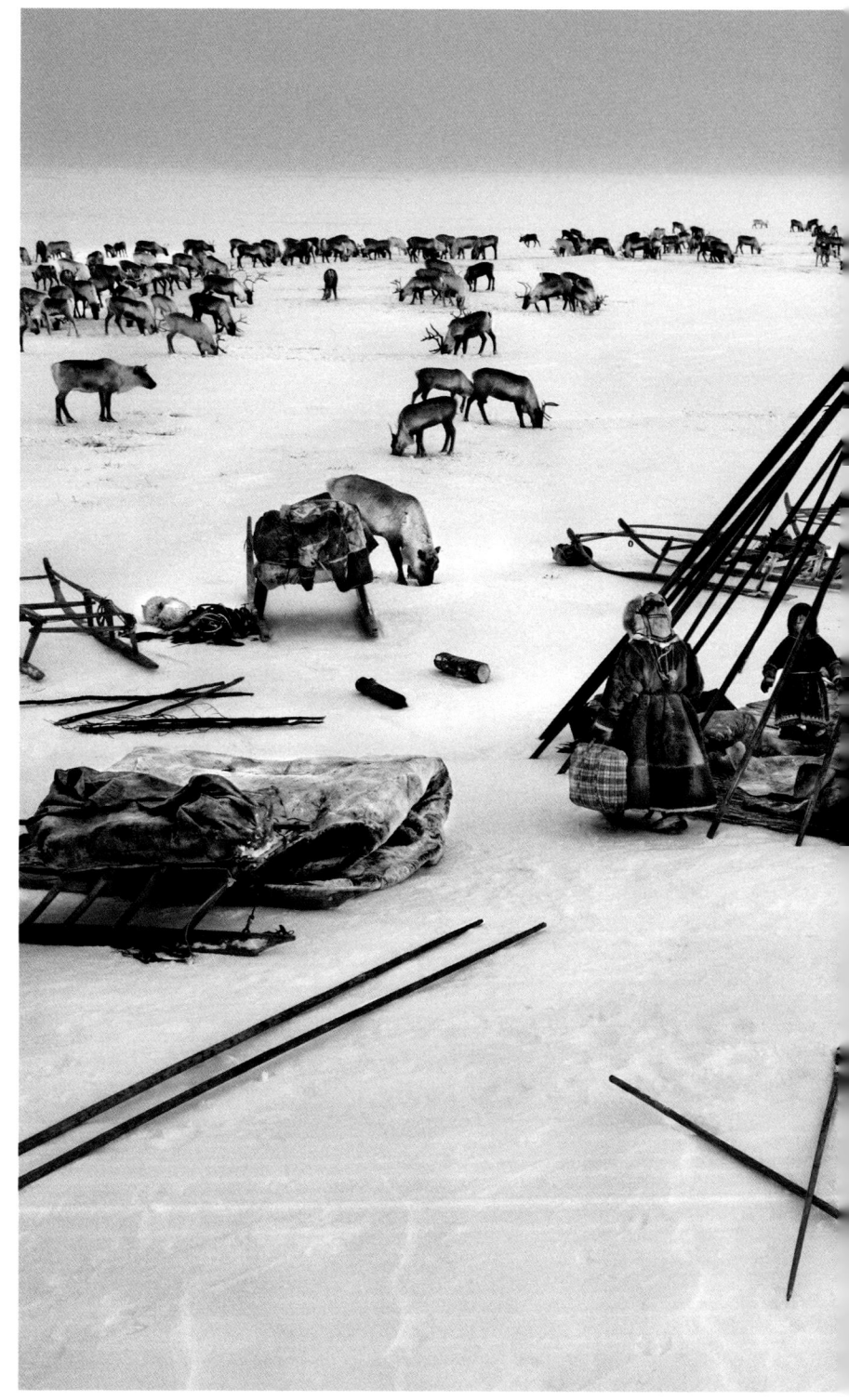

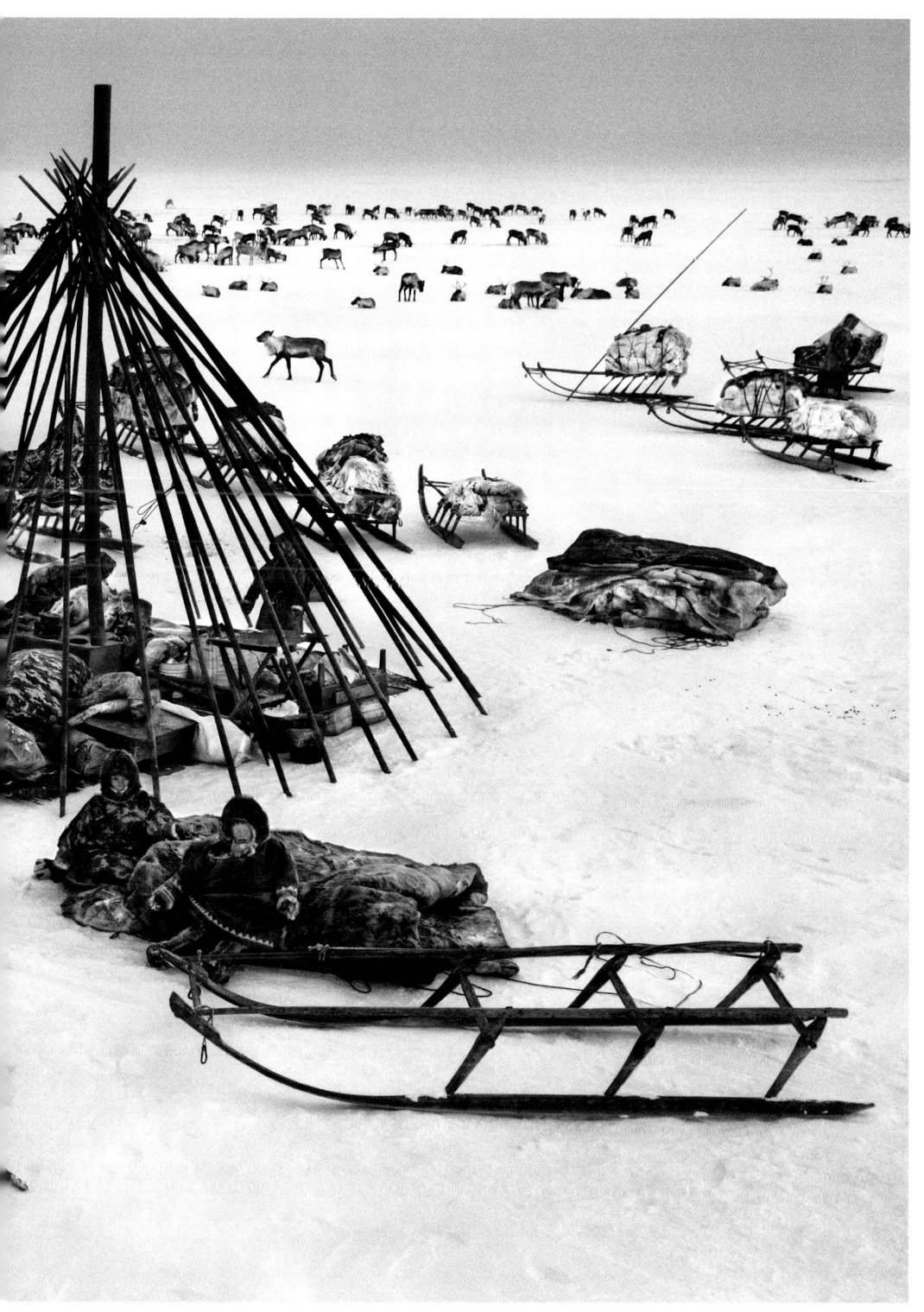

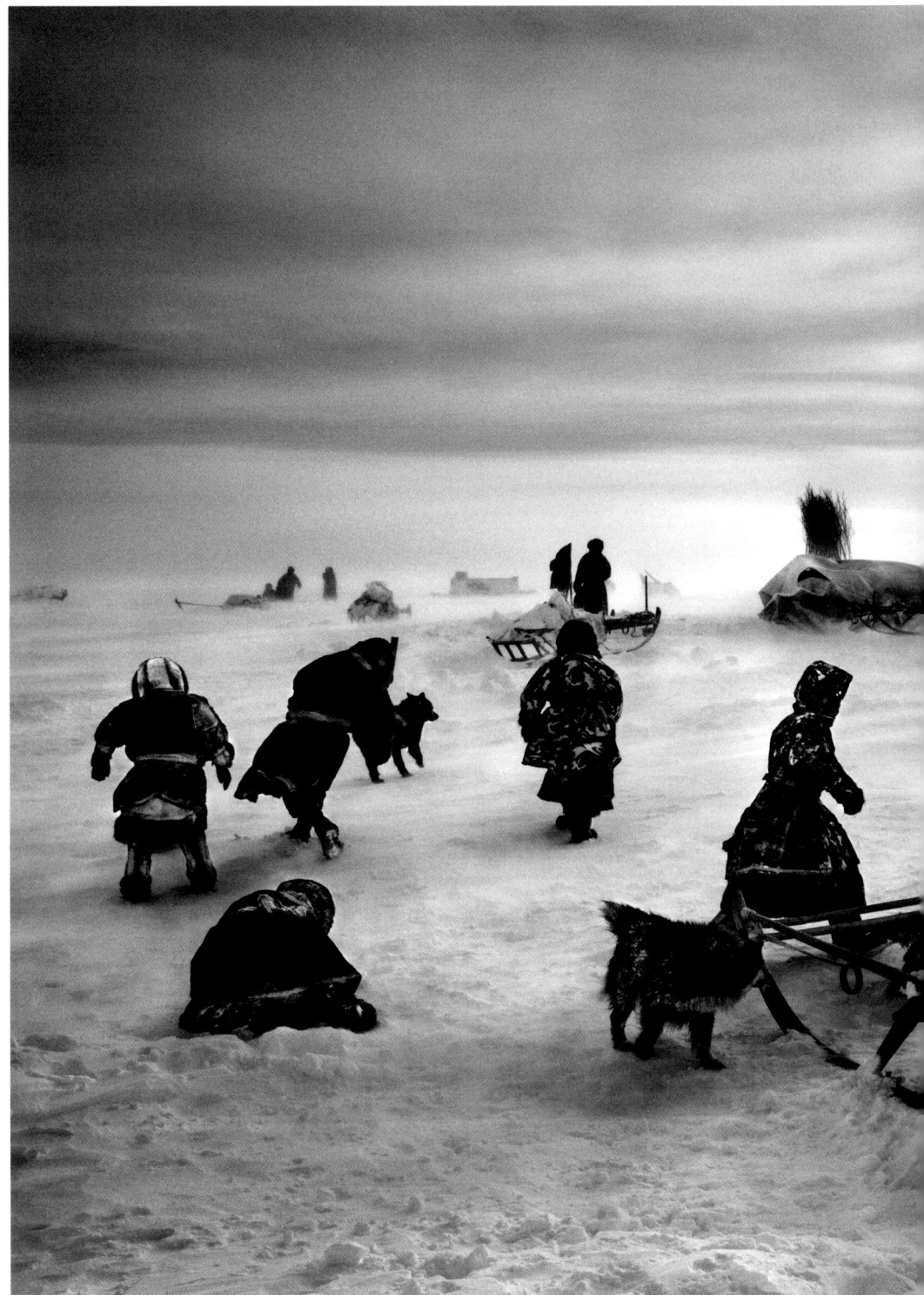

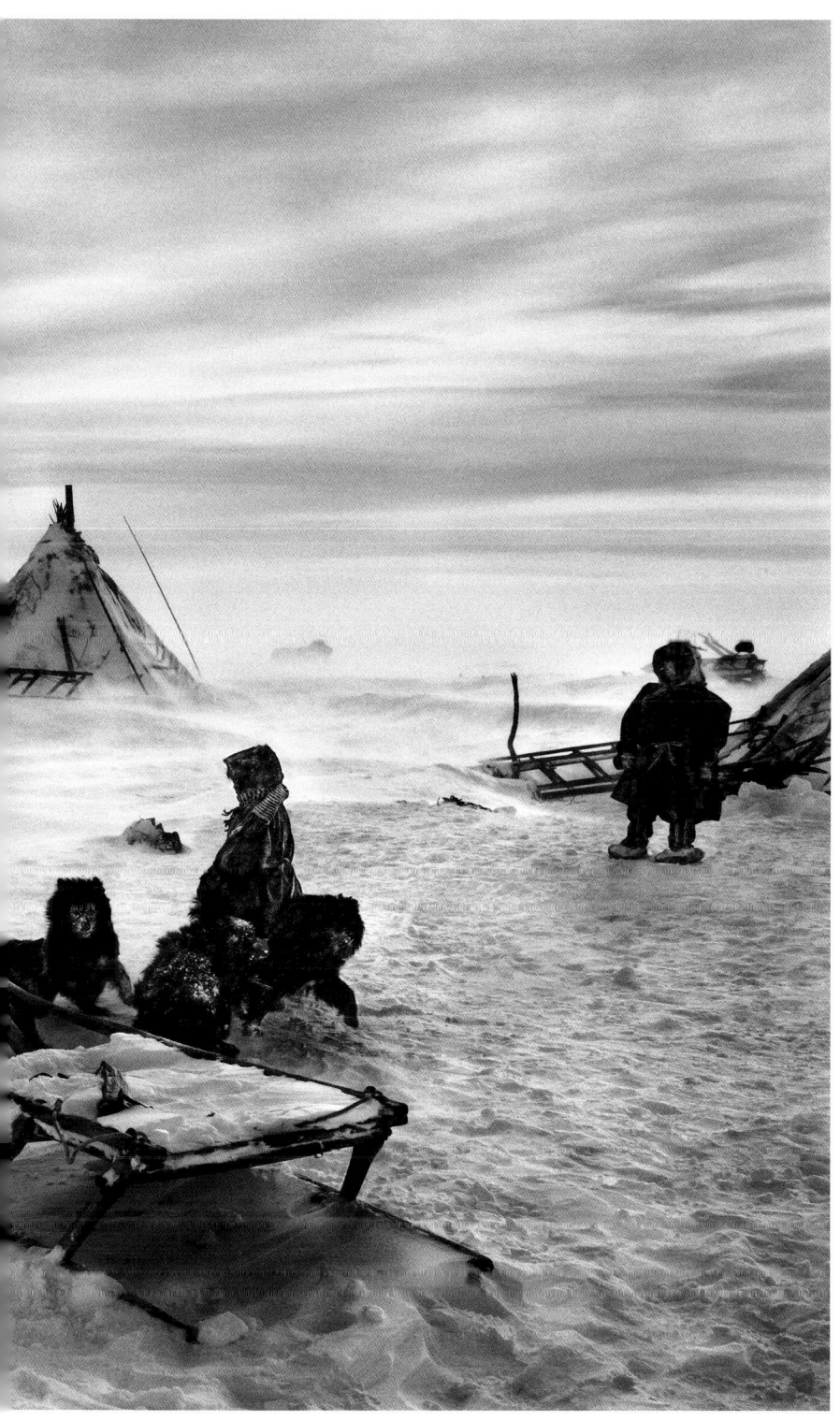

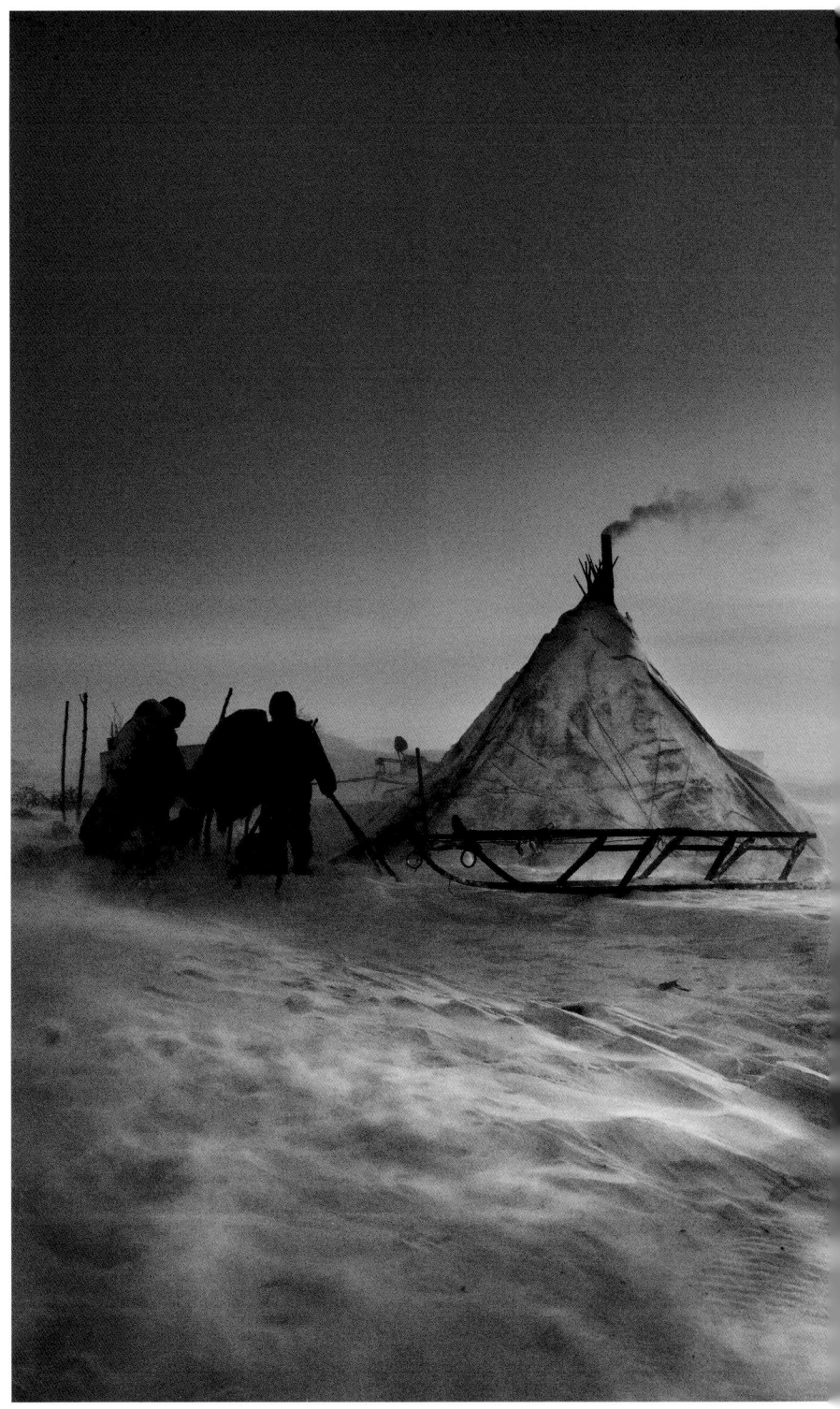

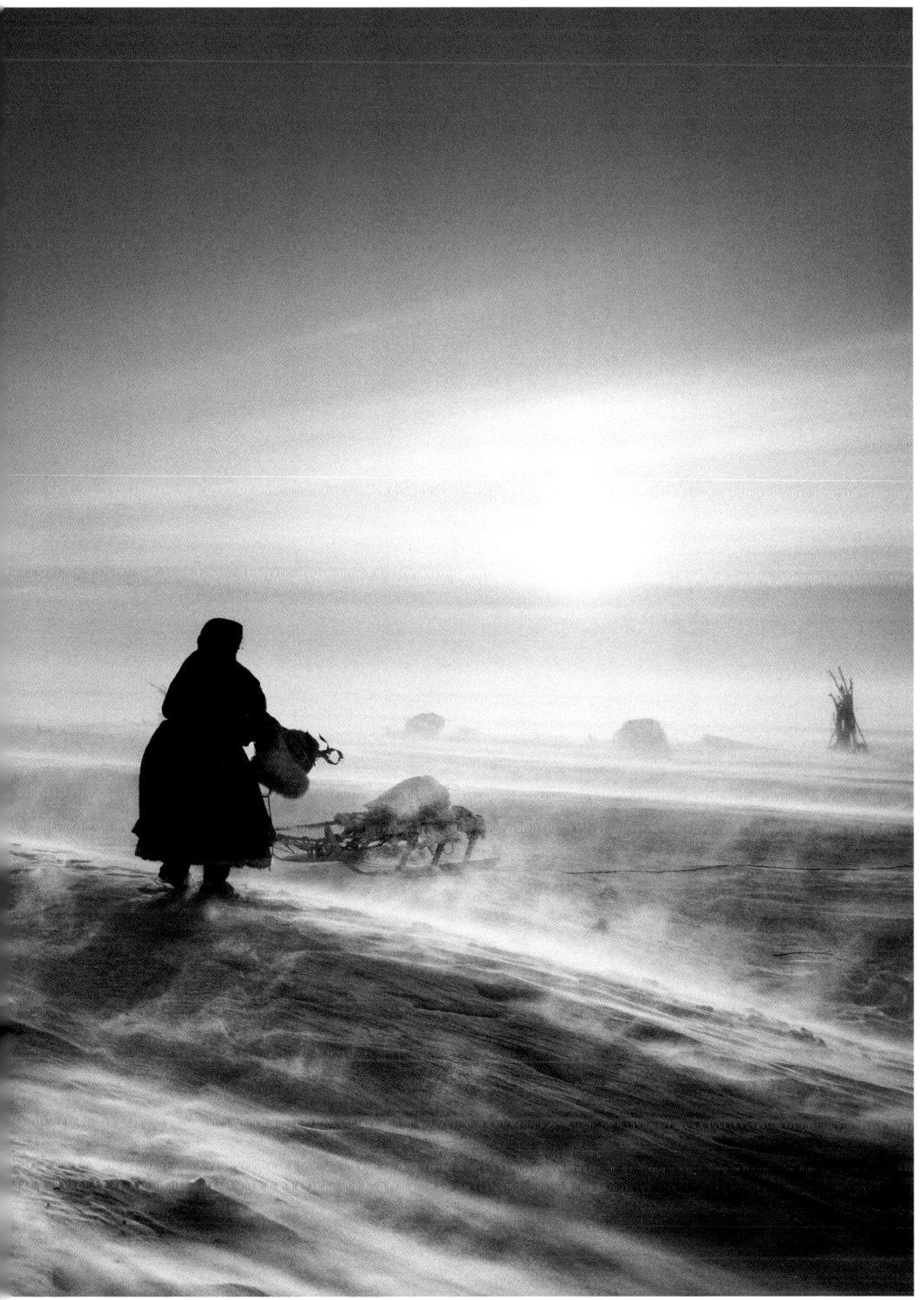

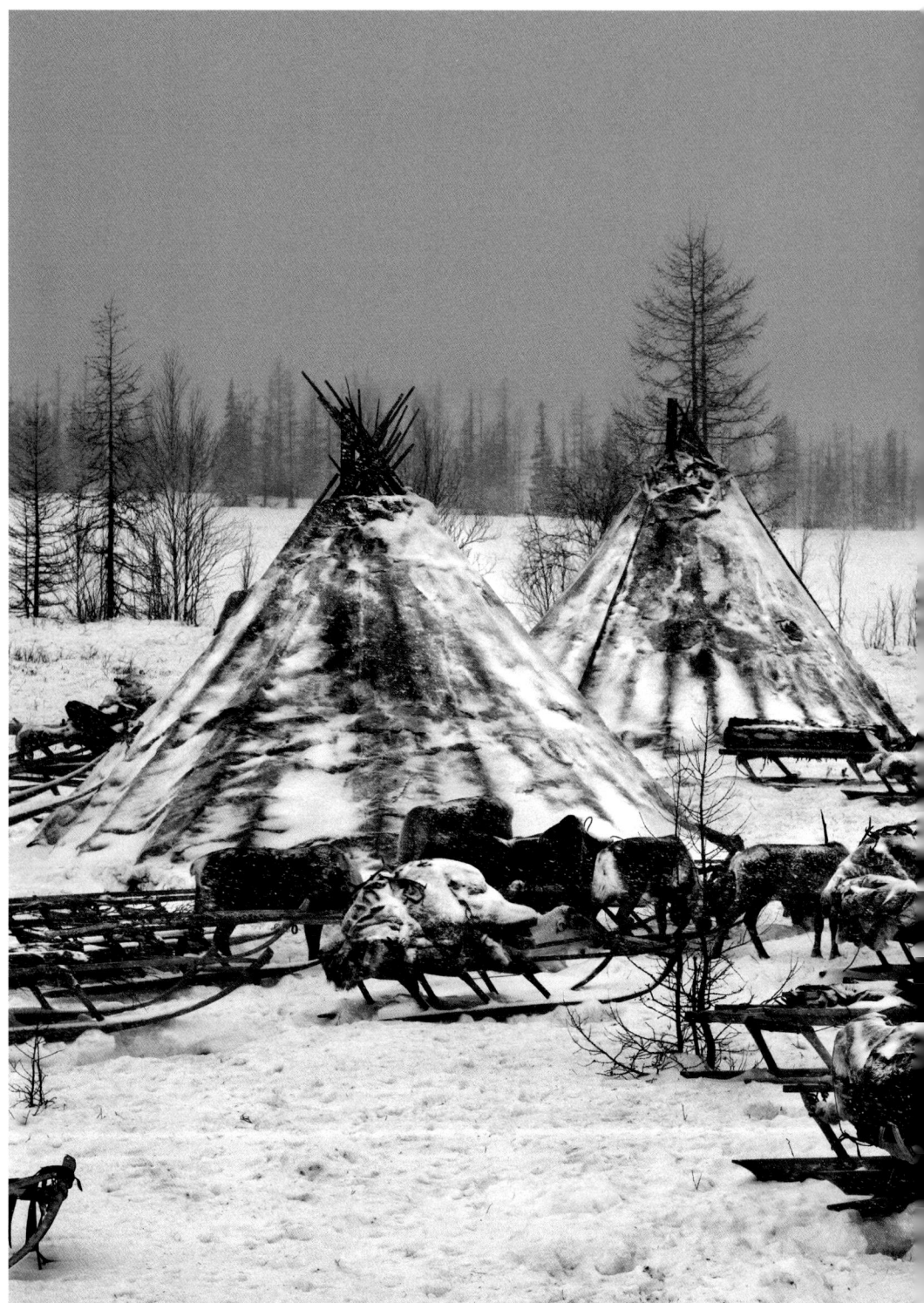

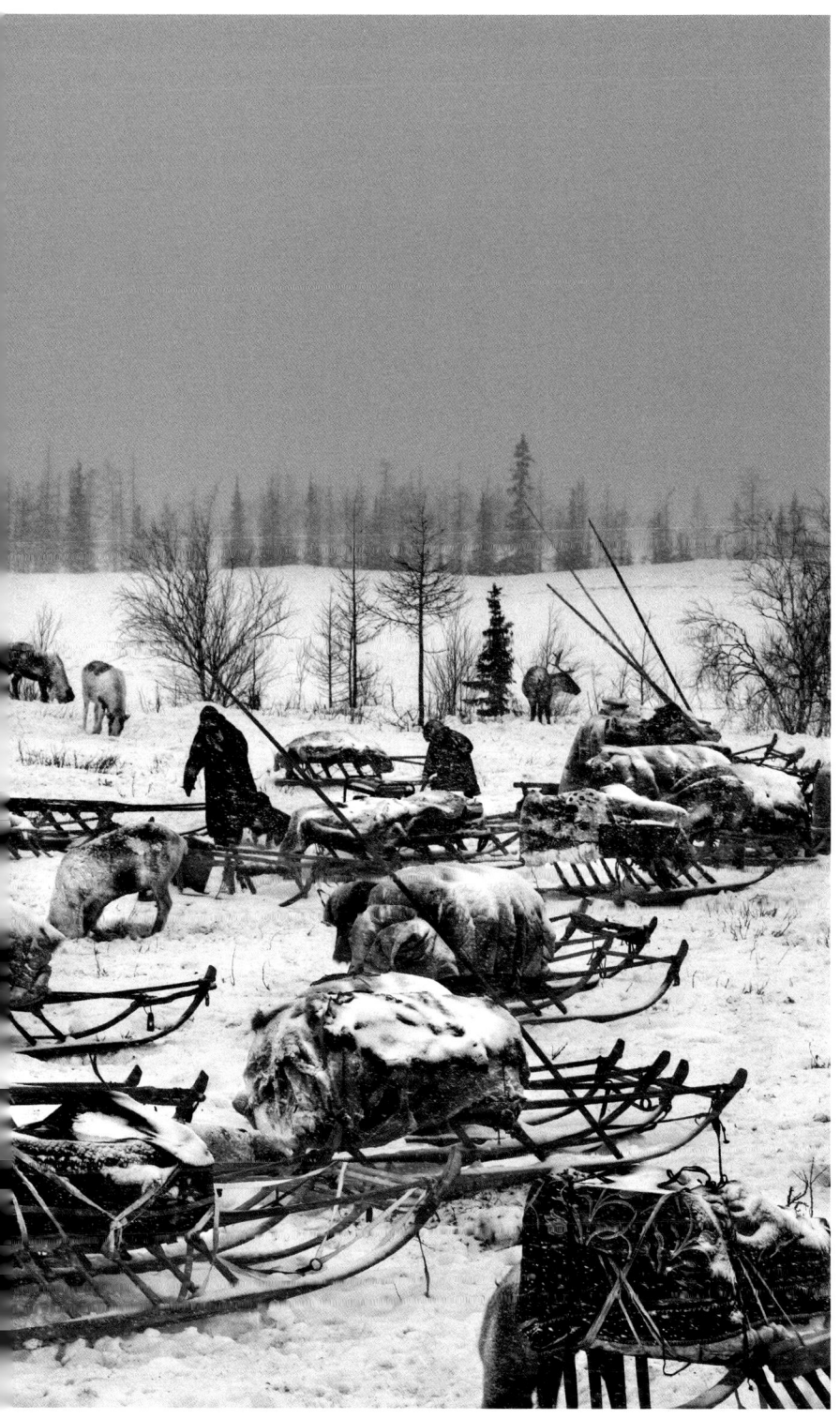

Pages 394/395, 396/397, and 402/403 North of the Ob River, about 62 miles (100 kilometers) inside the Yamal Peninsula, fierce winds keep even daytime temperatures low. When the weather is particularly hostile, the Nenets and their reindeer may spend several days in the same place, doing repair work on sledges and reindeer skins to keep busy. The deeper they move into the Arctic Circle, the less vegetation is to be found. Inside the Arctic Circle. Yamal Peninsula. Siberia. Russia. March and April 2011.

Pages 398/399 This photograph was taken after a very cold night south of the Ob River, on the edge of the Arctic Circle. In this region, the Nenets can still find wood needed to repair sledges. These sledges carry very heavy loads but, if carefully maintained, they can have long lives; a light sledge, for example, may last for 50 years. South of Ob River. Siberia. Russia. March and April 2011.

Opposite The Nenets need exceptionally warm clothing to survive their long migration into the Arctic Circle. Traditonally, all is made by the group's women. Each man wears a coat known as a *malitsa* comprising four layers of reindeer skin. It includes an integrated hood while even gloves are made of reindeer fur. Strips of reindeer skin in turn become lassos used to round up those reindeer chosen to pull the sledges. Yamal Peninsula. Siberia. Russia. March and April 2011.

Pages 404/405 The larger sledges are driven by the women, with as many as 10 sledges forming a long caravan. The men drive smaller sledges since they go faster: it is the men's job to regroup the herd around the camp each morning and, often with the help of dogs, to keep the reindeer moving in a single direction throughout the day. Yamal Peninsula. Siberia. Russia. March and April 2011.

Pages 406/407 These caravans of sledges carry all the belongings of the families in the group. Usually the men take care of the reindeer, herding them with smaller sledges and sometimes with snowmobiles; the women and children ride on the caravans, which may be composed of as many as 10 sledges tied to each other, with one woman in charge. Yamal Peninsula. Siberia. Russia. March and April 2011.

Pages 408/409 Crossing the Ob River to enter the Arctic Circle involves traveling some 31 miles (50 kilometers) over ice. Yamal Peninsula. Siberia. Russia. March and April 2011.

Pages 410/411 The way of life of the Nenets of the Siberian Arctic is inseparable from the reindeer. Every spring, they move enormous herds of reindeer from winter pastures on the Russian mainland, traveling over 620 miles (1,000 kilometers) northwards to summer pastures in the Arctic Circle. This ritual is so old that to this day it seems unclear whether the Nenets follow the reindeer or vice versa. The migration starts in mid-March in freezing temperatures and is immediately challenged by the need to cross the frozen Ob River. But the Nenets take this in their stride, bolstered by a regimented work ethic and a robust culture. They survived early Russian colonization of Siberia and the dark years of the Soviet regime, but are now being exposed to the perils posed by rapacious development of oil and gas fields in the far north. Ob River. Siberia. Russia. March and April 2011.

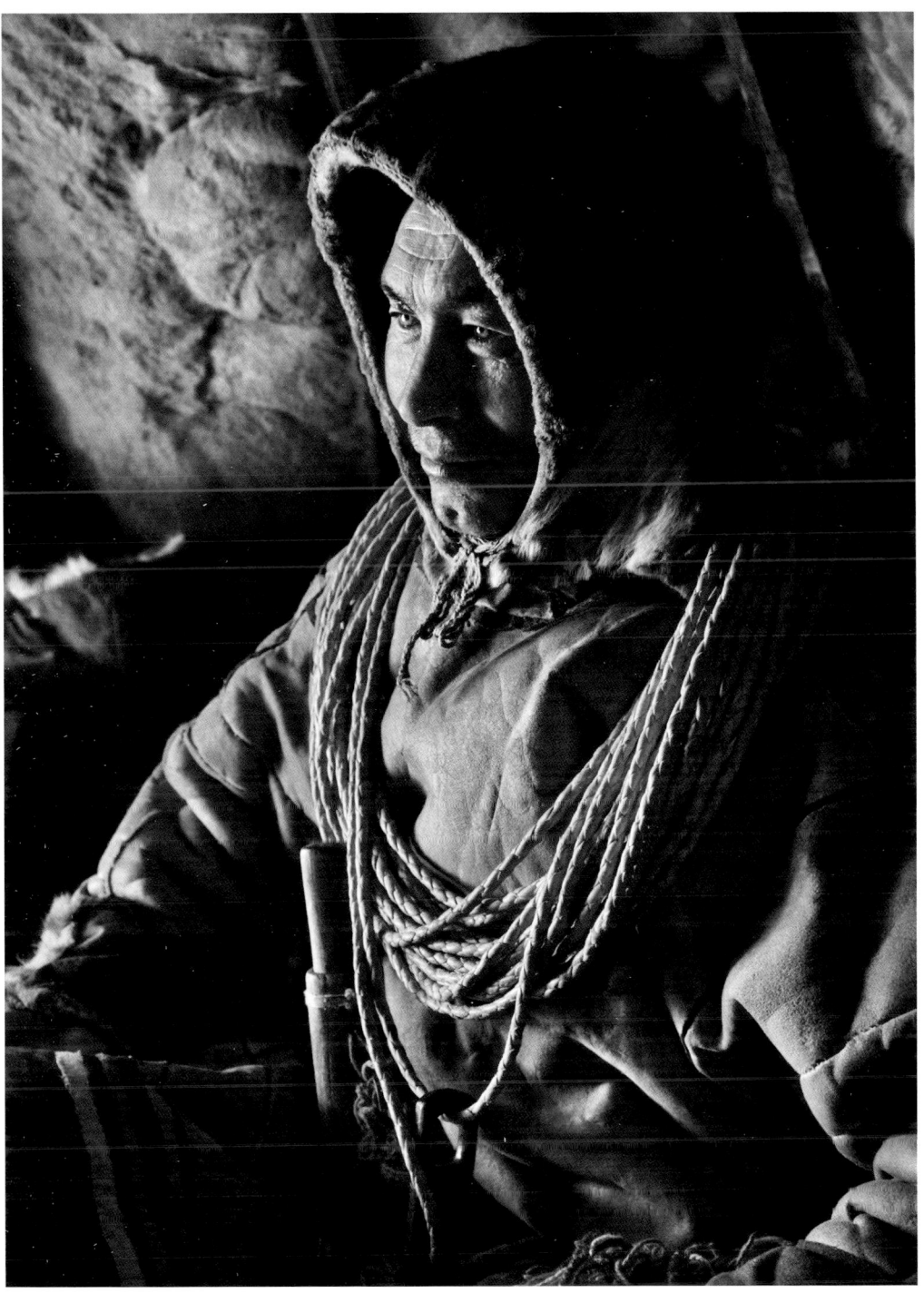

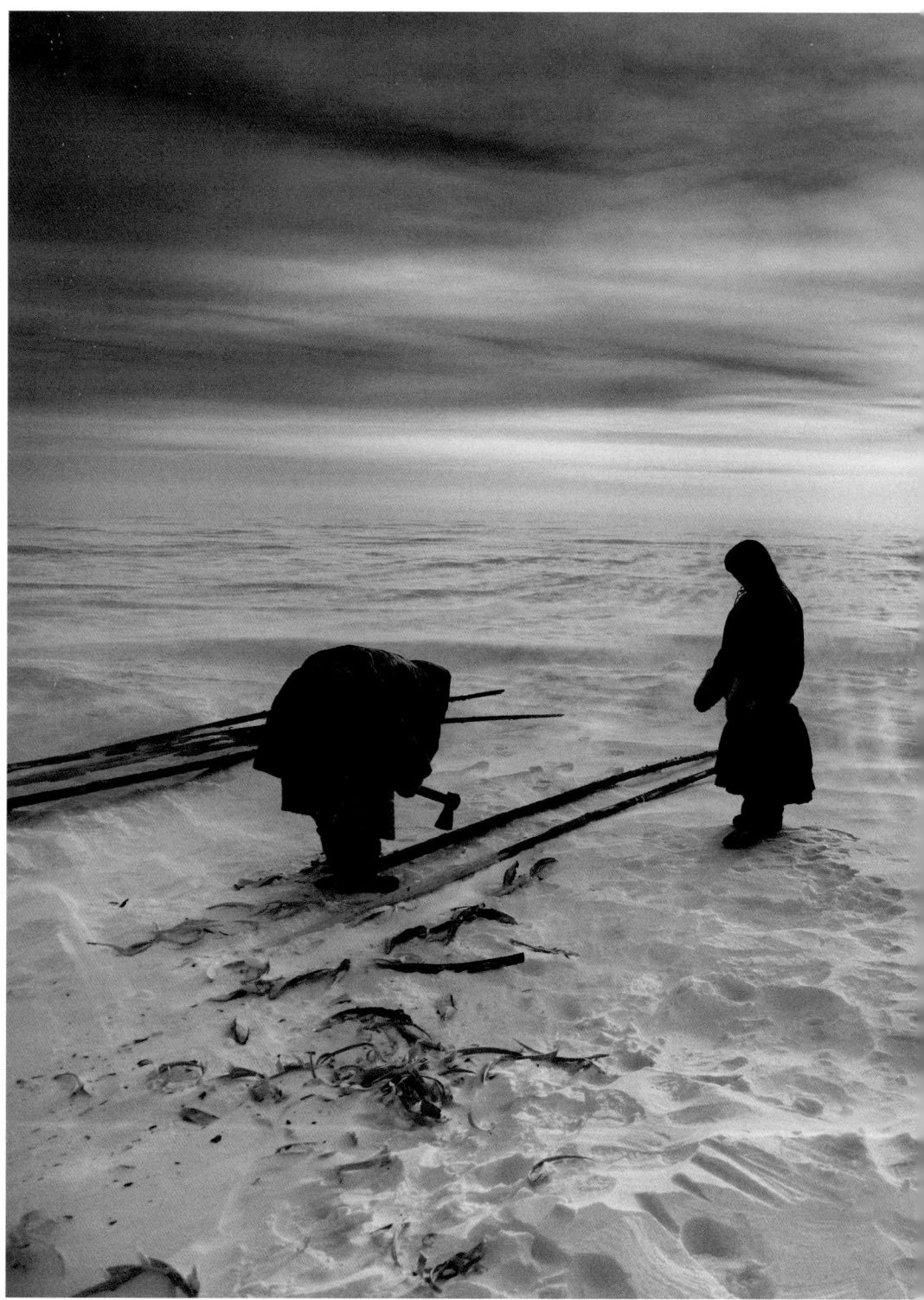

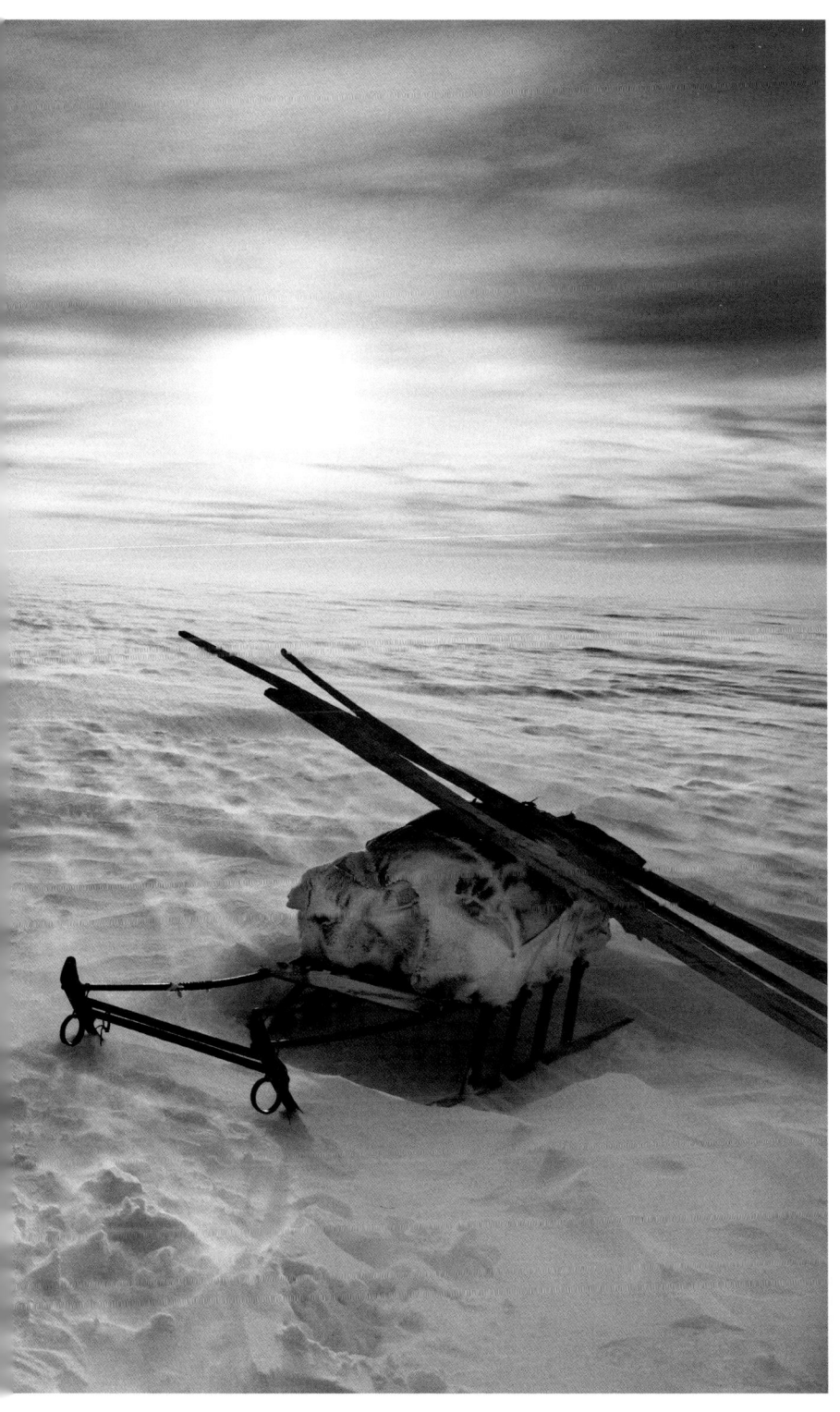

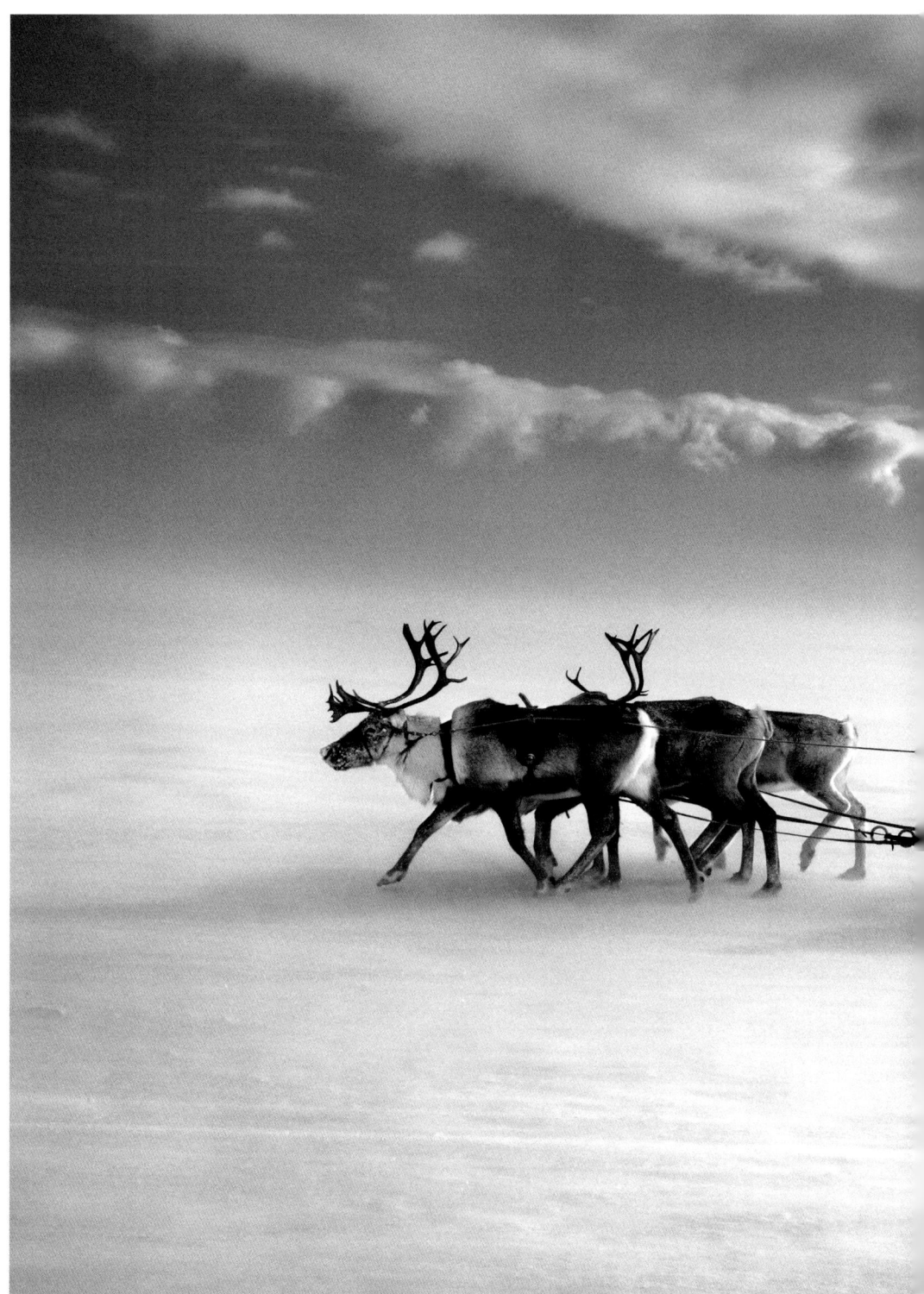

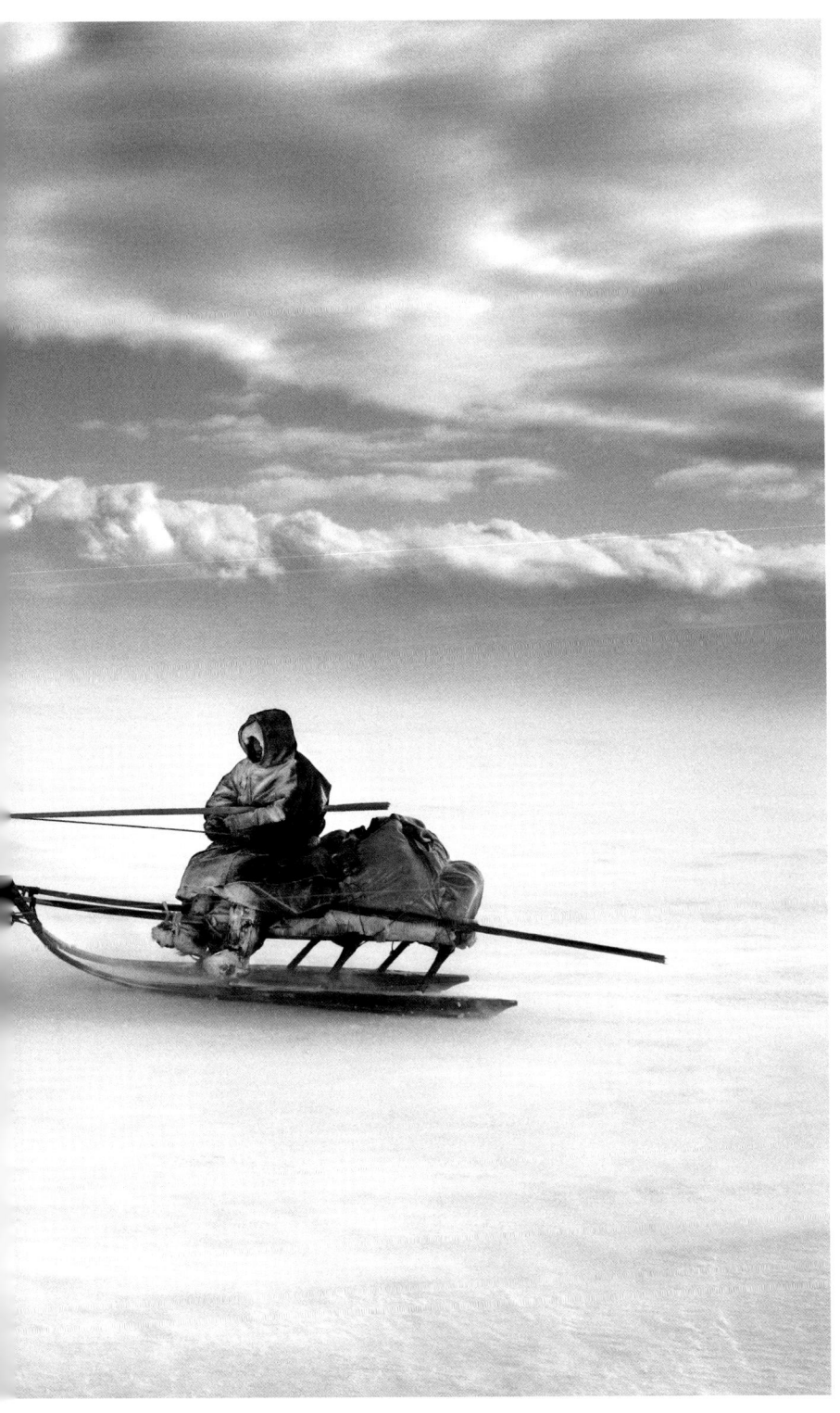

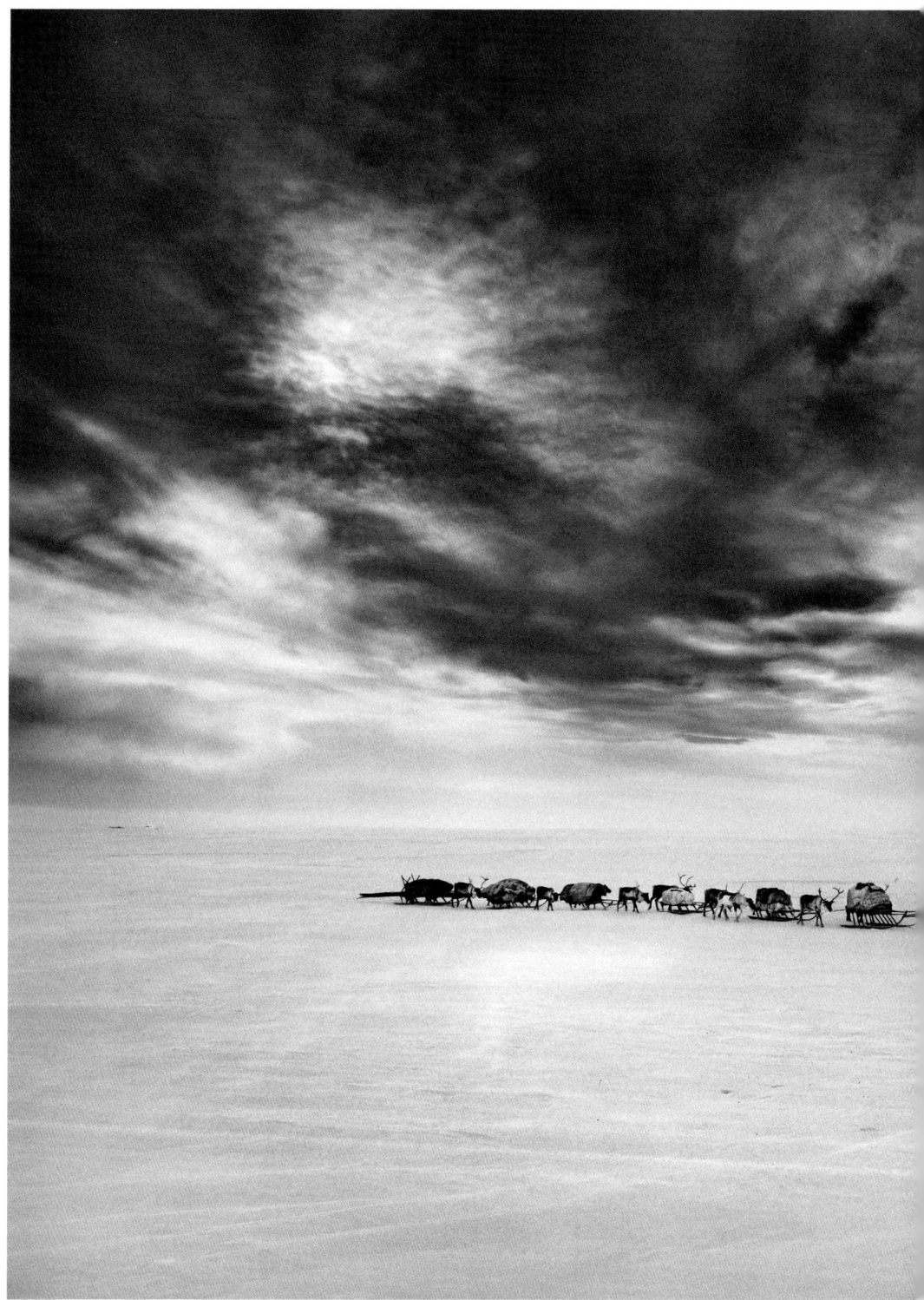

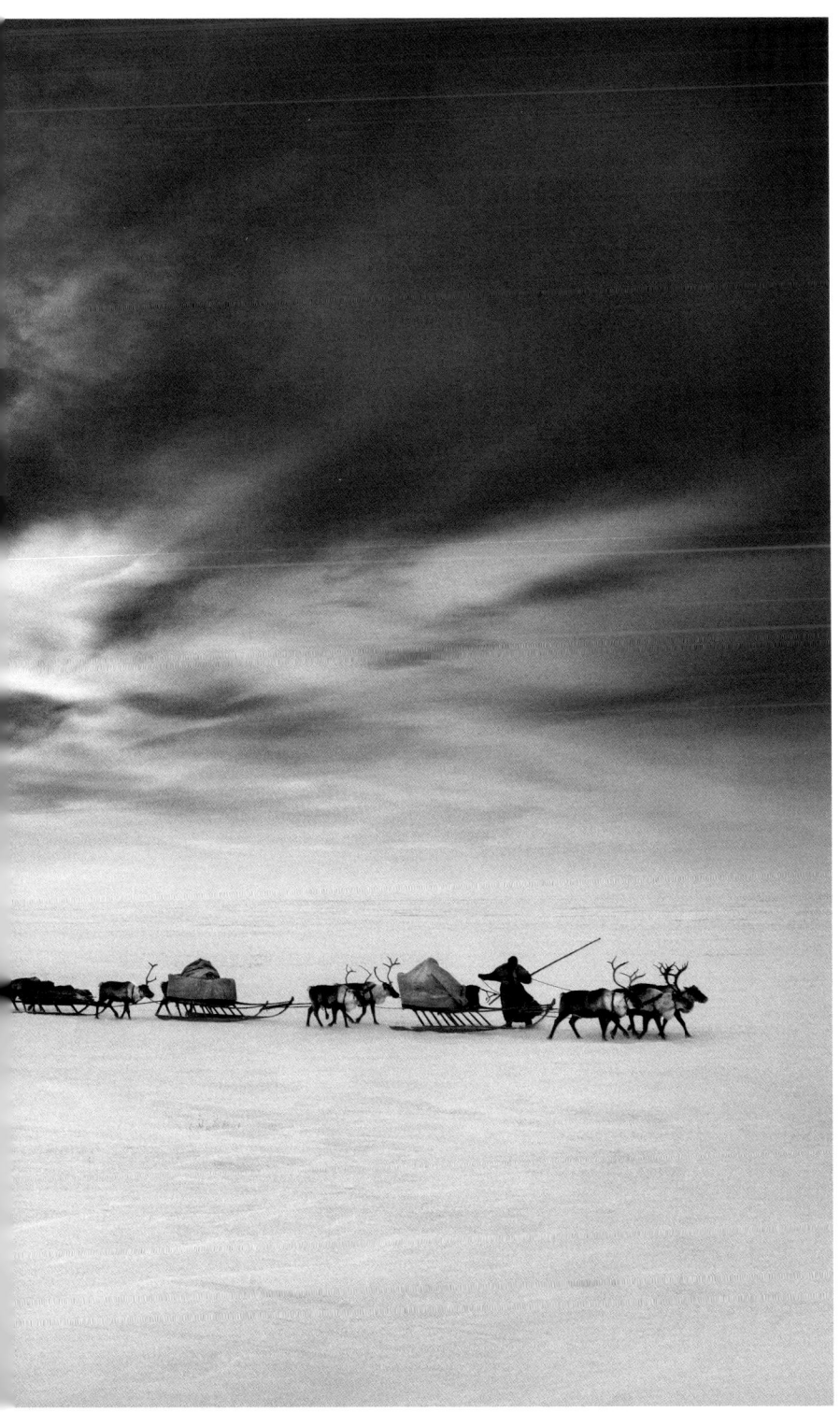

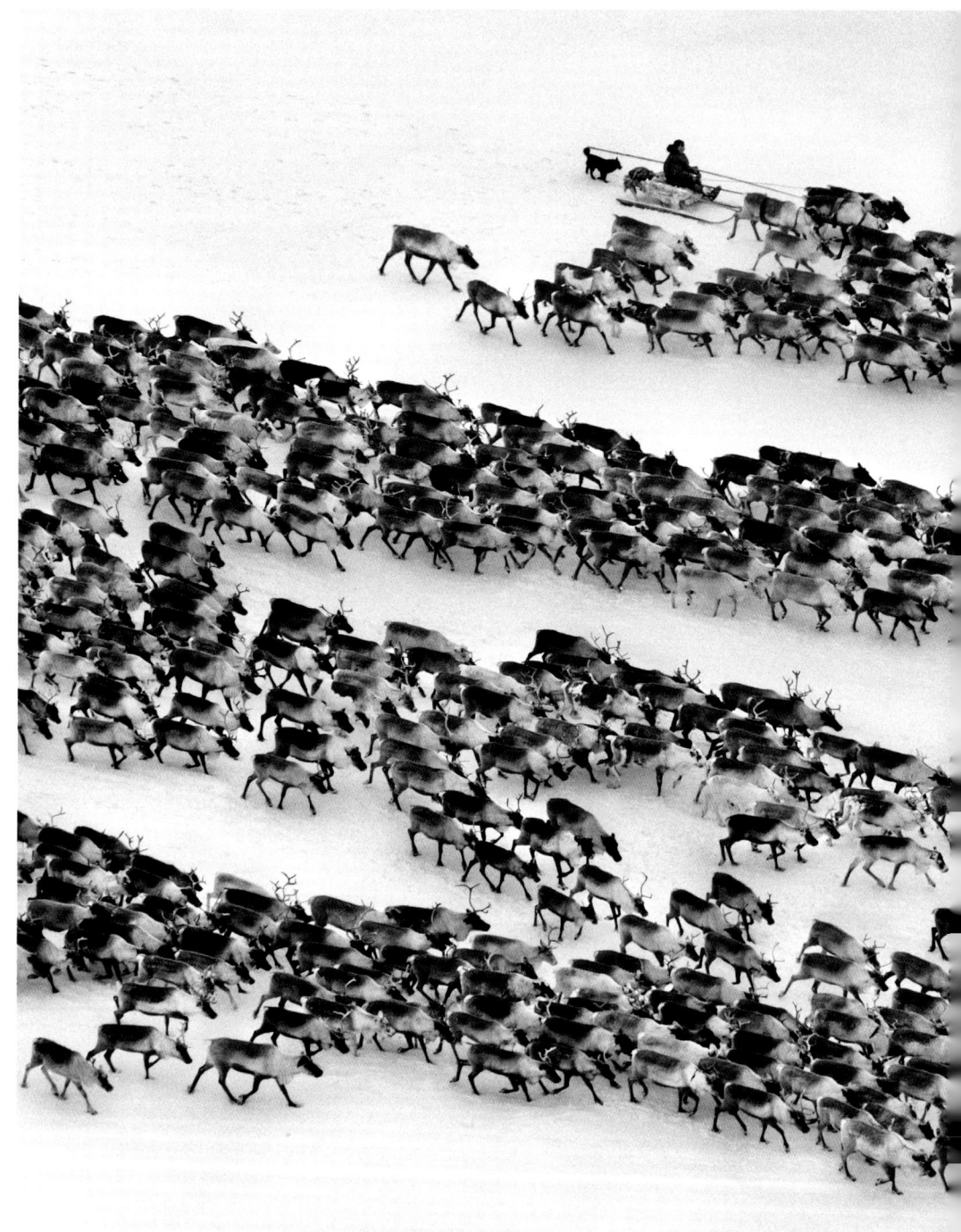

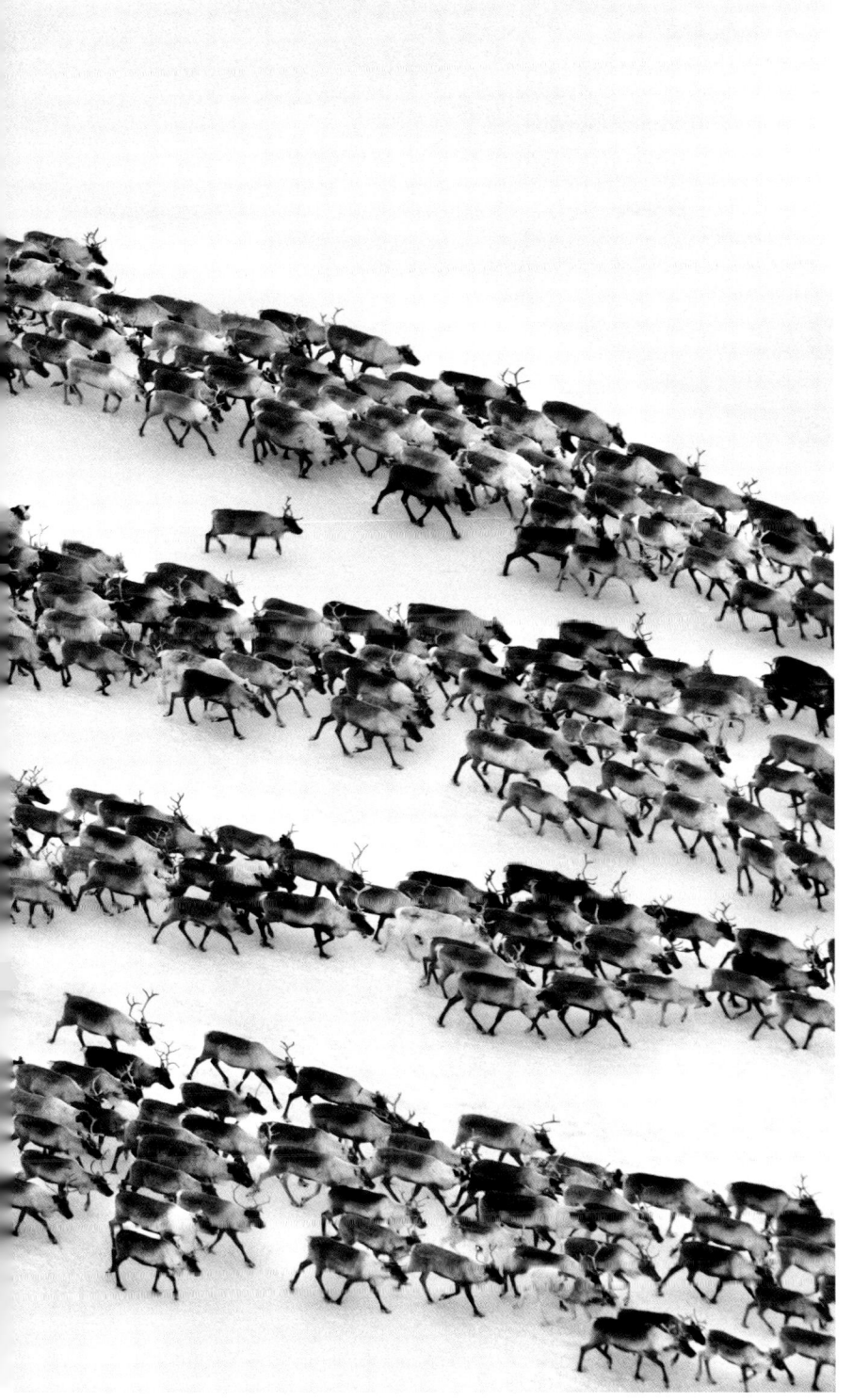

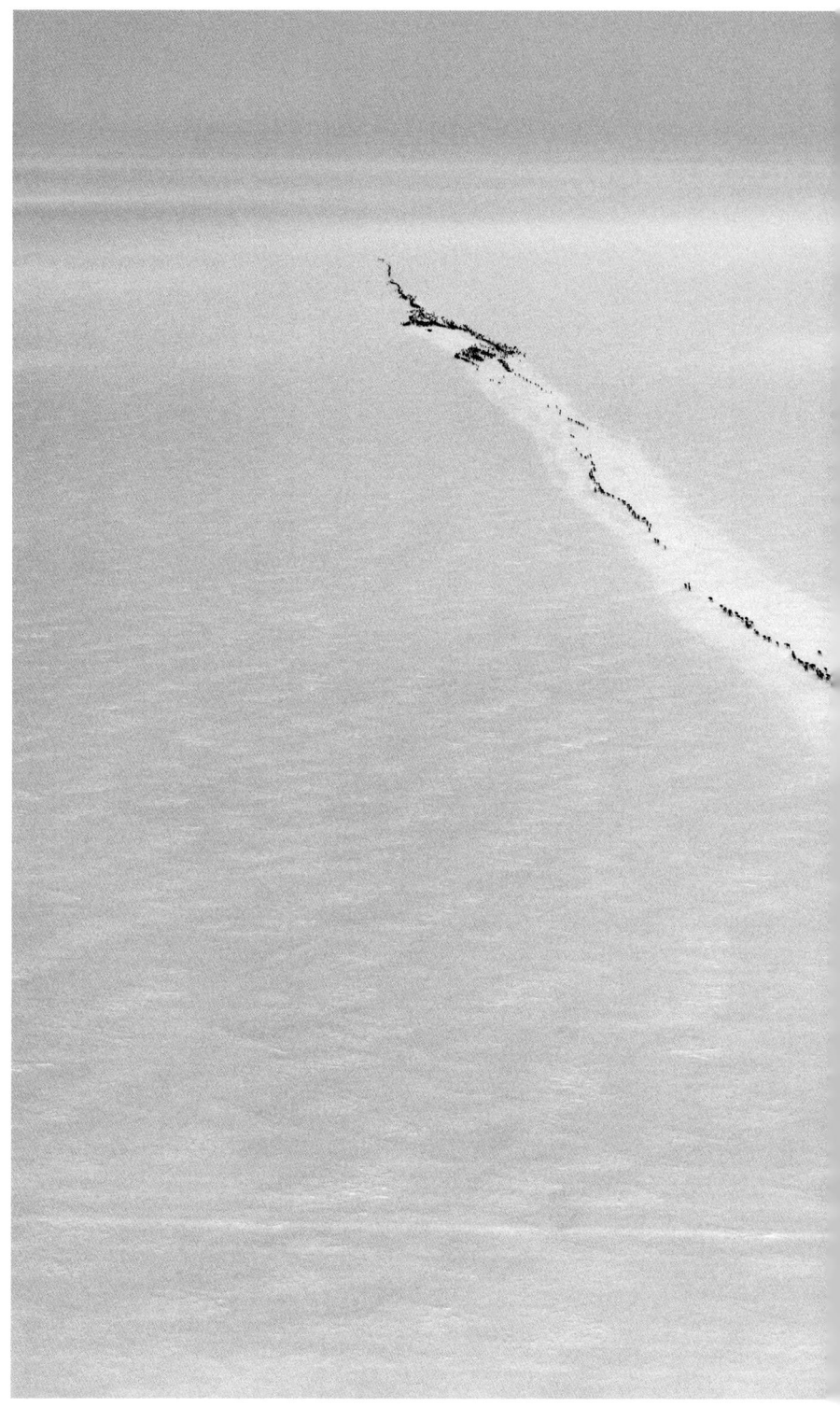

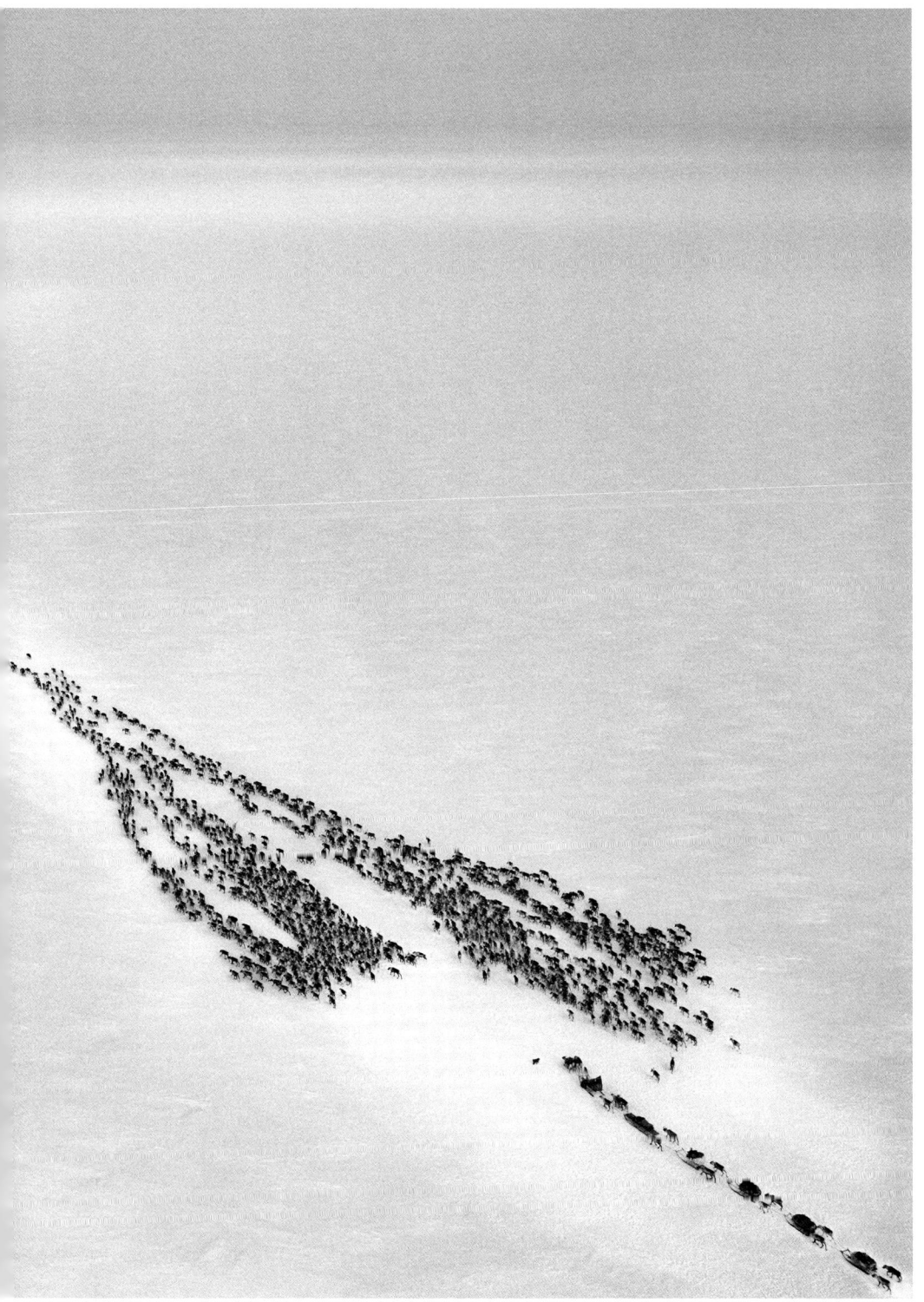

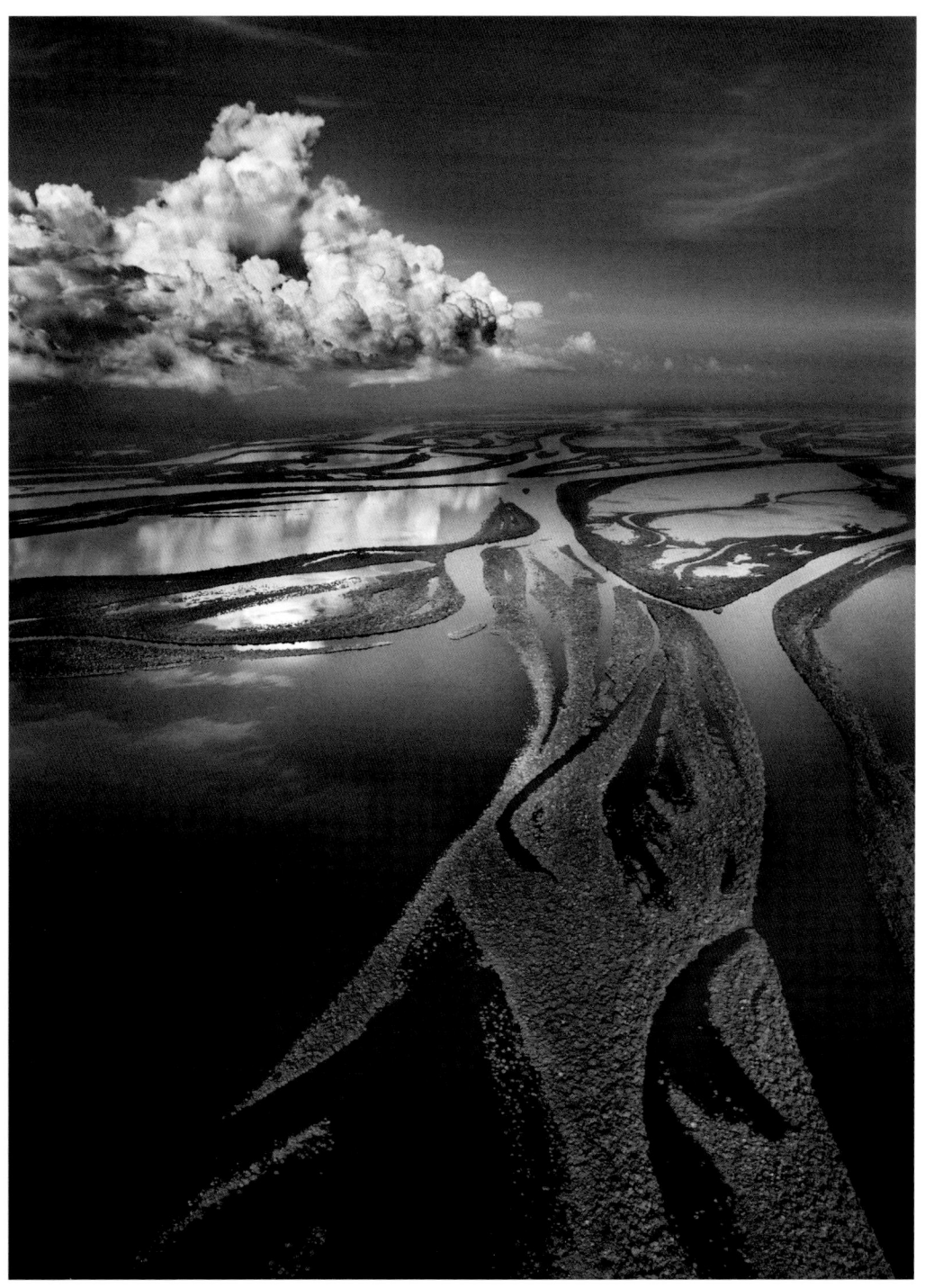

AMAZONIA AND PANTANAL

From space, the Amazon River and its tributaries resemble a giant tree of life. Indeed, the entire Amazon basin represents life in myriad ways: as a global lung, as the source of 20 percent of the world's fresh water, as home to uncounted species of flora and fauna, and as a refuge for scores of Indian tribes. On its peripheries, though, logging, cattle farming, mining and urbanization are slowly eating away at the jungle. Burned forest and cleared land have now left vast scars on what was once an uninterrupted carpet of green.

I know and love the Amazon region. This time I wanted to fly over the river which Brazilians only call the Amazon after the dark Rio Negro and the paler Rio Solimões meet at Manaus. From there, we headed northwest up the Rio Negro over land so flat that the river is sometimes 12 miles (20 kilometers) wide, leaving long fingers of islands covered by dense vegetation. What may appear in a photograph to be a static landscape is in fact ever-changing, depending on the changing seasons and the flow of water coming down from the Andes.

The Amazon rainforest spreads far beyond Brazil's borders, but what drew me to the Canaima National Park in southeast Venezuela were tabletop mountains known as *tepuis*, nearly 10,000 feet (3,000 meters) high, which rise abruptly from the jungle. Formed some four billion years ago, they are among the world's oldest geological formations. Climbing to the top of several *tepuis*, I was stunned to see how erosion had carved rocks into ghostly shapes, some evoking prehistoric animals, others deserted cities. And everywhere, there are waterfalls, as if the very mountains were weeping. At the Angel Falls, the highest on Earth, the water plunges more than 3,200 feet (970 meters). No wonder Arthur Conan Doyle chose this setting for his 1912 novel, *The Lost World*.

Opposite The Anavilhanas, the name given to around 350 forested islands in Brazil's Rio Negro, form the world's largest inland archipelago. Covering 390 square miles (1,000 square kilometers) of Amazonia, they start 50 miles (80 kilometers) northwest of Manaus and stretch some 250 miles (400 kilometers) up the Rio Negro, as far as Barcelos. Their formation dates back to the last Ice Age, when changes in the flow of rivers entering the Rio Negro produced accumulations of sediment that, over time, formed sandbars and islands. Since water levels change with the seasons by as much as 65 feet (20 meters), the Anavilhanas are themselves ever-changing, with channels, sandbars and lagoons appearing during the dry season and some small islands vanishing when waters rise. This often makes it very difficult for boats to identify the main navigation channel. Many of the larger islands, though, are self-contained parcels of rainforest. Amazonas, Brazil. May 2009.

People have lived in the Amazon forest for more than 10,000 years, although many tribes have disappeared in the wake of road-builders, loggers, missionaries and imported diseases. One exception are the Zo'é, first "contacted" only two decades ago. Thanks to Brazil's National Indian Foundation (FUNAI), I had the good fortune of being allowed to spend several weeks observing a way of life that has changed little over millennia. These gentle hunter-gatherers live in small communities and wear no clothes. Adults have a small wooden plug piercing their lower lip. I followed them into the jungle when they went hunting for monkeys and fish with bows and arrows, and watched them grind manioc root into flour. They now own a 2,400-square-mile (6,250-square-kilometer) reserve; even so, curious about the outside world, a few tribesmen have recently visited nearby towns.

Some 930 miles (1,500 kilometers) away, on the southern edge of Amazonia, Indian tribes in Mato Grosso state have more contact with modern society, although they enjoy the protection of living in the Xingu Indigenous Park, a reserve the size of Belgium created in 1961. My interest was to see how much of their traditional way of life had survived. I concentrated on three tribes living in the Upper Xingu Basin—the Waura, Kuikuro and Kamayura—who speak different languages and have distinct ethnic backgrounds. Some tribesmen understand Portuguese and wear Western clothes, but they also take immense pride in their rituals and ceremonies.

The two months I spent in the Xingu coincided with preparations by the Kuikuro and Waura tribes for the funeral ritual of the *Kuarup*, which celebrates life, death and rebirth. For this, a large amount of food and drink is prepared for guests from other villages, while near-naked bodies are painted and intricate feather headdresses are worn. The *Kuarup* climaxes with day-long chanting, dancing and wrestling. The Kamayura tribe was holding the *Amuricumã*, an annual festival in which women assume power and, along with preparing the food, engage in the Dance of the Women. The Kamayura also boast the only female shaman in the Upper Xingu.

Still further south is the Pantanal, the world's largest wetland, which is mainly in Brazil but also spreads into Bolivia and Paraguay. During the rainy season, 80 percent of the region floods, and streams and rivers disappear into lakes. We traveled mostly by boat through a world owned by a remarkable variety of animal life, from river otters, anteaters, marsh deer and tapirs to capybaras, anacondas, caimans and jaguars.

The air, in turn, belongs to crowned eagles, macaws, parrots, toucans, herons, hawks and giant storks known locally as the *tuiuiu*. Cattle have been introduced in some places, although nature occasionally protests. Where rain has washed away soil from cleared land, silted rivers have now permanently flooded pastures and bankrupted cattle farmers.

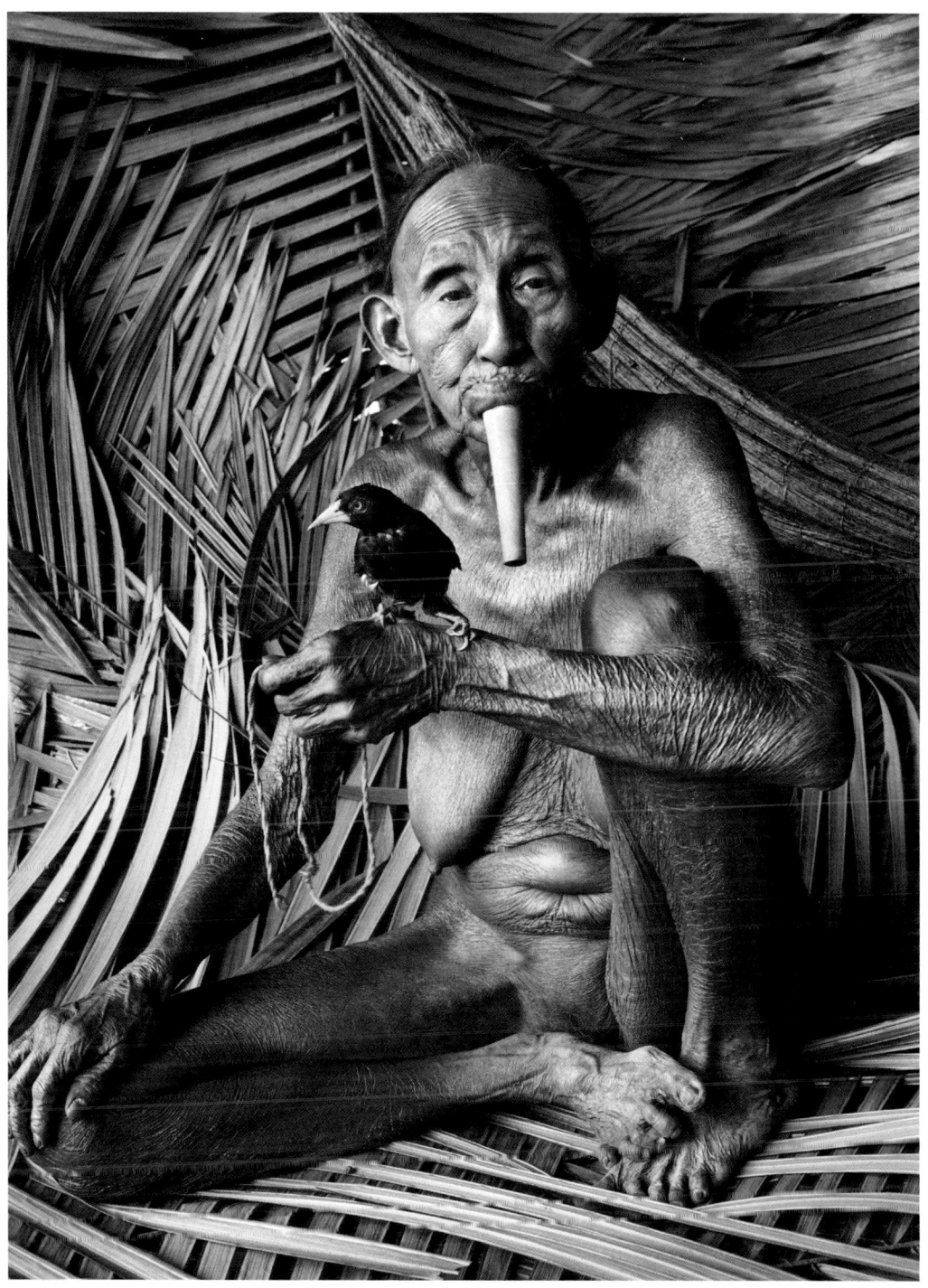

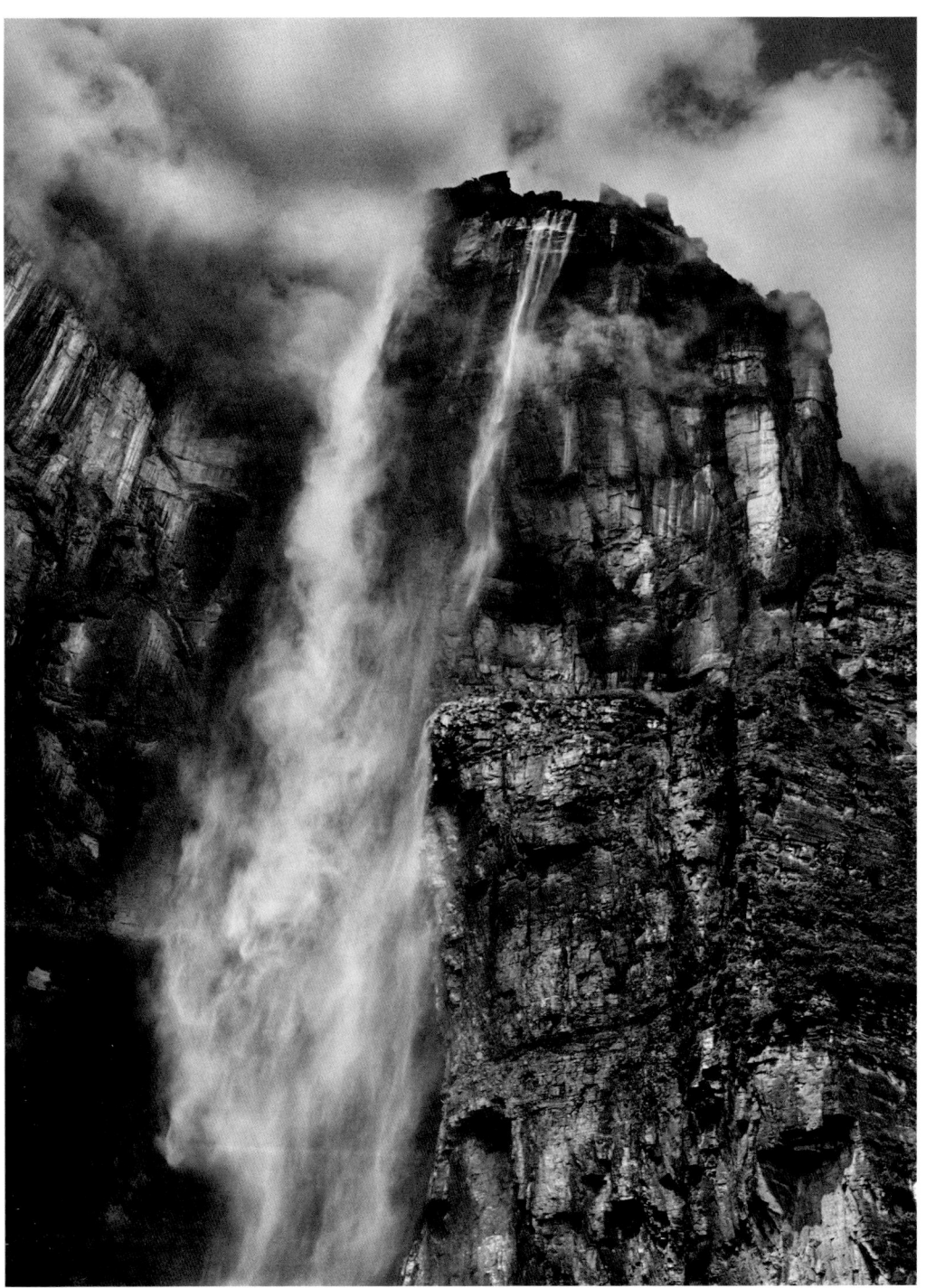

Page 415 Some birds, monkeys and turtles are kept as pets by the Zo'é. Pará, Brazil. March and April 2009.

Opposite Known in English as the Angel Falls, the Salto Ángel is the world's tallest waterfall, tumbling 3,200 feet (979 meters) from a flat-topped mountain called Auyantepui, or Devil's Mountain, in the indigenous Pemon language. The waterfall is in the central portion of this *tepui* and drops into what is known as the Cañón del Diablo, or Devil's Canyon, with the water flow eventually reaching the Churún River. The waterfall takes its name from an American bush pilot, Jimmie Angel, who flew over the falls in 1933. Four years later, he landed on Auyantepui's plateau in a four-seat plane while searching for gold. Unable to take off from the marshy terrain, Angel, his wife and two companions trekked across the *tepui* before climbing down an almost vertical cliff to safety. Their widely publicized 11-day odyssey drew attention for the first time to the existence of the waterfall. Venezuela. November and December 2006.

Pages 418/419 Close to Brazil's border with Venezuela, where the Amazon rainforest suddenly gives way to the Imeri mountain range, Brazil's highest peak, the Pico da Neblina, rises to 9,823 feet (2,994 meters). This jagged, pyramid-shaped rock towers over the jungle, although it is often shrouded in clouds, as its name suggests: *neblina* is Portuguese for mist. Amazonas, Brazil. August 2009.

Pages 420/421 On the plateau of the Kukenan *Tepui*, wind and water erosion has sculpted bizarre shapes from the ancient rocks. *Tepui* is the Pemon Indian name given to the 115 or so flat-topped mountains in a region straddling southeastern Venezuela, southwestern Guyana and northern Brazil. This *tepui* covers an area of 8 square miles (20.6 square kilometers) and stands 8,800 feet (2,680 meters) above sea level. In the background, partly hidden by clouds, the Roraima Tepui rises to a height of 8,933 feet (2,723 meters). Venezuela. November and December 2006.

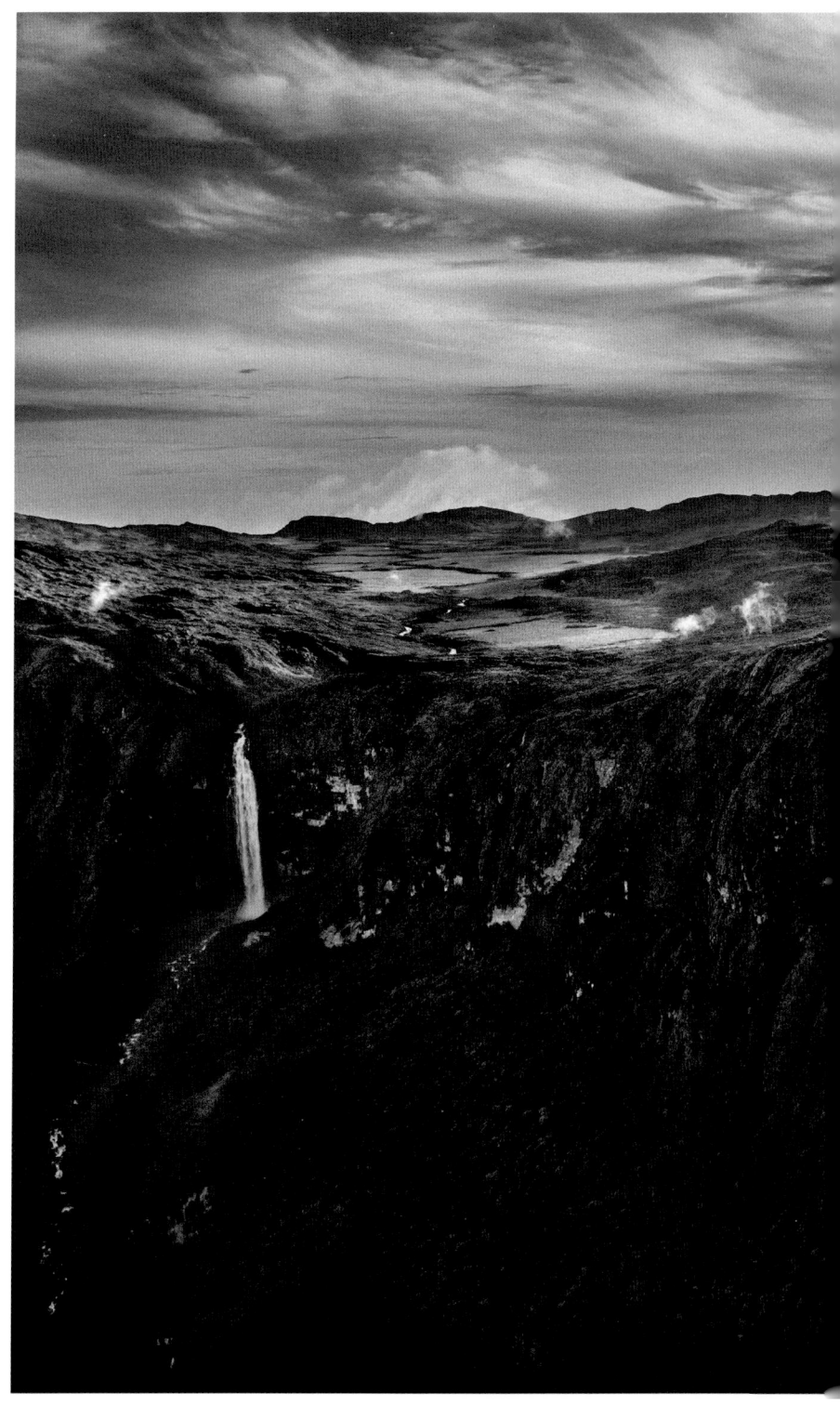

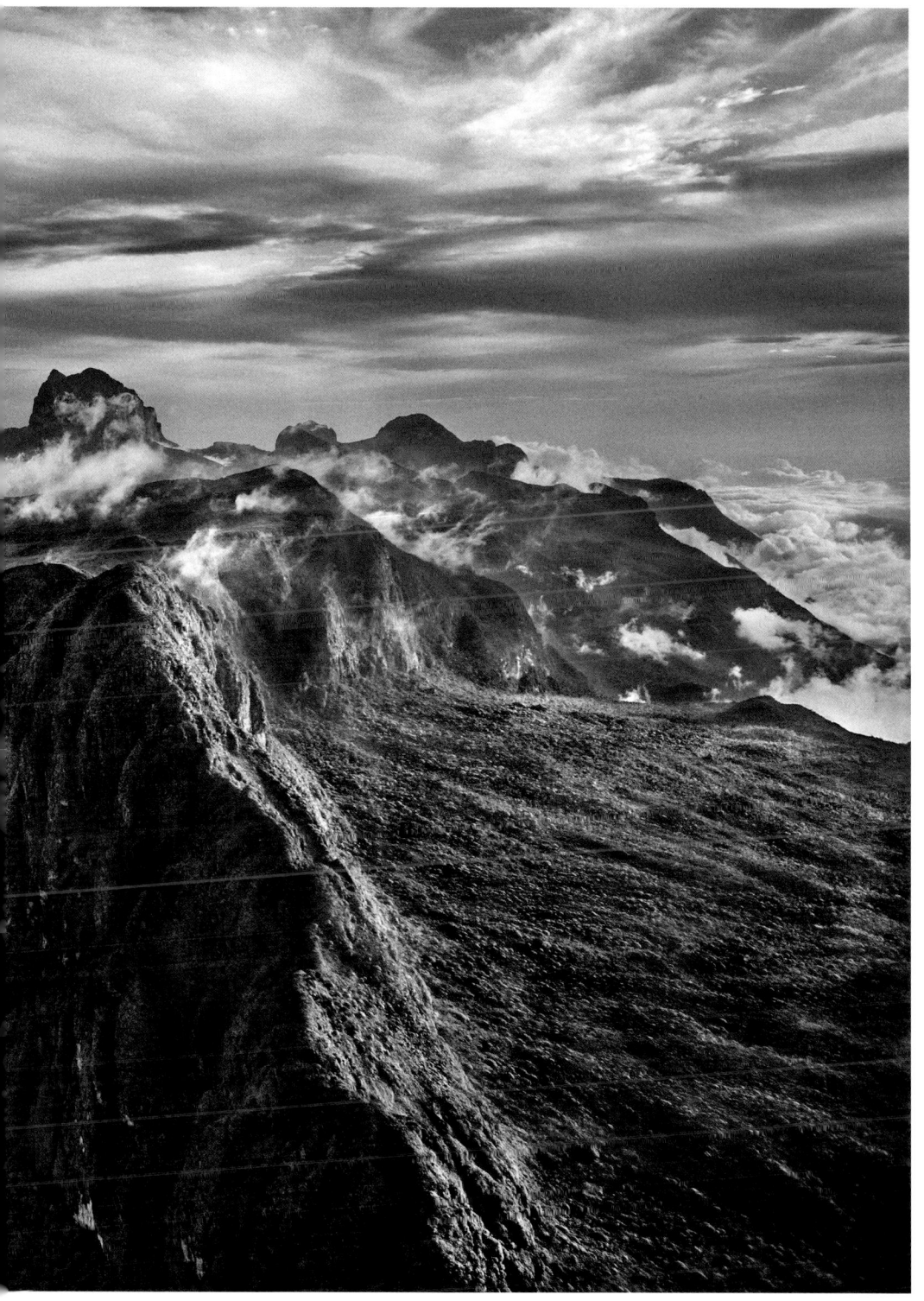

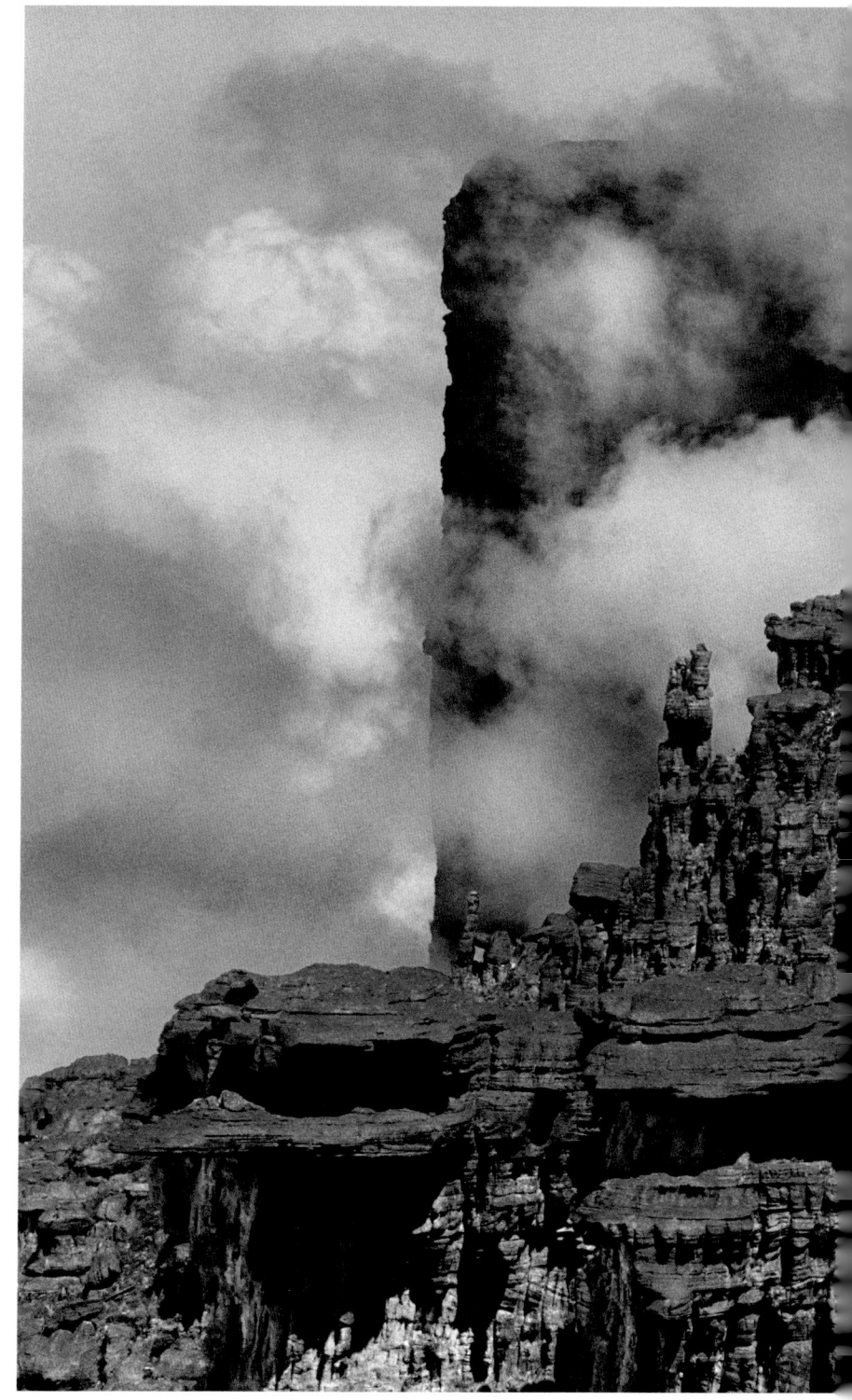

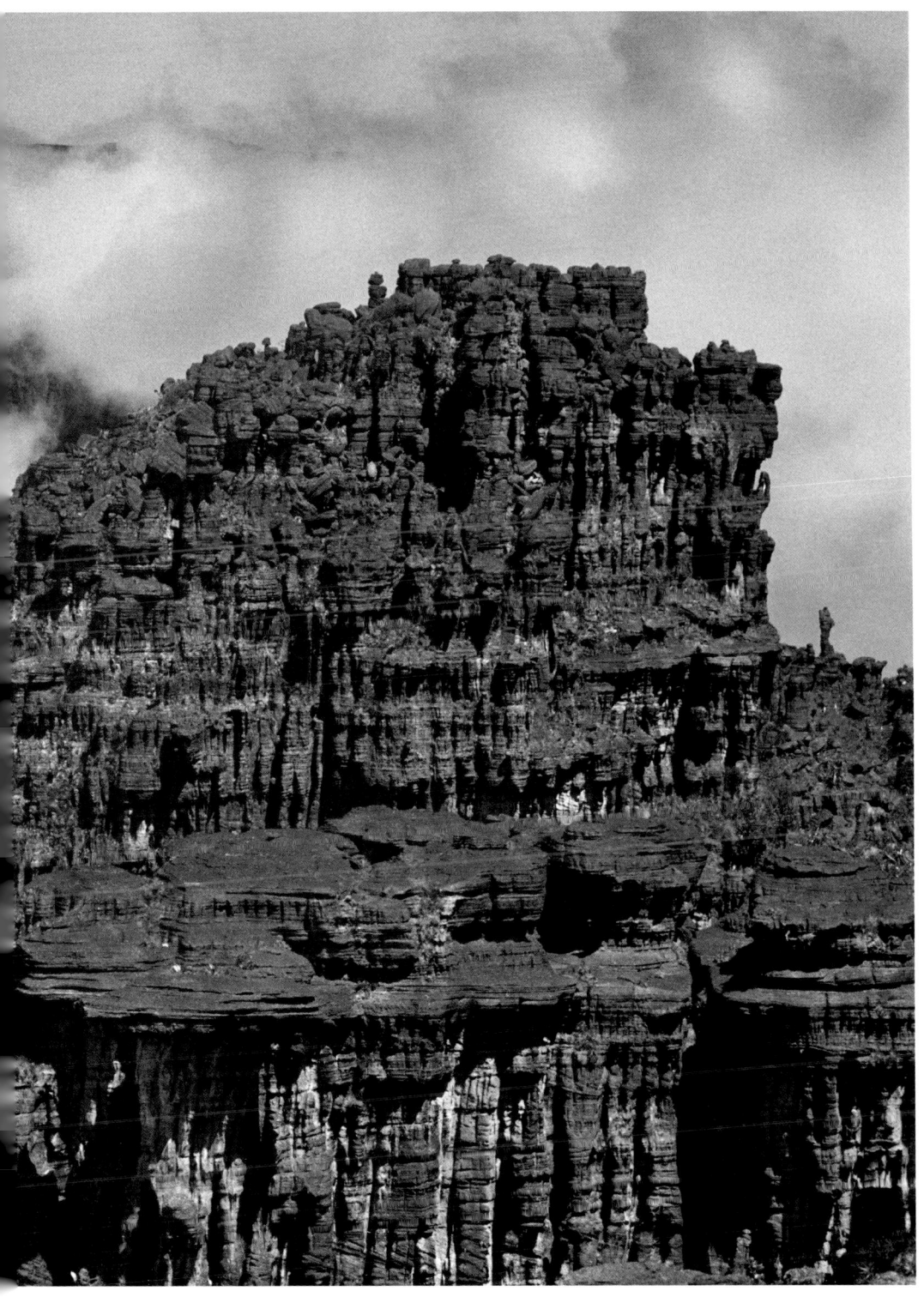

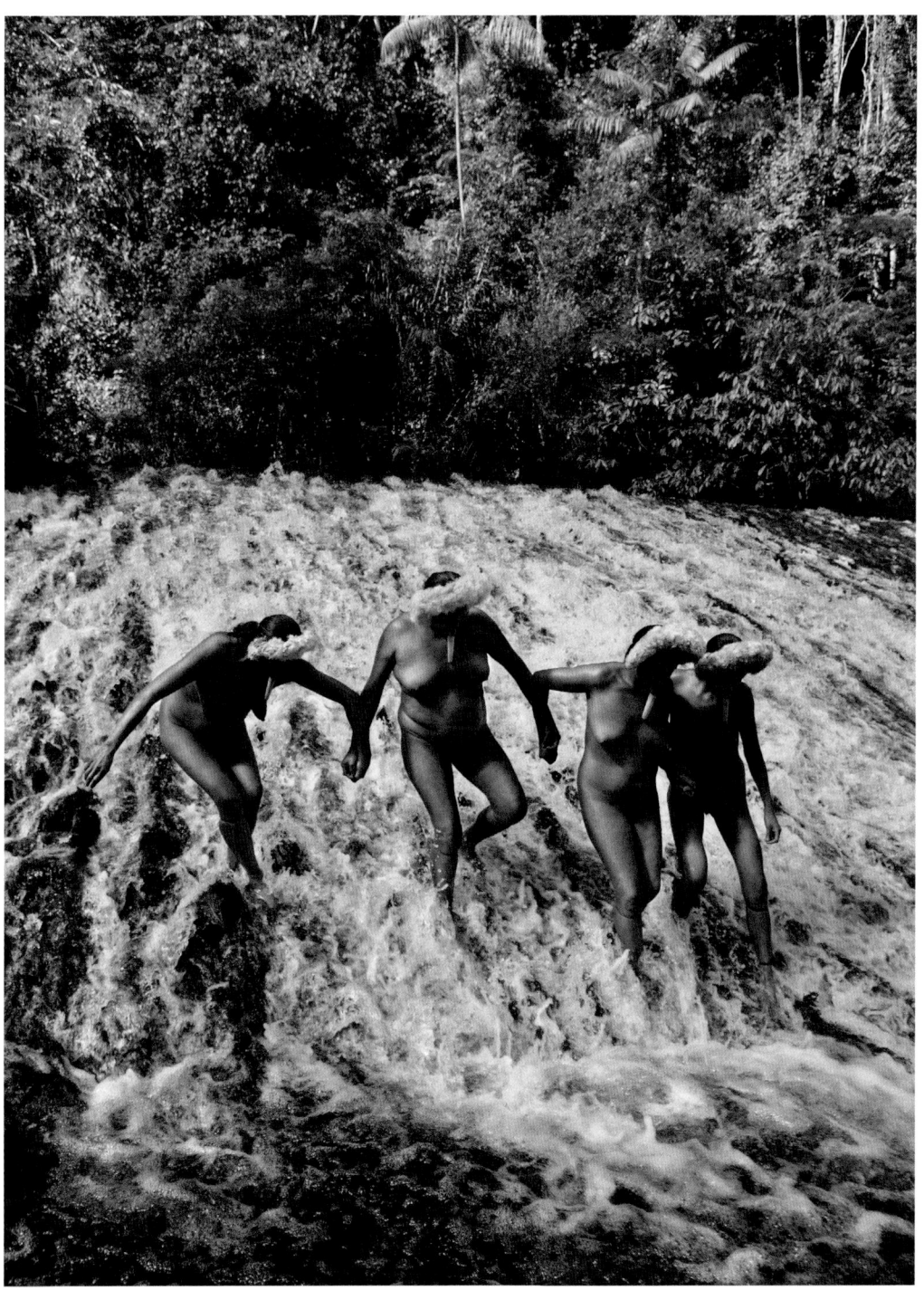

Opposite The Zo'é, an isolated indigenous people in the northern Amazon region, place great importance on their cleanliness. All the paths and trails from their settlement lead to water sources; their excursions, whether for hunting, fishing or gathering, are regularly interrupted by breaks for bathing in brooks and streams. Pará, Brazil. March and April 2009.

Pages 424/425 The Pantanal, one of the world's largest wetlands, covering a vast area of western Brazil and spilling into Paraguay and Bolivia, is home to an estimated 10 million yacare caimans (*Caiman yacare*). At the end of the dry season, they concentrate in small lakes, such as seen here at the Porto Alegre estate in the region of Porto Jofre, where 5,000 to 8,000 are gathered. Measuring between 7 and 10 feet (2 and 3 meters) long, they feed on fish, mollusks and shellfish. Although the Pantanal boasts the largest population of caimans on Earth, they have been declared a threatened species because of uncontrolled hunting, mainly in Paraguay and Bolivia. Pantanal. Mato Grosso, Brazil. September and October 2011.

Pages 426/427 The Amazon forest and a tributary of the Rio Negro in the region of São Gabriel da Cachoeira in the state of Amazonas. Brazil. August and September 2009.

Pages 428/429 The jaguar (*Panthera onca*), the largest cat of the Americas, is to be found mainly in the Amazon rainforest although also in the Pantanal and its adjoining plain known as the Gran Chaco. Jaguars vary in size between 44 and 73 inches (112 and 185 centimeters), with the average male weighing 265 pounds (120 kilos) (although some in the Pantanal weigh as much as 330 pounds / 150 kilos). In the cat family, only lions and tigers are larger. This jaguar was seen beside the Tagoarira River, in the region of Porto Jofre. Encontro das Águas National Park. Pantanal, Mato Grosso, Brazil. September and October 2011.

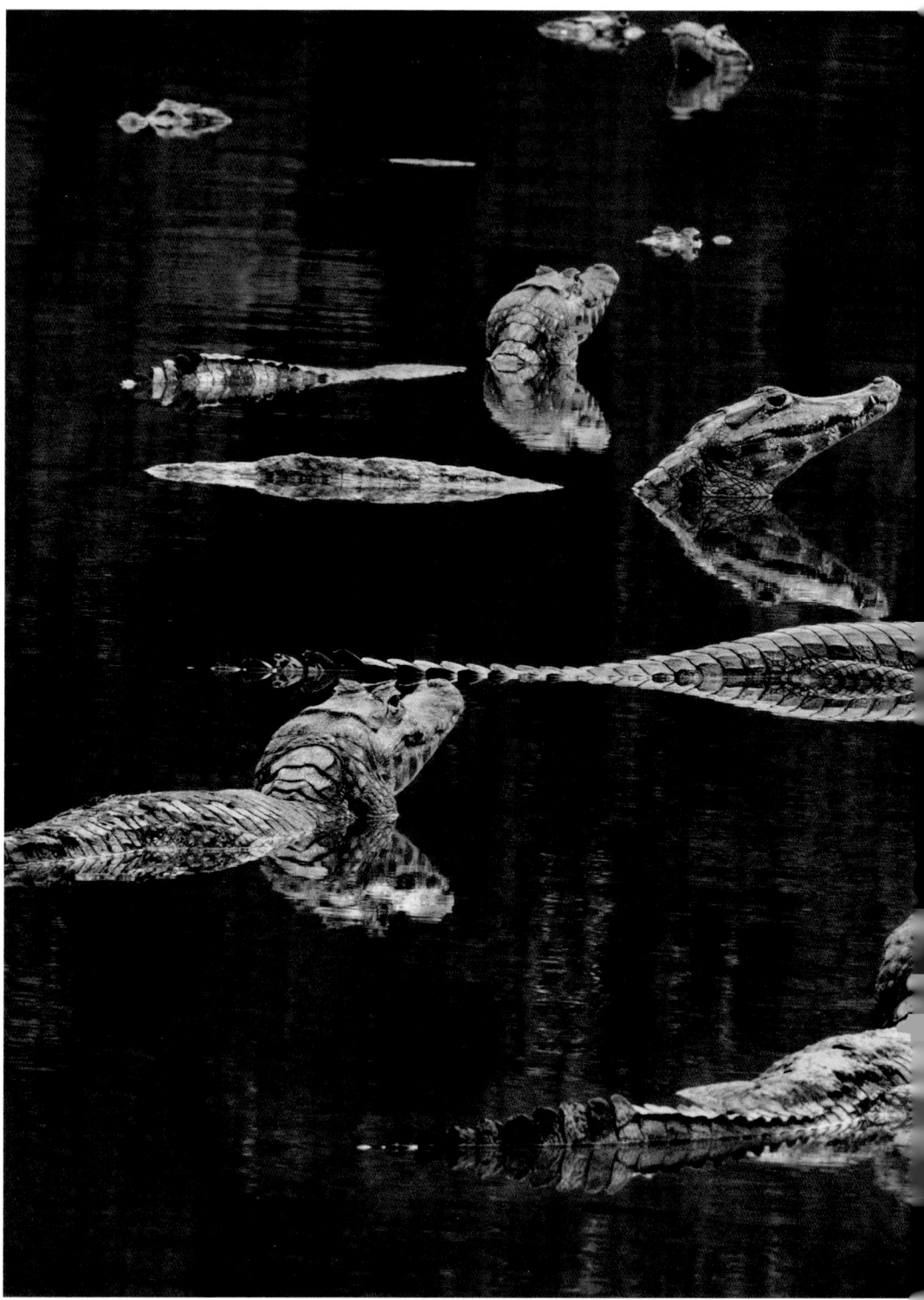

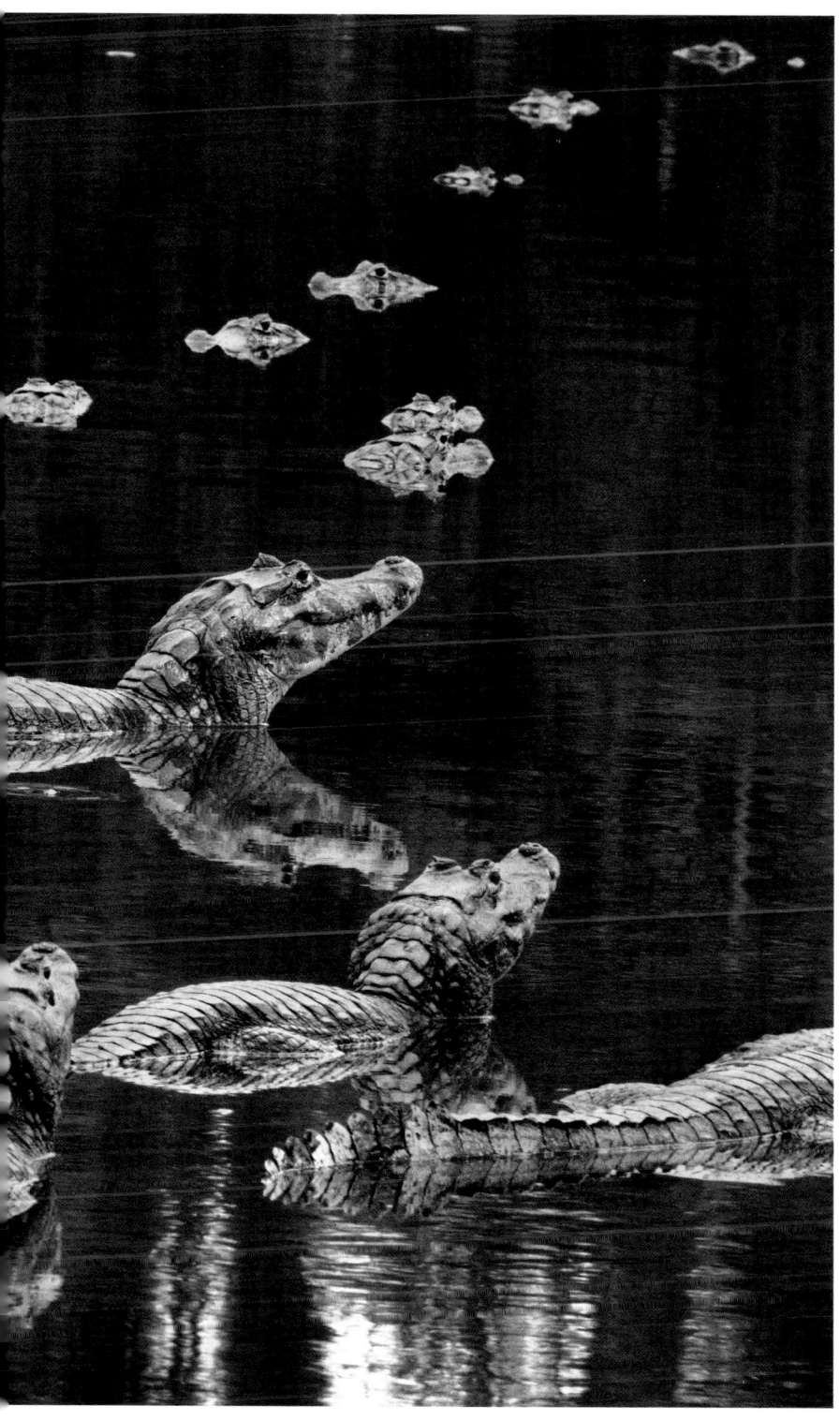

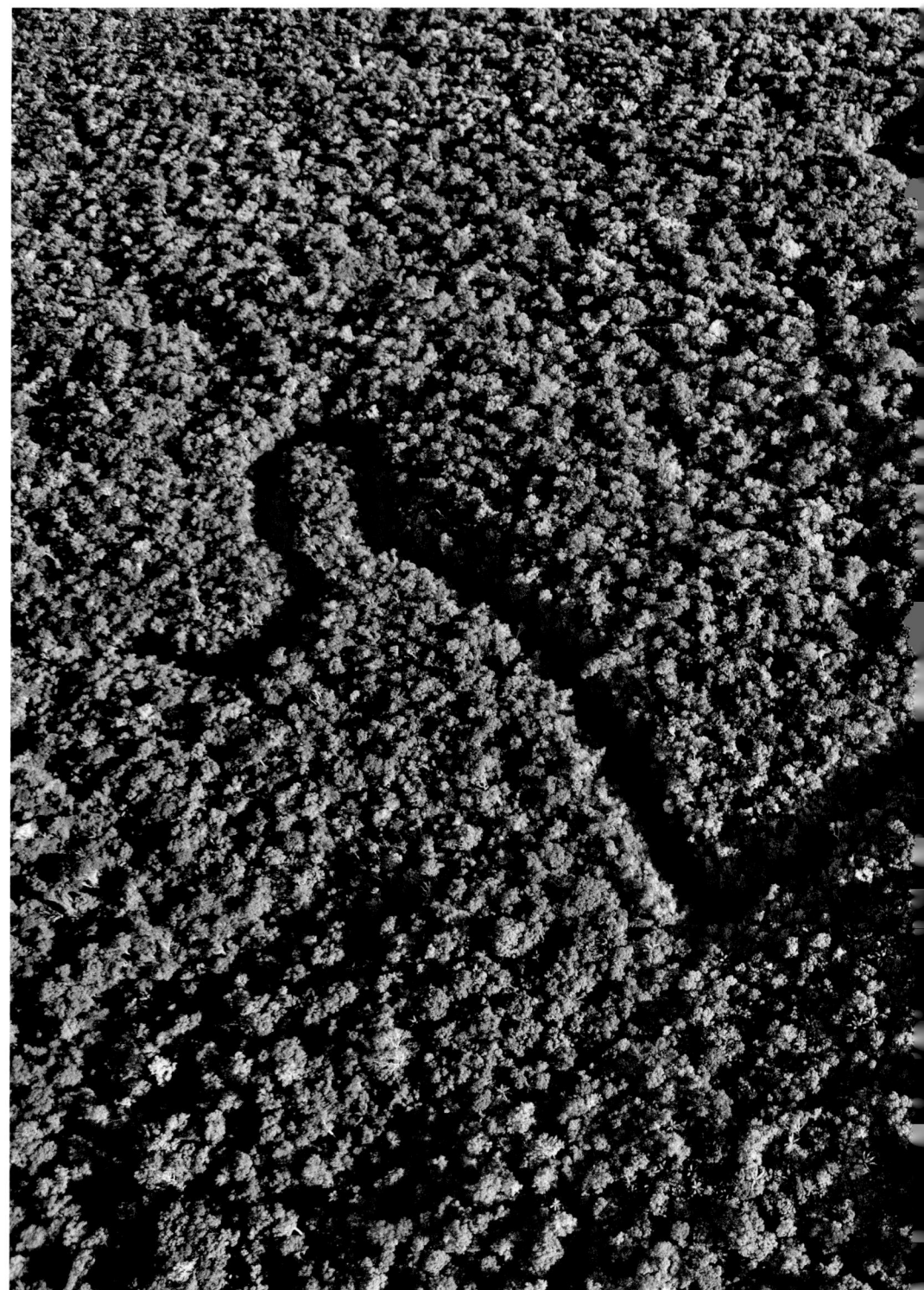

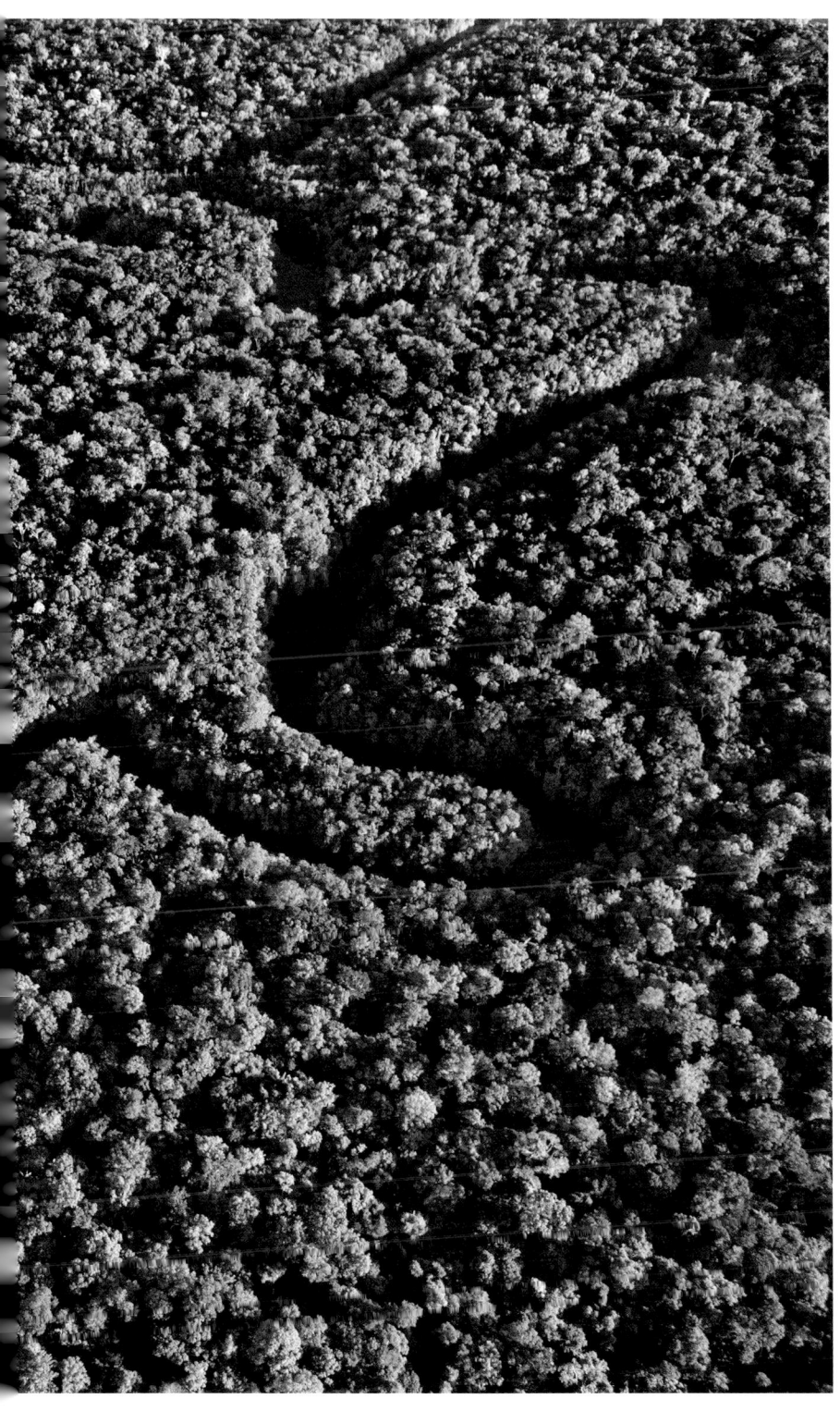

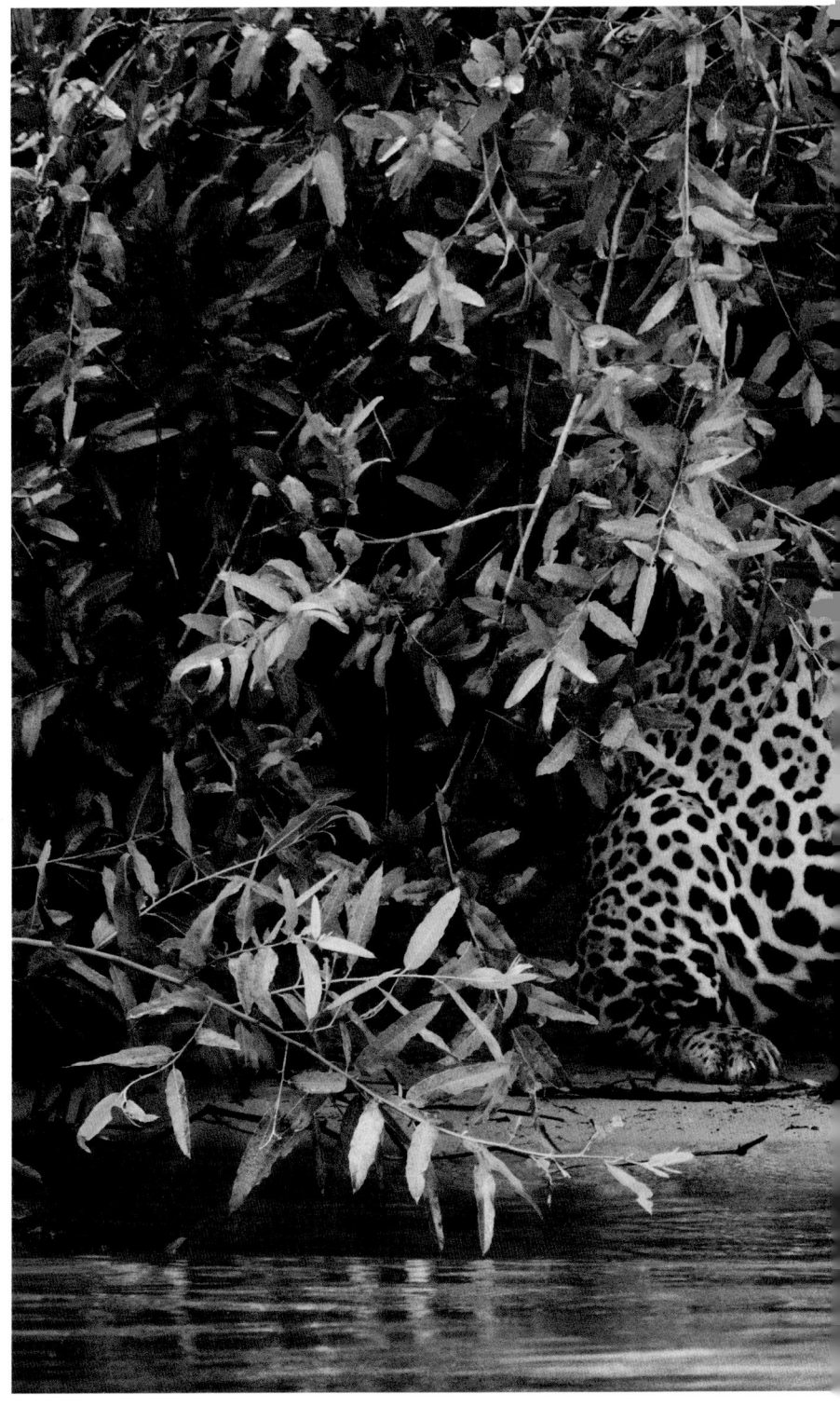

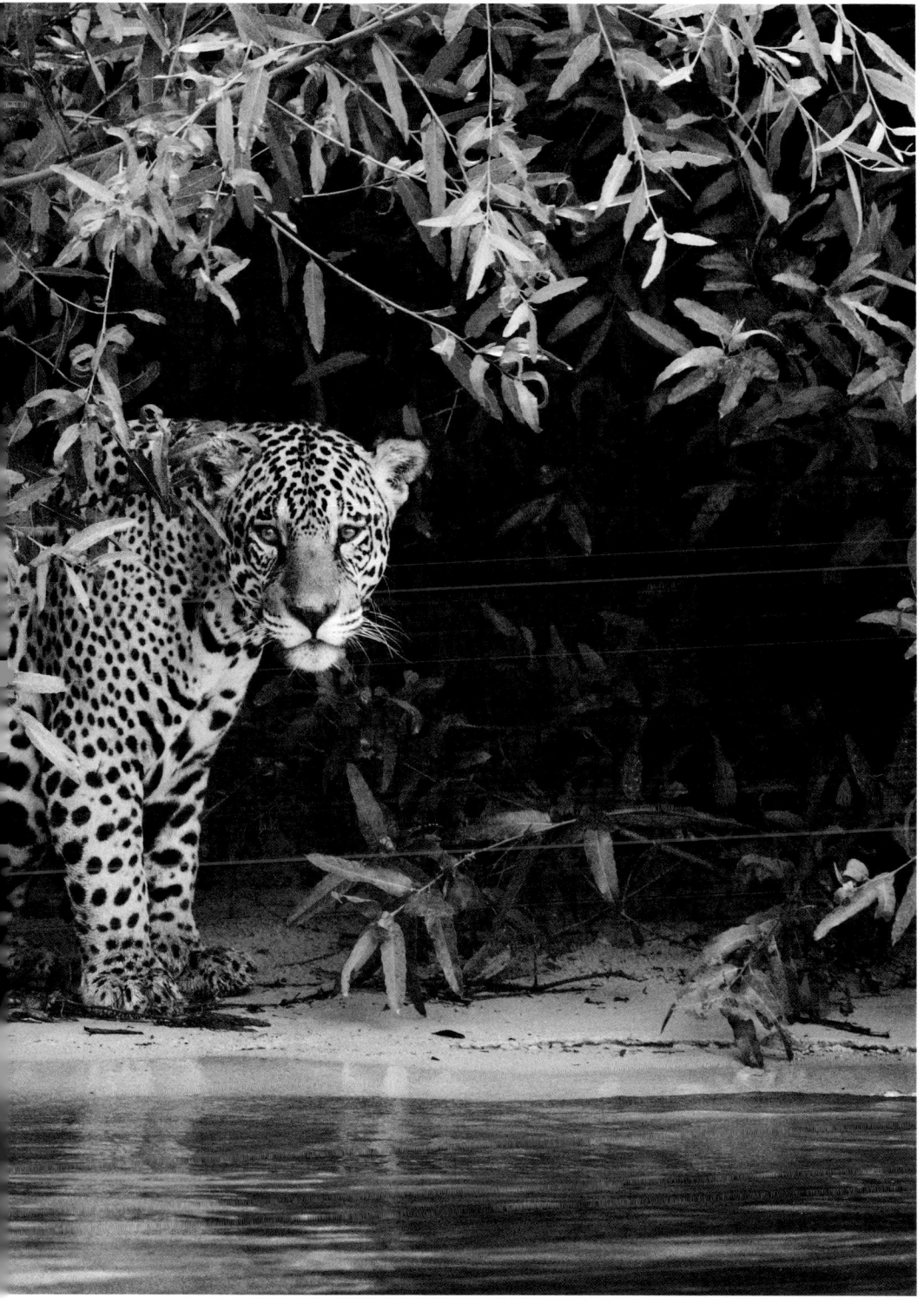

THE ZO'É

Pages 431 through 439
The Zo'é live deep in the rainforest of the northern Brazilian state of Pará in an area stretching between the Erepecuru and Cuminapanema rivers, both northern tributaries of the Amazon. Since they belong to the Tupi-Guarani linguistic group, traditionally settled near the Atlantic coast, it seems likely that the Zo'é migrated west several thousand years ago. They were contacted in 1987 by American evangelists from the New Tribes Mission. Intent on converting the Indians to their version of Christianity, they began by handing out presents such as clothes, machetes and mirrors, and by building the first landing strip in the area.

But within three years, the FUNAI, the Brazilian government agency responsible for protecting indigenous peoples, expelled the New Tribes Mission from the Zo'é lands. FUNAI subsequently created the so-called Ethno-environmental Front for the Protection of Cuminapanema with the specific mandate of preventing any further invasion of Zo'é territory.

In 2009, the Zo'é were granted ownership of 2,400 square miles (6,240 square kilometers) of land in the form of a protected reserve. Further protection is provided by a 12-mile (20-kilometer)-wide band of land around the perimeter of the reserve, which can only be crossed with special permission. Pará, Brazil. March and April 2009.

Opposite The Zo'é capture very young wild pigs when they hunt adult females. These piglets are then raised as pets, which also provide villagers with protection from jaguars. Pará, Brazil. March and April 2009.

Pages 432/433 Some birds, monkeys and turtles are kept by the Zo'é as pets. Pará, Brazil. March and April 2009.

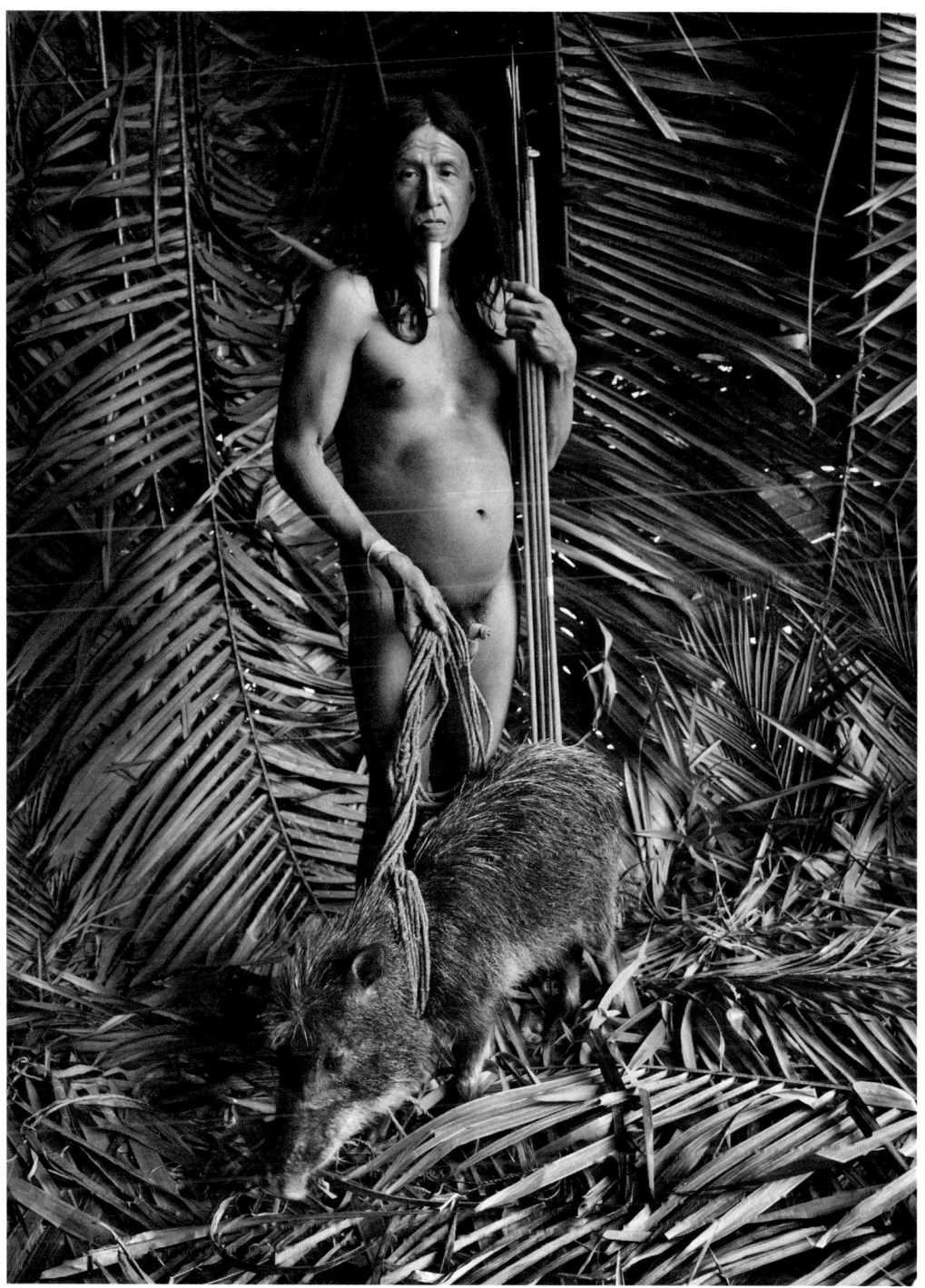

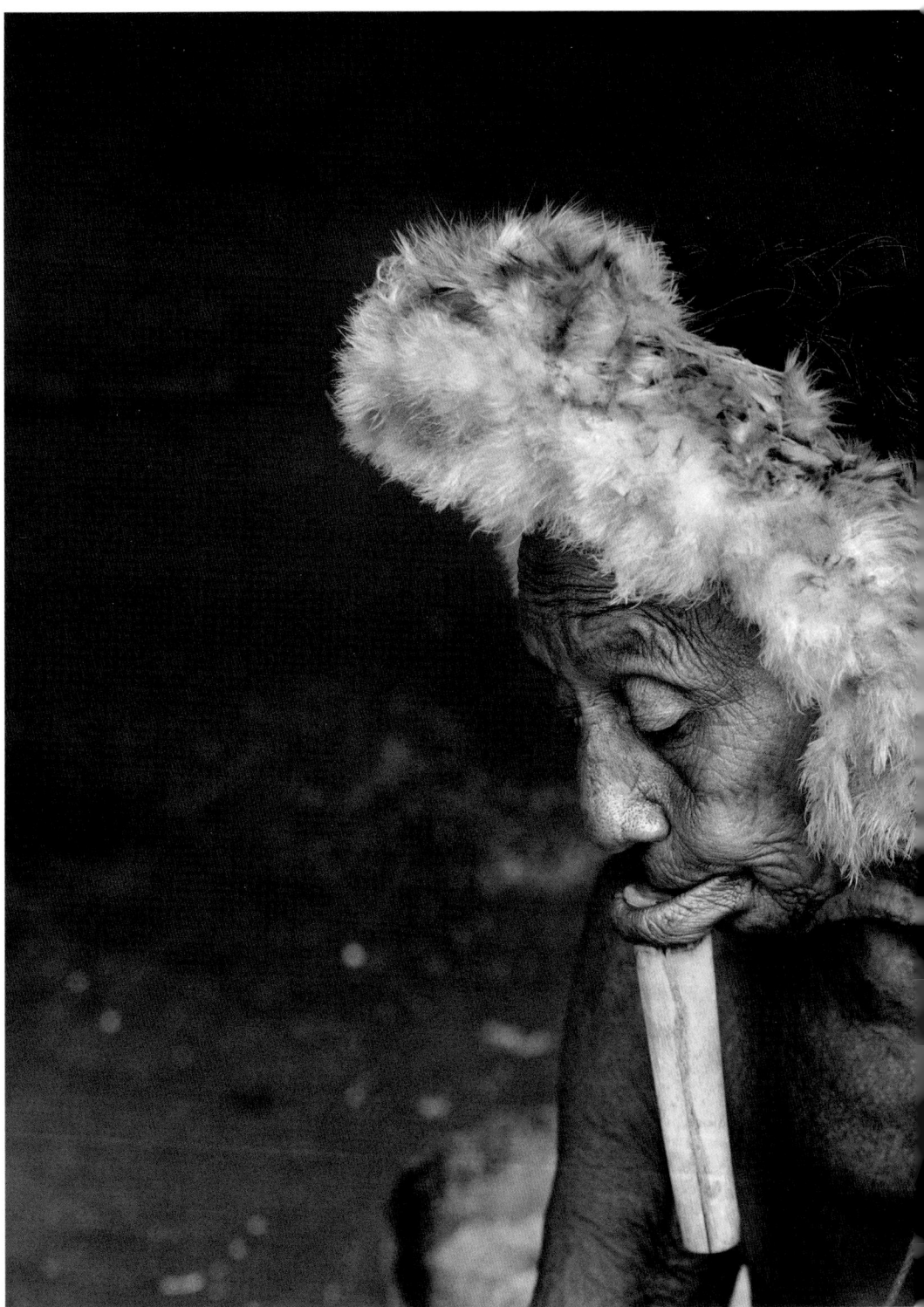

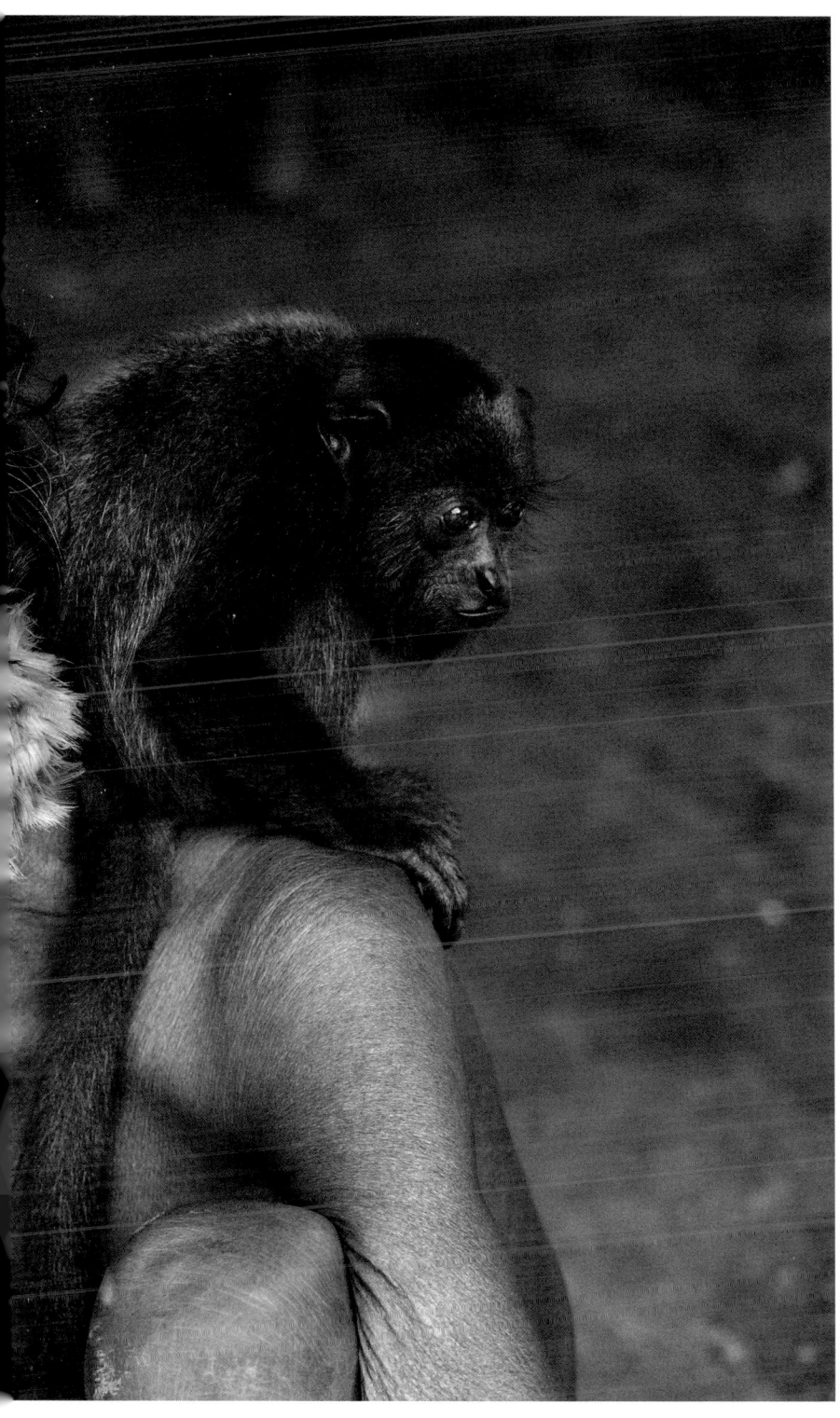

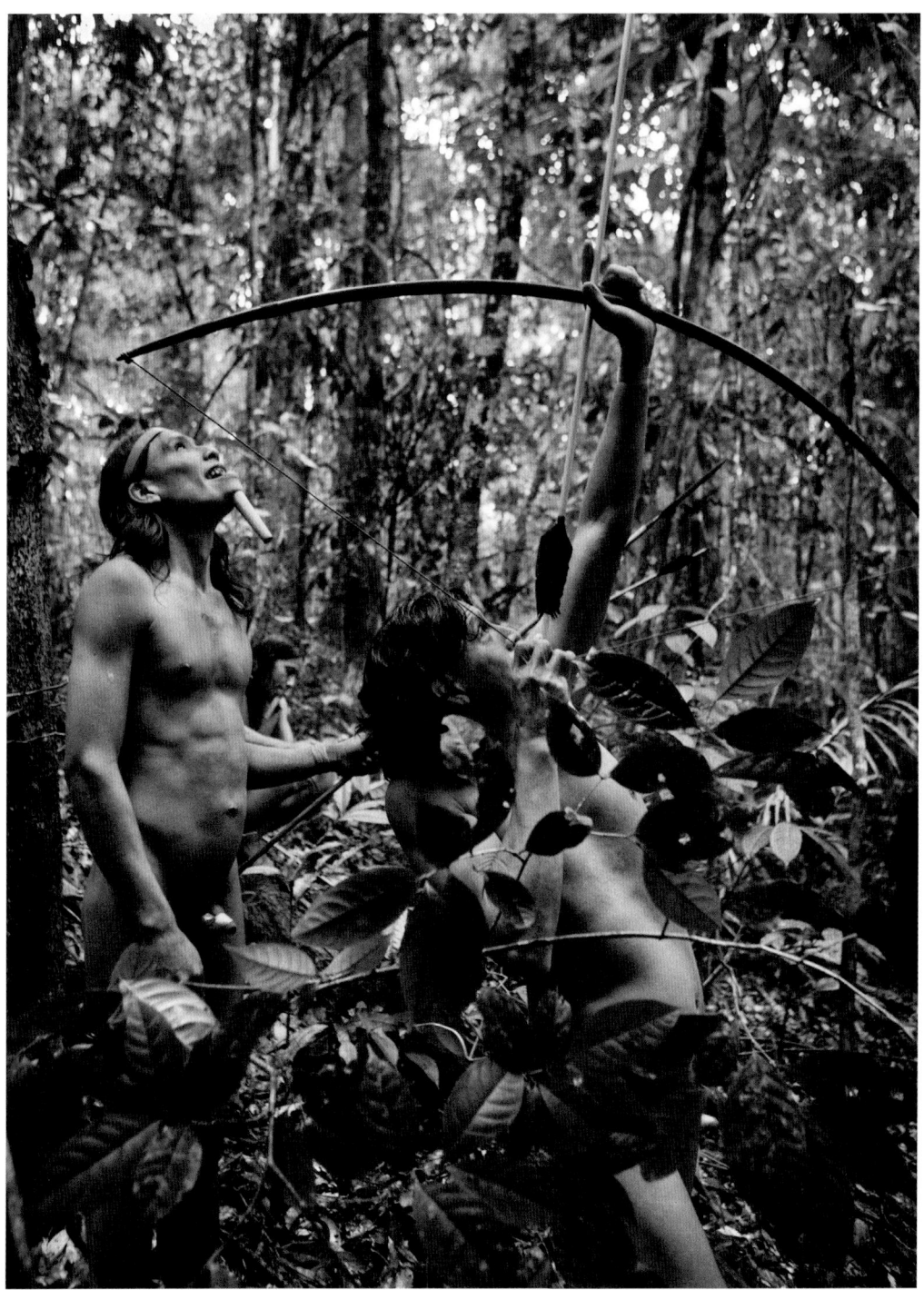

Opposite Zo'é hunting practices vary with the season. This photograph was taken during the rainy season in March and April. Since this is not a good time for fishing, the Zo'é hunt monkeys, who are much sought after for their meat. Then, in June, they begin hunting wild pigs. Pará, Brazil. March and April 2009,

Pages 436/437 Even after a monkey is shot by an arrow, it may not fall from the tree, so the hunter must be ready to climb up to collect it and, if it is only wounded, to kill it. In this photograph, with his bow and arrow at the ready, the hunter is hurriedly climbing to follow his prey, a monkey, who has already leapt to an adjacent tree. Pará, Brazil. March and April 2009.

Pages 438/439 The Zo'é, an isolated Indian people in the northern Amazon region, give great importance to their cleanliness. All the paths and trails from their settlement lead to water sources; their excursions, whether for hunting, fishing or gathering, are regularly interrupted by breaks for bathing in brooks and streams. Pará, Brazil. March and April 2009.

Pages 440/441 The Pantanal, one of the world's largest wetlands, covering a vast area of western Brazil and spilling into Paraguay and Bolivia, is home to an estimated 10 million yacare caimans (*Caiman yacare*). At the end of the dry season, they concentrate in small lakes, such as seen here at the Porto Alegre estate in the region of Porto Jofre, where 5,000 to 8,000 are gathered. Measuring between 7 and 10 feet (2 and 3 meters) long, they feed on fish, mollusks and shellfish. Although the Pantanal boasts the largest population of caimans on Earth, they have been declared a threatened species because of uncontrolled hunting, mainly in Paraguay and Bolivia. Pantanal. Mato Grosso, Brazil. September and October 2011.

Pages 442/443 The Roraima Tepui, which straddles the borders of southeastern Venezuela, Brazil and Guyana, has a surface of almost 14 square miles (35 square kilometers) and rises to a height 8,933 feet of (2,723 meters). The photograph shows its best-known feature, its so-called prow, which reaches into Guyana. *Tepui*, a Pemon Indian word for mountain, is now commonly used to describe a particular type of flat-topped mountain to be found in this region of South America. Varying in height between 3,300 and 9,800 feet (1,000 and 3,000 meters), the mesa or plateau of tepuis often have a unique ecosystem characterized by endemic animals and plants. Venezuela. November and December 2006.

Pages 444/445 Carnivorous plants. The *Drosera roraimea*—sundew. On the plateau of *tepuis*, large expanses of rock offer harsh conditions for plant life. With extreme changes in temperature and precipitation, only hardy algae, lichens and mosses survive on rock surfaces. But larger plants can grow in crevices or in hollows where small amounts of soil and other debris provide root substrates. The poor soil on *tepui* summits even prompts some plant species to capture and digest small insects to supplement their diet. Venezuela. November and December 2006.

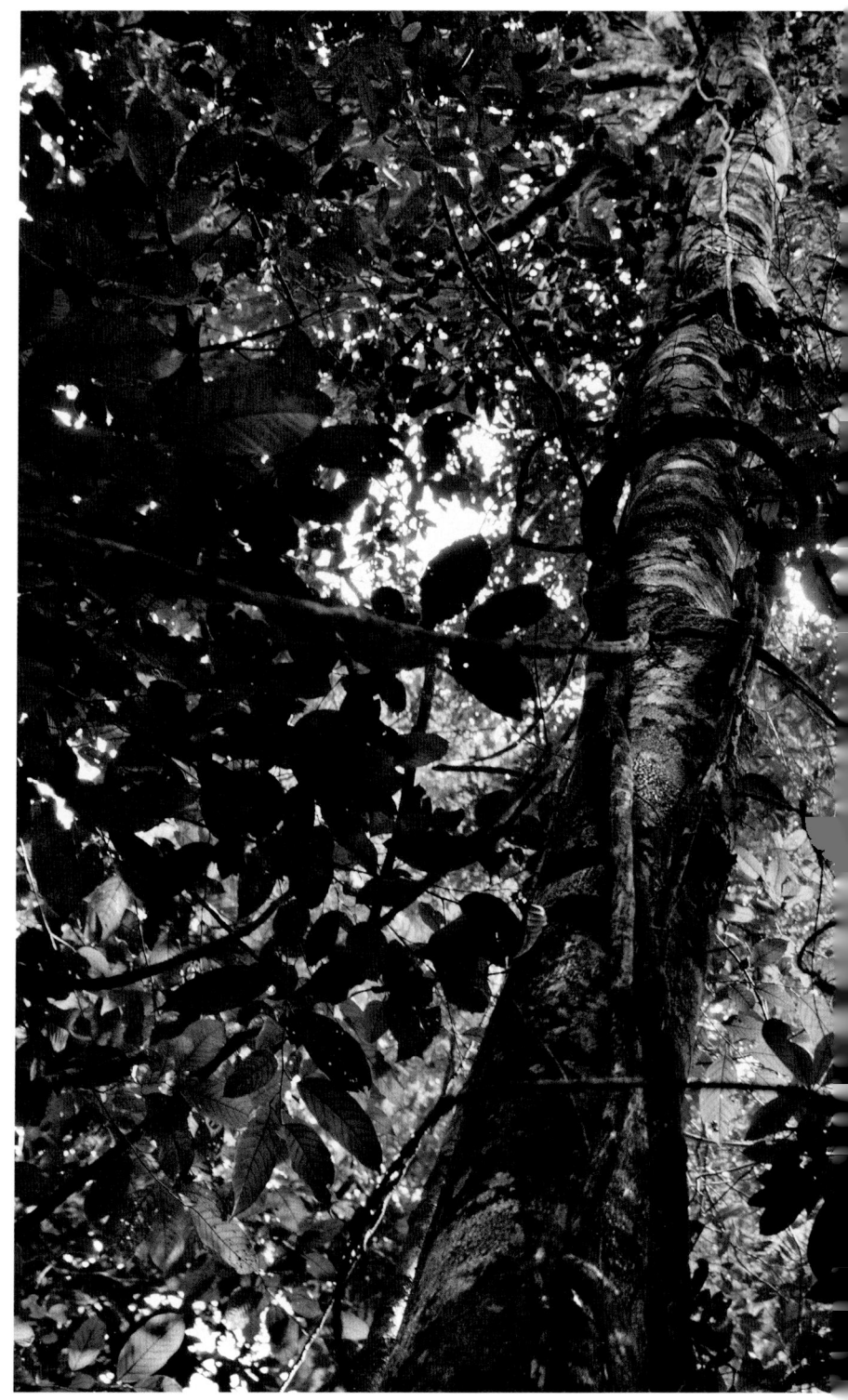

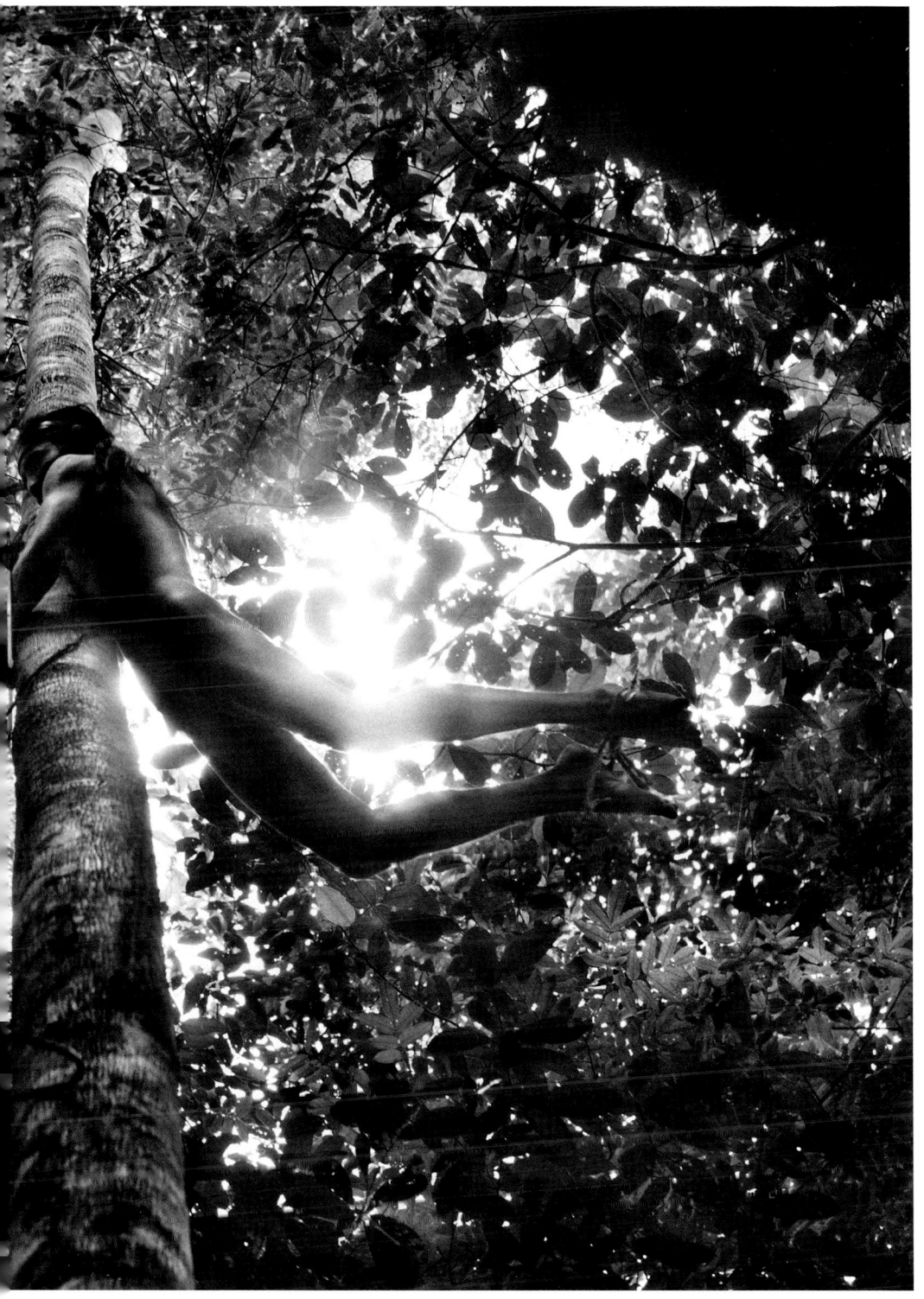

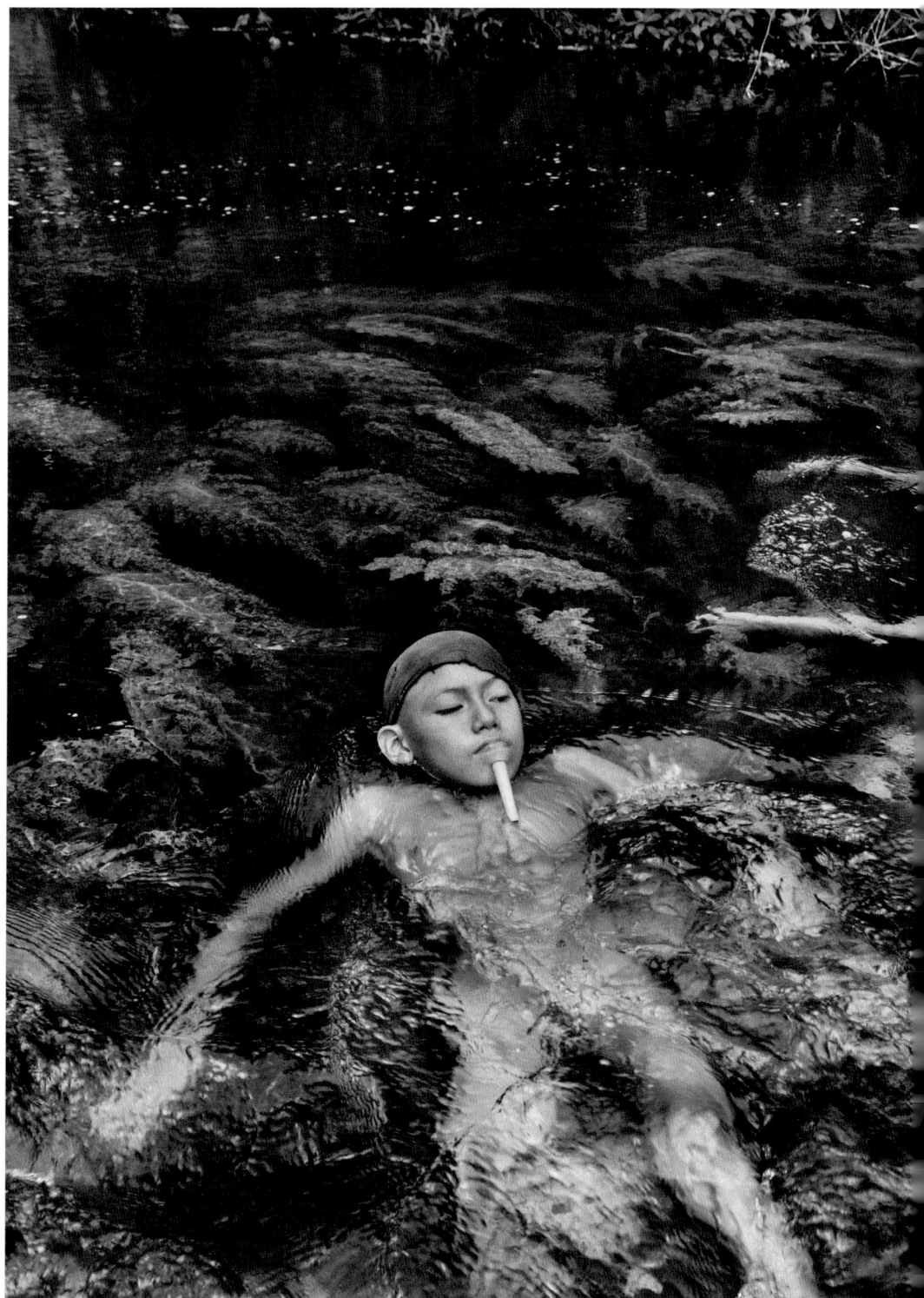

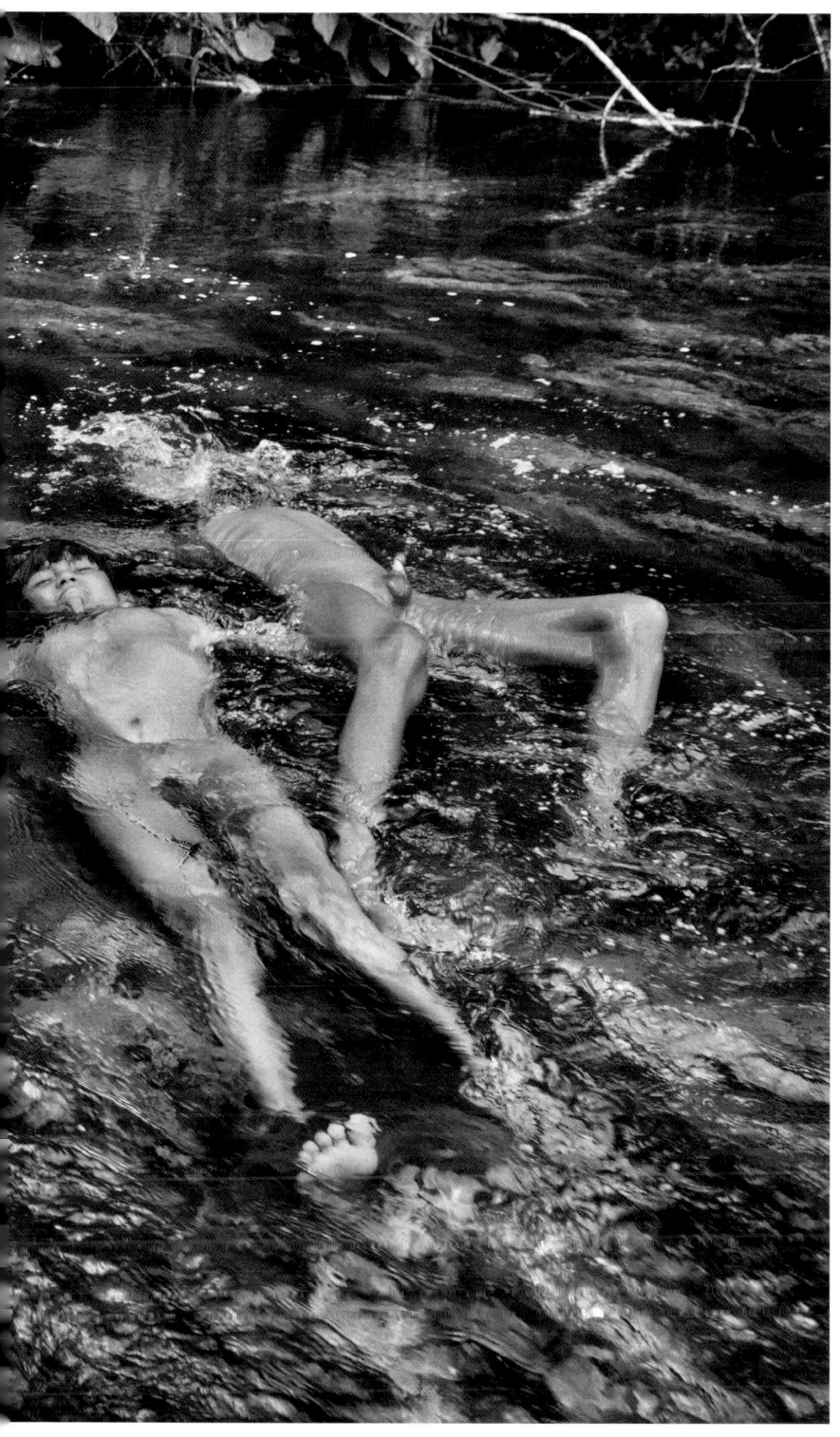

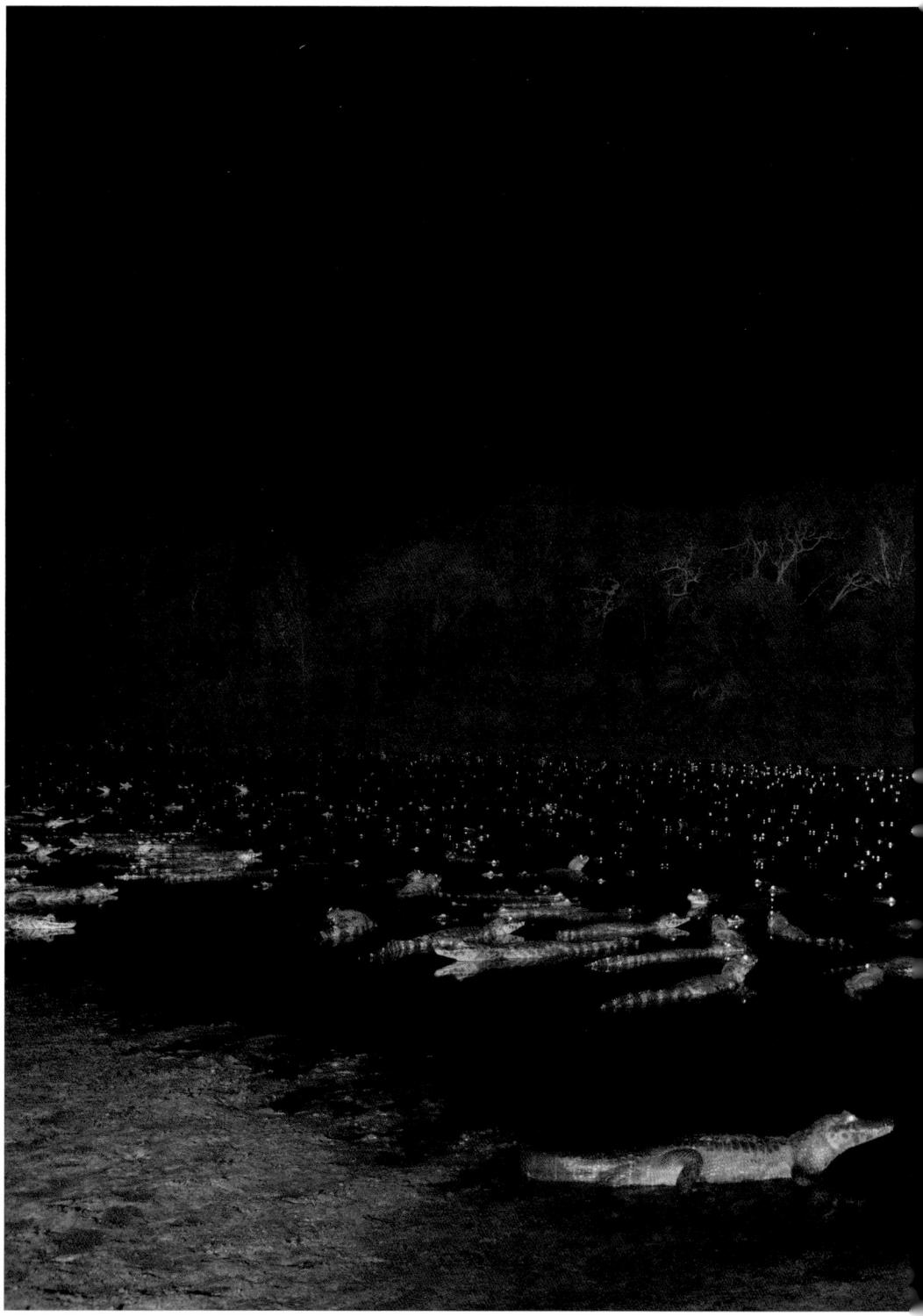

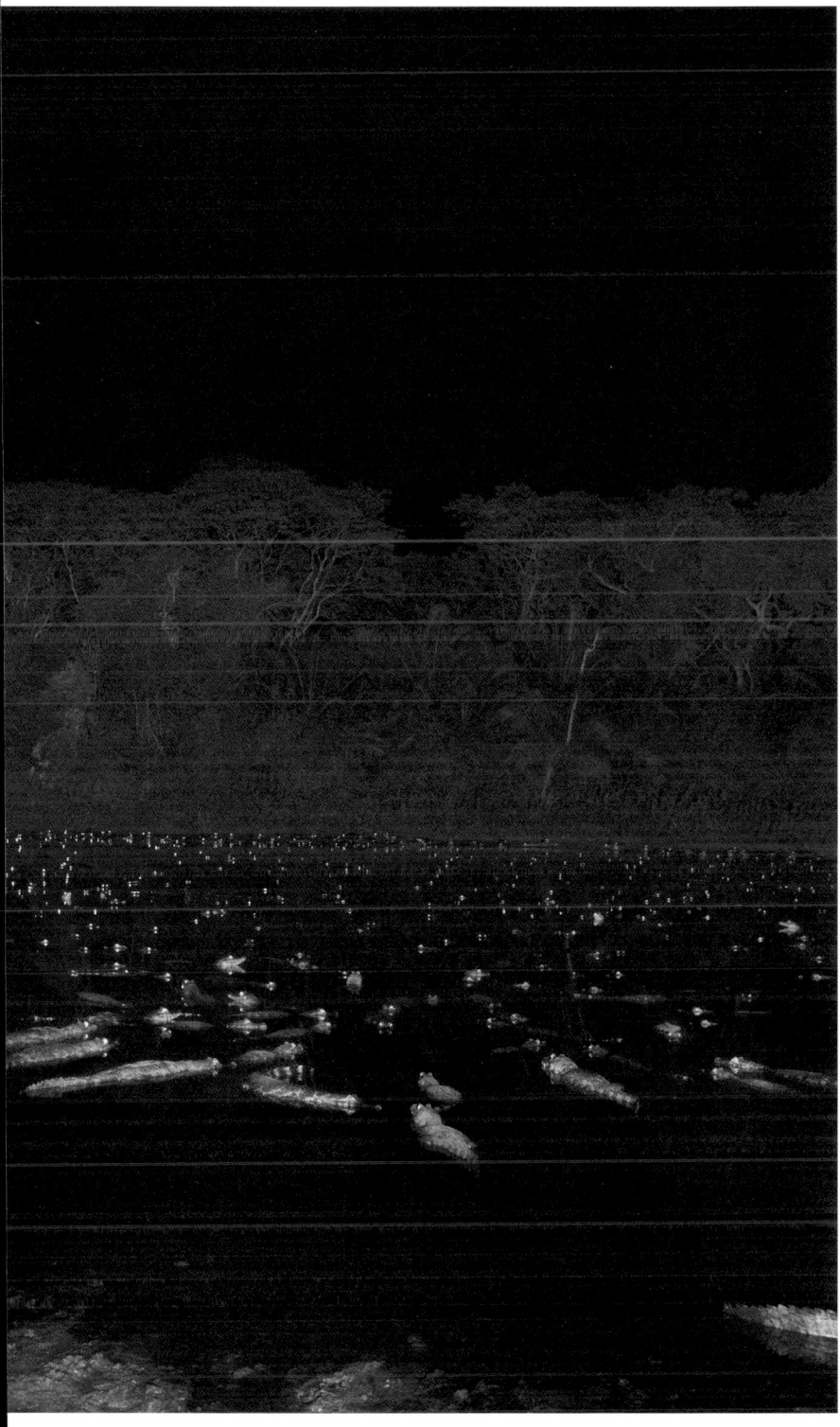

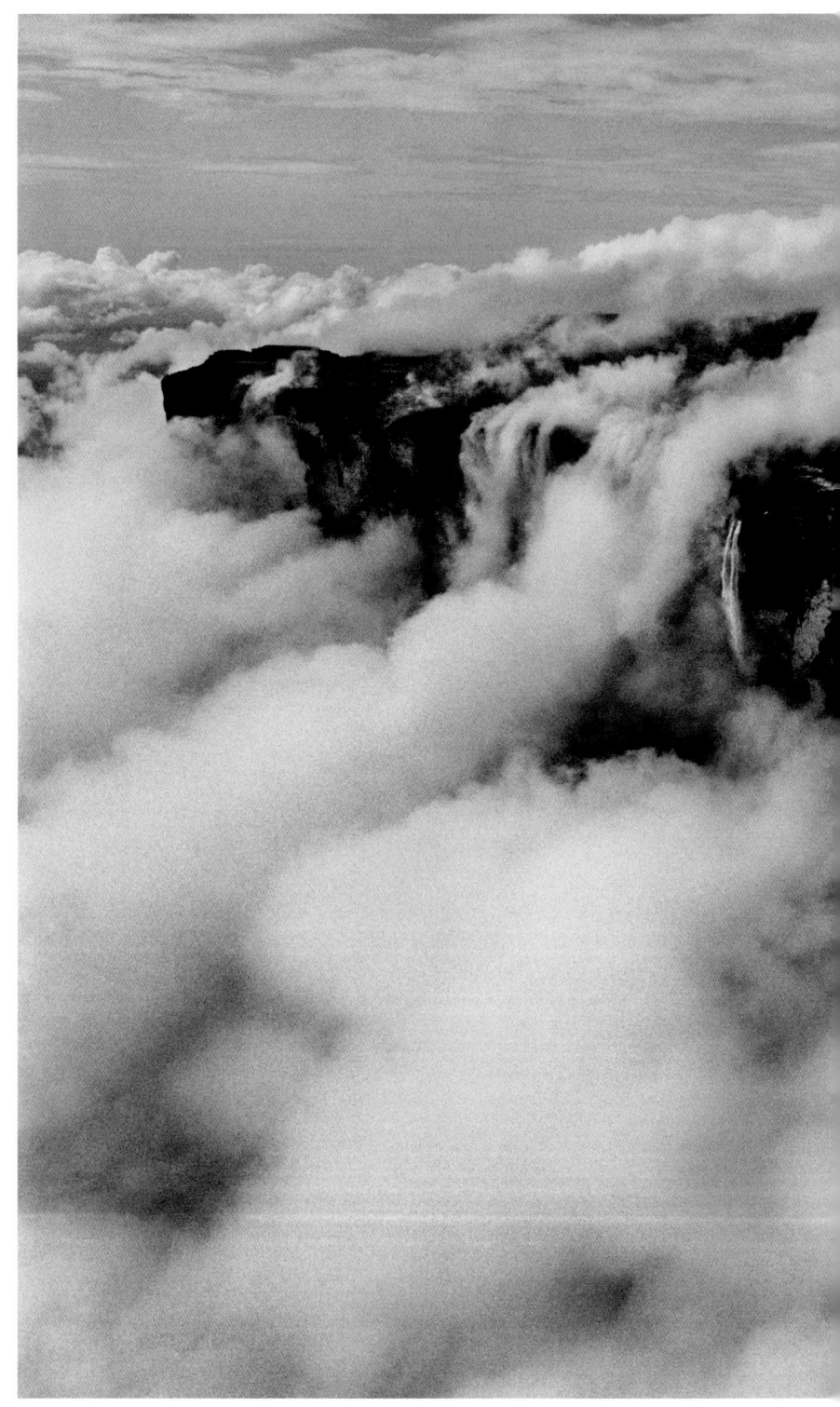

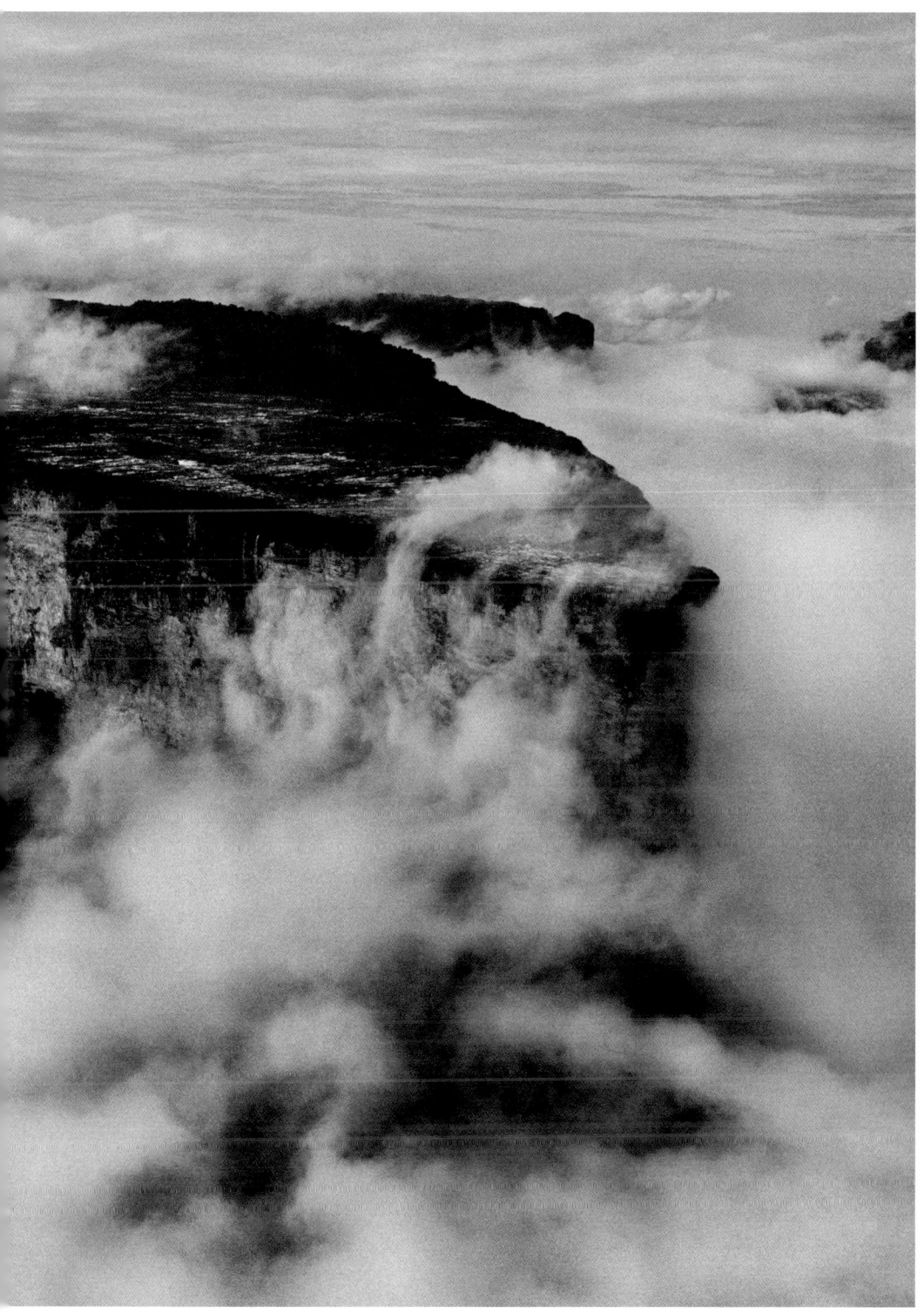

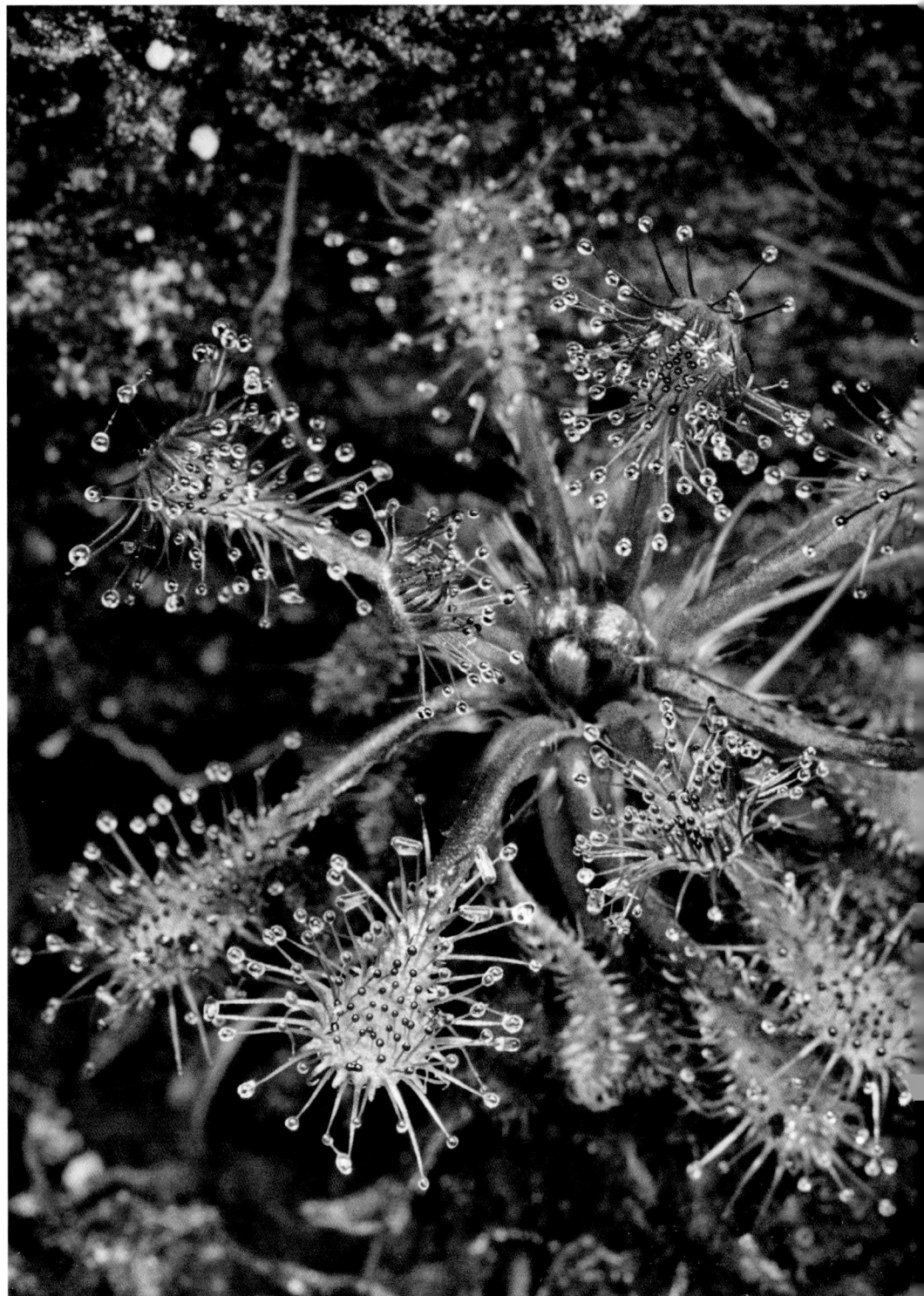

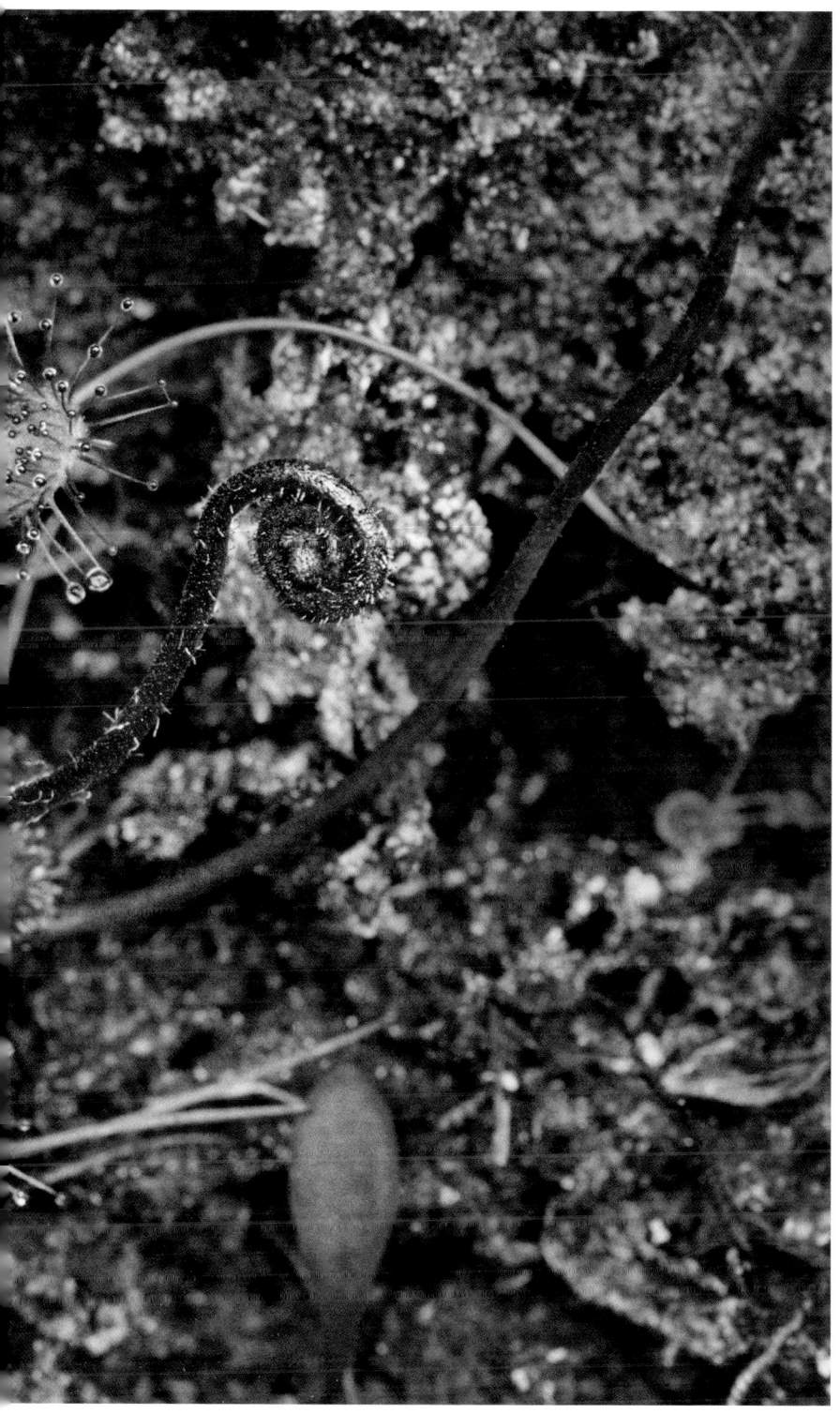

445

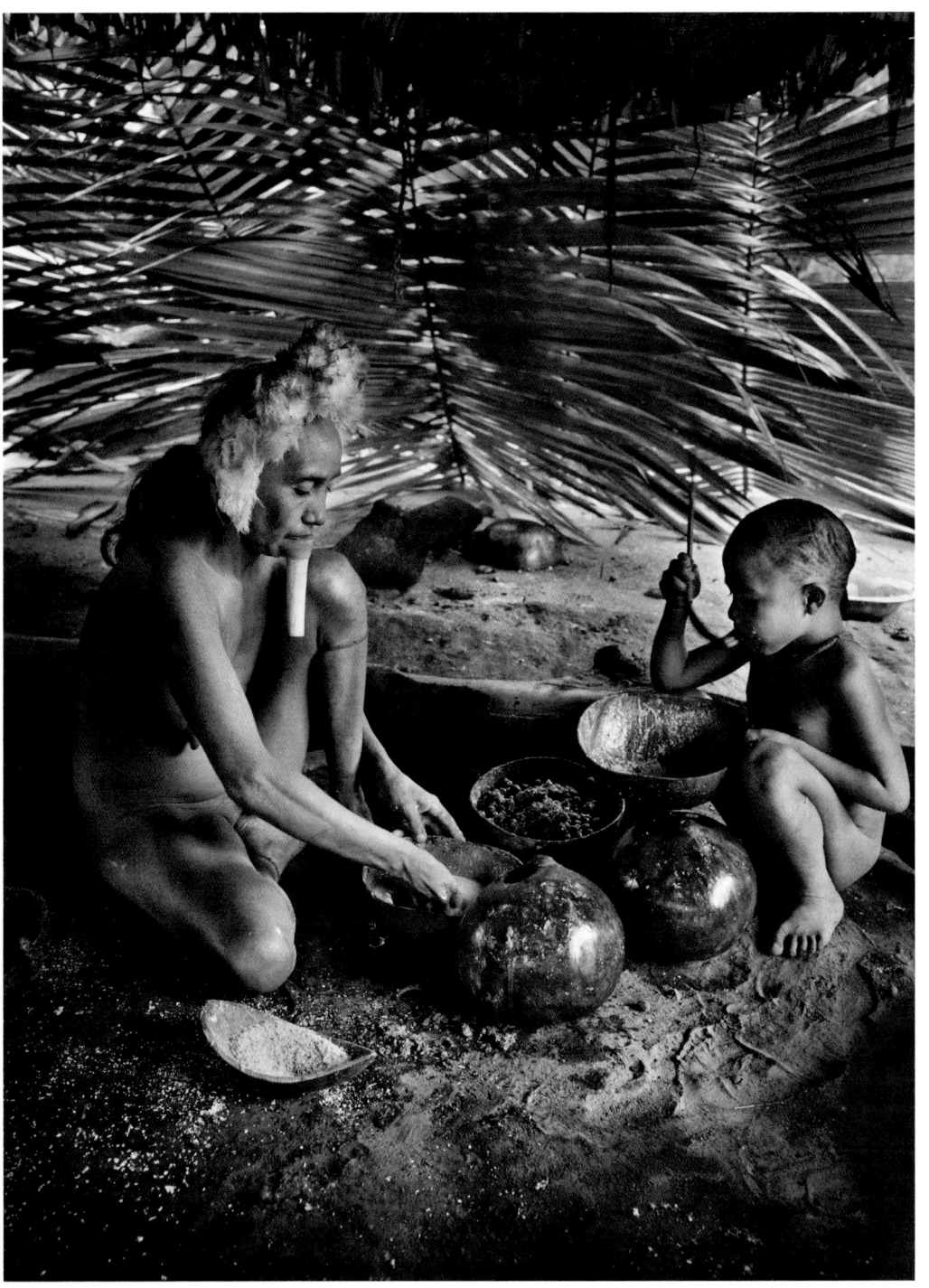

Opposite To mix or prepare their food, the Zo'é use a variety of utensils, such as gourds, the shells of nuts and the skulls and bones of monkeys. Pará, Brazil. March and April 2009.

Pages 448/449 Seen from on high, the jungle seems impenetrable, but the reality on the ground can be different. The Zo'é people, who number between 250 to 275, live in some 10 small villages which are connected by numerous trails, giving them easy access between communities. Pará, Brazil. March and April 2009.

Pages 450/451 The *garça moura*, or Cocoi heron (*Ardea cocoi*), with its stunning 4-foot (1.2-meter) wingspan, is common across the Pantanal, and is often to be found fishing alone in coastal estuaries and mangroves as well as on riverbanks and in marshes and oxbow lakes. One is shown here on the Mata Cachorro River. Pantanal, Mato Grosso do Sul, Brazil. September and October 2011.

Pages 452/453 Ariranha or giant otter (*Pteronura brasiliensis*). Giant otters—males can measure 5 feet (1.6 meters) long—live along rivers with exposed banks, where they dig dens for family groups of five to nine members. Excellent swimmers, they dive for fish and also eat crustaceans, mollusks, snakes and baby caimans. Gestation takes from 60 to 70 days, with one to five babies born; the young leave the group after their first year of life. This region has two other species of otter, the neotropical and the tayra. Pantanal, Mato Grosso, Brazil. September and October 2011.

Pages 454/455 Typically, the women in the Zo'é village of Towari Ypy use the red fruit of the *urucum* (*Bixa orellana*) to color their bodies. It is also used in cooking. The *urucum* is a shrub or small tree originating from tropical regions of the Americas. It has long been used by American Indians as body paint, especially for the lips, thus earning the nickname of "lipstick tree." Pará, Brazil. March and April 2009.

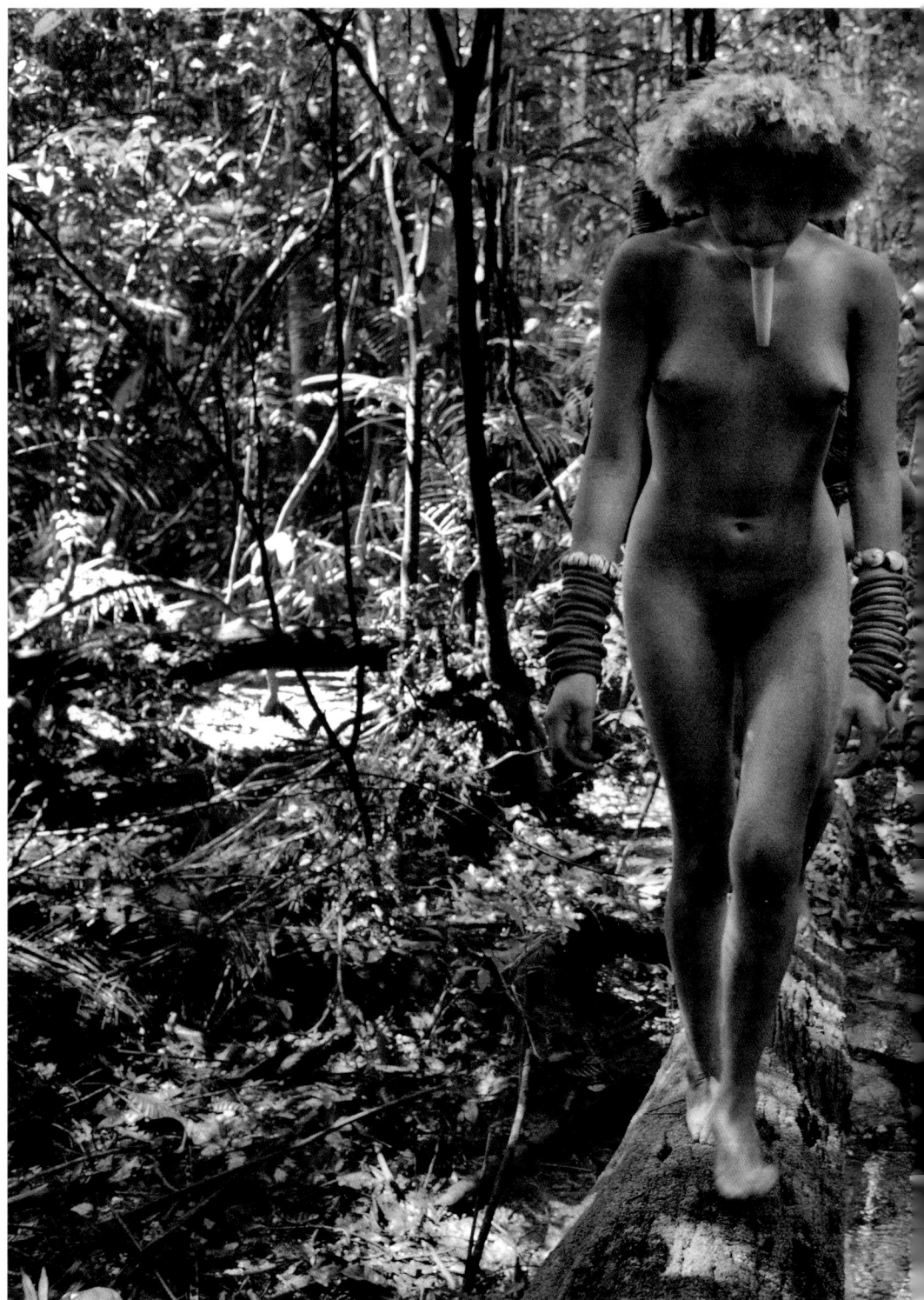

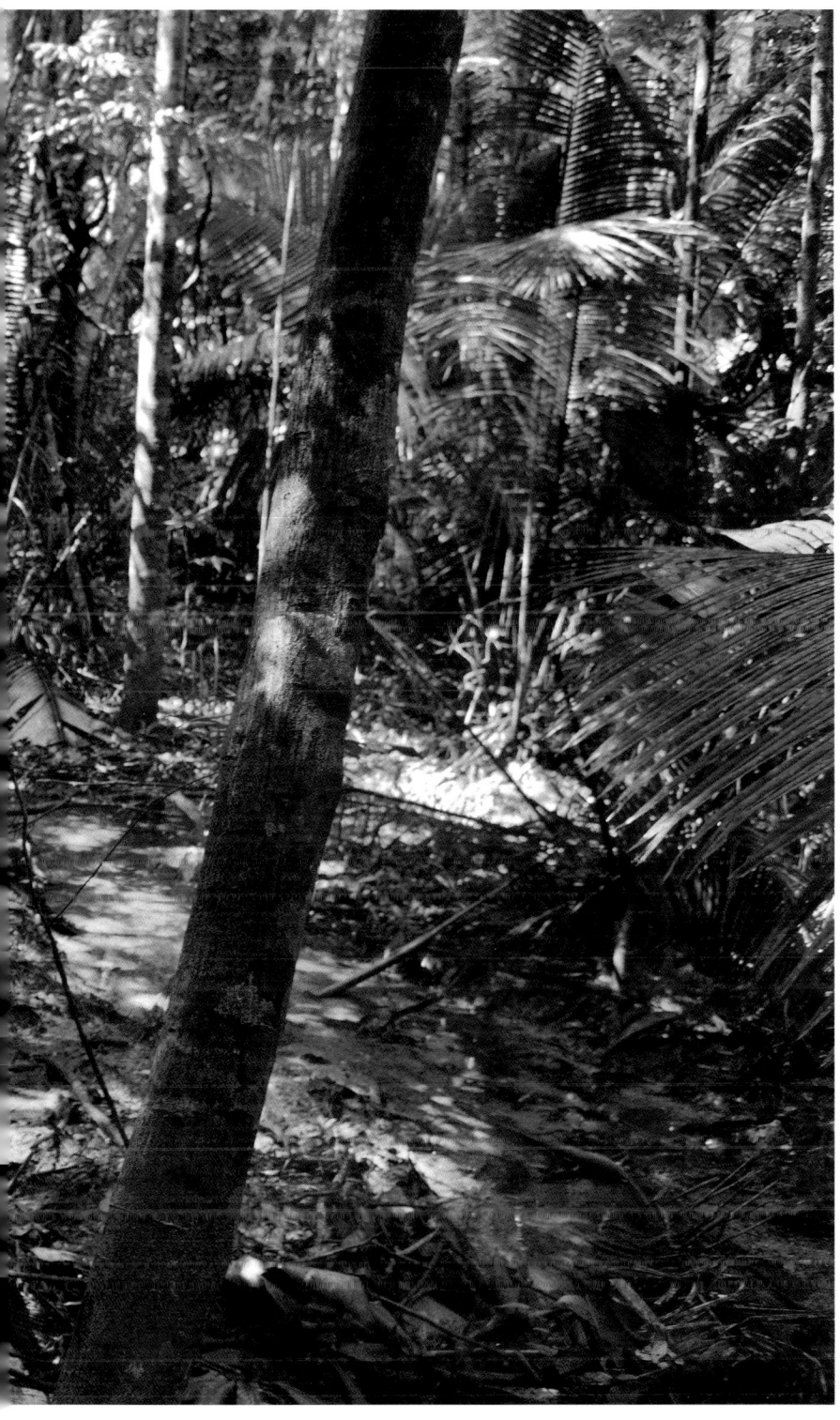

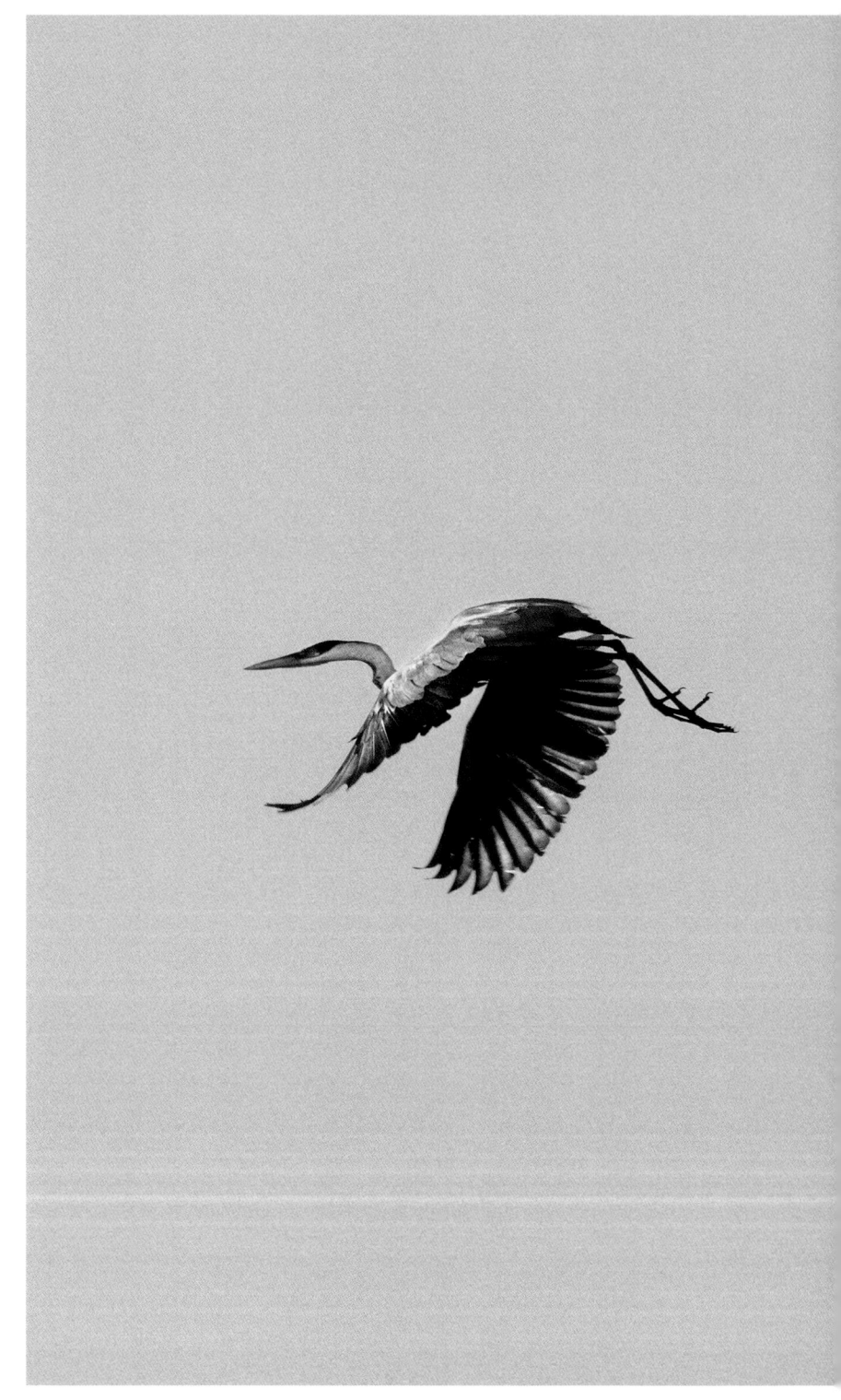

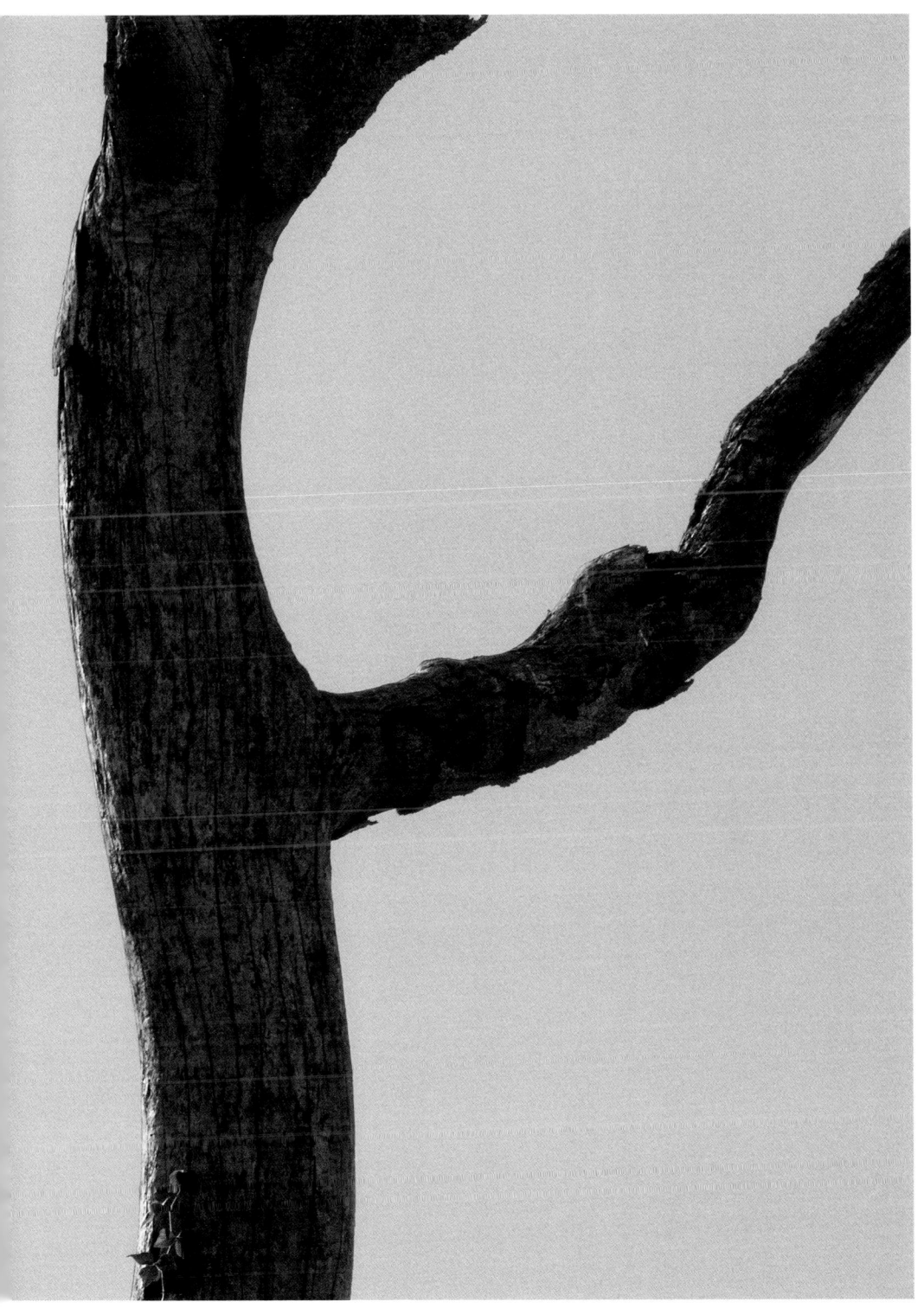

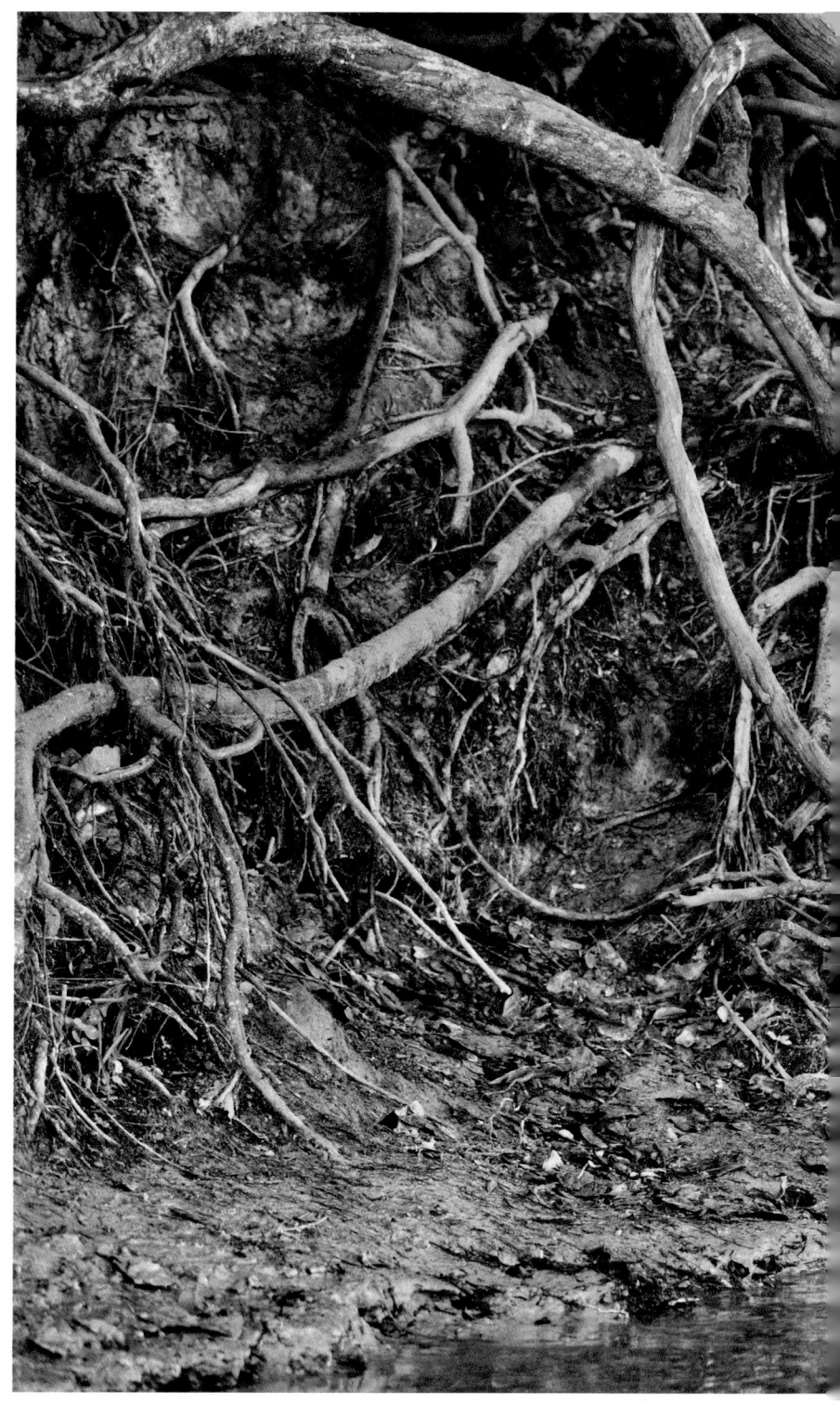

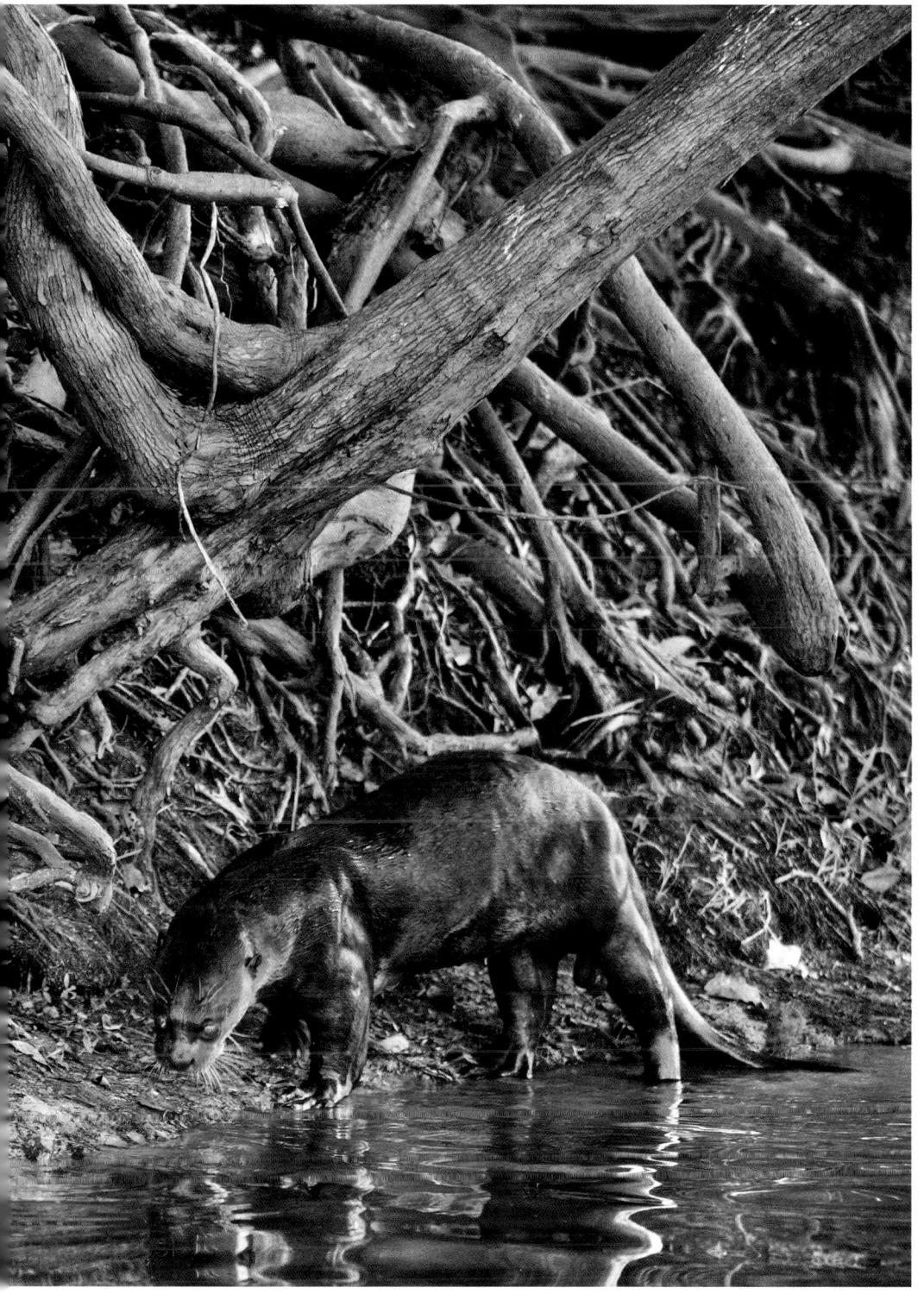

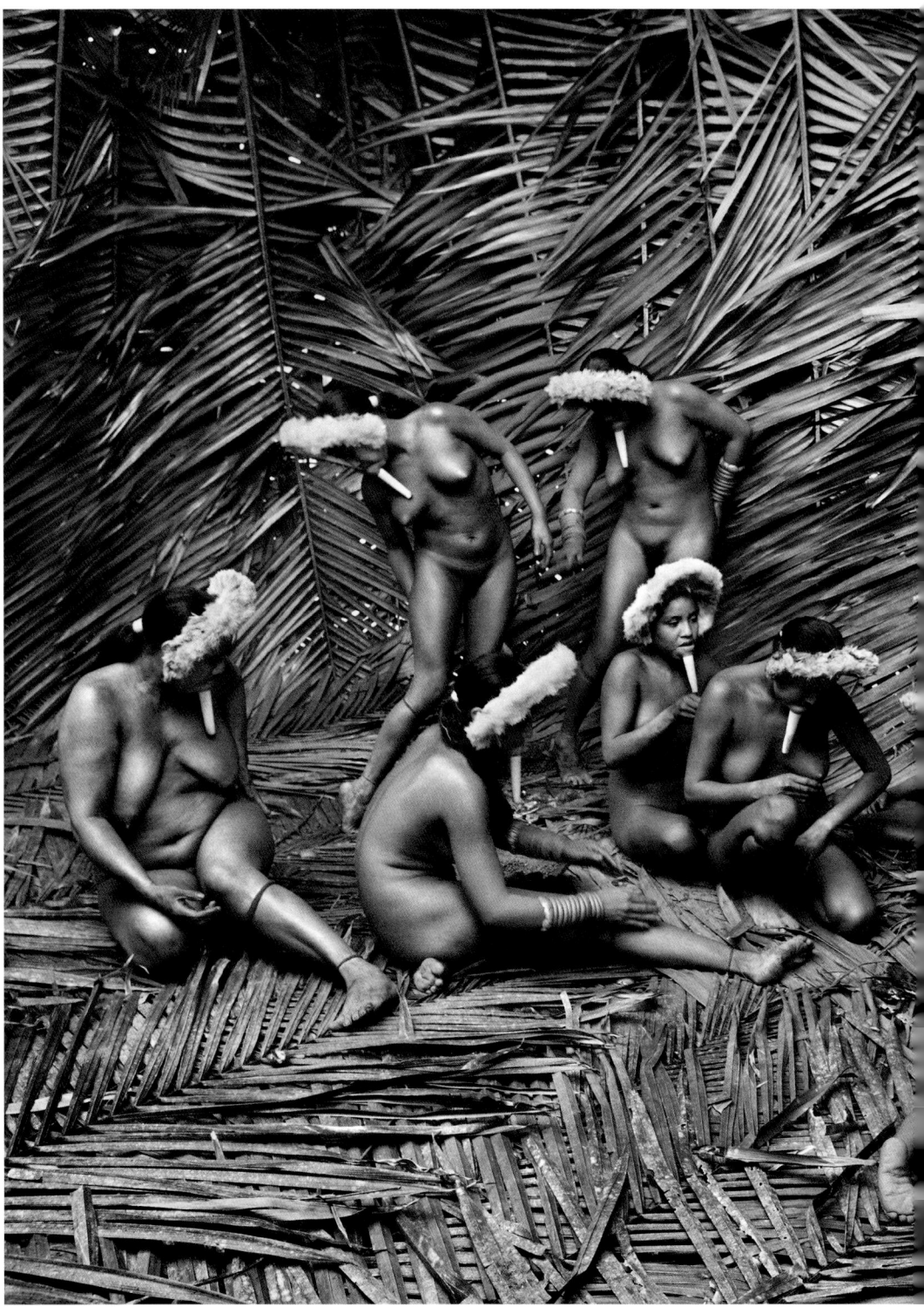

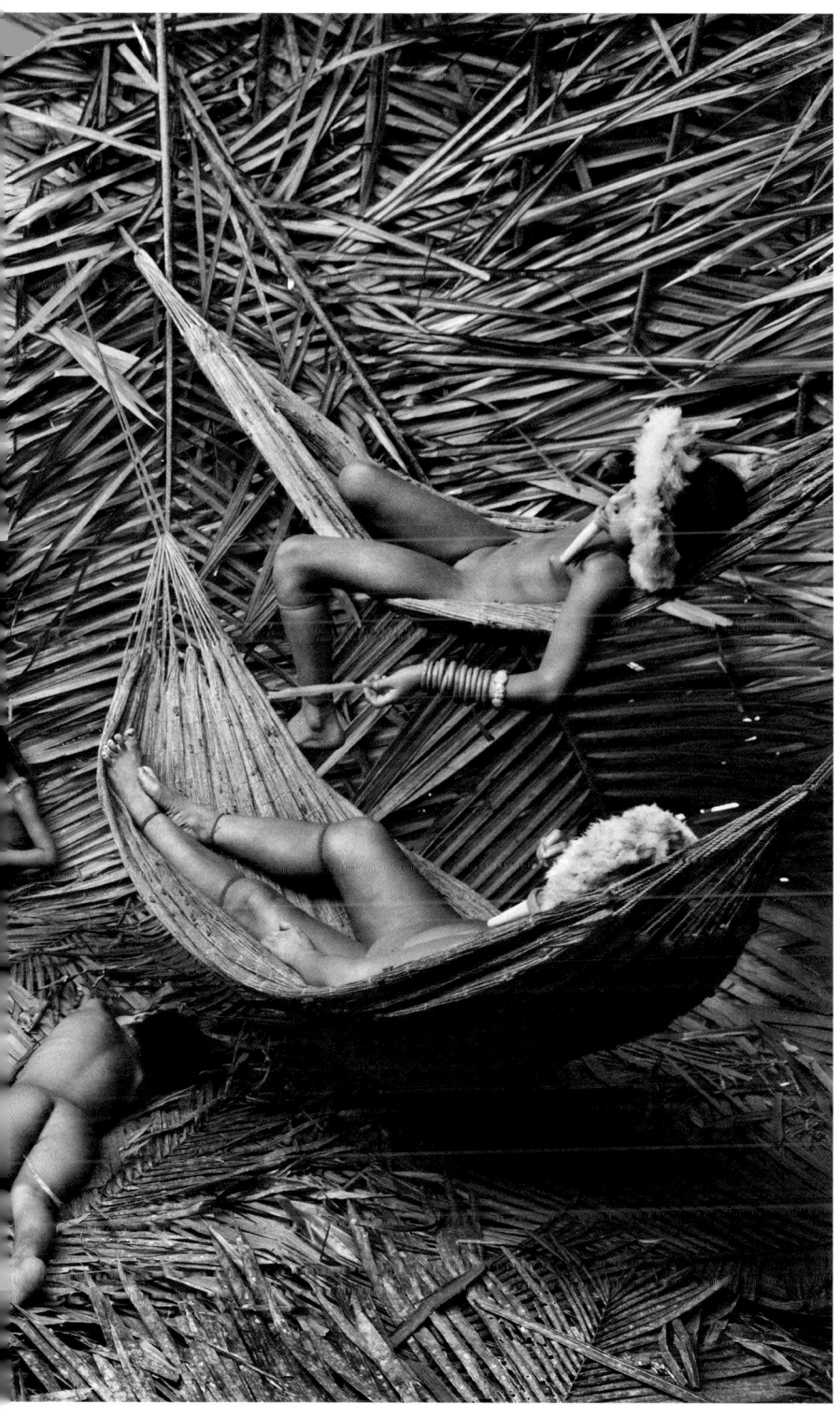

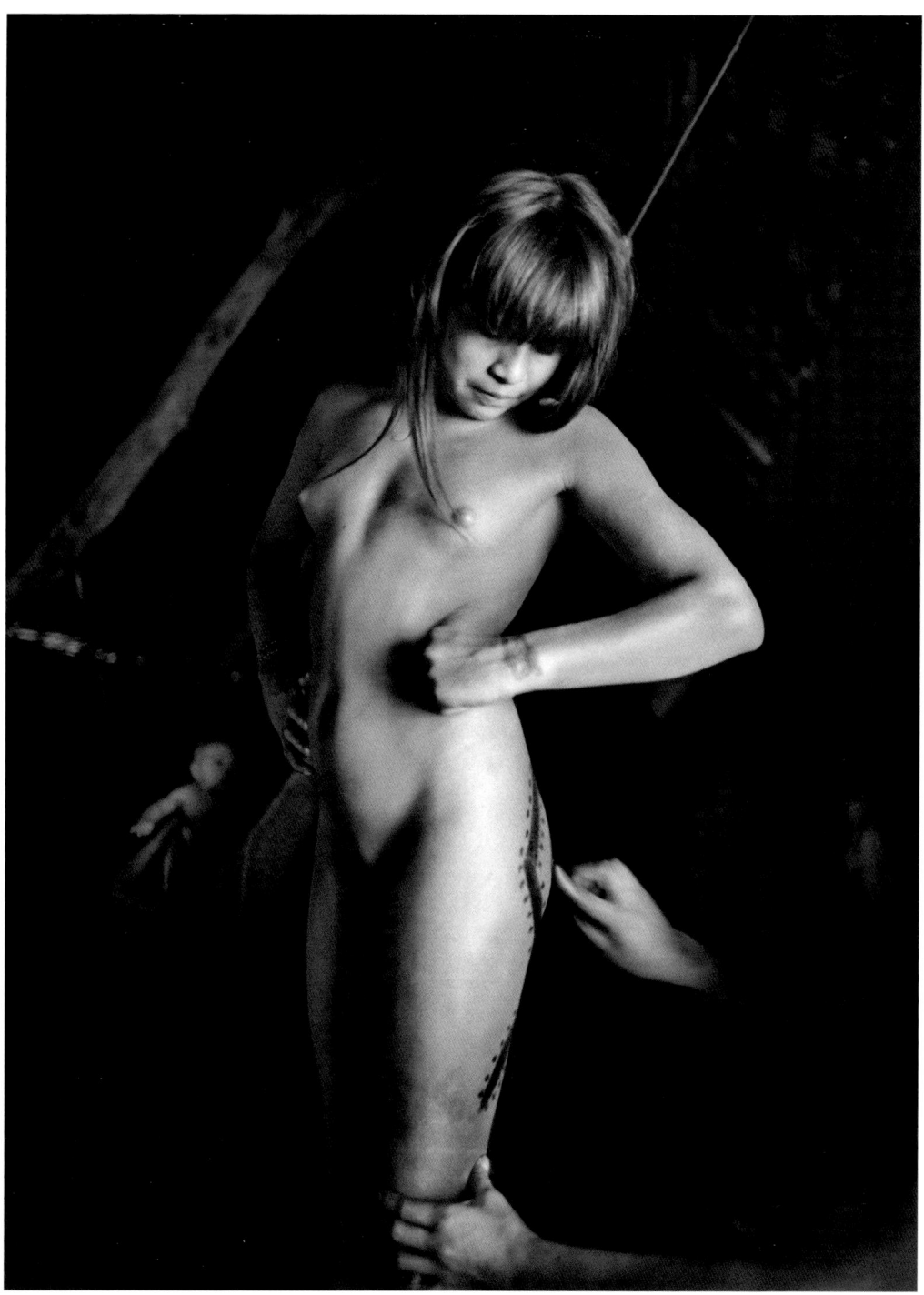

456

THE ALTO XINGU INDIANS

Pages 456 through 460

The Upper Xingu Basin in the state of Mato Grosso lies between the equatorial forest of southern Amazonia and the savannah of central Brazil. The Xingu River, which flows north into the Amazon near Belém, gives its name to this beautiful region in which flora, fauna and soil present all the characteristics of Amazonia even though it lies more than 620 miles (1,000 kilometers) to the south.

The Upper Xingu Basin is home to an ethnically diverse population, with the 2,500 inhabitants of 13 villages speaking languages with distinct Carib, Tupi and Arawak roots. While they occupy different land and preserve their cultural identities, they coexist in peace. Even more unusually, they join each other's important ceremonies, such as the *Kuarup*, the *Amuricumã*, the *Takuara* and the *Jawari*, with their ritualistic dancing, chanting and speeches.

Unfortunately, this cultural and environmental harmony is threatened by damage to the areas adjacent to the National Xingu Park. The biggest worry is pollution of streams, which pass through soya plantations and carry toxic chemicals into the Xingu River. This is already affecting fishing by the region's indigenous peoples, for whom fish is a central part of their diet. In fact, the Mehinaku tribesmen believe their fish diet accounts for their passivity: "We do not eat animals that have hot blood so our food is sweet and as a result our guts are never warmed up for aggression." No less alarming, the Upper Xingu region is recording among the highest rates of deforestation in Brazil. In addition, construction of several hydroelectric dams upstream on the Xingu could decimate the ecosystem of the river and its tributaries and undermine an entire culture that depends on the purity of its waters. Brazil. July, August and September 2005.

Opposite Preparing a young girl for the final stage of the *Amuricumã* ceremony at the Kamayura village. Upper Xingu, Mato Grosso, Brazil. July, August and September 2005.

Pages 458/459 A young Kuikuro girl prepares for the following day's *Kuarup* ceremony. She has spent one year in isolation inside the large family hut, learning everything she will need to know as an adult woman. She went into seclusion immediately after her first menstruation and, until now, she was kept away from the daylight. She is seen here accustoming her eyes to the light, although her hair still covers her face; only the next day, after the *Kuarup* wrestling is over, will she reveal herself in public and signal that she is ready to find a husband. Upper Xingu, Mato Grosso, Brazil. July, August and September 2005.

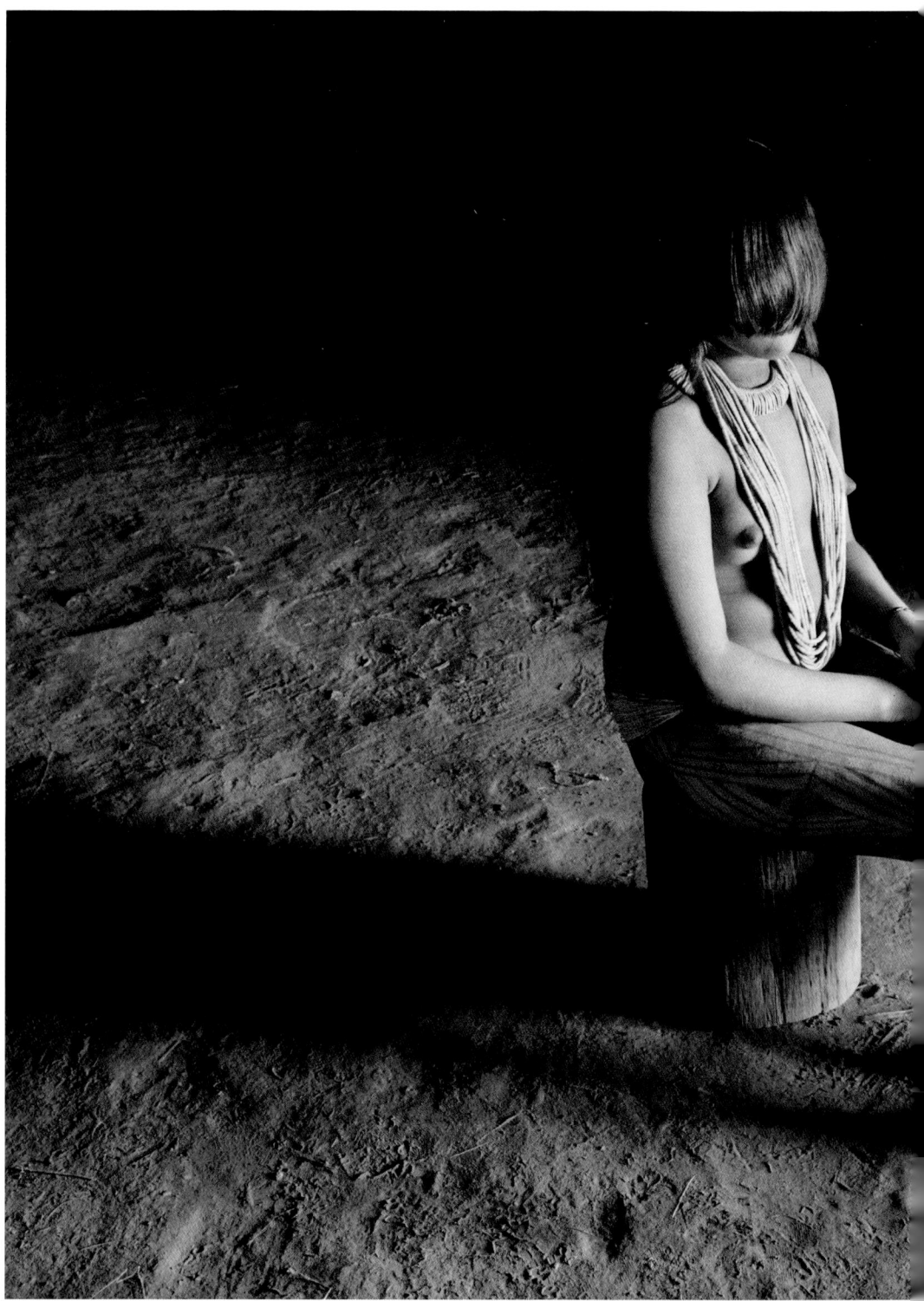

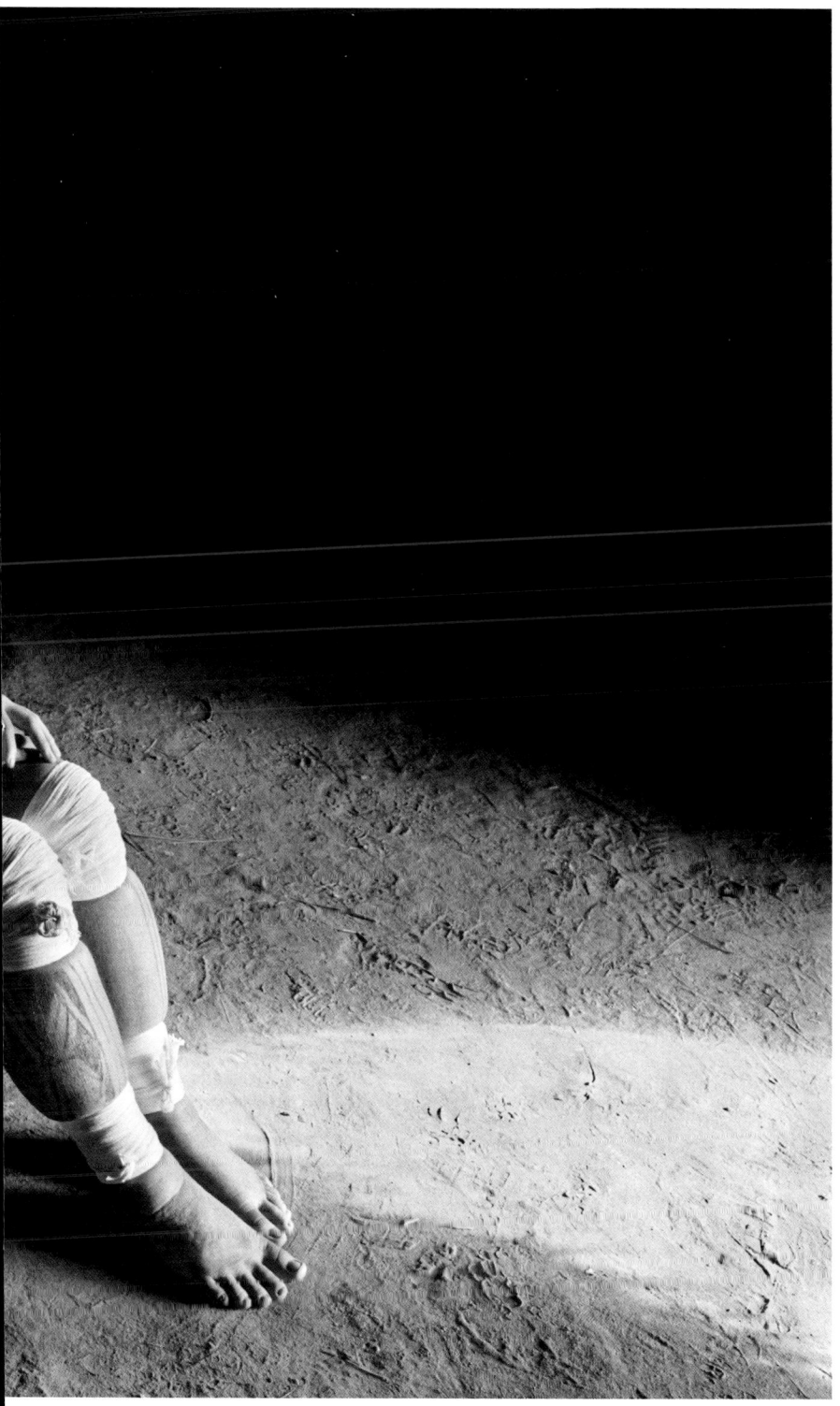

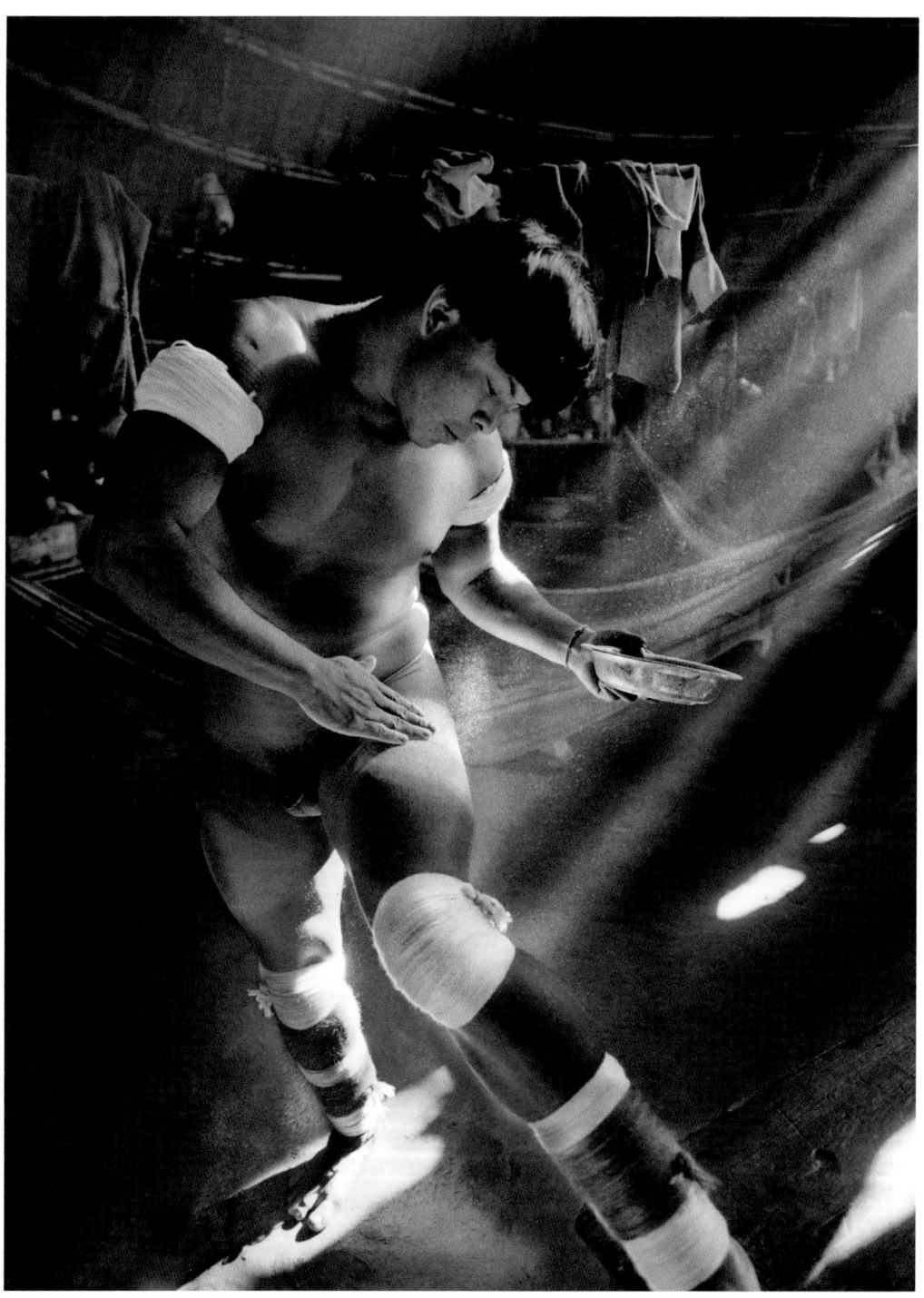

Opposite A Kamayura athlete paints his body to participate in the final day of the *Kuarup* as a guest of the Waura group village. Upper Xingu, Mato Grosso, Brazil. July, August and September 2005.

Pages 462/463 The *Arara azul* (*Anodorhynchus hyacinthinus*) or hyacinth macaw. With their 3-foot (95-centimeter) wingspan, these stunning macaws can be seen gliding in pairs over the forest canopy, their eyes alert to their favorite food, palm-tree fruits. Their feathers are a rich violet-blue, with bare skin below their beak and around the eyes providing little splashes of yellow. Caiman Ecological Reserve, Pantanal, Mato Grosso do Sul, Brazil. September and October 2011.

Pages 464/465 The waterfalls of Ichun-Prarara, located on the Ichun Plateau in the heart of Venezuela's Amazon rainforest, are very isolated and difficult to reach. Venezuela. November and December 2006.

Pages 466/467 Seen from on high, the jungle seems impenetrable, but the reality on the ground can be different. The Zo'é people, who number between 250 to 275, live in some 10 small villages which are connected by numerous trails, giving them easy access between communities. Pará, Brazil. March and April 2009.

Pages 468/469 The Garça Branca Grande or great egret (*Ardea alba*), which has a 3-foot (1-meter) wingspan, is at home in the swamps and rivers of the Pantanal. These birds sometimes group together in their hundreds. Pantanal, Mato Grosso do Sul, Brazil. September and October 2011.

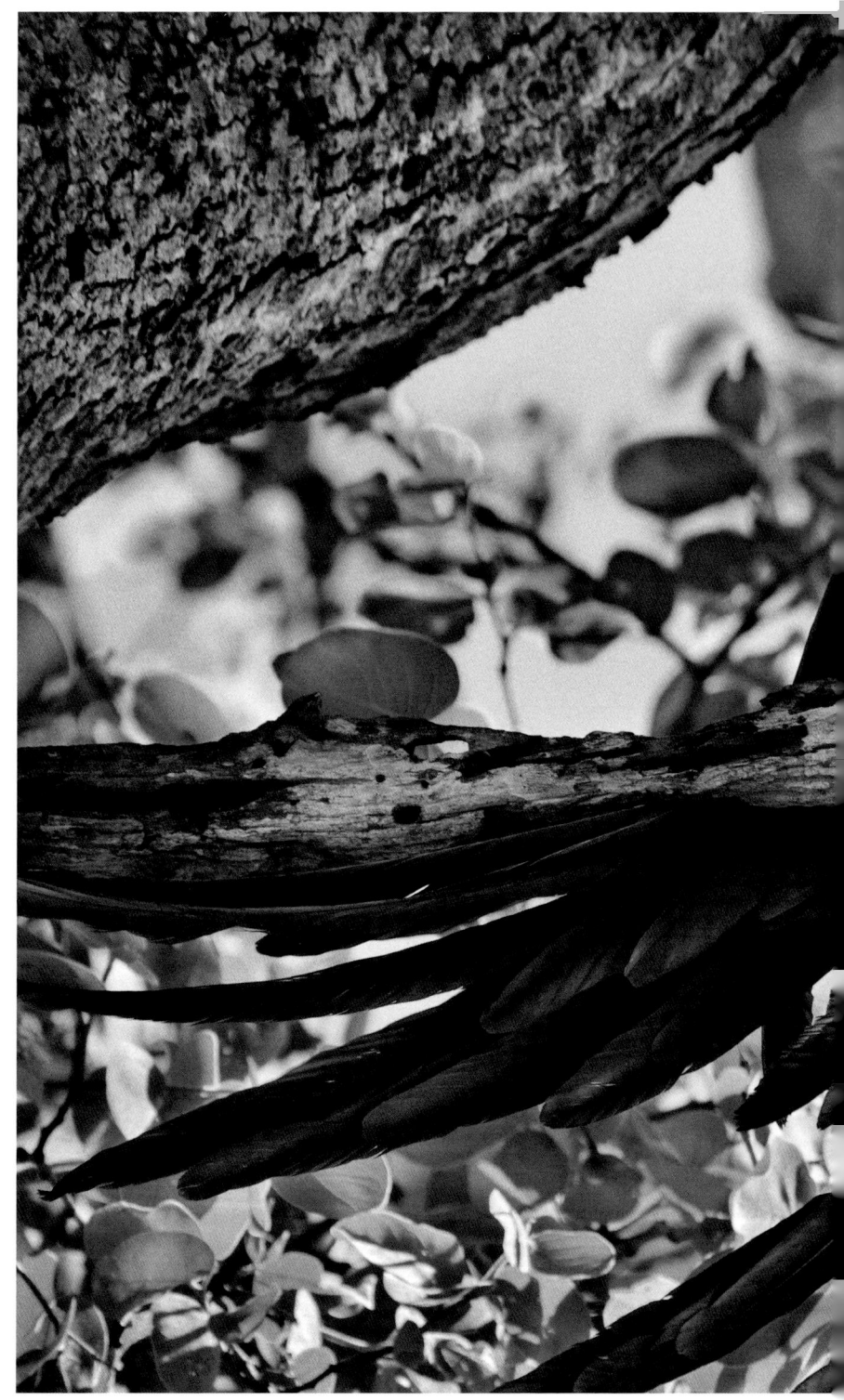

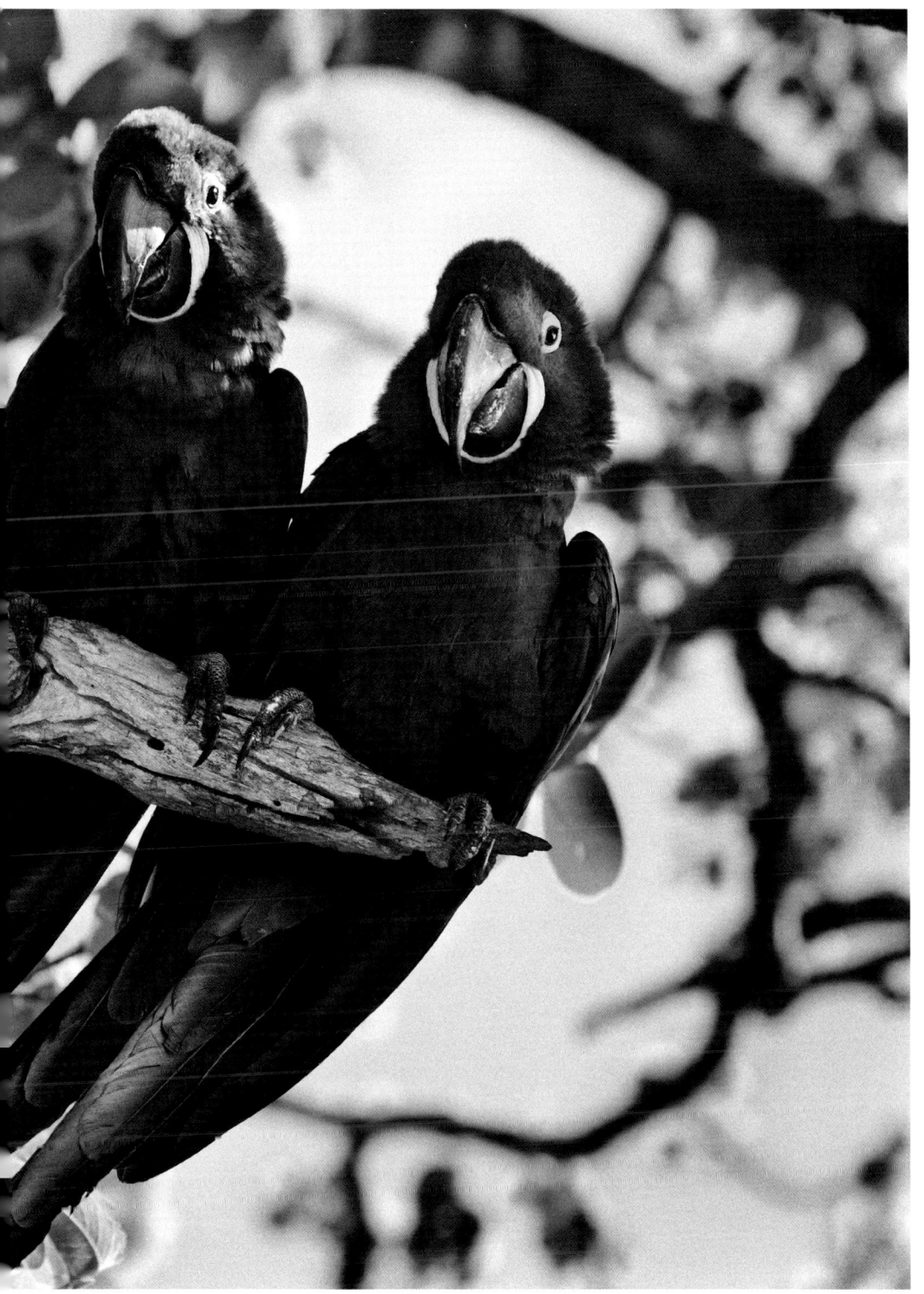

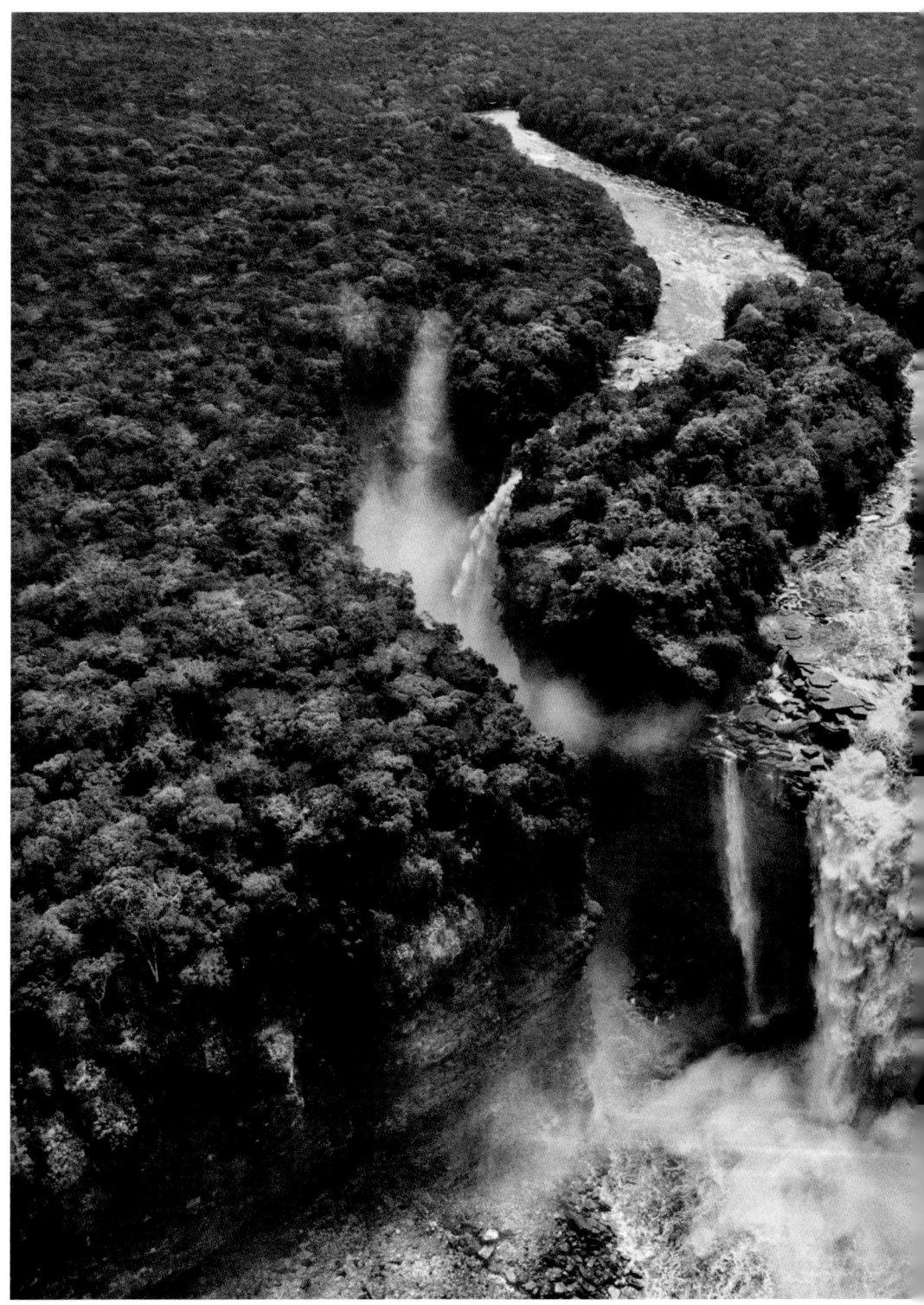

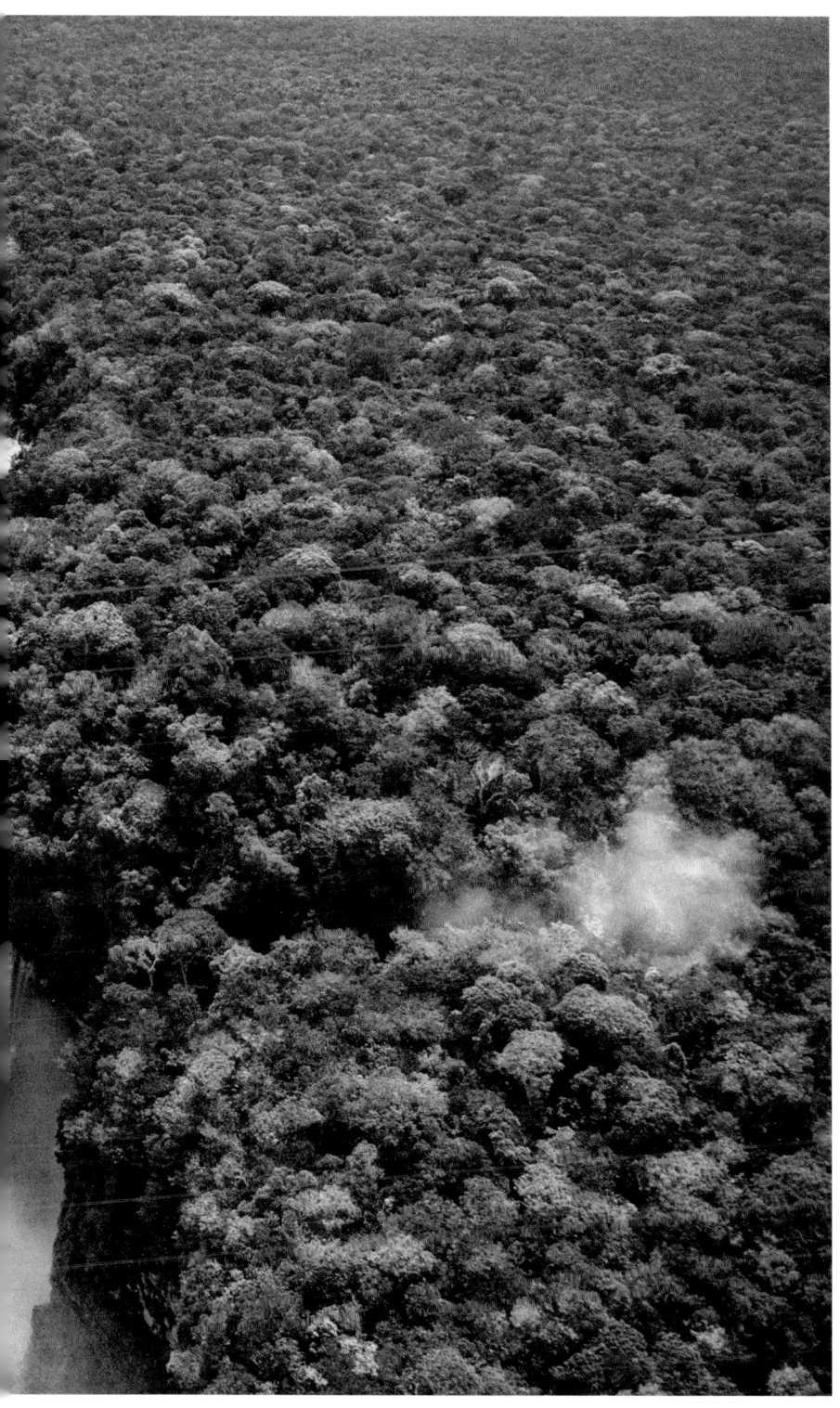

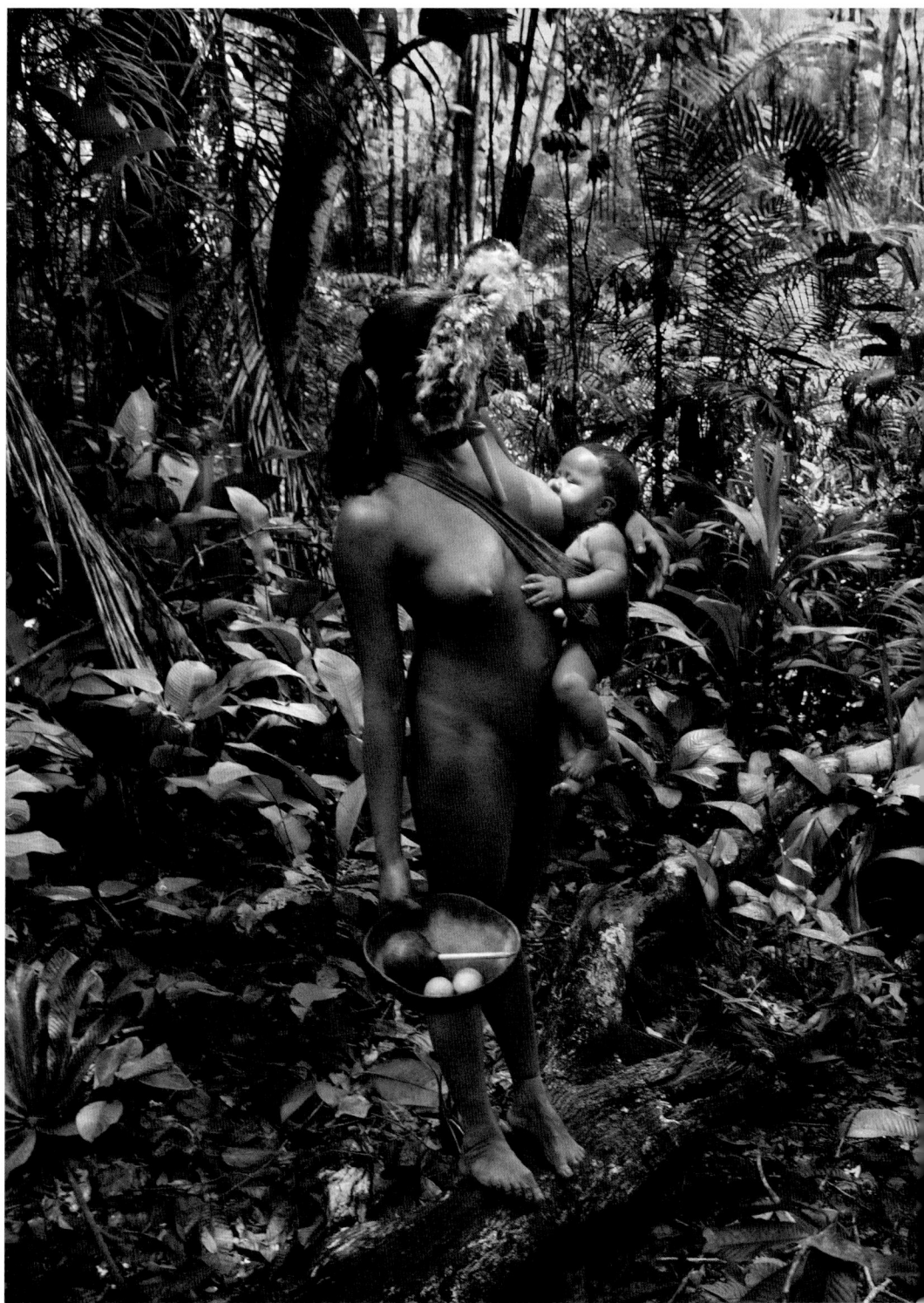

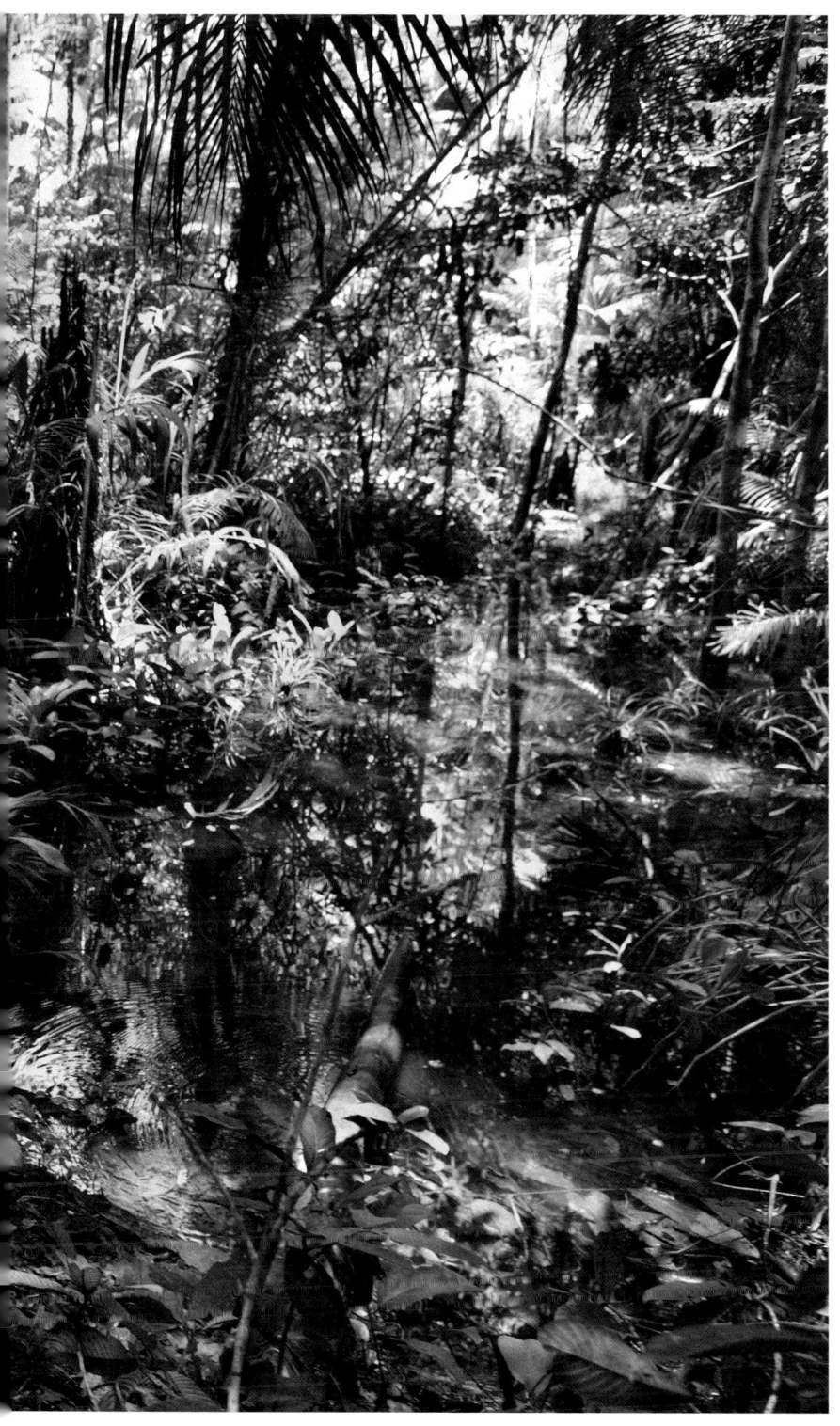

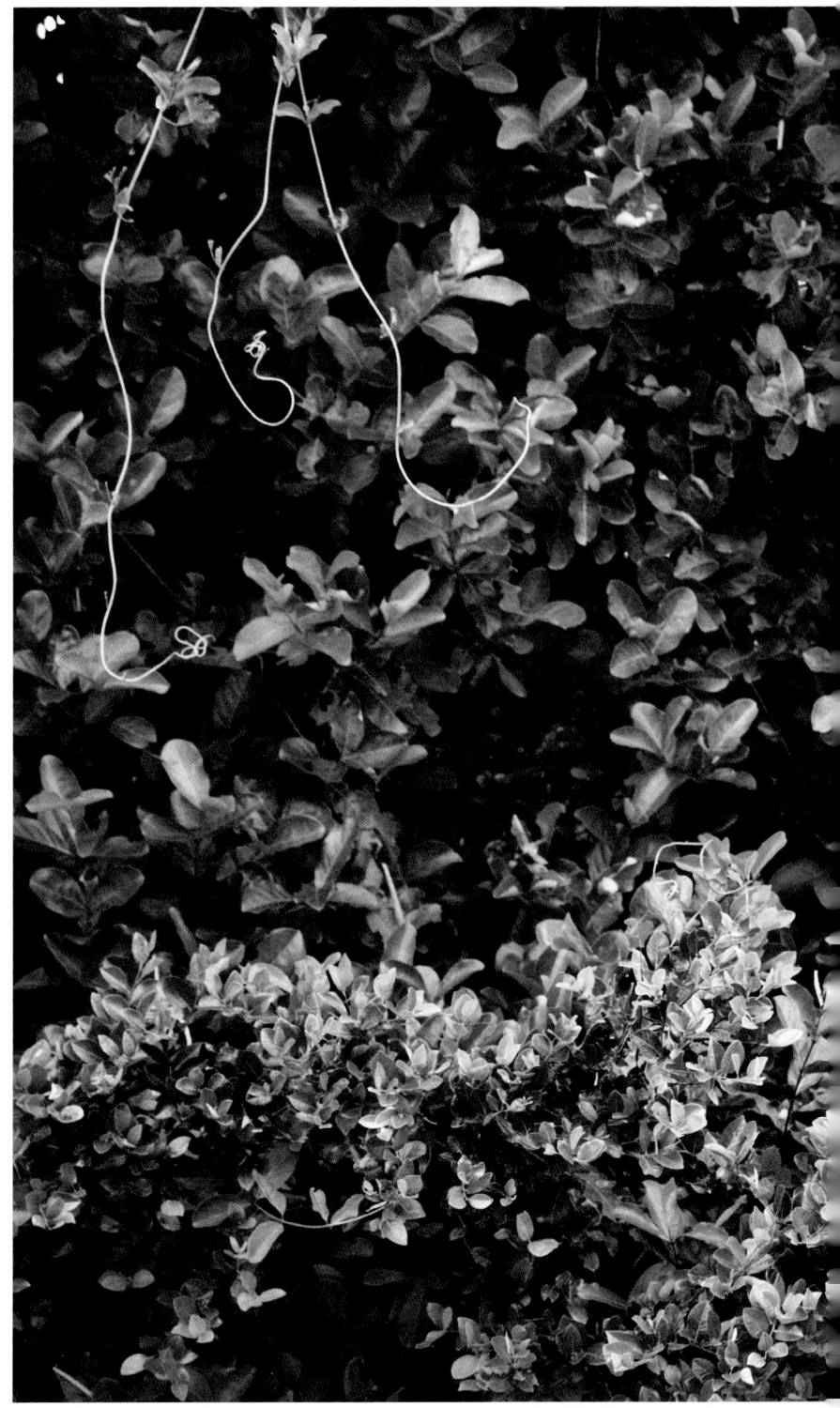

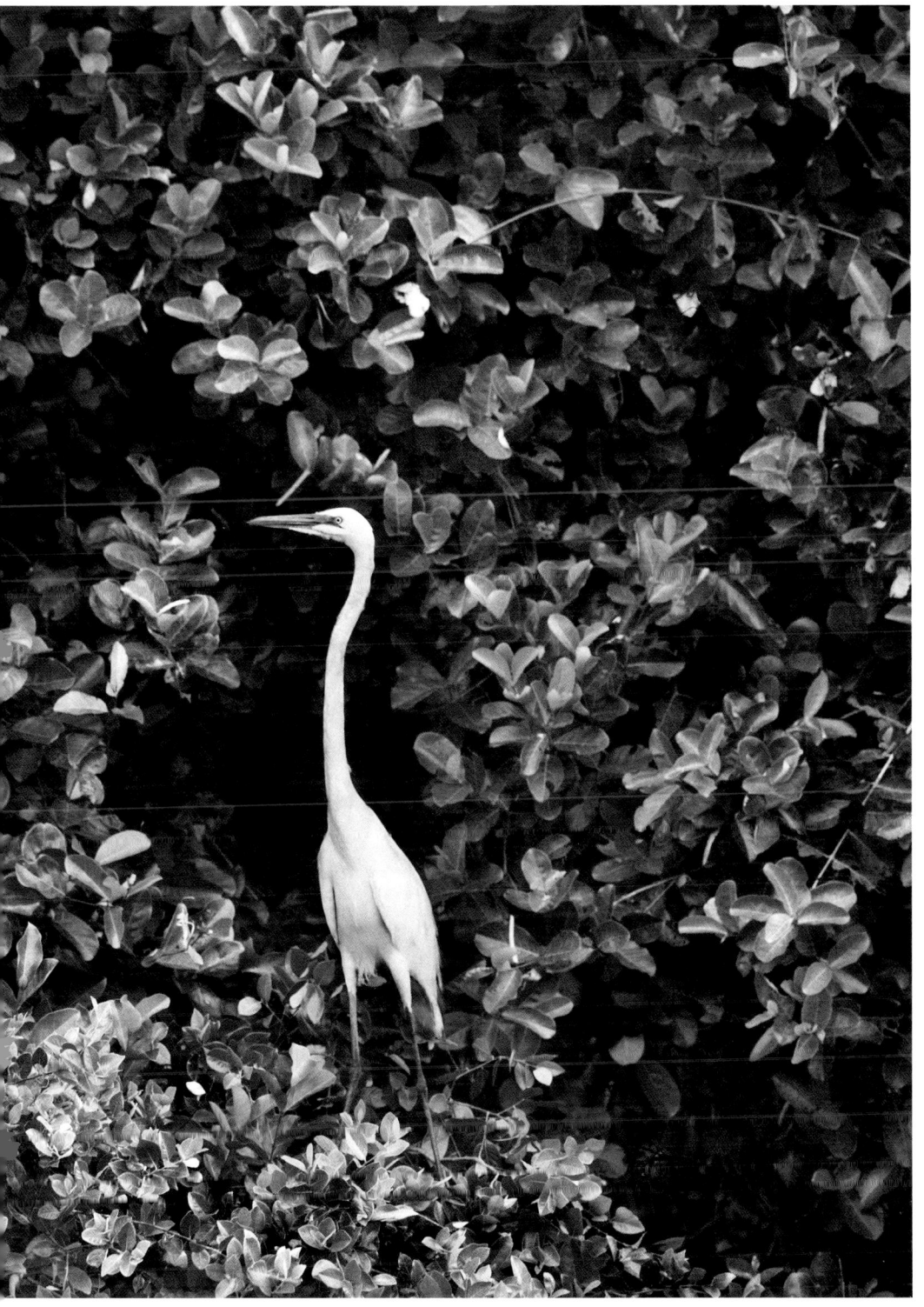

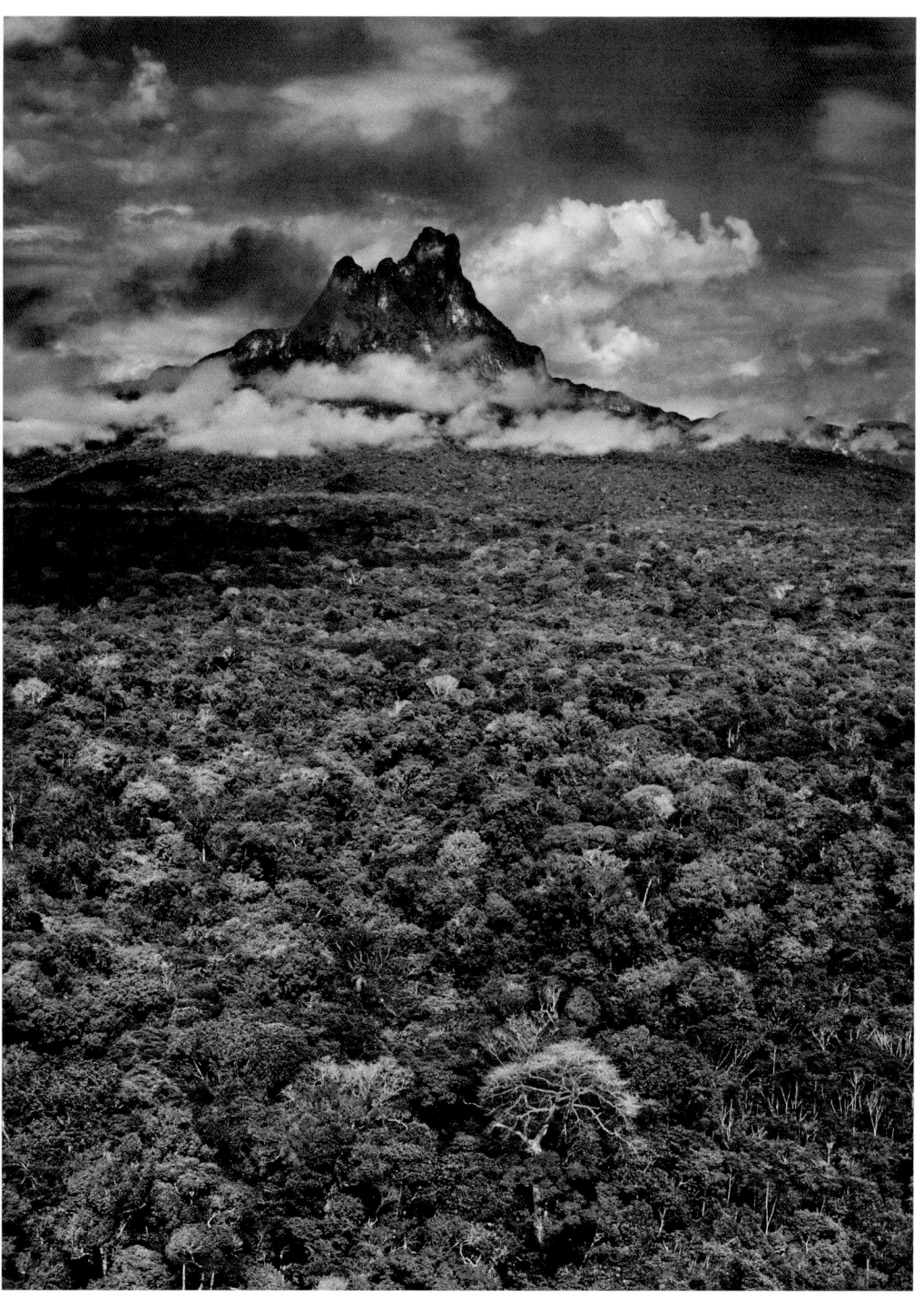

Opposite This peak rising out of the Amazon rainforest marks the beginning of the Serra do Imeri, a section of the Guyana Highlands on the Brazil-Venezuela border, which also includes the Pico da Neblina, Brazil's highest mountain. Brazil. August and September 2009.

Pages 472/473 and 478/479 The Pantanal, one of the world's largest wetlands, covering a vast area of western Brazil and spilling into Paraguay and Bolivia, is home to an estimated 10 million yacare caimans (*Caiman yacare*). Measuring between 7 and 10 feet (2 and 3 meters) long, they feed on fish, mollusks and shellfish. Although the Pantanal boasts the largest population of caimans on Earth, they have been declared a threatened species because of uncontrolled hunting, mainly in Paraguay and Bolivia. Pantanal, Mato Grosso do Sul, Brazil. September and October 2011.

Pages 474/475 La Cueva de Auyan. Just as Auyantepui means Devil's Mountain in the indigenous Pemon language, the Cave of Auyan is thought to be the home of the devil, a place to be entered with fear and respect. It is located in Uruyen, west of Auyantepui. Venezuela. November and December 2006.

Pages 476/477 After three days in a canoe on the Akakan River and then the Carraro River, we finally reach the Churún River. Mirroring the forest and the Auyantepui in the background, its water is black because tree sap seeps through the sandy soil of the region. Venezuela. November and December 2006.

Pages 480/481 The Rio Negro, the largest blackwater river in the world, loses its name at Manaus, where it joins the Solimões River and becomes the Amazon. Spread out like a fan, its sources are to be found in both Venezuela and far to the west in Colombia, where it receives water from the northern Andes. For Brazil's neighbors and most geographers around the world, however, the Amazon does not begin at Manaus, but rather at the confluence of the Marañón and Ucayali rivers in Peru, more than 1,200 miles (2,000 kilometers) to the west. Amazonas, Brazil. August and September 2009.

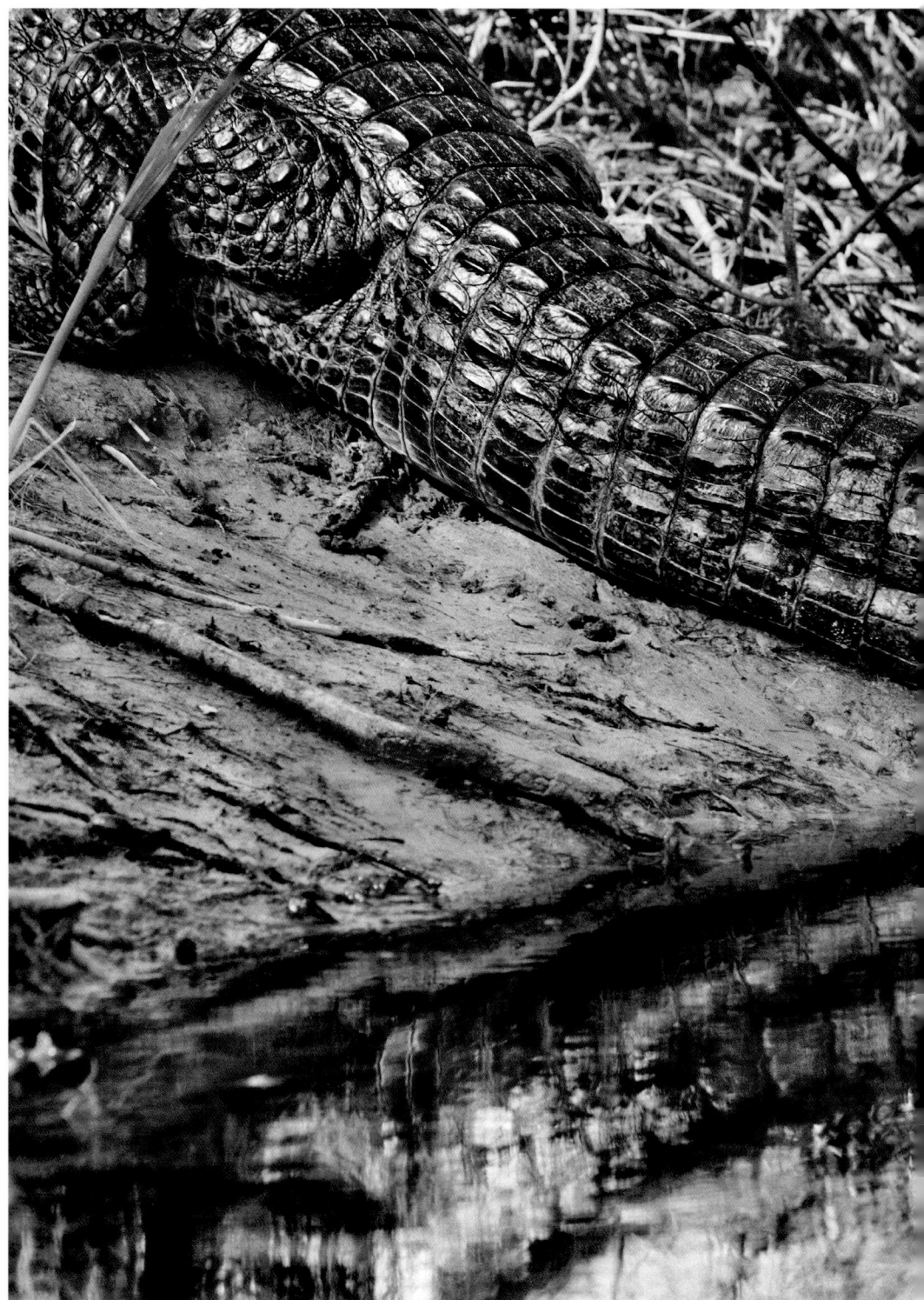

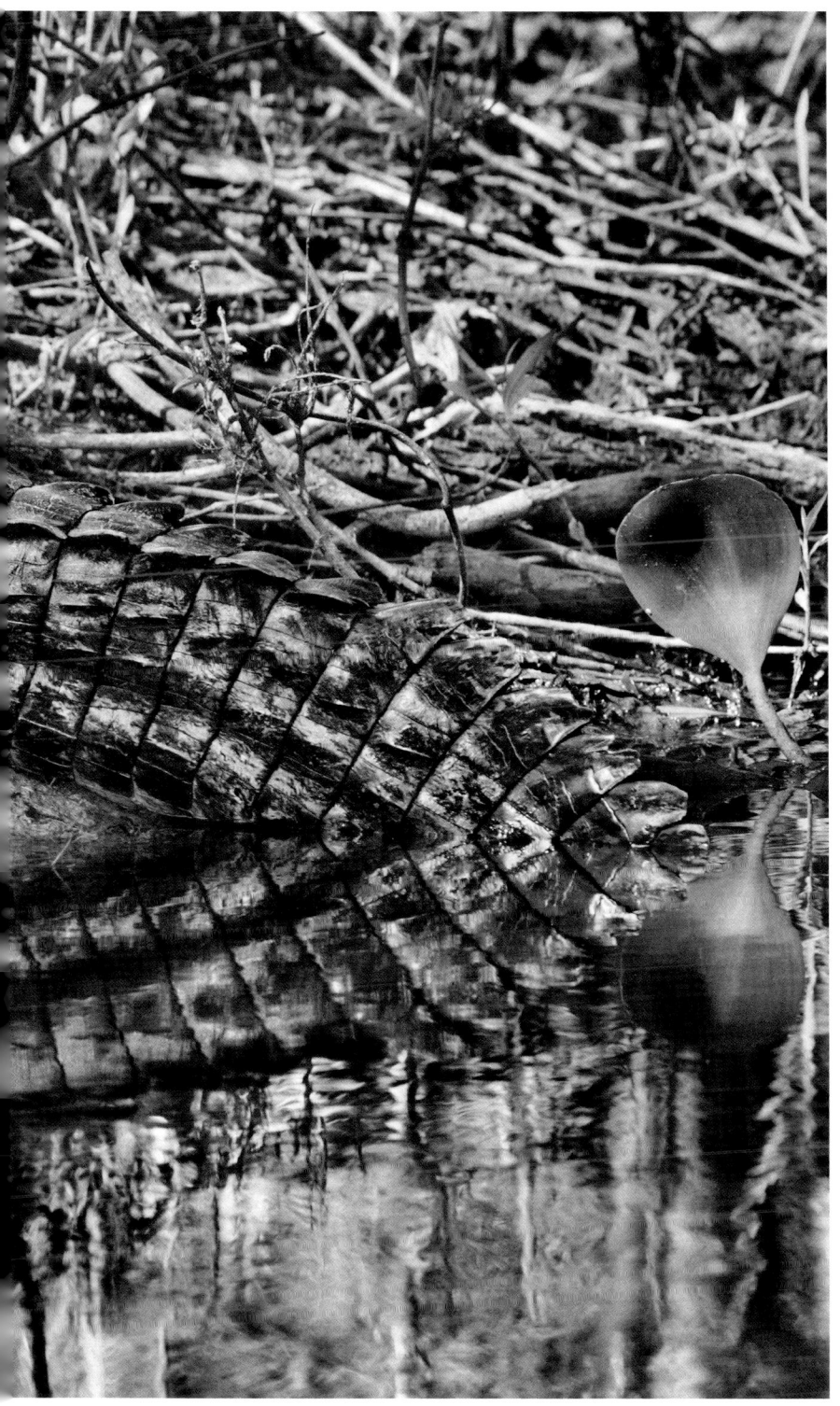

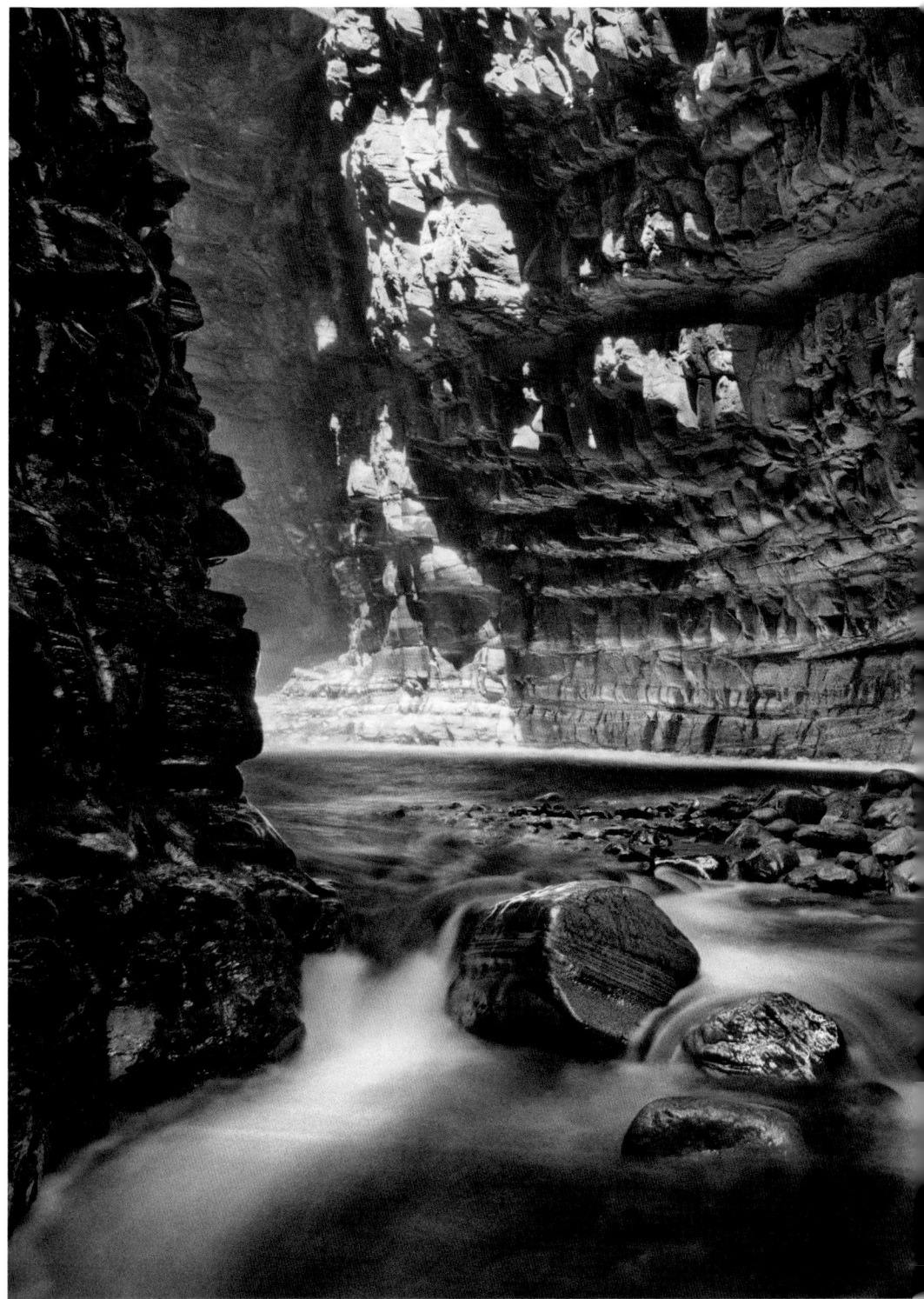

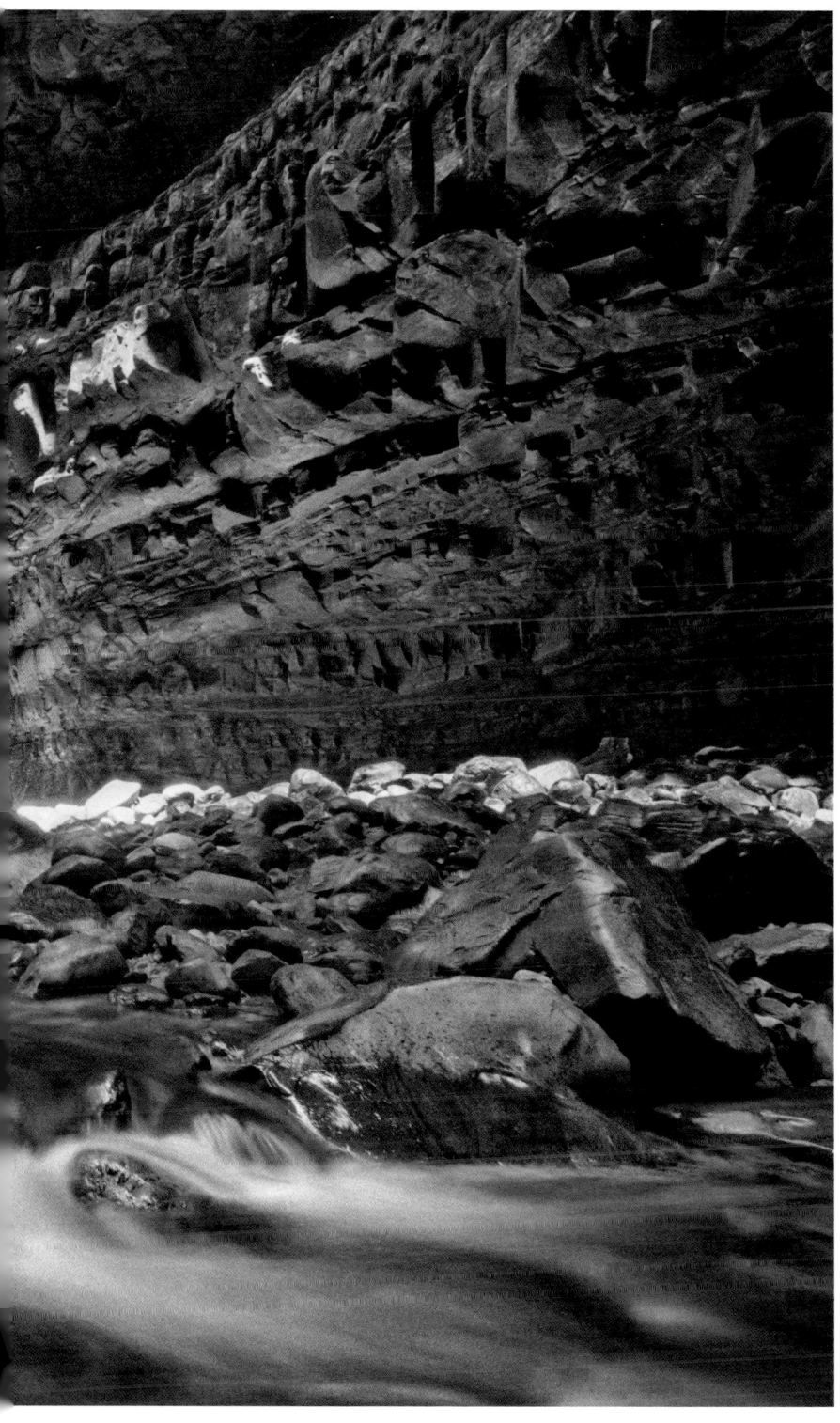

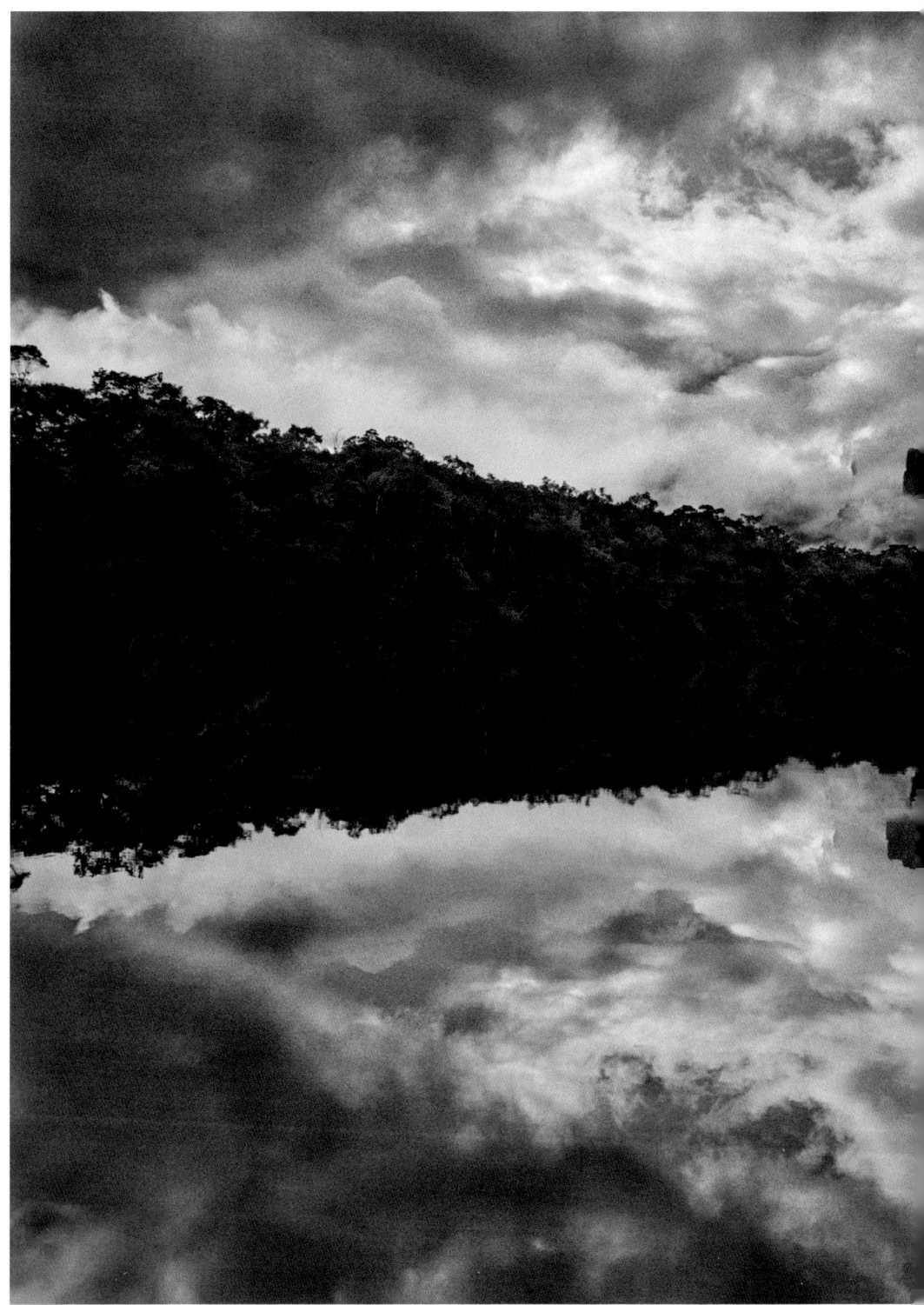

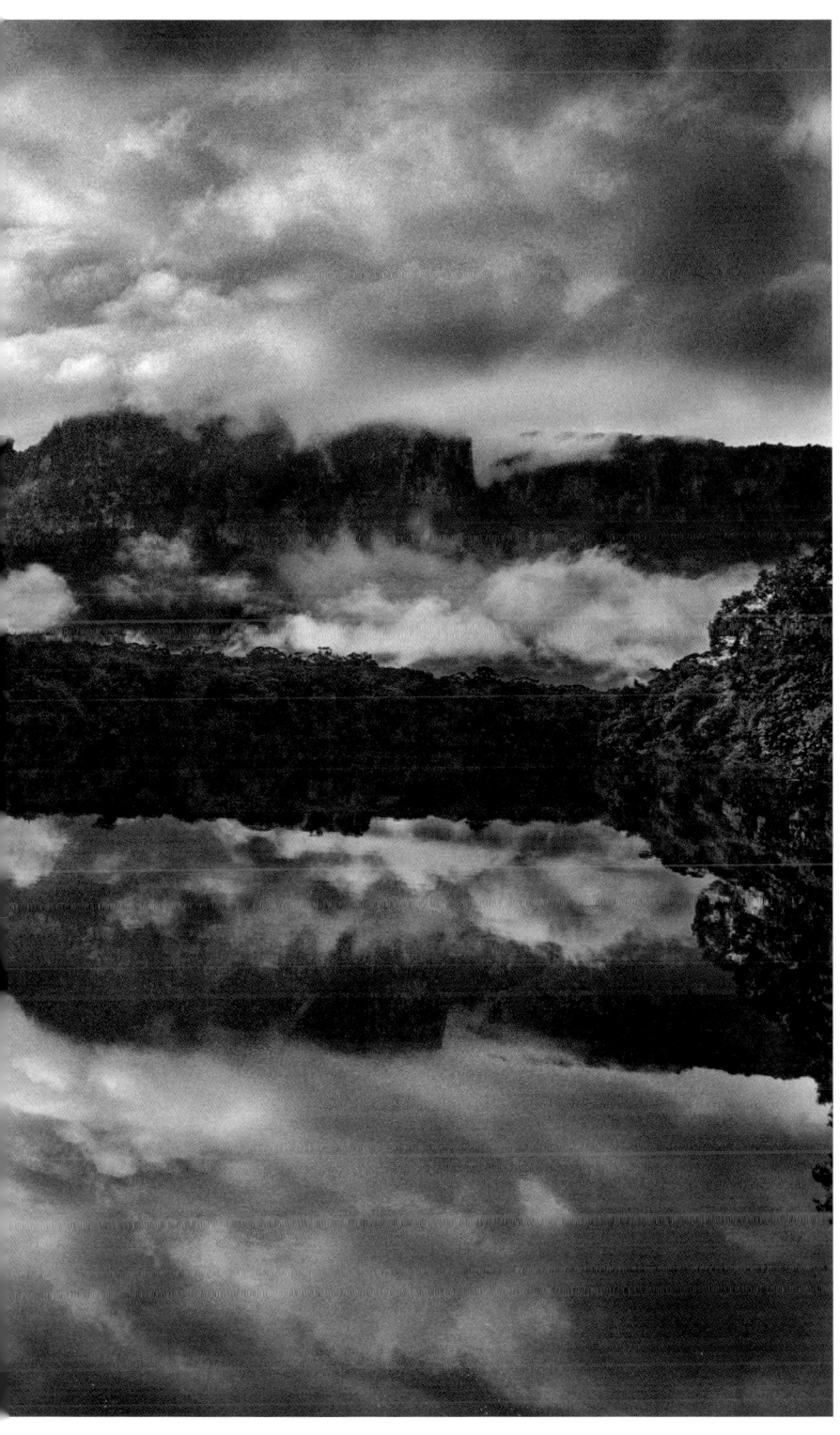

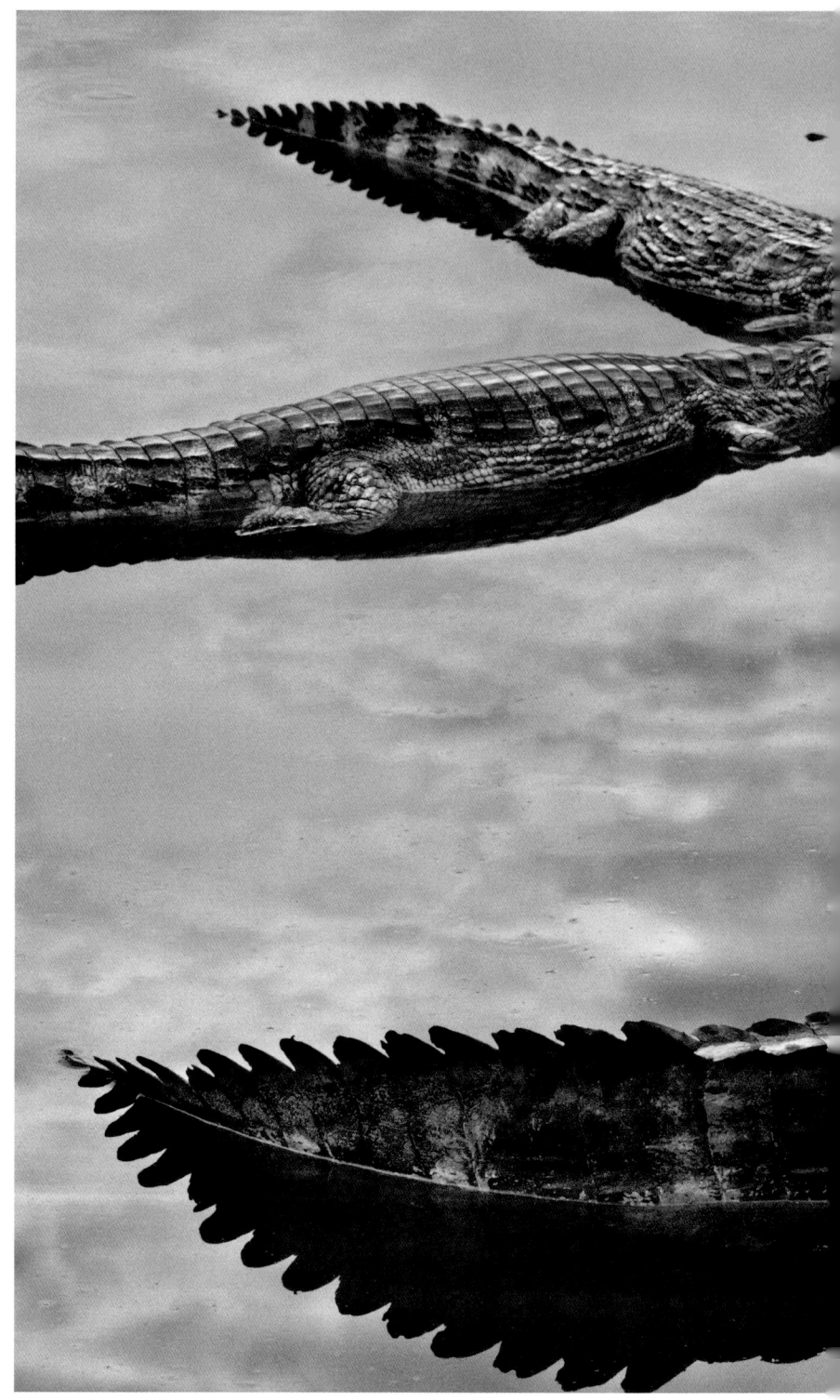

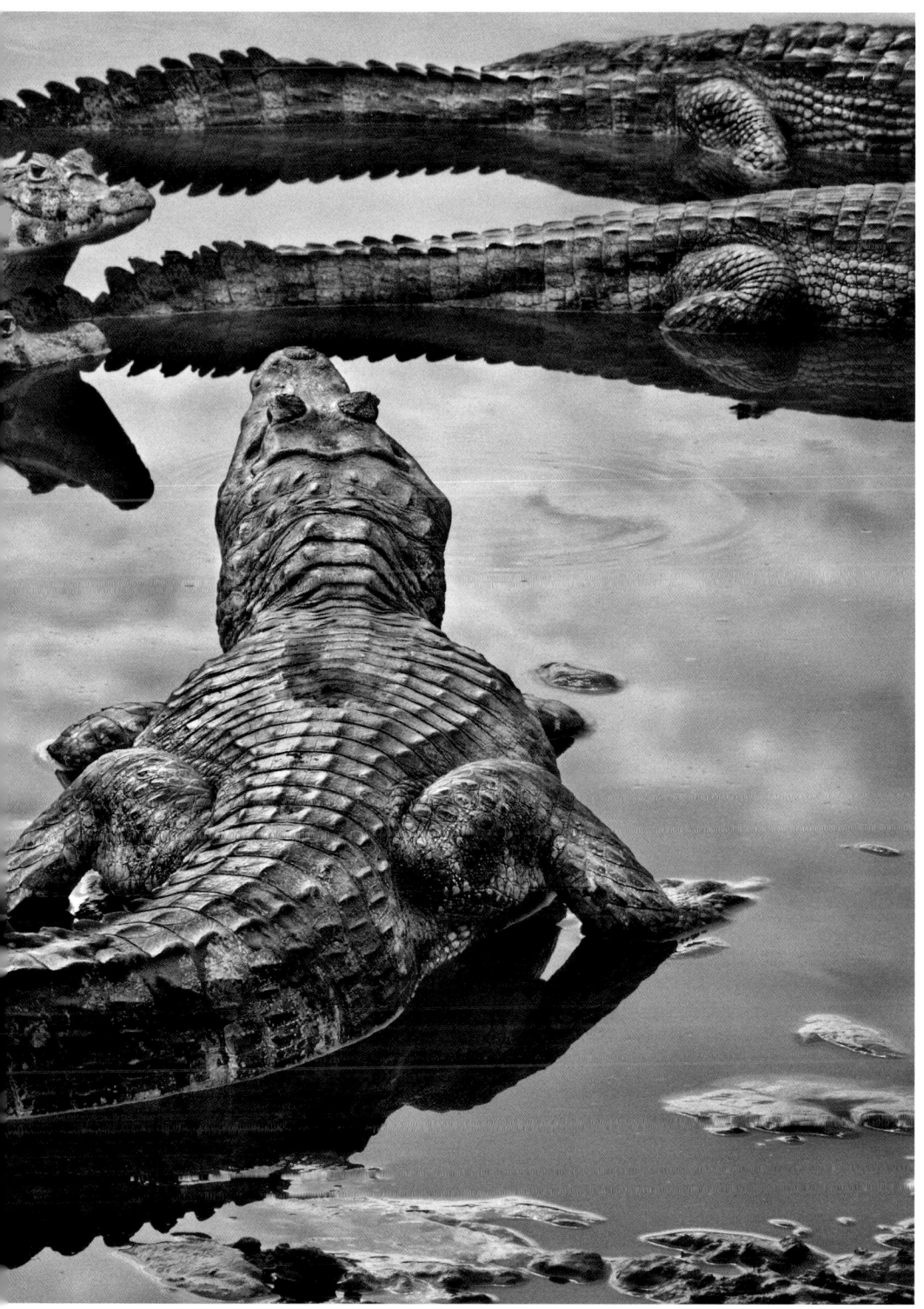

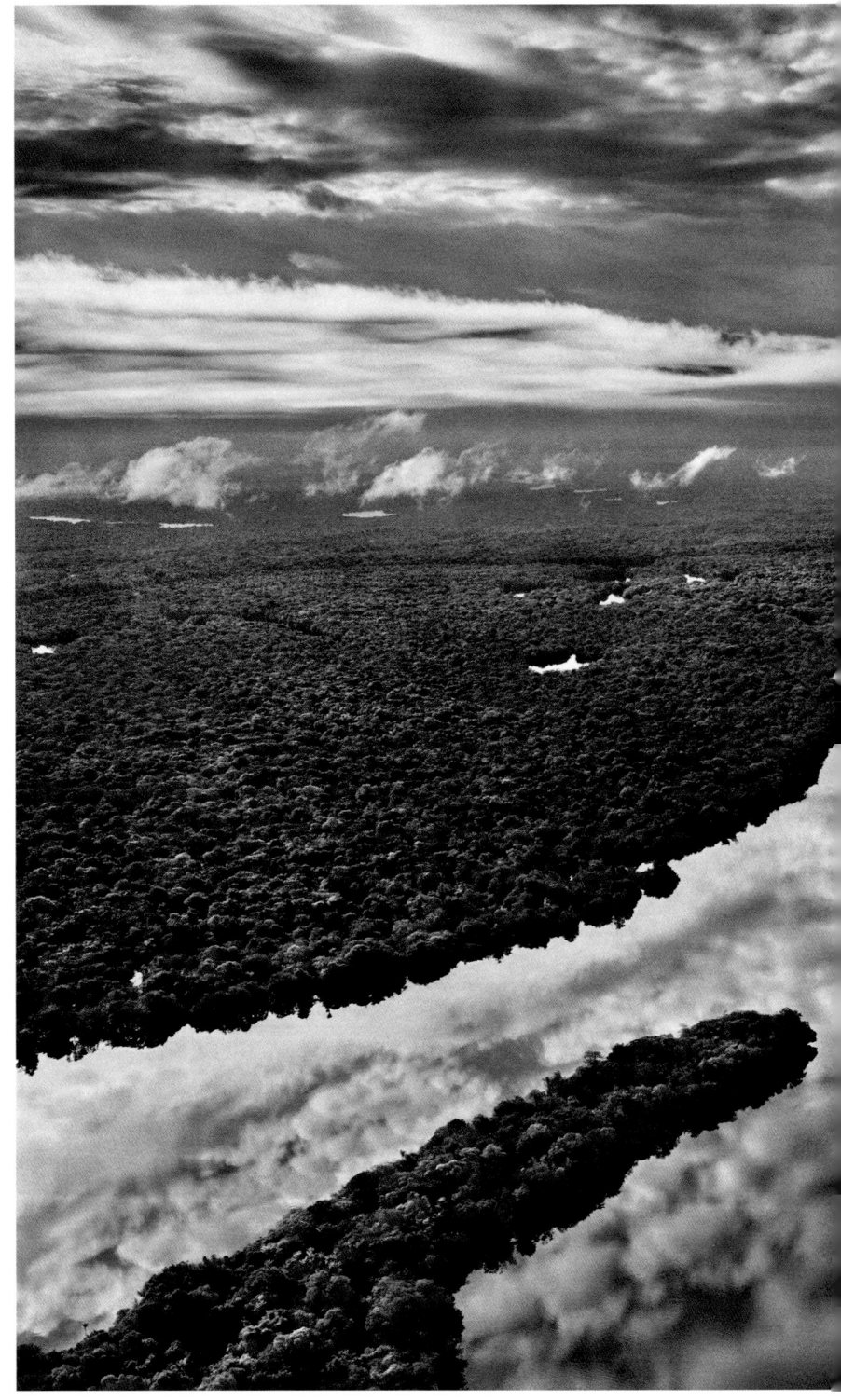

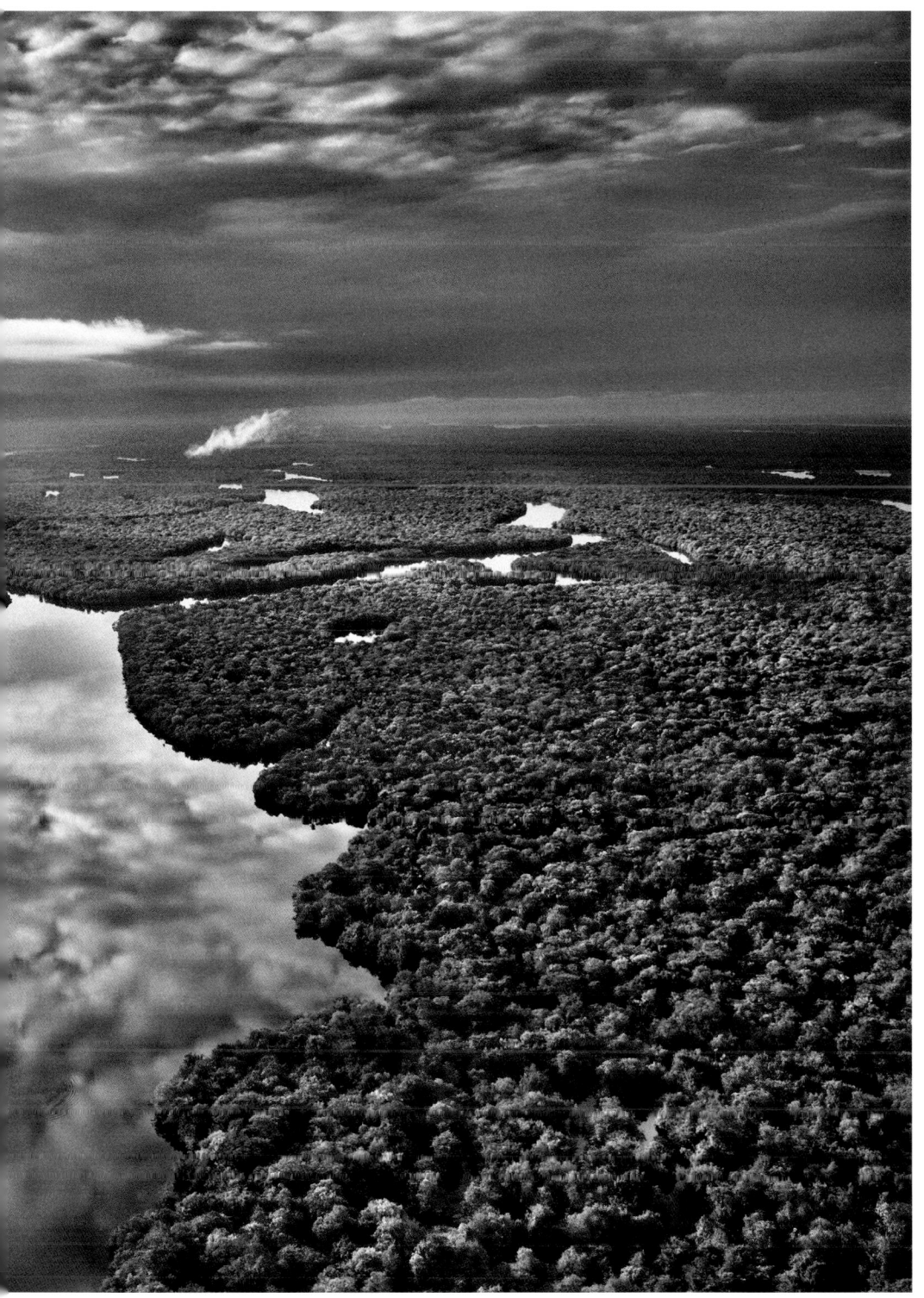

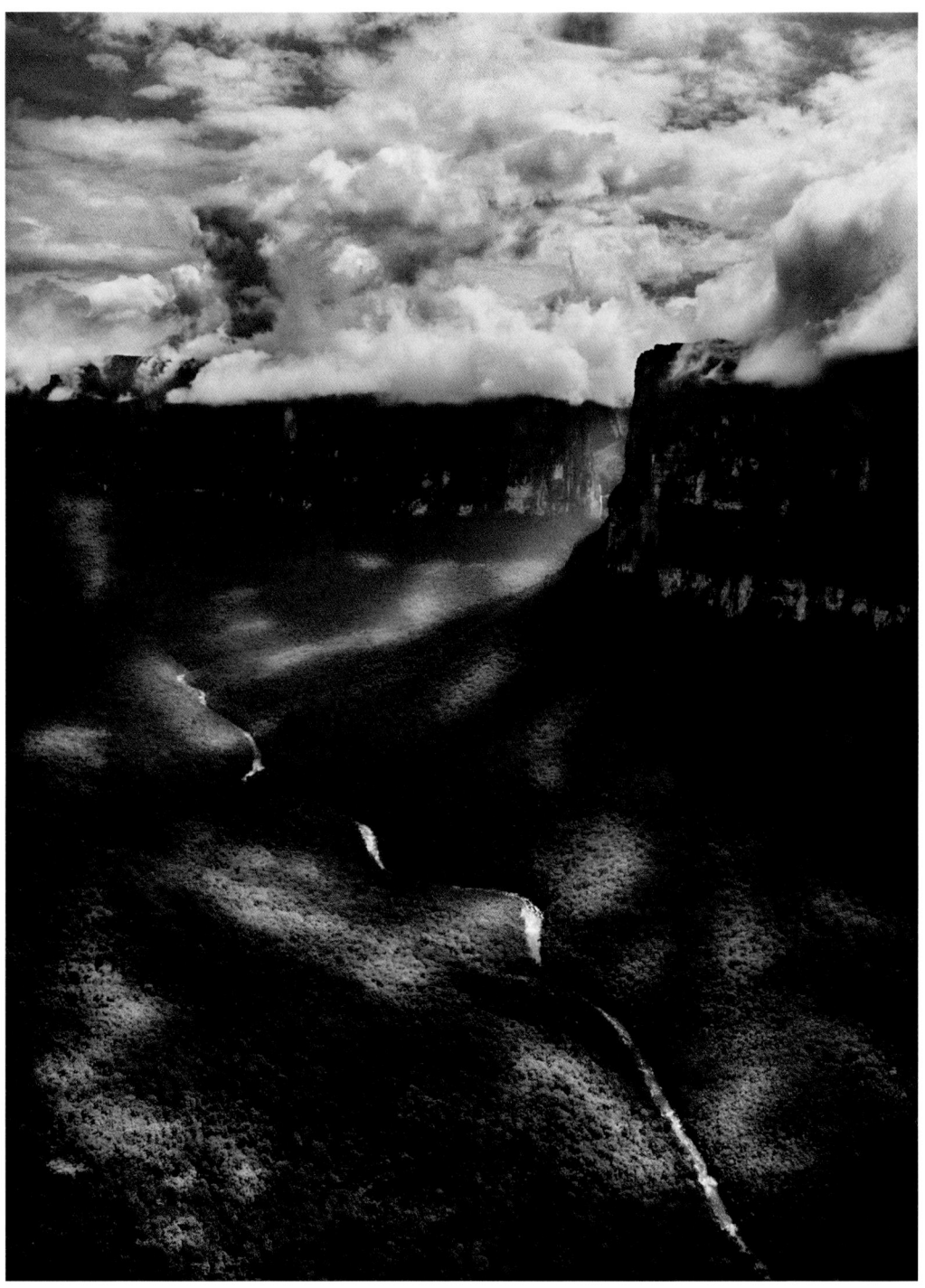

Opposite Surrounded by Amazonian rainforest, the Churún River cuts a wide valley beside Auyantepui. The water from the Angel Falls drops into the "Devil's Canyon" and eventually joins the Churún River. Venezuela. November and December 2006.

Pages 484/485 The Roraima Tepui, which straddles the borders of southeastern Venezuela, Brazil and Guyana, has a surface of almost 14 square miles (35 square kilometers) and rises to a height of 8,933 feet (2,723 meters). *Tepui*, a Pemon Indian word for mountain, is now commonly used to describe a particular type of flat-topped mountain to be found in this region of South America. Varying in height between 3,300 and 9,800 feet (1,000 and 3,000 meters), the mesa or plateau of *tepuis* often have a unique ecosystem characterized by endemic animals and plants. This photograph was taken as we climbed down the 3,000-foot (900-meter)-high "wall" of the *tepui*, a venture that took us the best part of two days to complete. Venezuela. November and December 2006.

Pages 486/487 The *Warime* ceremony of the Piaroa people in Venezuela symbolizes the birth of the world. It portrays earlier times of humanity and demonstrates how, thanks to their strength and vitality, they have survived until today. This ceremony, which takes place once a year, is also a harvest festival. This *Warime* is being held in the basin of the high Carinagua River. Venezuela on the border with Colombia. November and December 2006.

Page 488 Afukaka Kuikuro, chief of the Kuikuro people, with his youngest daughter. Upper Xingu, Mato Grosso, Brazil. July, August and September 2005.

Page 489 As with this Kamayura villager, the indigenous groups of the Upper Xingu attribute their pacifism to their overwhelming diet of fish. Mehinaku tribesmen explain. "We do not eat animals that have warm blood so our food is sweet and as a result our guts are never heated up for aggression." Mato Grosso, Brazil. July, August and September 2005.

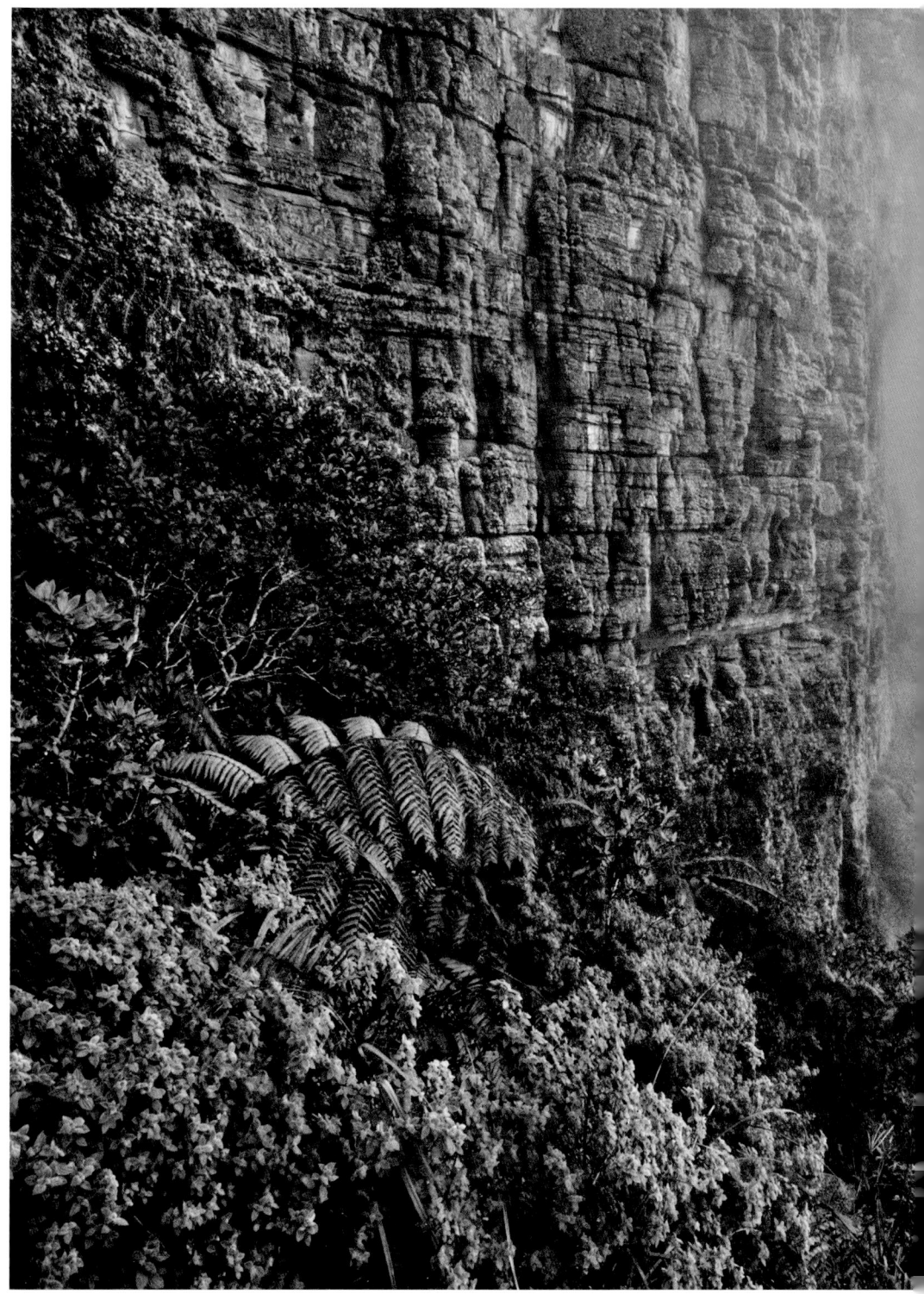

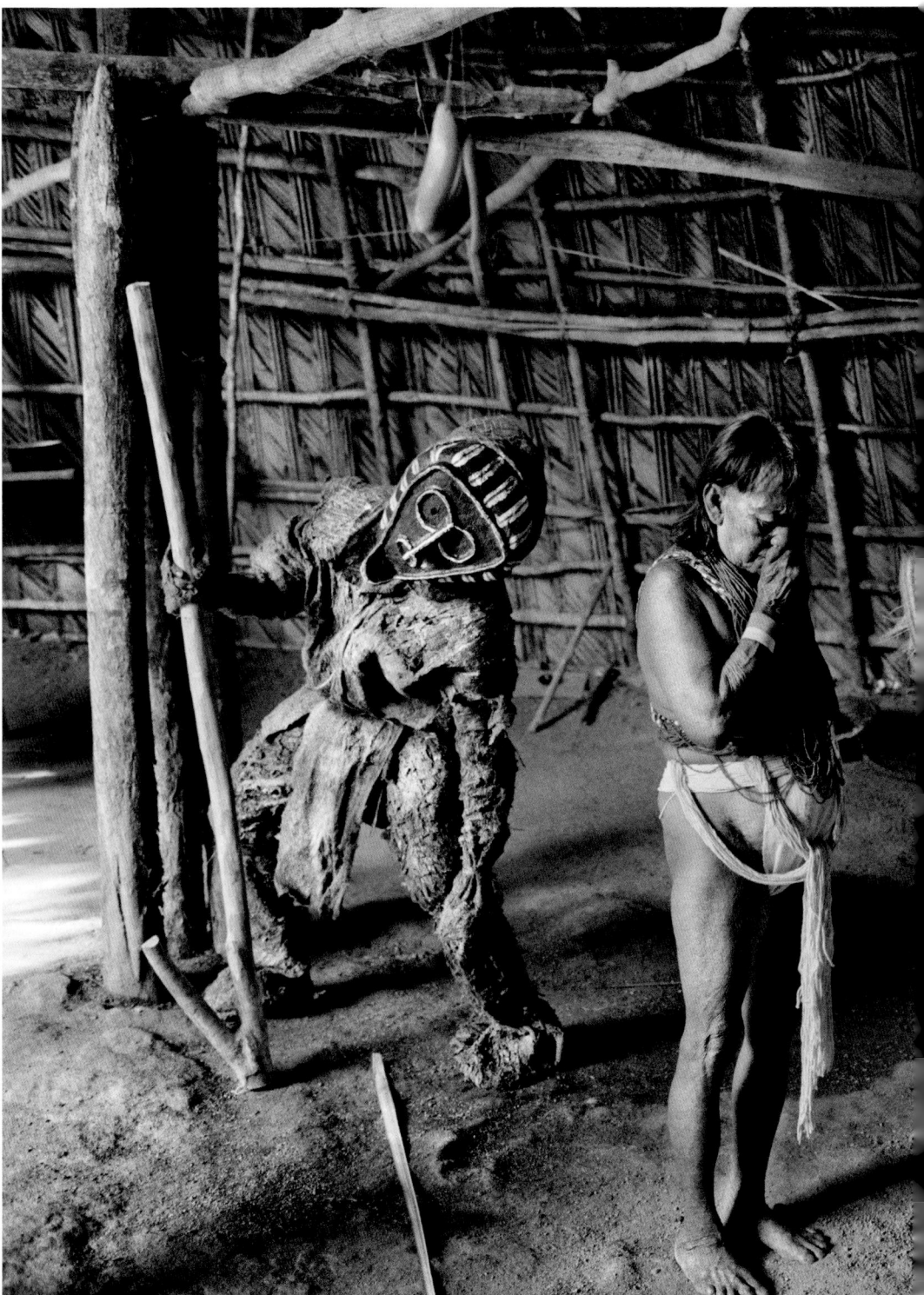

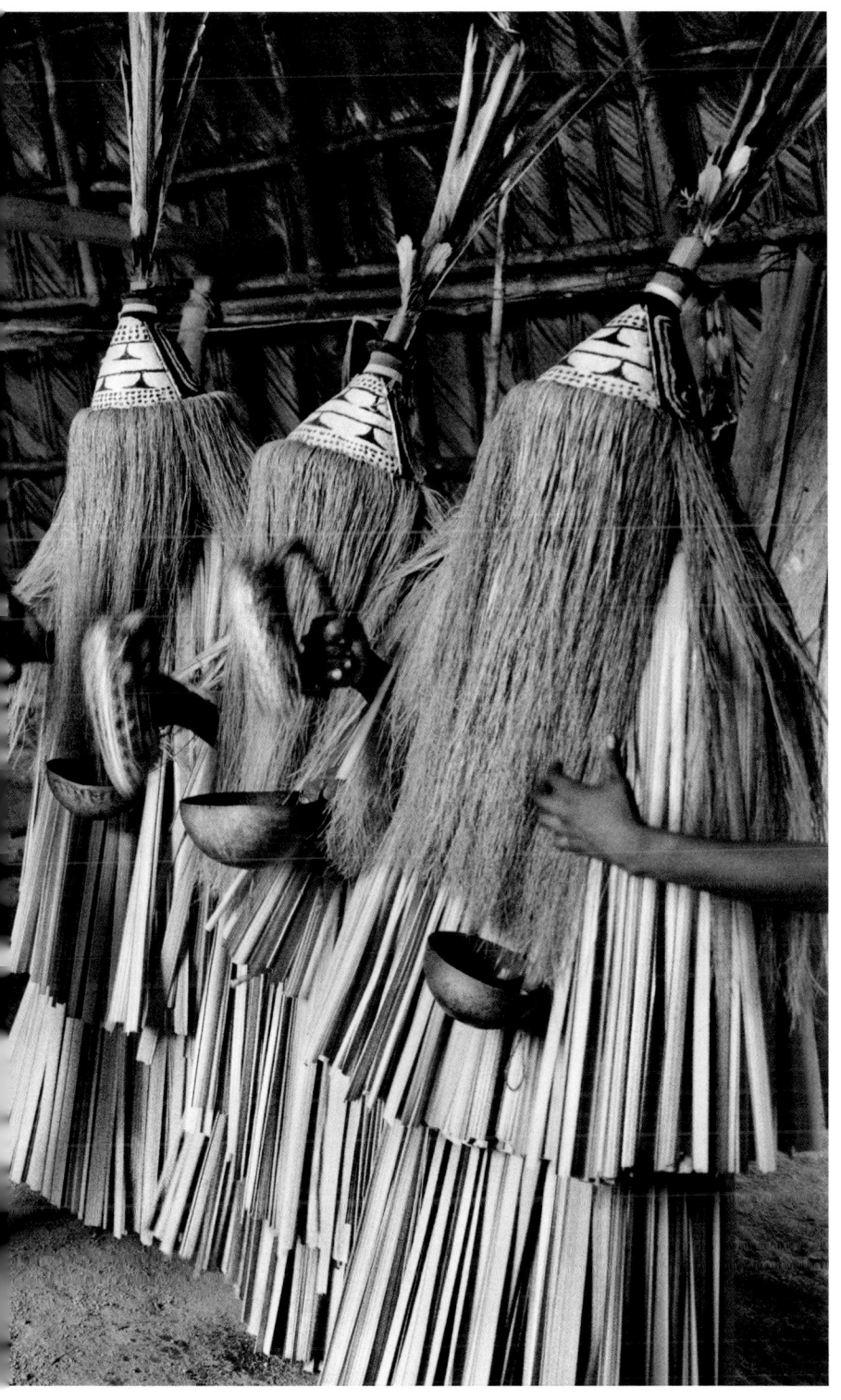

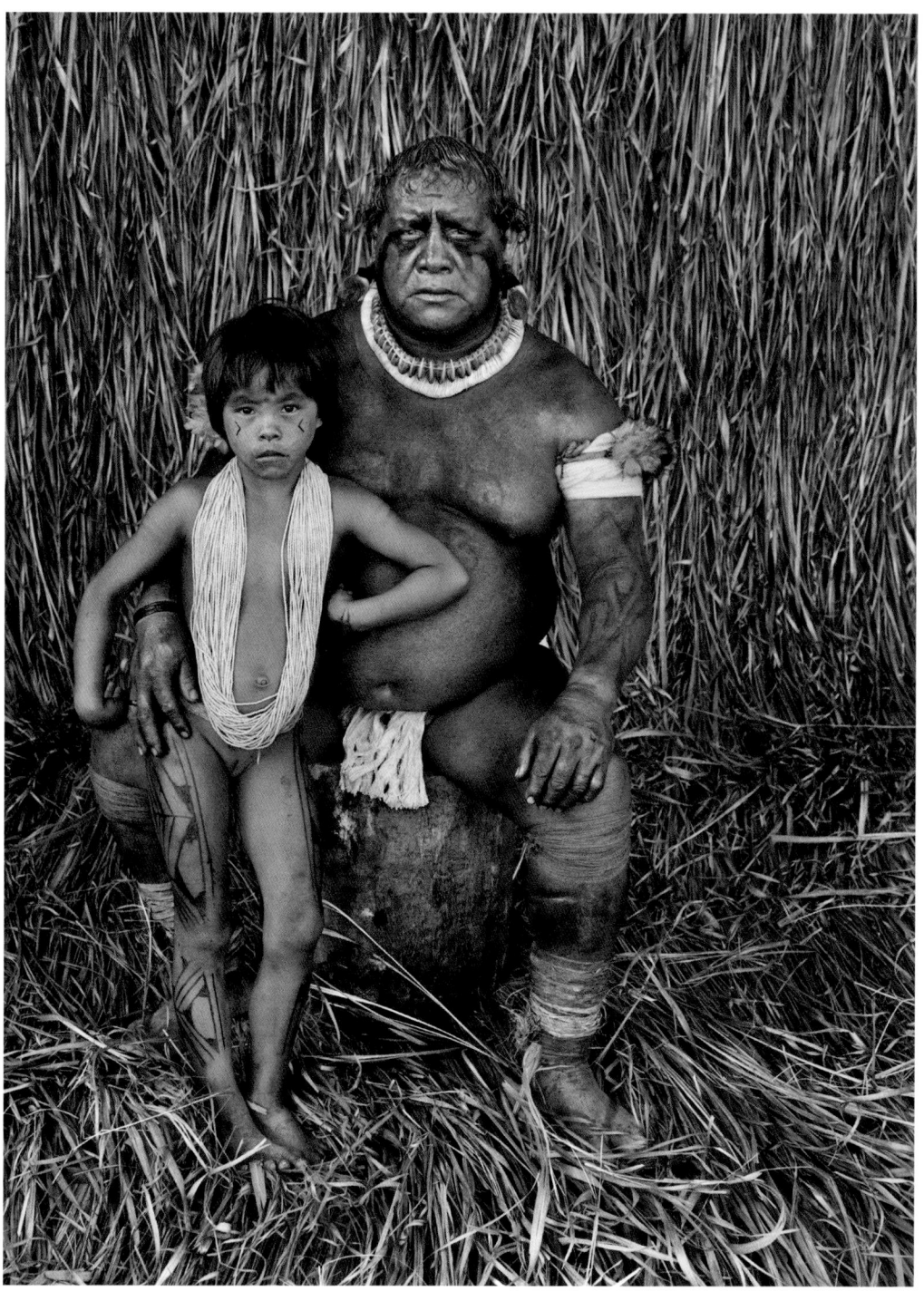

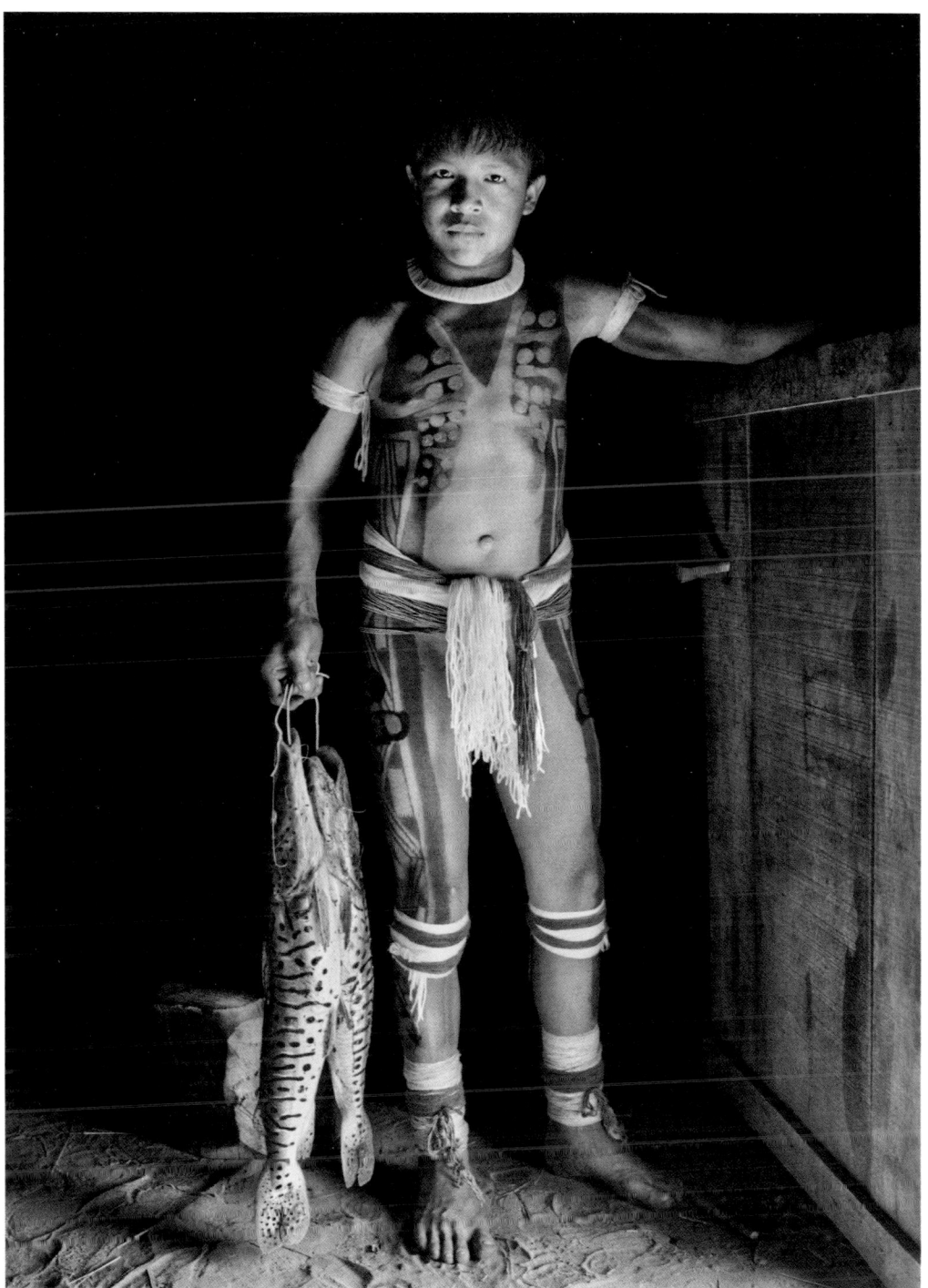

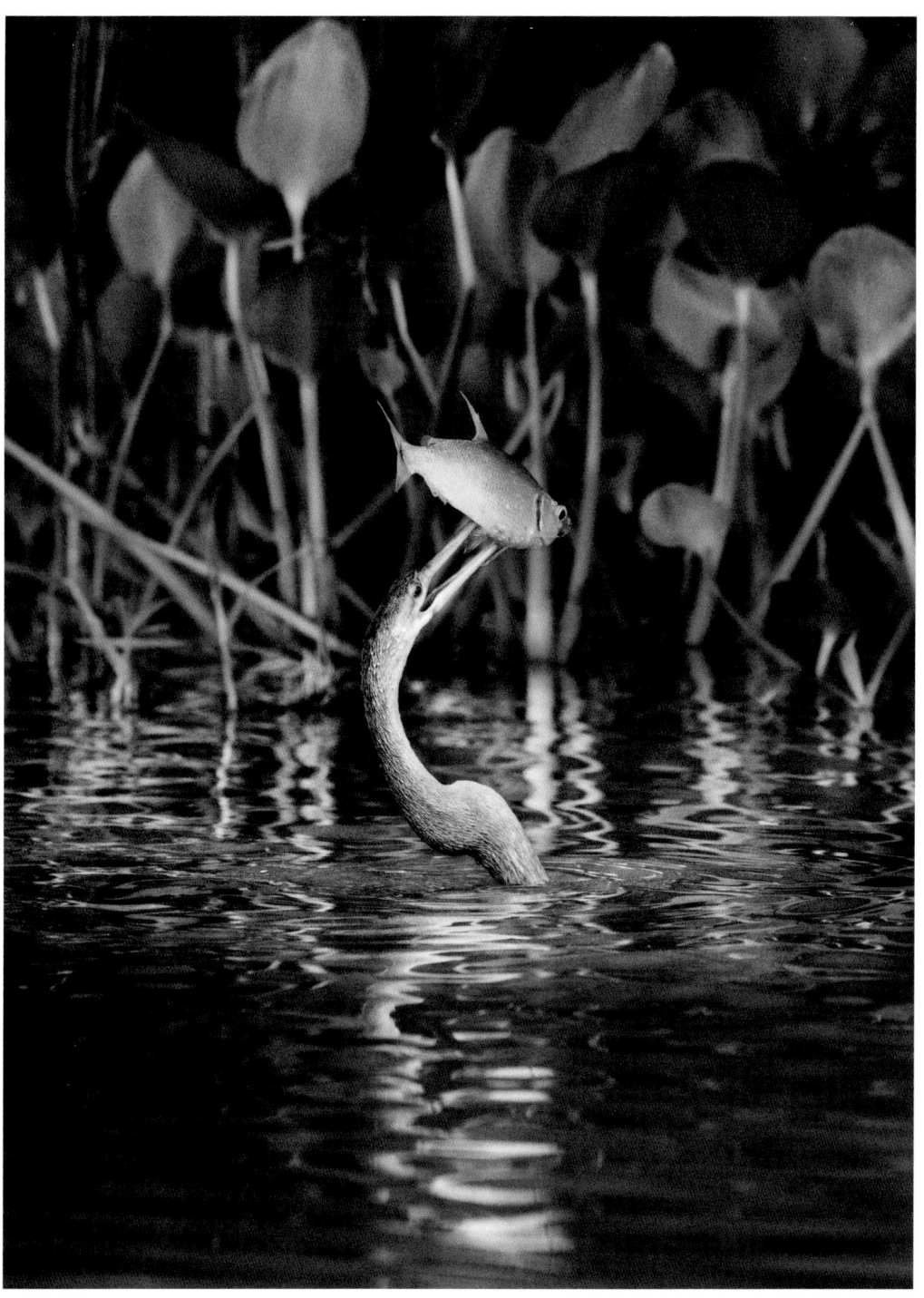

THE PANTANAL FAUNA

Pages 490 through 496

The Pantanal, which takes its name from the Portuguese word *pântano*, meaning bog, swamp or marsh, is a region bursting with natural life. One of the world's largest wetlands, it sprawls across the Brazilian states of Mato Grosso and Mato Grosso do Sul, spilling into Bolivia and Paraguay and covering an area estimated at between 54,000 and 75,000 square miles (140,000 and 195,000 square kilometers). Because the level of its waters rises and falls with the seasons, the Pantanal's cycles of life are also constantly in flux. During the rainy season, flooding of about 80 percent of the area nurtures an astonishing diversity of aquatic plants and animal species. Its ecosystem hosts some 1,000 bird species, 400 fish species, 300 species of mammal and 480 different kinds of reptile.

Among its rarest fauna are the marsh deer (*Blastocerus dichotomus*) and the giant river otter (*Pteronura brasiliensis*). Endangered animals include the maned wolf (*Chrysocyon brachyurus*), the bush dog (*Speothos venaticus*) and the yacare caiman (*Caiman yacare*), while the hyacinth macaw (*Anodorhynchus hyacinthinus*) and the crowned solitary eagle (*Harpyhaliaetus coronatus*) are also threatened. In contrast, several species prosper. The jaguar (*Panthera onca*) is very much at home in the Pantanal, while the yellow anaconda (*Eunectes notaeus*), the red-footed tortoise (*Chelonoidis carbonaria*) and the green iguana (*Iguana iguana*) are relatively common. Brazil. September and October 2011.

Opposite The *biguatinga*, or anhinga (*Anhinga anhinga*), is a large aquatic bird with an 33-inch (84-centimeter) wingspan as well as a long, straight bill and a very slender neck, which make it an effective fisher. Here, a *biguatinga* has just caught a *lambari* (*Astyanax bimaculatus*) in the Cuiabá River, close to Porto Jofre in northern Pantanal. Mato Grosso, Brazil. September and October 2011.

Pages 492/493 The *capivara*, or capybara (*Hydrochoerus hydrochoeris*), the world's largest rodent, is a semiaquatic mammal that lives in groups of as many as 40 animals. It measures between 40 and 50 inches (100 and 130 centimeters) in length and can weigh close to 175 pounds (80 kilos). It is hunted for its meat. Encontro das Aguas National Park. Pantanal. Mato Grosso, Brazil. September and October 2011.

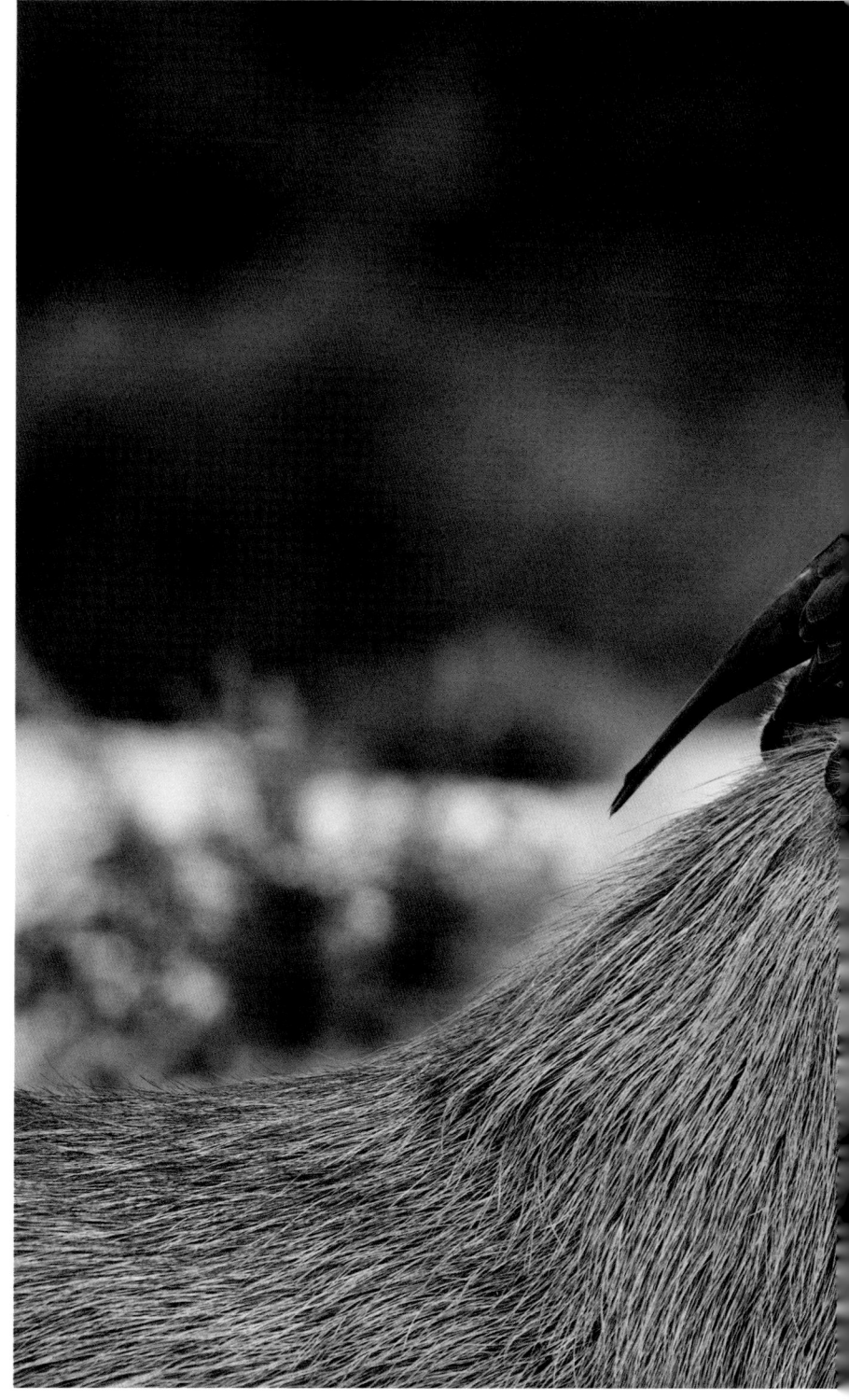

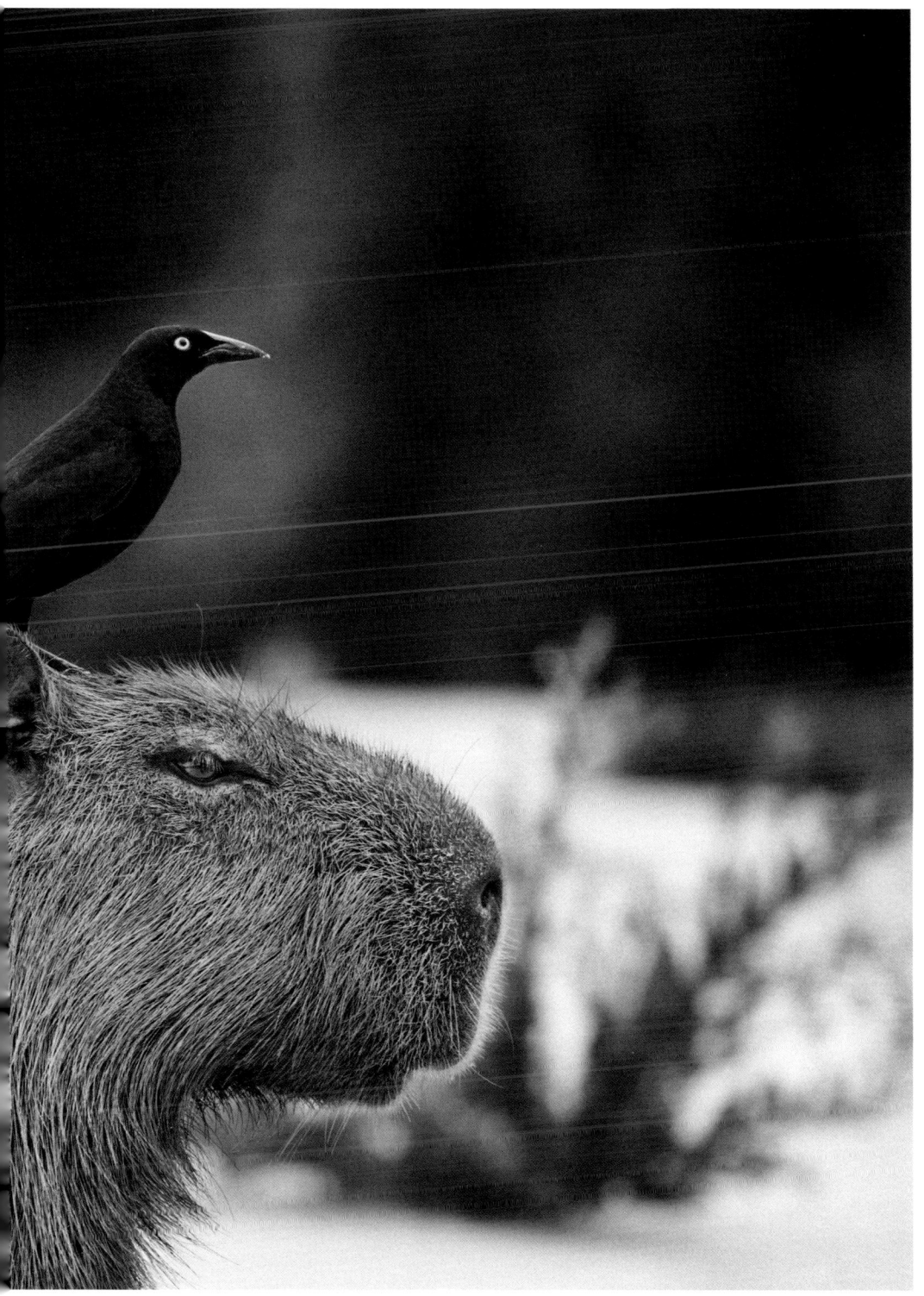

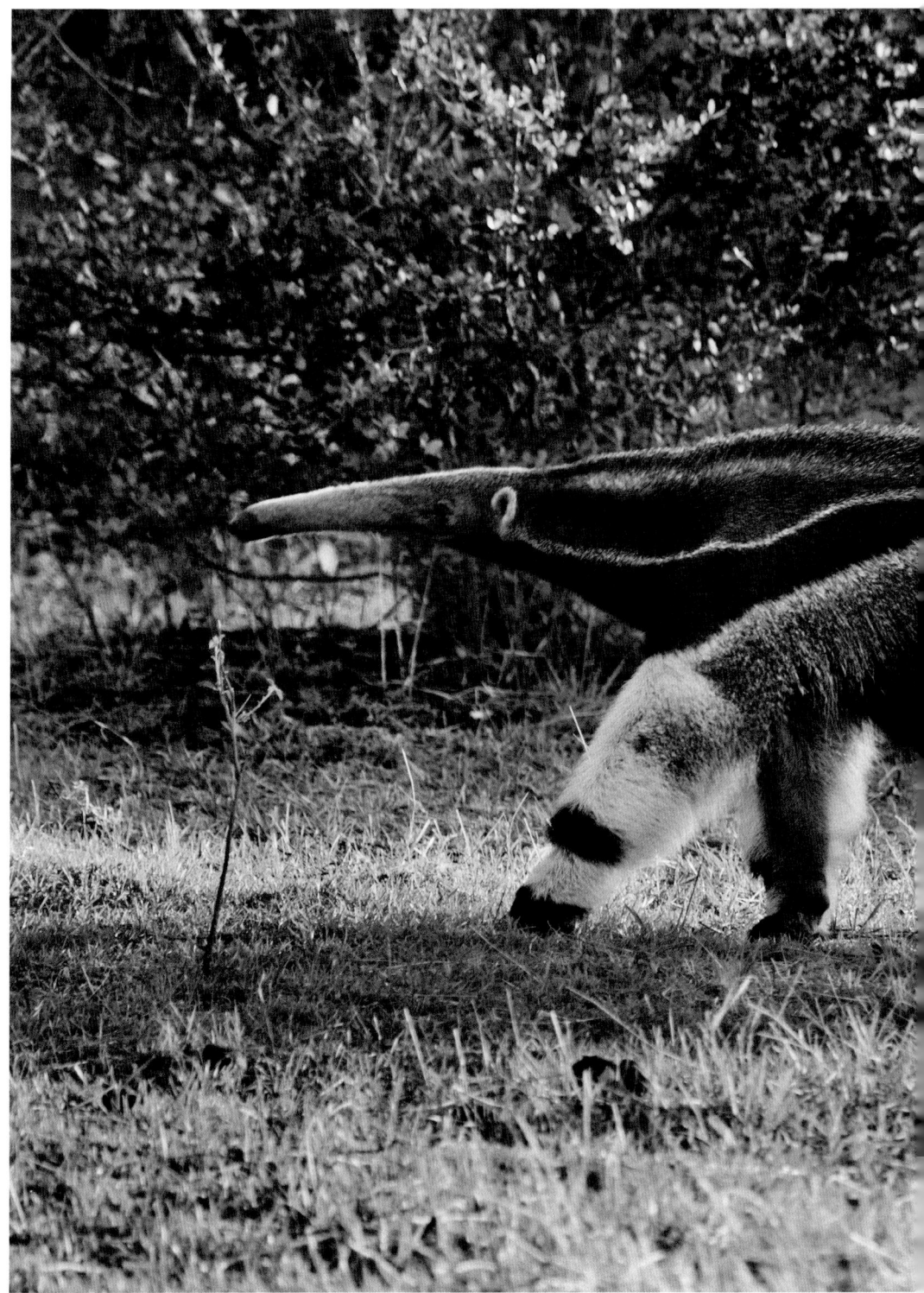

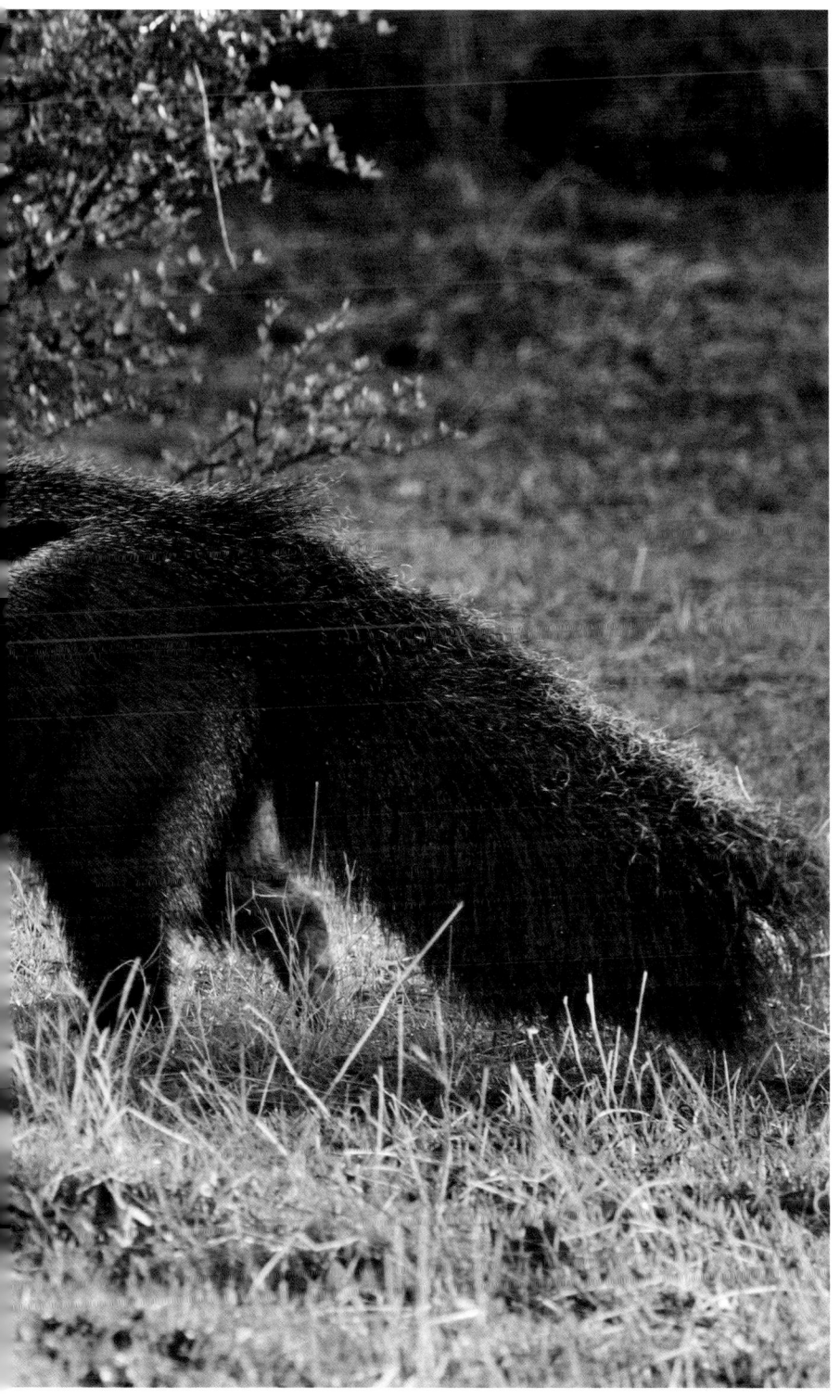

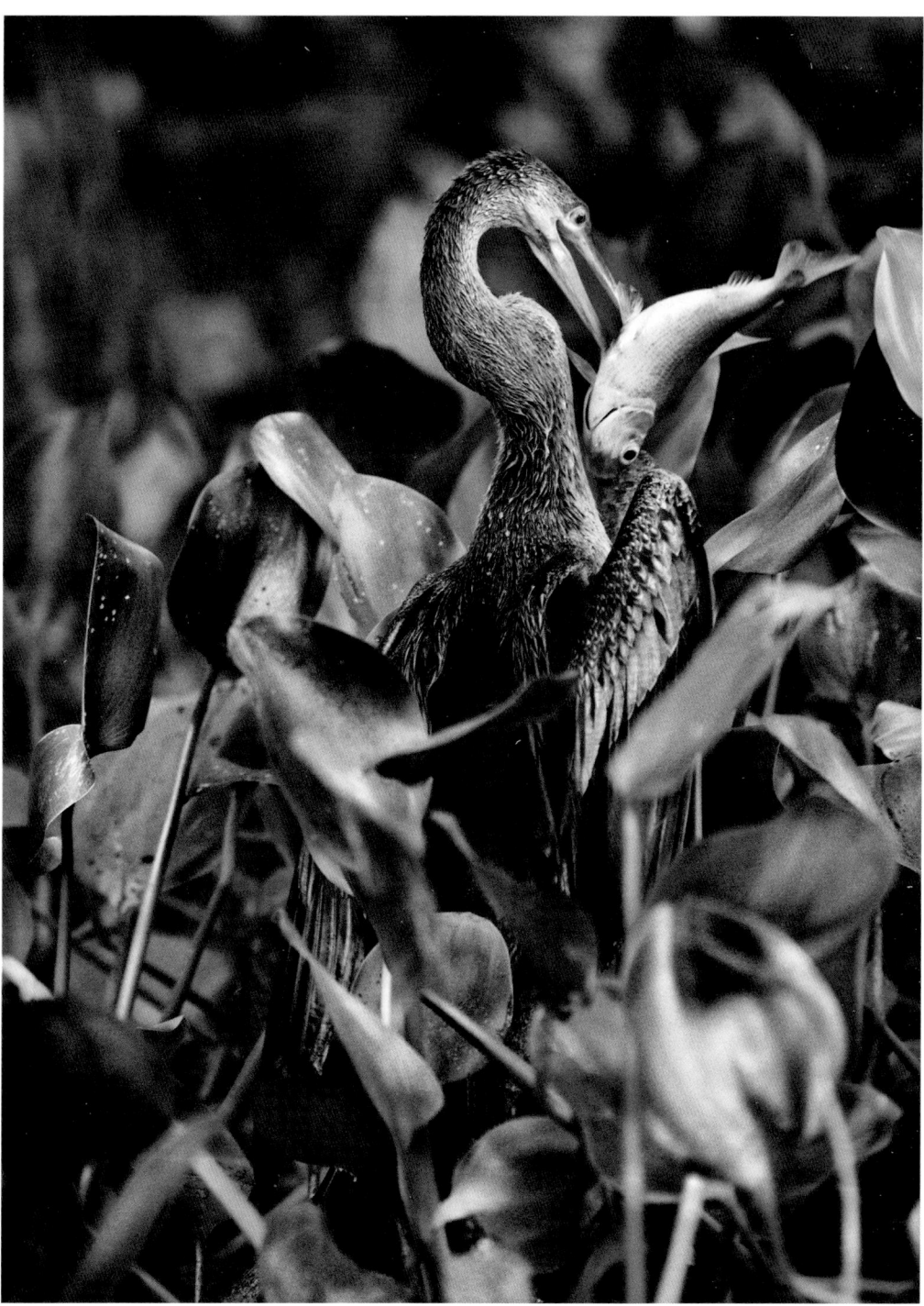

Pages 494/495 *Tamanduá-bandeira*, or giant ant-eater (*Myrmecophaga tridactyla*). This strange-looking animal has evolved to suit its diet of ants and termites, with fiercely powerful claws on its forelimbs designed to rip open insects' nests. It has no teeth, but its long, sticky tongue slips into the galleries to catch the prey, which are then swallowed whole. Its poor eyesight is compensated by a sharp sense of smell. The anteater can measure between 4 and 7 feet (1.2 and 2 meters) long, with its featherlike tail adding a further 30 inches (75 centimeters). Caiman Ecological Refuge. Mato Grosso do Sul, Brazil. September and October 2011.

Opposite The *biguatinga*, or anhinga (*Anhinga anhinga*), is a large aquatic bird with an 33-inch (84-centimeter) wingspan as well as a long, straight bill and a very slender neck, which make it an effective fisher. Here, a *biguatinga* has just caught a *lambari* (*Astyanax bimaculatus*) in the Cuiabá River, close to Porto Jofre in northern Pantanal. Mato Grosso, Brazil. September and October 2011.

Pages 498/499 *Mutum de penacho*, or bare-faced curassow (*Crax fasciolata*). Among the most striking birds of the Pantanal, male curassows are black with white bellies, while females have a streaked back and a cream-colored belly (as seen here). Although they can fly, they prefer to scour the ground for seeds, fruit, insects and frogs; for safety, they spend nights hidden in trees. Ecological Park of Baia Bonita. Mato Grosso do Sul, Brazil. September and October 2011.

Pages 500/501 Approximately 1,500 miles (2,400 kilometers) long, the Juruá River is one of the Amazon's longest tributaries. It rises in Peru's Ucalayi Highlands and is navigable for 1,120 miles (1,800 kilometers) before it joins the Solimões River. But once it enters the flat, forested lowlands known as the Amazon depression to the west of Manaus, it wiggles like a worm, curving to the left and right in order to advance barely half a mile. Even traveling downstream, boat skippers need immense patience. Amazonas, Brazil. August and September 2009.

Pages 502/503 Sometimes the mesas of the *tepuis* resemble well-cultivated gardens. *Tepui*, a Pemon Indian word for mountain, is now commonly used to describe a particular type of flat-topped mountain found in southeastern Venezuela and across its borders with Brazil and Guyana. Seen on top of the Roraima Tepui, the *Orectante sceptrum* (of the *Xyridaceae* family) is a plant common to *tepui* plateaus. Venezuela. November and December 2006.

Pages 504/505 The Anavilhanas, the name given to around 350 forested islands in Brazil's Rio Negro, form the world's largest inland archipelago. Covering 390 square miles (1,000 square kilometers) of Amazonia, they start 50 miles (80 kilometers) northwest of Manaus and stretch some 250 miles (400 kilometers) up the Rio Negro, as far as Barcelos. Their formation dates back to the last Ice Age, when changes in the flow of rivers entering the Rio Negro produced accumulations of sediment that, over time, formed sandbars and islands.

Since water levels change with the seasons by as much as 65 feet (20 meters), the Anavilhanas are themselves ever-changing, with channels, sandbars and lagoons appearing during the dry season and some small islands vanishing when waters rise. Many of the larger islands, though, are self-contained parcels of rainforest. Amazonas, Brazil. May 2009.

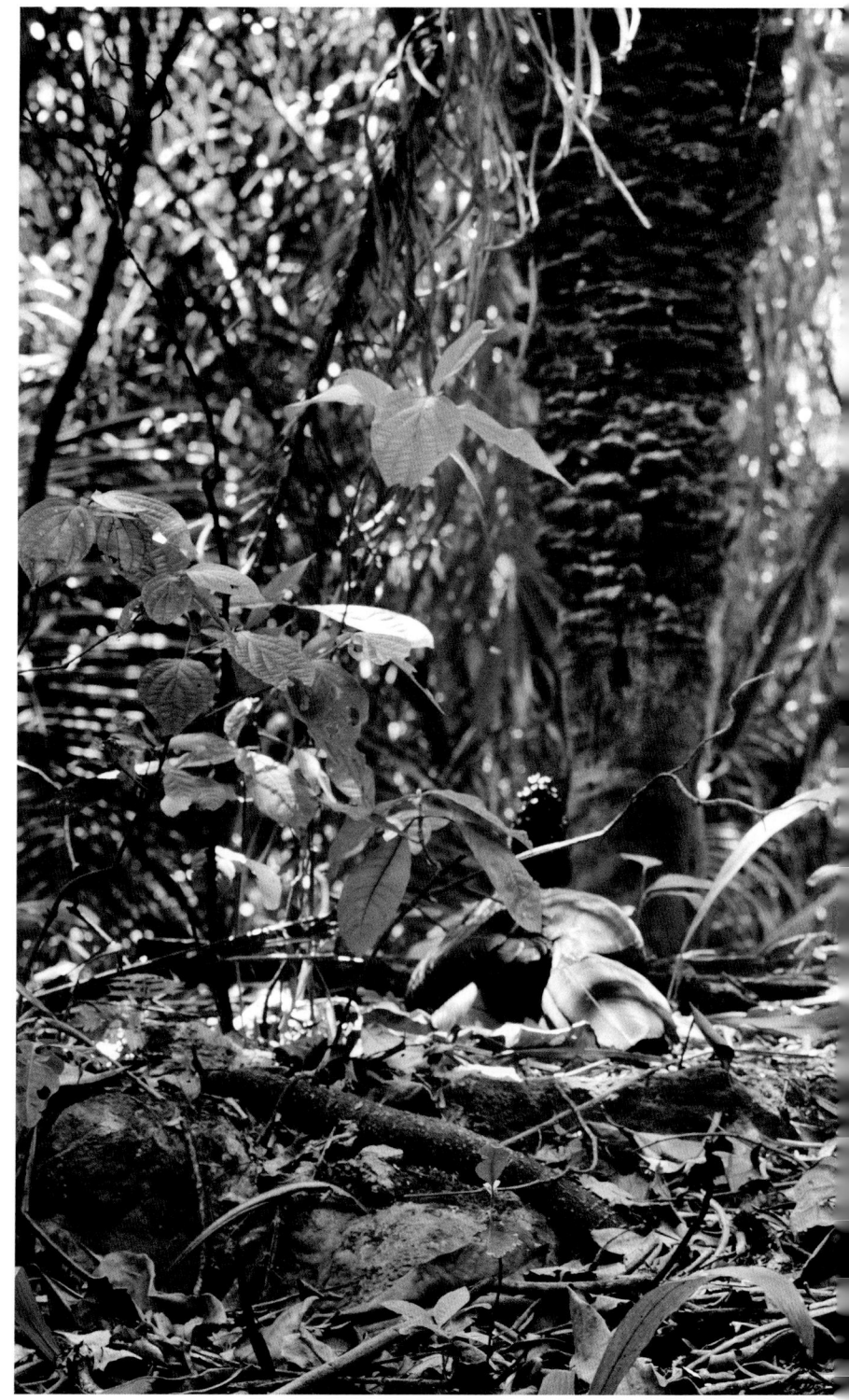

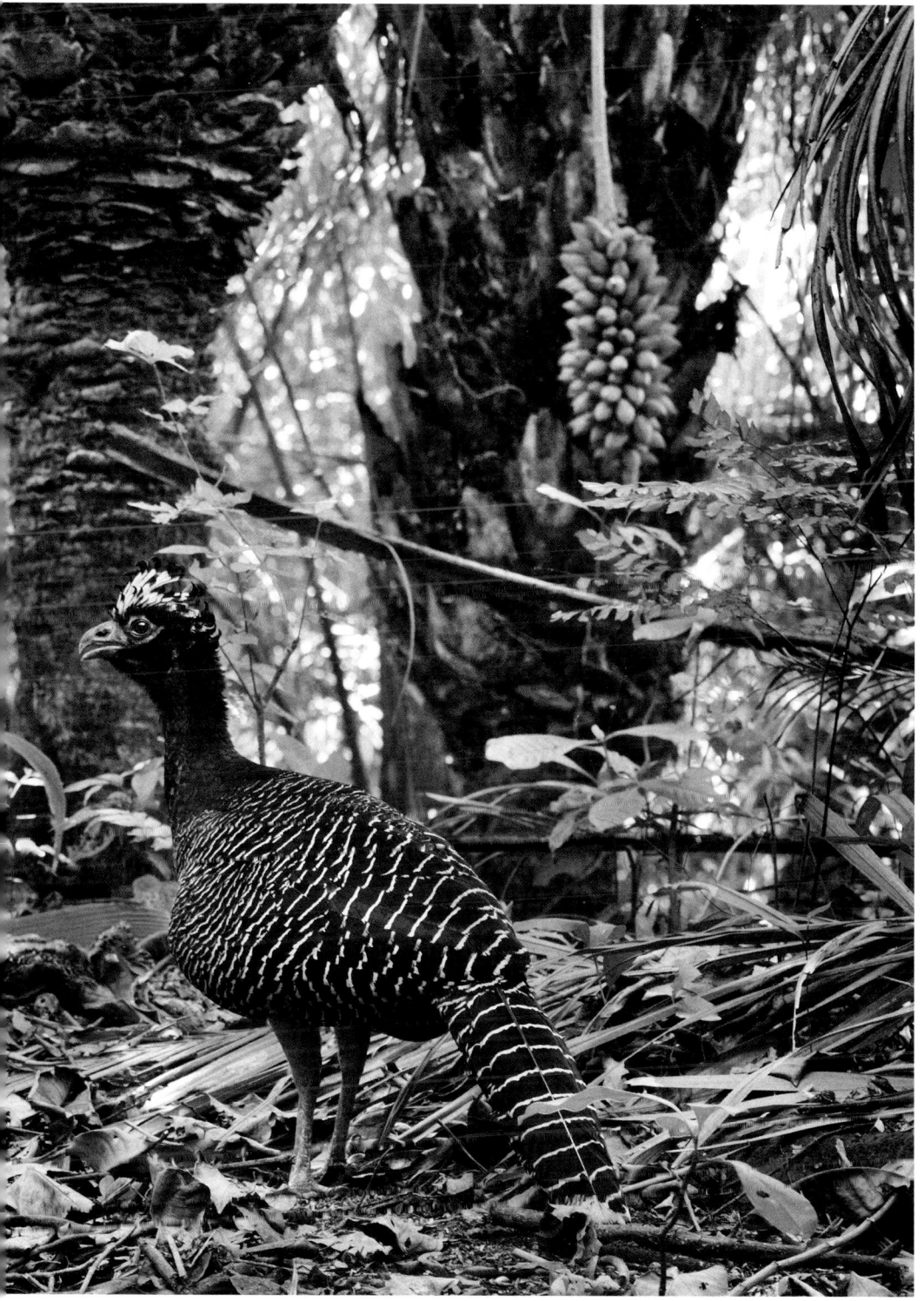

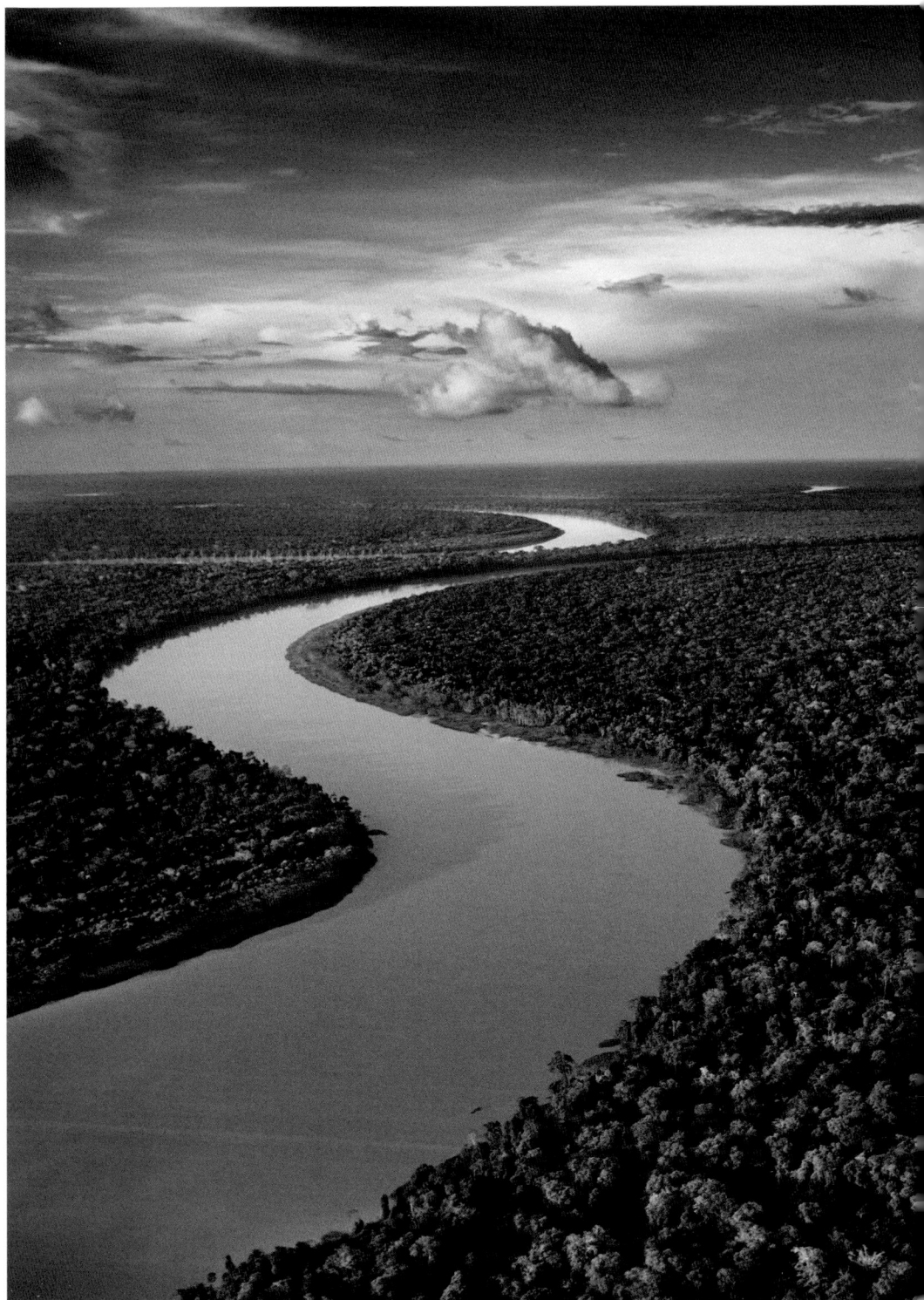

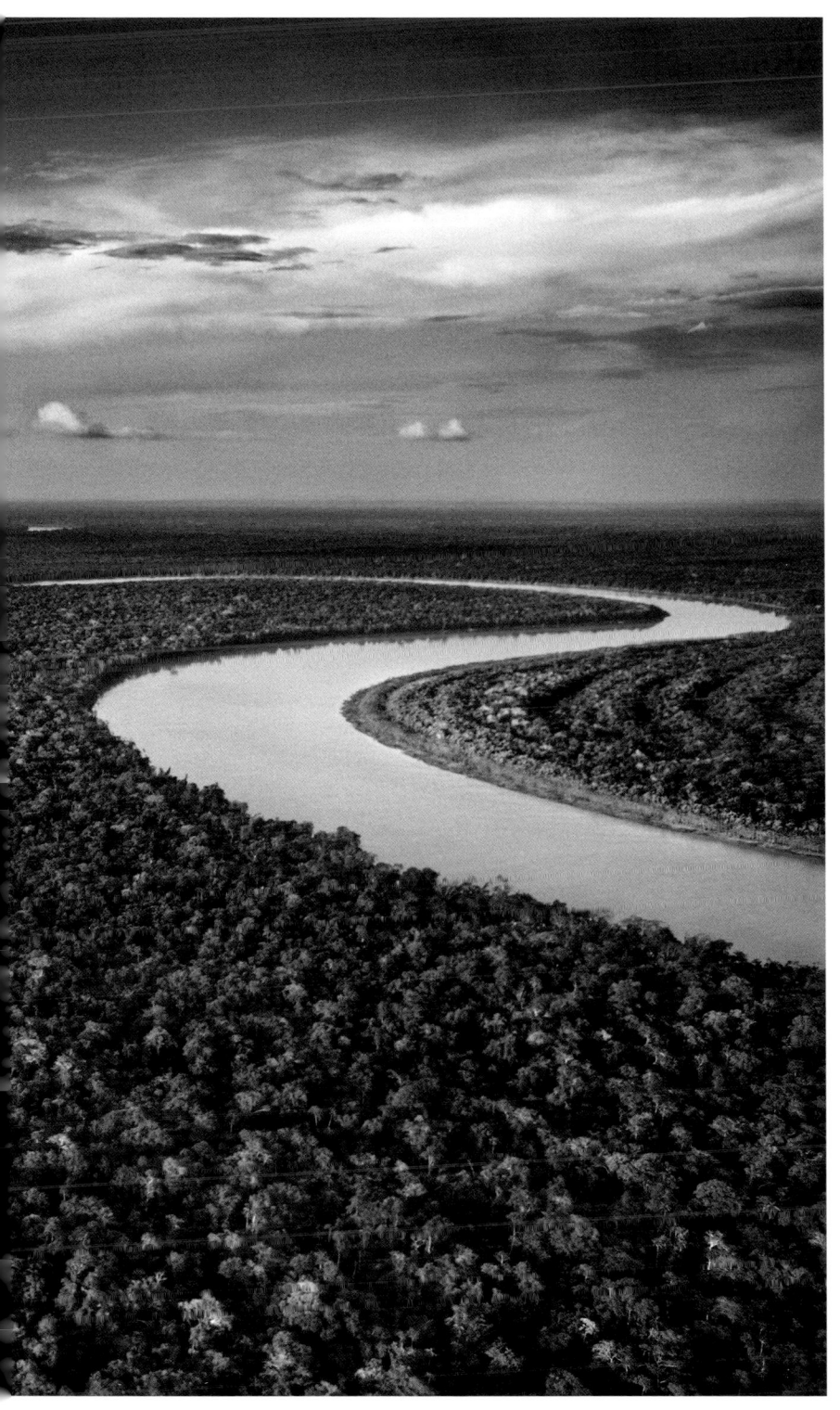

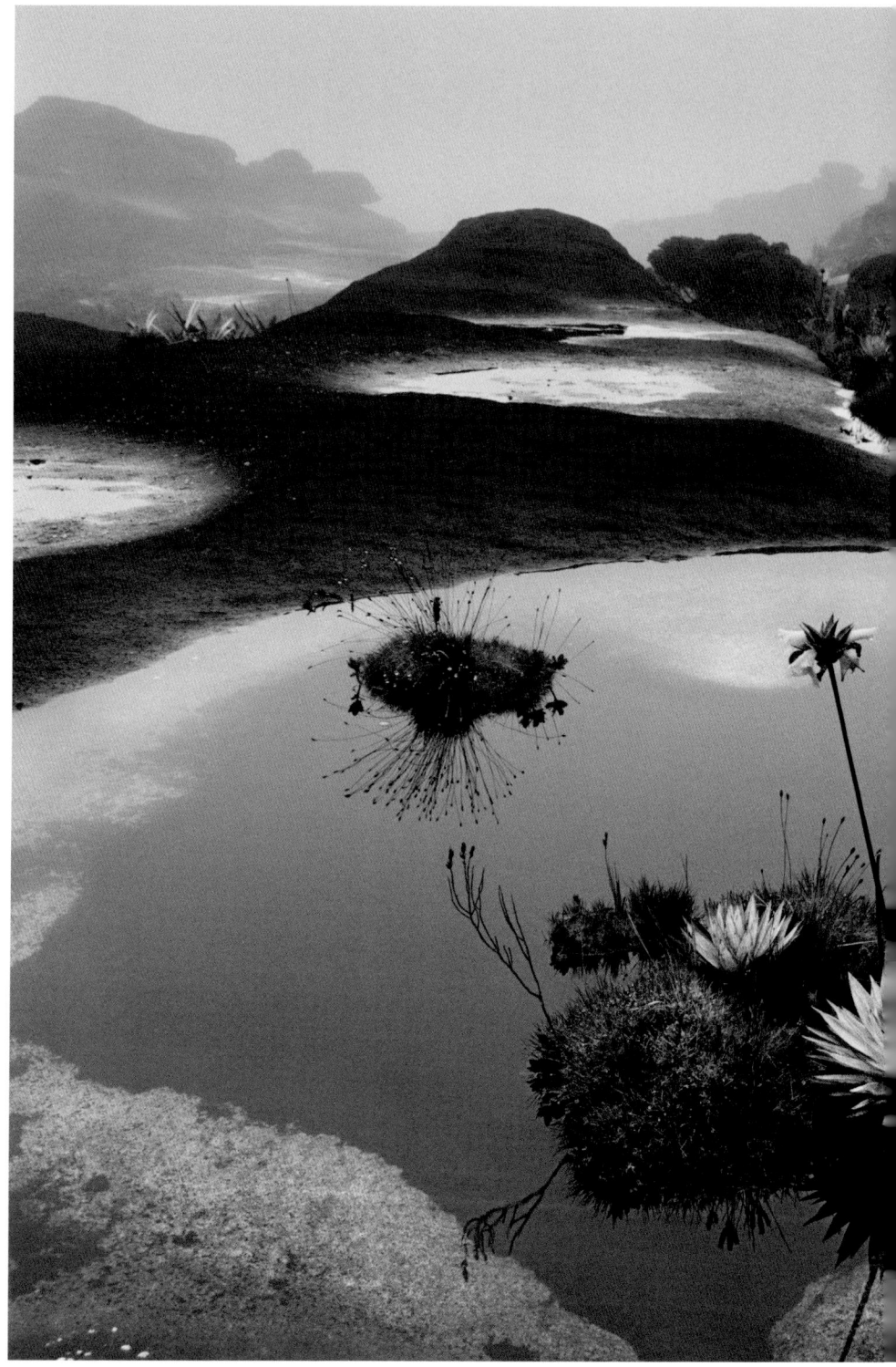

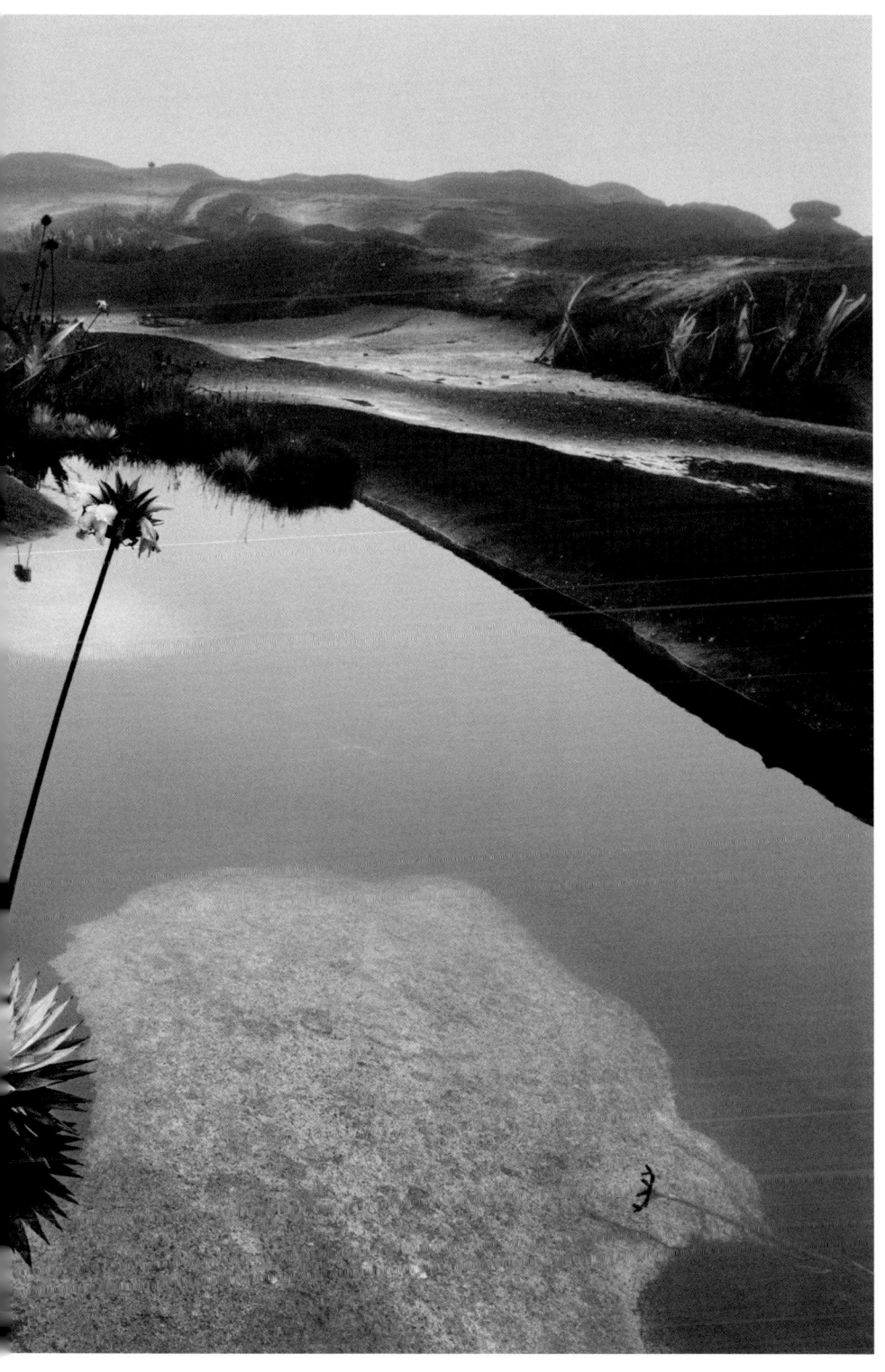

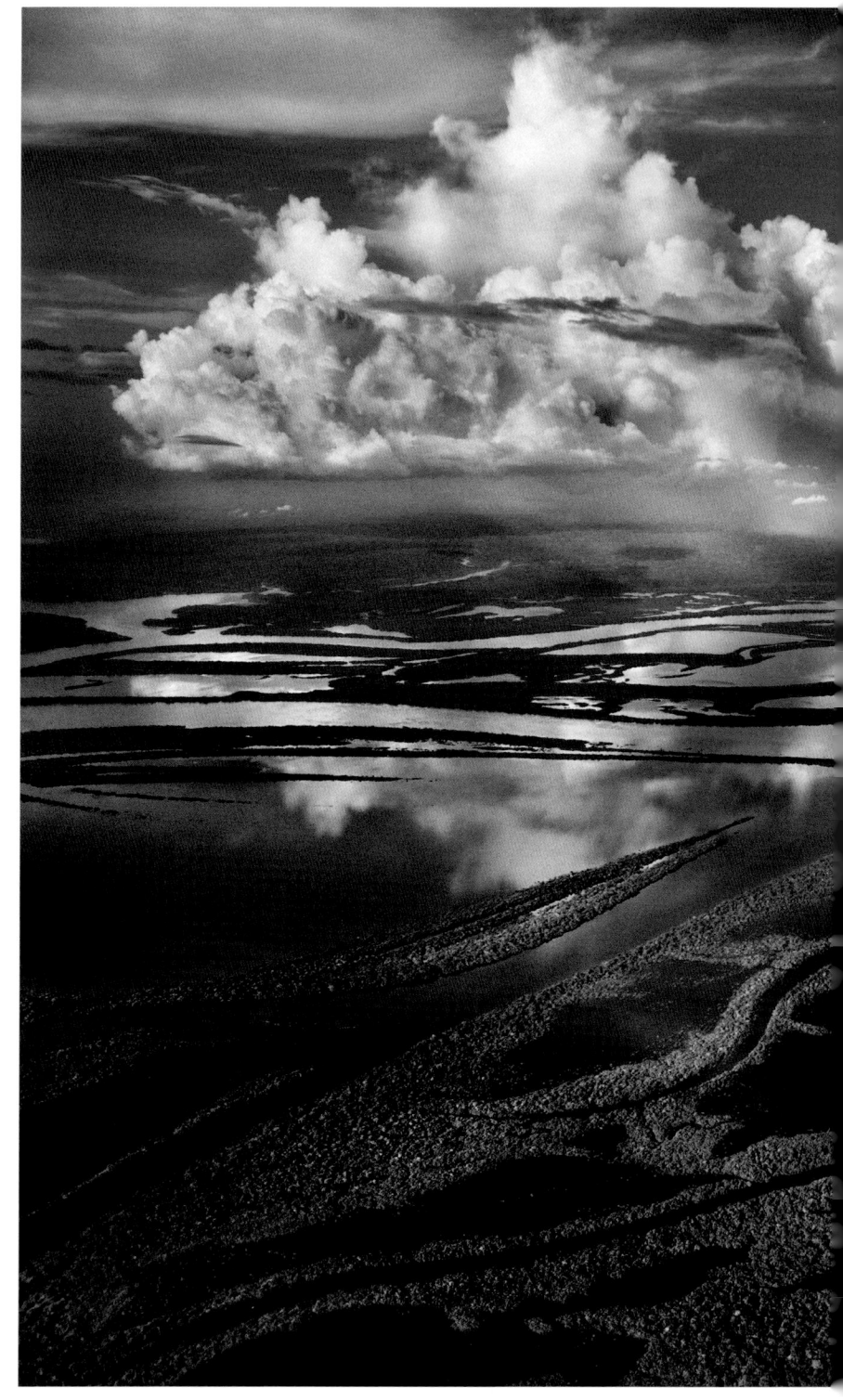

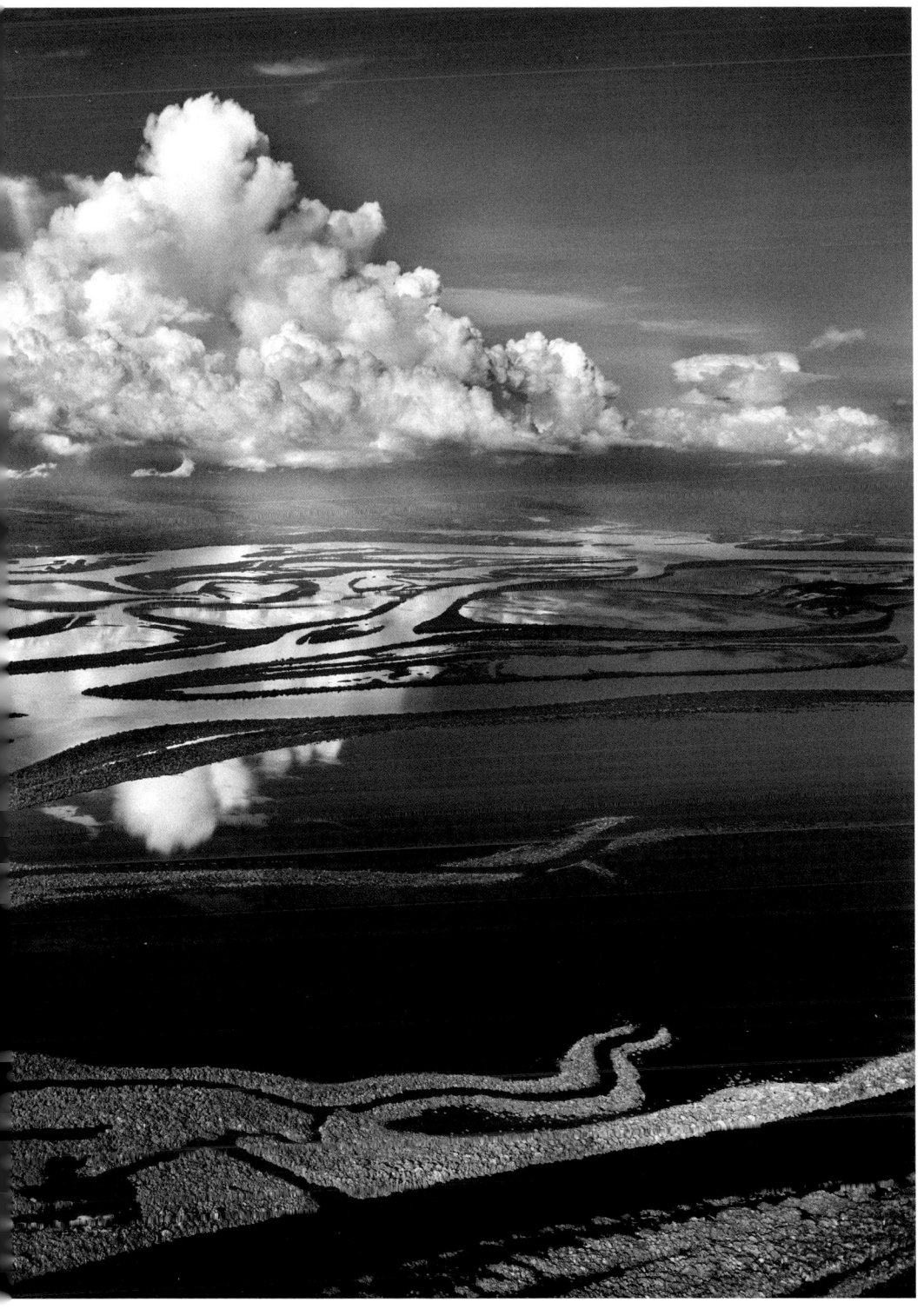

BIOGRAPHY

1944 Sebastião Ribeiro Salgado, born on February 8, in Aimorés, MG, Brazil, is the only boy out of eight children.

1964–69 Earns a master's degree in economics at the Universidade de São Paulo, Brazil. Economist in the Department of Finance for the city of São Paulo. He marries Lélia Deluiz Wanick on December 16 1967.

1969–71 The couple moves to France. Salgado studies at the École nationale de la statistique et de l'administration économique at the Université de Paris, France.

1971–73 Economist for the International Coffee Organization in London, England.

1973–74 Upon his return to Paris, Salgado opts for a career in photography, working as a freelancer before joining the Sygma photo agency. In February 1974, Lélia and Sebastião's first child, Juliano, is born.

1975–79 Salgado joins the Gamma photo agency.

1979 Joins the Magnum agency. In August, Lélia and Sebastião's second child, Rodrigo, is born with Down syndrome.

1984–85 Documents the devastating effects of the drought in the Sahel in Africa for Médecins Sans Frontières. From this work comes his book entitled *Sahel. L'Homme en détresse.*

1986–92 Documentary project on the end of manual labor, photographed in twenty-six countries. This project is presented in the book *Workers* (1993).

1994 Leaves Magnum. With Lélia Wanick Salgado, he founds the Paris-based Amazonas Images, an agency exclusively devoted to the management of his oeuvre.

1994–99 Completes a long-term project on the theme of population migration worldwide. This includes thirty-six photographic investigations of the mass movements of migrants, refugees, and displaced peoples. It forms the basis of his new book, *Migrations.*

1998 With Lélia, founds the Instituto Terra, a non-profit civil organization focusing on reforestation, environmental education and sustainable rural development in the Rio Doce Valley, in the state of Minas Gerais, Brazil.

2001 Completes a series of reportages on the global campaign to end polio, an initiative led by a partnership between UNICEF and the WHO, among other organizations.

2004–11 Concludes the *Genesis* project, which, through black-and-white photographs of landscapes, human settlements, and wildlife, seeks to provide a portrait of aspects of nature and humanity that remain intact.

2013–19 Photographic project on the theme of the Brazilian Amazonian Forest and the indigenous communities living in these regions, their territory. Released in 2021 as *Amazônia.*

2025 Sebastião Salgado dies on May 23. His photography and dedication to an ecologically and socially just world remain a lasting legacy of a life committed to values essential for both the planet and humanity.

BOOKS

Autres Amériques, published by Éditions Contrejour, France, 1986, and by:
Other Americas, Pantheon Books, USA, 1986.
Otras Americas, Ediciones ELR, Spain, 1986.
Outras Américas, Companhia das Letras, Brazil, 1999.

Sahel. L'Homme en détresse, Prisma Presse and Centre National de la Photographie, for Médecins Sans Frontières, France, 1986.
Sahel. El Fin del Camino, Comunidad de Madrid, for Médicos Sin Fronteras, Spain, 1988.
Sahel. The End of the Road, University of California Press, USA, 2004.

Les Cheminots, Comité Central d'Entreprise de la SNCF, France, 1989.

An Uncertain Grace, published by Aperture, USA, 1990, and by:
An Uncertain Grace, Thames & Hudson, UK, 1990.
An Uncertain Grace, SGM, Sygma Union, Japan, 1990.
Une certaine grâce, Nathan, France, 1990.
Um Incerto Estado de Graça, Editorial Caminho, Portugal, 1995.
Un incerto stato di grazia, Contrasto, Italy, 2002.

The Best Photos/As Melhores Fotos, Sebastião Salgado, Boccato Editores, Brazil, 1992.

Photo Poche, **Sebastião Salgado**, nº 55, Centre National de la Photographie, France, 1993.
FotoNote *Sebastião Salgado*, nº 02, Contrasto, Italy, 2004.
Photofile *Sebastião Salgado*, Thames & Hudson, UK and USA, 2006.
Photo Pocket *Sebastião Salgado*, Edition Braus, Germany, 2006.
Photo Poche *Sebastião Salgado*, Lunwerg Editores, Spain, 2006.
Poche *Sebastião Salgado*, Cosacnaify, Brazil, 2011.

Workers, published by Aperture, USA, 1993, and by:
Workers, Phaidon, UK, 1993.
La Main de l'Homme, Éditions de La Martinière, France, 1993.
Trabalho, Editorial Caminho, Portugal, 1993.
Trabajadores, Lunwerg Editores, Spain, 1993.
Arbeiter, Zweitausendeins, Germany, 1993.
Workers, Iwanami Shoten, Japan, 1993.
La mano dell'Uomo, Contrasto, Italy, 1994.
Trabalhadores, Companhia das Letras, Brazil, 1996.

Terra, edited by Lélia Wanick Salgado and published by:
Éditions de La Martinière, France, 1997.
Editorial Caminho, Portugal, 1997.
Zweitausendeins, Germany, 1997.
Contrasto, Italy, 1997.
Phaidon, UK, 1997.
Companhia das Letras, Brazil, 1997.
Alfaguara, Spain, 1997.

Migrations, edited by Amazonas Images and published by:
Exodes, Éditions de La Martinière, France, 2000.
Éxodos, Editorial Caminho, Portugal, 2000.
Migranten, Zweitausendeins, Germany, 2000.
In Cammino, Contrasto / Leonardo Arte, Italy, 2000.
Migrations, Aperture, USA, 2000.
Éxodos, Companhia das Letras, Brazil, 2000.
Éxodos, Fundación Retevisión, Spain, 2000.

The Children, edited by Amazonas Images and published by:
Les Enfants de l'Exode, Éditions de La Martinière, France, 2000.
Retratos de Crianças do Êxodo, Editorial Caminho, Portugal, 2000.
Kinder, Zweitausendeins, Germany, 2000.
Ritratti, Contrasto / Leonardo Arte, Italy, 2000.
The Children, Aperture, USA, 2000.
Retratos de Crianças do Êxodo, Companhia das Letras, Brazil, 2000.
Retratos, Fundación Retevisión, Spain, 2000.

The End of Polio, published by Bulfinch, USA, 2003, and by:
La Fine della Polio, Contrasto, Italy, 2003.
O Fim da Pólio, Companhia das Letras, Brazil, 2003.
O Fim da Pólio, Editorial Caminho, Portugal, 2003.
L'Eradication de la polio, Le Seuil / Turner & Turner, France, 2003.

L'Homme et l'eau, Éditions Terre Bleue, France, 2005.

The Cradle of Inequality, UNESCO, Brazil, 2005.

Africa, TASCHEN (international), 2007.

Genesis, TASCHEN (international), 2013.

De ma Terra à la Terre, Presses de la Renaissance, France, 2013.
Dalla mia Terra alla Terra, Contrasto, Italy, 2014.
De mi Tierra a la Tierra, La Fábrica, Spain, 2014.
Da minha Terra à Terra, Companhia das Letras, Brazil, 2014.

Profumo di Sogno, Contrasto, Italy, 2015.
Terres de Café, Éditions de La Martinière, France, 2015.
The Scent of a Dream, Abrams, USA, 2015.
Perfume de Sonho, Paisagem, Brazil, 2015.

Duft der Träume, Knesebeck, Germany, 2015.
The Scent of a Dream, China Photographic Publishing House, China, 2015.

Kuwait. A Desert on Fire, TASCHEN (international and Collector's Edition), 2016.

GOLD. Serra Pelada Gold Mine, TASCHEN (international and Collector's Edition), 2019.

Amazônia, TASCHEN (international and Collector's Edition), 2021.

Amazônia Touch, TASCHEN (international), 2023.

Des Oiseaux, Atelier EXB, France, 2024.

MAIN EXHIBITIONS

Swahel. L'Homme en détresse. Canon Photo Gallery, Amsterdam, The Netherlands, 1986. Palais de Tokyo, Paris, France, 1986. Festival International d'Arles, France, 1986. Musée de l'Elysée, Lausanne, Switzerland, 1987. Museu de Arte de São Paulo, Brazil, 1988. National Gallery of Art, Beijing, China, 1989. Biennale de Cétinié, Montenegro, Yugoslavia, 1997.

Other Americas. Museo de Arte Contemporáneo de Madrid, Spain, 1986. Maison de l'Amérique Latine, Paris, France, 1986. Musée de l'Elysée, Lausanne, Switzerland, 1987. Palace of Youth, Shanghai, China, 1989. Royal Library, Copenhagen, Denmark, 2007. Cultural Center, Brazilian Embassy, Buenos Aires, Argentina, 2008. Corporación Cultural Las Condes, Santiago, Chile, 2016.

Retrospective. Hasselblad Center, Gothenburg, Sweden, 1989. Bienal de Cuba, La Havana, Cuba, 1989. Stills Gallery, Edinburgh, Scotland, UK, 1990. Royal Albert Memorial Museum, Exeter, England, 1991. Glasgow Arts Centre, Scotland,

UK, 1992. National Museum of Modern Art, Tokyo, Japan, 1993.

An Uncertain Grace. San Francisco Museum of Modern Art, USA, 1990. International Center of Photography, New York, NY, USA, 1991. Corcoran Gallery of Art, Washington, D.C., USA, 1992. Städtisches Museum, City of Schleswig, Germany, 1996. Victor Barsokevitsch Valokuvakeskus, Kuopio, Finland, 1997. EFDI, Madrid, Spain, 1999.

Workers. Philadelphia Museum of Art, Philadelphia, PA, USA, 1993. Palais de Tokyo, Paris, France, 1993. Centro Cultural de Bélem, Lisbon, Portugal, 1993. Biblioteca Nacional, Madrid, Spain, 1993. The JB Speed Art Museum, Louisville, KT, USA, 1993. National Gallery Slovakia, Bratislava, Slovakia, 1993. Royal Festival Hall, London, England, UK, 1993. Palazzo delle Esposicioni, Roma, Italy, 1994. The University of Iowa Museum of Art, Iowa City, IO, USA, 1994. Musée de l'Elysée, Lausanne, Switzerland, 1994. Museu de Arte Moderna, MAM, Rio de Janeiro, Brazil, 1994. Museu de Arte de São Paulo, MASP,

Brazil, 1994. Museu Metropolitano de Arte de Curitiba, Brazil, 1994. The Bunkamura Museum of Art, Tokyo, Japan, 1994. Arberjdermuseet, Copenhagen, Denmark, 1994. Nederlands Foto Instituut, Rotterdam, The Netherlands, 1994. Bibliothèque Méjanes, Aix-en-Provence, France, 1994. Palazzo Affari ai Giureconsulti, Milan, Italy, 1994. The National Musem of Photography, Film and Television, Bradford, England, UK, 1994. Kulturhuset, Stockholm, Sweden, 1995. International Center of Photography, New York, NY, USA, 1995. Onomichi Municipal Museum of Art, Hiroshima, Japan, 1995. The Art Gallery of New South Wales, Sydney, Australia, 1995. Basilica Palladiana, Vicenza, Italy, 1995. Palais de Beitaddine, Le Chouf, Lebanon, 1995. The John & Marble Ringling Museum of Art, Sarasota, FL, USA, 1995. Georges Eastman House, Rochester, NY, USA, 1995. Palmer Museum of Art, University Park, PA, USA, 1996. Museo dell'automobile, Movimento Sviluppo e Pace, Turin, Italy, 1996. Honolulu Academy of Arts, Hawaii, USA, 1996. Deichtorhallen, Hamburg, Germany, 1996. «Hall Victor Hugo», Limpertsberg, Luxembourg, 1996. Elvehjem Museum of Art, Madison, WI, USA, 1997. Museo de Bellas Artes, Caracas, Venezuela, 1997. Museo de Arte Moderno Jésus Soto, Bolivar, Venezuela, 1997. Grand-Hornu Images, Hornu, Belgium, 1997. Museu de Arte da Pampulha, Belo Horizonte, MG, Brazil, 1997. Museo de Arte Moderno, Mexico City, Mexico, 1998. The Old Kornhaus, Berne, Switzerland, 1999. Städtische Gallery, Iserlohn, Germany, 1999. Contemporary Art Center Zamek Ujazdowski, Warsaw, Poland, 2000. Norsk Industriarbeider Museum, Rjukan, Norway, 2000. Festival Schichtwechsel 2000, Saarbrücken, Germany, 2000. Ghetto Degli Ebrei, Cagliari, Sardegna, Italy, 2001. On a train touring throughout the country, Czech Republic, 2005. Zourab Tsereteli Gallery, Fine Art Academy, Moscow, Russia, 2006. The Royal Library, Copenhagen, Denmark, 2007. Théâtre Forum Meyrin, Meyrin, Switzerland, 2008. Austin Museum of Art, Austin, TX, USA, 2008/2009.

Palazzo Pardi, Colonnella, Italy, 2010. Ecomuseu de Itaipu, PR, Brazil, 2014. Folkart Gallery, Izmir, Turkey, 2015.

Migrations. Maison Européenne de la Photographie, Paris, France, 2000. Sesc Pompéia, São Paulo, Brazil, 2000. Parque das Nações, Pavilhão de Portugal, Lisbon, Portugal, 2000. Scuderie Papali al Quirinale, Roma, Italy, 2000. Circulo de Bellas Artes, Madrid, Spain, 2000. La Pedrera, Barcelona, Spain, 2001. Deutsches Historisches Museum, Berlin, Germany, 2001. Berkeley Art Museum, California, USA, 2002. Bunkamura, Tokyo, Japan, 2002. Barbican Gallery, London, England, 2003. Ludwig Museum, Budapest, Hungary, 2004.

Africa. Tokyo Metropolitan Art Museum, Japan, 2009.

Genesis. Natural History Museum, London, England, 2013. Royal Ontario Museum, Toronto, Canada, 2013. Ara Pacis, Rome, Italy, 2013. CaixaForum, Madrid, Spain, 2014. SESC Santo André, SP, Brazil, 2014. Casa dei Tre Oci, Venice, Italy, 2014. National Museum of Singapore, 2014. Palácio das Artes, Belo Horizonte, MG, Brazil, 2014. Palazzo della Ragione, Milan, Italy, 2014. International Center of Photography, New York, USA, 2014. Museu Oscar Niemeyer, Curitiba, PR, Brazil, 2014. A Cordoaria Nacional, Lisbon, Portugal, 2015. Amerika Haus, C/O, Berlin, Germany, 2015. Forti di Bard, Aosta, Italy, 2015. Natural History Museum, Shanghai, China. 2015. Kunst Foyer, Munich, Germany. 2015/2016. Mouravieff-Apostol House & Museum, Moscow, Russia, 2016. Palazzo Ducale, Genoa, Italy, 2016. Museum & Galleries of Ljubljana, Slovenia, 2016. Center for the Meetings of Cultures, Lublin, Poland, 2016. Erarta, St Petersburg, Russia, 2016. Belveder, Prague, Czech Republic, 2017. MOPA – Museum of Photographic Arts, San Diego, CA, USA, 2017. Nederlands Fotomuseum, Rotterdam, The Netherlands, 2017. Kunsthalle, Budapest, Hungary, 2017. Palazzo Arti Napoli – PAN.

Naples, Italy, 2017-2018. Museum für Gestaltung Zurich, Switzerland. 2018-2019. La Sucrière, Lyon, France, 2020.

Amazônia. Philharmonie de Paris, France, 2021. MAXXI, Roma, Italy, 2021. Science Museum, London, England, UK, 2021. SESC Pompeia, São Paulo, Brazil, 2022. Science and Industry Museum, Manchester, England, UK, 2022. Palais des Papes, Avignon, France, 2022. Museu do Amanhã, Rio de Janeiro, Brazil, 2022. California Science Center, Los Angeles, CA, USA, 2022.

Fabbrica del Vapore, Milan, Italy, 2023. MAAG, Zurich, Switzerland, 2023. Fernán Gómez - Centro Cultural de la Villa, Madrid, Spain, 2023. Salone degli Incanti, Trieste, Italy, 2024. National Museum of Singapore, 2024. Museu Marítim de Barcelona, Spain, 2024. Museu Nacional de Antropología, Mexico City, Mexico, 2025. Tour & Taxis, Bruxelles, Belgium, 2025.

Glaciers. Museo d'Arte Moderna e Contemporanea di Trento e Rovereto, Trento, Italy, 2025.

FILMOGRAPHY

Contacts: Sebastião Salgado, **1989**. Directed by Sylvain Roumette for CNP/La Sept/Riff Productions, France. 13 minutes, series.
Sebastião Salgado: Entretien avec Frank Horvat, **1990**. Directed by Bruno Tompier for La Vidéothèque de Photographes series, Paris Audiovisuel, France. 26 minutes.
Sebastião Salgado: Looking Back at You, **1993**. Directed by Andrew Snell for Omnibus series, BBC, UK. 51 minutes.
L'Aventure Photographique: Sebastião Salgado, **1998**. Directed by Philippe Azoulay for Rosebud Productions, France. 26 minutes.
Les 100 Photos du Siècle: Sebastião Salgado, **1998**. Directed by Marie-Monique Robin for Capa Production /Arte, France. 6 minutes, series.

Visionen zum Millennium: Sebastião Salgado, **1999**. Directed by Thomas Bogensberger for DoRo Produktion/Arte/ORF, Austria. 13 minutes, series.
Exodes, **2000**. Directed by Alain Taïeb for Riff Productions/Canal+/Amazonas Images/Sogecable, France. Series of 30 films, 3 minutes each.
The Spectre of Hope, **2001**. Directed by Paul Carlin for Minerva Picture Company, UK. 52 minutes.
Le Sel de La Terre, **2014**. Directed by Wim Wenders and Juliano Ribeiro Salgado for Decia Films, France, Italy, Brazil. 109 minutes.

MAJOR HONORS

1982 Awarded a grant by the W. Eugene Smith Memorial Fund in Humanistic Photography.
1984 Receives the Prix de la Ville de Paris et Kodak, used for the publication of his first book of photographs on Latin America, *Autres Amériques*.

1985 World Press Photo Award, the Netherlands, and the Oskar Barnack Award, West Germany, for his work on the Sahel.
1986 Following the publication of his projects on Latin America and the Sahel, earns several distinctions, including the Premio Iberoamericano de Fotografía, Spain; Photojournalist of the Year

Award, the International Center of Photography, USA; the Prix du Livre, for *Sahel. L'Homme en détresse*, Rencontres de la Photographie d'Arles, France; the Grand Prix and Prix du Public for the presentation of *Other Americas*, during the Mois de la Photographie, Paris, France.

1987 Prix Villa Médicis, Ministry of Foreign Affairs, France.

1988 Erich Salomon Prize, West Germany. Premio de Fotografía Rey de España, Spain.

1989 Erna and Victor Hasselblad Award for lifetime achievement, Sweden. Artist of Merit, Josef Sudek Medal, Czechoslovakia.

1990 Visa d'Or Award, International Festival of Photojournalism, Perpignan, France.

1991 Grand Prix de la Ville de Paris, France.

1992 Elected Foreign Honorary Member of American Academy of Arts and Sciences, Massachusetts, USA.

1993 Prize for Best Photography Book of the Year for *La Main de l'Homme*, Rencontres de la Photographie d'Arles, France. Trophée Match d'Or, for lifetime achievement, France.

1994 Grand Prix National, Ministère de la Culture et de la Francophonie, France. Award of Excellence and Gold Medal, Society of Newspaper Design, USA.

1997 Prêmio Nacional de Fotografia, Ministry of Culture, Funarte, Brazil. Prêmio A Luta pela Terra, Personalidade da reforma agrária (Movement of Landless Peasants), Brazil.

1998 Principe de Asturias Award for the Arts, Spain.

1999 UNESCO Prize in Culture, Brazil.

2000 Medal of the Presidency of the Italian Republic, Pio Manzù International Research Center, Italy.

2001 Honorary Doctorate, Universidade de Evora, Portugal. Honorary Doctor of Fine Arts, The New School, New York, USA. Honorary Doctor of Fine Arts, Art Institute of Boston at Lesley University, USA. UNICEF Goodwill Ambassador.

2002 Honorary Doctor of Letters, University of Nottingham, UK.

2003 International Award, Photographic Society of Japan, Tokyo.

2004 Comendador da Ordem de Rio Branco, Ministry of Foreign Affairs, Brazil.

2007 Michael Horbach Stiftung Award, Cologne, Germany.

2011 PSA International Understanding Through Photography Award, Photographic Society of America, New York, USA.

2014 Honor: Commandeur de l'Ordre des Arts et des Lettres, Ministry of Culture and Communication, France.

2015 The Cherry Kearton Medal and Award for excellence in Amazonian photography as a record of natural history. The Royal Geographical Society, with IBG, UK.

2016 Member of the Académie des Beaux-Arts of the Institut de France, elected to the seat previously occupied by Lucien Clergue, France. Chevalier (Knight) of the Legion of Honour. France. Doctor Honoris Causa, Universidade Federal do Espírito Santo, Vitoria, ES, Brazil. The International Primo Levi Prize for year 2016, Genoa, Italy.

2018 Chevalier (Knight) of the Order of Cultural Merit, Principality of Monaco.

2019 Elected Foreign Honorary Member of the American Academy of Arts and Letters, USA. Peace Prize of the German Book Trade, Germany.

2021 27th Annual Crystal Award, the World Economic Forum, Davos, Switzerland. Honorary Doctor of Arts, Harvard University, Cambridge, MA, USA. The Praemium Imperiale Award, Japan Art Association, Japan.

2022 International Center of Photography's Infinity Award, International Center of Photography (ICP), USA.

2023 Named among *Time Magazine*'s 100 Most Influential Climate Leaders in Business, 2023.

2024 Outstanding Contribution to Photography Award, Sony World Photography Awards, London, UK. Golden Plate Award, American Academy of Achievement, Washington, D.C., USA.

© 2025 TASCHEN GmbH
Hohenzollernring 53, D–50672 Köln
www.taschen.com

Photographs
© Sebastião Salgado

Text
© Sebastião Salgado, Lélia Wanick Salgado and Irina Bokova

Editing, conception, and design
Lélia Wanick Salgado

Staff
Françoise Piffard
Marcia Navarro Mariano
Olivier Jamin, *digital prints*
Valérie Hue, *digital prints*
Jacques Barthélemy, *field assistant*

In collaboration with
Gérard Lamarche, Bernard Dumas, *graphic designers*
Adrien Bouillon, *contact sheets, work prints*
Philippe Bachelier, *consultant*
Dominique Granier, *silver prints*

Editorial coordination
Simone Philippi

Printed in Bosnia-Herzegovina
ISBN 978–3–7544–0335–8